NO
CONTEST

CONTEST

CORPORATE LAWYERS AND THE
PERVERSION OF JUSTICE IN AMERICA

Ralph Nader
and
Wesley J. Smith

RANDOM HOUSE

NEW YORK

Grateful acknowledgment is made to the following for permission to reprint previously published material:

THE APPLESEED FOUNDATION: "The Appleseed Foundation Statement of Purpose." Reprinted by permission of the Appleseed Foundation, Washington, D.C.

CORPORATE LEGAL TIMES: Excerpt from "Purge Your Files Now or Pay for Bad Documents Later" by Philip A. Lacovara (*Corporate Legal Times*, January, 1994). Copyright © 1994 by *Corporate Legal Times*. Reprinted by permission of *Corporate Legal Times*.

Library of Congress Cataloging-in-Publication Data
Nader, Ralph.
No contest: corporate lawyers and the perversion of justice in America/Ralph Nader and Wesley J. Smith.
p.   cm.
Includes index.
ISBN 0-679-42972-7
1. Corporate lawyers—United States.   2. Justice and politics—United States.   3. Law reform—United States.   I. Smith, Wesley J. II. Title.
KF299.I5N33   1996   347.73'53—dc20 [347.30753]   95-25432

Random House website address: http://www.randomhouse.com/

Designed by Michael Mendelsohn

Printed in the United States of America on acid-free paper

9 8 7 6 5 4 3 2
First Edition

RN: To my father and brother,
for their inspiring, lifetime dedication to justice,
community, and civic engagement.

WJS: For Debra J., wife and total sweetheart.

RN/WJS: To all lawyers and their clients—past, present,
and future—who make the ethical pursuit of justice
under law a pillar of our democracy.

Acknowledgments

THIS BOOK IS THE PRODUCT OF MORE THAN TWO YEARS OF research and writing. It would not have been possible without the cooperation of literally hundreds of individuals, who shared so selflessly with us: Lawyers, including corporate lawyers, who sent us volumes of case material to review, and who gave so freely of their time and expertise. Clients, who shared their often painful experiences with us. We also appreciate the many others who assisted with this work, legal observers in the media, ethicists, academics, legal secretaries, young associates, and other staff members from some of the world's largest firms, who were an invaluable source of insight into the working and mind-set of the corporate legal world. We also appreciate family and friends who have been so supportive and understanding.

Special thanks to Peter Smith, Olga Seham, David Halperin, and David Gehrig, whose dedication and commitment to this book made such a difference.

Contents

CONTENTS

Introduction

T WAS SATURDAY MORNING IN APRIL 1995 WHEN VIRGINIA Coleman, a partner in the Boston-based corporate law firm Ropes & Gray, chaired a reunion gathering of her Harvard Law School class of 1970. Hers had been a rebellious class, attending the law school during the tumultuous years from 1967 to 1970. Many participated in protests over the Vietnam War, civil rights, and law school educational policies. They also protested what large law firms were not doing, namely, free (pro bono) work on behalf of the needy. They even sent a questionnaire to firm partners who came to Harvard to recruit asking about the nature and amount of free legal services their respective firms provided. This was unheard-of assertiveness for law students.

Coleman introduced a panel of classmates to the gathering. They spoke about their respective careers during the past quarter century. Though many of the graduates in the crowded room had gone on to more traditional practices, some of the panel still pursued work grounded in those active and idealistic early years, and their provocative words stimulated attorney Coleman to offer a moving, even poignant confession of sorts. She wondered about spending so many years of one's life in a practice that essentially was about "making rich people richer." Yes, she said, speaking in measured tones, she found her work intellectually challenging, but . . .

She told a story about a lottery winner who came to her firm, which has 285 attorneys, for advice on how to obtain a large bank loan based on future installment payments due him. Soon, there were assembled around her firm's conference table a bevy of specialists that included attorneys, bank loan officers, tax accountants, and other financial experts. She wondered whether this was a very productive use of all that brainpower.

The audience murmured in acknowledgment, as if their own memories and feelings were similar. Yet, no one truly dealt with the issue. No one started a discussion on the relationship of lawyers to democracy and why so much of the popular demand for justice is ignored, if not rejected. No one criticized the imbalances in the system that too often benefit the rich and powerful at the expense of the rest. No one confronted the psychic costs of serving money rather than ideals.

In actuality, law schools are not often forums for such discussions before or after alumni return home. Still very vocational in emphasis, law schools' teaching and research heavily reflect the existing job market for attorneys. Whatever passes for intellectual ferment, whether practical or theoretical, is usually quite remote from debate over the law as a system of justice for people who are not rich or powerful. Nor is much thought given to developing new roles and organizing modes with which to serve unmet community or individual needs.

Returning alumni at law schools like Harvard largely mirror the comfortable though recently less stable life at the nation's business law firms. These classmates swap family anecdotes, tell "war" stories, and talk a little politics as they catch up with one another. But underneath their successful careers there lies an unease, perceptible in the lawyers' reaction to attorney Coleman's musing: Our society is in trouble, and most lawyers have not done their part to help right the many wrongs.

Big-time attorneys of all ages are worrying about this state of affairs, but few press too insistently for answers to their private doubts. The polls and surveys are so consistent as to be tedious: Far too many lawyers are bored, dissatisfied, depressed, or burned out. Many younger attorneys are regretting ever going to law school, while middle-aged attorneys yearn for early retirement, despite earning record amounts of money and exercising more power over our political economy than their predecessors ever did. The glorious vision of lawyers working with others to shape a just society seems very distant on their horizons.

Given the palpable public consternation over abuses of power, lower standards of living, and a loss of civic control over events and conditions affecting our lives, why do so many attorneys in those law firms that the media unthinkingly label "prestigious" find their labors unsatisfying and empty? Could their ennui have anything to do with idealism frustrated because their work is so detached from the serious questions of justice to which the law should respond? Could it be related to the highly pressured and competitive service rendered to ever-demanding corporate clients whose power is currently at a historical peak? Is law practice really just "another business"—to use a frequent cliché of the daily disillusioned?

In the early 1970s, another member of that Harvard class of 1970, Mark Green, set out to appraise the workings of some of Washington's leading lawyers: the firm of Covington & Burling and attorney Lloyd Cutler, who cofounded the firm of Wilmer, Cutler & Pickering. At that time, there were no publications that closely examined the inner workings of large law firms or the stresses and moods of their attorneys. Lawyers generally were not accustomed to justifying their conduct in public. Green had such a difficult time gaining even routine information from these firms that humor turned to farce. During one interview, a Covington & Burling lawyer declined to say what law school he graduated from (it was Yale) on the basis that any reply would be self-touting and thereby a violation of the canons of ethics. Before submitting to questioning, Cutler insisted that Green obtain an American Bar Association opinion declaring that it would not be considered unethical advertising or soliciting for Cutler to accede to Green's request for an interview.

Green's pathbreaking experiences in writing his 1975 book, *The Other Government*, illuminated how these megafirms avoided examination of their exercise of immense power over society for so many decades. Working in secretive surroundings, behind the screen of attorney-client privilege, led to practices that stretched ethical boundaries beyond even what their big-business clients demanded of them and narrowed the constraints that belonging to a supposedly learned, independent profession was expected to instill.

Before Green's book and the 1972 best-seller *Super-Lawyers* by journalist Joseph Goulden, most of the books about business law firms, other than a few sociological studies, were authorized biographies. But one book, entitled *The Washington Lawyer*, written in 1952 by a thoughtful Covington & Burling attorney, Charles Horsky, contained cogent advice to his colleagues:

> We have an obligation to do more than tell clients how they can lawfully do what they want to do. I do not refer only to the clients who want to urge positions so outrageous that no lawyer could advocate them and still maintain his self respect. We should go beyond that. The public position of the bar suffers, and properly so, when it becomes apparent that there are Washington lawyers who are quite willing to ignore entirely the larger interests of the country and the basic standards of decency in the process of stringing together sets of legal loopholes to achieve some inordinate advantage! Because this is an area in which canons of ethics and Grievance Committees cannot operate is the more reason why all lawyers should be alert to the implicit, as well as the explicit, responsibilities which distinguish law as a profession, not merely a highly technical trade.

Like the proverbial wise man speaking to the assemblage that listened and then drifted away, Horsky the writer has had little effect on his colleagues, then or now. Neither Horsky's own firm, one of whose specialties is lobbying for tobacco industry immunities, nor others in the corporate legal community broke stride in their rush to curry their clients' every favor. Their conscientious brethren admonish corporate attorneys that they should be willing to balance the requirements of two worlds—*attorneys* for their clients and *lawyers* for the larger goal of advancing systems of justice in society. The terms *lawyer* and *attorney* denote different functions required of the legal profession. *Attorney* describes the role of representing a client. *Lawyer* describes the public role of the professional, whose duties extend beyond his or her client to the justice system and the public interest. These imperatives are often described by the phrase "officer of the court."

In today's legal profession, the attorneys have eclipsed the lawyers. The big-client imperative, driven by the petrochemical, automobile, oil, steel, tobacco, drug, insurance, banking, real estate, agribusiness, genetic-engineering, telecommunications, nuclear, food-processing, and other industries, is the decisively dominant claimant on the time, talent, and allegiance of too many members of the profession.

Even given the demands of zealous client advocacy, attorneys cannot dismiss the need for maintaining a somewhat independent status, as at least some leaders of the bar have acknowledged. Earlier in this century, a prominent New York corporate lawyer, Elihu Root, told a client, "The law lets you do it, but don't. . . . It's a rotten thing to do." Compare this proper and lawyerly admonition with how, according to Mark Green's book *The Other Government,* a Covington & Burling attorney instructed an associate who learned that their client, the Electronic Industry Association, was dividing up markets in a manner that violated federal criminal antitrust laws. He told him to burn the information. Unfortunately, as we will detail in this book, such attitudes are disturbingly common.

Eminent tax lawyer Randolph Paul wrote in 1950 about the public obligations of private lawyers:

> The responsibilities of the tax advisor [lawyer] . . . may be said to end at the point of faithful attendance to his client's interest. But this is not, in my opinion, the end of the tax advisor's responsibility. He is a citizen as well as a tax advisor. He is more than the ordinary citizen; he is a specially qualified person in one of the most important areas of common interest. His experience equips him with a peculiar knowledge of what is wrong with tax laws and makes especially valuable his objective opinion about what should be done—and sometimes what should

not be done—to remedy defects. Special qualifications which may not be passively discharged.

No enforcement agency stands behind Paul's important words, only the self-enforcement of professional duty—the ultimate professional dignity.

The exercise of this duty should not be seen as an irresolvable conflict between the tasks of attorneys on one hand, and the mission of lawyers on the other. Former Harvard law professor Donald Turner told a group of antitrust attorneys in the mid-sixties, when Turner was the Justice Department's antitrust chief, that "service to a client, even continual service to a client, does not prevent a lawyer . . . from taking positions on public issues in opposition to the views of the client."

Henry L. Stimson, the twentieth-century doyen of the modern corporate attorney, who served in high government positions under six presidents, wrote passionately of the necessity of the American lawyer to be a defender of the laws and Constitution. "I felt," he wrote in his co-authored book *On Active Service in War and Peace*, "that if the time should ever come when this tradition faded out and the members of the Bar had become merely the servants of business, the future of our liberties would be gloomy indeed."

That time may have come. Thanks to the ingenious advocacy of corporate attorneys, in conjunction with the stiffening matrix of corporate power, there is an accelerating imbalance between individuals and corporations, both within and outside formal legal frameworks. The growing double standard between the procedural and substantive rights and powers of artificial persons—corporations—and real persons is one of the most momentous and disturbing handiworks in the history of American law and its counselors.

Lawyers have never been able to escape the standards for their ideal behavior precisely because of their central place in promoting the rule of law and the tenets of democracy and justice. They can, and do, violate these standards, or they uphold them "in theory" but not in practice. But they cannot wish them away and remain who they claim to be—semiofficial participants in the public administration of justice. The corporate bar does not deny the validity of such noble expressions of the exalted statures of attorney and lawyer. But where it really counts, in the trenches of actual law practice, attorneys find these precepts a luxury at best and a business suicide course at worst. A lot is at stake in corporate legal maneuverings, and, they believe, the lawyer who cleaves to the ideals of the profession may soon be out of work as an attorney, or at least as a corporate attorney.

Although they are disinclined to renounce standards of conduct publicly, corporate attorneys have been discomforted enough by their actual day-to-day standards to create rationalizations for a lower level of practice, expressed in the mantra we have already cited, "zealous representation of the client." This is taken to mean that for the system to work according to its ideals, attorneys for each side of a controversy or legal transaction should unhesitatingly advocate their client's position with competence, integrity, and unflagging zeal. From this confrontation between supposed equals, justice is expected to prevail—may the best argument win. Moreover, continues the creed, attorneys merely bring skills to their client's needs, not any inherent or self-asserted power. (This modesty reached proverbial levels in the long career of former White House counselor and secretary of defense Clark Clifford, the quintessential power lawyer. For more than forty years in practice, he would calmly declaim, "I have no influence." This phrase became the title of a chapter in Douglas Frantz's and David McKean's recent biography of Clifford, suitably titled *Friends in High Places*.) Thus, the attorneys bear no moral responsibility for outcomes. There are of course examples of corporate law firms refusing to represent particular clients or types of clients. For example, Boston's second-highest-grossing firm, 237-attorney Hale and Dorr, has a policy of not representing any tobacco company, one of the firm's partners told us. And in the early 1970s, Washington, D.C., attorney Robert Wald dropped tobacco maker Lorillard, Inc., as a client when he became convinced of the health risks of smoking and the company's failure to address them. Such instances demonstrate that it is perfectly appropriate and ethical to exercise moral judgments in the practice of law. Principled stands such as these should be commended where they occur, but they are far from the norm.

The "zealous representation" rationale has a plausible ring. Until, that is, a persistent reality is considered: a structural inequality of power. Corporations have spent a great deal of time, effort, and money establishing privileges and immunities, through their attorneys, that real people do not possess, thus creating uneven playing fields that allow corporations to maneuver and dominate in a way that individuals never could. For example, imagine a group of workers announcing they will leave the country unless they receive demanded wage and benefit concessions, as corporations almost routinely are able to do because of the ways in which their lawyers have helped structure the governing statutes.

On a more individualized level, people in legal disputes with corporations and insurance companies frequently do not have counsel representing them, allowing corporate attorneys free rein, often resulting in profound injustice. Average people often do not have the money to hire a lawyer or finance a lawsuit. How many people are forced to forgo or abandon access to legal redress simply because they lack the resources of their corporate adversaries?

Faced with these and other inequalities, leading corporate attorneys have become adept at keeping their professional self-image and status intact while engaging in activities that allow their ample fees to continue to flow. But there is another set of historically affirmed standards that keep testing, at least abstractly, the ability of these attorneys to have it both ways—both the money and the majesty. Passing the bar confers a legal monopoly to practice law, and especially to represent clients in courts of law. Additionally, lawyers are deemed "officers of the court." The American Bar Association (ABA) Model Rules of Professional Conduct provide this celebrated elaboration of these two central privileges:

> A lawyer is a representative of clients, an officer of the legal system and a public citizen having special responsibility for the quality of justice. . . . As a public citizen, a lawyer should seek improvement of the law, the administration of justice . . . A lawyer should be mindful of deficiencies in the administration of justice . . .

How many lawyers think of these words even once a year? The gap between this profession's idealism and reality is vast and replete with difficult contradictions. Our society would be far better off if all attorneys endeavoring on behalf of their clients were also mindful of their duties as lawyers to labor for broader missions of the law to enhance justice for all.

The various rules of professional conduct affecting millions of people are more than sonorous phrases of professional self-edification. They delineate, however generally, important public interests that the legal profession is expected to advance, in return for the distinct privileges and monopoly it has been accorded by law. Yet the overwhelming economic incentives of the legal workplace put zealous advocacy for paying clients far ahead of the civic duties that the Model Rules of Professional Conduct assign to lawyers.

The distinction between the respective obligations of attorneys and those of lawyers rarely is discussed in law school courses or at bar association meetings. There is a great deal of tension and conflict that would arise if these two roles were exercised seriously. The very structure of the profession would have to change, as would the distribution and administration of justice in America. So the discussion forums and institutions of the profession have generally avoided the subject, along with the expanding corporate firm "law factories" that have managed to avoid facing up to this duality.

At Harvard Law School in the 1950s, students were urged to question everything, even the opinions of the revered judge Learned Hand. Everything, that is, except the culture and strategies of the corporate law firms. This vital segment of the legal landscape was beyond the analytic boundaries of legal education, although that was where most of the students were heading. Later, in the 1970s, Steven Brill, the aggressive founder of modern legal journalism, also found formidable the walls surrounding these corporate firms and shielding them from scrutiny. But as editor of the journal *The American Lawyer*, Brill, aided by diligent reporters, cracked those walls to obtain a consistent flow of internal law firm information whose disclosure in earlier decades would have sent the partners into exile.

Brill tells us a story of what it took to obtain data merely on the gross annual revenues of these large firms. One of his reporters told him that she could not get these figures from Sidley & Austin, which then had about 175 partners. Brill asked, "How many partners have you called?" She replied, "One hundred thirty-seven." "Call the rest," he said. She did and finally reached a partner who divulged the figures.

The firms are changing. Compared with the sedentary old days, they are caught in a maelstrom of mergers, diversity pressures, bankruptcies, partner raiding by competitors, and eviction of older brethren. The turmoil does not, however, normally extend to wrestling with the dual life of attorney and lawyer, other than to evade the issue by stressing that "this firm will be run like a business," as if making money were the end-all and be-all, explaining away all faults and failings.

Facing increasing scrutiny by their corporate clients striving to manage them more closely on the one hand and growing public cynicism on the other, these law firm partners seem caught in a commercial rat race that allows little respite for reflection. Yet, if lawyers are indeed members of a learned profession, the absence of reflection on the effects of raw commercialism in the practice of law amounts to professional delinquency of grave import to the rule of just laws.

Those attorneys who do harbor doubts about the direction of their practice and profession are more likely to remain quiet or depart than are their supercharged, business-oriented colleagues. Increasing firm discipline tends to wrap the skeptics with invisible chains. "The

giant law firms have become like business corporations in their structure, management and goals," writes Peter Megargee Brown, former
partner in charge of litigation with Cadwalader, Wickersham & Taft.
In his insightful little book *Rascals: The Selling of the Legal Profession*,
Brown recounts the conversion of the New York law firm White &
Case by managing partner James Hurlock. One of Hurlock's partners, Raynor Hamilton, observed that the firm became "a business by
emphasizing that each of us is a profit center." A saddened Brown
commented:

> A precipitous change of this character may bring with it deep
> troubles to the Bar as a whole. Becoming an efficient machine
> and urging every partner to be a "profit center" has its own spe-
> cial consequences on how the partners behave, how they go
> about counseling clients and how they serve community inter-
> ests. It is not the salient purpose of the law profession to focus
> so specially, so exclusively on *profits* and on *efficiency* (the same
> concept, euphemistically). Indeed to do so is directly counter
> to the essence of what the profession is about.
> [Emphasis in original.]

What are corporate attorneys about at their core? Is it, as business
lawyer, author, and diplomat Sol Linowitz urges, to be the keepers of
the corporate conscience, or, as novelist Scott Turow put it as a young
law student, "to be the chief custodian of justice"? Is it to heed the
words of then corporation attorney Louis D. Brandeis back in 1905
when he told a gathering at Harvard:

> Instead of holding a position of independence, between the
> wealth and the people, prepared to curb the excesses of either,
> able lawyers have, to a great extent, allowed themselves to be-
> come adjuncts of great corporations and have neglected their
> obligation to use their powers for the protection of the people.
> We hear much of the corporate lawyer and far too little of the
> "people's lawyer."

And that was said ninety-one years ago! Imagine Brandeis's reaction to
the raw mercantilist ethic so prevalent in today's modern corporate law
culture.

Throughout the twentieth century, occasional, powerful critiques
and admonitions by prominent lawyers, law professors, deans of law
schools, and bar association leaders have gained wide notice among

members of the bar, who nod approvingly and then return to the daily realities of their marketplace. This is not a difficult choice given the lucrative temptations on one side, weak state bar disciplinary commissions on the other, and codes of ethics that can be read to support placing client interests above the broader interests of the legal system or the public. This explains, in part, how many large law firms can justify rather limited pro bono work—representing a handful of indigents, for example—while avoiding a more systemic pro bono leverage on agencies and institutions of power, pleading conflicts with their business clients.

The two pillars of affirmative professional obligations—a licensed monopoly for practicing law and being an officer of the court—turn out to have few concrete manifestations beyond what the criminal law forbids members of the general public from doing. In 1989, University of Kentucky law professor Eugene R. Gaetke searched the legal literature in preparing a law review article on "Lawyers as Officers of the Court." He found little of substance flowing from this privileged status. "Lawyers," he wrote, "like to refer to themselves as officers of the court. Careful analysis of the role of the lawyer within the adversarial legal system reveals the characterization to be vacuous and unduly self-laudatory. It confuses lawyers and misleads the public. The profession, therefore, should either stop using the officer of the court characterization or give meaning to it."

Gaetke believes that the conflict between "officer of the court" and "zealous advocacy" can be accommodated by requiring lawyers' duties to include assuring the efficient operation of the judicial system and the protection of innocent people from harm. To achieve these commitments, the law, Gaetke reasons, must require lawyers in certain concrete instances to subordinate their own interests and the interests of their clients in favor of the interests of the judicial system or the public. This would mean starting at home plate, since, presently, the legal codes of ethics "do not obligate lawyers to provide free legal services to the poor for the benefit of the fair and efficient operation of the judicial system," nor, Gaetke writes, "must lawyers protect innocent persons from harm by disclosing even unprivileged information showing conclusively that the wrong person has been arrested or convicted of a crime even when the best interests of the client would not be harmed by this disclosure."

In 1983, the ABA rejected a recommendation by a commission it had established for mandatory pro bono. Some attorneys angrily called the concept "involuntary servitude." A broader objection by many lawyers is that any obligations on them that compromise their zealous advocacy for clients undermines the strength of the adversary system that provides for attorneys on both sides to argue before an impartial judge. What is so repeatedly ignored is that the heavily skewed deployment of attorneys—where the money and power are—leaves millions of people and thousands of constituencies without the legal representation to even constitute a credible adversary process.

The debate regularly misses another major point. Legal systems are supposed to prevent or punish or restrain abuses of raw power. Lawyers are official participants in these arenas, apart from their clients' interests. The courts, agencies, prisons, and other public institutions rely vitally on this professional involvement. Indeed, it can be said that their role is so crucial as to be a sine qua non, given the attorneys' monopoly to practice law. Judges and agency heads most often wait upon the filings and arguments of lawyers before they act. And attorneys, in Sol Linowitz's words, "can command corporations and governments to testify, to produce documents, to defend their actions." They are truly invested with unique "public citizen" responsibilities. When a legal system begins to break down due to bias, corruption, or inaccessibility, the members of the privileged legal profession must act.

Attorney excesses on behalf of clients thrive when there is an imbalance of advocacy and power on one side of the case or negotiation. The coal company attorneys who created the notorious "broad-form deeds" by which they obtained from the impoverished and desperate Appalachian rural people, for fifty cents per acre, the right to all coal, oil, gas, metals, and minerals, the right to divert and pollute water, and immunity from all liability, did not pause to consider their obligations as lawyers. Nor did attorneys for banks, hospital chains, and employers who developed the compulsory arbitration clauses in the fine print of bank signature cards, insurance policies, hospital consent agreements, and employment contracts that take away the legal remedies of unsuspecting people. Nor did the attorney-lobbyists who damaged the equity of the tax laws for a quick retainer, knowing that the harm extended well beyond anything required to meet their clients' interests. Nor did the attorneys for the savings and loans or other financial firms who aided, abetted, or condoned the looting of savers and investors by management. Nor did the attorneys who, with investment bankers, pushed for huge fee-generating leveraged buyouts, loaded with debt, knowing that the top executives would reap the largest riches while workers, communities, and shareholders would be made to suffer. Nor did the attorney–union busters, whose crude and cruel tactics destroyed not just the prospect of decent livelihoods for working families but also the workers' belief that the law could work for, not against, them.

There is a reason for this. In the power-attorney view of law, to hesitate, to get into "lawyer mode," is to endanger their big fees and to be labeled by their business clients as hesitant, unreliable, and disloyal. Power attorneys crush the powerless populace and smaller businesses to assure that their clients prevail. The tools they use and the places they control twist the nation's political economy to serve corporate purposes. Corporate firm partners and associates alike would view as hopelessly naive Elihu Root's observation that "about half the practice of a decent lawyer consists in telling would-be clients that they are damned fools and should stop."

To the contrary, big law firm business-getters, "rainmakers," in legal parlance, are often steps ahead of their future clients—touting tactics, strategies, and a take-no-prisoners reputation against weaker adversaries. These attorneys do not have to go on television to advertise—their image precedes them on the corporate grapevine.

In a society officially dedicated to the rule of law, economic power needs its counselors to legitimize, mystify, facilitate, extend, immunize, shield, and entrench. For these services, attorneys are the central organizers and catalysts for the entry of other professions, such as accountants and even scientists, advancing corporate agendas. The complex systems and structures that corporate attorneys have constructed over the past 130 years are intellectual as well as practical achievements. Hardly a fraction of the brainpower of the profession was ever arrayed on the side of shareholders or small businesses, much less workers, the environment, consumers, citizens, voters, or the poor.

Corporate attorneys developed dazzling techniques of raising and investing capital, avoiding accountability and disclosure, concentrating power within and outside of companies, limiting liability from the early stages of corporate chartering to the recent maneuvers of voluntary Chapter 11 bankruptcy. Rarely do historians attribute to the work of these attorneys the difficulties faced by labor, consumers, suppliers, franchisees, shareholders, and local communities dealing with corporate management. Simply stated, these attorneys are masterminds of choreographing contests that are, in fact, no contest at all. To many corporate lawyers such deeds are their finest hour.

A no-contest world invites overreaching. As this book describes, whether in litigation or regulatory proceedings, tactics that delay or obstruct proceedings and obscure or destroy evidence send a clear message to future would-be challengers: Take us on and be prepared for attrition, or far worse. In legislative lobbying, the scope of changing the very rights and rules of contention systematically in favor of business further erodes attorneys' self-restraint. It is easy enough to observe that elected representatives passed the proposals. Meanwhile, corporate clients and attorneys themselves send the campaign money and other inducements that grease these skids.

The corporation is emerging as a private legislature—imposing private legal systems under one-sided agreements of "fine print" between sellers and consumers, employers and employees, companies and government departments, and in the burgeoning taxpayer subsidy areas, between corporations and communities. The incremental nature of this process obscures the advancing surrender of Americans' rights as they have been delineated by our nation's unequaled system of civil law torts (personal injuries and other civil wrongs such as fraud) and contracts. Contractual "gag rules" reach public notice only after a rare company whistleblower (a vanishing breed these days) goes on an intrepid television news magazine and risks his or her lifetime assets and future job prospects. The imbalance of power thus leads to isolating the powerless from the very legal rights designed to give them the chance to assert their causes on a legally meritocratic playing field. Since the Bill of Rights applies to arbitrary government action rather than corporate conduct, the basis to challenge these private corporate legislatures is not available. Gag rules on citizens by state action are unconstitutional, while gag rules by corporations are deemed a matter of private contract, enforced by courts with no effective constitutional remedy.

The legal architecture is moving closer to creating a quasi-governmental model. Utilities shift the costs of managing radioactive wastes to government and taxpayers, a kind of lemon socialism. Weapons makers secure by law the "sovereign immunity" defense usually available only to government. The Walt Disney Company's 22,000 acres near Orlando, Florida, are a private government with taxing, police, and zoning powers over a territory as large as San Francisco. The private corporate domains, such as giant shopping malls, "business improvement districts," and their counterparts in the housing area, the so-called gated communities, continue to break legal ground, stretching corporate sovereignty and shrinking public places. The state or city can condemn private property, as Detroit did in 1980–81 for a General Motors plant, justifying the demolition of hundreds of homes, small businesses, schools, and churches by declaring this private corporation's operations to be a "public purpose." Few ambitions were greater than those of the corporate trade attorneys who conceptualized the charter of the World Trade Organization (WTO) within the new General Agreements on Tariffs and Trade (GATT). This international autocratic system of governance, to which the United States adheres, allows companies through their proxy governments to bypass our open judiciary and administrative procedures entirely. They can take disputes, for example, about health and safety laws and rules (called "nontariff trade barriers") to closed and secret WTO tribunals in Geneva, Switzerland, from which there is no independent appeal, forcing the government either to repeal the laws or pay perpetual trade fines to the winning country. Even more creative corporate legal strategies are being designed to help companies escape national jurisdictions, allowing them to choose the most favorable rules, including those of brutal or corrupt regimes, under which to operate.

Following a single decade, 1965–75, when consumer, environmental, and other laws protecting individuals were enacted and judicial decisions rendered to hold corporations more accountable, corporate power domestically and internationally has been in ascendance for the past twenty years. If there is a thematic meaning to the consequences of spreading corporate commercial culture over the young, of weakening trade unions, of increasing government subsidies, of reducing government safety and antitrust enforcement, of restricting the common law of torts, of expanding business political action committees, together with an ever-concentrated mass media, it is this: The imbalances between real people and artificial persons called corporations are growing fast. The privileges and immunities of the large international corporations are constantly being expanded by the creativity of their attorneys. The one-sided franchiser-franchisee impositions and health maintenance organization (HMO) managed-care contracts with physicians, nurses, and patients, recently in the news, illustrate how attorneys can give a cruel and cutting edge to the industries they represent.

But the dominance of these corporations can perhaps best be sensed by the absence of society's corrective reaction and reform to documented patterns of corporate crime, corporate welfare abuses, and the suppression of industrial workers' attempts to form trade unions. Indeed, the momentum in Congress and state legislatures has been in reverse—to weaken the very laws that restrained the abuses of companies and channeled their energy toward less destructive paths or, at best, into more singularly productive outcomes such as adopting safety technologies. The government's weakening of the nation's banking laws only a half decade after enacting huge bailouts and indirect subsidies for both criminal or mismanaged savings and loans and commercial banks is just one illustration.

Corporate attorneys are at the nerve center of these trends—creating and facilitating practical frameworks for business interests bent on taking more power into their own hands. Indeed, even within the company structure itself, the carefully crafted division between ownership and control has shredded the very authority of shareholders and members of mutual financial institutions in favor of management control.

Can power attorneys continue to escape the professional responsibilities that arise from the immense advantages that their clients have vis-à-vis other people in society? At what point do the realities of their practice push them to say no, to counsel restraint, to criticize their colleagues in other industries? Even in a period of record corporate profits, stock prices, and executive compensation, the silence of these prosperous lawyers is extraordinary. For example, while the behavior of the tobacco industry's attorneys has been criticized in the press, members of the corporate bar have chosen not to speak out regarding the ethical boundaries beyond which their zealous advocacy should not tread.

When a profession seriously fails at internal examination, not to mention self-discipline, of the questionable conduct of its members, the initiative needs to shift externally. This is usually how professions have had to endure reform—from the outside. Corporate law firms are losing what independence they once had to the frenzy of underbidding, competition, and also to more insistent scrutiny by in-house counsel, whose status is on the rise inside their companies. Such a state leads to serious disintegrating forces that erode the public interest. For if the law in all its dimensions means anything, it is that access, fairness, and efficiency need to come as blends so as to enlarge opportunity and the fulfillment of human possibilities in the context of peace and justice. Without the raising of voices in support of greater exercise of responsibilities of lawyers to society, the supremacy of the service-only-to-client model will continue to make the profession more pretense than practice.

This book strives to demonstrate how power lawyers can harm innocent and vulnerable people and undermine the rule of law. What we describe is not rare; it is conduct all too representative of many corporate attorneys who react to the pressures and rewards that drive the large-firm and in-house corporate law practice. When so many attorneys are privately despairing or even quitting because lawyering has become just another business, when a partner at the 538-attorney Los Angeles–based firm O'Melveny & Myers tells us that many veteran corporate attorneys are looking back on their careers and experiencing "a feeling of emptiness," when surveys show a majority of attorneys believe that there is widespread overbilling, they are reacting to work environments that resemble the various cases and circumstances reported in the following pages. Our interviews indicate that some tenured attorneys resist such pressures, but these individuals are rarely able to influence their colleagues. Indeed, the firms pressure dissenters to submit to the "profit center" model. Most of these internal firm struggles do not surface publicly, but they feed the more abstract condemnations and warnings that the elders of the bar issue from time to time.

It is only when these excesses breach firm walls and come to public attention due to court sanctions or the occasional media exposé that the public is able to see the tip of the iceberg. This book presents a number of such cases—cases where attorney misconduct or oppressive behavior was revealed and, sometimes, punished or overcome. Given the skill of power lawyers and the layers of secrecy that shield the dealings between these attorneys and their corporate clients, these cases represent rare peeks at a complex system—the corporate-legal establishment. Though much of this establishment's labors are intricate and routinized, the changes that emerge for society are anything but humdrum. The failure of the bar and the government to invoke or enforce ethical standards or civil and criminal prohibitions produces over time its own accepted pattern of entrenched and immunized misconduct.

So long as corporate attorneys maintain that they are not vitally influential, that they are simply doing their job, that they are fighting to protect their besieged corporate behemoths from the twin Goliaths of big statism and the frivolous hysteria of the masses, they will continue to shirk the demands and betray the aspirations of their profession; they will, instead, wallow in its trade. That is why citizens need to organize to demand that power lawyers attain the level of conduct they have set for themselves. External jolts in such directions lead to internal courage and creativity that institutes long-overdue changes.

We hope that this book, addressed to the American people, including lawyers, will move both groups toward activism that may someday produce a better balance of power, advocacy, and justice.

RALPH NADER, Washington, D.C.
WESLEY J. SMITH, Oakland, California

CONTEST

CHAPTER 1

THE POWER LAWYERS

LOYD N. CUTLER, FOUNDING PARTNER OF THE WASHINGTON, D.C., law firm Wilmer, Cutler & Pickering, is not your typical corporate attorney. He is the consummate power lawyer, a man so systematically dedicated to expanding his influence that he could have come straight out of central casting. Born in 1917, Cutler seems to have wanted it all at least from 1962, when he opened Wilmer, Cutler, which now has 230 lawyers and is one of the nation's highest-earning law firms. To say simply that Cutler touched all the bases and made all the right tactical moves is to fail to note bases and moves that he invented. His tracks illustrate both the pathways to power and the costs to society and people that result from the maneuvering of skilled power lawyers, driven by the twin towers of ambition and acquisitiveness.

Cutler wanted to build a law firm that would represent the largest, most powerful corporations in the land. He wanted to take their agendas to the courts, the regulatory agencies, and the Congress. He needed capable attorneys from pedigree law schools and former high officials in agencies such as the Securities and Exchange Commission and the Department of Justice. He needed to have it known that his young firm had a close relationship with the venerable New York law firm Cravath, Swaine & Moore, where he had once toiled as a junior attorney. He sought a high profile at his alma mater, Yale Law School, whose alumni included leading corporate executives, attorneys, and politicians, so he led a fund-raising drive and spent a semester teaching a course at the school on "the limits of regulation." What he needed he got. But there was more.

Cutler had to be more than a lawyer-lobbyist for many companies and trade associations, more than just a corporate attorney. He sought, both personally and for the firm's growth, to appear as a statesman, as a person so influential and well connected that he could, at times, transcend individual contesting parties and represent "the situation," as the

3

legendary Washington criminal defense attorney Edward Bennett Williams liked to describe his own role.[1] The concept of the "lawyer for the situation" is associated with Louis Brandeis, who considered himself to have served in such a role in at least one matter before he became a Supreme Court justice in 1916. But this representation was attacked by critics during Brandeis's confirmation process. University of Pennsylvania law professor Geoffrey Hazard, Jr., says the "lawyer for the situation is advocate, mediator, entrepreneur, and judge, all in one. He could be said to be playing God." He adds, "Playing God is tricky business."[2] Cutler strove to be praised by presidents, senators, and cabinet secretaries, to serve on presidential commissions, to be published regarding his "detached" reflections on governmental reforms, and to become, as one of his clients, *The Washington Post,* described him in 1994, "a pillar of the Washington legal establishment."[3]

To Cutler, the quests for power and position were of a piece. In a town where "social is political," he was and is a frequent presence in the city's salons. He befriended the reporters, columnists, editors, publishers, and politicians who count for his purposes. He took them to Baltimore Orioles baseball games, appeared at their dinner functions, and ended up representing quite a few of them as clients, including CBS, ABC, the *Los Angeles Times,* James Reston of *The New York Times,* and syndicated columnist Joseph Kraft. Officially a member of the Democratic party but aggressively bipartisan when the need arose, Cutler made sure his circle included the Democrats' mother of all political networkers, Pamela Harriman, Republican Secretaries of State Henry Kissinger and George Shultz (both clients), and Katharine Graham, publisher of *The Washington Post.* He had the right combination of meticulous patience and ego to connect with the powers that be and ride on their shoulders. Cutler's socializing with such influential persons doubtlessly made them less inclined to take seriously the substantive criticisms made about his work.

High-and-mighty society was but one important dimension of Cutler's presentation of self. There had to be more to him than just a wealthy attorney on the make. In 1968, sensing the mood of the street demonstrations, Cutler brought many in his firm down to the District of Columbia criminal courts during the night rioting after the slaying of Martin Luther King to provide counsel to the detainees. The resultant publicity, along with his enduring Democratic party credentials, led President Lyndon Johnson to appoint Cutler to be executive director of the National Commission on the Causes and Prevention of Violence. In 1979, President Jimmy Carter appointed Cutler to be White House counsel. In 1988, during the Reagan administration, he was chairman of the President's Quadrennial Commission on Executive, Legislative and Judicial Salaries, which was designed to take the public heat off Congress and the president on the touchy subject of pay increases. Cutler came through with a very vocal recommendation to raise the salaries of the president, cabinet members, members of Congress, and federal judges by at least 50 percent. Was there a better way to become popular with the branches of government, each of which is crucial to your law firm's success?

Once again, in 1994, Cutler let it be known that he was available for White House service. President Bill Clinton had seen his White House counsel, Bernard Nussbaum, resign in the wake of the Whitewater investigation and the suicide of Nussbaum's deputy, Vince Foster. Clinton needed the reassuring influence of an old Washington hand whose confident voice and friendly, high-level media contacts could be translated into instant political capital. He was looking for, as he put it, "a Lloyd Cutler type."[4] The man himself was available, but he laid down distinct terms never witnessed in White House history. He would serve as a "special government employee" (SGE) without compensation for 130 working days, the maximum period permitted under this designation. SGE status was developed years ago to allow federal agencies to bring in scientific or other technical specialists for a short period without obligating these experts to sever all relationships with their employers. It was never remotely applicable to top, sensitive positions like White House counsel. Until, that is, power lawyer Lloyd Cutler conceived of that application.

As an SGE he could remain as a senior counsel to his law firm and continue to draw a salary (Cutler said that his earnings, reportedly $450,000 annually, would be reduced to account for the time spent at the White House[5]), be exempt from some of the more stringent government ethics regulations and would continue working for undisclosed private clients whose needs did not conflict, in his judgment, with his White House duties. Imagine, for a moment, if an experienced attorney for the AFL-CIO retained his position there and at the same time became White House counsel. The corporate and media uproar would be loud and explicit. But few complaints were heard when Cutler, a key legal representative of major corporations, assumed a dual role. Cutler had spent a lifetime laying the groundwork that led the Washington publication *Legal Times* to write, "Full-time White House counsel have never been able to conduct any outside work, but no one has raised questions about Cutler's arrangement—perhaps partly because of his stature."[6]

Having established this dubious precedent that blurred the separation between the public and the private, Cutler then grandly announced that, though he did not have to, he would voluntarily disclose information about his clients and would voluntarily comply with the Clinton administration's postemployment guidelines, such as a five-year ban on official appearances before the agency he would serve and a lifetime ban on lobbying for foreign interests. Such promises may matter very little, since it is difficult to envision an "appearance" before the White House, and other attorneys at Wilmer, Cutler can continue to lobby for foreign interests attracted to the firm by the Cutler name. Such unenforceable self-restraint nevertheless appeared to impress President Clinton, who described Cutler as a "man of seasoned judgment . . . and the highest ethical standards."

There are three vital functions that a White House counsel is expected to perform: screen nominees for sensitive executive branch positions, supervise the selection of federal judges, and keep the president out of legal difficulties. With this portfolio, on March 9, 1994, Cutler was at large in the White House while his law firm, retaining his name and senior counselship, was on the prowl for more business and more success for its clients.

Cutler's SGE coup was all the more remarkable because his past "seasoned" advice had not always worked out. He was a strong supporter of a controversial Reagan nominee to the Supreme Court, Robert Bork, whom the Senate rejected; he was an unyielding backer, until her withdrawal, of Aetna Insurance Company's general counsel, Zoe Baird, to be Clinton's attorney general, though she plainly lacked the experience and judgment for this top cabinet post; and he advised Clinton not to seek a special counsel to investigate Whitewater, again a losing position as Clinton soon acceded to congressional and public pressure and asked for such an appointment.[7] So Cutler was at least a three-time loser on crucial matters. But the privileges of power overcome such liabilities.

Some forms of influence in Washington are priceless. One of them is for a law firm to have its senior counsel in the cockpit position at the White House passing on scores of federal court nominees, including an appointee to the Supreme Court. Among a group of semifinalists, Stephen Breyer was Lloyd Cutler's friend and ideological match, especially in their shared opposition to effective regulation of business. Breyer was Cutler's choice for the job, and he got it. In their private, jocular moments, litigators, those lawyers who specialize in going to court rather than simply advising clients, have been heard to say that they do not practice law, they practice judge. For corporate attorneys and their high-earning clients, Cutler had scored the touchdown that won the Super Bowl.

On the occasion of being named White House counsel, Cutler said, "In government, as in other aspects of life, trust is the coin of the realm, and I pledge myself to do what I can to assure that trust is maintained." A few reporters, not so trusting, were asking questions about his continuing ties with his law firm. Cutler warded them off by referring them to ethics officials in the White House who had approved his unique arrangement as an SGE. To an unusual degree, Cutler's sensitivity to what he does and how he does it leads him to refer repeatedly to approval by government ethics officials, despite the fact that the history of ethics offices—one of providing ethical sheens for improprieties or worse—should raise cautionary signals.

Indeed, few in public life so regularly find it necessary to describe their own integrity in public. Journalist Andrew Ferguson wrote of Cutler's testimony before a House committee on Whitewater that Cutler "is a dignified, highly skilled lawyer whose integrity is unimpeachable. I know this because he kept saying it himself all day long."[8]

When, as director of President Johnson's Violence Commission, Cutler was asked by a law professor if he had recused himself from the commission's review of violence in the media, since he represented media clients, Cutler scolded him, "I do not think it appropriate for you to question my ethical judgment in the matter."[9]

While many of his colleagues embrace the response of Henry Ford II to the public—"never explain, never complain"—Cutler, to his credit, is driven to explain his behavior. He complains about any media criticism, through letters to the editor, op-ed articles, or, more often, through well-placed phone calls to publishers and top editors.

Implausibility has rarely daunted Cutler. Testifying before the House Banking Committee on July 26, 1994, on Whitewater, Cutler tried to behave like an impartial judge rather than an advocate for his boss, the president. He told the legislators, "I am not here as a special pleader for the President of the United States. I am here to report to you about a factual investigation that I conducted. I didn't ask for this job, I came in, and I took it, and I reported, frankly, to the best of my ability as a lawyer and a person of integrity."[10] Earlier that day Cutler had appeared on morning network television shows vigorously defending the president. (Trusting Cutler is not always a good idea. The day before Harry A. Blackmun announced he was resigning his Supreme Court seat, the one that went to Stephen Breyer, Cutler told a reporter that the White House knew "nothing beyond the rumors" of Blackmun's plans. Yet the very next day Cutler said that Blackmun had previously called Cutler's deputy, Joel Klein, to discuss the timing of his resignation announcement.[11])

Before the Senate Banking Committee in August 1994, Cutler declared that the Office of Government Ethics had concluded there were no ethics violations by White House staff in their numerous contacts with Treasury officials over Whitewater. But fifteen months later, before the same committee, Cutler admitted he "may have gone too far . . . may have transgressed" in making that statement, since the ethics office had neither investigated the matter itself nor reached any conclusions about violations.[12]

Constant concerns about image and the appearance of propriety may help explain the frequently observed physical suggestions of tenseness that punctuate Cutler's otherwise calm, composed manner. As well described twenty years ago by Mark Green, "As he speaks his fingers do a digital dance, waving in the air like some upside-down caterpillar. His feet twitch and jerk this way and that, as his elbows flap up and down, as if unconnected to his body."[13]

Sometimes such tenseness turns to anger. At an August 1983 American Bar Association meeting in Atlanta, Joan Claybrook, the president of the nonprofit consumer group Public Citizen[14] and a former head of the National Highway Traffic Safety Administration, spoke about how the automobile companies and their attorneys were working to undermine or block the installation of air bags both before and after the unanimous Supreme Court decision that year to reinstate this important crash protection standard.[15] Cutler, who was to follow Claybrook on the podium to speak about an entirely separate Supreme Court decision, became furious and launched a laborious response on the technical deficiencies of air bag systems—a misguided view he held after years of representing major auto industry clients. The minutiae and defensiveness puzzled other attorneys in the room. After the program ended, a major attorney-lobbyist for the oil industry, J. D. Williams, turned to Claybrook and drawled, "I don't know why Lloyd Cutler is so embarrassed about what he does."

Maybe this attorney did not know, but many consumer, environmental, and labor advocates who have been on the opposing side of Cutler's corporate clients think they know.[16] In 1966, the major U.S. automakers hired Cutler to gut the proposed motor vehicle safety legislation that was beginning to move through Congress. He began his moves, mostly unsuccessful in this case, to turn the bill into his specialty, a toothless, no-law law. His principal success was to defeat a provision, customary in safety laws, that would have made it a crime to knowingly and willfully violate federal auto safety standards or regulations. He defended his action by saying his clients—General Motors, Ford, and Chrysler—would never stoop to such criminal behavior.

Apart from such touching fealty to his paying clients into the distant future, Cutler's work absolved not only those companies from criminal liability but also thousands of other domestic and foreign vehicles and parts manufacturers, wholesalers, and retailers who might commit intentional, deliberate violations of this federal safety law. Cutler lobbied legislators to give all of these corporations immunity from criminal sanctions in a perverse kind of pro bono advocacy in order to service his few clients.

More than 100,000 Americans lost their lives and many more were seriously injured while Cutler masterminded years of delay for his auto industry paymasters to keep air bags out of any federal safety standards. Cutler even represented Ford Motor Company in the early seventies against air bags when General Motors, however briefly, was touting the devices. Cutler worked against air bags even as they were installed in some twelve thousand (mostly GM) automobiles in the seventies and demonstrated their reliability during actual crashes. (Cutler now protects himself and his family by driving a vehicle equipped with the very air bag technology he once derided.)

Representing the Automobile Manufacturers Association back in the late 1960s, Cutler persuaded the Justice Department's antitrust division to drop a pioneering criminal prosecution of the automobile industry for "product fixing"—namely, conspiring to restrain competition by agreeing to freeze technological innovations related to vehicular smog controls. Even after the antitrust division had convened a grand jury and concluded that it had "evidence to prove beyond a reasonable doubt the existence of [a] conspiracy among the auto manufacturers," Cutler managed to resolve the matter by means of a civil consent decree with the government, under which his clients admitted no wrongdoing but promised not to violate the law in the future.[17]

Cutler has bristled at being labeled a "lawyer-lobbyist" because of the term's odious association with the run-of-the-mill influence peddlers who cavort around Capitol Hill.[18] He calls attention to his support of campaign finance reform and his work representing the citizen group Common Cause years ago on this issue. He tells author Hedrick Smith that contributions to politicians by political action committees are "one step away from bribery. PACs contribute because they count on you to vote with them. You've got to take the money from PACs to survive, and then you're under obligation to them."[19] But meanwhile, when Cutler and his firm lobby to weaken the Drug Safety Act of 1962, to block auto safety standards, to advance the interests of banks, telephone companies, broadcasters, steel companies, airlines, and chemical manufacturers, their efforts are aided by political action committees and other corporate campaign contributors every step of the way. Members of Congress give Cutler their attention not just because of the wealth of his clients but also because these same clients grease the legislative wheels with their campaign dollars. Having it both ways— accepting praise for advocating reform while quietly earning big fees from the very system in need of reform—is a measure of Cutler's dexterity.

Wanting to have it both ways has led Cutler to many a paradox. One involves his association with the Lawyers Committee for Civil Rights Under Law, of which he was co-chairman at the same time that his firm represented the Lloyd Corporation before the Supreme Court, where it won a decision barring protesters from peacefully distributing leaflets on the "private property" of a large, enclosed shopping mall occupying a sprawling fifty-acre site.[20]

Many corporate attorneys appear to find nothing troubling about such inconsistencies. "In a society where [having] a lawyer matters" so much, it is "perfectly appropriate for a lawyer to represent clients whatever they may do," an ex-Food and Drug Administration official turned corporate attorney, who declined to be quoted by name, told *The Washington Post* in an article about how two former Food and Drug Administration (FDA) legal heavyweights, Richard Cooper and Arthur Levine, left their jobs and went into private practice, where they represented tobacco companies.[21]

But Cutler does not hide behind the rules of legal ethics that permit such a stance, such as Rule 1.2 of the American Bar Association's Model Rules of Professional Conduct, which provides: "A lawyer's representation of a client, including representation by appointment, does not constitute an endorsement of the client's political, economic, social or moral views or activities." On more than one occasion, Cutler has coolly declared the position he once gave an interviewer: "Listen . . . There is one point I want to make clear: We believe in the arguments that we make."[22]

Cutler's stance opens up interesting opportunities for evaluation. Did Cutler believe the argument he made on behalf of Parke, Davis and Company before a Senate investigating committee that his client had the right to avoid placing a warning in international advertisements for Chloromycetin that the drug had risks of fatal side effects for certain users—as would have been required in the United States?[23] Knowing that several hundred Americans had died in the 1950s, before the warning information was required by U.S. law, Cutler nevertheless said that his client could avoid printing the warning in any country that had no such requirement (failing to heed Elihu Root's advice to his

client: "The law lets you do it, but don't. . . . It's a rotten thing to do").
At the end of a day of hearings, which included a physician's testimony
about his own ten-year-old son's death from Chloromycetin's side effects,
Senator Gaylord Nelson, Democrat of Wisconsin, pointedly said
to Cutler, "It shocks me that you do not even blush." Somehow, Cutler's
experience running a presidential commission on street violence
could not generate a comparable concern about corporate violence.

Earlier, in the sixties, Cutler represented the Pharmaceutical Manufacturers
of America's (PMA) drive to block the McKesson and Robbins
Company's agreement to sell the government of Colombia
lower-priced generic drugs—from 80 to 90 percent cheaper than the
brand-name medicines for some important antibiotics. Senator Nelson's
investigator, economist Benjamin Gordon, believed that the effect
of the PMA's opposition to generic drug marketing would be to
deny necessary medicines to large numbers of impoverished people in
South America. More than ten years later, Cutler was asked what had
finally happened with respect to McKesson's proposed deal with
Colombia. He replied, "I don't know; you see, I was only outside counsel
to PMA."[24] In Cutler's long career and within his large firm of attorneys,
this episode is only one of dozens that are handled in routine
daily work, where a situational ethic of amorality is just part of being a
"professional."

In the case of the National Commission for Housing Partnership
(NCHP), Cutler adroitly spotted an opening to gain a long-standing
client. In 1967, President Johnson established the Commission on
Urban Housing to develop ways to increase low- and moderate-income
housing. He asked Edgar Kaiser, head of Kaiser Industries and a Cutler
client, to be the chairman. Kaiser then asked Cutler, who sat on the
Kaiser board of directors, to be the committee's special counsel. Over
the objections of the committee staff, Cutler pushed through a proposal
whereby wealthy investors in housing efforts would receive very large
tax write-offs. In a short time Congress passed the NCHP, whose promotional
brochures then attracted partnerships by openly touting the
"tax savings generated." Although Cutler presented his firm's efforts in
this matter as pro bono publico, in reality he simply reduced his hourly
billing by about 30 percent during the gestation period. By 1971,
NCHP was paying Wilmer, Cutler & Pickering the firm's standard
rates. Cutler had conceived and lobbied into law an institution that became
a client, built on the activities of another client, Edgar Kaiser.
Cutler subsequently became a paid director of NCHP. Paul Nelson,
chief of staff for the House Banking Committee for more than 20 years
(through 1987), was not impressed with NCHP, which he called "only

a gimmick, a subsidy for big corporations, another tax write-off, some-thing they could put in their public relations brochure to the effect, 'Look how we are helping the poor people.' "[25] But to his competitors in Washington's legal business, Cutler's work was a masterstroke—con-verting, as one attorney put it, *pro bono publico* into a permanent *pro bono privato* client propped up by an ongoing corporate welfare scheme.

Another form of giveaway of the public's assets emerged with Cut-ler's recent Canadian client, Barrick Goldstrike Mines, Inc., which lo-cated $10 billion worth of gold on federal public land in Nevada. Prior to joining the Clinton administration, Cutler pressed Bruce Babbitt, Clinton's secretary of the interior, to sell the land above the gold de-posits for the tiny sum of $9,765—a price of about five dollars per acre, authorized by the antiquated 1872 Mining Act. Babbitt denounced the giveaway of the people's gold and urged the passage of pending reform legislation in Congress to give the government a more realistic value for such lucrative public properties. But Congress did not act and, in May 1994, while Cutler was serving his dual roles as White House counsel and an attorney with Wilmer, Cutler, Secretary Babbitt had to sell the billions in gold to Barrick Goldstrike at lower than fire sale prices.[26] We were unable to determine whether Cutler recused himself or played a role in the matter. Apparently, Cutler, who favored Stephen Breyer over Babbitt for the Supreme Court vacancy, believes in his arguments here because he has never spoken out against the ridiculous policy of surrendering what belongs to all Americans to do-mestic or even foreign companies essentially for nothing in return—other than leaving taxpayers with the burden of cleaning up the environmental wreckage after such hard rock mines are exhausted.

An overview of Cutler's cumulative impact, along with that of other corporate attorneys working similar territories at the seat of the national or state governments, involves more than simply describing client-by-client advocacies. With relentless focus and resources, the Lloyd Cutlers of the legal world work to indenture government and the people to large corporations, to have government subsidize in many ways entire industries, to compromise the arm's-length relationship be-tween government and business by systemically undermining the rule of just law that is supposed to protect wronged or harmed citizens. By complex means, public assets, from natural resources to medical re-search and development, are given away to private monopoly owner-ship and/or control. Neutering the purpose of the law vis-à-vis corporations—as with health and safety regulations—yet keeping its pretense to mislead public expectations—as he has done particularly in the auto and drug areas—is a specialty at which Cutler has excelled, but he has had many imitators and competitors. All the while, innocent people, many of whom have never heard of Cutler or his colleagues, have suffered in the workplace, marketplace, and environment. Michael Pertschuk, the normally reserved former chairman of the Federal Trade Commission, once said of Cutler after years of dealing with him when Pertschuk served as general counsel to the Senate Commerce Committee, "He is clearly a very skilled advocate and a real technician at drafting amendment after amendment. He's a genius, but an evil genius. The role Lloyd Cutler plays reflects poorly on the legal profession. . . . It is not in the best tradition of the practice."[27]

Attorneys like Lloyd Cutler matter intimately and often adversely to the health, safety, and economic well-being of many people here and abroad. They matter to the quality of the air, water, soil, and food. They matter to the state of our democracy and the integrity of the law and its enforcement. They matter to future generations, who will inherit the harmful results of their labors.

In calling for a more vigorous public interest law commitment back in the 1970s, Antioch Law School co-deans Edgar and Jean Cahn made the point that law firms "already operate as the makers of public policy—with regard to the operation and design of the legal system, and with respect to official government policy."[28] They might have added that hundreds of these corporate lawyers go into government, where they directly shape policy, during a few years of on-the-job training and influence gathering, before returning to corporate practice with more salable skills and contacts.

Corporate power lawyers are not just any citizens equipped only with the influence of their facts and arguments. They are paid to be what *Fortune* magazine once called Lloyd Cutler, "the very model of a modern legal conduit,"[29] for the greatest powers in the private sector—the giant, multinational corporations spanning the globe and transcending national jurisdictions and gaining unaccountable advantages. The paradoxes and seeming contradictions of Cutler's fluctuations between commercial lucre and his shorter government service and pro bono stints have one singular theme—the supremacy of his law firm's role as an architect of the corporate state from whence he derived his power, his wealth, and his status.

THE POWER LAW LANDSCAPE

We refer to the subjects of this book as "power lawyers" because, like Lloyd Cutler, they serve the interests of society's most powerful entities and therefore are themselves extremely influential. Some of these at-torneys work in the in-house legal departments of major corporations and others labor at relatively small, specialized firms, but many congregate in giant law firms with hundreds of attorneys. The power of these major corporate firms is measured by their size, the money they make, the clients whose purposes they further, and, frequently, how far their attorneys are willing to stretch the ethical envelope.

For example, Baker & McKenzie, the world's largest law firm, has 1,642 lawyers, with more than fifty offices throughout the United States and the world: New York, Chicago, San Francisco, Mexico City, Caracas, London, Frankfurt, Warsaw, Cairo, Bangkok, Hong Kong, Sydney—the firm even had offices in Ho Chi Minh City and Hanoi, Vietnam, before U.S. trade restrictions were lifted. Another corporate powerhouse, Jones, Day, Reavis & Pogue, boasts 1,072 lawyers in eighteen offices across the globe, while Skadden, Arps, Slate, Meagher & Flom has 968 lawyers in twenty-one offices, with 552 of them in Skadden, Arps's New York headquarters alone. About twenty U.S. firms have five hundred or more lawyers, and 150 firms have two hundred or more lawyers.[30] And these figures don't include the thousands of paralegals, secretaries, librarians, business managers, clerks, messengers, dining room cooks, and other personnel who work for the big firms.

The clients of the major corporate law firms are among the more substantial companies in the world. Skadden, Arps has represented, among others, Mobil, Dupont, Bethlehem Steel, Scott Paper, Honeywell, Union Pacific, Bell Atlantic, Nynex, Time Warner, Colgate-Palmolive, Kmart, Pepsi Co., and Tyson Foods. The clients of New York's 262-lawyer Cravath, Swaine & Moore have included IBM, Ford, Bristol-Myers Squibb, Nestlé, Chemical Bank, Morgan Stanley, Time Warner, Westinghouse/CBS, General Electric, Shell Oil, and Ashland Oil. The client list at Chicago-based, 401-attorney Kirkland & Ellis includes General Motors, Amoco, Dow Chemical, Motorola, Federal Express, and Colgate-Palmolive. And in Washington, D.C., 301-lawyer Covington & Burling has represented clients like Exxon, AT&T, IBM, Procter & Gamble, Boeing, United Technologies, Goodyear, Archer-Daniels-Midland, Eli Lilly, and Dupont, plus a who's who of the tobacco industry: the Tobacco Institute, the American Tobacco Company, Brown & Williamson, Liggett & Myers, Lorillard, Philip Morris, and R.J. Reynolds.[31]

Big money is made practicing power law. Legal services in the United States produce more than $108 billion in revenue annually,[32] and the one hundred largest-grossing law firms earn about $15 billion of that total.[33] The latest annual figures from Skadden, Arps, the top-earning firm, show $582 million in gross revenues, producing $820,000 in profits per partner—*partner* is the term most law firms use to describe a lawyer with an ownership interest in the firm, while the term *associate* refers to a lawyer working at the firm who has no such ownership interest but instead is a wage-earning employee. ("Profits per partner" means the firm's net operating income divided by the number of partners.) Cravath, Swaine & Moore had $186 million in gross revenues, creating $1,225,000 in profits for each of the firm's sixty-nine partners. (More revenue figures are provided in Chapter 7 and Appendix 1.)

In-house corporate counsel—lawyers who work full-time for the corporations they serve, rather than for outside law firms—can do even better. Stephen L. Hammerman, general counsel at the investment firm Merrill Lynch & Company, earned $2,800,000 in 1994. The general counsel for media conglomerate Viacom, Philippe P. Dauman, earned $2,270,692. Peter R. Haje, general counsel for another media giant, Time Warner, received $1,650,000. Benjamin W. Heineman, Jr., general counsel at weapons maker General Electric, made $1,427,500. Murray H. Bring, general counsel for cigarette maker Philip Morris, got $1,135,962. And these figures do not include additional compensation such as stock options or executive perquisites.[34]

By contrast, federal trial judges earn $133,600 per year, with state trial judges generally making between $95,000 and $125,000. Meanwhile, lawyers working for nonprofit public interest organizations earn as little as $20,000 and rarely earn more than $75,000, even after decades of work on behalf of civil rights, environmental safety, or economic justice.

Even the youngest and least experienced power lawyers make a lot of money. Attorneys hired directly out of law school by big law firms generally receive very high pay for an entry-level position, with beginning lawyers at top New York firms earning about $85,000.[35] In addition, they often receive special perquisites, such as expensive meals (billed to clients) and memberships in clubs, as well as benefits such as insurance and pension plans.

Law firm associates usually have to work very hard for this money, sometimes putting in six or seven twelve-hour days a week. The carrot that keeps them toiling so intently is the promise of a partnership, where the real influence and money await. Because there are fewer partnership positions than there are associates, only the most industrious—which mostly has come to mean the highest-billing—associates find this pot of gold at the end of the rainbow. In this intensely competitive atmosphere, idealism and rigorous adherence to professional ethics can easily take a backseat to simply getting the job done.

Which brings us back again to money. That is what the world of corporate lawyers and the law they practice is essentially about. Making money by helping clients make it and making money by helping clients keep it. There is, of course, nothing inherently wrong or unethical in making money, nor in representing businesses that exist to make a profit. However, there is a trap here for the unwary. When money and power become the central pursuits of one's work, when the problems and yearnings of average people are rarely encountered (except, perhaps, in opposition on the other side of a courtroom or conference table, or in representing the occasional client pro bono), as is often the case with big business lawyers, it is easy to lose sight of the fundamental values of fairness and equity that our system of laws is designed to foster. When lawyers push these values aside, justice is reduced to a disposable commodity.

A CYNICAL CLIMATE

Why is all of this important? As we shall discuss in the following pages, the legal talent, depth of resources, and the willingness, if not eagerness, of many power lawyers to do whatever it takes to win is a potent tool. Their tactics are a primary cause for the scandalously high costs associated with the legal system, and the often unreasonable and frustrating delays in bringing legal controversies to closure. These tactics also foster the worrisome disdain and animus of the public toward a profession that in a better world would be looked to as defenders of freedom and justice.

It is no secret that the legal system, whose quarters are drawn by unbridled power, is in disarray. Indeed, courts and government agencies are increasingly seen by the public, commentators, cultural observers, and lawyers alike as dysfunctional and in need of reform. Michael S. Josephson is a lawyer who runs a Southern California–based ethics institute that advises federal and state governments, among others, on ethics issues.[36] He believes that the way some attorneys approach their work is a major cause of the problem. "Lawyers are competitors," he told us. "They tend to look at what they do as a sport. The way law is practiced today is to get away with what you can. Why? Because money is the only way to judge." This is especially true for the large corporate firms. "The big firms are doing the bad things because the big firms have the big cases," Josephson said.[37] Money has become the mother's milk of systemic abuse of the legal system, and corporate lawyers deal with issues involving the largest amounts of money.

Others share Josephson's concern. Attorney Steve France is the editor of *Bank Lawyer Liability*, a professional journal directed at lawyers and executives in the banking industry. He has thought and written extensively about issues relating to legal ethics and the big firms. He is disturbed by the ethical atmosphere not only in the major firms but also among the corporate managers who hire them. "It is vital to the efficient working of the capitalist system that there be some sense of honor and ethics," he told us. But, he says, business executives instead "want lawyers with guts of steel and no morals. Under this theory, lawyers are machines—you just point them in the direction you want and away they go."

France says that such attitudes "sap the vitality of the business world in the long term" and "take advantage of people in the short term."[38] This stick-it-to-the-other-guy approach to law, especially if the other guy is weaker and perceived to have fewer resources, creates an attitude that often condones misbehavior and thereby extracts a terrible price, often in the lives of ordinary people made unjustly miserable by the blitzkrieg methods of power lawyers.

Harvard law professor Mary Ann Glendon has written about these important issues in her book, *A Nation Under Lawyers*,[39] in which she reflected, perhaps too nostalgically, on the old virtue of practicing law "in the spirit of public service," a virtue that has largely been replaced by an ethic that places "zealous representation" as the lawyer's principal responsibility. According to Glendon, this approach allows lawyers to follow "the course of least resistance" by subordinating their public-service duties, transforming lawyers into "friends-of-the-client." Consequently, the lawyer becomes a "virtuoso of single-mindedness—like a professional soldier or the surgeon who drapes all but the affected part of the patient under a sheet." Substantially relieved of the abstract obligations attendant to being an officer of the court, the lawyer is free to be self-serving or, to put it more tactfully, pragmatic. He or she can unquestioningly pursue the client's bidding, regardless of its propriety, and still, seemingly, get a good night's sleep. As this book will show, her description is particularly apt when applied to today's power lawyers, whose scale of temptations could only be in the avaricious dreams of yesterday's counselors.

This is cause for alarm. Unless tempered by adherence to the higher calling of professional honor and restraint, unquestioning client loyalty can cause profoundly adverse consequences. The lawyer devolves into the proverbial hired gun, where, as in the old Westerns, an ethic of might-makes-right prevails. Reputations are made, not by doing right, not by avoiding wrongdoing, not by wise counsel, but by winning. The system descends into legal Darwinism, as natural selection increasingly favors those clients with the most money to spend on lawyers willing to do whatever it takes to please the patron.

In such an atmosphere, those without wealth or influence simply cannot compete, and they avoid using the legal system. Justice grows scarce and cruelties abound. A good place to test this proposition is the decades-long struggle by health advocates and cancer victims to hold tobacco companies accountable for their promotion and marketing of cigarettes.

THE CASE OF THE OUTRAGED JUDGE

Peter F. Rossi, a Wayne, New Jersey, business executive, began smoking cigarettes at age fourteen and continued for forty-one years, until his 1982 death from lung cancer. In 1984, his daughter, Susan Haines, filed suit in the United States District Court for the District of New Jersey against Liggett Group, Inc., Loew's Theatres Incorporated, R.J. Reynolds Tobacco Co., and Philip Morris, Inc., the makers of the various brands Rossi had smoked over the years, alleging that they had misled smokers like Rossi about the risks of tobacco.

The case was assigned to Judge H. Lee Sarokin, who had been appointed to the federal bench in 1979. Haines's attorneys, Marc Edell and Cynthia Walters, charged that the tobacco industry had for many years engaged in fraudulent conduct by actively concealing known dangers associated with smoking. The tobacco industry lawyers, from several New Jersey corporate firms, waged a fierce fight, as tobacco lawyers have in suits brought by smokers all over the country. Conceding nothing, they fought particularly hard to avoid the disclosure of documents.

As lengthy pretrial proceedings in the case went forward, Edell and Walters began to examine the role of the Council for Tobacco Research (CTR), an organization created and funded by tobacco interests. CTR presented itself to the public as an independent research institute that objectively investigated the health impact of smoking. Edell and Walters contended that, in fact, the CTR had only one goal: to cover up the truth about the harmful effects of tobacco use.

To substantiate their contention about the CTR, Edell and Walters sought access to internal tobacco industry documents that they believed would reveal that the industry itself saw the CTR as a propaganda organization. Specifically, they contended that the documents would show that CTR established a "special projects" section, directed by industry lawyers rather than scientists, where data considered to be harmful to tobacco interests would be placed and protected from public disclosure through claims of "attorney-client privilege"—a legal doctrine that protects communications between a client and lawyer from disclosure. The purpose of this doctrine is to encourage clients to be candid and thereby allow lawyers to provide informed advice, but Edell and Walters claimed that in this case the industry abused the privilege by bringing in lawyers to "special project" efforts solely to take advantage of the doctrine and keep records sealed. They claimed, in effect, that the tobacco industry, in its careful structuring of CTR, wanted to have it both ways: For purposes of publicly releasing credible studies on smoking and health, it was an independent, scientific research organization. For purposes of keeping unfavorable research results and communications secret, it was, instead, a law firm, bound by privilege to avoid disclosure.

Indeed, the tobacco industry lawyers argued strenuously that records concerning the "special projects" section *were* protected from disclosure by the privilege, because tobacco lawyers in the past had influenced decisions as to which CTR research efforts should be funded by industry contributions.

But the attorney-client privilege is not absolute. The law recognizes a so-called crime/fraud exception, which holds that a claim of privilege must be rejected where an attorney's advice was obtained for the purpose of furthering an ongoing criminal or fraudulent scheme.[40] Edell and Walters argued that the CTR special projects group was established precisely to hide evidence of the harmful effects of smoking and that, therefore, the crime/fraud exception applied to the documents in dispute.

The two sides wrestled over the issue for more than a year. The dispute was so complicated and time-consuming—involving more than fifteen hundred documents—that the court appointed an outside lawyer as a "special master" to examine the materials and make recommendations. The master's findings were then reviewed by a magistrate judge, a judicial officer who often handles pretrial matters for federal district judges. The magistrate judge concluded that the crime/fraud exception did not apply and, accordingly, that Haines's lawyers could not see the documents. Haines appealed to Judge Sarokin. By now it was 1991—seven years after she had filed the lawsuit.

Sarokin was no newcomer to tobacco litigation. In addition to the Haines case, he had presided over the case of *Cipollone v. Liggett Group*, in which Rose Cipollone, a smoker for forty-two years, had raised similar claims against the industry, pointing to decades of industry assertions about the safety of smoking cigarettes.

In a deposition, Cipollone testified that from 1942 to 1955 she smoked Chesterfield brand cigarettes, made by Liggett, in part because Chesterfield advertisements stated that the cigarettes were "mild," which she took to mean safe. Indeed, the tobacco companies sued in the case did not dispute that Rose Cipollone had heard the following claims made in Chesterfield advertising in the 1950s:[41]

—"PLAY SAFE Smoke Chesterfield.

NOSE, THROAT, and Accessory Organs not Adversely Affected by Smoking Chesterfields. . . . A responsible consulting organization has reported the results of a continuing study by a competent medical specialist and his staff on the effects of smoking Chesterfield cigarettes. . . . The medical specialist, after a thorough examination of every member of the [study] group, stated, "It is my opinion that the ears, nose, throat and accessory organs of all participating subjects examined by me were not adversely affected in the six-month period by the cigarettes provided." (Print ad, 1952)

—"[Chesterfields contain] PURE . . . MOISTENING proved by over 40 years of continuous use in U.S.A. tobacco products as entirely safe for use in the mouth. . . . Scientists from Leading Universities Make Sure that Chesterfield Contains Only Ingredients that Give You the Best Possible Smoke." (Print ad, 1952)

—"After 8 months, the medical specialist reports that he observed no adverse effects to the nose, throat and sinuses of the group who were smoking Chesterfields. I'd say that means real mildness." (Television ad, 1950s)

—"You hear stuff all the time about 'cigarettes are harmful to you' this and that and the other thing. [The medical specialist's study] ought to make you feel better if you've had any worries at all about it. I never did. I smoke two or three packs of these things every day. I feel pretty good. I don't know, I never did believe they did you any harm and now, we've got the proof. So—Chesterfields are the cigarette for you to smoke, be they regular or king-size." (Arthur Godfrey, on the "Arthur Godfrey and His Friends" radio show, sponsored by Chesterfield, 1952)

In 1955, Rose Cipollone switched to another Liggett brand, L & M filter cigarettes. Liggett advertised this brand as having a "miracle tip" that was "just what the doctor ordered!" The filter tip, according to ads, "removes the heavy particles, leaving you a Light and Mild smoke." Cipollone changed brands several times after that, smoking one to two packs per day. In 1981 she was diagnosed with lung cancer, and in 1982 her lung was removed. She continued to smoke in secret because, she later testified, she was "addicted." She died in October 1984, at age fifty-eight, from the lung cancer.

Cipollone's husband, Antonio, also represented by Marc Edell and Cynthia Walters, prevailed after a four-month 1988 trial on some claims, winning a $400,000 verdict. It was the first products liability verdict ever against the tobacco companies, after decades in which they had not only avoided any judgments but also refused to pay a single dollar to settle any case against them brought by smokers. But the Third Circuit Court of Appeals, buying the arguments of aggressive power lawyers from firms like 200-attorney Shook, Hardy and Bacon of Kansas City and 329-attorney Arnold & Porter of Washington, D.C., ordered a new trial.[42] The case was pending before the Supreme Court of the United States.

Reviewing the materials examined by the magistrate judge in the Haines case, as well as materials he knew well from the Cipollone case, Judge Sarokin came to a firm conclusion: The evidence did tend to prove that the tobacco industry had perpetrated a fraud on the public when it claimed that CTR was an independent organization. Attorneys for the tobacco industry had indeed established a special projects division connected to the CTR with the intent to use claims of attorney-client privilege to shield documents deemed harmful to tobacco interests. The special projects records supported Haines's contentions about the explicit and pervasive nature of the alleged fraud.

In a decision issued on February 6, 1992, Judge Sarokin ruled that the crime/fraud exception compelled the release of, at the very least, five CTR-related documents he had reviewed. He also announced that he would appoint a new special master to determine what additional CTR documents should be released.[43]

In support of his ruling, Judge Sarokin quoted from some of the very documents the tobacco lawyers wanted so desperately to keep secret. One document, minutes of a September 10, 1981, meeting of the Committee of General Counsel—top tobacco-industry attorneys—included a discussion of the CTR and the various projects it commissioned dealing with the relationship between smoking and health. According to Sarokin's opinion, the document quoted one participant as saying:

When we started the CTR Special Projects, the idea was that the scientific director of CTR would review a project. If he liked it, it was a CTR special project. If he did not like it, then it became a lawyers' special project. . . . We wanted to protect it under the lawyers. We did not want it out in the open.

Concluding that "no evidence could be more damning," the judge proceeded to quote from other CTR documents he had reviewed. One such document, a memorandum in a CTR file from one R. B. Seligman, recounted a November 1978 presentation in New York:

> CTR began as an organization called Tobacco Industry Research Council (TIRC). *It was set up as an industry "shield" in 1954.* That was the year statistical accusations relating smoking to diseases were leveled at the industry [and] litigation began. . . . *CTR has helped our legal counsel by giving advise and technical information, which was needed in court trials. CTR has provided spokesmen for the industry at Congressional hearings. The monies spent on CTR provides a base for introduction of witnesses . . .*
> *On these projects, CTR has acted as a front;* however there are times when CTR has been reluctant to serve in that capacity . . .
> [Emphasis in original.]

Judge Sarokin held that, in light of this evidence

> A jury might reasonably conclude that the industry's announcement of proposed independent research into the dangers of smoking and its promise to disclose its findings was nothing but a public relations ploy—a fraud—to deflect the growing evidence against the industry, to encourage smokers to continue and non-smokers to begin, and to reassure the public that adverse information would be disclosed.

Judge Sarokin was clearly outraged by the apparent systematic plan pursued by the tobacco industry and its power lawyers to shield materials from disclosure, a plan that the industry, through its lawyers' skilled advocacy, was now seeking to bring to fruition by claiming attorney-client privilege. Thus his opinion began with the following emphatic statement:

> All too often in the choice between the physical health of consumers and the financial well-being of business, concealment is chosen over disclosure, sales over safety, and money over morality. Who are these persons who knowingly and secretly decide to put the buying public at risk solely for the purpose of making profits and who believe that illness and death of consumers is an appropriate cost of their own prosperity!

As the following facts disclose, despite some rising pretenders, the tobacco industry may be the king of concealment and disinformation.

Judge Sarokin did not rule conclusively that the tobacco interests and their lawyers actually had perpetuated a fraud on the public. That would be a matter for the jury. But, in order to decide whether the crime/fraud exception applied to the disputed documents, he had been required to make—he had no choice but to make—a preliminary determination regarding the defendants' conduct. And his decision opened the way for Haines to obtain industry documents about the CTR that presumably would assist her at trial.

It was an important victory for Haines, and a major blow to the tobacco industry's effort to keep their activities a secret. But it was short-lived.

The defendant cigarette makers decided to pursue an extraordinary remedy called mandamus—asking the U.S. Court of Appeals for the Third Circuit to immediately reverse Judge Sarokin's pretrial ruling. Appellate courts rarely grant requests for mandamus; the normal procedure is to let a case run its course and review the decisions of the trial judge only after a judgment has been issued by the judge or jury. But there was much at stake: If Haines's lawyers obtained the documents it might hurt the tobacco companies' defense severely—and the same files, once introduced in open court, could cause the industry harm in some of the other fifty to sixty tobacco suits that were pending across the country.

But the tobacco makers wanted more than just the extraordinary mandamus order. They wanted finally to achieve a goal they had been pursuing for five years: to get rid of Judge Sarokin by claiming he was biased against them, even though he had ruled in their favor on many of the key issues in the tobacco cases.[44] They had tried to get Sarokin removed from the Cipollone case, but there the Third Circuit had rejected their claim that Sarokin was biased.[45] This time, however, they had something firm to latch onto: the judge's words crowning the industry "the king of concealment and disinformation." The judge had expressed judicial outrage at what he had seen in the confidential tobacco company documents. Now, the tobacco lawyers were going to use his anger to argue that he could not be trusted to be fair and impartial in the case.

To pursue their "fire the judge" strategy, the tobacco companies brought in new lawyers, the 190-attorney Philadelphia firm Schnader,

Harrison, Segal & Lewis. A firm spokesperson recently described Schnader, Harrison to us as "a full service litigation firm with clients from every segment of commerce, ranging from tobacco interests to transportation companies to the asbestos industry." (The firm also represents the government in cases involving the savings and loan scandal aftermath, charging taxpayers more than $10 million in fees and expenses in 1993 alone.[46]) The man to argue the case was Schnader, Harrison partner Arlin M. Adams, who had recently retired as a federal judge serving on . . . the Third Circuit Court of Appeals.

By the time the Third Circuit heard arguments in the Haines case on August 7, 1992, a dramatic development had occurred in the Cipollone suit. The Third Circuit had previously ruled that health warning labels on cigarette packages and advertising, required by federal law since 1965, barred Cipollone from claiming that the defendants had failed to warn her, after that date, of the risks of smoking. But on June 24, 1992, the U.S. Supreme Court ruled, by a 7–2 vote, that the federal warning labels did not excuse tobacco companies from liability to smokers for their injuries.[47] (Both Peter Rossi and Rose Cipollone started smoking long before the 1965 imposition of warning labels, so some of their claims did not even depend on winning this issue.) The ruling was somewhat complicated—it held that smokers could pursue some types of claims but not others—but it strengthened the case not only of Antonio Cipollone but also other plaintiffs, like Susan Haines. The stakes had been raised, and the companies appeared, for the first time, to be in danger of losing some ground. But it was not to last.

The appellate court decision in the Haines case, issued on September 4, 1992, gave the tobacco companies and their lawyers everything they wanted. Writing for the court of appeals, Judge Ruggero J. Aldisert ruled that Judge Sarokin, in applying the crime/fraud exception, had improperly relied in part on documents he had obtained in another case—the Cipollone matter—rather than simply reviewing the record that was before the magistrate judge in the Haines case. And while the appellate court rejected the notion that Judge Sarokin was "incapable of discharging judicial duties free from bias or prejudice," it granted the tobacco industry's request to remove him from the case because, the court concluded, the opening sentences of Judge Sarokin's opinion destroyed the "appearance of impartiality" expected of federal judges. The court ordered the case assigned to a new judge, who would be charged with redeciding the dispute over the special project documents.[48]

For Haines and her lawyers, it was a devastating loss. After years of effort to get the right to review the documents, they were back to square one, facing more months or even years refighting a battle over document review that they thought had already been won.

Harvard law professor Laurence Tribe, a leading constitutional law expert who had successfully represented the Cipollones before the Supreme Court (rejecting a seven-figure offer, conveyed by an Arnold & Porter lawyer, to instead represent the tobacco companies in the case), told *The New York Times* that nothing in Judge Sarokin's decision in the Haines case warranted the Third Circuit's decision to remove him. He added, "Judge Sarokin's familiarity with the details means that replacing him with a relative novice is likely to be good news for the industry, not because he is biased but because he's harder to deceive than someone who's new to this material."[49]

Soon the industry got more good news. On September 11, 1992, Judge Sarokin issued a memorandum announcing that, in light of the Third Circuit's order removing him from the Haines case, he was voluntarily recusing himself from the Cipollone case. He defended his previous decisions, stating, "I sincerely believe that all of the rulings I have made in these cases involving the tobacco industry have been based upon the evidence presented to me over a decade, and not upon any predisposition or bias." Commenting on the Third Circuit's decision to remove him from the case, he wrote that he could not understand how merely expressing his legal conclusions "in strong terms" could demonstrate bias. He added, "I fear for the independence of the judiciary if a powerful litigant can cause the removal of a judge for speaking the truth based upon the evidence." He said that, in the end, he was recusing himself from the Cipollone matter, "not because of any bias or lack of impartiality, but out of my profound respect for the law and our judicial system."[50]

These decisions proved to be the last straw for the law firm in which Marc Edell and Cynthia Walters were partners, the seventy-six-attorney firm Budd Larner Gross Rosenbaum Greenberg & Sade. The New Jersey firm had taken on eight cases on behalf of smokers, working, as lawyers for victims often do, on a contingency basis—that is, the firm would receive no payment from the clients until and unless the tobacco defendants paid them compensation, at which time the firm would get a percentage. The Budd Larner firm had already incurred more than $500,000 in out-of-pocket expenses and another $3.75 million in attorney and paralegal hours working on the cases. Four years of lawyer time were spent on witness depositions—taking of pretrial testimony—alone.

With the tobacco industry's power lawyers continuing their tenacious efforts to resist disclosure of damaging information, one partner foresaw a "bottomless pit" of litigation. The only judgment obtained so far, $400,000 in the Cipollone case, had been sent back for a new trial. The Supreme Court's *Cipollone* decision offered hope, but also guaranteed litigation over the complex legal issues it raised. Judge Sarokin was out of the picture, and new judges would have to be brought up to speed. Moreover, a former Budd Larner partner told a reporter, the tobacco cases were damaging the firm's entire practice, which focused mainly on work on behalf of defendants, like manufacturers sued for asbestos-related diseases. "There was a direct relationship between what I had in my [bank account] and Marc Edell," said the former partner, who claimed that tobacco companies had influenced the decision of two Fortune 500 companies not to hire Budd Larner.[51]

At the firm's urging, six of its eight tobacco case clients, including Rose Cipollone's son (whose father had died in 1990), promptly agreed to drop their lawsuits voluntarily—forever terminating their right to seek damages from the tobacco companies. A seventh client refused to drop her case, but, over her objections, a New Jersey state judge allowed Budd Larner to withdraw from representation.[52]

The tobacco companies had once again gained the upper hand, and their attorneys gloated over their renewed good fortune. Charles Wall, vice president and associate general counsel of Philip Morris, said, "Edell has said [pursuing the tobacco cases] is not economically feasible, and I take him at his word. He doesn't believe there is a return on his investment." He expressed confidence that Budd Larner's decision would influence plaintiffs' attorneys in the remaining sixty or so tobacco suits around the country.[53] Liggett Group's general counsel and senior vice president, Josiah Murray, bragged about the industry's firm stance against compensating victims of smoking: "The decision to dismiss the Cipollone case does not surprise us. For four decades the cigarette industry has been successful in defending itself in these cases, never settling nor paying any damages or compensation."[54]

But Susan Haines refused to go away quietly. The Philadelphia woman saw no reason to retreat from her claims, backed by the document excerpts Judge Sarokin had revealed, that the tobacco companies had deliberately deceived its customers. And she saw no justification for Budd Larner backing out—the firm had been promised a substantial share of any judgment in exchange for its representation, and a deal was a deal. It couldn't bail out just because the deal no longer seemed like a good one. But instead of Budd Larner seeing it her way and assisting her continued fight against the tobacco companies, the firm fought Haines. Over Haines's objection, Budd Larner demanded to be relieved from the case.

On January 26, 1993, district judge Alfred Lechner, Jr., who had re-placed Sarokin, issued an opinion siding with Haines. Budd Larner could not withdraw from the case.[55] The firm filed an appeal with the Third Circuit, in which it complained that the legal firepower of the tobacco industry was simply too great to defeat:

> The tobacco industry's defense strategy is to resist discov-ery, appeal virtually every adverse decision and avoid settle-ment. The industry does everything it can to cause plaintiff's attorneys to spend a great deal of money. This is revealed by the tobacco companies' own statements.

The Budd Larner brief quoted from an April 1988 speech by an R.J. Reynolds attorney, one Michael Jordan, who boasted about ten Cali-fornia lawsuits that smoking victims were about to dismiss voluntarily. Jordan said:

> The aggressive posture we have taken regarding depositions and discovery in general continues to make these cases ex-tremely burdensome and expensive for plaintiffs' lawyers, par-ticularly sole practitioners. To paraphrase General Patton, the way we won these cases was not by spending all of Reynolds' money, but by making the other son of a bitch spend all of his.

The power lawyers had won another round. The Budd Larner firm had surrendered, worn down by the litigation tactics of its opponents. Six of its eight clients had acquiesced in the firm's withdrawal, and the other two had ended up fighting Budd Larner, rather than the tobacco defendants, in court. The special projects documents, except for the few partially exposed by Judge Sarokin, remained locked in industry vaults. The Budd Larner cases, and perhaps many of the others filed against the industry, would be decided not on the merits of the claims but rather on the balance of legal firepower between individual smokers and big to-bacco companies, which, unlike their mortal human challengers, have perpetual lives (called corporate charters). In short, no contest.

The Budd Larner cases are no anomaly. They fit squarely within the tradition of decades of legal battles fought over tobacco liability. The industry's fierce legal tactics were well described in a 1987 *Wall Street Journal* article:[56]

> Tobacco companies have put a legion of lawyers on their pay-rolls. At last count, more than 70 law firms had been hired, in-

cluding some of the most prominent in the country. Tobacco companies also have retained psychologists, economists, physicians and medical researchers to testify at trials. . . .

[T]he industry's forces resemble an army perpetually on red alert. Investigators comb plaintiffs' neighborhoods and workplaces for gossipy tidbits that might be useful to the lawyers. Lawyers stage secret full-dress mock trials to test the reaction of lay people to the industry's legal arguments. Before actual trials, pollsters take the public pulse on issues such as cigarette advertising, information that might be helpful to lawyers in picking a jury.

The *Journal* article reported on the case of Dolly Root, who sued General Cigar & Tobacco Company after her husband, a pipe smoker, died of heart failure and lung cancer in 1983. She dropped her suit after a two-year struggle because she could no longer bear the oppressive litigation tactics of General Cigar. The company's lawyers spent days questioning her about such personal topics as her infertility and her son's 1986 suicide. They also asked Root how she felt when she found out that her daughter-in-law had been pregnant when she married Root's son, a fact, if true, of which Root was not even aware. General Cigar's attorney on the case, Charles Breyer (brother of Supreme Court Justice Stephen Breyer), told the *Journal* that it was "entirely proper to ask questions about any stressful or potentially stressful situations in this family" because stress might have caused Mr. Root's death.[57] But such limitless interrogations also have the undeniable effect of making it burdensome and stressful for tobacco victims to press on with their lawsuits.

As of this writing, the tobacco companies still have not paid a dollar—any judgments against them have been reversed on appeal or are presently being appealed.

This is the reality of our legal system that the public rarely sees in any detail. Notwithstanding the extravagant claims of advocates of restrictions on personal injury or tort law, corporations aren't victims of the legal system. Far from it. The reverse is often the case. The legal playing field is tilted steeply in favor of corporate wealth and power. Big corporations have more resources than sick or injured individuals and small businesses. Corporations are artificial legal entities; time delays usually work to their advantage, weakening and demoralizing the mortal opposition. A good power lawyer with enough resources to spend can delay a case for years, or even decades. Indeed, as may happen in the case of Susan Haines, corporate lawyers can keep a case from ever coming to trial.

This disparity of influence suits power lawyers just fine, and not only because it makes their jobs easier. Usually, corporate lawyers are paid by the hour, with fees ranging up to more than $500 per hour for top big-firm partners.[58] That means the more work the lawyers do, the more complicated they make a litigation, the more money they make. Attorney John W. Toothman, who owns a Virginia company, the Devil's Advocate, that audits law firm bills for the benefit of clients, says, "Typically, big law firms in a civil dispute will file motion after motion. Some of these motions can pend for years. Such delays encourage disputes which, in turn, lead to further delay and further disputes." By gumming up the works, corporate lawyers can turn their litigation cases into perpetual billing machines. (See Chapter 7.)

Postscript: Susan Haines ended her appeals court fight with the Budd Larner firm in 1995 when she hired a new lawyer. The case is back before the district court.

Notwithstanding its victory over the Budd Larner attorneys, the tobacco industry continues to face damaging disclosures and pressure on a number of other fronts. In 1992, federal prosecutors launched criminal investigations of the industry, and press sources say these probes were initiated after law enforcement officials read the excerpts of industry documents revealed for the first time in Judge Sarokin's opinion in the Haines case.[59] This federal investigation is continuing, with grand juries impaneled in five jurisdictions. On August 10, 1995, the Food and Drug Administration for the first time announced plans to regulate cigarette companies, issuing proposed rules aimed at reducing sales to minors. (The industry, in aggressively challenging these regulations, was represented by Richard A. Merrill, a partner at Washington's Covington & Burling—and formerly the FDA's general counsel. When *The Wall Street Journal* asked Merrill why he was now representing the tobacco industry, he said, "I have absolutely no comment on that." According to the *Journal*, at least four other former top FDA lawyers now at D.C. corporate firms—Richard N. Cooper, Thomas Scarlett, Arthur N. Levine, and Donald O. Beers—have been recruited to represent tobacco companies.[60]) Nine states—Connecticut, Florida, Louisiana, Maryland, Massachusetts, Minnesota, Mississippi, Texas, and West Virginia—have sued the tobacco industry to obtain compensation for health care expenses under Medicaid incurred treating smoking victims. A federal judge in New Orleans agreed to hear a class-action lawsuit filed on behalf of smokers nationwide charging the tobacco companies with deception about the health effects of smoking. The industry, represented by Kenneth W. Starr, a partner at

the 401-lawyer firm Kirkland & Ellis (and the special prosecutor prob-
ing the Whitewater affair), appealed the judge's decision to certify a
national "class" of plaintiffs. In May 1996, the tobacco makers won
their appeal before the Fifth Circuit Court of Appeals, but lawyers for
smokers vowed to file similar suits in state courts. In March 1996, the
fifth-largest tobacco maker, Liggett Group, had announced tentative
agreements to pay millions of dollars to settle the New Orleans suit and
most of the cases brought by the states, but the other industry members
denounced Liggett's action and vowed to continue to fight. Whatever
the results of these various efforts, it is clear that conscientious public
officials are at last taking some meaningful action in response to strong
public concerns about smoking and health.

In addition, documents obtained from tobacco industry files continue to build the case that the big tobacco companies hid evidence of
health risks while they schemed to expand their markets. A detailed
study of industry files published in the July 1995 *Journal of the American
Medical Association* demonstrated that CTR was indeed an industry
propaganda tool and that tobacco lawyers indeed selected CTR projects based on their potential value in litigation or public relations campaigns.[61]

Thousands of documents from tobacco maker Brown & Williamson,
apparently leaked by an ex-employee, suggest repeated efforts to shield
from disclosure damaging internal studies about the health effects of
smoking. The preferred means: a familiar one—get the lawyers involved,
and thereby be in a position to invoke attorney-client privilege if the files
are ever demanded in litigation or by government authorities.[62] A front-
page story in the October 18, 1995, *Wall Street Journal* reported on two
leaked Brown & Williamson documents, dating from 1991 and 1992,
that indicate that the company adds ammonia to its cigarettes in part to
improve delivery of physically addictive nicotine to smokers. Brown &
Williamson, as well as other tobacco makers, have denied that a purpose
of adding ammonia is to enhance nicotine delivery.[63]

Leaked documents have also called into question the responsibility
of R.J. Reynolds. A 1973 memo by a Reynolds executive, provided to
The Washington Post in October 1995, proposed a plan for marketing
cigarettes to young people aged "21 and under." The memo recommended nicotine levels that would appeal to "learning smokers" and
outlined a marketing plan that promoted cigarettes as a remedy for the
"stress . . . awkwardness, boredom" of the teenage years and as a way to
boost self-esteem. The memo argued that health warnings on the package "may be a plus"—since " 'older' establishment . . . preaching
against smoking . . . would cause the young to want to be defiant and

smoke."[64] A 1976 R.J. Reynolds memo stamped "secret," obtained by *USA Today*, also in October 1995, includes this passage[65]:

> Evidence is now available to indicate that the 14 to 18 year old group is an increasing segment of the smoking population. [R.J. Reynolds] must soon establish a successful new brand in this market if our position in the industry is to be maintained over the long term.

Although R.J. Reynolds executives denied that the memos were ever acted upon, their thrust appeared consistent with the company's "Joe Camel" campaign of the 1980s and 1990s, which uses a fun-loving cartoon camel to sell cigarettes, and 1990 Reynolds memos advising sales representatives to focus on stores "close to colleges [or] high schools."[66]

In March 1996, the FDA released affidavits from former officials of Philip Morris alleging that the company carefully adjusted nicotine levels to satisfy smokers' physiological needs—in apparent contradiction to the sworn congressional testimony of Philip Morris's top executives.

As the tobacco industry continued its efforts to avoid legal liability, President Clinton nominated Judge Sarokin to the Third Circuit Court of Appeals, the same court that had ordered him removed from the Haines case. Republican senators, led by the Judiciary Committee's ranking Republican, Orrin Hatch of Utah, charged that the judge was an overaggressive activist. Their main piece of evidence: Sarokin's *Haines* decision, which so angered and frightened the tobacco industry. Appearing at his confirmation hearing before the Senate Judiciary Committee on August 3, 1994, Judge Sarokin was forced to express regret for the words he used: "I concede that the language was strong, and probably unduly strong, and I would take it back if I could."[67] On October 5, 1994, the Senate confirmed Sarokin for the appellate judgeship by a vote of 63–35, with most Republicans voting against him. In the first six months of 1995, the tobacco industry contributed more than $1.5 million to national Republican party coffers, five times as much as in the same period the previous year.[68] In June 1996, Sarokin announced he would retire. In doing so, he again expressed concerns about judicial independence.

THE CASE OF THE UNWANTED MOTHER

The abusive tactics of power lawyers are not limited to cases of national or international importance. They occur in the courthouses of communities everywhere, in many cases in which a citizen is involved in a law-suit against a powerful corporation.

"Dealing with the defense lawyers was one of the worst experiences of my life," says Lana Ambruster. "It was worse than the trauma of being fired."[69]

According to a jury, Lana Ambruster lost her job for committing the terrible sin of getting pregnant.

In June 1990, Ms. Ambruster became a claims adjuster for the California Casualty insurance company in its San Jose, California, office. She received achievement awards for her work on two separate occasions. Despite these honors, Michael Cross, manager of the San Jose office, put her on "oral probation" for performing in a less-than-satisfactory manner.

Ambruster contends that Cross ordered the probation to avoid giving her a scheduled raise, a practice she says was utilized in her department, along with other abusive practices such as forcing employees to work ten- to twelve-hour days and not paying overtime, to keep the department within its budget. For these and other reasons involving the quality of management, morale in Ambruster's department in 1991 was very low, so low in fact that the company's head office ordered an investigation. The executive who looked into the matter later wrote a memo stating that morale problems in Cross's office were bad, growing worse, and "spreading like a cancer."

In the spring of 1991, despite this workplace unhappiness, Ambruster's personal life was happy. She was engaged and about to be married. But Cross did not share her joy. Three women in the office had been pregnant the year before, and Cross bluntly told Ambruster that she had better not come back from her honeymoon pregnant because he didn't have any room in his budget for any more pregnancies. He allegedly repeated such statements many times. He later claimed not to remember making the statement, but the denial was so unbelievable that the company's lawyer decided to argue instead that Cross meant the statement as a joke.

In July 1991, a few months after her marriage, Ambruster received some good news: Cross told her that she was doing a much better job and was off oral probation. That relieved her so much that she told her boss what she had been keeping to herself for fear of job recriminations: She and her husband were expecting their first child.

Cross did not smile at the news. In fact, according to Ambruster, he glared. He looked so angry, she actually apologized for being pregnant. To make matters worse, *within an hour* Cross told Ambruster that he had changed his mind. Instead of going off oral probation, she was to be placed on written probation, the first formal step in a process that could—and eventually did—lead to her firing.

The company fired Ambruster on September 24, 1991, allegedly for failing to sufficiently improve her work during her formal written probationary period.

The firing was extremely traumatic for Ambruster. She was humiliated at having been fired and worried that she could again have the rug pulled out from under her at her next job. She slipped into a significant depression.

To make matters worse, her husband also lost his job. The couple was now threatened with a financial free fall, exacerbated by the fact that they had to pay for health coverage out of their dwindling resources or face Lana giving birth without insurance benefits to pay for it. After the birth of their baby, they lost their insurance altogether, unable to afford a $500-per-month premium. Soon, the pair were forced by financial pressures to move in with Lana's mother. Tensions between Ambruster and her husband grew, and for a while it seemed the marriage might be headed for a breakup. Eventually, the family left their home in the San Francisco Bay area to try to find work in Southern California.

Lana Ambruster was convinced that her pregnancy, rather than her job performance, was the real reason California Casualty had fired her. Under California law, as well as the 1978 federal Pregnancy Discrimination Act, it is unlawful to fire or demote a woman for being pregnant. So Ambruster filed suit in California state Superior Court, alleging pregnancy discrimination and claiming that her firing caused severe emotional distress. California Casualty refused to acknowledge that the pregnancy was the cause of the firing. Instead, they furiously fought back, claiming that she had been a poor worker. A protracted and difficult litigation process began.

Such controversies are what make many lawsuits. However, California Casualty's lawyers did not limit their defense to contesting the facts surrounding Ambruster's dismissal. Instead, they questioned the cause of Ambruster's post-firing depression. There was little doubt that she suffered from depression after the firing, experiencing a precipitous loss of self-confidence and finding it difficult to cope. That would not have been California Casualty's problem—if the firing had been justified. Indeed, the company's lawyers, from the firm Fox & Grove of San Francisco, could have acknowledged that her depression was caused by the termination and still maintained their client had done nothing wrong. Instead, they decided to attack Ambruster at a very personal level.

In one of Ms. Ambruster's depositions, she was asked whether she had ever been abused by a family member. She answered, truthfully, that she had been abused when she was ten. Once this painful episode was uncovered, the lawyers tried to use Ambruster's childhood tragedy against her, claiming that her emotional distress was not caused by the firing, but rather was due to her childhood abuse. They pursued this course despite a complete lack of evidence that Ambruster had ever experienced emotional problems related to the abuse. This was defense by cruel innuendo rather than fact.

"It was humiliating," says Ambruster. "They threw it out in front of the jury. I thought I was going to black out I was so upset. And what was the purpose? There was no evidence that I was permanently messed up by the abuse. They were trying to make me look like a liar when I testified I had been traumatized by the firing."[70] Ambruster's attorney, Gary Gwilliam of Oakland, denounced the tactics: "It was harassment, pure and simple, a vendetta to punish her for standing up for her rights."[71]

In the end, seeking to blame Ambruster's depression on a difficult childhood event appears to have done California Casualty more harm than good with the jury. Before trial, Ambruster sought $149,999 in settlement. The defense initially offered $30,000, ultimately upping the ante to $100,000. After trial, the jury was so incensed by the conduct of California Casualty and its personnel that, on November 19, 1993, it awarded Ambruster $1.2 million for compensatory damages (including emotional distress) and $1.5 million punitive damages. The trial judge subsequently reduced the compensatory damage award to $350,000, but he nevertheless allowed the $1.5 million in punitive damages to remain intact—a notable decision since punitive damages are designed to punish a defendant for intentional or malicious wrongdoing.

Even after the resounding verdict against it, California Casualty took the position that it had done nothing wrong. Three days after the jury's decision, unrepentant company chairman Thomas R. Brown sent a memo to all company employees stating that management was "completely convinced that pregnancy discrimination did not take place" and adding that Ambruster "went through several months of performance counseling and disciplinary action prior to her pregnancy" and was fired "based solely on performance." Perhaps most telling of all, Michael Cross, the supervisor who warned Ambruster not to get pregnant, was promoted.

After the verdict, one of the jurors was so angry at the cavalier manner in which California Casualty sought to justify its treatment of

Lana Ambruster that she took an unusual step. She sent a letter to the head of the company about the case. "It is my intent," she wrote, "to get the upper management of California Casualty to begin taking a good, hard look at the way we put profits before people. . . . How would you have liked your mothers, wives, daughters or granddaughters to be tormented and threatened as Mr. Cross did to Mrs. Ambruster and others?" She added, "If we all approach one another with respect and always remember to treat others as we want to be treated . . . what your company just went through would not have occurred."

While the appeal was pending, in July 1995, Ambruster and California Casualty agreed to an out-of-court settlement. Although Ambruster attorney Gary Gwilliam tells us that "justice was done," California Casualty admitted no liability, and the terms of the settlement, including the amount the company paid Ambruster for her claims, are confidential. As Chapter 2 will demonstrate, corporate lawyers frequently demand confidentiality as the price of settling cases, a practice that keeps information that is embarrassing or potentially damaging to the company buried in corporate vaults—sometimes at the expense of the public's right to be informed about critical conditions affecting their health, safety, or other interests.

A Cincinnati-based leading employment-law attorney, Paul Tobias, says that reasoned approaches to employment litigation are growing increasingly rare: "Employers are fearful that settlements will set a bad precedent and encourage other lawsuits. So, they frequently give their lawyers the green light to be fierce gladiators and use whatever means are necessary to defeat the employee in court. The objective thus becomes total victory."

This damn-the-torpedoes attitude on the part of the powerful and wealthy is not lost on the lawyers who represent them. Says Tobias, "Defense lawyers feed upon the combative emotions of their client. They know that employers do not like a 'bad news' lawyer who tells them their case is weak, that they have broken the law and should pay damages. They sense that to be retained [hired], they must be supportive of the employer's macho-militant posture. They perceive that the clients welcome an expensive war and vicious posture, intended to destroy the plaintiff and his or her counsel and teach them a lesson. Often, this results in more money being spent on fees than it would have cost to settle the matter."[72]

Indeed, corporations seem inclined to fight harder, and with less scruples, in the labor law area than perhaps in any other. A look at some of the tactics pursued by one large corporate firm, San Francisco–based Littler, Mendelson, Fastiff, Tichy & Mathiason, is instructive. The firm, founded in 1942, does almost nothing but labor law. Its clients have included Exxon, Chevron, Texaco, American Airlines, JC Penney, and Safeway. As of March 1996, it had over 250 lawyers spread over twenty offices around the country, and it had announced plans to double in size to 500 lawyers by the year 2000. The firm earned $320,000 in profits per partner in 1994. Littler's managing partner, J. Richard Thesing, told a reporter, "We're the largest labor and employment law firm in the country by far."[73]

Some of the methods Littler has employed during its ascendancy, however, are disturbing. A 1984 AFL-CIO publication states, "Ask any organizer on the West Coast who the biggest and most ruthless union busting law firm is and they'll tell you it is Littler, Mendelson . . ."[74] What kind of tactics gave Littler this reputation?

- In April 1984, a California federal district judge imposed sanctions of $5,625 against Littler for bringing a frivolous lawsuit. Littler had filed suit on behalf of a corporate client, Huettig & Schromm, Inc., against the Landscape Contractors Council of Northern California and a local of the International Union of Operating Engineers. In its complaint, Huettig & Schromm claimed it was entitled to damages arising out of *its own breach* of a collective bargaining agreement! The court found the corporation's claim to be "utterly without merit." It held that Littler's reliance on a 1972 decision of the National Labor Relations Board, a decision that, in fact, undermined its client's position, "is indicative of [the Littler attorneys'] lack of understanding of their obligation as officers of the court." The court further ruled that Littler's position "was not warranted by existing law or a good faith argument for extension or modification of existing law" and that Littler attorneys "could not reasonably have believed it was." The Littler attorneys, according to the court, "knew or should have known that . . . their client had neither a cause of action nor any claim to invoke this Court's jurisdiction." Noting that Littler "holds itself out as preeminent in labor law," the judge concluded that "a strong inference arises that their bringing of an action such as this was for an improper purpose." The court specifically ordered Littler, which maintained that it had acted appropriately, to pay the fine itself rather than pass the expense on to its client, and it further directed that a copy of its decision be distributed to every partner and associate in the Littler firm.[75]
- In May 1985, another California federal district judge fined the Littler firm for bringing a "wholly frivolous counterclaim . . . with the full weight and resources of the employer behind it." Littler's client,

Moore Business Forms, had been sued for $4.2 million by Ida Hudson, who alleged sex discrimination. Littler responded by filing a $4.2 million counterclaim against Hudson, an unemployed woman in her fifties. The judge, Marilyn Patel, warned Littler that if its attorneys "persist in stepping over the line of permissible advocacy, more severe sanctions must be considered." She added, "Opposing parties and their counsel, the firm's own clients and the court should not be forced to expend time and money on these lawyers' reckless adventures." Littler responded by filing an appeal. The Ninth Circuit Court of Appeals ruled that the counterclaim itself was at least plausible but that the amount of damages Littler claimed, $4.2 million, was indeed "frivolous and brought to harass Hudson." After the district court recalculated sanctions, Littler again appealed to the Ninth Circuit, which upheld Judge Patel's award of more than $6,000.[76]

- In April 1987, yet another California federal district judge ordered sanctions against Littler attorneys for improperly removing an employee's sexual harassment lawsuit from state court, where the plaintiff filed it, to federal court. The court concluded that there was no legal basis to shift the case from state to federal court and that the analysis of prior court decisions in Littler's court papers was "completely unreasonable and meritless." The judge added that the Littler attorneys' "experience in labor and employment law only compounds the severity of the violation of Rule 11," the federal court rule that prohibits the filing of frivolous claims.[77]

- In February 1990, Fresno, California, meatpacker Edwin O'Neill sued the Littler firm for malpractice when an apparent union-busting scheme backfired. In 1977, after O'Neill had hired Littler, he closed his businesses and laid off all his workers. One month later, he opened a new company. The National Labor Relations Board determined that O'Neill had committed unfair labor practices aimed at getting rid of labor unions. The board ordered O'Neill to reinstate the fired workers, pay them back wages, and negotiate with their unions. Asked by a reporter about the case in 1994, with the suit still pending, Littler partner George Tichy denied that he advised O'Neill to try to bust the union. He called the case "entirely a bogus matter."[78]

- In April 1993, lawyers for Jacqueline Bass, who had filed a wrongful discharge lawsuit against American Eagle airlines, claimed that Littler attorneys had deliberately withheld evidence in order to raise the costs of litigating. Littler firmly denied the charge, but the California state court judge presiding in the case, James Lambden, held American Eagle in contempt and fined the company and its lawyers (Littler and another firm) $4,940. American Eagle, represented by Littler, had twice failed to provide documents to the court after Lambden ordered them to do so.[79]

- In December 1993, Terry Haynie, a former employee of Pacific International Rice Mills, Inc. (PIRMI), sued Littler in California state court, claiming legal malpractice. According to Haynie, he went to his supervisors to report sexual harassment complaints he received from two female coworkers. The women subsequently left PIRMI and filed suit against the company. PIRMI hired Littler to represent it in the case. According to Haynie, a Littler partner asked him to sign a statement alleging that the women had used "profane language" and that PIRMI management had handled the complaints appropriately. Haynie refused. Soon after, his performance ratings dropped precipitously, and he was fired. When Littler, which denied misconduct, moved to dismiss the malpractice claim, the firm's motion was rejected by the trial judge, then by the California Court of Appeal, and finally by the California Supreme Court.[80]

- In March 1994, the Ninth Circuit decided an appeal brought by Littler on behalf of Security Experts, Inc. (SEI), an airport security firm. Alfred Tonry prevailed in a federal district court lawsuit against SEI for breach of an employment contract. In presenting SEI's appeal, Littler made several references to an earlier decision in the dispute by a court-appointed arbitrator, who attempted to decide the matter out of court. The Ninth Circuit not only affirmed the judgment in favor of Tonry but also ruled that Littler's references to the arbitration violated both the rules of the district court and the Federal Rules of Appellate Procedure.[81] (The court, however, declined to impose sanctions, because it had never previously addressed the propriety of citing an arbitrator's decision in this manner.)

- In May 1994, the Ninth Circuit criticized Littler for "inappropriate and misleading appellate advocacy." The court's order did not specify Littler's misconduct in the case, Campbell v. U.S. District Court, in which Littler represented a law firm being sued by a discharged attorney for disability discrimination.[82] (Again, no sanctions were imposed.)

- Also in 1994, a California woman, Jennifer Kobylka, sued Littler attorneys in federal district court, claiming that they arranged to have her arrested on phony embezzlement charges after she filed a sexual harassment case against her employer, Willetts Brewing

Company, a Littler client. Police arrested Kobylka at the very moment a Littler attorney was taking her deposition in the case. Kobylka won the harassment suit, and authorities subsequently dropped the criminal charges against her. U.S. District Judge Charles Legge refused to dismiss Kobylka's emotional distress claim against Littler attorneys. Managing partner Thesing has called Kobylka's charges "inflammatory" and "outrageous."[83]

Indeed, Littler has repeatedly denied engaging in improper tactics. "There is no such thing as a union buster," partner Wesley J. Fastiff once said. "Unions beat themselves."[84] Thesing told a reporter that the judicial rebukes against the firm are the price of "creative legal thinking."[85]

Unfortunately, hardball tactics are found across the depth and breadth of corporate litigation practice. The pain such behavior causes to the already victimized can be extreme, making even the winners of lawsuits feel like losers. Moreover, these scorched-earth tactics harm society at large. They add to court congestion, increase the cost of litigation, and foster a public view of courts as an arena of unfair combat rather than a forum for determining the truth and delivering just outcomes.

POWER LAW BEHIND THE SCENES

When most of us think of law, we think of lawsuits: courtrooms, judges, juries, and verdicts. And, indeed, several sections of this book focus on how aggressive power-lawyer tactics subvert the litigation process, destroying meritorious claims through attrition, harassment, and obfuscation. But, as the case of Lloyd Cutler shows, some of the most harmful acts inflicted on society actually occur quietly, behind the scenes, when corporate lawyers act as counselors to corporate executives and lobbyists before government bodies. Following are two examples, each involving some of the biggest and richest law firms in the country.

COUNSELING THE CON ARTISTS

The savings and loan crisis of the late 1980s and early 1990s is probably the worst banking scandal in U.S. history. Taking advantage of the federal government's promise to insure S & L deposits, scoundrels and reckless incompetents, pursuing risky investments or cynical Ponzi schemes, ran many of these institutions into the ground, frequently lining their own pockets in the process. More than one thousand S & Ls closed their doors forever, requiring the federal government to create a new agency, the Resolution Trust Corporation, to manage the cleanup.[86] The cost of this debacle to taxpayers, who are forced to bail out this wave of crime, irresponsible speculation, and mismanagement, is in the hundreds of billions of dollars, with bills that will extend into the next century.

One of the notorious S & L "entrepreneurs" was Charles H. Keating, Jr., head of American Continental Corp. (ACC), the parent of a California institution called Lincoln Savings & Loan. Keating and his underlings swindled thousands of small investors, many of them elderly, by selling them uninsured and ultimately worthless bonds. ACC's ethics are crystallized in one internal document, entitled "Capitalize on This," that offered the following advice for the company's sales force: "Always remember the weak, meek and ignorant are always good targets."[87]

One defrauded Lincoln Savings bondholder is a woman named Evangeline Ivy. She and her husband were planning to retire. He gave up the lease on his barbershop. They sold an apartment house they owned and took their money to Lincoln, planning to deposit it into a certificate of deposit.

But that is not how things turned out. "We were talked out of depositing our money and into investing it in Lincoln bonds," Ms. Ivy told us. "The salesperson absolutely insisted that the money was so safe that we couldn't lose. We were promised that we could get our money back within a year. I told him I didn't want to take *any* risk with our money, that it was our entire life savings. He said not to worry, it was absolutely safe and paid a higher interest. We were so happy. Then, the bottom fell out."

Jeri Mellon had a similar experience. "Lincoln had been my family bank for years," she told us. "I knew all the tellers. It was just like one big happy family." Mellon recalled the takeover of Lincoln by Charles Keating during the 1980s. "When Keating took over, everyone at my branch was happy. He gave people bonuses, raises. The morale was very high. Everyone seemed to think that he was the best thing since television." When Mellon's $40,000 government-insured certificate of deposit matured, Lincoln offered her a bond that paid 1.5 percent higher interest than the CD but lacked government insurance backing. Bank employees, says Mellon, "were really pushing it. I assumed I would have the same protection as my CD did. When I asked about safety, I was told that the United States would go bankrupt before ACC would. No one even mentioned the bond investment would not be insured.

"The gentleman who sold me the bond gave me a prospectus," Mellon continued. "It stated that ACC was worth five billion."

That was a falsehood. ACC was, in reality, an empty shell headed for financial collapse.

Federal authorities, who took over Lincoln Savings in 1989, estimate total losses from the institution's collapse at $3 billion, requiring the most expensive S & L bailout in history. In 1993, a Los Angeles federal judge sentenced Keating to nearly thirteen years in prison after a jury convicted him on seventy-three counts of racketeering, conspiracy, and fraud. He is serving this sentence concurrently with a ten-year term imposed by a California state superior court judge in 1991 after a jury convicted him on seventeen counts of securities fraud.

Some of the nation's largest law firms served this scoundrel. Why? Money. While Charles Keating was riding high, American Continental and Lincoln had plenty of it, and Keating was smart enough to know that blue-chip law firm assistance could help legitimize and protect his crooked schemes.

In order to sell ACC bonds legally at Lincoln Savings local branch offices, Charles Keating needed a formal legal opinion letter stating that ACC/Lincoln lawyers had reviewed the firm's records and financial affairs, and that all was in appropriate financial and legal order. Keating's accountants, from the national firm Arthur Andersen & Co., had refused to involve themselves in the matter, apparently because of concerns about the institution's viability. Enter Jones, Day, Reavis & Pogue, the 1,072-attorney law firm mentioned earlier in this chapter.

According to a class-action lawsuit filed by defrauded Lincoln Savings bondholders, beginning in March 1986 Jones, Day conducted a regulatory compliance review of ACC and Lincoln Savings during which it had unfettered access to ACC/Lincoln's books and records. The lawsuit alleged that as a result of reviewing the records of ACC/Lincoln Savings, Jones, Day learned that ACC/Lincoln corporate records and minutes of meetings had been backdated and forged; that ACC/Lincoln records on real estate loans had been altered; and that ACC/Lincoln's conduct did not comply with Federal Home Loan Bank Board regulations. Despite the alleged knowledge of ACC/Lincoln's improper practices, Jones, Day did not suggest disclosure of any of these items in ACC's 1986 prospectus offering the bonds for sale.

Jones, Day contended otherwise. In response to the lawsuit, the firm said that its attorneys orally advised the officers of ACC/Lincoln to halt these improper practices and that the firm even threatened to withdraw as ACC/Lincoln's attorneys. However, Jones, Day lawyers never went above the heads of the Lincoln in-house lawyers to complain to the S & L's board of directors about the practices. If Jones, Day threatened to withdraw, it was not in writing, and the firm continued to represent Keating's companies on various legal matters.

Why would an influential law firm risk its reputation and its finances by associating itself with the likes of Charles Keating, while he perpetuated a fraud on the public? Money. Keating had written an unsolicited check to Jones, Day for $250,000 as a retainer—an advance against legal fees—and then a few weeks later sent another $250,000, telling the firm it could bill liberally. An internal Jones, Day memo reported that ACC did not care how much its legal services would cost.[88] In other words, in Charles Keating and ACC/Lincoln, Jones, Day had found a legal-fee cornucopia. In the end, Jones, Day received $1,000,000 in fees for legal services provided to Keating's empire between March and June 1986.[89] (Jones, Day now generates $384 million in annual gross revenues and $375,000 profits per partner.)

Another major firm that reaped the financial benefits of an association with Charles Keating's empire was New York's 311-lawyer Kaye, Scholer, Fierman, Hays & Handler (which now produces $153 million in annual gross revenues and $490,000 profits per partner). The firm received fees of $3 million from ACC/Lincoln in 1987, $5 million in 1988, and a total of $13 million between 1985 and 1989.[90] Kaye, Scholer also advised ACC/Lincoln on the sale of bonds to the public. The defrauded bondholder suit alleged that Kaye, Scholer helped set up the fraud by designing the bond offering "to mirror the customary practice for CDs in an attempt to confuse, deceive, or mislead the investing public."[91]

Kaye, Scholer also stepped into the bank examination process in mid-1986, apparently after Jones, Day voiced its concerns about irregularities.[92] In an unusual move that surprised federal bank examiners in San Francisco, Kaye, Scholer immediately directed the examiners to communicate all requests for information to the law firm, rather than through Lincoln. In April 1987, federal regulators issued a report outlining numerous legal violations by Lincoln. Kaye, Scholer fired back with a 768-page rebuttal, with ten thousand attached exhibits, portraying Lincoln as a secure and prudently run institution. It included assurances such as "Lincoln unquestionably is not in an unsafe and unsound condition" and "Lincoln prudently manages and thus minimizes the risks associated with real estate lending" and Lincoln "has always undertaken very careful and thorough procedures to analyze the [loan] collateral and the borrower."[93]

The defrauded bondholders alleged in their complaint that Kaye, Scholer "participated in a series of misrepresentations and deceptions upon regulators" and "applied political pressure" so that "government enforcement proceedings against, censure of, cease and desist orders relating to and/or seizure of Lincoln were delayed."

Federal regulators sided with the bondholders. In 1992, the federal Office of Thrift Supervision (OTS) sued both law firms. The regulators claimed that Jones, Day knew that Keating was looting Lincoln Savings and should have taken action to stop this wrongdoing. In a separate complaint, the regulators charged that Kaye, Scholer lawyers had conspired with Keating's companies to hide evidence of wrongdoing from federal bank examiners. According to OTS, Kaye, Scholer knew that Lincoln had engaged in improper practices but failed to report this information to the examiners; instead, the firm vouched for Lincoln. The OTS complaint alleged that Kaye, Scholer lawyers "knowingly disregarded the facts that Lincoln had fabricated and backdated documents, issued false and misleading statements to bank examiners," and "provided [federal bank examiners] with Lincoln files and documents . . . knowing the files and documents to be false and misleading." In addition, according to OTS, Kaye, Scholer had also submitted to examiners a document in which Lincoln stated that the Arthur Andersen accounting firm's resignation did not result from any concerns by the accountants about Lincoln's operations, when in fact Kaye, Scholer knew that Andersen did have such concerns.[94] The OTS cited federal regulations that forbid anyone making representations to regulators to make false statements or to make "material omissions"—that is, to fail to tell regulators about factual matters when such failure makes one's statements misleading.[95]

The OTS action sought a $275 million fine from Kaye, Scholer. To show it meant business, OTS froze the firm's assets, although the freeze did not prevent the firm from spending money for usual and routine business expenses. Even so, Kaye, Scholer feared the reaction of its banks and clients.

On March 8, 1992, Kaye, Scholer, which had turned for representation to Bernard Nussbaum, partner at the New York firm Wachtell, Lipton, Rosen & Katz, agreed to pay the federal government $41 million to settle claims over Lincoln Savings. (Nussbaum became the White House counsel in 1993 when President Clinton assumed office.) Kaye, Scholer's top Lincoln lawyer, Peter M. Fishbein, and another partner at the firm, Karen Katzman, also agreed as part of the settlement with OTS never again to represent a federally insured financial institution. That same year, Kaye, Scholer paid $20 million to settle claims brought against it by Keating's defrauded investors.

On April 19, 1993, Jones, Day, too, settled, agreeing to pay the government $51 million in fines—the largest payment ever made by a law firm to settle claims of professional liability. The firm, in 1992, had settled Lincoln bondholders' claims by paying $24 million.

Despite these huge payouts, Kaye, Scholer and Jones, Day continue to insist that they did nothing wrong.

Kaye, Scholer and Fishbein say that they only agreed to the settlement with federal regulators because the government freeze on the firm's assets threatened to shut it down. Fishbein told *The New York Times* that he and his colleagues had "acted properly as lawyers."[96] Fishbein told us that his firm settled with the bondholders to avoid substantial risk: "We were being sued for $3 billion. There were going to be a lot of elderly people saying that their life savings were lost. Under those circumstances, no one can predict what a jury is going to do." He added that malpractice insurance paid every dime of the settlement with bondholders.[97] However, insurance covered only about $26 million of the $41 million fine paid to federal regulators, with the rest coming from firm partners.[98]

Jones, Day partner Brian Toohey, who helped resolve the firm's Lincoln Savings difficulties, gives a similar explanation for why his firm settled: "We would have been sitting in the courtroom with Charles Keating," Toohey says, "and caught up in the problem of a ninety-year-old woman telling the jury she had lost her life savings."[99]

The assumption that juries give large awards in nonmeritorious cases and that judges stand idly by is not rooted in the evidence of courtroom experience. (See Chapter 8.) The two law firms may have settled because they feared that the courts would find substantial merit in the claims against them.

Perhaps not surprisingly, the legal establishment officially backed up the position of the corporate lawyers that there had been no misconduct. In February 1993, an American Bar Association panel issued a report concluding that federal regulators had attempted to hold Kaye, Scholer to "standards of lawyer conduct that appeared to go beyond or conflict with traditional principles of professional responsibility."[100] The ABA panel was chaired by John Curtin, Jr., partner at Boston's 220-attorney corporate law firm Bingham, Dana & Gould. The vice-chair was Robert H. Mundheim, general counsel to the giant financial services company Salomon, Inc. In August 1993, the ABA's House of Delegates unanimously approved the panel's recommendations to curb the RTC's ability to discipline lawyers.[101]

On August 9, 1993, a New York state court legal ethics committee, charged with reviewing and punishing attorney misconduct, issued an opinion in the form of a three-and-one-quarter-page letter to Fishbein stating that it had investigated several of the charges against Fishbein—those that were "among the most provable . . . and also appeared to be the most egregious"—and concluded that there was "no basis for taking any disciplinary action."[102] The letter to Fishbein, signed by Hal R. Lieberman, chief counsel of the ethics committee, noted that the committee staff's conclusion that no disciplinary action was warranted was submitted to the committee chairman, Haliburton Fales II, Esq., who assigned the matter to John R. Horan, Esq., another committee member. Horan, who approved the staff recommendation, is a partner at the twenty-attorney corporate law firm of Fox & Horan. Fales is a retired partner at the five-hundred-attorney corporate firm of White & Case.

How could these pillars of the legal establishment disagree so profoundly with government agencies about whether the law firms representing Lincoln had done wrong? The answer goes to the tension at the heart of the contemporary debate about lawyer responsibilities and duties. On the one hand, legal codes of ethics prevailing in every state direct a lawyer to act zealously to represent clients and to maintain a client's secrets. On the other hand, under these same rules, the lawyer has responsibilities to the legal system and the public to tell the truth and otherwise avoid becoming an instrument of ongoing dishonesty, fraud, or criminal conduct.[103] (The concluding chapter of this book, Chapter 9, will revisit these issues.) The corporate attorney–dominated ABA and New York ethics panel appeared to elevate the requirement of zealous representation of the client and protection of client secrets far above these other concerns. In Fishbein's view, "federal regulators said that Kaye, Scholer had a duty to investigate our own client and tell the government about what we found. I suppose we learned things here and there that [regulators] would have liked us to have made known. But that is not the role of a lawyer. We can't lie but it was not up to us to do the agency's job."

Others took a different view. Carolyn B. Lieberman, the OTS chief counsel, said that the New York ethics board erred in limiting its investigation to only a portion of the allegations against Fishbein. She added that by aggressively interposing itself between federal examiners and Lincoln Savings, Kaye, Scholer assumed greater responsibility to be candid with the federal officials.[104] Harris Weinstein, Lieberman's predecessor at the OTS and now a partner at the Washington, D.C., law firm of Covington & Burling, rejected the suggestion that, although Lincoln was obviously required to tell federal regulators the truth, Lincoln law firms like Kaye, Scholer had an ethical obligation to avoid disclosing such truths: "I am hard pressed . . . to understand how we can claim that a lawyer is free to deceive a third party when the client could not. If that were the rule, if a lawyer were permitted to do that, what would be left of the liability risked by the client's deception? Any client could overcome that liability simply by hiring a lawyer to do the dirty work for him."[105] Weinstein charged that Kaye, Scholer had in its hands specific evidence of irregularities that undermined the broad, general statements the firm presented vouching for Lincoln's stability and diligence.

Harvard law professor David B. Wilkins concludes that, although lawyers representing banks in federal examinations should be granted "some leeway to resolve questions of fact in favor of their clients," they should not "be entitled to withhold information properly requested by regulatory examiners," nor do they "have any special permission to mislead the regulators into thinking that harmful information does not exist." He adds: "The extensive web of federal regulations governing [S & Ls] makes it quite clear that the examiners should have free access to all . . . records—particularly those that may indicate wrongdoing."[106] The type of obstructionist tactics utilized by corporate lawyers in litigation are not appropriate in the context of a bank examination.

Steve France, editor of *Bank Lawyer Liability*, notes that there is a difference between court litigation and the bank regulation process, in which federally insured institutions are supposed to cooperate with the government that insures and subsidizes its ventures: "Litigation is an elaborate game where two adversaries attempt to convince a neutral third party [a judge or jury] about the righteousness of their respective client's cause. But that is not what was going on in the Lincoln audit. A bank and its regulators are partners. You can't come into a partnership with daggers drawn. Fishbein was a litigator, a dagger man. That is why he was hired."[107] Charles Keating may have wanted his lawyers to engage in an adversarial approach to the audit, but that does not mean he had the right to have that kind of representation, or that Kaye, Scholer acted appropriately in giving it to him. France says that Kaye, Scholer should have advised Lincoln to tell the truth, and, if Lincoln refused, should have resigned from the case.

Which view is the majority view among corporate executives and lawyers? While we don't know for sure, when asked how he and his firm were viewed by peers in the wake of the scandal, Peter Fishbein confidently told us, "We have gotten a tremendous amount of support from lawyers, judges, the bar, and the financial community. They have been truly sympathetic to what happened to us. The general feeling in the world we deal with is that there are a bunch of Nazis at the OTS who took advantage of a public crisis situation and abused the powers of its agency to coerce an unjustified settlement." When we asked Fishbein whether the firm suffered damage to its reputation with clients, he answered, "Let me put it this way. We know we haven't lost any clients. We have gotten a lot of new business. The firm is very healthy and very prosperous. Our clients are bigger and more prosperous than they have ever been."[108] So it appears that in the corporate and corporate law communities in which Kaye, Scholer operates, the firm's conduct was viewed as standard, acceptable, even commendable legal work. (In 1992, the Federal Deposit Insurance Corporation issued rules that require a lawyer who believes that a client bank is making a fraudulent and risky loan to direct the client to desist. If the client refuses, the lawyer must report the matter to federal regulators.)

Note: Following is a list of some of the firms who have paid to settle professional liability lawsuits or administrative proceedings brought against them for acts and omissions arising out of their legal representation of failed savings and loans. (These figures only represent amounts paid by these firms to settle claims brought by federal regulators. They do not include payments made to settle private lawsuits.)

Jones, Day, Reavis & Pogue paid $51 million to the RTC in connection with the Lincoln Savings case. In addition, partner William J. Schilling agreed to be barred from holding any position in the banking industry and was suspended from practice before the OTS.

Paul, Weiss, Rifkind, Wharton & Garrison of New York paid $45 million to the RTC for conduct arising from the 331-attorney firm's representation of a Miami S & L, CenTrust. Former partner Peter R. Haje (the same lawyer who is now Time Warner's highly paid general counsel) was enjoined from representing any insured depository institution for five years and suspended from practicing before the OTS for the same time span.

Kaye, Scholer, Fierman, Hays & Handler paid $41 million in the Lincoln Savings case. In addition, partners Fishbein and Katzman were prohibited from representing federally insured financial institutions in the future.

Troutman Sanders of Atlanta, Georgia, paid $20 million in connection with its representation of Lincoln Savings.

Kirkpatrick & Lockhart, a 351-lawyer Pittsburgh-based firm, paid $9 million to resolve claims arising from its representation of American Savings Bank of Miami. In addition, partner Alan J. Berkeley agreed to a prohibition against representing any depository institution for three years.

Sidley & Austin, a 608-lawyer Chicago-based firm, paid $7.5 million to settle claims arising from its representation of Lincoln Savings.[109]

The lawyers and law firms who paid such unprecedentedly large penalties, of course, admitted no wrongdoing.

THE CASE OF THE FAITHFUL BUTLER

In the eyes of many corporate lawyers, New York's Cravath, Swaine & Moore stands at the pinnacle of legal practice. Its attorneys are among the highest paid, its clients among the most powerful. The firm, whose origins go back to 1819, has, among other notable accomplishments, bested the U.S. government in monumental 1970s antitrust litigation involving the International Business Machines Corporation (IBM) and obtained a $500 million settlement for the U.S. government against investment banker Michael Milken and Drexel Burnham Lambert. (See Chapter 7.) Its attorneys are influential in politics and affairs of the bar. According to *The American Lawyer* magazine, from 1988 through 1995 Cravath has been the most profitable of the one hundred top-grossing U.S. law firms, measured by profits per partner. The firm has traditionally maintained a much-envied ratio of at least three associates toiling for each partner.[110] (Cravath's history also has a darker side. For example, Hoyt Augustus Moore, one of the partners who gave the firm its name, once approved of hundreds of thousands of dollars in bribes paid by the Bethlehem Steel Company to a federal trial judge. Years later Moore admitted the deed in congressional testimony, and he was indicted in 1947. But the indictment was dismissed because the court ruled that the applicable statute of limitations had expired. Moore's partner, Robert T. Swaine, wrote, "No lawyer ever unreservedly gave more of himself to a client than Hoyt Moore gave to Bethlehem."[111])

At the top of the current Cravath hierarchy is Samuel C. Butler. A graduate of Harvard College and Harvard Law School and a former law clerk to U.S. Supreme Court Justice Sherman Minton, Butler joined Cravath in 1956 and became a partner four years later. In 1980, at age fifty, Butler became the firm's presiding partner. Among other high-profile matters, he represented Time, Inc. in its merger with Warner Communications, Capital Cities/ABC in its acquisition by the Walt Disney Company, and CBS in its acquisition by Westinghouse.[112] Other longtime clients have included Bristol-Myers Squibb and Paine Webber. In 1989, *Forbes* magazine listed Butler as one of the ten "best paid corporate lawyers" and estimated his 1988 income as around $2.4

million.[113] "Butler," according to a 1995 article in *The American Lawyer*, "has come to symbolize the phenomenal success of [Cravath]."[114] *The National Law Journal* has included Butler in every one of its periodic lists of "the most influential lawyers in America" and called him "the undeniable leader of one of the nation's most influential law firms" and "the epitome of the big-firm establishment."[115]

Butler has found time outside of his busy Cravath schedule for several other important pursuits. He served on the Board of Overseers of Harvard College from 1982 to 1988, and as that board's president from 1986 to 1988. He has been on the board of trustees of the New York Public Library and the American Museum of Natural History.

Butler has also served on the boards of directors of several corporations, including the U.S. Trust Corporation, GEICO Corporation, and the Olin Corporation. In the years Butler served as an Olin Corporation director, 1972 through 1981, the Stamford, Connecticut–based company, a diversified business with interests in chemicals, metals, electronics, aerospace, and defense, received some bad press. In 1978, Olin pleaded no contest to federal charges that it falsified license applications to sell 2,200 guns to South Africa in violation of export restrictions. The Internal Revenue Service and federal prosecutors also investigated Olin in connection with $6.5 million in deductions on its 1974, 1975, and 1976 tax returns, deductions that investigators charged were for bribes to foreign officials. The bribery investigation was terminated, in part because Congress did not specifically outlaw foreign bribes until it passed the Foreign Corrupt Practices Act (FCPA) in 1977.[116]

But another company on whose board Butler has served and still serves,[117] Ashland Oil, Inc., was not so lucky when allegations arose that it had bribed foreign officials.

Since 1970, Butler has been a director of Ashland, a Kentucky-based oil and gas business. Butler also represents Ashland as legal counsel. Ashland's most recent annual revenues were $10.4 billion, making it the twelfth highest-earning U.S. oil company.[118] But Ashland is also a company with a troubling record. In 1983, the *Charleston* (West Virginia) *Gazette* said that Ashland "may be the most indicted corporation in America."[119] Recounting the years in which Orin Atkins served as Ashland's chairman and chief executive officer until his 1981 resignation, the *Gazette* later wrote: "[Ashland] was caught repeatedly in bid-rigging, fraud, price-fixing, overseas bribes and political payments such as the illicit $20,000 Ashland sent in a satchel to [West Virginia] Gov. Arch Moore."[120]

Indeed, in 1975 Ashland executives admitted that they handed Moore $20,000 during a visit to his office.[121] Two years earlier, in another case, Atkins had pled no contest to criminal charges of making $633,000 in illegal campaign contributions. He paid a $1,000 fine. Ashland and one of its subsidiaries pleaded guilty and paid a $30,000 fine. And Ashland's troubles did not end with Atkins's departure.

In April 1982, the company's Ashland-Warren subsidiary pleaded guilty to antitrust violations and paid a $6 million fine—at the time the largest criminal antitrust penalties ever assessed. Sixteen Ashland officials were convicted in related cases. Ashland-Warren vice president G. William Jones was convicted in July 1984 of bid-rigging and served a sixty-day sentence. Soon after his release, Ashland hired Jones back. By 1988, he was running the company's $1 billion construction operation.[122]

In January 1988, an Ashland storage tank, built with forty-year-old steel, ruptured while being filled with oil, and 3.2 million gallons of diesel spilled into the Monongahela River near Pittsburgh, resulting in $60 million to $70 million in cleanup and damage costs. Ashland had failed to obtain a state permit for the tank or to adequately test or protect it.[123]

Between 1988 and 1990, at least sixteen hundred West Virginians sued Ashland for alleged health problems and property damages caused by emissions from Ashland's refinery complex near Catlettsburg, Kentucky. In February 1993, Ashland settled the claims of 709 of these plaintiffs for an undisclosed sum; the company continued to deny liability.[124]

(In September 1989, Orin Atkins, who remained an Ashland consultant from 1981 to 1984, pleaded guilty to federal criminal charges of conspiracy and wire fraud. His offense: attempting repeatedly between 1982 and 1988 to sell confidential Ashland documents to the National Iranian Oil Company, which was in a dispute with Ashland. A federal district judge sentenced Atkins to two years' probation and six hundred hours of community service.[125])

But one of the most notorious chapters in Ashland's history concerned a series of payments made, on attorney Samuel Butler's watch, to foreigners connected to the governments of certain oil-producing nations.[126]

In 1975, a federal investigation of Watergate-era political contributions developed evidence of questionable conduct by Ashland, including more than $4 million in secret payments abroad. Ashland, advised by Butler, entered into a consent decree with the Securities and Exchange Commission. The company agreed never to use corporate money for "unlawful political purposes or other similar unlawful purposes" or to engage in unlawful financial or record-keeping activities. But soon, it appears, notwithstanding the 1977 passage of the Foreign Corrupt Practices Act, the company returned to its old ways.

In November 1979, Ashland agreed to pay a business consultant, Sadiq Attia, a commission of $2 a barrel—several times what was standard—to try to preserve an existing agreement to obtain oil from Abu Dhabi's state-owned oil company. Attia had previously worked for the Abu Dhabi government. Abu Dhabi nevertheless broke the agreement, but by then Ashland had paid Attia $17 million. A federal jury later concluded that Ashland made these payments knowing, or having reason to know, that the money would be used to bribe a government official of Abu Dhabi.

In March 1980, Ashland paid James T. W. Landon, a former British army officer who had become a special adviser to the sultan of oil-rich Oman, $25 million for a 75 percent share in a chrome mine in Rhodesia (now Zimbabwe). Nine months earlier Landon had purchased the 30 percent of the mine he and his family did not previously own for $135,000, suggesting that the entire mine was worth $450,000. Ashland wrote off the $25 million within two years without ever opening the mine. Notes from a January 1980 Ashland board meeting referred to the mine purchase as the "price of getting crude."

In December 1980, Ashland paid $1.3 million to Yehia Omar, who held a diplomatic passport from Oman. Ashland vice president Bill McKay, Jr., complained to John Hall, Ashland's vice chairman and chief operating officer, that Omar's diplomatic passport indicated that he was a foreign government official and that such a payment violated the Foreign Corrupt Practices Act. Atkins, however, insisted that Omar was not a government official and that the payment was compensation for Omar's efforts to facilitate an October 1980 crude oil contract between Ashland and Oman. Ashland had also made a $2.3 million investment in a project to develop reusable sausage casings, a venture in which Omar was a one-third owner. Ashland wrote off that investment, like the Landon mine, in short order.

At a January 7, 1981, meeting with top Ashland officials, Butler raised both the Omar payments and the Landon purchase. He reviewed a January 5, 1981, letter from former CIA director Richard Helms to Atkins that called Landon "the most influential individual on policy matters with the sultan" and said that Landon chaired the sultan's military planning committee. But Atkins insisted that neither Landon nor Omar was an Omani official. According to a chronology of events Butler later prepared for an internal investigation, Butler concluded, "If they were government officials, clear questions would be raised under the FCPA." Butler later warned Atkins that the CEO "might have to spend time in jail if McKay took his story to the SEC or the Department of Justice."

Butler began gathering information aimed at determining whether Omar and Landon were government officials. He was aided in this effort by Lloyd Cutler—the same Lloyd Cutler described earlier in this chapter—whose firm, Wilmer, Cutler & Pickering, had close ties with Cravath and who was personally close to Butler. The evidence Butler obtained did not support Atkins's position. A 1980 diplomatic communication described Omar as a "counselor" to Oman's United Nations delegation. An August 1980 U.S. State Department diplomatic list described Omar as "Counselor (Political Affairs)" to Oman's Washington, D.C., embassy. According to Butler, Richard Helms and then-deputy CIA director Bobby R. Inman told Cutler that "Omar should probably be regarded as a foreign government official for FCPA purposes."

In April 1981, Ashland chief operating officer Hall met with Landon. Afterward, he wrote a memo reporting that Landon "said, as far as he is concerned, Yehia Omar is a government official but that American lawyers might decide otherwise. [He] emphasized the benefits received by Yehia Omar as an official of Oman and said he was certain that Mr. Omar would not begin to be giving up those benefits. . . . He also said he believed that any reasonable person in the government would consider Yehia Omar a government official."

Ashland attorneys even prepared a plea to the sultan of Oman, asking him to certify that Omar was not an Omani official and that Omani law had not been violated. But the sultan never signed the papers.

Butler concluded that Ashland "could not satisfactorily demonstrate to the Department of Justice that Omar was not a foreign government official." According to his chronology, Butler urged Atkins to get the $1.3 million back from Omar. After some resistance by Omar, Atkins managed to do so.

But there was still the problem of Landon. Atkins told Butler that the chrome mine purchase was "directly related" to the October 1980 oil deal, indicating that Landon had received a payoff greater than the value of the mine. And Atkins described Landon in a letter to Butler as "probably the most influential, powerful man in the Omani government."

To resolve the matter internally, in May 1981 Butler convinced his colleagues on the Ashland board of directors to hire an outside lawyer to conduct an "independent" investigation. At Butler's suggestion, the board selected Charles Queenan, Jr., a partner at the Pittsburgh-based law firm Kirkpatrick & Lockhart (which, as noted above, later paid $9 million to settle federal claims in the savings and loan scandal).

The appointment of Queenan might have raised a few eyebrows. He was a law school classmate and friend of Butler's. Queenan had performed a similar investigation for Ashland at the time of the earlier, 1975 controversy. The report had been quite critical of Ashland, and Kirkpatrick's business with Ashland dropped from $247,000 in billings in 1975 to only $12,000 by 1978. However, by 1980, the firm's billings to Ashland were up to $293,000. In 1981, the year of the "independent" investigation, they were up to $711,000. (By 1983, Kirkpatrick was doing $865,000's worth of business for Ashland, including work on the Monongahela River spill.) Ashland's in-house general counsel, Arloe Mayne, later testified that he had consulted Queenan about the $1.3 million deal with Omar before it was consummated. Queenan had also attended the January 7, 1981, Ashland management meeting.

At the time he commissioned Queenan's report, Butler also recommended a law firm for Bill McKay, the Ashland v.p. who was raising questions, to hire as his personal attorneys—Wilmer, Cutler & Pickering.

As the Queenan investigation proceeded, Atkins and Butler clashed over the foreign payments issue, and each tried to oust the other from the company. Butler later accused Atkins of fueling an investigation by the Federal Trade Commission into whether Butler's service on both the Ashland and the Olin Corporation boards constituted a conflict of interest. But the FTC never took action. On September 17, 1981, Butler prevailed. Atkins resigned.

Queenan's report, submitted on October 26, criticized the judgment of Ashland officials but concluded that the company had done nothing illegal. Queenan said that Ashland had no obligation to report the matter to its shareholders or government agencies. The board unanimously ratified this conclusion. McKay continued to press for disclosure, but he was rebuffed by his superiors.

Meanwhile, Hassan Y. Yassin, a McLean, Virginia–based Saudi Arabian businessman who had been an Ashland consultant for a decade, demanded a $5 million fee to improve Ashland's access to oil. John Hall concluded that Yassin "has done almost nothing to help us." Orin Atkins echoed that Yassin was "mainly a contact man." But Yassin, who had previously served as an official at the Saudi Arabian embassy in Washington, had a pretty good contact: the Saudi oil minister, Sheik Ahmed Zaki Yamani. In an April 1981 memo, Atkins wrote Hall that "we definitely need access to Yamani and . . . Hassan may be our best contact." In late 1981, Ashland agreed to pay Yassin $1.25 million.

In October 1982, the Internal Revenue Service, as part of a routine audit, sent questionnaires to Ashland officials. One question asked whether the company had made any "bribes" or "kickbacks." In coordinated responses drafted by Ashland attorneys, top Ashland officials provided a carefully crafted answer: Each man stated that he had made no effort to investigate or refresh his recollection. Each man stated that his response was based on "current recollection" and "personal knowledge." Each denied any violations.

McKay, bolstered by the advice of his attorney, Michael R. Klein of Wilmer, Cutler, refused to go along. McKay believed the coordinated response Ashland wanted him to ratify was an attempt to hide illegal payments. So Samuel Butler and Cravath, according to a report in *The Washington Post*, "began a campaign to persuade Wilmer, Cutler & Pickering . . . to get McKay to conform." This effort, according to the *Post* story, "created severe strains on the close personal and professional ties between" Butler and Cutler. One Wilmer, Cutler partner, Arthur F. Mathews, later testified that Cutler told him that "Sam Butler was particularly angered or incensed with Michael Klein" and "had stated he would never send me, Art Mathews, another piece of business again as long as he practiced law." Mathews testified that Butler made repeated calls to Wilmer, Cutler senior lawyers about the matter. He also testified that "there was always a concern by Lloyd Cutler, communicated to me, stemming from his conversation with Sam Butler at Cravath that we, Wilmer, Cutler, not become counsel to anybody, including McKay, in a lawsuit against Ashland offensively." (Butler later denied trying to undercut McKay's legal representation. In 1988, Cutler told *The American Lawyer*, "I have no criticism of Sam Butler whatsoever.")

McKay, undeterred, told the IRS about some of the questionable Middle East payoffs. In May 1983, the SEC launched an investigation. Soon after, McKay was fired, along with Harry Williams, another Ashland vice president who had supported McKay's position. John Hall, who had been promoted to become the new CEO, said McKay's fixation on the Omani matter had undermined his effectiveness. (As chief operating officer, Hall was the official who actually authorized the $1.3 million payment to Omar.) Williams's firing was credited to a necessary management downsizing.

In 1986, the SEC charged that Ashland's purchase of Landon's chrome mine violated the FCPA. The company promptly entered into a consent decree, agreeing to face criminal penalties for future violations, but admitted no wrongdoing. (Butler later referred to the consent decree as a "wrist slap" that was not worth fighting. But SEC enforcement division head Gary Lynch told *The American Lawyer* that the matter was "a high priority investigation." He also told *The Washington Post* that the reason the SEC did not pursue the Omar case, as well as the allegations involving Saudi Arabia and Abu Dhabi, was because the agency was seeking only an injunction—a court order barring Ashland from further questionable acts—rather than fines, and the Landon charges were sufficient to obtain that result. The IRS initiated no proceedings with respect to Ashland's foreign payments.)

Meanwhile, McKay and Williams sued Ashland and top company officials in federal district court in Kentucky for wrongful discharge. They claimed that they were fired for blowing the whistle on the Middle East payments. Their complaint alleged that the defendants had violated the FCPA, as well as the federal Racketeer Influenced and Corrupt Organizations Act (RICO). (Wilmer, Cutler did not represent McKay in the suit, because, according to attorney Michael Klein, he and one of his colleagues were essential witnesses in the case.)

Ashland's defense team included Sam Butler and Cravath. That didn't sit right with McKay and Williams, who asked the judge, William Bertelsman, to disqualify them as defense counsel. On August 6, 1985, McKay's new attorney, John McCall, told Judge Bertelsman, "It was Sam Butler who was trying . . . to get the sultan of Oman to make statements that Butler knew to be fraudulent. It was Butler who knew that the chief executive officer of Ashland had committed acts which would result in that chief executive officer's 'going to the slammer.' And then it was Butler who engineered the cover-up of those very activities." On January 29, 1986, the judge ruled that Butler was an essential witness in the case and granted the motion to disqualify Butler and his firm from representing Ashland.

When the case went to trial in April 1988, the plaintiffs sought to prove that, indeed, Omar and Landon were Omani officials—and that Ashland knew it. Ashland's central defense was that it had relied on the advice of Butler, Queenan, and its other lawyers. But the plaintiffs countered by contending that the Queenan report was a whitewash.

On the stand, Queenan insisted that his investigation was independent and unbiased. Although he acknowledged that he "was unable to conclude that [Landon] was not a foreign official," he contended that the chrome mine deal was genuine. The defendants offered evidence that the chrome mine might have been worth $25 million. The defendants also offered documents and expert testimony countering the claim that Omar was an Omani government official. They also proffered opinions from other power lawyers—Harvey Pitt of the 363-attorney New York–based firm Fried, Frank, Harris, Shriver & Jacobson and Milton Freeman of Washington's Arnold & Porter—that Queenan's report was conducted with professionalism and independence.

But these contentions were weakened by notes, introduced at trial by the plaintiffs, written by Ashland general counsel Mayne. One, dated April 1, 1981, stated, "CQ concludes Mr. X not an FO." Although Mayne testified that he did not recall this conversation, he acknowledged at trial that "CQ" would have referred to Queenan, "Mr. X" to Omar, and "FO" to "foreign official." Here was evidence that, even before he was hired to conduct his "independent" investigation, Queenan was promising to deliver the conclusion that would get Ashland off the hook. In another note, written just three days before Ashland hired Queenan, Mayne wrote that Queenan " 'will try hard' to give opinion of counsel no violation of the FCPA. . . . Conclusion— CQ indicated (reluctantly) he will be willing to opin[e] no violation of the FCPA are either (i) a finders fee or (ii) consulting arrangement if all the documents are signed." (A spokesman for Queenan later indicated that the phrase "if all the documents are signed" referred to the ultimately unsuccessful effort by Ashland to get the sultan of Oman to certify that Omani laws had been obeyed.)

Despite his notes, Mayne insisted at trial that he did not know what Queenan's conclusion would be. When Queenan testified, he denied that either conversation had occurred.

When the plaintiffs shifted their focus to Butler, they contended that he pursued the foreign payments issue only in order to get rid of Atkins. But once that was accomplished, the plaintiffs claimed, Butler saw McKay's complaints as nothing more than an annoyance. The plaintiffs introduced Butler's notes of the September 17, 1981, board meeting at which Atkins offered his resignation. According to these notes, "While [Atkins] would continue to have the title of chairman of the board and chief executive officer until September 30, 1981, he would act in that capacity during the period only with respect to the [Queenan] investigation." When a lawyer for the plaintiffs asked Butler, testifying at the trial, whether Atkins was left in charge of Queenan in order to ensure a favorable report, Butler offered a response that was, under the circumstances, remarkable for a man of his accomplishments and abilities: "For the life of me, I can't understand why I wrote those opinions that way, because I don't know what it means. I'm sorry."

On the stand, Butler also appeared to have trouble explaining certain other corporate documents. One Ashland attorney's notes of the January 7, 1981, meeting made this comment about Butler's view of Ashland's arrangements for managing consulting contracts abroad: "[Butler] fears leaving too many tracks—this leads the govt. to you. If you start a monitoring procedure what do you do if you find something afoul." Butler testified: "I don't really have a clear recollection of saying anything along those lines. What I said was that it would be undesirable to adopt a set of arrangements which would be too stringent, which if you didn't meet would . . . give the government a road map as to something you didn't do that you said yourself you should have."

Butler was also confronted with notes from a November 1980 Ashland board meeting that read, "Orin Atkins wants to use [Tradeco, another Ashland joint venture with Yehia Omar] to act in crude oil purchase. . . . Give us insulation from charges." The notes add that Butler indicated that "Foreign Corrupt Practices Act is a problem." "Does that help refresh your recollection about setting up a trade company to insulate Ashland Oil from charges of FCPA violations?" Butler was asked by McKay's attorney. "I don't know why," Butler answered. "That had nothing to do with avoiding the Foreign Corrupt Practices Act."

Butler also had to acknowledge that, in the spring of 1981, as it became clear that Omar's $1.3 million contract would have to be canceled, he and Atkins considered a new $3 million deal with Omar. But he insisted that the two deals were unrelated. The $3 million contract, for various business services Omar would perform for Ashland, was never concluded.

When the two-month trial ended, the six-member jury awarded $44.6 million to McKay and $24.9 million to Williams—one of the largest awards ever in a wrongful discharge case. (The primary component of the award was triple damages as provided under RICO.) On August 26, 1988, Ashland dropped its threat to appeal and settled the case by paying the two former vice presidents a combined $25 million.

Although Butler and Queenan were not defendants in the case, jurors interviewed after trial by The American Lawyer found fault with their behavior. The foreman, Robert Schworer, said, "I thought [Butler] originally started out convinced that what Ashland was doing was wrong; but once he found out he could hide behind the Queenan report, he changed horses in midstream." Another juror, John McGee, said, "We felt [the Queenan report] was more or less a cover-up," and added that "[i]t seemed like [Butler] was covering up." Another juror said that Queenan was "[a]bsolutely a liar. Butler was just as bad." A fourth juror also accused Butler and Queenan of lying.

In a 1988 interview with The American Lawyer, Butler denied any wrongdoing and suggested that Judge Bertelsman was biased. (In response to inquiries from the same publication, Queenan declined to comment.) But The American Lawyer's outstanding account of the case concluded by properly asking, "Does Butler, as the company lead attorney since the 1960s and a board member since 1970, bear some responsibility for the company's ethical shortcomings?"

As of 1996, Butler remained on the board of directors of Ashland Oil and continued to provide legal representation to the company.

As the Butler-Ashland case suggests, when a law firm member serves on the board of a corporation while that lawyer's firm represents that same corporation, a serious question arises: Can one person loyally serve the company as a board member without compromising the standards of an outside lawyer as an independent professional with duties to the legal system as well as to the client? Unfortunately, many of the most influential lawyers in the United States are not sufficiently troubled by this question to avoid such dual allegiances. In addition to Butler, there is former U.S. attorney general Benjamin Civiletti, a partner at Baltimore's Venable, Baetjer and Howard. He sits on the board of directors of Bethlehem Steel, a company his firm represents. The same is the case for former U.S. secretary of state Cyrus R. Vance, of the firm Simpson Thacher & Bartlett and the board of the New York Times Company. Washington lawyer and political power broker Robert S. Strauss sits on the board of agribusiness giant Archer-Daniels-Midland Co., a client of his firm, Akin, Gump, Strauss, Hauer & Feld. Strauss's partner at Akin, Gump, Vernon E. Jordan, Jr., a close associate of President Clinton, is a board member of both Union Carbide Corporation and Xerox Corporation, both clients of his firm. And there are many others, including: Thomas A. Reynolds, Jr. (Winston & Strawn and the Gannett Company); Nicholas D. Chabraja (Jenner & Block and General Dynamics Corporation); James R. Ukropina (O'Melveny & Myers and Lockheed Corporation); and Robert E. R. Huntley (Hunton & Williams and Philip Morris Co.).[127]

These are just some of the ways and means used in the corporate law trade. Subsequent chapters will examine in more detail the strategies and tactics power lawyers use to try to crush opponents representing shareholders, employees, customers, small businesses, and the public interest in corporate and government accountability. It will be seen how corporate attorneys scheme to hide corporate misbehavior by pressuring opponents for confidentiality orders and hiding or even destroying damning company files; how they try to force off the legal landscape witnesses, opposing lawyers, and even judges who stand in the way of victory for their clients; and how they use meritless but threatening lawsuits to strike back at opponents who dare to cross them. The corporate lawyer–directed drive to rewrite the liability rules in Washington and throughout the states to immunize big business clients from responsibility for their actions, even when such actions cause grave harm to individuals and society at large, will be tracked. And we will also describe the one area in which power lawyers dare to steamroll the corporate clients to whom they otherwise bow: over-billing for their legal services. As we proceed, changes that could transform the corporate attorney–dominated, no-contest legal world into one rooted more often in fairness, honesty, and fidelity to just principles should become apparent.

CHAPTER 2

I'VE GOT A SECRET

*I*N THE 1950S AND 1960S THERE WAS A POPULAR TELEVISION GAME show called *I've Got a Secret*. On the program, four celebrity panelists tried to discover a contestant's "secret" by asking a series of questions that could be answered yes or no. If the celebrities failed to guess the secret, the contestant won a cash prize. It was all great fun.

Today, big law firms and their corporate clients play their own version of the game. Only, the action isn't televised, there are rarely celebrities, and the game isn't fun at all. The corporate lawyer version of *I've Got a Secret* allows evidence of corporate wrongdoing, evidence relevant to public policy debates and consumer interests, to remain hidden, frequently from the public and sometimes even from victims of the wrongdoing. It is a dangerous strategy, with grave consequences for the public welfare.

THE PRICE OF SECRECY

Power lawyers use and manipulate the rules of law to play their secrecy game. This chapter examines three primary tools that corporate attorneys use to shroud litigation in secrecy: protective court orders, confidential settlements, and vacature agreements. Judges issue *protective orders* to prevent one side of a lawsuit from obtaining certain information in the possession of the other side or from taking information that *is* obtained from the other side during the development of a case (known as discovery; see Chapter 3) and sharing it with anyone else. In a typical *confidential settlement*, the party who sued is paid damages to resolve the claim, on condition that the facts of the case and the amount of the settlement be kept a secret. A *vacature* is an agreement, approved by the presiding judge after trial, to "vacate" the result, which has the legal effect of voiding it as if it never occurred and stripping the case of any precedential value in future lawsuits. Vacatures are usually accompanied by a confidential settlement, under which the parties agree to a court order sealing the records of the trial, with the result that no one has access to the evidence that was presented.

Such practices exact a heavy toll. Secrecy deprives people of the power to decide. In order for people to make informed decisions about how they will conduct their lives, about which products to purchase and which to avoid, about which companies to patronize, and the like, they need access to information. "Information is power," write attorneys Nicole Schultheis and Arthur Bryant. "Without information, the public is powerless to act. With information, the public can act to make sure that illegal conduct ceases, that victims are fairly compensated, that problems are appropriately resolved, and that future injuries are prevented."[1] Today, a parent may buy a child car safety seat unaware that other children have been severely injured or killed in that model due to a product defect. A secret settlement may have swept the potential danger under the rug. A doctor may prescribe medication unaware that there are potential side effects being kept from the public by the drug company, side effects that may take his patient's life. Why? Because a secret settlement buried information about the side effects. A woman may seek help from a mental health professional unaware that he has been repeatedly accused of sexually assaulting his patients, because he secretly paid his previous victims for their silence through confidential settlements.

The justice system is a public institution funded by taxpayers, and secrecy inhibits its proper working. The judicial branch of government is responsible for facilitating the peaceful redress of grievances, but secrecy prevents the public from adequately judging whether the judicial branch is performing effectively and efficiently. Moreover, because of court-endorsed confidentiality, people who have been injured due to circumstances similar to those being kept secret may remain unaware that they have a right to make a claim or that there is favorable legal precedent on their side. As a consequence, they may bear the entire burden of their injuries or other losses while the wrongdoer who caused their damages escapes unscathed. Secrecy also adds to cynicism about the justice system itself. When powerful interests are able to manipulate public courts to substantially shield wrongdoing from public scrutiny, people detect a double standard—openness for regular people involved in the courts and secrecy for the rich and powerful.

When corporations, unable to resolve their differences, sue each other, they avail themselves, for no fee, of assistance from judges and other resources of the courts. Yet when they wish to hide information unearthed through litigation, these same corporations often turn around and seek to turn the judiciary into a private sanctum for their damaging or embarrassing secrets.

Secrecy also undermines the proper functioning of government. Democracy shrivels without substantially free access to information. If government officials are kept in the dark, they are unable to perform their duty. When people do not know the facts, they cannot put pressure on government to pass laws necessary to promote the general welfare. Conscientious regulators, denied judicially produced information, cannot set proper safety standards or issue product recalls. Secrecy runs counter to the open processes and access to information envisioned by the Founding Fathers when they established the United States Constitution.

Secrecy is primarily the tactic of lawyers for corporations rather than lawyers for individuals, especially if the lawsuit is between an injured person and an alleged corporate wrongdoer. Washington State attorney Leonard Schroeter, who began his legal career practicing with Thurgood Marshall and later became a top products liability lawyer, knows well the power-lawyer tactic of imposing secrecy in civil cases. He says the reason corporate lawyers usually insist on secrecy is found in the nature of their representation: "Plaintiffs' lawyers represent real people. The representation is a onetime situation. The client hasn't done anything and usually has nothing to hide. On the other hand, corporate lawyers often are dependent on their major clients, who pay them huge amounts of money. This money talks, causing many corporate lawyers to abdicate professional judgment to the client. When corporations have something to hide, they often insist on secrecy and the lawyers are happy to go along."[2]

A GAME OF HIDE-AND-SEEK

When most people envision lawsuits, they imagine two dynamic trial lawyers duking it out over a matter of great public import in a majestic wood-paneled court in front of a crotchety judge with a droll sense of humor—in short, something out of *Inherit the Wind*. Indeed, trials can be very compelling affairs. That is why they are increasingly being televised.

Trials are public events, and only in unusual types of proceedings (such as juvenile criminal cases) can the public or the media be excluded. However, the trial itself is only a very small part of the total litigation story. Most cases never get to trial because they are settled or dismissed during the pretrial phase. Even those relatively few cases that are tried are largely shaped by the extensive work performed by the attorneys before they ever begin the process of picking the jury.

It is here, in the trenches of litigation practice, where corporate lawyers routinely use secrecy to delay justice, prevent their opponents from obtaining the information necessary to prove their case, and keep information damaging to their clients from ever reaching the public.

PRETRIAL PROTECTIVE ORDERS

Proceedings before trial are the meat and potatoes of litigation. This pretrial stage is largely devoted to *discovery*, where each side is allowed to investigate the case thoroughly and seek to discover relevant facts and information in the possession of the adverse party and others. Discovery activities include taking witness statements under oath (depositions), compelling parties to answer written questions under oath (interrogatories), and subpoenaing and reviewing documents, such as internal memos and technical reports. Discovery can facilitate settlements and eliminate disruptive and unfair surprises at trial. The more at stake in the case, usually the more pretrial workup performed. It isn't glamorous and it isn't fun, but it is where most lawsuits are made or broken. Winning the discovery war is often the key to winning the lawsuit, whether the case ends by voluntary dismissal, by negotiated settlement, or by the decision of the judge or jury.

Under the rules that govern discovery in federal and state courts, each side must permit the other to discover all evidence in its possession, even if such evidence would harm the disclosing party's case, except where the evidence falls within a few narrow categories that make it privileged. (For example, confidential communications between attorney and client, or between doctor and patient, or between husband and wife are often privileged.) Even evidence that would not be admissible in court is subject to disclosure through discovery, on the theory that such evidence might lead to other evidence that *would* be admissible.

Despite the broad reach of the discovery rules, there are often protracted and heated disputes among litigating parties over the extent and scope of discovery. (See Chapter 3.) Power lawyers routinely choreograph secrecy into the pretrial stage of lawsuits by obtaining protective orders from the judge either (1) preventing the other side from obtaining information or (2) preventing material that is provided to the other side during discovery from being disclosed to third parties. Efforts by power lawyers to obtain the first kind of protective order—keeping documents or witnesses away from the opposing side—are discussed in subsequent chapters. This chapter looks at the second kind of protective order—in which information is shared with the opponent but shielded from everybody else. This latter kind of protective order is sometimes called a secrecy order. When asked for discovery information, defense lawyers will often refuse to disclose it unless the other side agrees to a secrecy order preventing those involved in the case—the lawyers, parties, and witnesses—from sharing any knowledge obtained.

Under federal court rules and similar rules that apply in state courts, a party seeking a protective order must demonstrate "good cause" for its request.[3] Normally, a party must prove to the judge that the order is necessary to protect proprietary business information or an established privilege. That can take time and effort, which suits corporate lawyers just fine: The time and expense spent battling over discovery secrecy works against the interests of individual litigants, who may be badly injured, financially ruined, or otherwise in need of a quick resolution of the case. Power lawyers exploit this imbalance to coerce plaintiffs into agreeing to secrecy orders. They can be confident that plaintiffs and their lawyers will agree to keep the fruits of discovery secret in order to get on with the matter, and that judges, anxious to keep their dockets clear, will routinely sign stipulated secrecy orders rather than insist on carefully reviewing matters on which the parties agree. Thus, many cases against corporations are conducted with pretrial secrecy orders firmly in place.

What do these orders look like? The simplest of them bind the lawyers in a case to share confidential information disclosed through discovery only with persons whose input is required in the case—normally only parties, law firm employees, and expert witnesses. More elaborate secrecy orders impose complex systems for affirming adherence to the secrecy requirements—for example, demanding that a copy of the secrecy order itself, sometimes ten to twenty pages in length, be affixed to every single confidential document. Or requiring that every single time a document is viewed, the person examining it affirm compliance with the secrecy order by notarized signature. Some secrecy orders include threatening language warning readers that any violation of the order could result in a fine or imprisonment—since violations could amount to contempt of court, for which, indeed, a judge can send violators to jail. And most secrecy orders conclude with a demand that all confidential documents be returned at the end of the case to their corporate owners. To add insult to injury, sometimes corporations even demand that the secrecy order itself be sealed, thereby keeping from public scrutiny the elaborate measures the corporation insists on to hide its files.

This strategy usually has more to do with the big picture than with the individual case at hand. The company does not want one lawsuit to spark others or to weaken its position in similar pending cases. If a corporation has manufactured a defective product or engaged in an improper business practice, there are often multiple lawsuits filed all over the country by different people who have been affected. Secrecy in each case is designed to give the corporate lawyers a big advantage in defending all of the cases.

When a corporation faces many lawsuits over the same product or issue, its lawyers will establish a system of centralized advocacy, using in-house counsel or a big outside firm to coordinate all of the litigation around the country, with regional or local counsel retained to handle the day-to-day tasks. Thus, what a corporate lawyer in Michigan discovers during a case is soon shared with his or her colleagues representing the same client in California, Arizona, and Maine. A tactic that has worked in California will soon be utilized in Maine, Arizona, and Michigan.

There's nothing wrong or improper about sharing information. In fact, centralized coordination is a very effective litigation strategy, permitting maximum output and efficiency and reducing the need for extended periods of discovery. That's exactly why corporate lawyers use secrecy orders to prevent adversaries from enjoying a similar benefit. Take, for example, a protective order approved by a California Superior Court judge in Los Angeles in a case brought by Milton Green. Green's wife, Ester-Ruth Green, burned to death in January 1981 when her 1981 General Motors Chevrolet Chevette was rear-ended. Green's attorney contended that the Chevette was defectively designed, with an extremely vulnerable rear-location fuel tank, and he sought General Motors safety documents and crash test results that might prove his claim.[4] Such information might have been of interest to any Chevette owner or anyone considering purchasing a Chevette, as well as other victims of fires resulting from Chevette accidents. GM's attorneys crafted a draconian eight-page secrecy order. It expressly warns readers that failure to maintain the confidentiality of the GM records will put the violator "in contempt of court . . . subjecting the violating party to fine and imprisonment." And after stating again and again that GM information provided to Green's lawyer must be kept secret and not shown to anyone, GM feels compelled to single out perhaps its biggest concern:

> Under no circumstances shall any such information be disclosed or otherwise conveyed to parties, counsel or witnesses (including expert witnesses) in other actions (or claims which have not yet resulted in suit) against General Motors Corporation.

When the lawyers who are representing similarly injured individuals are prohibited by court order from communicating with each other about what information they have discovered, there can be extensive delay and duplication of effort. Each lawyer is forced to reinvent the wheel in each case. One lawyer must spend years trying to pry out information a corporation already has supplied another lawyer in a similar case, information that could lead to a prompt resolution of the case, to the benefit of the client and the court system.

In their book *Confidentiality Orders*,[5] authors Francis H. Hare, James L. Gilbert, and William H. ReMine demonstrate how secrecy orders delay justice, increase the costs of litigation, and create a cynical "catch me if you can" system of discovery where valid claims may be lost if one plaintiff's lawyer isn't able to obtain information already in the hands of another lawyer—even if that lawyer is suing the same company based on the same type of wrong. Moreover, as we will discuss in Chapter 3, there are cases of corporate lawyers improperly withholding or even destroying evidence adverse to their clients, sometimes after the evidence has been effective in an earlier case. Secrecy makes it easier for unethical lawyers to get away with such conduct because the opposing lawyer who obtained the information is prevented by court order from sharing this evidence with his or her colleagues, evidence that may never see the light of day again.

Secrecy orders can prevent the public from learning the truth about harmful products and conditions. For example, court-ordered secrecy can suppress information that, if made public in medical journals, would encourage doctors to stop prescribing dangerous medications.

Not coincidentally, pretrial secrecy orders also benefit power lawyers by generating extra discovery work. The discovery process is complex and time-consuming. In the legal system, matters that are complex and time-consuming usually add up to high fees for lawyers who charge by the hour. Thus secrecy orders in and of themselves produce profits for corporate litigation lawyers, keeping their billing meters running and running.

THE CASE OF THE DEPOSED DICTATOR

It isn't too often that the public gets to look behind the scenes at material blocked from view by pretrial protective orders. However, several years ago the curtain of secrecy was lifted in a case involving Westinghouse Electric Corporation and the Republic of the Philippines.

On December 1, 1988, the Philippine government of President Corazon Aquino filed a multimillion-dollar lawsuit against Westinghouse and the New Jersey engineering firm Burns and Roe Enterprises, Inc., in federal district court in New Jersey. The charges were serious, accusing Westinghouse and Burns and Roe of conspiring in the mid-1970s to bribe former Philippine dictator Ferdinand Marcos in order to secure a contract to build a nuclear power plant. The Philippine government contended that $17.2 million in sales commissions Westinghouse paid a Marcos crony named Herminio T. Disini, plus another $2.3 million Burns and Roe paid, were in fact bribes that were passed on to Marcos.

During the pretrial stage of the case, the Philippines and Westinghouse lawyers agreed, at Westinghouse's request,[6] to a protective order granting Westinghouse the power to declare which documents turned over in discovery were to be confidential. That maneuver effectively kept the evidence regarding the allegations against Westinghouse out of the public eye.

But then Westinghouse lawyers filed a written motion for summary judgment, an effort to convince the judge that there were no disputes as to the relevant facts and that the case could be decided, in Westinghouse's favor, without a trial. The Philippines filed a brief opposing the motion. The judge, Dickinson R. Debevoise, heard oral argument on the motion, and this hearing was open to the public. In arguing the motion, the lawyers quoted evidence from the court record.

On September 20, 1991, Judge Debevoise denied Westinghouse's motion. Thereafter, Westinghouse asked the judge to seal the briefs and the documents used to support the motion—that is, to lock up these items and keep them from the public. But by now the documents had been placed before a court as evidence. They concerned a matter of strong public interest—alleged bribery by Westinghouse, one of the United States' most powerful defense contractors and business conglomerates, as well as relations between the United States and the Philippines. Two civic groups, Public Citizen and Essential Information,[7] intervened in the lawsuit to seek public release of the documents.[8] They requested a court order unsealing the records on the basis that the protective order was inconsistent with the long-established public right of access to judicial records, as well as with the First Amendment to the U.S. Constitution. The judge agreed with the organizations and granted their request. Westinghouse appealed to the United States Third Circuit Court of Appeals.

The power lawyers representing the huge corporation in the case were the high-priced firms of Cravath, Swain & Moore of New York; Donovan, Leisure, Rogovin, Huge and Schiller of Washington, D.C.; Wolf, Block, Schorr and Solis-Cohen of Philadelphia; and Shanley &

Fisher of Morristown, New Jersey. That is a lot of expensive legal capacity. Why would Westinghouse spend such a considerable amount of
its stockholders' money to fight a battle that, as a formal matter at least,
had no bearing on the ultimate outcome of the case brought by the
Philippines?

Judge Debevoise's summary of the evidence that Westinghouse
wanted sealed provides a good clue. In his decision granting the request
to unseal the records of the motion, the judge wrote:[9]

> First, there is evidence that by decree President Marcos had
> placed NPC [National Power Company, the party that made
> the deal with Westinghouse] directly under the control of his
> office.
>
> Second, there is evidence that both Westinghouse and
> Burns & Roe believed that in order to obtain the PNPP
> [Philippines Nuclear Power Plant] contracts they sought, they
> would need the assistance of a powerful person having influ-
> ence with President Marcos. Disini was the person they se-
> lected to fill that role and there is evidence that both
> Westinghouse and Burns & Roe expected and knew that pay-
> ments they made to Disini would be passed on in whole or in
> part to the President or would otherwise be at his disposal.
>
> Third, there is evidence that Disini communicated with
> President Marcos and obtained from him authority to handle
> the PNPP contracts.
>
> Fourth, it is undisputed that both Westinghouse and Burns
> & Roe entered into commission agreements with companies
> controlled by Disini pursuant to which millions of dollars were
> paid to those companies. There is evidence that the amounts
> of the payments were far in excess of any amounts which simi-
> larly situated companies would normally pay in such circum-
> stances and that the payments were not made in the normal
> course but were transmitted to Swiss and other foreign bank
> accounts and were disguised by [payment-receiving companies]
> and by Westinghouse and Burns & Roe.
>
> Fifth, there is evidence that President Marcos personally
> intervened in the PNPP project to ensure that Burns & Roe
> [and] Westinghouse obtained the [contracts] and that the
> terms were satisfactory to Westinghouse . . .
>
> Sixth, there is evidence that both Westinghouse and Burns
> & Roe took steps to cover up the payments, suggesting guilty
> minds. . . . After 1977 reports in the press suggested that West-

inghouse may have made improper payments to obtain the
PNPP contract, Westinghouse burned the files in Manila relating to the procurement of the contract. Other records were destroyed and other efforts were made to avoid discovery of
the . . . agreement.

What Westinghouse's lawyers appeared to be interested in protecting with the secrecy order were not issues involving trade secrets, such
as power-plant design specifications, but facts that would be embarrassing to their client, facts that the public had an interest in learning. In
November 1991, a three-judge panel of the court of appeals upheld the
order of the trial court. Writing for the appellate court, Judge Dolores
Sloviter affirmed the strong public interest in ensuring that such proceedings are open to public scrutiny: "Certainly, the allegations of
bribes by a major United States corporation to the leader of a foreign
country is a matter of public interest, which could give rise to public
debate." Judge Sloviter concluded that openness should be the general
rule because "access to the judicial process reinforces the democratic
ideals of our society."[10]

The judges had made the right decision. Big corporations and their
power lawyers cannot turn public courts into private domains simply
because they are embarrassed about their own behavior.

(When the case finally went to trial in March 1993, the Philippines was unable to prove its charges of bribery. The jury ruled in favor
of Westinghouse and Burns and Roe.[11] The Philippine government appealed, claiming that Judge Debevoise's instructions to the jury mis-
stated the law. In October 1995, Westinghouse and the Philippines
finally settled their dispute over the power plant, which was completed
in 1985 but never went into operation due to alleged construction defects. The Philippines agreed to drop an appeal of the federal court suit
over the bribery charges as well as related fraud charges [concerning the
plant's construction] pending before an international arbitration panel
in Geneva. It also agreed to allow Westinghouse to resume business activities in the Philippines. In return, Westinghouse agreed to pay the
Philippine government $100 million in cash and equipment and ex-
pressed "deep regret" over the matter.[12])

Conscientious trial judges like Judge Debevoise take seriously their
obligation to approve protective orders only if such orders are genuinely
required to protect tightly held, legitimate secrets or privileges. Another
such jurist is Illinois federal district judge Robert J. Kauffman, who
presided over *Sieracki* v. *Ford Motor Company*, a case that arose when an
Illinois couple burned to death following a collision when the fuel tank

in their Ford Galaxie ruptured. In June 1978, Judge Kauffman was presented with a motion for protective order filed by the automaker. Ford argued, in effect, that allowing its auto design files to be made public would
be unduly burdensome because the plaintiff's lawyer would, in the judge's
words, "use discovery in the case to promote further litigation involving
[Ford]." In other words, Ford believed that if its secrets were exposed,
others harmed in Ford vehicle accidents might decide to sue Ford or
would gain an advantage in such litigation. Kauffman concluded that
this concern was not a legitimate basis for imposing a protective order.[13]

> It is difficult to complete discovery in complex and time con-
> suming products litigation such as this. We are concerned with
> specific automotive design defects which resulted in gasoline
> entering the passenger compartment upon impact. The mat-
> ters of discovery include corporate knowledge of the fact, the
> feasibility of alternative design, the cost of alternative design,
> the corporate decision-making process in selection of one de-
> sign alternative over another, the existence of documentary
> admissions regarding product safety, and corporate knowledge
> of the type of injuries caused by the design defect. None of
> these matters have been shown to be trade secrets or confiden-
> tial proprietary matter which should not be obtainable through
> discovery in this case or in other similar cases. Ford has not
> shown that it will be at any competitive disadvantage by re-
> vealing this information.
>
> I can find no good cause or compelling reason for denying
> public access to this information, including access by attorneys
> in similar proceedings. Quite the contrary, I believe this infor-
> mation should be available for use in a proper case. The avail-
> ability of such discovery may reduce time and money which
> must be expended to prepare for trial in those cases and may
> allow for effective, speedy and efficient representation.

THE CASE OF THE EXPLODING GAS TANKS

The decision in the *Sieracki* case came at a bad time for Ford—the cli-
max of the controversy over the safety of another Ford automobile, the
Pinto. The case of the Pinto, and of General Motors' efforts to hide
similar defects in its vehicles, provides insight into how power lawyers
use protective orders to strengthen a client's hand in court.

In 1971, Ford introduced the small, sporty Pinto. Unbeknown to
purchasers of the car, the Pinto had a dangerous safety problem: The lo-

cation of its gas tank, under the trunk and close to the rear bumper, and the manner in which it was installed rendered the Pinto susceptible to explosion and fire when hit from behind.

In 1973, the federal National Highway Traffic Safety Administration (NHTSA) was considering regulations to reduce the likelihood that automobile collisions would lead to fuel tank ruptures and resultant fires—particularly at speeds under 30 miles per hour. Ford opposed the regulations and prepared a secret internal memorandum that marshaled arguments against them. In the memo, entitled "Fatalities Associated with Crash Induced Fuel Leakage and Fires," Ford applied a cost-benefit formula to one part of the regulations: that aimed at reducing injuries and damage from fuel fires when vehicles rolled over. The formula worked as follows: Ford set the cost to society of a lost human life at $200,000, a burn injury at $67,000, and an incinerated Pinto at $700.[14] Ford estimated that the proposed government regulations would annually prevent 180 deaths, 180 burn injuries, and 2,100 incinerated vehicles from rollover fires in cars and light trucks nationwide. Multiplying and then adding these figures, the memo thus set the benefit to society from the regulations at $49.5 million. Ford then estimated that it would cost the company $11 per auto to meet the new standard. Applying this cost to all car and light trucks by all makers, the Ford memo calculated a total cost of $137 million to comply with the regulations. (In fact, however, another internal Ford memo from the same period estimated that the cost of compliance with the proposed NHTSA standards would be substantially less—$5.08 to $9.95 per vehicle.) Although the Ford memo examined fires only from rollovers, it contended that similar examination of costs and benefits for frontal, side, and rear impact crashes "would be expected to yield comparable results." Thus, Ford argued, the cost of the new regulations was far more expensive than the benefit.

In September 1977, an article in *Mother Jones* magazine disclosed the dangers of the Pinto fuel tank design.[15] The article used the Ford memo and other internal Ford documents to prove that Ford knew of the problem before it put the Pinto on the market. However, the cost-benefit study suggested it would be "cheaper" to compensate burn victims and their survivors than to modify the fuel tank to prevent fires in the first place. The *Mother Jones* article showed that Ford owned a patent on a better-designed gas tank but that cost and styling considerations ruled out any changes in the Pinto's tank design.

Soon after, in February 1978, an Orange County, California, jury awarded a man named Richard Grimshaw $3.5 million in compensatory damages and $125 million in punitive damages for injuries he sustained while a passenger in a 1971 Pinto that was struck by another car at an impact speed of 28 miles per hour and burst into flames. The jury's punitive damage award was $1 million more than the $124 million in profits Ford had made by not spending the few dollars for each Pinto's fuel tank modification since its introduction. (The trial judge later reduced the punitive damages to $3.5 million.)

In the wake of the *Mother Jones* story and publicity over the Grimshaw case, NHTSA granted a petition by the nonprofit Center for Auto Safety and launched an investigation into the Pinto. NHTSA crash tests of the Pinto resulted in significant fuel tank ruptures and leakage and, in some tests shown widely on television, enormous fireballs erupting from crashed Pintos.

Faced with much negative publicity and a dramatic drop in sales, Ford agreed to recall all 1971 through 1976 Pintos for modifications to the fuel tank. But the recall came too late for some Pinto passengers: At least twenty-seven people were killed, and many more were injured, as a result of Pinto fuel tank fires by the time of the recall.

The blow to Ford's reputation—exacerbated by the cruelly calculating tone of the cost-benefit memorandum—was serious, and Ford paid a price in lost sales, recall expenses, and lawsuits. But meanwhile, a strikingly similar internal memorandum, dealing with the same fuel tank issues, sat in the files of Ford's rival, General Motors. GM had placed the gas tanks in most of its cars in a vulnerable position—by the rear bumper—and, internal memoranda showed, on several occasions in the 1970s GM executives had rejected suggestions that the tanks be moved for safety reasons. But GM and its power lawyers succeeded where Ford had failed—not by making safer cars but by shielding the damaging memoranda from the public.

It was not until 1988 that a *Washington Post*[16] exposé publicized that GM's own fuel tank troubles had led to the preparation of a cost-benefit memo similar to Ford's. GM knew by the late 1960s from its own test data that its gas tanks were susceptible to rupturing in rear-end collisions. GM began to consider moving its gas tanks by mounting them over the rear axle. Successful crash tests supported the argument that the new location was far safer. But some GM officials objected, citing the resultant reduction in trunk space and a $8.59 to $11.59 cost increase per car. When in 1973 it appeared likely that the federal government would issue fuel tank regulations, GM took another look at the issues. This inquiry resulted in GM's own cost-benefit memo, which assumed the value of a human life to be $200,000 and estimated that at most five hundred people a year would die in GM vehicle accidents "where the bodies were burnt."

GM power lawyers, however, managed to keep this damaging information under wraps. When victims of fuel tank fires sued, GM disclosed documents to them only under confidentiality agreements. When claims proved meritorious, GM settled, but only on the condition that plaintiffs and their lawyers agreed to keep the information secret. Following one 1983 trial in Kansas, GM convinced the judge to seal the court transcript and exhibits—even though the proceedings had taken place in a public courtroom. The same year, GM power lawyers asked a Detroit judge to punish Darrell Peters, an attorney who five years earlier had won a $2.5 million verdict against GM in one of the few fuel tank cases that the giant automaker had allowed to go to trial. That case had settled following the verdict, with GM insisting on confidentiality as a condition of settlement. GM now claimed that Peters had violated the agreement by telling other lawyers suing GM about the existence of the cost-benefit memo. In 1986, Peters agreed to pay an $8,000 fine for the breach of confidentiality. (In 1988, a *Washington Post* reporter who was investigating this story contacted GM for comment, but the company declined, citing the confidentiality agreement.)

The safety standards that the federal government ultimately adopted permitted GM to keep the original tank location with some modifications. But by the early 1980s, GM had moved its car gas tanks to a safer location, under the backseat. Aggressive efforts to keep damaging secrets hidden for so long saved GM from the kind of public relations disaster Ford had suffered. The cost, however, was that millions of dangerous vehicles were put on the road—and many of these older models are still in circulation today, placing their occupants at continual risk. (As we shall see in subsequent chapters, GM tactics have not prevented major controversy over similar fuel tank problems with GM's pickup trucks.)

Chrysler Corporation, too, plays the secrecy game. Consider a 1987 protective order it demanded from a California Superior Court judge in a suit filed in Los Angeles. Shirley LoPrest sued Chrysler after her husband burned to death when his 1971 Dodge Demon was hit from behind and burst into flames. Her lawyer alleged that the Demon's fuel tank design was unsafe, creating a serious risk that fire would enter the passenger compartment on impact. Chrysler insisted that access to all documents it produced in response to LoPrest's discovery requests be limited to the parties, their attorneys, consultants, and expert witnesses. With the order in place, Chrysler crash test results and other company safety documents—information of strong interest to other Chrysler owners—remained hidden from public view. The case settled confidentially. The Chrysler files are still a secret.

THE CASE OF THE PAMPERED UTILITY

In the summer of 1990, Commonwealth Edison, the sole provider of electricity for the city of Chicago, experienced a severe problem delivering service to the city's West Side. Two separate blackouts, caused by power station fires, left a total of 65,000 residents without power for days. The blackouts occurred at the worst time for Chicagoans, when the heat and humidity off Lake Michigan turn the city into an inferno.

The blackouts raised significant doubts about the reliability of Commonwealth Edison and became a political issue of some significance in the city. As fate would have it, the blackouts occurred just as the utility giant's franchise contract with the city was up for renewal. Under public pressure, city political leaders decided that an investigation was in order.

Under Commonwealth Edison's franchise contract with Chicago, the city had the right to examine the utility's records. Thus Commonwealth Edison could not prevent city officials from reviewing internal documents. But the utility did not want the *people* of Chicago to gain access to the information. Accordingly, its attorneys, from the 608-lawyer Chicago-based firm Sidley & Austin (which paid a $7.5 million fine in the Lincoln Savings fiasco described in Chapter 1 and whose most recent annual gross revenues were $254 million), demanded and obtained a secrecy pact. Under the agreement, Commonwealth Edison had the right to stamp any document turned over to the city "confidential." Any document so stamped could not be disclosed to the public. Why a secrecy agreement about an issue of such clear public importance? "We made that agreement with the city to protect certain sensitive information from falling into the wrong hands," a Commonwealth Edison spokesman was quoted as saying.[17]

In this matter, as is often true when corporations seek secrecy agreements, the term "sensitive material" really meant embarrassing material. News media investigations revealed a poor record on safety matters: that Edison maintenance had declined significantly in the years prior to the blackouts; that the utility had been slow to turn off power so the fires could be adequately battled; that in the summer of 1988, Edison crews had used water from city fire hydrants to cool down overheated electrical equipment; and that Edison had failed to give the Chicago Fire Department a list of Edison sites that contained toxic chemicals.

James Ylisela, Jr., consulting editor for the *Chicago Reporter,* an investigative monthly that first broke the story about the confidentiality agreement, says, "This was a way to dilute city oversight by reducing public pressure on officials to be tough with Edison. It was also a way for Edison to avoid embarrassment. It was a real attack on public accountability."

Eventually, Edison relented on most of the confidential documents, and the media were able to take a look. "We found some problems and the public advocacy groups got on the case," Ylisela recalls. "The franchise was renewed, but there were some provisions in there that I don't think would have been had the confidentiality agreement held. For example, Edison is required to spend one billion dollars over the next ten years on infrastructure repair."[18]

Martin Cohen, director of the Illinois Citizen Utility Board (CUB),[19] says the secrecy agreement still sticks in his craw. "Nothing much came out of the investigation, and the shroud of secrecy made the outcome suspect," he says.[20]

So, even with respect to matters of intense public concern, too often, where power lawyers are involved, secrecy rules. People cannot effectively participate in public life and hold their elected representatives accountable if they are not allowed access to what is going on.

CONFIDENTIAL SETTLEMENTS AND VACATURE

Confidential settlements are even more damaging to the justice system and the public safety than are protective orders. This is the usual drill:

—A person is harmed, perhaps by a defective product, through medical malpractice, in an investment scam, or through wrongful termination from employment.

—The person sues, seeking redress in a court of law.

—Power lawyers are brought in by the defendant's insurance company or by the corporation itself.

—Years may pass as defense lawyers resist and avoid legitimate requests for discovery. (See Chapter 3.)

—Finally, if after years of wrangling the defense lawyers are forced to release the requested information, and if the now disclosed evidence proves the plaintiff's case, the defendant will offer a settlement.

—The settlement offered will come with one catch: In order to receive the money, the litigant and his or her lawyer have to agree to secrecy. The terms of the settlement will be kept secret, thereby preventing the public from knowing if the case was valid, while allowing the company to continue to insist that it did nothing wrong. (A million-dollar suit that settles for $750,000 was probably meritorious, while a case that settles for $5,000 probably was not provable.) Worse, the settlement offer will require that all the evidence discovered in the case be sealed against disclosure to other persons similarly injured, other lawyers representing such persons, the media, and government regulators—even if the secrecy serves no beneficial public purpose, and even if it endangers the public safety.

—Once the confidential settlement offer is made, the motivations of the litigants, once bitterly at odds, ironically merge. Each now has a vested interest in seeing the settlement go through. The corporation or insurance company can cut its losses and, more important, protect future profits and goodwill with the public by shrouding evidence of its own wrongdoing from public notice. Defense lawyers, having earned an ample fee, are able to resolve the matter successfully while retaining the confidence of the client. The plaintiff obtains money that is often desperately needed, without further delay or risk of losing the case in trial. If secrecy is the price to pay, most are willing to pay it. The plaintiff's lawyer, often working on a contingency fee, can collect his or her paycheck.[21] The court tends to rubber-stamp its approval since a large and cumbersome case is effectively taken off its hands.

There is only one loser: the American public.

Bill Lockyer, president pro tem of the California state senate, has sponsored legislation to limit confidential settlements. "The truth is," says Senator Lockyer, "corporations and their lawyers don't want corporate misdeeds made known to the public. They see the public courts as a private way for them to resolve their disputes. Confidential settlements promote that interest, sometimes at the expense of public safety."[22]

THE BREAST IMPLANT CONTROVERSY

There are so many secret settlements that hide defective products and poor performance by professionals, such as doctors and lawyers, that it is impossible to know the extent of human harm being perpetrated by the practice. However, in breast implant cases, court orders have recently lifted the veil of secrecy, exposing the very real harm caused by confidential settlements, not only to victimized consumers but also, ironically, to the long-term profitability of business enterprises.

Nineteen eighty-three was not a good year for Sybil Goldrich. That was the year the Southern California woman had a bilateral mastectomy to treat breast cancer. But she felt some consolation in the opportunity to have reconstructive surgery using silicone breast implants.

Goldrich wasn't worried about safety. As far as she knew, there were no health problems arising from implants. Her doctor, also unaware of any dangers, told her that the Dow Corning product salesman had bragged that the inserts should last a lifetime.

Unfortunately, manufacturers of silicone breast implants had a secret that they did not share with Sybil Goldrich and others considering breast implants. There were increasing signs that the prosthetic devices posed various health risks. But the power lawyers representing these companies had seen to it that the information about potential defects remained hidden.

Unknown to Goldrich, the year before she had her prostheses surgically implanted, a woman named Maria Stern had sued Dow Corning for damages caused when her own breast implants leaked. In 1976, Stern had implants inserted as part of a breast reconstruction after a mastectomy. Within two years she suffered from weight loss, joint pain, and hair loss. Stern's doctor searched for a cause of her health problems but was unable to make a diagnosis, much less find a treatment. Worse, Stern was growing increasingly ill. Finally, the doctor referred her to the Stanford Medical Center in Palo Alto, California.

It was now 1981. The Stanford doctors were equally puzzled. Then, one resident doctor recalled that he had read in a medical journal about the potential harm that could arise if a silicone breast implant ruptured. The doctors checked Stern's implants. Sure enough, both had ruptured, leaking silicone into her body.

The doctors removed the implants. Stern's symptoms were reduced but not eliminated. She began to exhibit symptoms similar to those associated with lupus, a chronic disease in which the body's own immune system attacks connective tissues, causing inflammation. Symptoms include rash, malaise, loss of appetite, fever, joint pain, nausea, and inflammation of the lining of the lungs. Stern approached the San Francisco law firm of Leroy Hersh and Nancy Hersh to see if Dow Corning could be held accountable for the harm her implants had caused her. Attorney Leroy Hersh recalls, "We knew we had a case. Ms. Stern was suffering from a serious disability and we believed it could be traced directly to the implant ruptures. But we had no idea of the level of knowledge of the problem that Dow Corning possessed."[23]

Stern sued Dow Corning in federal district court. Dow Corning's attorneys demanded a strict protective order requiring that all documents turned over in discovery be kept confidential. The judge granted a broad order, in essence giving Dow Corning the power to decide what information would be treated as confidential.

Despite the secrecy order, getting adequate discovery from Dow Corning was like pulling teeth. It took the Hersh firm more than a year to gain access to the information they would need to prove their case, with motions filed and court-ordered sanctions granted against Dow Corning and its lawyers for discovery abuse. "Finally, Dow Corning put us into a big room with one hundred boxes of material," Dan Bolton, then an attorney for the Hersh firm, says. "We spent one full week poring through the material and found 'smoking gun' memos. That was when we knew we could make out a good case for punitive damages."[24]

Discovery continued. Depositions were taken and other documents reviewed. Dow Corning offered $75,000 to settle the case, but the Hershes, confident that they had caught Dow Corning in serious wrongdoing, advised Stern to reject the offer.

The case finally went to trial in 1984. The trial took one month. At the end, the jury issued a "Special Findings" verdict, as follows:

1. Did the plaintiff establish by a preponderance of the evidence that the defendant manufactured a mammary implant which was defectively designed? YES.
2. Did the plaintiff establish by a preponderance of the evidence that the design of the product was the proximate cause of her injuries? YES.
3. Did the plaintiff establish by a preponderance of the evidence that the defendant manufactured a mammary implant which was defectively manufactured? YES.
4. Did the plaintiff establish by a preponderance of the evidence that the manufacturing defect of the product was the proximate cause of her injuries? YES.
5. Did the plaintiff establish by a preponderance of the evidence that the defendant breached an express warranty? YES.
6. Did the plaintiff establish by a preponderance of the evidence that the breach of warranty, if such you found, was the proximate cause of her injuries? YES.
7. Did the plaintiff establish by a preponderance of the evidence that the defendant breached an implied warranty? YES.

8. Did the plaintiff establish by a preponderance of the evidence that the breach of warranty, if any you found, was the proximate cause of her injuries? YES.
9. Did the plaintiff establish by a preponderance of the evidence that the defendant committed actionable fraud? YES.
10. Did the plaintiff establish by a preponderance of the evidence that the actionable fraud, if such you found, was the proximate cause of her injuries? YES.

The jury awarded $211,000 to Stern in compensatory damages and found the fraud of Dow Corning so egregious that it slapped the company with $1.5 million in punitive damages.

At the trial, documents kept secret during discovery were introduced into evidence. That made them part of the public record. But despite efforts by Nancy Hersh to interest the press in the dangers of silicone breast implants, the verdict and evidence received little media coverage.

Dow Corning immediately appealed. Handling its appeal was Shirley M. Hufstedler, once a federal district court judge and President Jimmy Carter's secretary of education, a woman who had once been touted as a possible nominee to the United States Supreme Court. (So zealous was Hufstedler in representing Dow Corning that the judges of the federal Ninth Circuit Court of Appeals accused her of misrepresenting, in her appellate brief, what had occurred at the trial. Hufstedler responded with a letter admitting an error of "draftsmanship" but not an intent to mislead the court.)

Meanwhile, all around the country the popularity of breast implants was growing. With little public indication that there were dangers to women's health associated with breast implants, tens of thousands of women were having them implanted. But thousands of these women were beginning to experience health problems. Soon, lawsuits began to multiply. A dark cloud was forming over the lives of implant recipients and the businesses of companies manufacturing the devices.

With the court of appeals decision in the Stern case expected shortly, the powers that be at Dow Corning decided that they wanted the case sealed and forgotten. The only way to accomplish that was to obtain a vacature and confidential settlement.

Dow Corning's lawyers called Nancy Hersh and offered a deal: If Stern agreed to join with Dow Corning to ask the trial judge to vacate the jury's verdict and to have the entire matter sealed by a secrecy order, and if Stern agreed to keep quiet the amount of money Dow

Corning paid to settle the case, then Dow Corning would pay the settlement and drop its appeal.

The case would not simply be over—*it would be as if it had never gone to court*. Consequently, no precedent would be set for future litigation, and all evidence introduced in the trial, all the wrongdoing uncovered by the Hersh firm, would be swept back under the carpet.

Stern wanted the information kept public, but she was in a bind. She needed the money. Her health was poor. She had suffered very real damage from the leaked silicone. Stern's lawyers also found themselves in a quandary. "The offer really created an internal conflict of emotions," says Dan Bolton. "On one hand, our highest loyalty is to our client. Yet there is the knowledge that secrecy may cause others to be injured."

In the end, Stern took the deal. Bolton felt horrible. He had read the evidence contained in Dow Corning's files and knew what it contained. Although he was barred by the agreement from disclosing what he knew—even to the government—he contacted the federal Food and Drug Administration (FDA) anyway. "During the course of the litigation, I had maintained a general dialogue with the FDA about these issues," Bolton says. "When it was over, I urged them to investigate."[25]

On November 22, 1988, Bolton traveled to Washington, D.C., to testify before the FDA General and Plastic Surgery Devices Panel meeting. He warned the panel that breast implants could cause severe consequences to the health of women. He testified that he had seen the documents in the Dow Corning files but added, "I am prevented from discussing these documents under the terms of a protective order requested by Dow. I can tell you, however, that the jury saw many of these documents and determined that Dow had committed fraud, misled the public and disregarded the safety of women in marketing silicone breast implants."

Members of the panel were skeptical. Because Bolton's hands were tied by the secrecy accord, his general allegations were not backed by factual data. One panelist, Dr. Norman Anderson, told Bolton that his testimony was "anecdotal" and not "scientific." He then asked Bolton, "Do you have any hard data? Do you have any evidence of fraud, falsehood and misrepresentation?"

Bolton wanted to tell Dr. Anderson and the panel all he knew. But he couldn't. He was prevented by the confidentiality agreement. All he could answer was, "We have the Stern case."

Meanwhile, more than 100,000 women each year, unaware of the danger, were having silicone breasts surgically implanted, some for reconstructive purposes, many more for cosmetic reasons. With the evidence revealed in the Stern case stuffed back in the vaults, Dow Corning initiated a new strategy for dealing with defective implants: a product replacement expense program, under which a woman who suffered from faulty implants would accept $600 from Dow Corning in exchange for the woman signing a general release freeing both Dow Corning and the doctor who performed the operation from further liability. Such callousness passed directly from executive suites to power-lawyer offices, as the fact that numerous women were experiencing health problems was systematically covered up by corporate attorneys through their strategy of obtaining protective orders and extracting a promise of confidentiality as the price of a fair settlement.

Back in July 1983, at a time when the Hersh firm was jumping through hoops trying to get access to Dow Corning's internal documents, Sybil Goldrich, following treatment for her breast cancer, received a breast implant. By December 1984, she was on her fourth prosthesis because of implant failures. At one point her implant began to break through her nipple graft. At the same time, she was experiencing pain, a body rash, fever, infections, and chronic exhaustion. She also had vaginal bleeding.

"It wasn't until 1986 that I began to put two and two together," Goldrich recalls. Unlike many breast implant victims, she was fortunate to be close to people who were in a position to get to the bottom of her health troubles. A friend of hers, longtime consumer advocate Mark Green, now New York City's elected public advocate, advised her to look into the silicone implants as a possible cause of her health problems. Goldrich's husband is an obstetrician-gynecologist. He conducted a search of the medical literature and found a handful of articles that addressed silicone implant problems. Goldrich was now convinced that the source of her illness was her implants. "And all that time," she says, "I had thought my problems were caused by the cancer.

"I wanted to sue," Goldrich recalls, "but could not find a lawyer. They simply did not know about the breast implant problems. They had no idea that there were other cases pending. They had no idea that other women were secretly settling cases."[26]

Later in 1986, Goldrich finally found a lawyer and brought suit in California state court. Lawyers for Dow Corning offered a settlement in exchange for a secrecy order and her promise that she would never speak publicly about health dangers associated with breast implants. This was one case where the corporation was particularly interested in buying silence: Goldrich had become an activist, speaking loudly and whenever she could against breast implants. Paying her off would help keep damaging information from the public. But Goldrich refused.

Dow Corning's lawyers responded by filing a motion to dismiss the case. Their claim was that Goldrich had waited too long to file the suit and that her claims were thus barred by the one-year statute of limitations. Goldrich filed her suit less than one year after discovering that her implant had ruptured. But the trial judge granted Dow Corning's motion to dismiss, holding that her implant problems had started more than a year before the filing date.

To add insult to injury, Dow Corning and other companies then sued Goldrich for costs associated with her failed lawsuit. The trial judge ordered her to pay $80,000 in costs. "They're going to punish me but good," Goldrich says. "Because I blew the whistle." Indeed, in 1988 Goldrich chronicled her implant difficulties in a Ms. magazine article[27] and cofounded the Command Trust Network, a national organization dedicated to supplying information to women regarding breast implants.

Also in 1988 Goldrich had a total abdominal hysterectomy for what turned out to be a benign tumor. However, upon biopsy, silicone was discovered in her ovaries and uterus. She also had a liver biopsy at the time of the hysterectomy because the surgeons saw spots on her liver. These proved to be silicone nodules.

Nearly ten years after filing suit, Goldrich's case remains unresolved. Unable to convince the California courts that she filed her suit quickly enough, she has asked a New York state court to hear her claims. "All I want is a few days in front of a jury of my peers," Goldrich says. "And a judge who is fair."[28]

Meanwhile, other women were falling ill after receiving silicone implants, and few of them knew why. The crucial information remained closely held by some breast implant manufacturing company executives, their power lawyers, and victims precluded from talking by confidential settlement agreements.

Ultimately, the lid blew off the cover-up. In one year alone, between July 1, 1992, and June 30, 1993, the FDA received 26,644 reports from women complaining of serious injuries associated with silicone breast implants.[29] More than five thousand of these women reported ruptures of one or both implants. There were 335 reports of lupus-type illnesses, and 113 reports of scleroderma, an autoimmune disorder that causes shortness of breath, palpitations, joint pain, and muscle weakness, and sometimes leads to heart, kidney, or respiratory failure.

So many breast implant lawsuits were filed that all cases were consolidated under the jurisdiction of one federal judge. In 1993, the judge, Sam C. Pointer, Jr., of Birmingham, Alabama, signed an order prohibiting breast implant manufacturers from enforcing confidentiality clauses in settlements and from seeking such clauses as part of future settlement agreements.

The implosion of the industry's secrecy strategy has opened the way for society to take a hard look at material that lawyers for Dow Corning and other implant manufacturers had fought so long and hard to keep from public view because of the story they tell. The documents that have been disclosed are voluminous. They reveal that Dow Corning employees repeatedly expressed concerns regarding the reliability of the implants. Following are a few examples.

In a May 16, 1975, memo to sales representatives, a Dow Corning executive noted that the company's silicone-gel-filled implants "have a tendency to appear oily after being manipulated." The executive claimed that "this is not a product problem," because the doctor performing the implant operation "will not see any appreciable oiling on the product removed from the package." But, the memo says, "[t]he oily phenomenon seems to appear the day following manipulation." The executive's solution to oil appearing on the outside of the implants? First, "change demonstration samples often," and second, "clean demonstration samples while traveling . . . wash with soap & water in nearest washroom, dry with hand towels. . . ." Frequent replacement and cleaning served the purpose of hiding the leakage from doctors who examined the prostheses tendered by Dow sales representatives. The memo provided no explanation to the sales force as to how women could wash and dry their implants once inside their bodies.

In another memorandum, dated January 15, 1976, a Dow Corning engineer complained forcefully about quality control problems with the company's implants. The engineer noted that there was "[d]isappointment that two of our units broke during augmentation surgery for the TV tape demonstrations." He mentioned meetings among Dow Corning employees to discuss the quality of implant outer envelopes: "We ended up saying the envelopes were 'good enough' while looking at gross thin spots and flaws in the form of significant bubbles. The allowable flaws are written into our current specifications. When will we learn at Dow Corning that making a product 'just good enough' almost always leads to products that are 'not quite good enough'?"

In a letter dated April 29, 1980, an angry Dow Corning salesman griped about quality control. He recounted a conversation with a doctor who was "very upset over the performance of our gel saline implants. To say that he was upset was putting it mildly [sic] actually he was downright indignant." The doctor, according to the letter, complained that the implant envelope was "to [sic] greasy" and that he was

"getting excessive gel bleed on all three pair that were given to him."
The salesman's letter added that the batch of implants that included
the ones about which the doctor complained "was put on the market
with prior knowledge of the bleed problem." The letter suggests that
the salesman was extremely frustrated. "I cannot begin to tell you," he
wrote, "how distressing this is to me . . . I have worked very hard for
over a year to bring [the doctor] back to Dow Corning. . . . The thing
that is really galling is that I feel like I have been beaten by my own
company instead of the competition. To put questionable mammaries
on the market is inexcusable." Referring to the Dow Corning implants
as "substandard products," he contended, "I don't know who is responsible for this decision but it has to rank right up there with the [Ford]
Pinto gas tank."

Evidence that Dow Corning knew that some of its product claims
were false is contained in a Dow Corning employee's internal memo,
dated September 15, 1983, addressing the quality of gels used in the implants. According to the memo, Dow Corning was selling one type of
implant gel as "Medical Grade," when in fact the company did not
"have adequate testing to qualify it as 'Medical Grade.' " The memo
called for "immediate action . . . to bring it into compliance with the
business definition of medical grade." Nor, according to the memo, did
the company have "valid long-term implant data to substantiate the
safety of gels for long-term implant use," although it had some data sub-
stantiating the safety of the type of material used in the gels. Dow
Corning, at the request of the FDA, released these and other documents on February 10, 1992. Company officials acknowledged that the
memos contained "inflammatory language," but said that the negative
memos were isolated complaints out of a long and favorable product
record. The same day, the company announced that its chairman, John
S. Ludington, would retire.

The dust has still not settled in the breast implant cases. In 1991,
the FDA, flooded with consumer complaints and having finally gained
access to what lawyers for breast implant victims had been able to discover in the files of manufacturers, authorized an advisory panel to review the problem. On January 6, 1992, the agency requested a
voluntary moratorium on the use of silicone-gel-filled breast implants
pending further review.

Desperate to head off the sheriff at the pass, one implant maker,
McGhan Medical Corp., sued in federal court seeking a restraining
order preventing the advisory panel from even considering the issue.
McGhan also asked the court to disqualify FDA chief Dr. David Kessler
on the ground that his continued questioning of the safety of the prod-

ucts showed that he was not an objective decision maker. A federal judge in Baltimore rebuffed these efforts.[30]

When the advisory panel met on February 18, 1992, attorney Dan Bolton, who had represented Maria Stern, was finally free to testify about what he knew. Bolton had represented Mary Ann Hopkins, another consumer injured by a breast implant. That case had gone to trial, and the evidence presented was in the public domain. In December 1991, Hopkins was awarded $7.34 million based on product defect, failure to warn, breach of warranty, and fraud. The jury in that case found Dow Corning's conduct "malicious and oppressive," warranting the imposition of punitive damages. Dow Corning appealed, contending that Hopkins had filed her claims too late, that the trial judge had admitted inappropriate expert testimony, and that the evidence at trial did not support a finding of fraud. It also contested the amount awarded. In August 1994, the Ninth Circuit Court of Appeals affirmed the jury verdict in all respects.[31] In 1995, the Supreme Court rejected Dow Corning's petition for review, and the case was over. Bolton told the FDA:

> Considerable evidence was presented during the Hopkins trial that Dow was aware of the risks of silicone as early as the 1960s and continued to market breast implants despite the absence of any studies demonstrating the long term safety of silicone in the human body. . . . During the trial, Dr. Robert Lavier [Dow's chief scientific officer] admitted that, by 1972, Dow was aware that silicone would migrate through the lymphatic system and to various organs of the immune system. . . . Dr. Lavier admitted at trial that this condition can be an auto immune response . . . Dr. Lavier admitted under cross examination that the longest testing on gel before Dow began to market its new implant in 1975 did not exceed 80 days. Further testing was halted due to marketing concerns. Significantly, the testing at 80 days showed chronic inflammatory response and evidence of granuloma formation, which can be a potential indicator of an immune response. . . . Dow privately acknowledged that it did not know the full range of hazards associated with silicone. In the mid-1980s, Dow scientists candidly admitted in confidential memos that Dow had no data supporting the long-term safety of silicone. . . . Rather than resolve this issue after selling breast implants almost 30 years, the head of research and development at Dow decided that it was best to "vigorously oppose" FDA efforts to require safety testing.

As a result of the hearings, the FDA required that women seeking breast implants for reconstructive purposes enroll in clinical studies to permit further evaluation of the health risks and that women who wanted implants for cosmetic purposes could do so only as part of FDA-approved research studies.

Meanwhile, in the litigation overseen by Judge Pointer, the industry created a $4.25 *billion* settlement fund made up of contributions from all major implant manufacturers to compensate victims. Dow Corning put up $2 billion of that amount.

Despite these developments, the American Society of Plastic and Reconstructive Surgeons continues to insist that silicone breast implants are safe. Also, a study partially funded by Dow Corning and the plastic surgeons group and undertaken by the Mayo Clinic found no link between breast implants and connective tissue disorders. But the Mayo study and a handful of other studies published thus far involved relatively small patient pools over short periods of time and cannot, says Commissioner Kessler, "rule out either a small but statistically significant increased risk in traditional connective tissue disease or the risk of atypical disease." And given, he notes, that an estimated one million women have received silicone breast implants, even a 1 percent causation rate would affect ten thousand women.[32] Research continues, including a major National Institutes of Health study that may at last provide some solid answers.

Whatever the result of these studies on connective-tissue issues, it is abundantly clear that breast implants rupture or, as Commissioner Kessler puts it, "fall apart," and that such rupturing poses a separate and widespread health problem. According to Kessler, a ruptured implant "can cause local symptoms. It can cause pain, it can cause nodules. No one wants a foreign substance leaking throughout one's body." And, Kessler reports, widely diverging published studies so far suggest that the implant "rupture and bleed rate is somewhere between 5 percent and 71 percent."[33] The concerns about rupturing expressed in the long-concealed internal Dow Corning memos were clearly well founded. (On November 27, 1995, at the annual meeting of the Radiological Society of North America, Dr. Michael S. Middleton of the University of California at San Diego summarized research findings that put the Dow Corning memos, especially the one about the doctor's complaint of "excessive gel bleed," in stark relief. According to Dr. Middleton, "Often, implants are called 'normal' when silicone gel is seen on the surface of the implant, and that gel is referred to as 'bleed.' In our experience, silicone gel on the surface of an implant is a sign that silicone gel has migrated through a hole or tear in the shell, and therefore that implant has ruptured. . . . To call a ruptured but uncollapsed implant 'gel bleed' may be a disservice to the patient."[34])

So, what does the implant case tell us about the power-lawyer game of "I've Got a Secret"? Maria Stern's attorney Nancy Hersh says that it is clear that unwarranted secrecy hurts people: "Confidential settlements and secrecy prevents the dissemination of information that could prevent injury to the public." And what about allegations from business interests that eliminating secrecy will only create unnecessary litigation? "I never intended to make a career of these cases," says Hersh. "I had a desire to right a public wrong and make public the fact that the breast implants were defective and to prevent other people from being injured. I was unable to do that effectively because of confidentiality agreements."[35]

How many women would have been spared a lifelong nightmare of health problems had secrecy not been imposed in these cases? Part of the responsibility rests with the media, which ignored the Stern case. But where one case can slip between the cracks, multiple cases of women suffering great harm from silicone breast implants would have generated tremendous media attention, as it eventually did. However, media scrutiny was delayed for years because of a deliberate secrecy strategy designed by lawyers to protect their clients from the consequences of their actions and to keep cash pouring in by leaving potential customers in the dark about the dangers.

In the end, secrecy backfired on the manufacturers. Because their lawyers had so successfully kept the lid on the potential dangers of implants for so long, two million implants were eventually sold. Each implant recipient is now a potential victim, entitled to compensation for the manufacturers' wrongdoing. More than 400,000 women have made claims under the settlement of the class action litigation before Judge Pointer, and there are many others, like Maria Stern and Sybil Goldrich, whose cases predated the settlement or who chose to opt out of that settlement and pursue their claims individually. Dow Corning, by far the leader in breast implant sales, filed for bankruptcy on May 15, 1995.

By then, it had become clear that the $4.25 billion settlement fund was nowhere near enough to compensate victims. On October 1, 1995, three of the breast implant makers, Bristol-Myers Squibb, Baxter, and 3M, reached an eleventh-hour tentative agreement with plaintiffs' lawyers to avert a total collapse of the settlement. The agreement would reduce the maximum amount injured women could receive in damages but eliminate the ceilings on overall contributions by the three participating defendants. However, obstacles remained: The agreement was subject to approval by corporate directors; another manufacturer, Union Carbide, rejected it; Dow Corning's bankruptcy apparently precluded it from raising its own contribution; and there was no telling how many of the most seriously injured victims would be spurred by the lower payments to pursue their claims individually.

A confidential settlement also helped delay public awareness of the dangers of General Motors' notorious Corvair automobile, introduced in 1959. John Petry, a Pennsylvania man, purchased a 1961 Corvair Greenbriar station wagon and used it to drive more than one hundred miles a day in his job. The Corvair heating system was based on an approach that other designers had long rejected, for obvious reasons: Air used to cool the engine was diverted into the passenger compartment to provide the heat. This process allowed lethal carbon monoxide fumes to enter the passenger space. Petry developed permanent brain damage. He hired Philadelphia attorney Edward Wolf, who, in 1962, filed suit in federal court against GM, alleging that the heater design was defective.

Although GM initially claimed that it did not know the design was dangerous, a GM engineer admitted in a 1966 deposition in the case that, in fact, the company considered the risks but decided to proceed with the design anyway. Following this deposition, GM and Wolf negotiated a settlement, one that, at GM's insistence, buried the facts about this hazardous design defect and its potentially lethal impact on GM customers. GM paid Petry $125,000. In return, Wolf acceded to GM's demand that he sell the company his entire case file, including all the depositions in the case and all expert witness reports. GM even bought the station wagon. Wolf and his client also had to agree not to discuss the case. Finally, GM demanded that Wolf amend the original 1962 complaint to change the basis of the case from design defect—which would implicate all similar Corvair cars—to manufacturing defect—which might cover only Petry's car. According to Wolf, at the time of the settlement, GM representatives told him that the company had received only one other customer complaint regarding fumes in the Corvair Greenbriar wagons.

In spring 1971, press accounts revealed that, in fact, GM had by 1966 received hundreds of customer complaints about fumes in Corvair passenger compartments. (To read about how GM disposed of these complaints, see Chapter 4.) The previous year, 1970, the United States Department of Transportation had launched an investigation of the Corvair heater. In November 1971, the day before scheduled hearings on the matter, GM entered into an agreement with the department to notify all 1961–69 year Corvair owners of the problem. But GM denied in the letter that there was a defect, and it refused to pay for modifications. The response to the notification was light, owing in large part to the age of the vehicles affected. But the confidential agreement with Petry and Wolf had kept the matter suppressed for nearly a decade.[36]

LET THE SUNSHINE IN

Public pressure is beginning to build against confidential settlements and, to a lesser degree, protective orders. This is not a matter of arcane legal procedure best left to the legal profession. The public is the ultimate victim of secrecy. Citizens must act to prevent power-lawyer games of hide-and-seek—or really, seek-and-hide—from continuing to harm innocent victims.

Refusing Confidential Settlements: One way to end confidential settlements is for litigants to refuse to participate in them. This, of course, is asking a lot of individuals who may desperately need the money from an offered confidential settlement to cope with their injuries. Confidential settlements recall the "offer you can't refuse" from the movie *The Godfather.* If someone is seriously ill and in desperate need of compensation, it is very hard to turn down settlement money for the greater good, i.e., to prevent others from being similarly injured or to promote the democratic principle that government processes and procedures should be held in the open. That is why confidential settlements should be outlawed. But in the meantime, some determined citizens have refused to accept secret settlements, as one courageous family did a few years ago.

THE CASE OF THE PRINCIPLED PLAINTIFFS

On a quiet Sunday afternoon, February 13, 1988, Jim Miller was driving the family's 1986 Ford Escort near his home in Escondido, California. His wife, Patricia, was sitting next to him in the front passenger seat. In the back were their thirteen-year-old twin sons, James and Richard.

They all had their seat belts securely fastened. But in the Escort, some safety belts were safer than others. The belts that Jim and Patricia were wearing were shoulder belts. However, the backseat passengers, James and Richard, had only lap belts.

About a mile from home, as they drove around a curve in the road, an approaching car suddenly veered into their lane. There was a horrible crash. The cars had collided head-on.

The Escort withstood the impact quite well. Jim and Patricia, although hurt, escaped grave danger. Jim suffered a broken ankle, his ribs were compressed, and he had a cut over his eye. Patricia suffered a broken collarbone and compressed ribs. Their shoulder belts had literally saved their lives.

In the backseat, however, it was a different and tragic story. Both boys suffered terrible abdominal injuries and broken spines. James was killed. Richard became a paraplegic. And every injury the boys received would have been greatly reduced had they been wearing shoulder belts instead of lap seat belts.

Why weren't shoulder belts installed in the backseat? When the car was built, there was no government regulation requiring that it be done. The National Highway Traffic Safety Administration had at one time sought to require auto companies to provide shoulder belts for backseat passengers. The agency had even published a Notice of Proposed Rule Making announcing its intention to require rear seat shoulder belts beginning in 1972.[37] But the proposed rule never made it to final promulgation, due, in part, to intense lobbying by Ford and other members of the automobile industry. The auto industry message was "Don't regulate the issue. We will do it voluntarily."

Unfortunately, talk is cheap. Ford never installed shoulder belts in its Escorts. (The federal government finally required backseat shoulder belts in 1990.)

"The hatchback we owned had a fold-down backseat," Jim Miller says. "When Ford started to make the hatchback, it found that the seat belts would disappear under the seat. To cure the problem, they made a buttonhole in the seat with rubber loops around the belt. This raised the belt above the pelvis so that it cut across the abdomen, which created a deadly hazard, especially for children like our sons."[38]

The Millers discovered that there had been an almost identical case in Maryland two years before their accident with almost identical injuries. A lawsuit had followed, and Ford lost. The Millers were incensed that the car company had not recalled the vehicles and installed shoulder belts or otherwise warned Escort owners of the hazard. "Ford had installed anchor points in the vehicle so that shoulder belts could have been put in," Jim Miller recalls angrily. "In fact, at the very time Ford sold my family a car without shoulder belts, the same car was being sold *with* shoulder belts in Europe. That was inexcusable!"[39]

The Millers sued. "We weren't in this for the money," Patricia Miller recalled. "We had determined to do this to protect other families from suffering a tragedy like ours. We wanted as public a trial as we could get. They knew this seat belt design was faulty. But they had done nothing about it."[40]

Ford offered $2.5 million to settle. The Millers, sticking to their principles, refused. The offer was raised. Again, the Millers refused. Finally, they decided to counteroffer at $6.5 million on the theory that the offer would be so high that Ford's lawyers would know that they would be going to trial.

Amazingly, Ford countered at $6 million. But, there was one catch. Ford insisted on a confidential settlement.

"We thought about it," Jim told us. "But there was no way we could be in complicity with them in keeping news about this unsafe product from the public."

"We had lost our son," Patricia added. "Our other boy was in a wheelchair for life. We couldn't have lived with ourselves if other parents lost their children because we took the money and kept quiet."

The Millers instructed their attorney, Craig R. McClellan of San Diego, to make Ford a counteroffer. "The Millers will agree to keep the amount of the settlement confidential," McClellan wrote to Ford's lawyers on March 20, 1990, "if Ford will agree to notify all existing Ford Escort and Mercury Lynx owners (of pre-1990 models) of the availability and desirability of rear seat, outboard shoulder harnesses, *and* if Ford will agree to make such shoulder harnesses easily and inexpensively available at its dealerships."[41] (Emphasis in original.)

Attorney Rosewell Page III of the Virginia law firm McGuire, Woods, Battle & Boothe wrote back declining the offer of a public safety campaign in return for confidentiality. In his letter, dated March 25, 1990, he cited the following reasons for Ford's continued insistence on any settlement being agreed upon and executed in secret.[42] First, he said that "some plaintiffs' lawyers interested in publicity for themselves have all too willingly distorted the nature of cases, reasons for settlement, and other matters." Second, Page wrote, because each lawsuit has unique facts, the amount for which one case settled, if published, could mislead the public about the value of claims in other pending cases. Finally, he said, publicity about a settlement might make it more difficult for a company to get an impartial jury in subsequent cases. Page added that any Ford product safety action would be taken only if "determined to be appropriate . . . not because of the settlement of this lawsuit."

The Millers, primarily interested in public safety, would have none of it. McClellan wrote back to Page on March 29:[43]

> When the Millers realized that even a large judgment against Ford could not compel a recall, then they looked for other ways of informing the public of the necessity for rear seat shoulder harnesses and ensuring their availability from Ford.
>
> There were only two ways to accomplish that. One way was to see if the confidentiality that Ford desired was dear enough to the company to cause it to spend the money necessary to educate its customers and retrofit their vehicles. Unfortunately, that alternative has now been eliminated.
>
> The second option, which is still available, is to make the public aware of what happened to the Miller family, why it happened, and what consumers can do to protect their families. The solace the Millers will take in the exposure will come from being able to sleep at night knowing that the death of one son and the crippling of another may have resulted in the saving of many other young lives and limbs. . . .
>
> You also understand that hundreds of thousands of lawsuits are settled around the country everyday. The fact that a lawsuit has settled is not ordinarily newsworthy. What makes a settlement newsworthy is normally the amount paid. If this case had settled with Ford for $50,000, I am sure that the press would not take note, concluding that Ford had paid a "nuisance value" to get rid of the case. On the other hand, a multi-million-dollar payment tends to get attention, because the press and the public quite logically conclude that a defendant does not pay that kind of money in the absence of liability. Thus, it lends credibility to the claims of the lawsuit and the things that the Millers have to say.

The two sides were eyeball-to-eyeball, the only issue separating them, Ford's insistence on confidentiality. Ford, unwilling to conduct its own public safety campaign but obviously anxious to avoid a public trial, blinked first. It agreed to an open settlement of $6 million.

The Millers, true to their word, did everything in their power to alert the public to the dangers of the pre-1990 Ford Escort and Mercury Lynx. They hired a public relations firm. They were interviewed in newspapers and on television. They sought as much media attention as possible, accomplishing their safety goals sooner rather than later by accepting a very public settlement.

"These companies think in terms of cost versus benefit," Jim Miller told us. "It would have cost twelve dollars per car to install shoulder belts. Secret settlements allow them to save money by unnecessarily risking safety. Without secrecy, the cost of instituting lower standards of safety rises."[44]

Jim and Patricia Miller were the recipients of the 1993 Community Champions Award from the Civil Justice Foundation, a nonprofit organization formed by plaintiff lawyers to recognize grassroots heroism.

Courts Should Refuse to Accept Most Confidential Settlements: Cases cannot be kept secret without the cooperation of judges. It is the judge who reviews the proposed settlement. It is the judge who must approve it. It is the judge who signs the order sealing the case from view from the American public. Since it is the courts that grant secrecy, it can also be the courts that take it away.

It is difficult for judges to refuse to apply secrecy when litigants on both sides agree to it. Judges are loathe to interfere with settlements or other agreements between litigants, believing that if the parties are satisfied, the judge should not get in the way without a compelling reason. In addition, settlements obviously reduce the workload of the court. If the parties are ready to settle, why should the court add to its caseload by carefully scrutinizing the settlement terms and possibly forcing the parties to continue to litigate? Each case can cause a judge to have to plow through piles of paperwork, reviewing legal briefs, documents, and transcripts. Big cases can fill court file cabinets with thousands of documents for a judge to review. Many judges are likely to accept secrecy to make such cases go away.

But judges, like lawyers, have public responsibilities too. They do not preside over a private system of dispute resolution. They are government officials. Every time they act in their official capacity, whether it is issuing a ruling on a motion, signing a judgment, or sealing a court record, they are invoking the authority of the government behind their acts. When those actions hurt the public welfare, judges abuse their power.

Some courts have assumed a broader responsibility, as in the following Georgia case.

THE CASE OF THE JUDGE
WHO WENT TOO FAR

One of the most egregious examples of the ease with which corporate lawyers can obtain secrecy arose after a man in Georgia was killed in 1979 in a 1976 Jeep manufactured by American Motors Corp.

The man's widow, Barbara Wilson, claiming the vehicle was defective, sued American Motors in federal district court. The case went to trial, and for two weeks the litigants presented evidence, took testimony, and otherwise conducted a completely open and publicly accessible proceeding. The trial was transcribed by a court reporter.

After the evidence and arguments concluded and the jury began deliberations, the judge attempted to help the parties reach a settlement. There is nothing improper about a judge trying to get the parties to settle a case; judges often intervene in such a manner. But there was something odd about the terms of the settlement. The parties agreed and the judge ratified by order that all records of the public trial were to be retroactively sealed. Under the judge's order, information that would have been available to anyone who had attended the trial was stripped of its public nature, preventing those interested in the proceeding from obtaining information that had already entered the public domain.

One person interested in the trial testimony was Ron Bain, a lawyer representing the family of another man killed in a separate accident involving a 1977 Jeep.[45] Bain, whose client's case was pending in California state court, wanted to obtain court transcripts, affidavits, trial exhibits, and other materials from the Wilson trial. American Motors' attorneys fought him every step of the way. When Bain filed a motion before the judge in the Wilson case to obtain the documents, the judge denied it.

When Bain appealed, the Eleventh Circuit Court of Appeals saw things differently. In a decision issued on May 13, 1985, the court firmly held that information presented in trials is the property of the public and that, absent "exceptional circumstances," the people have the right to see the records of a public trial. The unanimous appellate court stated that "simply showing that the information would harm the company's reputation is not sufficient to overcome the strong common law of presumption in favor of public access."[46] The court determined that the trial judge's decision to seal the record was an abuse of authority.

The court's decision stands for important principles: Embarrassment is not grounds for sealing public trial records. A desire to keep the public from learning the truth about potential defects in products is not grounds to seal public records. And the desires of the parties alone are not sufficient either, because as the court put it, judges must "keep in mind the rights of a third party—the public." More judges should keep the rights of the public in mind when they rubber-stamp requests to seal the records of public trials.

Fortunately, courts increasingly are recognizing the harm created by confidential settlements and secrecy orders. They are addressing the problem more systematically.

Amending Court Rules

Texas Supreme Court Justice Lloyd Doggett (who now serves in the U.S. House of Representatives) had seen one secrecy order too many. "There are a number of cases in which the general public health and safety is seriously undermined by secrecy," he told a reporter.[47] With Justice Doggett as the driving force, in 1990 the Texas Supreme Court amended the state's court rules to create a presumption that all court records are to remain open. A lawyer seeking secrecy has the burden of showing that a serious and substantial interest clearly outweighs any likely adverse effect on the public health and safety. Further, the public has a right to be notified of a hearing before documents are sealed, allowing third parties such as public interest organizations or the press to intervene in the case to argue against sealing.

Not surprisingly, the Texas rule, which the state high court approved by a slim 5–4 margin, is under attack. As this is written, parties are waging protracted battles in Texas courts over how to apply it. Only time will tell if the rule will ultimately have its desired effect of protecting the public safety.

Local courts are also beginning to attack secrecy rules. San Diego, California's Superior Court has enacted a local rule stating:

> It is the policy of this Court that confidentiality agreements and protective orders are disfavored and should only be approved by the Court when there is a genuine trade secret or privilege to be protected. Such agreements will not be recognized or approved by this Court absent a particularized showing (document by document) that:
> 1) Secrecy is in the public interest;
> 2) The proponent has a cognizable interest in the material, i.e., the material contains trade secrets, privileged information, or is otherwise protected by law from disclosure; and
> 3) That disclosure would cause serious harm.

This rule places a burden on defendants to prove the need for secrecy and restricts the circumstances under which the protection of secrecy will be available. According to Judith McConnell, the presiding judge of the San Diego Superior Court when the rule was instituted, the rule supports a vital public policy. "As a general principle," she says, "public institutions should be open to the public, and the records kept as the basis for decisions should be open to the public. That includes the courts. Public trust in the courts is not going to be there unless the courts are open to scrutiny. That is the reason we adopted the rule: to make sure that what we do is open to scrutiny."

But, we asked, "What about the argument often made by corporate lawyers that open settlements will clog the courts because litigants won't settle?"

According to Judge McConnell, the five-year experience disfavoring secrecy has not resulted in increased court congestion. "We have seen no difference at all in the amount of settlements," she told us. "When lawyers come in with confidential settlement clauses and are told that secrecy violates our local rules, the confidentiality clause is usually stricken and the case proceeds to resolution. In fact, I know of no settlements that dissolved because of our rules."[48]

Several other states—including Idaho, Georgia, Michigan, and Delaware—have enacted similar court rules. These jurisdictions are to be applauded for their efforts to pry open the strongboxes in which power lawyers seek to lock their clients' dirty secrets. But the problem is much bigger than can be addressed through amending court rules, so some states have enacted comprehensive antisecrecy legislation.

Passing New Laws

In 1990, Florida adopted an antisecrecy law, the Sunshine in Litigation Act. The law prohibits courts from entering orders that conceal a public hazard or information about a public hazard. The law also makes any agreement to conceal a public hazard unenforceable and allows the public or news media to contest court orders or contracts that conceal public hazards. And the law prohibits the government from obtaining secrecy agreements: All records relating to agreements to settle tort claims against the state must be maintained as public records.

In 1993, Washington State passed the Public Right to Know Bill, sponsored by State Senator Marlin Applewick, despite heated opposition from the giant Boeing Aircraft company and other businesses in the state. The law follows Florida's in most respects. "What we have done," Senator Applewick says, "is create a right for the public to know about risks from products and hazards. The right is formulated as the amount of information necessary for a member of the lay public to understand the nature, source and extent of the risk."[49]

Defense lawyers in the state have already tried to circumvent the anticonfidentiality provisions of the law. Power lawyers drafted slyly worded "sample orders" aimed at getting around the law when crafting settlements. For example, one such sample order stated, "The parties agree that there is no public hazard." Another, that "Both parties agree that the defects alleged by plaintiff in this lawsuit shall not be deemed a public hazard." Notwithstanding such efforts to derail the law, Senator Applewick reports that "things have tightened up to the public's benefit."

In June 1995, Louisiana passed a similar law, despite heavy lobbying against it from industry groups.

In many states, however, corporations have succeeded in preventing such laws from passing. Nevada came close to passing one before industry efforts won out. The California state legislature has passed such a right-to-know measure several times, only to have it vetoed by Republican Governor Pete Wilson.

No progress has been made to adopt antisecrecy legislation at the federal level. Senator Herb Kohl, Democrat of Wisconsin, has introduced watered-down legislation, and even that has gone nowhere.

This suits corporate lawyers just fine. Secrecy adds to their power, their advantage in court, and their billable hours, while detracting from the power of consumers. But such tactics make it more likely that people will be injured by hazardous products and activities.

In opposing antisecrecy laws, power lawyers accuse legislators who promote openness of an unwarranted intrusion into the judicial arena. They claim that antisecrecy laws are unnecessary because current law adequately protects the public. Or, as stated by the American Tort Reform Association, an organization funded by manufacturers, insurance companies, and tobacco interests, "the public has nothing to gain . . . but everything to lose in terms of its right to 'privacy.' "[50] But these lawyers' conception of the public interest is, at best, strained— they and their clients are the same people who for years have been lobbying Congress and state legislatures to weaken severely the substantive rights of people injured by defective products and services. And while there may be circumstances where extremely personal matters, with little or no implications for the public, are appropriately shielded from public scrutiny, along with genuine trade secrets and materials subject to legal privilege, the state laws already passed allow for such protections.

Another argument offered by the prosecrecy forces is that antisecrecy legislation will impair the ability of the legal system to resolve disputes—without confidentiality there will be fewer settlements and thus greater court congestion. But the experience in San Diego belies that argument. Moreover, ending secrecy would ultimately reduce the amount of litigation. Openness deters misconduct or, to use Justice Louis Brandeis's phrase, "Sunlight is the best of disinfectants."

Increasingly, commentators are urging an end to the confidential settlement agreement and unnecessary protective orders. Here's a sampling:

> All judges should disavow secrecy pacts except on narrow points involving legitimate trade secrets. Disclosure should be the rule, not the exception.
>
> —Business Week[51]

> [The proposed California law to reduce secrecy agreements,] which has been unfairly painted as anti-business, is actually pro-business and pro-consumer legislation that deserves support. . . . Protecting evidence of fraud or consumer hazard under the guise of trade secrets or maintaining economic competitiveness is not in the best interests of California business.
>
> —Los Angeles Times[52]

> Imagine a cozy legal system that allows a company to conduct business as usual after its faulty products or toxic wastes were exposed as hazards. The public lives with this cynicism every day, as judges sign secrecy orders that seal the results of lawsuit settlements involving threats to the public safety.
>
> —The Seattle Times[53]

> If fear of public disclosure discourages companies from writing off certain levels of pain and death, and if it exposes inaction on the part of federal agencies charged with protecting public health and safety, the [antisecrecy] laws will have done their job.
>
> —The Wisconsin State Journal[54]

> Who does [secrecy] hurt? It can hurt you:
> —Government regulators don't see data that could help protect consumers.
> —Manufacturers have less incentive to change harmful products.
> —Other victims are denied helpful evidence, and potential victims remain unaware.

Consumers clearly need federal and state laws so judges will
forbid secrecy if public safety or health is at stake.
—*USA Today*[55]

It's time to end the secrecy, to open up the process. The disgraceful power-lawyer game of "I've Got a Secret" should be shut down, so that justice is not rationed.

CHAPTER 3

THE OBSTRUCTIONISTS

EW WHO HAVE SEEN IT COULD FORGET THE 1982 PAUL Newman movie, *The Verdict*. Newman plays a down-on-his-luck lawyer, working alone, who takes on a Boston power law firm in a medical malpractice case. The firm, led by a ruthless senior partner played by James Mason, employs every weapon in its arsenal to wear down Newman, the attorney for the family of a woman who died during a routine operation. In the dramatic courtroom conclusion, a hospital nurse, tracked down out-of-state by Newman, reveals, rage in her voice, how a doctor ordered her to alter the patient's chart to conceal obvious negligence on the doctor's part.

Not many moments in real-life civil litigation are so dramatic. But the kind of conduct portrayed in *The Verdict* is far from imaginary. In the real world, corporate lawyers can and do conceal the truth. And unlike in *The Verdict*, where Newman prevailed, in the real world the obstructionists often get away with it.

THE IMPORTANCE OF DISCOVERY

To understand how some power lawyers manipulate and even violate the rules of lawsuits, we need to take a quick look at those rules, particularly the arcane procedures of pretrial fact-finding known as "discovery."

Until the late 1930s, lawsuits in the United States were pursued under the "sporting theory of justice," where trials were often a game of chance rather than a search for the facts.[1] A party to a lawsuit did not have the right to discover facts and evidence in the possession of its opponent. This situation reduced settlement opportunities, limited the ability to effectively contest disputed evidence, caused many trials to take unexpected twists and turns, and generally interfered with the search for the truth.

Modern discovery rules, both at the federal and state court levels, were enacted to reform the justice system on the theory that, as the Supreme Court put it in a 1947 opinion, "[m]utual knowledge of all relevant facts gathered by both parties is essential to proper litigation."[2] The aim of the modern rules, according to the Supreme Court, is to "make a trial less a game of blind man's bluff and more a fair contest with the basic issues and facts disclosed to the fullest practicable extent."[3] In discovery, each party in a lawsuit is permitted to obtain information and evidence in the possession of its opponent—even if the facts disclosed hurt the case of the party providing them. For example, a woman involved in an auto accident who sues contending that the accident caused continuing back pain must disclose her past medical records to the defense, even if they reveal that she had a preexisting back problem with symptoms identical to those she claimed were caused by the accident. Similarly, a business accused of racial discrimination can be forced to reveal internal memos, even if they disclose a policy to prevent African-Americans from advancing in the company. Litigants may not be happy when their lawyers tell them they have a duty to permit discovery, but that does not reduce their duty to comply with the rules. Parties are also entitled to obtain information from third parties not involved in the litigation.

Corporate executives and their lawyers often disparage discovery and support proposals to curtail its application. To them, discovery rules are often an excuse for attorneys to go on a fishing expedition in the hope that something will turn up to support a lawsuit. While some unprincipled lawyers no doubt sometimes attempt to conduct unwarranted fishing expeditions, the real reason big corporations oppose current discovery rules is that these rules help equalize access to relevant evidence. Discovery helps level the playing field between the haves and have-nots, giving less wealthy parties genuine hope that the legal system will resolve their claims or defenses based on the truth. Often, that means that large corporations are held accountable for their wrongdoing—wrongdoing that is proved by material contained in their own files.

Discovery is deemed so essential to the smooth functioning of justice that special rules have evolved to ensure that each side is open and forthcoming in its discovery duties—an obligation owed not only to the other side but to the system of justice itself.

Each state has its own discovery rules, as does the federal court system. Generally these rules embody the following principles:

- *Discovery is to be broad:* Every party in a lawsuit has an affirmative duty to disclose information. As stated above, this is true even if disclosure will win the case for the other side.

- *Relevance is to be broadly interpreted:* In discovery, litigants are entitled to information in possession of the other side or third parties, even if it would not be admissible as evidence at a trial, so long as the information is, as the federal rule puts it, "reasonably calculated to lead to the discovery of admissible evidence."
- *Uncertainties are to be decided in favor of allowing access to the information:* If cases are to be justly resolved, litigants must not be cheated out of access to evidence. Thus, an asking party is generally entitled to the benefit of the doubt when seeking discovery.

Of course, discovery rights are not absolute. If a party seeks information not possibly relevant to the matter at hand or if the information sought is privileged—for instance, if it involves a request to see a communication between a client and an attorney—the opposing party can object. If the parties disagree as to whether an objection is valid, they can file motions and let the judge decide.

In theory, discovery should lead to a prompt understanding by both sides of the issues in the case and the evidence available to prove or disprove claims. This, in turn, is supposed to improve the efficiency of the justice system by shortening trials and promoting settlements of cases.

But what works in theory is often frustrated by tactics that subvert discovery and liberal disclosure policies. These strategies can be boiled down to one word: *stonewalling.* As the cases below suggest, some corporate lawyers routinely make specious objections, withhold documents, reinterpret questions asked of their clients, ignore those parts of questions they would rather not answer, and twist the common meaning of language to avoid disclosing documents. These tricks force their adversaries to go to court repeatedly to obtain information to which they are entitled under the law.

Such stonewalling serves three primary purposes: It makes corporate lawyers a lot of money, it exhausts the legal opposition, and it keeps discoverable information from being disclosed.

Obstructing discovery is a powerful revenue generator because it takes a lot of time and effort. Although some efforts are under way to reform the method of legal billing (see Chapter 7), most corporate lawyers continue to bill by the hour. Robert Aronson, who teaches professional ethics at the University of Washington School of Law, says, "Lawyers who bill by the hour have a very strong incentive to obfuscate. If they can spend three thousand hours doing what should have been able to have been done in five hundred hours, the lawyers benefit. It is an amazing situation."[4] Billable hours can add up quickly. There are letters to read, letters to write, files to review, motions to file, motions to answer, internal conferences to hold. There are also repeated court appearances to make, phone calls to place, legal research to conduct, younger firm lawyers to train—corporate law firms, with employees working around the clock, keep going and going in a manner that would make the Energizer Bunny envious.

Beyond attorney self-interest, power-lawyer stonewalling during discovery often benefits willing corporate clients. Because individuals and small businesses who sue or are sued by big corporations rarely have equivalent financial resources, all the fussing and fighting over discovery serves the same purpose as a war of attrition: It exhausts the resources and energy of the "enemy," often leading to its collapse. The result can be unfairly low settlements or meritorious cases being dropped simply because the litigant can't afford to go on. And when discovery abuses actually prevent litigants from gaining access to information to which they are legally entitled, and with which they could prove their case, the stonewallers are often able to win cases they should lose.

Stonewalling often succeeds because of court-imposed time limits by which discovery must be completed. Such discovery schedules, properly intended to promote efficiency by keeping cases moving through the system, often have the unintended effect of enabling stonewalling lawyers to accomplish their desired ends. "Deadlines are music to obstructionists' ears," Georgia attorney Jim Butler, who has been fighting the discovery wars for years, says. "They string it out, and you run out of time, and the judge runs out of patience. The strategy works like a charm."[5]

A CULTURE OF QUESTIONABLE ETHICS

Of course, not every discovery dispute involving a corporate lawyer involves stonewalling. Some discovery disputes are legitimate and brought in good faith. But when lawyers create a dispute where one should not exist, as they often do, it is merely a tactic to circumvent the law rather than legitimate representation of a client. It is an abuse of the legal system and a breach of legal ethics. The American Bar Association (ABA) Model Rules of Professional Conduct, adopted in 1983, set ethical standards that are followed by many state legal disciplinary committees. One of these rules, Rule 3.2, provides, "A lawyer shall make reasonable efforts to expedite litigation consistent with the interests of the client." But do the words "consistent with the interests of the client" constitute an enormous loophole that excuses much power-lawyer delaying? What if the client knows it has done wrong and faces liability and therefore wants to delay? Rule 3.2 comes with an explanatory comment that rejects such a loophole:

Dilatory practices bring the administration of justice into disrepute. Delay should not be indulged merely for the convenience of the advocates, or for the purpose of frustrating an opposing party's attempt to obtain rightful redress or repose. It is not a justification that similar conduct is often tolerated by the bench and bar. The question is whether a competent lawyer acting in good faith would regard the course of action as having some substantial purpose other than delay. Realizing financial or other benefit from otherwise improper delay in litigation is not a legitimate interest of the client.

Most people are unaware of the real damage discovery abuse causes to both individuals and the legal system itself. The subject receives little attention in the media, who generally view it as an arcane topic, of interest only to law professors and judges, one guaranteed to make the eyes of "real people" glaze over with boredom. But discovery abuse is one of the central ailments of the legal system, and, as the cases in this chapter will show, is not always boring. Indeed, it can be shocking. However, discovery abuse is now so entrenched that even some legal ethicists have become desensitized and wink at the practice.

The depth of the problem and the severity of its consequences do, however, receive the attention they deserve in some quarters. Stephen Gillers, a leading legal ethicist and professor of law at New York University, says that discovery abuse is one of the two worst ethical problems currently facing the legal profession. (The other, billing abuses, is the subject of Chapter 7.) What is particularly troubling about discovery abuse is that it is not only the lawyers who transgress; the client often supports or even demands the abuse. As Gillers explains, "The client's incentive is to avoid loss. The lawyer's incentive is to avoid displeasing the client. It is consensual wrongdoing between the lawyer and the client, with the victim being the 'other,' the person or entity on the other side of the lawsuit."[6]

In this vein, Ted Schneyer, law professor and legal ethicist at the University of Arizona School of Law, zeroes in on discovery abuse by lawyers representing major corporations: "There are strong forces at work that induce corporate and defense lawyers to satisfy the managers in the company who hire them and can fire them. Sometimes this comes at the expense of ethical practice. Their general inclination is to not go out of their way to poison their relationship with their people by 'beating them into rectitude.' "[7] In other words, corporate lawyers may be loathe to ethically advise their clients to observe rules and turn over documents that will be harmful to their case.

Another ethics specialist, University of Pennsylvania law professor Geoffrey Hazard, paints a similar picture: "It is the attorney's responsibility to rise above the feeling that they don't wish to disclose embarrassing or harmful material. But, when the consequences of telling the truth are severe, when telling the truth may make the situation worse for your client, an inherent tension develops."[8]

But gentle handling of misbehaving clients can run afoul of ethical standards. ABA Model Rule 3.3 requires a lawyer "to disclose a material fact to a tribunal when disclosure is necessary to avoid assisting a criminal or fraudulent act by the client." Similarly, the older ABA Model Code of Professional Responsibility, an earlier ABA ethical code (adopted in 1969), which some states still follow, contains a provision forbidding lawyers from concealing any evidence that the lawyer or client "has a legal obligation to reveal."[9]

But even though discovery abuses can violate ethical obligations, such conduct is rarely punished by the disciplinary arms, or ethics committees, of state bars. Why? As Gillers notes, because attorney and client collude in the wrongdoing, such abuses are "virtually subterranean and hidden when it comes to ethics enforcement. The client approves so it doesn't get reported."[10]

Discovery abuse is a major drain on our system of justice. Constant and unremitting fights over discovery are a major cause of court congestion. According to Professor Aronson, "An overwhelming amount of time is spent by judges and their clerks in dealing with these discovery disputes. Judges are always complaining about the problem. They worry about all the time it takes away from their being able to conduct actual trials."[11]

When the orderly process of discovery goes awry, it can delay a case for years. Basic struggles over access to documents or answers to questions can eat up months. When one side attacks the other for misconduct and asks the judge to impose sanctions, even more time can pass before resolution. And it isn't that most judges are lazy, either. Many are so overburdened by work that they don't have the time to plow through the thousands of documents that may be required reading if they are to make a just and proper decision on a discovery motion.

Discovery wars create a chain reaction that is inimical to the purposes of justice. The disputes keep cases from getting to trial, but they also delay settlements of cases. According to Professor Aronson, such delay usually benefits large business concerns, especially if they have been accused of selling unsafe products. "If it takes two or three years to get a judicial ruling that a product isn't safe," Aronson says, "the company will be able to continue to market its unsafe or problem product while it switches to a new and improved product. They don't lose market share while this is ongoing. Then, when the old product is found to be unsafe, they will have substantially completed the transition into the new product." Add to Aronson's observation the secrecy tactics discussed in the last chapter, which can delay knowledge of a hazardous product for many years, and it is easy to understand why big companies pay attorneys so much money to throw monkey wrenches into the workings of the justice system.

With many hours of judicial time going to resolve discovery disputes, less time is available for trials and other judicial activities. This, in turn, helps create a backlog of civil cases on court dockets, which are already overloaded with criminal cases. The huge backlog, and the resultant inability to get a prompt day in court, causes frustration with the legal system, raising the allure of such destructive solutions as the current movement to "reform" the tort system by severely restricting the rights of individuals. (See Chapter 8.)

As the following cases suggest, the place to start reforming the system is not with individual rights but with corporate stonewalling and power-lawyer tactics that support it.

THE CASE OF THE DOCTORED DIARY

Kathryn Anderson, MD, was a well-respected surgeon on staff at the Children's National Medical Center (CNMC) in Washington, D.C. From 1981 to 1991, she held the position of vice chairman, department of surgery. In 1991, CNMC's surgeon-in-chief decided to retire. Dr. Anderson became acting surgeon-in-chief, and CNMC launched a national search to fill the position permanently. Anderson sought the post, along with another CNMC staff surgeon, Dr. Martin Eichelberger. Ultimately, however, neither Anderson nor Eichelberger received the coveted position; it went instead to Dr. Marshall Schwartz from the University of California, Davis.

Anderson resigned from the hospital staff in July 1992 and accepted a position as chief of surgery at Children's Hospital in Los Angeles. But, in her view, sex discrimination was all that kept her from receiving the appointment she wanted at CNMC. In February 1993, Anderson sued CNMC for sex discrimination in the federal district court in Washington.

Anderson alleged that CNMC's chief executive officer, Donald Brown, wanted to rig the chief of surgery search so that he could appoint his friend, Dr. Eichelberger, even though, she claimed, her qualifications were superior. Anderson further contended that the search for the surgeon-in-chief was so thoroughly marred by sex discrimination that a man was going to be appointed even if Eichelberger did not get the position. The search committee, she discovered, had characterized her as too "aggressive," "forceful," and "abrasive."

Anderson retained Bernabei and Katz, a small Washington, D.C., firm that specializes in employment discrimination cases.[12] CNMC hired the 378-lawyer corporate firm Paul, Hastings, Janofsky & Walker.

Anderson's lawyers learned that Eichelberger had kept a diary during the search. It took several months of legal wrangling for Anderson's lawyers to obtain this diary. Once they had it, they noted a March 11, 1992, entry in which Eichelberger described a conversation he had had with his friend Frank Ziegler, a CNMC board member. Ziegler told Eichelberger of a prior conversation he had had with Brown. As Anderson's lawyers received it, the diary entry read:

> Ziegler - (T.C.) Spoke [with] Brown on Sat at retreat
> Wants to select one but in bind:
> create difficulty for several people.

Anderson's lawyers suspected that this entry might have been altered. It looked as though it had originally read "Wants to select *me*," meaning Dr. Eichelberger, not "one." They questioned Eichelberger about it at a December 1, 1993, deposition. Eichelberger denied altering the diary. Anderson's attorneys suggested that it might be appropriate to have an expert examine the diary to see if it had been altered.

Five days later, Bernabei and Katz received a letter from Mary Dollarhide, a Paul, Hastings attorney. It read in part:

> It has just come to our attention that Dr. Eichelberger's response to your deposition question about a suspected change in the March 11, 1992, entry, on that document was inaccurate. Dr. Eichelberger testified that he did not recall changing the document so that it now reads "Wants to select one but in bind," rather than "Wants to select me but in bind."
>
> We now understand that Dr. Eichelberger did change the word "one" from "me" some time ago.

The difference was dramatic. In its original form, the diary entry supported Anderson's allegation that Brown wanted to hire Eichelberger. As altered, the entry suggested a more fair and impartial search process.

Anderson's lawyers did not accuse the Paul, Hastings law firm of involvement in the actual alteration of the document. But they did contend that the hospital's lawyers put up a smoke screen, first to prevent them from learning of the very existence of the diary and, when that failed, to keep them from discovering that the diary's wording had been changed. In a court motion,[13] Dr. Anderson's attorneys alleged:

> The conduct of defendant and its counsel appears to have been designed to suppress evidence crucial to Dr. Anderson's case. . . . First, defendant failed to identify or produce Dr. Eichelberger's journal at the earliest stages of this litigation even though the journal was clearly responsive to plaintiff's discovery request . . . Next, defendant deliberately redacted critical portions of the journal . . . Defendant provided a complete copy of the journal only after plaintiff threatened to move for . . . sanctions and demanded to see the original.
>
> At some point, and again, only upon threat of court involvement, defendant's counsel informed plaintiff that Eichelberger intentionally altered at least one critical and damaging entry in his journal. Defendant's counsel have refused to inform plaintiff about the date and circumstances under which Dr. Eichelberger made this alteration.

United States District Judge Royce C. Lamberth granted Anderson's request for an evidentiary hearing to determine what had happened and whether CNMC or its lawyers should be penalized. Federal judges have the authority to impose a range of sanctions on parties and their attorneys for violation of court discovery orders and for other discovery-related misconduct.[14] Among the available punishments are fines, payment of the other side's litigation expenses, an order barring the disobedient party from offering certain legal claims or defenses, and, the ultimate sanction, an entry of judgment in the case in favor of the opposing party—as if the opposing party had proved the case on its merits. Anderson's lawyers sought this last and most severe sanction; they contended that the seriousness of the alleged misconduct justified Judge Lamberth blowing the whistle, stopping the game, and giving the victory to Anderson.

The hearing took place in two sessions in early 1994. It did not go well for CNMC or its counsel, with the judge focusing quite specifically on the allegations of misconduct against the defense attorneys themselves. Defense attorney Dollarhide admitted on the witness stand that she had, in effect, concealed the whereabouts of the original of the altered diary when she had personal possession of it:

THE COURT: It's a different question of whether you turn [the diary] over than whether you conceal it.

THE WITNESS: Well, I wasn't trying to conceal it. I mean, I was willing—

THE COURT: I don't know what else you were doing. You're sitting there with it in your possession; your client is saying, "I don't have the original," and you've got it in your possession, and you don't say anything? . . .

THE WITNESS: Well, I strictly construed the question, I admit. It was hypertechnical and hindsight being 20/20, I suppose I should have said, "I've got the original."

BY MS. BERNABEI:

Q: Ms. Dollarhide, isn't it true that after I asked the question and Dr. Eichelberger looks at you, you prevent him from answering the question by asking the question to him, "Have you got the original of this?"

A: Yes, I did come in with a question to get him to go ahead and respond. I actually thought you would follow up, but you didn't.

THE COURT: No. Your ploy worked, didn't it? That was the purpose of the question, wasn't it?

THE WITNESS: I was trying to get him out of a jam, yes.

THE COURT: I think you got yourself into one.

THE WITNESS: I realize that.[15]

Judge Lamberth took the motion under advisement. Power-lawyer discovery tactics had forced the already-overworked judge, at taxpayers' expense, to pore over hundreds of pages of documents and transcripts to decide an issue—when a diary entry was altered and who knew about it—that had nothing to do with the merits of Anderson's discrimination claim or the hospital's defense.

In November 1994, before Judge Lamberth had announced a decision, the parties settled the case. The terms of the settlement were made confidential. But an intervening incident may have spurred the hospital to come to the table with a fair offer. Judge Lamberth had granted a default judgment for discovery violations by the defense in another case, this one involving allegations of discovery abuse by an even bigger defendant and an even more powerful defense law firm.

THE ABC'S OF DISCOVERY ABUSE

Michele Shepherd and LaRue Graves worked as graphic artists in the Washington, D.C., bureau of the American Broadcasting Company's news division. Both are African-American.

On October 9, 1985, Shepherd and Graves participated in a meeting of minority employees of the ABC bureau. The purpose of the meeting was to discuss minority employee grievances. The grievance session was conducted with the knowledge of ABC management. Its organizers had posted notices announcing the session, which took place in an ABC conference room. Such a grievance meeting is a protected activity under federal labor law, and the participants had the right to believe the meeting was private. At the meeting, Shepherd and Graves complained about alleged mistreatment on the job. Indeed, their complaints were two of the meeting's most important agenda items.

Soon after the meeting, ABC fired Graves. Shepherd remained with the network, but she claimed that her supervisors refused her requests to ease an overly demanding work schedule.

On January 31, 1986, Shepherd and Graves, represented by their attorney, solo practitioner Mark Lane, filed suit together in the District of Columbia Superior Court. They charged ABC with violating the District of Columbia's Human Rights Act, which protects employees against employment discrimination. Specifically, they alleged that ABC had given them unfair work assignments and had improperly retaliated against them for attending the minority grievance meeting.

Representing ABC was one of the most powerful law firms in Washington: 230-attorney Wilmer, Cutler & Pickering. Wilmer, Cutler, which represents the interests of many large corporations in the nation's capital, is led by Lloyd N. Cutler, who, as earlier described, served as the chief lawyer to the president of the United States—the White House counsel—under Jimmy Carter and temporarily returned to the same job under Bill Clinton in the wake of the Whitewater investigation.

Wilmer, Cutler promptly exercised ABC's right to transfer the case from the D.C. court to the federal United States District Court.[16] The case was then assigned to Judge Lamberth.

After three and a half years of discovery and delay, Judge Lamberth was set to hold a hearing on a motion by ABC for summary judgment, that is, an effort by ABC to have the judge resolve the case on the legal issues and the undisputed facts and thereby avoid a trial. But on the day of the hearing, plaintiff's attorney Lane filed an emergency motion for sanctions, alleging that ABC and Wilmer, Cutler had altered a document produced in discovery and had harassed two potential witnesses.

Judge Lamberth put the summary judgment motion aside and conducted a four-day hearing on the sanctions motion. At the hearing, Lane contended that ABC management induced Robert Sam, who worked in the ABC personnel department, to attend the minority meeting and then report back to management on what had occurred. Evidence presented at the hearing showed that Sam did indeed recount the meeting to the bureau's personnel manager, Carol Ornes, and that Ornes, in turn, wrote a memorandum to her superiors. Through the discovery process, Lane had obtained a copy of the memo. It made no mention of Shepherd or Graves having attended the meeting. But Ornes's secretary, who typed the memo, testified at the hearing that she recalled that it did mention Shepherd.

The plaintiffs also presented evidence that a Wilmer, Cutler attorney, partner Stephen Hut, had approached a potential witness in the case, another employee in the ABC graphics department. Although the woman had told other lawyers for ABC that she did not want to talk about the case, Hut came to her office at lunchtime, with her coworkers around her, asked for a meeting with her, and used words and demeanor that she perceived as harassing.

Shepherd and Graves waited almost three years for Judge Lamberth's ruling, a delay that is, unfortunately, typical for some overworked federal judges. But when the decision finally came, it vindicated their contentions. Indeed, Judge Lamberth's opinion was a blistering attack, alleging "flagrant misconduct" by ABC and its lawyers. On nearly every key point, Judge Lamberth agreed with the plaintiffs. The judge held that the conduct of ABC and Wilmer, Cutler "mandates imposition of the most severe sanctions for abuse of the judicial process." So Judge Lamberth granted the relief Shepherd and Graves sought: a default judgment, a victory on the merits of the case.

ABC and its power lawyers were not finished, however. They loaded up more legal firepower and resumed the battle. They filed an extensive motion asking Judge Lamberth to reconsider his ruling. But now new lawyers, from the Washington firm Miller, Cassidy, Larocca & Lewin, had joined Wilmer, Cutler on the legal team.

Miller, Cassidy is a relatively small firm, with about forty lawyers. But it has a reputation for being able to get a client—often a major corporation or a powerful politician—out of a tight jam, whether a criminal indictment or a troublesome civil claim. Its list of clients over the years has included former president Richard Nixon (in his battle to assert control over the infamous Watergate tapes—see Chapter 4), former attorney general Edwin Meese, presidential adviser Michael Deaver, and three onetime chairmen of the Senate Judiciary Committee, Edward Kennedy, Joe Biden, and Orrin Hatch. One Miller, Cassidy partner, Jamie Gorelick, was once president of the District of Columbia Bar and became deputy attorney general, the number-two official in the U.S. Justice Department, under President Bill Clinton. Also added to the legal team, to take over representation of two ABC management officials named in the suit, was Kevin Baine of the legendary D.C. 135-lawyer firm Williams & Connolly (earning $645,000 annually in profits per partner—the highest of any big D.C.-based firm), which, like Miller, Cassidy, excels at "white-collar" criminal defense work as well as representing major corporations.

On September 2, 1993, Judge Lamberth resolved ABC's motion to reconsider. In several respects he retreated, concluding that the overall evidence failed to bear out some of his conclusions. But the core of his ruling held, as did the result: misconduct by the defense still required him to grant a default judgment. Specifically, Judge Lamberth found that:[17]

- ABC had "knowingly and purposely alter[ed] the Ornes memorandum to remove Ms. Shepherd's name" and acted improperly by failing to preserve all copies of the memo—four copies were missing from the files;
- Attorney Hut had harassed the coworker witness—Judge Lamberth concluded that "ABC's counsel, who are the perpetrators of the harassment at issue, must conform their conduct not to the standards governing mafia enforcers but to the higher norms of the legal profession";
- ABC and its attorneys had concealed from the court the fact that ABC management sent Mr. Sam to the meeting and asked him to take notes;
- ABC had acted improperly in submitting answers to plaintiff's written questions (interrogatories), because the person who verified these answers, Carol Ornes, later testified that she could not remember verifying them and that some of the answers were inaccurate.

He concluded:

The court might have been able to assume that ABC and its attorneys, as respected members of the community, would never have engaged in such misconduct. The facts are not ambiguous, however. The facts instead clearly demonstrate that ABC and its attorneys engaged in a pattern of misconduct ranging from document alteration to witness harassment. There comes a time when the parties' reputations no longer matter and only the facts do. That time has come.

Judge Lamberth had carefully considered ABC's plea to reconsider and admitted his own misapprehensions in several respects. But he reaffirmed the essence of his decision. And Judge Lamberth was no left-wing judge. Appointed by President Ronald Reagan in 1987, Lamberth had spent six years as an army lawyer, first in Vietnam and then at the Pentagon. He then joined the United States Attorney's office in the District of Columbia, where he specialized in defending the army and the Central Intelligence Agency.

Instead of taking stock, accepting the result, and moving on, ABC and its lawyers continued to fight. It took another twelve months for the parties to litigate and Judge Lamberth to determine an appropriate award of damages and attorney fees and court costs. Judge Lamberth awarded Graves $184,293.33 and Shepherd $125,000.[18]

ABC headed straight to the higher court, the United States Court of Appeals for the District of Columbia Circuit. There, ABC and its lawyers finally obtained the result they wanted. On August 25, 1995, the appellate court delivered its opinion, authored by Judge David Tatel, whom President Clinton had nominated to the bench in June 1994, during the six-month period that Lloyd Cutler served as the White House counsel and advised the president on judicial appointments. (Before his appointment, Judge Tatel was a partner at 401-lawyer Hogan & Hartson, whose 327-lawyer D.C. office is the largest in the city.[19]) Tatel flatly overruled most of Judge Lamberth's key factual findings. The only one of those findings that he did not reject outright was the conclusion that ABC had altered the Ornes memorandum. But Judge Tatel's opinion cast doubt on even that finding and held that Judge Lamberth could not impose severe sanctions, such as a default judgment, on ABC unless he concluded, after yet another review, that the plaintiffs had proved the misconduct by the demanding standard of "clear and convincing evidence." Unless plaintiffs met that difficult burden, the most Judge Lamberth could impose was some minor sanction, "such as finding that ABC knew Ms. Shepherd attended the minority employee meeting." And even if plaintiffs could meet the "clear and convincing" standard, there could be no default judgment unless Judge Lamberth offered a better explanation for why lesser sanctions were insufficient, something that the appellate court appeared to doubt he could accomplish.[20]

So, ten years after the fateful minority grievance meeting, Shepherd and Graves were essentially back to square one. They appeared to have little hope of obtaining the default judgment they sought. They could look forward to another protracted struggle over the sanctions issue, to be followed, most likely, by an even more hotly contested struggle over the actual merits of their claims.

Tellingly, the appellate court decision in *Shepherd* v. *ABC* came just four days after ABC had settled defamation lawsuits brought against it by cigarette makers Philip Morris and R.J. Reynolds. As part of the settlement, ABC, which two weeks earlier had agreed to be acquired by the Walt Disney Company, announced that it would pay the tobacco giants' attorney fees, which ultimately reached $15 million.[21] In a public statement, ABC stood by the "thrust" of a report on tobacco makers, but it apologized for reporting that Philip Morris "spikes" the tobacco in its cigarettes by adding significant amounts of nicotine from outside sources. The ABC correspondent on the story, John Martin, and the producer, Pulitzer Prize–winner Walt Bogdanich, insisted their reporting was accurate and refused to sign the apology.

Many First Amendment experts and consumer advocates complained that the network was sacrificing principles of freedom of the press—and the truth—just to avoid additional litigation costs. "This is a triumph of bottom-line thinking over news judgment," charged Richard A. Daynard, law professor at Northeastern University in Boston and chairman of the nonprofit Tobacco Products Liability Project. "Philip Morris has bullied a major television network into apologizing for what was essentially a true story."[22]

Indeed, power-lawyer tactics ensure that litigation decisions are often made not on the merits of cases but on the resources of the opponent. It was worth trying to wear down two former employees and their solo practitioner attorney, even after a federal judge had found egregious conduct on ABC's part. But it was not worth fighting another tenacious corporate opponent, even where ABC's position was solid and a grave matter of public health was at issue. So Philip Morris got an apology, while Shepherd and Graves got a fight.[23]

THE CASE OF THE DANGEROUS SAMURAI

Other compelling displays of discovery abuse come from the world of product liability lawsuits.

In the case of *Malautea* v. *Suzuki Motor Co.*, the plaintiff asked the court to punish the defendant's discovery abuse by ordering the same sanction sought by Dr. Anderson against CNMC and by Shepherd and Graves against ABC: a default judgment. But this time, the trial judge agreed, and his decision was upheld on appeal.[24]

Fati F. Malautea was driving his 1988 Suzuki Samurai four-wheel-drive vehicle. After a collision with another car, the Samurai rolled over. Malautea suffered severe head and spinal cord injuries.

With Malautea incapacitated, his wife, Gayle White Malautea, was appointed his guardian. Mrs. Malautea, believing that the rollover was caused by a defect in the Samurai, hired Jim Butler of the Atlanta firm Butler, Wooten, Overby & Cheeley, and, in December 1990, sued Suzuki, a Japanese firm, in the federal district court for the southern district of Georgia. The automaker was represented by Philip A. Siracuse, national counsel for Suzuki, of the Los Angeles firm Crosby, Heafy, Roach & May, along with the Georgia law firm Freeman & Hawkins.

The discovery wars began. Suzuki and its attorneys stubbornly withheld information requested by the plaintiffs. Suzuki offered repeated objections to plaintiffs' written interrogatories. The answers Suzuki did provide appeared to Butler to be incomplete or misleading.

Plaintiffs filed a motion to compel the defendants to be more forthcoming. At a hearing, the trial judge, B. Avant Edenfield, agreed with the plaintiffs and sternly warned the defendants to comply or face severe sanctions. But six months later, in December 1991, after Judge Edenfield had warned Suzuki's lawyers a second time, the parties were back in court. Following this second hearing, Judge Edenfield granted the default judgment and ordered Suzuki and, personally, lawyers for Suzuki to pay the plaintiffs' court costs and attorney fees. He also fined Suzuki $5,000 and fined each defense lawyer $500.

What had Suzuki and its lawyers done to merit the severe sanction?

A key piece of information that Malautea's lawyers wanted had to do with the proposed marketing of the Samurai by General Motors Corporation. The plaintiffs had information that General Motors had refused to participate in marketing the Suzuki because its own safety testing showed that the auto was unstable and subject to rolling over. This was important evidence for the plaintiffs since it would support their allegation that the Samurai was defectively designed and manufactured and was responsible for the horrible injuries to Fati Malautea.

At first, Suzuki's attorneys had refused to answer the interrogatories, arguing that certain words and phrases were undefined. "The Defendants and their lawyers . . . have managed to inject ambiguity into . . . ordinary words," Judge Edenfield ruled. These words included "tests, research or other investigation," "risk of rollover," "risk of personal injury," "substantially similar," "change, alteration, or modification," and "engineer."

In subsequently attempting to justify Suzuki's evasive answers to the Malauteas' interrogatories, Suzuki attorney Joe Freeman told Judge Edenfield that a vehicle test was, in fact, not a test: "When we say that General Motors did not do any testing with rollover, there are tests that are done like the circle test and the S-turn, and all of those sorts of things, and impact tests that in some instances will . . . be more predictive of the road stability of the vehicle." But such an exercise, according to Freeman, "is not a test. It is simply a calculation. . . ."

Another tactic of the defendant's lawyers was to answer a general question by pretending it was a limited one. Thus, when plaintiffs asked questions about rollover problems with the Samurai over several model years, the defendant limited its answer to the 1988 model year. Judge Edenfield concluded, "By restricting their answers in this manner, the Defendants avoided revealing a great deal of discoverable information." Suzuki also failed to turn over deposition transcripts taken in other cases, although the court specifically ordered it to do so.

But Suzuki and its lawyers went beyond refusing to answer questions fully. When the Malauteas asked Suzuki to provide information about General Motors' refusal to market the Samurai, Suzuki answered that it was "unaware of any decision by General Motors not to market the Samurai." As at least some Suzuki officials well knew, this was untrue.

Stymied in his attempt to get information he was entitled to discover from Suzuki, attorney Jim Butler had tried a different tack. Rather than rely on lawyers for Suzuki to provide the documents, he subpoenaed the documents directly from General Motors. After a fight in court, he received many GM documents damning to Suzuki's defense and proving that Suzuki had not been truthful when it professed to be unaware that General Motors had refused to market the Samurai. For example, a 1984 memo from GM to Suzuki stated that tests of the Samurai, indicating the vehicle's "perceived rollover tendencies," led to GM's decision to decline to market the vehicle.

After the documents were disclosed, the head of Suzuki's legal department admitted to Judge Edenfield that Suzuki executives must have known about the 1984 memo. And attorney Siracuse, Suzuki's national counsel, admitted knowing of the memo at least since 1989.

Judge Edenfield concluded that Suzuki and its lawyers were guilty of committing discovery abuses willfully and in bad faith. "If the Court," he wrote, "allowed the Defendants their way in this litigation, the Plaintiff would be completely unable to find the truth. . . . If the Defendants do not deserve the most severe sanction available, then no one does." Having entered a default judgment, Judge Edenfield ordered a proceeding before a jury to determine the Malauteas' damages.

However, Suzuki and its lawyers, who themselves were now parties to the case because their conduct was at issue, delayed a jury proceeding by appealing the default judgment and sanctions to the Eleventh Circuit Court of Appeals. When the appeal was argued, Suzuki continued the process of obfuscation. Its appellate lawyer told the panel of three appellate judges that Suzuki was unable to meet discovery deadlines with respect to the material relating to General Motors because of the time required to translate Japanese documents and ship them to the United States. In its April 1993 decision, the appeals court concluded that it was "difficult to believe that this highly relevant information has not already been translated and provided to Suzuki's defense counsel in the United States." And, the court added,

> If our suspicions regarding the General Motors information are true, then counsel's oral argument statement regarding Suzuki's inability to comply was a bold falsity. Of course, the defendants' appellate counsel may have fully believed his representation to this court; he may have just been the innocent lamb which the defendants led to slaughter.

The court of appeals unanimously upheld Judge Edenfield's decision in all respects. Writing for a unanimous appeals panel, Judge Peter Fay concluded that Suzuki "richly deserved the sanction of a default judgment" because the company and its lawyers "engaged in an unrelenting campaign to obfuscate the truth." Judge Fay added:

> [W]e feel compelled to remark on the disturbing regularity with which discovery abuses occur in our courts today. . . . The discovery rules . . . were intended to promote the search for truth that is the heart of our judicial system. However, the success with which the rules are applied toward this search for truth greatly depends on the professionalism and integrity of the attorneys involved. Therefore, it is appalling that attor-

neys, like defense counsel in this case, routinely twist the discovery rules into some of "the most powerful weapons in the arsenal of those who abuse the adversary system for the sole benefit of their clients." . . . Too many attorneys, like defense counsel in this case, have allowed the objectives of the client to override their ancient duties as officers of the court. In short, they have sold out to the client.

Suzuki, unpersuaded by the unanimous, decisive judgment of one trial judge and three appellate judges, pressed on. It hired Kenneth Starr, a former federal appeals judge and solicitor general (the federal government's chief lawyer before the United States Supreme Court) and now a partner at the corporate firm Kirkland & Ellis (and the special prosecutor investigating the Whitewater affair). Starr sought review in the United States Supreme Court, but in October 1993 the high court rejected Suzuki's petition to hear the case. The Malauteas had won. Facing a proceeding on damages before a jury in Judge Edenfield's court, Suzuki settled the case. The automaker's misconduct forced it to pay damages without a trial. The lawyers who facilitated Suzuki's obstructionism saw their tactics fail but, unfortunately, never faced an ethics investigation.

According to Jim Butler, 147 people died in Samurai rollover accidents between 1985 and 1992. In 1995, another case involving the Samurai went to trial. Kathryn Rodriguez, left quadriplegic following a Samurai accident, sued Suzuki in Missouri state court. According to one of her lawyers, Robert Cheeley (of Jim Butler's firm), Suzuki, which by then had settled many of the Samurai cases, tried in the Rodriguez case to send a message to victims' lawyers by "waging an all-out war." Said Cheeley, "Suzuki never made an offer to settle. They pulled out all the stops and threw everything they could at us."[25] But Cheeley and his colleagues had something to throw back: Suzuki internal documents that showed management concern about the Samurai's tendency to roll over. On July 7, 1995, the jury awarded Rodriguez $30 million in compensatory damages and $60 million in punitive damages. Suzuki said it would appeal.

General Motors, meanwhile, has not learned much from watching what happened to Suzuki in the Malautea case. Jim Butler has for years also represented victims of fires caused by exploding GM truck fuel tanks. He says corporate lawyer obstructionist tactics are deliberate and have a specific purpose: "The strategy is to avoid disclosing the truth or at least delay doing so as long as possible so that the truth, when it comes out at all, is dribbled in such a way that it can't be put together coherently for trial. You end up running out of time or judicial patience and having to go to trial without the evidence you're entitled to. Then, in the next case, you start the effort all over again. . . . No single case is sufficient to extract the evidence needed to get to the whole truth."

But recently, in one of Butler's cases, the judge called a halt to GM's cynical game. On November 24, 1993, twenty-two-year-old Shawn Bishop burned to death after his GM pickup struck the side of a bridge near Kellyville, Oklahoma. In May 1994, Butler filed suit against GM in federal court in Muskogee, Oklahoma, on behalf of Shawn Bishop's parents.

One of Kenneth Starr's partners at Kirkland & Ellis, John T. Hickey, represented GM, and familiar power-lawyer obfuscation soon reared its head. The trial judge was forced to resolve numerous discovery disputes from the outset. In November 1994, pursuant to the judge's order, GM submitted a list of its exhibits for trial. Butler complained that GM had failed to provide him with many of the exhibits, though he had requested them. Judge Michael Burrage admonished the parties to reduce their exhibits to those that would actually be used at trial and make them available to the other side. Instead, at the next courthouse meeting, GM increased its number of exhibits, failed to produce copies of some of the listed exhibits, and, as Judge Burrage later found, "obfuscated the identity of numerous exhibits." GM informed Butler that some of these exhibits were available only at GM's "reading room" in Detroit. On the eve of trial, six months after promising to deliver copies of its exhibits to Butler, GM had still failed to do so. When the parties met with the court clerk to present their exhibits, it was immediately clear that GM had failed to prepare its exhibits in accordance with the court's instructions. Then, without seeking the court's permission, GM removed its exhibits from the courthouse.

Butler moved for sanctions. According to Butler, Judge Burrage had been "just frighteningly patient with GM in this case. They just violated his orders left and right."[26] Judge Burrage finally had had enough; rejecting GM's characterization of the dispute as a "misunderstanding," he found, by order dated September 6, 1995, that GM had repeatedly violated his discovery orders, thereby making it difficult for Butler to prepare for trial, and that GM's "disobedience . . . was both willful and intentional." The judge concluded that, in light of GM's wealth, a fine "would be ineffective and consequently serve as a tacit approval of GM's disobedient conduct in regard to its exhibits." Instead, he stopped just short of ordering a default judgment—he barred GM from introducing any exhibits at the trial, a ruling that would have made it difficult, to say the least, for GM to prevail.[27]

On September 11, 1995, the day trial was to begin, the parties announced that they had settled the case, as well as three other pending suits involving Butler clients killed in GM truck fires. The terms of the settlements are confidential.

Another notable case of obstructionism is *Rozier v. Ford Motor Company*. It arose in March 1973. William Rozier was riding on a Georgia highway in a 1969 Ford Galaxie 500 when the vehicle was hit from behind by another car. The Galaxie burst into flames, and Rozier died of severe burns. In August 1974, his widow sued Ford in Georgia federal district court, alleging that Ford had been negligent in designing the Galaxie fuel tank. The case went to trial in 1976, and the jury found for Ford. Mrs. Rozier appealed. Meanwhile, her lawyers learned about a Ford document regarding fuel tank design that fell within the scope of a court order in the case directing Ford to turn over files. Once confronted with the document, a Ford in-house attorney admitted that he learned about the document a week before trial. Yet he did not disclose it or even seek a ruling from the court as to whether it had to be disclosed. In June 1978, the United States Court of Appeals ordered a new trial, stating: "Through its misconduct in this case, Ford completely sabotaged the federal trial machinery, precluding the 'fair contest' which the Federal Rules of Civil Procedure are intended to assure."[28] Following this ruling, Ford settled the case for an undisclosed sum.

So improper corporate lawyer discovery tactics do not always benefit clients who demand them. And at least one corporate lawyer has gone to jail for such obstructionism. As recounted in James B. Stewart's 1983 book *The Partners*,[29] the big New York firm Donovan Leisure Newton & Irvine defended Eastman Kodak in a 1978 antitrust action brought by a smaller competitor. Unsurprisingly, Donovan Leisure's strategy was to drown the opposition in documents and endless depositions. More surprising was a sworn statement by one of the firm's partners, Mahlon Perkins, Jr., that he had destroyed several briefcases full of relevant documents. And even more surprising was Perkins's subsequent admission that, in fact, the documents were never destroyed but remained in a suitcase in his office. Kodak lost the antitrust trial and fired Donovan Leisure.[30] Later that year, Perkins pleaded guilty to misdemeanor criminal contempt of court. His attorney, former federal judge Harold Tyler, Jr., told the sentencing judge, "there, possibly but for the grace of God, go I, because of the pressures which come upon men and women who practice law in big cases." Perkins served twenty-eight days in jail. (Supported by friends, such as retired federal appeals court judge Walter Mansfield, who called Perkins "the epitome, the acme, the paradigm of integrity," Perkins avoided being disbarred. By 1985 he had launched a new career as a volunteer attorney for the non-profit Center for Constitutional Rights, which handles civil rights, freedom of speech, and criminal justice cases.[31])

Before considering what can be done to halt the blatant abuse of the discovery process, we consider one more case where outrageous corporate obfuscation was caught and punished—but, this time, not before a horde of lawyers, presented as "expert witnesses," came forward to claim that the conduct at issue was entirely ethical.

THE SMOKING GUNS THAT WOULDN'T STAY HIDDEN

Dr. James Klicpera is a pediatrician. One of his patients was two-year-old Jennifer Pollock. Jennifer had asthma. Dr. Klicpera prescribed Somophyllin Oral Liquid, a drug marketed by Fisons Corporation, a British-owned pharmaceutical firm. On January 18, 1986, after taking the medication, Jennifer suffered seizures that caused permanent and irreversible brain damage. The seizures were caused by theophylline, the key ingredient in Somophyllin. Jennifer's parents were devastated. So was Dr. Klicpera.

But, as Jennifer's parents and Dr. Klicpera learned much later, Fisons Corporation could not have been too surprised: It had known for at least five years about the dangers of using Somophyllin, the very dangers that attacked Jennifer Pollock. As Fisons knew, if a child had a viral infection with an accompanying fever, as Jennifer did, the medication would become more powerful, causing the equivalent of an overdose. A child with a fever taking the medicine could go into convulsions leading to brain damage. Despite Fisons's awareness of this danger, it continued to market the product and failed to warn many pediatricians about it.

Jennifer's parents sued Dr. Klicpera for medical malpractice and Fisons for product liability in an Everett, Washington, state court. Dr. Klicpera filed a cross-claim against Fisons for violation of Washington's Consumer Protection Act and for emotional distress. The drug company's defense alleged, among other things, that the doctor had misprescribed the medication.

A discovery battle commenced. One of Seattle's most well known corporate law firms, 200-lawyer Bogle & Gates, represented Fisons.

In 1989, after three years of discovery, Klicpera settled his case with Jennifer's parents for $500,000, with the proviso that if Fisons was not found liable, he would increase his payment to the parents to $1 million, the limit of his medical malpractice insurance policy. Klicpera and the Pollocks continued the legal fight with Fisons.

In 1990, fate, in the form of a Good Samaritan, intervened. The Pollocks' attorneys received an envelope in the mail from an anonymous source. Inside was a Fisons document that Fisons had not turned over despite discovery requests that appeared to ask for just such a record. If ever a document could be called a "smoking gun," this was it.

It was a "Dear Doctor" letter sent by Cedric F. Grigg, Fisons's manager of marketing and medical communications, and dated June 30, 1981. Bruce Schafer, senior vice president for Dr. Klicpera's malpractice insurer, Physicians Insurance Exchange, says, "The letter had been sent to a limited number of what the company called 'influential physicians.' But it had not been sent to all doctors, and the letter had not been turned over despite discovery requests that communications between Fisons and other doctors about the medication be revealed."

The letter warned of the *very side effect* suffered by Jennifer. It noted a recent article in a journal that doctors "might not normally receive." The article dealt with a study that confirmed reports "of life-threatening theophylline toxicity when pediatric asthmatics on previously well-tolerated doses of theophylline contract viral infections." Grigg wrote that if theophylline "is not to fall into disrepute as it did formerly, the physician needs to understand that it can be a capricious drug." The study, according to Grigg, reported that six asthmatic children who became acutely ill during a flu epidemic "developed signs of toxicity . . . while receiving previously well-tolerated doses of theophylline" and that three others "developed signs of acute toxicity on generally recommended dosages, with one developing seizures and respiratory arrest." One purpose of the memo, which was approved by top Fisons executives, was to promote another Fisons asthma medication, Intal, which did not contain theophylline.

Dr. Klicpera had never received this warning from Fisons, nor was there a warning in the medication's box insert. He prescribed the medication to Jennifer more than four years after the letter had gone out. The letter proved that Fisons knew its medication had a potentially lethal defect that could disable or kill children and yet continued to market the drug without warning most doctors of the danger. It was an inexcusable decision that cost Jennifer Pollock a normal life.

The letter turned the case on its head. Fisons could no longer deny blame or try to shift responsibility to Dr. Klicpera. Fisons risked a large jury award, because of the cost required to take care of Jennifer for the rest of her life. (Fortunately for Fisons, but unfortunately for consumers, Washington State law does not permit punitive damages. Otherwise Fisons would have undoubtedly faced a substantial financial punishment for its callous behavior.)

But there was more to come. One of the Pollocks' 1986 discovery requests to Fisons had stated: "Produce genuine copies of any letters sent by your company to physicians concerning theophylline toxicity in children." The 1981 letter fell squarely within this request, yet Fisons had not produced it. The Pollocks and Klicpera filed a motion for sanctions against Fisons for discovery abuse. At the hearing on the motion, the trial court ordered Fisons to produce all documents the other parties had requested related to theophylline. Fisons responded by turning over ten thousand additional documents to the Pollocks' and Klicpera's lawyers.

Among these documents was another smoking gun. It was a July 11, 1985, Fisons internal memorandum, also written by Cedric Grigg, that noted "a dramatic increase in reports of serious toxicity to theophylline in 1985 medical journals." The memo called the traditional recommended dosage of the ingredient "a significant 'mistake.'" The memo alluded to the "sinister" fact that the physician considered the "pope" of theophylline-dosage recommendation was a consultant to the leading manufacturer of theophylline and was "heavily into" that company's stocks. The memo also noted that the relevant toxicity reports had not been reported in the medical journal read by doctors who most often prescribed the drug, and concluded that those doctors might not know of the "alarming increase in adverse reactions such as seizures, permanent brain damage and deaths." In light of these risks, Grigg wrote, "I find it absolutely incredible that theophylline is still widely recommended as the first-line drug for the treatment of asthma . . ." He concluded that the " 'epidemic' of theophylline toxicity provides strong justification for our corporate decision to cease promotional activities with our theophylline line of products."

This memo was truly damning. Fisons had no valid excuse for failing to inform physicians about the dangers of its products. Despite the alleged "corporate decision" to stop promoting theophylline to which the memo alluded, the court record demonstrated that Fisons continued to promote as well as sell theophylline drugs after the date of the memo. Indeed, Jennifer Pollock took her tragic dose six months afterward. Nor did there appear to be a good excuse for failing to produce the Grigg memo in response to previous discovery requests. Seeing the writing on the wall, the drug company quickly settled with the Pollocks for $6.9 million.

Normally, that would have been the end of it. But Dr. Klicpera and his insurance company were not ready to let matters rest. The doctor pressed his claims against Fisons, not only on the merits of the case but also on the discovery-abuse issues, with his insurance company picking up the legal tab.

Why would an insurance company, with its doctor vindicated and the case resolved, decide to finance further litigation? "We saw two things that were clearly outrageous," Bruce Schafer, senior vice president of Physicians Insurance Exchange, recalls. "One, our doctor felt that there would be doctors in a similar position as he was who did not know of the dangers of the drug. He worried that other children would suffer a similar fate. Second, our concern from an insurance company standpoint was the discovery abuse. We felt that the attorneys or the drug company—we didn't know which—had engaged in litigation fraud and that they came very close to getting away with it. We believed the conduct had become typical and it wasn't right. We felt the courts needed to say, 'This conduct is wrong and shouldn't be tolerated.' "[32]

James Lobsenz, the attorney who represented Klicpera, agrees. He says, "In this case we were very fortunate to have a progressive insurance company willing to litigate sanctions. They understood that this type of misconduct makes litigation more expensive for everyone. Everyone benefits from early and full disclosure."[33]

Klicpera, his insurer, and his attorney didn't know it, but to get a court to condemn Bogle & Gates for unethical conduct would be a lot more difficult than they ever expected.

First, Klicpera's case on the merits, for consumer protection law violations and emotional pain and suffering, went forward. "Before we went to trial, Bogle & Gates approached us about settlement. We were willing but with one nonnegotiable demand," Schafer recalls. "It was important to the doctor that the dangers of the medication receive a lot of publicity. We wanted Fisons to alert all of the doctors in the country to the danger. They thought we were kidding. To them, everything was about money. But we weren't kidding, so the case didn't settle."[34]

In July 1990, Dr. Klicpera finally got his case to a jury, which, after a one-month trial, awarded him $3.3 million. (The Washington state Supreme Court later reduced this award to approximately $1.1 million, concluding that under the circumstances the law did not allow the doctor to receive damages for emotional distress.)

Klicpera and his insurance company also sought sanctions against Fisons and Bogle & Gates based on the discovery abuse. The essence of the defense? Three words: "Everybody does it."

Fisons acknowledged that its own internal searches turned up the smoking gun documents, and Bogle & Gates later admitted to having reviewed them by 1987. They argued, however, that those documents did not directly concern the specific product Somophyllin, but instead concerned only Somophyllin's primary ingredient, theophylline. When the plaintiffs in 1986 had asked for materials related to *theophylline* toxicity, Fisons had replied that no such documents existed "regarding Somophyllin Oral Liquid." Fisons and Bogle & Gates contended that by referring in their answer to Somophyllin they were signaling to the plaintiffs that Fisons objected to producing documents, like the two smoking gun memos, that were not filed in Fisons's Somophyllin files, even if those documents discussed theophylline. In sum, Fisons and its lawyers insisted that the plaintiffs had simply failed to ask and pursue the precise questions needed to elicit the documents. They told the court that discovery is an adversarial process and that good lawyering required them, under the circumstances, to withhold the documents. Never mind that any responsible corporation would have promptly disseminated evidence that recommended doses of its products were potentially lethal to children, quite apart from any litigation or discovery request.

Everybody does it. Other lawyers warmed to that credo. Esteemed members of the bar, including purported experts on legal ethics, rushed to support Bogle & Gates. "The attorneys who handled the case for us took a lot of heat from other lawyers in town," Bruce Schafer told us. "They would ask, 'Why are you trying to change the way we do business? Why don't you let it drop?' They were as passionate about it as we were."[35]

Three members of the trial court denied Klicpera's motion for sanctions—first a special master (a court official, akin to a magistrate, who deals with pretrial matters like discovery) and then two trial judges.

Before the trial court, Bogle & Gates mounted a state-of-the-art defense, producing a daunting array of lawyer-experts who signed written affidavits in support of their position that discovery obfuscation was merely a standard operating procedure that violated no discovery rules or ethical principles.

- F. Lee Campbell, a former head of the Washington State Bar Association, wrote that the "practical side of the discovery process" had to be considered, that discovery is "an adversarial process" and that

"Fisons' attorneys owed an ethical duty to their client to zealously defend the case." He found nothing wrong with Bogle's conduct in not disclosing the smoking gun documents.

- Thomas J. Greenan, another prominent Washington lawyer, agreed, writing, "Based on the documents I have reviewed, and upon my background and experience as a trial lawyer for more than thirty years, I have formed the opinion that [the special master and first trial judge] were undoubtedly correct in their rulings denying . . . the motions for sanctions." Greenan's opinion was largely based on his contention that the opposing lawyers had not sought the appropriate remedies from the court when Fisons had refused to produce documents.

- Geoffrey C. Hazard, Jr., then a Yale Law School professor and one of the leading, and highest-paid, authorities on legal ethics, weighed in supporting Fisons and Bogle & Gates. He stated, "An award of sanctions is reserved for clear abuses of the discovery process where reasonable minds cannot differ on the issue. In responding to discovery requests, the rules do not require the responding party to be generous or to volunteer information that may be helpful to the other side."

In all, fourteen noted lawyers and ethicists supported Bogle & Gates. Only two offered affidavits backing Dr. Klicpera's contention that Fisons and its lawyers had violated the discovery rules and deserved sanctions. One was professor Robert Aronson of the University of Washington School of Law. He recalls, "I was reluctant to get involved because a former student of mine works at Bogle & Gates. But when I reviewed the file and saw what had happened, I was outraged. There were kids out there dying because they were hiding information so they could win a lawsuit."[36]

Aronson is amazed that his opinion seems to be in the minority in the legal world. "When a company comes to a lawyer and says that we've got these documents showing that our product can be harmful that we want to hide, the lawyers should simply say, 'No way! I will do what I can to limit the damages, but hiding your wrongdoing is just not an option.' "

Legal commentator Stuart Taylor, Jr., has also lamented this astonishing show of support for wrongdoing, writing, "I fear [that] the discovery process has been clogged by a culture of evasion and deceit that accounts for much of its grotesque wastefulness, and the adversary system has been perverted from an engine of truth into a license for lawyerly lies."[37]

Fortunately, the Washington Supreme Court was not as cynical or complacent about discovery obstructionism as were some of Bogle & Gates's supporters. Moreover, its opinion was the one that counted, and the court, in its September 1993 decision, unanimously denounced Bogle & Gates for its improper tactics.[38]

The court dismissed Bogle & Gates's specious "everybody does it" defense and the affidavits that supported it by stating, "Conduct is to be measured by the spirit and purpose of the rules, not against the standard of practice of the local bar." The court rejected Bogle & Gates's tortured arguments that it had, in fact, technically complied with plaintiffs' discovery requests. Instead, the court determined, what had occurred was a prolonged shell game, replete with "misleading" answers that were "contrary to the purposes of discovery and . . . most damaging to the litigation process." The court added, "Having read the record herein, we cannot perceive of any request that could have been made to this drug company that would have produced the smoking gun documents."

The court noted Bogle & Gates's claim that "they were just doing their job, that is, they were vigorously representing their client." But the court responded that the job of being a lawyer must not include violating the rules, thereby encouraging opponents to do the same: "Misconduct, once tolerated, will breed more misconduct and those who might seek relief against abuse will instead resort to it in self-defense."

The court sent the case back to the trial court with directions to impose sanctions "severe enough to deter these attorneys and others from participating in this kind of conduct in the future."

Bogle & Gates now faced a big problem. The attorneys for Dr. Klicpera wanted to conduct discovery, explore the depth of abuse practiced by the Bogle firm, and present their evidence in a public court hearing. That could have proved embarrassing. Instead of submitting to this inquiry, Bogle & Gates and Fisons agreed to settle by paying $325,000. Bogle & Gates admitted that its attorneys advised Fisons not to produce the smoking gun documents and that such advice violated court discovery rules.

"We settled for less money than fighting Bogle & Gates cost us because it was never about the money," says Bruce Schafer. "We accomplished everything we set out to do. Our doctor was completely vindicated. Information about the dangers of theophylline was publicized, we got the Supreme Court to say unequivocally that discovery abuse is wrong, and we did some behavior modification on Bogle & Gates and the rest of the legal community."[39]

Two years after the Washington Supreme Court's decision, Dr. Klicpera's lawyer James Lobsenz believes there has been a marked impact on the practice of law in the state. "My impression is that the benefit of the doubt is being given to disclosure," Lobsenz says. "I know that lawyers are telling me they notice a difference and believe that judges are taking discovery abuses far more seriously."[40]

ENDING THE ABUSE

Too often power-lawyer strategies are aimed at one goal: delay. That word describes so much of what many corporate lawyers do. They delay the truth from coming out by obstructing the fact-finding process before trial. They delay their client's day of reckoning by preventing cases from coming to trial. They delay final resolutions of lawsuits by filing questionable appeals. As a consequence, it often takes many years, occasionally a decade or more, for a civil case to reach its ultimate conclusion.

When justice moves at the pace of continental drift, it contributes mightily to the public's current crisis of confidence in attorneys, judges, and, indeed, the entire civil justice system. And with some power lawyers going even further and deliberately concealing evidence, it is evident that dramatic changes are needed.

Justice was obtained for Jennifer Pollock and Dr. Klicpera only because an anonymous whistle-blower had the courage to expose wrongdoing by revealing a smoking gun document. More often, evidence of misconduct is exposed only through determined and expensive discovery litigation, or never turns up at all. For every case where the wrongdoing finally comes out, how many cases are there where smoking gun documents remain buried in the files or damning eyewitness testimony never comes to light? Presently, there is no way to know.

If lawsuits are to be decided on their merits, and not on the vagaries of the discovery wars, professional integrity must be restored to the legal process.

Change won't happen overnight. It took years for the system to get to a place where the term "zealous representation of a client" is often synonymous with "obstruct, lie, obfuscate, and abuse." But the system can be brought back into balance. It will, however, take work.

Judges Must Get Tough

Jim Butler, the lawyer who took on Suzuki and GM, says that obstructionist tactics will not disappear unless more judges begin entering default judgments for discovery abuse. "Otherwise," he says, "there will be no deterrence."[41]

Entering a default or, if the abuse comes from a plaintiff, dismissing the case is the ultimate sanction. It deprives a party of the right to defend or prosecute the case. By increasingly invoking default and dismissal, judges can send a powerful message to lawyers and their clients that obfuscation does not pay. That should reduce the temptation to attempt to win cases through impropriety rather than on the facts and the law.

Professor Aronson, who testified for Dr. Klicpera in the Fisons case, agrees with Butler: "There is so much evidence that when judges intervene, when they get tough, this stuff stops. Unfortunately, too many judges still take a hands-off attitude. They assume lawyer goodwill. So they tell the lawyer to knock it off and assume that will take care of the problem. But that only emboldens those who would abuse the system. They know they have a couple of free bites of the apple."[42]

Some contend that fining the parties or their attorneys is a sufficiently tough sanction for discovery abuse. But to giant corporations and lawyers earning millions in fees, even a six-figure fine could be a slap on the wrist, a cost of doing business. In the case of egregious, willful violations, the only kind of money sanction that can work is one that is tantamount to the defendant's ultimate liability in the underlying lawsuit.

The past experience of a firm and client should also be taken into account when determining the sanction. "One of the reasons all of this goes on," Professor Aronson says, "is that with the growth of big city practice and the number of lawyers, wrongdoers feel anonymous. They figure they may never again appear in front of a particular judge or against a particular lawyer. That emboldens them and encourages wrongdoing."

If judges held the conduct of a firm or a client in past cases to be relevant to current controversies—if a firm that obstructed discovery in Georgia could not come into Maine or Montana with a clean slate—the system would be less lenient to repeat offenders, creating a strong incentive for proper behavior.

The Rules Must Be Tightened

Another way to reduce obstruction and deceit in the discovery process is to change court rules to strengthen and clarify the obligations of parties and their lawyers.

But a recent experiment at the federal level illustrates the challenges faced in achieving this result. The federal Judicial Conference, overseen by the U.S. Supreme Court, recently acted to reform the discovery process. Amendments to federal court rules, made effective in December 1993, provide for a new regime of mandatory disclosure. Under the new rules, a party to a lawsuit must turn over lists of potential witnesses, copies of "relevant" documents, and other information—without waiting for any discovery request from the other side.

Predictably, corporate power lawyers howled in protest. They mounted a furious, but ultimately unsuccessful, effort to convince Congress to overturn the rules. Judge Ralph Winter of the U.S. Second Circuit Court of Appeals suggested one reason for opposition to the changes: Opponents prefer a system that requires "extensive and unnecessary paperwork"—the rounds of motions that make up the discovery wars—"for which they get paid."[43]

Whether this new approach will do much to curb discovery abuses remains to be seen. For one thing, by its terms the rule is optional: Each of the ninety-four federal district courts nationwide can decide for itself whether to implement it, and even where it is in force, in any given case the trial judge can suspend it. Many district courts have so far avoided adopting the new rules.[44]

Second, much will turn, and much litigation will occur, on the definition of "relevant" documents in the new rules. Without a discovery request, it may be hard for a party to determine which records will be considered relevant in a given case.

Third, the new rules place a rather arbitrary ceiling on discovery exchanges. The ceiling, which judges have the authority to waive in any given case, limits parties to ten depositions and twenty-five written interrogatories per case. For this reason, and because of concern that the new procedures will simply add another unnecessary layer of work to the litigation process, many public interest advocates and plaintiffs' lawyers also opposed the new rules.

Fourth, at the same time the Judicial Conference acted to provide for full, honest exchanges of information through mandatory disclosure, it weakened one of the key tools judges have used to punish attorney misconduct, Rule 11 of the Federal Rules of Civil Procedure. Rule 11 provides for punishment of attorneys for making unwarranted assertions or bringing frivolous claims. Where punishment for violations was once mandatory, under the amendments, judges now have discretion to impose no punishment at all on offending attorneys. And the amendments give lawyers a new twenty-one-day grace period to withdraw offending court papers before risking punishment.

Only time will tell whether the new rules, on balance, will reduce the obfuscation and free judicial resources for more productive work. But the federal and state courts should continue to review the discov-

ery rules and their operation in practice and look for ways to deter obstructionism.

Ethics Boards Must Act

Tough judges and new rules will not be enough to stop discovery abuse.
Lawyers need additional reason to stiffen their backbones in the face of
client demands to win at all costs. States must be equipped to investigate lawyer misconduct and prepared to suspend or disbar those found
to have violated state codes of legal ethics.

Each state has an agency responsible for disciplining lawyers for
misconduct. The agency receives complaints from clients, lawyers, and
others about the conduct of a particular attorney. It will then conduct
a preliminary review, interviewing witnesses, reviewing records, and
seeking a response from the accused lawyer. If the agency finds reason
to proceed, it will hold a formal hearing. A typical hearing panel consists of three members. An official called the bar counsel serves as
"prosecutor," and the accused lawyer has the right to be represented by
another lawyer and to cross-examine witnesses.

If it determines that the attorney has violated the state's legal ethical rules, the hearing panel can recommend various mild sanctions,
with names like "reprimand" or "censure." If the conduct is more egregious, it can recommend a more severe sanction like temporary suspen-
sion of law practice or disbarment. The panel's decision is then
reviewed by the agency's governing board, and then by the state's highest court.

At least in theory, state bar ethics boards have real power over
lawyers. Discipline deters misconduct. Reputation counts a lot in the
legal world. Lawyers, like others in society, are loathe to be embarrassed
in front of colleagues, clients, and the general public. "If a lawyer faces
adverse publicity or a fine that will not be paid by malpractice insurance," legal ethicist Stephen Gillers says, "he or she is more likely to be
conscientious about obeying the rules."[45] Thus, even if state bars
brought few disciplinary actions and rarely suspended anyone, the real
likelihood of lawyer discipline for discovery abuse could go a long way
toward cleaning up the system.

But obstructionism will not be brought under control until ethical
rules are sharpened and ethics boards are emboldened to make it more
likely that violations of discovery rules are grounds for discipline. The
failure of disciplinary committees to take such ethical wrongs seriously,
especially in the discovery area, is illustrated by Bogle & Gates's wrongdoing in the Fisons case. Despite the well-publicized decision of the

Washington Supreme Court that Bogle & Gates practiced law in an inappropriate manner, the state ethics enforcement office has taken no action against the attorneys involved. That result sends a powerful and disturbing message: If you get caught it might cost you money, it might even cost you a case, but it will not endanger your right to practice law. That message needs to be amended.

The failure to discipline discovery abuses is part of a larger failure of state bars and courts to discipline attorneys for dishonest behavior. Robert C. Fellmeth, director of the Center for Public Interest Law and the former bar discipline monitor for the State of California,[46] writes, "The Bar must begin to search for ways to deter attorney deceit, particularly in the practice of civil law. The level of attorney dishonesty in representations to the court, . . . in dealings with adverse counsel, and perhaps especially in . . . legal briefs, is embarrassing to anyone with a measure of intellectual pride."[47]

Unfortunately, state ethics boards, which are usually funded entirely by annual bar membership dues, generally do not have the resources to go after the big fish in their particular pond. "Increasingly, state bar ethics enforcement officers are tenacious, making that work their career," Professor Schneyer says. "However, that has not altered the historic pattern that lawyers in big firms are not subjected to a sufficient level of ethical enforcement. Perhaps that is because state bars are simply overmatched in resources by the big firms."[48]

One area where reform is surely needed is in the composition of bar disciplinary committees. These bodies are dominated by lawyers, often from the top corporate firms in the state. The American Bar Association recommends that one third of the members of state ethics boards and hearing panels be nonlawyers, but in most states that goal is not met.[49] Instead of being shocked by the misconduct of their colleagues, or driven to uphold the highest standards of the profession, the lawyers who dominate the ethics boards appear to be more of the mind-set invoked by attorney and former federal judge Harold Tyler in defending the Donovan Leisure partner who lied to the court about destroying documents: "There, possibly but for the grace of God, go I, because of the pressures which come upon men and women who practice law. . . ."[50] More nonlawyer representation on these bodies might help improve attorney discipline.

It would be nice to believe that lawyers—educated, privileged men and women—could step back from the litigation wars, look inside themselves, own up to their ethical obligations to the justice system, and solve this crisis. As the Eleventh Circuit Court of Appeals stated in its opinion in the *Malautea* v. *Suzuki* case, "We must return to the original principle that, as officers of the court, attorneys are servants of the law rather than servants of the highest bidder. We must rediscover the old values of our profession. The integrity of the justice system depends on it." But such rousing hortatory rhetoric, while admirable, is not enough. Not in a world where a former lawyer at Covington & Burling, one of the most powerful firms in Washington, D.C., can recall from his experience at the firm that "the intent of a lot of discovery is to break the other side financially," and another attorney remembered presenting to a federal agency "long arguments knowing that we'd lose. But the bigger the pile, the more time bought . . . The purpose is obstructionism while the client continues to make a profit."[51] Not in a world where Bruce Bromley, a top partner at New York's Cravath, Swaine & Moore, once bragged to an audience at Stanford Law School, "I was born, I think, to be a protractor . . . I could take the simplest antitrust case and protract the defense almost to infinity . . . [One case] lasted fourteen years. . . . Despite fifty thousand pages of testimony, there really wasn't any dispute about the facts. . . . We won that case, and, as you know, my firm's meter was running all the time—every month for fourteen years."[52] The way to create a just legal system is for the people to keep a close eye on the lawyers and see to it that the various available punishments are used to make sure that this corporate legal culture of obstructionism doesn't pay.

CHAPTER 4

BURNING THE TAPES

O NE OF THE MOST DRAMATIC MOMENTS IN THE 1970S Watergate scandal occurred in the summer of 1973 when former White House aide Alexander Butterfield told a hushed Senate hearing room about an automatic taping system that had recorded nearly every word uttered in President Richard Nixon's Oval Office. Surely these tapes would answer the question that, as Nixon himself admitted, so many people were asking: whether their president was in fact "a crook."

New York Times columnist William Safire, a former Nixon speechwriter, wrote that Nixon should burn the tapes. With both the Senate investigating committee and Archibald Cox, the special Watergate prosecutor, seeking access to the tapes, White House officials like special adviser John Connally (a former Texas governor and U.S. treasury secretary) and communications aide Patrick J. Buchanan (later a candidate for the 1992 and 1996 Republican presidential nominations) were privately urging the president to do the same thing. Connally reportedly advised Nixon to have White House press secretary Ron Ziegler "assemble the White House press corps in the Rose Garden, pile up all the tapes, set a match to them, and let them film the bonfire."[1]

Nearly twenty years later, Nixon's White House counsel, Leonard Garment, recalled in a television interview a meeting between aides and Nixon at Bethesda Naval Hospital, where the president was hospitalized with pneumonia:[2]

GARMENT: I think the foremost question was whether the tapes constituted material or evidence that had to be kept.

Q: Well, did anyone in that room that day suggest, "Why don't we just burn the tapes?"

GARMENT: Well, I don't think it was put in those terms. The

134

question was, "Do these have to be delivered? Do they have to be maintained—retained?"

Q: Did someone argue in that room that, no, they don't have to be preserved?

GARMENT: Well, that question was raised, and I can't associate it with one person or another.

Q: And what did you argue?

GARMENT: Well, I said that it would constitute a felony to destroy the tapes.

Instead of burning the tapes, Nixon stalled. He offered a compromise under which Senator John Stennis would listen to the tapes. There were no takers for this deal; Stennis was hard of hearing. He offered transcribed excerpts, but this did not satisfy the investigators. He fired special prosecutor Cox, but this action only increased opposition and led to talk of impeachment. He finally released some of the tapes, but the new special prosecutor, Leon Jaworski, subpoenaed more. So Nixon fought the subpoenas in court. He claimed that, as president, he was not subject to normal court processes. But on July 24, 1994, the United States Supreme Court, ruling unanimously and emphatically, held that even the president was not above the law and that Nixon would have to obey the subpoenas.

Many feared that the president would defy the Supreme Court, precipitating a profound and destructive constitutional crisis. Patrick Buchanan said in 1996 that, even after the Supreme Court's decision, he advised Nixon, "Sir, you should burn those tapes."[3] Instead, Nixon produced the tapes. He did so despite the extremely damaging revelations the tapes contained, evidence that indicated that Nixon was personally involved in the cover-up of the Watergate affair and that he had lied to the American people. This evidence led directly to his resignation shortly thereafter, on August 8, 1974.

The unanimous decision of the Supreme Court, led by a Nixon appointee, Chief Justice Warren Burger, and Nixon's subsequent decision not to defy the Court's ruling reaffirmed the importance of law and legal procedure in resolving even our most heated and controversial disputes.

But after Nixon's resignation, an undercurrent of dissatisfaction arose among those who, angry at the outcome of the scandal, claimed that Nixon's only crime was "getting caught." More destructively, some renewed the argument that Nixon should have destroyed the evidence by "burning the tapes." The fact that such an act might have been a felony and a shredding of the rule of law was not important to these commentators. For them, winning was the be-all and end-all.

This mentality guides the behavior of too many corporate lawyers. Indeed, one of the most powerful of all Washington power lawyers, the late Edward Bennett Williams, boasted many times after Watergate that, had he been in charge of Nixon's defense, the president would have beaten the rap. How would Williams have saved Nixon? Before any subpoenas could issue, "I would have told him to burn the tapes."[4]

This win-at-any-cost mentality has not disappeared. Nor does it apply only to historic disputes like Watergate; it also infects many legal battles, both large and small, civil and criminal, involving America's giant corporations. Like dry rot it has quietly grown, corrupting the conduct of business, the operation of the civil justice system, and the ethics of lawyers.

THE NATURE OF THE PROBLEM

It is a settled matter of law that litigants have a duty to preserve discoverable evidence once a lawsuit has commenced, for, as one New York federal trial judge wrote in an opinion, "Our adversarial system of civil justice rests upon access of all parties to all evidence bearing on the controversy between them, including that in control of adverse parties. This, of course, requires the absolute honesty of each party in answering discovery requests and complying with discovery orders. Destruction or concealment by a party of relevant documents in its files threatens the viability and public acceptance of the system."[5]

And the duty also applies before litigation, if a party reasonably should foresee that a lawsuit will be brought or if government regulatory agencies require such information. In their book *Combating Stonewalling and Other Discovery Abuses*, Frances Hare, Jr., James L. Gilbert, and Stuart A. Ollanik write that a broad conception of the duty "is necessary because, as courts have recognized, a pattern of stonewalling can begin well before discovery, and before [lawsuit] filing, when defendants try to purge their files of inculpatory evidence to prevent the truth from ever surfacing."[6]

In the law business, destruction or defacement of evidence has a name: *spoliation*. "I believe spoliation is an effective and growing litigation practice that threatens to undermine the integrity of civil trial process," writes Harvard Law School professor Charles R. Nesson. "It is a form of cheating which blatantly compromises the ideal of the trial as a search for truth."[7]

As we shall see, the truth is the last thing on the minds of some power lawyers seeking victory for their corporate clients.

THE CASE OF THE POLLUTING TENANT

Lorraine McGuire and her husband, Jack Valley, were part owners of a twelve-acre tract of land in Harvey, Louisiana. They leased their property to Sigma Coatings, Inc., from 1976 to 1991. Sigma, a division of the Fina Oil and Chemical Company, operated a paint manufacturing plant on the property. Fina was ranked 145th on the 1994 Fortune 500 list of industrial companies.[8] It is a company valued at $3.4 billion.

As the expiration of their lease grew near, McGuire and Valley discovered to their horror that their land had been ruined by chemical pollutants. They blamed Fina, which, they contended, allowed toxic heavy metals and volatile organic compounds used in their paint manufacturing plant to be spilled onto the land. Among the toxins released on the property were fifteen hundred gallons of chemicals from leaking tanks that Fina had not properly maintained or repaired, resulting in contamination at more than one hundred times the maximum level allowable under applicable laws.

Fina refused to admit its responsibility, and in 1991 McGuire and Valley, represented by Jonathan B. Andry, sued in federal court. Fina responded by blaming previous users of the property dating back to the 1950s for the pollution and suing these parties for any cleanup costs.

Discovery began. During depositions, Andry elicited testimony from Fina employees about audit reports they had prepared. Andry believed that these reports, as well as supporting documentation that had been prepared in conjunction with Fina's environmental audits of the property, might contain relevant information about the quality of the operations of the paint manufacturing plant and whether the procedures used were sufficient to prevent the contamination of the property.

Andry also requested document production, including "material safety data sheets" that would have identified the types of chemicals present on the site, preaudit questionnaires prepared by employees as part of audits, personal notes, and draft audit reports.

Fina's attorneys, the New Orleans defense firm Deutch, Kerrigan & Stiles, objected to producing the requested material, so Andry was forced to seek a court order compelling discovery. That resulted in court hearings in front of a federal magistrate, who ordered the materials produced. Fina's attorneys then appealed the order to United States District Judge Edith Brown Clement, who affirmed that the audit reports and supporting information had to be produced.

Judge Clement's order presented a big problem for Fina's attorneys. They could not obey the court order because the documents no longer existed. Someone had destroyed them.

Again, the matter was brought into court. The magistrate angrily demanded that Fina's lawyers explain why the documents had been destroyed and under whose orders they had been purged from Fina's files. The answer came in the form of a sworn affidavit from a Fina executive stating that the reports and supporting documents had been destroyed pursuant to the legal department's documentation retention policy.

But Andry wasn't buying that excuse. He believed the documents had been destroyed specifically because they would have proved very harmful to Fina in the pending litigation and for the specific purpose of limiting Fina's liability to his clients. He filed a motion seeking sanctions and a default judgment.

After a two-day evidentiary hearing, the magistrate unequivocally agreed with Andry, finding that the documents had been "deliberately and intentionally destroyed by Fina." The magistrate further found:

> As the court understands it, the cleanup procedure as well as the apportionment of fault could be greatly enhanced if everyone could be certain of exactly what chemicals or toxics were present on the property at any given time. The material safety data sheets addressed this issue. . . .
>
> [C]ompletely impossible to condone is the action of Fina's chief in-house counsel for environmental matters, James Veach, who ordered the destruction of the documents specifically responsive to discovery requests. The fact that counsel personally was involved is all the more distasteful as it brings into question matters of ethics and professionalism over which this profession has been so soundly criticized in recent years. . . .
>
> The documents that counsel has destroyed go directly to the issue of the condition of the property at the conclusion of the lease and at various times prior thereto. It was extremely relevant to this litigation . . .[9]

The magistrate recommended that sanctions be imposed, including raising Fina's burden of proof concerning its claims of contribution, making it much more difficult for Fina to blame others for polluting the property. The magistrate also ordered that Fina pay the attorneys' fees that plaintiffs incurred seeking to track down the attorney wrongdoing.

Judge Clement reviewed the magistrate's recommendation and accepted most of what she had proposed. But the judge, in an October 1993 decision, went further, making an extraordinary ruling:

> This court finds Fina in civil contempt of court for failing to comply with a discovery order of this court and enjoins Fina from utilizing its in-house counsel in any way until Fina demonstrates . . . that in-house counsel it seeks to utilize is not connected in any way with prior discovery or with gathering and/or destruction of evidence . . .
>
> Further, this court finds that James L. Veach flagrantly disregarded the authority of this court and the rules of discovery. As a result, criminal contempt proceedings will be instituted against Mr. Veach by forthcoming order of court.[10]

Facing heavy sanctions, Fina personnel began to produce documents not disclosed earlier in the case. Not just a few documents but boxes and boxes of documents. "They produced an additional twenty boxes of documents," Andry recalls. "These papers were not organized in any particular fashion, forcing the magistrate to order Fina to comply with the rules requiring indexing. Pursuant to this order, Fina produced an index that took up a box in and of itself."[11]

Information about other destroyed evidence also came to light. A valve that McGuire and Valley contended caused some of the spillage of toxic materials was unavailable for inspection. The reason? It had been destroyed and sold to a junk man. "We believed we could prove the valve had been kept open for fifteen years and that it had rusted open," Andry says.

Andry filed a second motion for sanctions. As the matter was coming up for hearing, Fina began energetically to attempt to settle its case with all concerned. McGuire and Valley finally received what Andry describes as a fair settlement, the terms of which, by agreement, are confidential.

We contacted Veach about the lawsuit and the charges made against him. He admits destroying documents both before and after discovery requests, but states that they were preliminary documents and that it was Fina's standard policy always to destroy them. Also, he claims that at the time the documents were destroyed, he did not believe they were covered by the plaintiffs' discovery requests. According to Veach, he and other Fina attorneys were "astonished when the judge ruled that the discovery request, in fact, covered the environmental compliance audits."

We also asked Veach about Fina's claim during discovery that all copies of the documents had been destroyed, when in fact, they had not. He said, "This hurt us in the litigation more than anything else. At the corporate level, we had destroyed all the documents. But at the plant site, nothing had been destroyed. We didn't know that until a few days before the hearing when the people who were going to swear under oath [that they did not have the documents] discovered that they actually did have them. So, we showed up at the hearing and had to tell [Judge Clement] we actually had the documents. She was not pleased. I can understand why, but it was a good-faith mistake."[12]

Veach ultimately escaped formal punishment. First, in March 1994, the State Bar of Texas, of which Veach is a member, concluded an ethics investigation into the matter by informing Veach, "The panel has found that you have not committed professional misconduct as defined in the [Texas] Code and this matter has been dismissed."[13] Then, two weeks later, Louisiana federal prosecutors advised Judge Clement that they would not prosecute Veach for criminal contempt because (1) Veach was not an attorney of record in the litigation; (2) Veach had destroyed the documents in another jurisdiction (Texas); and (3) there was insufficient evidence that his destruction of documents violated an outstanding court order, as the contempt statute requires.

On March 25, 1994, however, Judge Clement fined Veach $5,000 for the less serious offense of civil contempt of court. She stated:

> Although Mr. Veach's conduct does not rise to the level of criminal contempt because the documents he has admitted destroying were the subject of a valid discovery request at the time of destruction rather than an [court] order compelling production, this Court has found that James L. Veach flagrantly disregarded the authority of this Court and the rules of discovery. Such recalcitrant and willful misconduct is in complete disregard for the sanctity of the judicial process and cannot be condoned if other litigants are to be deterred from engaging in similar activity.[14]

Veach appealed, and in March 1995, the Fifth Circuit Court of Appeals vacated the contempt citation on the procedural ground that the trial court did not have jurisdiction over Veach since he was not a party to the case and had not been formally served with process. The reversal is not an exoneration of Veach; the appeals court specifically stated: "We understand the district court's frustration with the course of discovery in this case, and we certainly do not intend our opinion to be construed as in any way approving of dilatory or abusive discovery tactics."[15]

Thus the question of whether Veach's actions constituted deliberate misconduct was never fully resolved on the merits. But on their face the actions seem highly questionable. Moreover, there can be no question that the Fina case is a good example of why the court system is so bogged down and distrusted today. Months of judicial time were wasted reading inch-thick motions and responses, reviewing documents, and holding court hearings, all because Fina had destroyed documents relevant to the case.

Fina's stockholders also lost. First, because the trial court found that Fina's attorneys acted improperly, Fina was unable to defend the case effectively. Second, Fina was out more than $200,000 when the court ordered it to pay the plaintiffs' attorneys' fees incurred during the dispute over the destroyed documents. "It should have taken two thousand hours at most to completely resolve this case," Andry says. "But because of Fina's obstructionism, we spent more than fifty-eight hundred hours on the matter, not to mention the other firms, which also spent thousands of hours of attorney time." Third, Fina had to pay its *own* retained lawyers' fees, which had to go well into six figures, if not more. Finally, the settlement probably ended up costing Fina more money than it would have had the matter been addressed in an ethically appropriate way. "I won't say what the terms of the settlement are," Andry told us. "However, I can say we achieved a far better settlement for our client than the original offer we made to resolve the case."[16] Ironically, according to Veach, the cleanup of the land cost Fina only about $120,000.

THE WESTINGHOUSE FILES

The Fina case is not a rare occurrence. Crucial corporate documents seem to be disappearing with increasing and alarming frequency. Methods of implementing systematic document-destruction policies in anticipation of possible litigation are the subject of more than a few legal publications and lawyer symposia.

New Jersey attorney Christopher Placitella provided us with a copy of a document he had received in litigation he was conducting against Westinghouse Corporation over injuries allegedly caused by asbestos. It was a 1987 memo written by one Jeffrey J. Bair, a Westinghouse in-house attorney, to C. Wayne Bickerstaff, Manager, Corporate Industrial Hygiene and Environmental Affairs, that specifically recommended destroying smoking gun documents that might prove harmful to Westinghouse's litigation interests.

The memo reported on a review of files, some dating back to the 1930s, in the company's "Industrial Hygiene Department." According to the memo, "The majority of the documents in Industrial Hygiene's files are *potential* smoking gun documents. . . . The files are filled with documentation which critiques and criticizes, from an industrial hygiene perspective, Westinghouse manufacturing and non-manufacturing operations" (emphasis in original). These files, said the memo, discuss deficiencies in company operations and recommendations to correct them. The files also detail "inadequacies in Westinghouse's use and handling of [various chemical] substances" and "many years of employee test results, some of them unfavorable." Thus, according to the memo, "Industrial Hygiene, by performing its job, creates daily, potential smoking gun documents."

A 1960 letter in the files "might show early knowledge of the corporation to certain health hazards associated with epoxy resin dissolving agents. What use did the corporation make of this knowledge to protect employees and the public? If none or very little, then this document might become a 'smoking gun.'" The memo notes that if air sampling and radiation test results "exceed allowable limits, the possible consequences as far as litigation is concerned are apparent." It adds, "[T]he fact that the corporation performed, for example, air sampling for certain substances as early as 1940 (which it in fact did) might be used to prove early knowledge on the part of the corporation of hazards associated with such substances." As to safety data sheets in the files, "Again the smoking gun possibilities of these documents are clear." If the files show that safety information "was not conveyed to customers, the public, etc. again the potential future problems are readily apparent."

The memo offers the following guidelines for dealing with the above-described records: "[T]he risks of keeping the files must be balanced against the advantages of maintaining the records. Similarly, the disadvantages of not having records needed by the corporation in litigation must also be balanced against the cost and inefficiencies associated with maintaining valueless records." In fact, as the memo itself notes, Westinghouse kept most of the records described on microfiche, so the costs of maintaining them could not have been substantial, especially for a company the size of Westinghouse.

The memo proceeds to make recommendations as to what to do with the troublesome files. As to general plant correspondence files, the memo asserts that they are not required by law to be maintained. Thus it recommends that all files created before 1974 be "discarded."

The memo then adds that these files "are filled with technical product and chemical information, hazard information and safe-handling information, *most of it generated by the Industrial Hygiene Department in an 'editorializing' and opinionated manner*" (emphasis in original). Corporate lawyers dislike "editorialized" statements in corporate reports—e.g., "I think this condition is unsafe"—because of the harm such opinions can cause corporations in litigation. The memo concludes that the risks of keeping these files "substantially exceed the advantages."

As to post-1974 correspondence files, the memo recommends retention for the following reason: "[T]hese files might be of value to the Corporation. . . . It might be possible to use these files, as well as test record files, to establish that industrial hygiene and employee safety were and are promoted by Westinghouse as routine and indispensable requirements of daily operation." A similar approach informs the memo's discussion of testing records: "Based on our review of the data, it appears that at least a *substantial* portion of it is favorable. This information has in the past been used to respond to union requests for information . . . *and to defend workmen's compensation claims*" (emphasis in original).

In other words, the attorney thought the pre-1974 files had the potential to hurt Westinghouse in litigation. Consequently, he recommended that the material be destroyed. But when he found records he thought might prove helpful in litigation and workers' compensation claims, he recommended that they be maintained. Thus, any future jury or court decision or government investigation might be faulty, based only on partial information that had been skewed by Westinghouse for the benefit of Westinghouse. The memo concludes by noting that lawsuits involving injuries from toxic materials "show no signs of abating in the near future" and that legislation then pending in Congress might increase litigation. "Consequently," the memo argues, "well reasoned and conceived document retention and destruction programs for departments such as Industrial Hygiene, and in fact the entire corporation, are imperative." Based on this memo, a "well reasoned and conceived document retention program" would appear to be one designed to stack the deck in Westinghouse's favor in future litigation.

Were "smoking gun" documents at Westinghouse actually destroyed? Westinghouse says no, but there is evidence to the contrary. For example, electronic mail from Bair to Bickerstaff dated January 22, 1988, advised Bickerstaff that the "plant correspondence files generated prior to 1974 will be discarded. The remaining correspondence will be maintained." This advice would have been consistent with the smoking gun memo. In a memo dated January 29, 1988, Bickerstaff outlines the destruction policy originally set forth in the smoking gun memo. In addition, a March 3, 1988, handwritten note on Westinghouse stationery with the name of Jeffrey J. Bair at the bottom reads: "Informed Wayne begin discarding documents in nos. 5, 6 & 7." And a typewritten memo from Bair dated March 8, 1988, to S. R. Pitts, vice president, environmental affairs, reads, "Wayne Bickerstaff and his staff are currently discarding documents as per our retention guidelines. We will notify you when the process has been completed." Finally, there is a memo from Bickerstaff promising to have the destruction project completed by June 30, 1988.

On January 14, 1993, New Brunswick, New Jersey, Superior Court Judge L. Jack Lintner, who was handling an asbestos lawsuit brought by attorney Christopher Placitella against Westinghouse, held a hearing to consider the Bair memorandum and the possibility that Westinghouse had destroyed evidence relevant to the case. In the following excerpt from the court transcript, Westinghouse attorney Ray Tierney of the New Jersey law firm Shanley & Fisher tries to explain away Bair's handiwork:

MR. TIERNEY: . . . And let me tell you how I read that memorandum. I've read it and I looked at it, and I must tell you that except in some unfortunate words in there, I think it's fairly benign. . . . But when you read it as a layperson, you can't get any sense at all for example that it is dealing with asbestos, none whatsoever.

THE COURT: I don't think you can get any sense that it's dealing with any specific litigation.

MR. TIERNEY: I agree with that. But if there's a problem articulated, it is not asbestos. I read that and said well, these guys are talking about nuclear waste, and that's what I read.

THE COURT: Well, I quite frankly read it in a sense, and I can tell you how I read it—I read it in the sense of general environmental and toxic litigation and knowledge of conditions of the plant and/or chemicals that are being utilized by Westinghouse, and destroying if you would at least some documentation, at least a suggestion of destroying some documentation of material that goes to knowledge on the part of Westinghouse of these conditions. Now, the only reason that material would be destroyed, or be suggested to be destroyed, would be because of litigation in general. That comes through that memo a hundred percent.

Now, perhaps that memo doesn't talk about specific litigation. . . . But on its face, doesn't it talk about the destruction of material that could otherwise be utilized in a litigation?

MR. TIERNEY: There is nothing improper about that. Respectfully, Judge, taking documents that were created in 1935 or 1940 or 1950, simply because they have a generic connection with litigation is not improper.

THE COURT: Oh, it's not generic. It goes to an issue—it's talking about documents that go specifically to the issue of knowledge on the part of Westinghouse. How is that generic?

MR. TIERNEY: Because you have to hook up the knowledge with something specific. You've got to say, look, the fact that we knew something in 1935 is germane to a piece of litigation that exists whenever. Simply to say I had knowledge of something, or some guy wrote a memorandum saying this quote could be harmful end quote, doesn't deal with anything, and you don't have to keep that kind of stuff, as long as you don't—as long as you're not destroying things that are connected with specific ongoing or potentially reasonably anticipated litigation.

THE COURT: Well, let me ask you the next question . . . If I am a lawyer, and I know that there is a material that would be discoverable in future litigation, relative to specific knowledge of my client with regard to a toxic environmental problem, and I suggest that material be discarded because it does show knowledge and notice, you're telling me that because there's no specific litigation, that the lawyer has every right and obligation or can do that without being unethical?

MR. TIERNEY: Well, I'm not sure I could answer that yes or no. I have to—I think I have to do that by example. I think my answer to your question is yes. . . .

THE COURT: And I think the key . . . is discoverable information. . . . Let's say I build Chevrolets, and I realize that there is a potential defect in the Chevrolet. And there's been no litigation yet. But I know there are people out there driving that Chevrolet and may be subject to that defect. I can destroy the material?

MR. TIERNEY: I think you can. . . . I don't think you can do it to avoid the litigation process, since the issue is not a problem, you simply allow the document destruction program to take its toll. . . . If I have a document where one of my employees says there may be a problem or whatever, I don't think you've got to keep that stuff.

Is Mr. Tierney's description of the duties of corporate counsel correct? "A party's spoliation of evidence is not excused merely because it occurs before a complaint is filed," attorney and author James Gilbert, an authority on the subject, says. "If the party knew or reasonably should have foreseen that the subject litigation would be commenced, or where the party engaged in document spoliation primarily to suppress unfavorable evidence, it is sanctionable."[17] But requiring that litigation be pending or foreseeable before any duty is imposed provides for some corporate wiggle room. According to Ted Schneyer, legal ethicist and law professor at the University of Arizona, "It is only clearly unethical for a document to be destroyed where production is already required by discovery order or where destruction would constitute the obstruction of justice. Obstruction of justice laws in many jurisdictions are very limited and may only apply to cases that are pending or known to be about to be filed."[18]

What do the actual rules governing legal ethics say? The American Bar Association's Model Rules of Professional Conduct, which are the basis for some state legal ethics codes, don't quite settle the matter. The rules provide that a lawyer must not "unlawfully alter, destroy or conceal a document or other material having potential evidentiary value." The rules note that "[a]pplicable law in many jurisdictions makes it an offense to destroy materials for purpose of impairing its availability in a pending proceeding or one whose commencement can be foreseen."[19] So it comes down to provisions of individual states' laws and, again, the question of whether the corporation could see the litigation coming.

The issue on which courts and state bar disciplinary committees should focus is intent. Destroying a document *because* it would provide evidence of wrongdoing, whether in a pending or future litigation, undermines the fairness and integrity of our system of justice.

There can be little doubt that the Westinghouse memo clearly related to potential litigation. First, the term *smoking gun* is commonly used in the law business to refer specifically to documentary or other evidence that proves wrongdoing. For example, Fisons Corporation's "Dear Doctor" letter discussed in Chapter 3 was a smoking gun because it proved that Fisons knew that its asthma medication could cause serious side effects in children. The fact that Westinghouse's lawyer repeatedly used the term indicates that at least one purpose for the recommendation to destroy records was to benefit Westinghouse in pending or future litigation. Further, while urging that smoking gun materials be destroyed, the lawyer specifically recommended retaining evidence that could help Westinghouse make favorable factual showings. A generic "housecleaning" of obsolete material would not be concerned with such issues. Finally, the memo specifically refers to litigation. Note the language in the conclusion: "Toxic tort litigation, including toxic tort-related workmen's compensation litigation, show no sign of abating in the near future."[20]

The purpose of the memo is clear. That a lawyer could try to justify it with a straight face is astonishing indeed.

Recognizing that the Bair smoking gun memo was itself a smoking gun, Westinghouse attempted to persuade Judge Lintner that the document was subject to attorney-client privilege and thus could not be used in the asbestos litigation. On February 23, 1993, the judge rejected Westinghouse's argument. Two weeks earlier a Texas judge had rejected the same Westinghouse argument in another case. Austin-based state district judge Paul R. Davis found that the memo outlined a scheme "to commit fraud on the courts of this nation."[21]

CORPORATE POLICIES OF DOCUMENT DESTRUCTION

The problem of spoliation is such that much of this book could be spent describing the many cases under which corporate and defense lawyers and, less frequently, plaintiffs' lawyers,[22] have engaged in the wrongdoing. To take one other example:

In 1959, General Motors introduced the Corvair, a sporty new passenger car. Within months, GM began to receive customer complaints about the Corvair's stability, as well as about exhaust fumes entering the passenger compartment. Between 1959 and 1964, thousands of complaints regarding the Corvair reached GM headquarters. As discussed in Chapter 2, hundreds of these complaints concerned the fumes, which contained lethal carbon monoxide—a defect that GM sought to sweep under the rug by sealing the evidence in a lawsuit brought by a man who claimed that the Corvair defect caused him permanent brain damage. The letters were potent evidence that GM had been alerted to the shortcomings of the Corvair. And victims of Corvair accidents began filing lawsuits against the company. In the late 1960s, some junk dealers from the Detroit suburbs came across nineteen boxes of such complaints on microfilm—complaints that GM management had ordered discarded in August 1966. According to John DeLorean, who was then a GM executive, the discovery sent GM officials "into a panic." They quickly acted to buy the microfilm back from the junk dealers, who were wily enough to hold out for $20,000. GM subsequently devised new methods for more effectively disposing of firm records.[23] Another alleged GM effort may have been more successful. In December 1972, DeLorean, then a GM vice president, was on the verge of leaving the company as a result of several disputes. DeLorean sent a memo to GM's vice chairman, Thomas Murphy, in which, among other complaints, DeLorean said that he had been told by an executive of GM's Pontiac division, which DeLorean had once headed, that the company had destroyed Pontiac correspondence files relating to air bags after GM curbed its research on air bag technology in the 1960s. (Murphy read the memo and handed it back to DeLorean without comment. DeLorean resigned in March 1973; in 1974, Murphy became GM's chairman.)[24]

But such incidents are only part of the story. Today, corporate lawyers are moving beyond destroying documents once a litigation has commenced or appears ready to commence; they are now recommending that corporations, as a matter of regular procedure, purge their files before any lawsuit so that documents that would prove corporate wrongdoing will never come before a jury's eyes.

Advocacy of prelitigation discarding of files by corporate lawyers is open and direct. For example, the January 1994 issue of *Corporate Legal Times*, a monthly publication for corporate lawyers, includes an article entitled "Purge Your Files Now or Pay for Bad Documents Later." Its author is Philip A. Lacovara, a partner in the New York office of the 570-lawyer power firm Mayer, Brown & Platt ($263 million annual gross revenues, $365,000 profits per partner). Lacovara's résumé includes stints as chief in-house litigator for General Electric, general counsel of the large investment banking firm Morgan Stanley, and, ironically, a member of the Watergate prosecution team that sought the Nixon tapes. In the article, he advocates just what the title suggests: a purging of documents that might hurt a corporation in a future litigation.

Lacovara writes that a corporation's "Achilles' heel in almost every case involving a complex dispute is the paper found in the company's own files. Nothing is quite as dismaying—or as inevitable—as finding a memorandum written by some employee that seems to prefigure the opposing party's theory of the case." Lacovara recommends action by corporate attorneys before a dispute ends up in litigation. While there is, he says, "no vaccine that will inoculate against the creation of every troublesome document . . . there is a regimen which at least can substantially reduce the risk." What is that regimen? A "document retention" program that will protect against "the discovery of a nettlesome document in the midst of a lawsuit." And what is such a program? One that "helps to mitigate the danger from 'bad documents' that came into existence and wound up being saved."

Lacovara writes that an experienced corporate general counsel should be able to identify the types of business transactions that pose a risk of litigation or require "special handling." He advises that in those situations, the corporation lawyer should carefully monitor the files on an ongoing basis "from a litigator's perspective . . . for potential problems." Such review, he says, "allows counsel to implement an immediate 'document retention' screening." Although Lacovara's article warns that corporate files contain "careless or baseless comments" authored by employees who are "too busy to have mastered all the facts," he never writes that the goal of "document retention" is simply to root out false or misleading statements. And although he alludes to ethical responsibilities when he worries that a poorly administered retention program "may destroy documents which are actually subject to a current disclosure obligation," attorneys less sophisticated than Lacovara would be excused if they came away with only one clear message: Corporate lawyers should actively cleanse corporate files to improve the odds of winning lawsuits in the future.

When we asked Lacovara if, indeed, that was his message, he told us, "I don't have much to add to what I have written." He then added, "The point of the article is that the fewer documents a corporation has, the better, with or without regard to impact in future litigation." We did not find that statement in the article itself, however. Lacovara continued, "Lawsuits are more likely to reach an accurate result if not papered by tens of thousands of documents that are not accurate or warranted which become inflammatory when in front of a jury. They distort the results."[25]

But how can we be assured of more accurate trial results if eagle-eyed corporate lawyers actively purge damaging materials, while leaving more favorable and self-serving accounts in the files? In such circumstances, a "retention policy" could be nothing more than a way to ensure that the corporation distorts its own history—corporate historians, take note—and escapes accountability for its wrongdoing.

Lacovara is not alone in his advocacy. Prelitigation file-purging is increasing in popularity. Articles like Lacovara's are written, lawyers counsel their clients on the issue, and corporate interests even conduct seminars designed to teach corporate executives how to inoculate their corporations against smoking gun documents.

One such seminar took place in April of 1992. It was sponsored by the Drug Information Association and entitled "Legal Liability in the Pharmaceutical Industry." Among the topics covered was document destruction before litigation. One speaker was Timothy Pratt, a partner in Kansas City's 200-lawyer Shook, Hardy and Bacon, an aggressive corporate law firm that represents, among others, tobacco and drug companies. Pratt presented a talk he called "The Ten Commandments on How the Pharmaceutical Industry Can Minimize Legal Liability." In his talk, Pratt spoke of commandments that came not from the mountaintop but from "nightmares—the nightmares of pharmaceutical lawyers like myself who have seen how violation of these commandments can complicate the defense of lawsuits against the industry."

Pratt's first commandment was "Thou Shalt Not Participate In The 'I Can Create A Worse Document Than You' Sweepstakes." He was referring, he said, to documents "that can be taken out of context by a plaintiff's attorney and misconstrued [including] documents in which the author expresses opinions about which he or she may not have all the information necessary to form such an opinion." Although Pratt's speech did not advocate file-cleansing, those who do frequently say that their only goal is to eliminate documents that "editorialize" or "express unwarranted opinions." But these polite terms may be taken by overeager students as euphemisms for those documents about which corporations are most concerned—documents that prove what the corporation knew and when it knew it, documents that suggest the company is culpable, not only in product liability cases but also in regulatory controversies with government, employment cases, whistle-blowing disputes, stockholders' actions, and the like. One wonders how often these document retention experts advise clients to destroy "opinion documents" that make the company look good.

Pratt's second commandment was "Thou Shalt Create A Responsible and Responsive Management Style." He gave an example: "If an employee creates a bad document in a surge of ill-conceived originality, what a supervisor should do is to go to that employee's office, close the door, quietly lay the memorandum on the desk, and say, 'What in the heck are you doing here?' " Pratt advised that management should hold regular meetings, with "no minutes required," to allow "for communication for employees making unnecessary provocative comments." He also urged that employees be held "accountable—accountable for their mistakes in judgment and their bad memoranda." A less benign interpretation of this second commandment would be: Create an atmosphere where employees are afraid to document the truth about lack of safety, ethics, or other forms of inappropriate corporate conduct.

Pratt's third commandment was that employers "Not Succumb To The Pack Rat Syndrome." He advised that they "[f]ollow the same philosophy that Al Capone followed, and if Geraldo kicks in your vault on national television, be sure that all he finds is a bunch of dusty junk, nothing that's going to embarrass you or your company."

Another of Pratt's ten commandments advised, "Thou Shalt Clean Your House Before Inviting Company In." What did he mean? "Before placing a new product on the market, audit your files and iron out any problems that surface." Attorneys for plaintiffs, Pratt warned, seek "evidence that information was not submitted to the FDA or data was misreported to the FDA, or the company did not conduct all appropriate tests." So, he advised, a company should ensure that its "paper trail represents the company's dedication to the safety of the product. If necessary create factually accurate memoranda telling that part of the story. . . . [I]f you find a mistake has been made, bring it to the attention of the FDA. . . . All I am saying is beat the plaintiff's attorney to the punch." Bringing mistakes to the attention of the FDA is well and good, but, in the context of his speech, Pratt's advice appears to approve creating and selectively adding to and subtracting from corporate records to convey the corporate line, rather than to convey what actually took place. (Then, when our publisher wrote to Pratt seeking his permission to quote his speech at greater length, he replied with a letter refusing consent and adding, "I cannot authenticate these comments.")

As several episodes related so far in this book indicate, documents from the vehicle-design and safety-testing files of automakers, sometimes even decade-old documents, are often highly relevant to claims of accident victims that their injuries were caused by vehicle defects. Yet we have obtained a memorandum that suggests that at least one of the U.S. Big Three automakers, Chrysler Corporation, has viewed discarding such records quickly and systematically as business as usual. The memo is dated August 7, 1981, and its author is one W. L. Shollenberger, the manager of Chrysler's "Impact Test and Development Department 5320." It discusses company records relating to product development and testing. Shollenberger writes that he had spoken to three company officials—R. W. Johnson, Engineering Services, W. R. Kittle, Corporate Safety, and J. H. Dudley, Insurance Office—and learned that "there is no Corporate need for this type of file system."

Instead, federal law and company needs required only that the department "file information concerning the current model year and maintain records for the preceding five years." Due to space construction
and labor cost considerations, the memo says, the department would
save test and development records for only five years, beginning with
the 1982 model year. "The obsolete material," the memo says, "will be
destroyed by shredding at the Proving Ground."

Remember when Lee Iacocca used to tout Chrysler's "Five Year
Protection Plan"? You probably didn't know that, back at the office,
there was also a "Five Year Destruction Plan," a corporate mandate to
shred safety records more than five years old. Never mind that government auto-safety regulators have many times sought files more than
five years old pursuant to investigations. Never mind that many injured
automobile accident victims or next of kin of people killed in automobile accidents were able to determine whether their vehicles had
design defects by reviewing files more than five years old. Never mind
that microfilm storage—not to mention modern technologies such as
computer disks—permit concentrated storage of millions of documents. Never mind that the corporation's own employees might need
the data to advance their understanding of product improvement.

Corporations certainly cannot be expected to retain every record
they create. But there is something very wrong with corporate policies, approved by corporate lawyers, aimed at rooting out those specific documents that would make a corporation look bad in litigation
while retaining those records that make the company look good.
Such deliberate distortion, aimed precisely at winning legal battles, is
not innocent document management but a power game that can
transform legitimate airings of grievances against a corporation into
unjust slam-dunk corporate victories. Where corporations stack the
deck by purging their files of damaging information, there is, indeed,
no contest.

But if such purging offends one's sense of fairness, does it also violate the legal and ethical obligations currently imposed on lawyers? "A
lot of document retention policies are euphemisms for destroying embarrassing or inculpatory material," legal ethics expert Ted Schneyer
believes. But, as discussed earlier in this chapter, the rules provide some
leeway for such selective destruction. Schneyer says that "it is probably
not technically unethical" to advise clients to destroy incriminating
documents unless there is ongoing or foreseeable litigation or a specific
law or regulation requiring the company to keep the documents.[26]

Whether "ethical" or not, such policies have the potential to cause
real harm. For example, the 294-attorney Atlanta-based law firm King

& Spalding was recently called to task by U.S. District Judge Louis
Bechtle, Jr., in a case involving allegedly unsafe screws used in bone
surgery. King & Spalding represented Biometric Research Inc. of
Alexandria, Virginia, which compiled data for a study that was instru-
mental in obtaining FDA approval for use of the screws. According to
the judge, King & Spalding's "document retention policy" appears to
have, in fact, been a "document destruction policy," for it called for destruction of materials associated with the study, such as minutes of
meetings, correspondence, drafts of medical protocols, and other materials that the firm decided should not be saved.[27] The fact that the FDA
approved use of the screws has since been used as a defense by the manufacturers to allegations made by injured consumers that the screws,
used in spine fusion surgery, broke, causing serious health problems
ranging from sexual dysfunction to limb numbness. Due to the King &
Spalding policy, many documents that might have proved or disproved
some of these allegations are not available. Such are the consequences
of corporate document-cleansing policies. To paraphrase Elihu Root,
the rules may not prevent it, but that does not make it right.

WHAT CAN BE DONE?

Harvard law professor Charles R. Nesson says, "Spoliation is growing
steadily in sophistication and has become such a serious threat to the
very integrity of the civil justice system that an aggressive response is
needed to push it back."[28]

You don't have to be a legal scholar to realize that spoliation undermines justice. It is destructive of truth-finding. Deliberate destruction of evidence relevant to litigation is a form of corruption and can
also be criminal conduct, although it is rarely prosecuted. Once proved,
it should be grounds for taking away the guilty attorney's license to
practice law. Unfortunately, lawyers who destroy evidence, or acqui-
esce in its destruction, are rarely investigated by state lawyer ethics
boards.

There should be adverse consequences for falsifying the record, especially when it can be shown that the purpose of destroying documents was to affect the outcome of existing or reasonably anticipated
litigation. Of course, saying it is not as easy as doing it. "Completely
stopping spoliation may be impossible," says Professor Nesson. "From
the point of view of the spoliator, it all comes down to a cost benefit
analysis: Will the potential cost of destroying evidence be worth the
potential benefit? If a case is going to be lost anyway, many spoliators
feel there is nothing to lose. Thus, some way has to be found to increase

the risk."[29] Professor Stephen Gillers of NYU agrees, telling us, "The only way you are going to stop such discovery abuse is to make it too expensive to get caught."[30]

One way to make it more expensive is for judges to get tougher. "Judges haven't taken enough interest in the problem," Professor Nesson believes. "Too often they treat it as a hassle, a nuisance issue. They view lawyers as being above spoliation. But that view is naive." Nesson believes that such judicial softness promotes misconduct. He contends that, when spoliation is not adequately punished, "ethics of the profession are undermined. It is very discouraging for a lawyer to see an opponent win by being unethical."[31] When misconduct is winked at, when it helps a lawyer win, it creates a contagion that induces other lawyers to engage in similar conduct.

What can judges do? They can be quicker to order default judgments when such egregious wrongdoing is proved. That would send a powerful message that spoliation would have severe consequences to the client. Such a policy would provide an especially powerful deterrent to lawyers, because a client who lost a case because its lawyer destroyed evidence might sue for legal malpractice. Punishing a litigant for destroying relevant evidence before foreseeable litigation would also deter corporate lawyers from instituting or recommending overly aggressive or slanted corporate document-destruction policies.

Judges could also impose significant fines on lawyers who engage in spoliation or who cover up the practice. These sanctions should be set quite high so that they are real deterrents and not merely slaps on the wrist.

State bar ethics committees should also take a more active role in punishing spoliation. But that won't be easy. "Spoliation has moved into a category of 'the way things are done,' " worries Professor Nesson. "It's like professional football. The players know the rules but don't consider a breach of the rules a foul unless it is seen and flagged by a referee. Thus, they are willing to break a rule if they feel they won't get caught." Nesson believes that ethics committees, made up primarily of lawyers, would be unwilling to sanction a technical breach that is "part of the way the game is played."[32]

But if ethical rules were tightened to reduce wiggle room—and made it clear that deliberate efforts to destroy damaging client records were impermissible—most attorneys would think more carefully about falling prey to temptation or client coercion. Such a reform would have beneficial application beyond the corporate context and improve attorney behavior in all law practice.

Still, the threat of punishment for ethical lapses is one that is too often empty. Thus, market forces also need to be brought to bear, not only to deter attorneys from destroying evidence but also to deter clients. Spoliation should be considered a civil wrong, or tort, punishable by compensatory and punitive damages from both the client and the lawyer, in the same way that fraud or misrepresentation can be so punished.

Spoliation is already recognized as a tort in the courts of seven states: Alaska, California, Florida, Illinois, Kansas, New Jersey, and North Carolina.[33] Other states should follow. Damage suits for spoliation are a potent weapon against destruction of evidence.

Indeed, we conclude our discussion of the practice of document destruction by looking at a case where the availability of the tort of spoliation in one state, New Jersey, may have helped ensure that justice was done.

THE CASE OF THE MISSING HOSPITAL RECORDS

Rashad Kelly was born with cerebral palsy. He is afflicted with severe and irreversible brain damage, mental retardation, and seizure disorder. He is totally dependent on others for all of his activities of daily living and will remain so for the rest of his life. Rashad's mother, Jacqueline, believed her son's problems were caused, at least in part, by medical malpractice at New Jersey University of Medicine and Dentistry Hospital.

On the morning of May 20, 1987, Jacqueline Kelly arrived at the hospital's emergency room with prematurely ruptured membranes. Jacqueline was placed on a fetal monitor, but hospital personnel removed it when they determined that she was not in labor. At 10:00 P.M., Jacqueline complained to hospital personnel of foul-smelling water leakage. She was placed on a fetal monitor, but after twenty minutes the monitor was again removed. Then, in the early morning of May 21, Jacqueline began to suffer labor pains. She was brought to a labor and delivery room at 1:30 A.M. and connected to a monitor, which showed poor fetal heartbeat. Yet it was not until twenty minutes later that a doctor, a first-year resident, arrived, and it was not until forty minutes after that, at 2:30 A.M., that a senior resident examined her. By then it was clear to the medical personnel that Kelly's fetus was suffering from severe and prolonged bradycardia, that is, slow heartbeat. Doctors prepared for an emergency cesarean section, which started at 2:50 A.M., almost five hours after the malodorous water leakage was first discovered.

The child was born with birth defects. The pathologist's report indicated that the placenta showed evidence of severe infection and that the umbilical cord was defective and inflamed.

Jacqueline retained attorney Trudy Maran of New Jersey to examine her legal options. In fall 1988, Maran wrote the hospital asking for copies of the medical records, including the fetal monitor strips that record information about the fetus. But the hospital failed to produce the fetal strips. Officials claimed that they couldn't find them. Maran then sent an investigator to the hospital, who, she says, met with the "same song and dance." The records were not produced. The excuse given was that the fetal strips had been sent out for microfilming and had been lost.[34]

With Maran representing her, Kelly sued the hospital for malpractice,[35] claiming that hospital staff failed to recognize quickly enough that Kelly was suffering from an infected uterus, the condition that led to Rashad's medical problems at birth. According to the suit, the malodorous fluid leakage should have alerted the doctors to the problem, and the cesarean should thus have been performed much earlier. As part of discovery, Maran subpoenaed the records of the birth, including the fetal monitor strips. But the hospital's attorneys, the New Jersey law firm Budd, Larner, Gross, Picillo, Rosenbaum, Greenberg & Sade,[36] insisted that the strips did not exist.

"That didn't ring true to me," Maran told us. "I had a gut feeling that something wasn't right. So, I decided to do my own legwork."[37]

Maran personally went to the hospital and reviewed the hospital's voluminous fetal monitor strips, strip by strip, for five hours. Nothing. Then she struck pay dirt. Maran found one of Jacqueline's strips stuck in the middle of another patient's file. "It was a record of the early stages of Jacqueline's labor when she was first admitted to the hospital," Maran says. "The rest of the file was gone. There was not even a separate cover for Jacqueline's file. The strip I found had been thrown in with another patient's file. I could easily have missed it." Maran judged from examining the microfilm that the seal had been broken on the package containing the strips and that several portions were missing.

Maran suspected a coverup. The broken seal implied that someone had opened and examined the package. She believed that the file had contained evidence harmful to the hospital and that it had been destroyed—in short, spoliation.

By chance, on October 2, 1991, just a few weeks before the case was set for trial, a New Jersey appellate court, ruling in another case,[38] established a right to sue under New Jersey law for spoliation. Maran decided to use the law to good advantage. Getting documents and evidence to which she was entitled was a frustrating ordeal. She brought motion after motion, invoking the appellate decision and trying to compel documents and other discovery. "I was asking for specific records that the hospital should have maintained," she recalls. "Lung maturity tests,[39] lab tests, invoices to get the name of the laboratories that might have tested tissue, anything and everything I could think of. The more they didn't have, the better my spoliation case became."

Maran's tactic dramatically changed the stance of the hospital and its attorneys at Budd, Larner. Before she discovered the misplaced fetal monitor strip and the extent of the missing records, she says that the defense had been very hard-nosed in its negotiations. "I thought the matter was going to trial," she says. "But then, once a good case in spoliation had been made and I was able to get past the discovery obstructionist tactics, their attitude changed. Suddenly, they were willing to seriously talk settlement."

The case settled before trial for $1.35 million, structured (based on the purchase of U.S. Treasury bonds) so as to ensure a yearly income of $60,000 for thirty years, followed by a lump-sum payment, plus free medical care for Rashad for the rest of his life. "Justice was done," Maran says. "But it almost wasn't. I am convinced that if I had not discovered the [strip], the case would have gone to trial and who knows what would have happened. Thank goodness their tactics backfired."[40]

The hospital denies that it destroyed records or that spoliation was a factor in the settlement.

CHAPTER 5

SLAPP: TAKING CARE OF BUSINESS

S AN FRANCISCO LAWYER RICHARD B. SPOHN SPECIALIZES IN REP-
resenting corporations in their dealings with the government.
His clients include some of the nation's largest health care corporations. He says, "The world is an extremely complicated
place. Our nation has more than 250 million people, who generate billions of dollars in economic activity. Without lawyers, the system would not work. We are engineers of order, counselors of the
ordered state. We are the weavers of social processes."

Spohn believes firmly that corporate lawyers must not fall prey to
client pressure to engage in improper conduct or questionable uses of
the legal system. "Corporate lawyers ill-serve their clients when they
accede to improper client demands, and they ill-serve themselves," he
says. "Lawyers have to be willing to lose clients rather than compromise their professional ethics."[1] Unfortunately, many lawyers don't ad-
here to the standards Spohn advocates. Yet, when their win-at-all-costs
tactics are questioned, these lawyers hotly assert that they are acting
ethically and within the parameters permitted by the law.

Are these lawyers following the rules or not? Legal ethics expert
Michael Josephson, an adviser to federal and state governments on
ethics issues, says that attorneys like to follow rules, "but they are competitors. They tend to look at what they do as a sport. So they will try
and bend the official rules and see that process as merely following the
'real' rules of the way the game is played. All lawyers do this, but the big
firms tend to do it better."[2]

Josephson has put his finger on an attitude and value system that
permits corporate attorneys to pillage opponents and still get a good
night's sleep. When litigation is perceived as sport, winning justifies
almost anything, including, as we have seen, improperly obstructing

discovery and hiding the truth about client wrongdoing behind walls of secrecy.

But corporate attorneys don't just play defense. They are quite adept at using the law as an offensive weapon to punish those who get in the way of a corporation's business strategies and agendas or to deter others from doing so. For those in the path of stampeding power lawyers, the law is all too real. Aggressive corporate legal strategies and tactics can place their jobs, their investments, their homes, and their piece of mind at risk.

SLAPP SUITS

"It was one of the most traumatic experiences of my life," says seventy-six-year-old Walter Mosher of Salinas, California, a farm city in the heart of the San Joaquin Valley.

"When we received the letter, our hearts fell down to our shoes," recalls Walter's wife, Alice. "We had no choice but to knuckle under and not pursue our democratic rights."[3]

"It" was a letter from a corporate lawyer threatening to sue them for hundreds of thousands of dollars.

The Moshers' ordeal began in 1989 when Alice saw a notice in the local paper stating that an application to build an electric cogeneration plant in Salinas would be available for public review. A cogeneration plant uses agricultural waste to generate electricity for sale to the local utility company. The Moshers were stunned to hear such a plant was going to be built in Salinas. This was the first they had heard of it. They decided to investigate. The application itself made the Moshers uneasy. In their view, the document was short on facts but full of assurances that the plant would create no negative effects whatsoever for the community.

That sounded a little too good to be true, so the Moshers did some research. They discovered, much to their dismay, that the cogeneration plant would contain large tanks of chemicals and water to be used in the generation of steam for sale to the Pacific Gas & Electric Company, the local utility, and for use by food processing plants nearby. Noise pollution was also a big concern. The sound emanating from the plant would be equal to that of a fully powered Boeing 747 jet engine, and the plant would be in operation twenty-four hours a day. The Moshers were also concerned about increased air pollution and the potential effects should the plant be destroyed by an earthquake. Worst of all, there hadn't even been an environmental impact report published to gauge the overall effect on the community.

The Moshers' concerns were all reasonable, addressing issues that must often be confronted by industries seeking to build major projects. Indeed, working through community concerns is a normal, appropriate part of doing business for industrial companies. But O'Brien Cogen Ltd. II, the firm behind the project, was anxious to get the plant built. Federal law at the time required PG&E to buy any electricity produced by the plant, whether it needed it or not, at a price that was considerably above the fair-market price of electricity prevailing at that time. Thus, the investors were almost guaranteed a substantial profit once the plant began operating.

The Moshers were determined to act. They began energetically to organize the community against the project, walking their neighborhood, knocking on doors, writing letters, circulating a petition signed by four hundred neighbors, and otherwise building a devoted campaign of opposition. They forced a public meeting, which received wide coverage in local media, alerting other potential opponents to the project. Then, local growers entered the fray, worried that the project would remove so much groundwater it would worsen the already troublesome problem of seawater seeping into the area's water tables.

The clash of wills was classic: On one side of the controversy was a company wanting to develop new industry. On the other side were determined locals wishing to maintain their community's quality of life. In between were hand-wringing politicians.

Seeing its project threatened, the O'Brien firm began to make concessions. It promised that only reclaimed water from vegetable processing would be used in the cogeneration process. That satisfied the growers. The company also offered to turn off the noisy generator between midnight and 6:00 A.M. To make up for the increased air pollution, the company proposed to buy old, polluting junk cars each year and take them off the road.

The Moshers and other grassroots opponents were not placated. They did not believe the offer to take cars off the road would make up for the increased air pollution the new plant would create. They continued to question whether the company could operate without adversely affecting a community as small as Salinas. Moreover, by this time, the energy crisis of the late 1970s had long since passed. Pacific Gas & Electric didn't need the extra electricity and was then selling electricity below the price projected for that generated by the project. Thus, opponents believed the project was more about taking advantage of a temporary law that would soon lapse rather than filling legitimate electricity needs of the community. Accordingly, they vowed to continue their opposition.

As the political controversy raged, O'Brien brought in a platoon of lawyers, engineers, and various consultants to push the project through. This show of power began to work. Despite the vocal grassroots resistance, community political leaders were on the verge of approving the project.

Jane Haines, a lawyer from nearby Pacific Grove who describes herself as "cause oriented," had earlier entered the fray as the lawyer for a local farmer. Then she began to represent the Moshers, for no fee. Haines recalls what happened next. "The accommodations that had been agreed to by O'Brien forced them to change the proposed site of the plant. Now, it would be located much nearer to residential areas, making the noise issue even more important. We felt that these material change of plans required a new noise study to determine how the racket from the generator turned on at five or six in the morning would impact the surrounding area. O'Brien disagreed. So, we hinted that we might seek an injunction against proceeding with the plant, which would allow a court to decide whether O'Brien had complied with the law."[4]

O'Brien lawyer Lloyd W. Lowrey, Jr., of the firm Noland, Hamerly, Etienne & Hoss wrote to Jane Haines on April 18, 1990, warning her not to pursue those plans.[5] The letter began by stating that comments made on April 17 in opposition to the plant were "without basis in law or in fact." It then warned that a review of applicable legal authority "leads us to conclude that a lawsuit by you and your clients at this time to delay construction activities on the cogeneration facility would necessarily be regarded as a bad faith attempt to interfere with O'Brien's legitimate expectations." The letter continued: "There are millions of dollars involved with the construction financing for this project. We would expect to pursue to the fullest any and all remedies available to O'Brien should damages result from your efforts." The letter claimed that any lawsuit challenging the location of the plant "would be premature." It concluded by citing a case in which a homeowners' association had been hit with "$600,000 in sanctions" for filing a lawsuit to block a real estate development, which the trial court held "was not filed in good faith."

The Moshers were stunned by this letter sent to their attorney. The letter seemed to be threatening to sue them, perhaps for hundreds of thousands of dollars. Alice told us, "When we saw the letter, we felt we could win the case, but we could not afford to defend a suit like that with the level of power arrayed against us. We were being told, 'Stand up for your legal rights at your own risk. Assert your First Amendment rights and get sued.' "[6]

Rather than risk litigation and incur the costs of defense, the Moshers made a very painful decision. They surrendered, immediately and unequivocally, ceasing their efforts to oppose the project. Indeed, fear that they could be sued for being politically active caused the Moshers to stop participating publicly in their community altogether.

Of course, getting the Moshers, the most active and visible opponents to the cogeneration plant, to back off was the point. O'Brien's lawyers realized that a threat of huge damages would scare the activism out of most average citizens. "Letters such as the one I wrote to Jane Haines can chill public participation," acknowledges attorney Lloyd Lowrey. "But I felt very strongly about the matter, and I wanted Jane to think carefully about what they were doing. I believe my letter was appropriate based on the law at that time."[7]

Haines disagrees. "The letter was sent out of the blue," she told us. "Lloyd and I had a conversation but I never said we were going to sue. The opposition was not a group ready to go to court." What the Moshers were ready to do, however, was to continue speaking out and organizing against the plant, much to O'Brien's displeasure. The Moshers, says Haines, "were saying things in a public forum that O'Brien did not appreciate."[8]

According to Haines, the impact of the letter was not limited to the Salinas controversy. "The news of the letter and the subsequent capitulation by the Moshers spread very quickly. I began receiving notes from activists involved in many different types of issues telling me they were now afraid to speak out."

Others, with different agendas, also received the same message from the Mosher affair. "The letter seemed to give ideas to the community's most powerful groups," Haines continued. "The whole Salinas and Monterey Peninsula seemed to become a breeding ground for legal threats and suits by the powerful used as a tactic to keep community activists running scared. There was a definite chilling effect on public participation in community affairs."

(Despite O'Brien's tough tactics, the plant was never built. The company ran into water-delivery and other problems that delayed construction. When the mandatory purchase requirement of the federal energy law expired, O'Brien abandoned the project.)

Alice and Walter Mosher were just two victims of a power-lawyer hardball approach: using legal threats or lawsuits to stifle public participation. It is known as the SLAPP suit. The term, coined by University of

Denver professors George Pring and Penelope Canan, stands for Strate-gic Lawsuit Against Public Participation. SLAPP suits are legally ques-tionable or meritless lawsuits aimed at intimidating critics into silence. SLAPPs punish people for exercising their right, guaranteed by the First Amendment to the Constitution, to participate in public discourse.[9]

SLAPPs come in many shapes and sizes. They are lawsuits brought by powerful interests, most commonly land development companies, against citizen activists who oppose pet projects. The corporations who file these cases do not, of course, call them SLAPPs in their court pa-pers. Most often, SLAPPs are dressed up as libel cases—claims that the corporate reputation has been harmed by false accusations—but they may also take the form of suits for business torts, such as interference with contract.

SLAPPs often begin when aggrieved citizens, either individually or as part of an organized group, speak out to any branch of government or the electorate to raise concerns about a situation or a proposed proj-ect. Such citizen activism often delays, forces changes in, or outright derails the plans of corporate executives, who then resort to frivolous litigation to obtain their goals. "Yes, it is true," Professor Pring says. "Today, you, your neighbors, your community leaders can be sued for millions of dollars, just for telling government what you think, want, or believe in."[10]

The impact of a SLAPP on an individual can be devastating. Pro-fessor Canan told us, "A SLAPP is one of the most life-changing expe-riences a target can go through. Victims experience intense pressure, leading to physical illness, divorces, and emotional dysfunction. Per-haps the worst part is a loss of idealism. That can be very depressing. Victims come to lose their belief in American justice."[11] That was cer-tainly true of the Moshers. The mere threat of a suit destroyed their willingness to participate in the public affairs of their community, a fear from which they still have not recovered years after the events.

When we told attorney Lloyd Lowrey about the devastating impact his letter had on the Moshers, he sounded stunned. He acknowledged that his letter could be interpreted as a threatened SLAPP but claimed that he had "no idea" of the emotional impact his correspondence had had on the Moshers. "Personally, I like the Moshers," he told us. "I wouldn't want to hurt them." Lowrey then added, "We lawyers are so used to the pushing and shoving of litigation, we tend to forget that most people are not used to it. We have to be careful. We have the power to intimidate. We can chill public participation. It is incumbent upon us to refrain from overstating our case, and to communicate based strictly on a careful and accurate reading of current law."[12]

Lowrey is right, but too late. The time for corporate lawyers to consider tempering their behavior is *before* they intimidate citizen-activists, rather than months or years afterward when the damage has already been done.

Perhaps for attorneys who spend their careers representing big corporations, lawsuits seem like no big deal. When an individual or small business sues or threatens to sue a large corporation, the impact is far less devastating than when the situation is reversed, as in a SLAPP. Corporate executives are used to the give-and-take of litigation, of threatening and being threatened with legal action, of having to spend time and effort involved in legal affairs. It goes with the territory. Indeed, for the corporation, unlike the individual citizen-activist, defending a lawsuit is a tax-deductible cost of doing business. Besides, it is not usually the corporate executive's money or property that is directly at stake in legal controversies involving a corporation. But when a big corporation threatens to or does take legal action against an individual, the opposite is true.

The broader consequences of SLAPP suits are profound: Truth can be held hostage by corporate lawyers threatening or filing suit. Publicity about SLAPPs and their impact on defendants may make other citizens—whatever their political concerns or views—afraid to participate in civic affairs. And because SLAPPs may deter corporate employees from divulging information, government regulators may be deprived of the facts necessary to promulgate fair and effective rules and to enforce those that already exist. The threat of legal attacks could ultimately place whistle-blowers and community activists under such a cloud of fear that they would cease their activities, which are one of the few effective checks and balances against corporate (and government) power. In short, SLAPPs are a danger to the democratic process and the American tradition of citizen involvement in civic affairs.

Disturbed by the steadily growing number of SLAPPs, Professors Pring and Canan have established an interdisciplinary project at the University of Denver to study them. They have found disturbing trends.

"People are being sued in all fifty states for exercising basic rights," Pring says. He reports that among the SLAPPs he has investigated are lawsuits brought for:

- Writing a letter to the president of the United States opposing a political appointment;
- Testifying against a real estate developer at a zoning hearing;
- Filing administrative agency appeals;

- Complaining to a school board about unfit teachers;
- Peacefully demonstrating against government action;
- Collecting signatures on a petition; and,
- Campaigning for or against a state ballot.

The situation has become so outrageous, according to Pring, that "one person was even sued after attending a public meeting and signing the attendance sheet!"

Pring and Canan both believe that SLAPPs pose a significant threat to politically active citizens and the political system. Their intensive investigation has shown that the usual victims of SLAPPs are not radicals on the fringes of public participation but middle-of-the-road Americans, often people who have become involved in civic affairs for the first time.

"Our study found that SLAPPs . . . are an attempt to 'privatize' public debate," they have written, "a unilateral effort by one side to transform a public, political dispute into a private, legal adjudication . . ." Thus, the citizen-activist who questions a company in a zoning dispute is sued for libel, or for interference with the company's prospective economic gain, or threatened, like the Moshers, with such a lawsuit. The choice becomes stark: Shut up or be sued.

According to Professor Pring, in 80 to 85 percent of SLAPP suits, the SLAPPer loses before trial: Either the SLAPPer dismisses the case voluntarily without any significant concessions from the SLAPPed defendant, or the judge grants the defendant's motion to dismiss the case. But winning a verdict isn't usually the point of these lawsuits, according to Bakersfield, California, attorney Ralph Wegis, who has gained a national reputation for successfully combating SLAPPs. "Filers are often bullies who use the law to achieve business results," Wegis told us. "The point is the chilling effect. Suits force victims to spend time and money defending themselves during a crucial time in a political campaign or development controversy. The prospect of having to hire a lawyer and pay expenses is often enough to get victims to drop opposition."[13]

So, many times SLAPPers win even though, as a formal matter, their lawsuits are failures. And, according to Professor Pring, of the 15 to 20 percent of SLAPP suits that are not dismissed outright, the overwhelming majority settle, on terms quite favorable to the SLAPPer. Typically, the defendants agree to stop their public activism. Some defendants offer an apology for their activism. And the corporate SLAPPer will often ask that the settlement be confidential, with the chastened activist agreeing not to discuss the lawsuit or the underlying dispute. According to Pring, very few SLAPP suits ever go to trial, and there are only a handful of cases where a SLAPPer has actually won a verdict.

Philip Berry is national vice president of the environmental group Sierra Club, which has been victimized by SLAPPs. Testifying before the California senate, Berry said, "SLAPPs are almost always filed against organizations or individuals who are attempting to serve a public purpose through utilization of their constitutional rights. SLAPPs are typically unsuccessful in their immediate aim of establishing liability, but they are frequently successful in their larger purpose of scaring off public participation."

SLAPPs can be expensive to defend, even if the defendants are successful in terminating them at the initial stage. The issues can be complicated, and the corporate lawyers bringing a case can, from the outset, drown the opponent in motions, discovery requests, depositions, and other time-consuming tasks. For this reason, Wegis believes that lawyers have a professional responsibility to work on behalf of SLAPPed victims to protect their rights to participate in community issues, even when the victim can pay little or no fee. "This is an issue of freedom," he says. "It is harmful to society when leaders are crushed by superior economic forces at the very time when so many pundits bemoan the lack of participation and worry about citizen apathy."[14]

THE CASE OF THE SLAPPED FARMERS

Ralph Wegis has repeatedly acted on his convictions, representing victims of SLAPP suits. His first SLAPPed clients were a small group of California Central Valley farmers. In 1982, a powerful corporation sued the farmers, who had vocally supported a state ballot initiative, Proposition 9, which concerned one of the state's most contentious issues: water rights.

California is the nation's most populous state and the third largest in size. The north and east regions of the state, much of them forested and green, contain most of its water. The snowpack runoff from the High Sierra Mountains also flows in the north through the Sacramento River and other tributaries. This area of the state is also the least populated.

Most of California's population is located in the southern part of the state, which includes the greater Los Angeles area and where, unfortunately, water is most sparse. In addition, most of the state's rich agricultural land can be found in the central valleys, the Sacramento and San Joaquin, areas that are naturally semiarid but which extensive irrigation has made some of the most productive farmland in the world.

California has managed the water disparity problem through projects that move massive amounts of water through the California Aqueduct from the north, by way of the rich agricultural central valleys, where farmers buy it at far-below-market prices—as little as 1 percent of market rates—courtesy of massive federal and state subsidies. Water that is not diverted to central valley uses flows on to reach the teeming population of the Los Angeles area.

In the early 1980s, drought, damage to the Sacramento River Delta and other watersheds caused by water diversion, together with the increasing need for water by city dwellers in the south, created a water crisis. Farmers demanded, and still demand, a continuing source of cheap water, while environmentalists want reduced diversion of water from sensitive habitats. Meanwhile, people in Southern California want more water from northern resources. To say the least, when it comes to California and water, compromise does not come easily.

This was the atmosphere leading up to the political fight over Proposition 9, which would have authorized the building of a new water project known as the "peripheral canal." This plan would have diverted water away from the San Joaquin Delta and into the main aqueduct by way of a forty-three-mile canal, substantially increasing the annual water flow to the south. The measure was very controversial, with many strange bedfellows and a great deal of money spent both in support and in opposition.

Many small farmers in Kern County, a rural area surrounding Bakersfield, strongly supported Proposition 9, while two large agribusiness corporations that operated in the area, the Salyer Land Company and the J. G. Boswell Company, opposed it and spent approximately $2 million to try to defeat it.

Two local farmers, Jack Thomson and Ken Wegis, a second cousin of attorney Ralph Wegis, decided to publicize the part being played by these two large corporations in the fight over the proposition. They formed a nonprofit organization called Family Farmers for Proposition 9. Soon they were raising money from other small farmers and planning an advertising campaign. "We thought it was essential that the television ads being paid for by Boswell and Salyer be countered," Jack Thomson recalls. "So we spent eight thousand dollars on two newspaper ads telling people exactly who were paying for much of the opposition and speculating why they were putting up so much money."[15]

The advertisement, run in local valley newspapers on May 10, 1982, seemed like a fairly typical statement published in the midst of a hard-fought political battle:

WHO ARE BOSWELL & SALYER?
And why are they trying to cut off our water?

GIANT LANDOWNERS

Most people have never heard of J. G. Boswell Company or the Salyer Land Company because they have deliberately maintained a low profile. Privately held companies, accountable to no one, Boswell and Salyer are the biggest agri-business corporations in California—owning more than 255,830 acres. They use more water than the entire San Francisco Bay area.

POLITICAL CONTRIBUTIONS

They are also among the biggest campaign contributors in the State. During the last three years, they have given more than $1,362,179 to politicians and political committees. Lieutenant Governor Mike Curb supported the Peripheral Canal when it was before the legislature, but is now serving as Salyer-Boswell's chief spokesman against Proposition 9. Curb has already received $43,595 (over the last three years) from Salyer and Boswell representatives and allies, to further cloud the issue.

AN UNLIMITED WAR CHEST

With the 1982 campaign just beginning, these two land companies have already spent more than $1,000,000 trying to defeat Proposition 9 and sabotage the construction of the Peripheral Canal which is needed to meet water demands in Southern California and much of Central California and the Bay area. And, Jim Fisher, President of Boswell, says that they will spend "whatever it takes" to defeat Proposition 9.

WHY?

TO ELIMINATE ENVIRONMENTAL PROTECTIONS?—Salyer and Boswell have repeatedly attacked Proposition 9 for giving too much protection to fish and wildlife and for guaranteeing Delta water quality standards! Their only interest is in getting cheap water for themselves, regardless of water quality or the environment.

TO FREEZE OUT THE COMPETITION?—Salyer and Boswell have enough water resources to outlast the next drought and the years when water delivery will be delayed if Proposition 9 is defeated. Smaller farmers don't have those resources and Boswell and Salyer know this. If the small farms go out of business, Boswell and Salyer will be able to totally dominate California agriculture—setting prices where they want them.

TO DOMINATE CALIFORNIA WATER POLICY?—Historically, Salyer and Boswell have been against responsible water development in California. In 1960, Salyer sued the State to prevent development of the State Water Project.

Salyer and Boswell have consistently fought every safe water development and management program which has ever been proposed. Now, they are peddling their own plan—a thru Delta proposal which would destroy Delta fish and wildlife and force California consumers to pay even higher water prices.

TO AVOID PAYING THEIR SHARE?—Boswell and Salyer have built their empires on cheap water. Under Proposition 9, they would have to pay full market rates for State Project water—something the Salyers and Boswells apparently aren't prepared to do.

Boswell and Salyer are opposed to Proposition 9 because they have a stake in delaying new water development. It is clear that Boswell and Salyer's interests and the interests of the people of California are sharply at odds. Proposition 9 is desperately needed to meet water demands in the Bay area, the San Joaquin Valley and Southern California. If Proposition 9 is not passed, water development will be at a standstill—small farmers and their farm lands will have to be taken out of production. For the sake of our families and farms, Proposition 9 must receive a strong YES vote—whether or not Salyer and Boswell like it.

YES ON 9

Within four days of the ad appearing, lawyers for the J. G. Boswell Company would attempt to financially ruin Wegis and Thomson by suing them in state court. Boswell's lawsuit was based on a single sentence in the Family Farmers' ad, the one that read, "If the small farms go out of business, Boswell and Salyer will be able to totally dominate California agriculture—setting prices where they want them." Boswell claimed the sentence was libelous, in that it somehow accused the company of entering a conspiracy to violate the Cartwright Act, a state law prohibiting price fixing. It asked the court for $2.5 million in damages from each defendant.

Boswell's lawsuit hit the farmers like a horde of locusts attacking a wheat field. The suit named not only Wegis, Thomson, and Thomson's son Jeff, but also one hundred "John Does." By suing a "John Doe" or "Jane Doe," a plaintiff reserves the right to add additional defendants to a case as discovery reveals more alleged wrongdoers. "All of our friends and fellow farmers who had contributed to Family Farmers were very upset," recalls Thomson. "They were afraid they too might be sued."

Not only were Boswell's libel claims without merit, but also the damages Boswell sought were far beyond any actual damages the company could have suffered even if the statement was libelous. According to Professor Pring, "It is characteristic of SLAPPs for the money demands to be all out of proportion to the realistic damages a filer could have suffered, which makes sense, since the idea is to chill participation, not win money."

The Boswell SLAPP quickly accomplished its political goals. Not wanting to face a process server's knock on their door, other Yes-on-9 participants dropped out of the campaign. Whatever time and energy Wegis and Thomson could have spent in the political process were now taken up with the lawsuit. Other political ads that had been planned were scrapped. Boswell's lawyer had succeeded in using the court system to completely stifle an effective public policy opponent in the last crucial days of an important political campaign.

On June 8, 1982, voters defeated Proposition 9 by a nearly two-to-one margin, mainly due to fears about the measure's impact on the environment.

Beyond stifling the farmers' right to engage in political debate, the Boswell suit brought more than four years of litigation hell down on the heads of the Thomson and Wegis families. "The pressure was terrible," Thomson recalls. "As farmers, we depend on banks to finance crops. We had to disclose the suit against us in the disclosure statements. We were scared we would be cut off. We worked awfully hard just to keep our sources of financing."[16]

The Wegis and Thomson families worried constantly that a loss in court would force them to sell their farms, land that had been in their families for generations. They lost sleep. Thomson's wife developed an ulcer. "There's no doubt about it," Thomson says, "times were real tough."

Adding to the worries of the sued farmers were disputes with their liability insurance carriers over coverage. The companies eventually agreed to provide a defense for Wegis and Thomson but not to pay damages if they lost the case. That left them personally exposed to financial ruin. Moreover, a loss in court would probably mean they would have to sue their own insurance companies. Then, the insurance carriers canceled their policies, forcing them to pay higher premiums for new policies that provided lower benefits.

In 1984, the farmers brought a motion to have the Boswell lawsuit dismissed. The judge granted their motion, agreeing that the advertisement was not libelous. But Boswell, determined to continue its feud with the Family Farmers even though Proposition 9 had already lost, appealed. In 1986, the California court of appeals finally terminated the SLAPP with a decision stating that no reader would believe that the ad was a "factual accusation that Boswell was guilty of a criminal conspiracy."[17] Four and a half years after it had begun, the Wegis and Thomson families' ordeal was finally over.

Boswell's quick resort to a lawsuit when confronted with political opposition illustrates the readiness with which many corporate lawyers and executives use SLAPPs as part of their business strategy—in this case, to deter the Family Farmers from continuing their advocacy of Proposition 9. Indeed, Boswell's in-house corporate lawyer would later testify that Boswell's chief executive officer, J. G. Boswell, did not even express concern about damage to the reputation of the company or its profitability, but instead worried that the ad was "effective." Neither Boswell executives nor the company's in-house counsel sought advice from lawyers who were expert in libel litigation to determine whether the company had a meritorious case.[18] Rather, the in-house lawyer, and the outside firm paid by the company to prosecute the suit, simply gave their client what it wanted, even though the suit was frivolous and completely unwarranted. (Boswell did offer other evidence that its CEO considered the ad libelous.)

Injured and outraged by Boswell's abuse of the justice system, Wegis and the Thomsons countersued against Boswell for malicious prosecution. In 1988, after a seventeen-day trial in Kern County Superior Court, it was clear that the jury shared their outrage. It awarded them a total of $3 million in compensatory damages, later reduced by the trial judge to $600,000, plus $10.5 million in punitive damages. Boswell mounted a series of appeals, first to the California appellate court, then to the California Supreme Court, and finally, with the legal firepower of one of the largest law firms in the country, New York–based Shearman & Sterling, to the United States Supreme Court. The California appellate court upheld the verdict, and the two higher courts refused to review it.[19] Its legal options exhausted, Boswell eventually paid the damages plus interest and costs, an amount Thomson puts at about $15 million. By then, analysts had agreed on an appropriate name for the type of counterattack mounted by the farmers: a SLAPP-back.

In the Boswell case, a wrong was righted. But think of the anguish for Thomson and Wegis, not to mention the huge financial penalty for Boswell, that could have been saved had Boswell's lawyers dissuaded the company from filing an unmeritorious case in the first place. Jack Thomson says that he hopes Boswell's humiliating defeat "will prevent other corporations from hitting people with a big lawsuit to shut them up and keep them from raising money for a cause."

Despite his win, Thomson says, his SLAPP suit experience "has limited my willingness to act on political issues. I am very careful about what I get involved with and what I say in a political campaign."[20]

The Family Farmers' case was an early SLAPP. Unfortunately, many more have followed, including the next example, in which a Nevada hospital company SLAPPed one of its top doctors for speaking out on company practices.

THE CASE OF THE GREEDY
HEALTH PROVIDER

Dr. George Hemmeter was the chief of staff at Nevada's largest hospital, Sunrise Humana Hospital in Las Vegas. Humana, Inc., a giant, nationwide health-maintenance-organization corporation with revenues of $3.7 billion in 1994, owns and operates the hospital.

Dr. Hemmeter had uncovered what he believed was an important secret. The hospital, along with another Humana-owned business, Humana Health Insurance of Nevada, was apparently engaging in a clever, but seemingly improper, scheme. The hospital would bill patients covered by Humana Health Insurance approximately $1,600 to $2,000 per day for hospitalization. But it would accept, as fully satisfying Humana Health Insurance's obligations, only $125 per day, an amount well under the usual and customary price for such care. However, this discount was not passed along to patients, who were forced to pay the hospital deductible payments and copayments based on the full $1,600 to $2,000 price. So if a patient incurred a $2,000 charge and was responsible for a 20 percent copayment, she would owe the hospital $400—more than three times what her insurer was paying. Patients might have expected instead that, if the real charge to the insurer was only $125, their copayment would be about $30. Instead they were paying more than thirteen times that amount.

Hemmeter believed that the hospital and the insurer were using their cozy relationship to rack up profits at the expense of consumers. Since Humana, Inc., owned both companies, it wouldn't care that the insurer was paying the hospital bargain-basement rates. Presumably it wanted it that way: The discounted payments from Humana Insurance meant lower annual revenues to Sunrise Humana Hospital, which could therefore justify price increases to state auditors. But Hemmeter believed the scheme was illegal, because under Nevada law, such agreed-upon discounts were supposed to be returned to policyholders in the form of lower premiums.

Hemmeter decided to go public with his contentions. He publicly testified before the Nevada state senate commerce committee on March 3, 1989, and wrote letters to hospital staff and other doctors in the state.

Humana responded by calling in its lawyers to punish Hemmeter for speaking out. Represented by the law firm Lionel Sawyer & Collins of Las Vegas, Humana sued him for defamation and sought punitive damages. That Humana sought to turn the financial screws on Hemmeter cannot be disputed. Early on in the litigation, Humana publicly stated that it was willing to settle the case for $10 million.

Humana was lashing out at a wave of adverse consequences arising from its financial practices and the resulting bad publicity, of which Hemmeter's accusations were just one part. At the time of the suit, Humana was one of three companies under investigation by the Nevada Insurance Commission to determine whether it was in compliance with the state's hospital cost-containment law. It had also settled an earlier dispute with the insurance commission by refunding $303,000 in overcharges to enrollees and paying $180,000 in fines.[21]

Humana's suit against the chief of staff at one of its own hospitals received abundant publicity. Within days of Humana's filing, accounts of the suit appeared in newspapers, health care publications, and on television. The entire community knew that Humana was accusing Hemmeter of being a liar.

Forced to defend himself, Hemmeter fought back aggressively. He filed a counterclaim contending that Humana sued him to counter negative publicity, to intimidate him into stopping his criticism of Humana, to retaliate against him for his criticism thus far, and to deter others from speaking out against Humana.

The case went to trial in 1991. The jury rejected Humana's defamation claims. (It did find that one of two letters written by Hemmeter and at issue in the case contained a false statement that defamed Humana. But it nevertheless ruled for Hemmeter, because it did not find by clear and convincing evidence, as the law requires, that Hemmeter made the false statement "with knowledge of falsity or reckless disregard of its falsity.") And the jury found in favor of Hemmeter on his claims. Specifically, the jury concluded that the doctor's "compensatory damages for fears, anxiety, mental and emotional distress, damage to reputation, humiliation and inconvenience" caused by "Humana's abuse of process" were $1.95 million. In addition, it awarded Hemmeter $373,956 for attorneys' fees and expenses incurred defending against Humana's claims. But the jury was not yet through with Humana. It awarded Hemmeter $7.5 million in punitive damages "for the sake of example and the purpose of punishing Humana, Inc."[22]

Humana filed an appeal but eventually decided to abandon its SLAPP strategy and revert to another favorite corporate law game: "I've Got a Secret" (see Chapter 2). Humana and Hemmeter worked out a confidential settlement. The amount Humana paid, if any, to Dr. Hemmeter is a secret. Dr. Hemmeter's lawyer told us that neither he nor Dr. Hemmeter is free to discuss the case or the doctor's previous allegations about Humana's alleged wrongdoing. Indeed, Humana seemed determined to sweep evidence of its practices under the rug. In a separate lawsuit, Humana went all the way to the Nevada Supreme Court to try to keep a state senate committee from disseminating documents that were introduced as evidence in open court at the Hemmeter trial. Fortunately for principles of openness, Humana lost that case as well.[23]

The Hemmeter case shows how a corporation and its lawyers can abuse the legal system and use its processes as a form of intimidation and coercion. "Hemmeter had tried to organize other Humana doctors into testifying about problems he perceived with Humana's cost containment policies," Professor Penelope Canan says. "Not only did they sue Hemmeter as a warning to other doctors, but also they sought to ostracize him. They even sent memos out warning other doctors that they could suffer the same fate."

Humana's SLAPP suit is also an important illustration of the insidious nature of these actions. Humana, a wealthy, multistate corporation, sought to use its lawyers to stifle a whistle-blower who sought only to warn the public and state officials about the corporation's questionable business policies. This legal bludgeoning not only adversely affected Dr. Hemmeter's life for a substantial period, but it may also have deterred other doctors and hospital employees from speaking out against irregularities in the health care industry.

THE CASE OF THE ANGRY OIL COMPANY

Before examining some long-range solutions to the problem of SLAPPs, consider a third SLAPP action that eventually compelled an outraged jury to SLAPP back. This one took place in Sacramento, California, where lawyer Raymond Leonardini found himself in a bitter dispute with one of the world's most wealthy and powerful international conglomerates, Shell Oil Company. The case is notable not only because it was one of the first SLAPP-back victories affirmed on appeal but also for its insight into the corporate power mentality and the willingness of many executives to use improper methods—tactics all too willingly carried out by compliant corporate lawyers.

In the early 1980s, a national controversy arose over the proposed use of plastic piping, which was then used only for carrying nonpotable water, to deliver drinking water into homes. This greatly expanded use of plastic pipes was expected to generate a tremendous increase in demand for the product. Shell stood to benefit substantially from this expected sales bonanza because it made polybutylene, the most common resin used in residential plastic water pipes. The company thus had a major stake in obtaining approval by authorities throughout the United States for the use of plastic drinking-water-delivery systems.

Leonardini, a sole practitioner, was a leader in the fight against the expanded use of plastic pipes in California. A former official with the California Department of Consumer Affairs, he represented the California Pipes Trade Council, an organization of plumbers' and pipe fitters' unions. The group opposed the legalization attempt. (Leonardini's concerns about plastic pipes were twofold: first, the potential effects on health and safety, and second, the potential negative economic impact on his client union members.)

In the spring of 1980, Shell told California public health officials that the plastic pipe system was "100 percent safe."[24] Further, Shell's representatives stated, the pipes were so safe that the system did not need to be independently tested by the state. These assertions proved to be false. Shell did not inform state authorities that the polybutylene pipe system included Celcon pipe fittings, made by the Celanese Corporation. When these fittings were used with polybutylene pipes, the system leached high levels of toxic chemicals into the water. As the California court of appeals later found, "Shell's policy was that if the state did not discover any health problems with the system on its own and did not specifically ask for that information, Shell would not volunteer it."[25] As was later revealed in court, Shell and Celanese had reached a secret agreement to keep these problems hidden.[26] (Shell said that it would have provided information on the joints if the state had asked.) In addition to leaching dangerous chemicals, the plastic pipes, when used with Celcon fittings, suffered repeated mechanical failures.

While unaware of the problems associated with the use of the Celcon pipe fittings, Leonardini, on behalf of his trade council clients, forcefully questioned Shell's blithe safety assurances to state officials. In late 1980, he commissioned California Analytical Laboratories, Inc. (commonly known as Cal Labs), an independent laboratory often hired by Shell, to test the polybutylene pipes. The tests uncovered the presence in the pipes of potentially cancer-causing chemicals.

Using this information, Leonardini convinced state officials to order an independent environmental impact report. But controversy swirled around the details of the coming environmental tests, with Shell seeking to restrict the depth and breadth of testing and Leonardini, using the Cal Labs test results as an advocacy tool, urging a much broader approach.

It was about this time that Shell decided that Leonardini was being too effective for its own good. Company lawyers decided that they would shut him up, not by winning the scientific debate over the environmental impact report, but by suing him into silence.

The decision to sue Leonardini was not one made by angry executives acting on impulse and in ignorance of the law. Rather, the Shell Oil legal department appears to have been the catalyst for the decision. Back in 1980, when a California state legislator introduced a resolution seeking a delay in the approval of plastic pipes, Shell told one of its representatives that the company had "a battery of attorneys to handle people like that and . . . they'll turn it over to their legal department."[27] Now Shell and its lawyers were ready to turn their wrath on Ray Leonardini. A consultant for one of Shell's lawyers later testified that the lawyer, William Holliman, had told him that Shell executives "hated Leonardini's guts." Holliman himself later testified that the suit was "the work of a group of lawyers in Houston," the location of Shell's corporate headquarters, and the legal group there "had really insisted on" suing Leonardini. A scientific consultant to the state related another conversation with Holliman:

> [T]here are some boys in Houston—that was his phrase—who were playing hardball, and that was also his phrase, and that they are very concerned about people, specifically Mr. Leonardini. . . . And that it was beginning to hurt Shell economically to have these discussions and that something was going to have to be done to dampen or quiet these kinds of outspoken statements.

Even though Leonardini had participated in the pipes controversy solely in his capacity as a lawyer, Shell's lawyers, in August 1981, sued him in the federal district court for the eastern district of California as an individual without suing his client, the trade council. Shell also sued Cal Labs. Both defendants were charged with "trade libel," that is, making false, disparaging, and harmful statements about the quality of a product or service.

Shell sought an injunction—a court order—preventing Leonardini from discussing the Cal Labs test results. Shell pursued this effort, as later trial testimony revealed, despite the fact that Shell's executives and in-house lawyers knew that the Cal Labs test results were already in the public domain and thus their distribution could not legally be enjoined.

Shell's lawyers soon dropped the suit against Cal Labs in return for a vague statement by the lab that its tests were preliminary. Leonardini moved to dismiss the claims against him, arguing that the injunction Shell sought would be an unconstitutional infringement on freedom of speech. Three days before a scheduled hearing on Leonardini's motion to dismiss the case, Shell dropped the suit against him.

But Leonardini was not about to let the matter rest at that. Incensed that Shell and its lawyers would wantonly abuse the legal system in order to prevent discussion of a public issue as important as the purity of drinking water, in April 1983 he SLAPPed back at Shell, filing a suit in California state court for malicious prosecution.

After a five-week trial, the judge concluded that, as a matter of law, Shell had no cause to file the suit against Leonardini. On April 22, 1986, the jury awarded Leonardini $197,000 in compensatory damages and $5 million in punitive damages.

Shell appealed but got no sympathy whatsoever in the California court of appeals, which agreed that Shell's lawsuit had no legal validity. In affirming the verdict, the appellate court summed up the depth of Shell's wrongdoing:[28]

> ... (T)he jury determined that Shell was guilty of maliciously bringing a lawsuit against plaintiff to silence and muzzle him. As found by the jury, Shell engaged in a continuous course of conduct to thwart the open governmental process of resolving conflicting claims on a subject of marked public interest. Seen in this light, Shell's conduct threatened the indispensable rights of all citizens to appear before their government and to speak out in matters of public health and safety without fear of legal retaliation. As the jury inferentially found, the pattern of reprehensible conduct also involved the continuous misrepresentation of the nature and safety of the polybutylene pipe system. This pattern, the jury could reasonably have concluded, included the continuous threats of litigation against anyone who dared make any adverse comment about the . . . pipe system.
>
> The use of superior fiscal position to silence opposing voices in public debate by the misuse of the legal process strikes at the very heart of the democratic process. . . . The game Shell elected to play was a legal game and the object of its suit the suppression of speech.

Shell sought to mount further appeals, but both the California Supreme Court and the United States Supreme Court refused to review the case. On October 23, 1990, Shell delivered to Leonardini a check for $7,547,643.10 in payment for the verdict plus interest. Nine years after his ordeal had begun, Ray Leonardini's victory was complete. Shell stockholders had lost millions of dollars solely because Shell lawyers and executives intentionally abused the law and the courts, using them as weapons to stifle political and legal opposition rather than as tools to peacefully redress legitimate grievances. Leonardini issued a statement that deserves repeating:

> This victory is a victory for the average citizen of this country who believes that someone must stand up to stop corporate abuse of the public trust.
>
> Shell abused the public trust by withholding vital public information from the State of California about the safety of their product. Their personal attack on me was a mere diversion of attention from the real issue: placing corporate profits over public accountability.
>
> It is my hope that by one small individual standing up to the second largest company in the world and saying "enough" maybe other average citizens will have the courage to speak up to defend the public trust as well.

Leonardini believes that lawyers have a special responsibility to stand up against the powerful on behalf of individuals. He credits his own lawyer, John Poswall of Sacramento, California, for his courage and professionalism in successfully combating Shell.

Postscript: The plastic-pipe water delivery system, eventually approved for home use in many parts of the country, simply did not work. Facing thousands of claims for property damage from leaky pipes, Shell, Hoechst, Celanese, and the Dupont Corporation, the principal manufacturers of plastic pipe materials, have engaged in repeated negotiations to try to resolve the claims by a national class-action lawsuit. The first effort, to settle the case for $750 million, was rejected by a Texas state judge. In August 1995, Shell and Celanese agreed to an $850 million settlement before a state judge in Tennessee, while Dupont accepted a $120 million settlement in a separate proceeding in an Alabama state court. The messy litigation and the inevitable large corporate payouts prove once again that secrecy and the stifling of free and open debate about product safety and effectiveness not only damage society but ultimately take money from corporate shareholders.

COMBATING SLAPPS

As encouraging as the Leonardini, Hemmeter, and Family Farmers victories are, SLAPP-backs are far from the perfect answer to discouraging SLAPPs.

In the first place, collecting damages in a SLAPP-back suit can take a decade or more. Often that is enough time for the SLAPP to accomplish its true purpose—to deter opposition during an ongoing political or business controversy. In these circumstances, resulting litigation expenses or damages incurred in the SLAPP and SLAPP-back might be viewed as useful—and tax-deductible—costs of doing business for the corporation. Indeed, at the time Shell lost the Leonardini case, its net worth was $12 billion, with annual net profits of $1.7 billion. The $5 million punitive damage award, then the largest in California history, hardly made a scratch.

Second, in order to SLAPP back by bringing a lawsuit for malicious prosecution or abuse of process, the SLAPPed defendant will have to do more than fight and win the original lawsuit. Liability will attach only if the SLAPPed party can prove that the other side filed the original suit knowing that it was unwarranted. Most people do not have the resources or the stomach to engage in the years of protracted litigation required to mount such evidence, especially after having faced prolonged persecution in the original case.

Third, suing and being sued are bankrupting events for people not backed by multimillion-dollar bank or corporate accounts. If a SLAPPed person has no insurance, he or she will be looking at spending perhaps tens of thousands of dollars in legal bills just to offer a defense. No wonder many citizen-activists bail out at the slightest threat of litigation. Then, unless they can obtain an attorney on a contingency basis, bringing the SLAPP-backs, including appeals, can cost hundreds of thousands more in fees and costs—with no guarantee that money damages will ever be collected.

Fourth, there is the seduction of allowing one's silence to be purchased. Many SLAPP-back litigants are willing to bail out of the fight in a secret settlement that puts some money in their hands—at the expense of stifled truth. Confidential settlements dilute the deterrent value of SLAPP-backs since, one way or the other, the SLAPPer may be able to clear away opposition or obtain the silence desired—first with a suit and then with a settlement.

Finally, there is the problem of the forest getting lost for the trees. "People got blinded by the money I won," Leonardini says. "The size of the award against Shell became the focus of the discussion rather than Shell's wrongdoing. The money was virtually all that the media cared about. They were much less interested in the fact that Shell had stifled free speech and covered up serious threats to the public health and safety. Ironically, the money I earned made it more difficult for people to come to grips with the fact that this corporate abuse does, in fact, go on."[29]

For these and other reasons, SLAPP-backs are only part of an effective anti-SLAPP movement. Many observers believe the ultimate answer lies with legislation. Oakland attorney Mark Goldowitz, director of the California Anti-SLAPP Project, spends much time and effort combating these lawsuits. He says, "The most effective way to combat the SLAPP industry is for laws to be enacted that prevent SLAPPs from getting off the ground," he told us. "Such legislation is needed in every state and at the federal level."

Fortunately, a growing legal reform movement is actively working to turn back the SLAPP threat. Professors Canan and Pring from the University of Denver have drafted a model anti-SLAPP law for consideration by legislatures. The model statute would provide absolute immunity from suit for anyone participating in speech or speech-related activities protected by the Constitution, except where the speech or activities, whether speaking in front of a city council, raising money for a political advertisement, or circulating a petition, are merely a subterfuge for some other purpose, such as seeking to secretly obtain an improper business advantage. (Maliciously spreading libelous or slanderous accusations is not normally protected by the Constitution and thus would not be protected under the model statute.) The model law also specifically authorizes a SLAPP victim to sue the person, entity, or government violating the anti-SLAPP law. The stated aim of this model law is to "strike a balance between the rights of persons to file lawsuits and the rights of persons to petition, speak out, associate, and otherwise participate in their governments."

Thus far in the 1990s, nine states—California, Delaware, Massachusetts, Minnesota, Nebraska, Nevada, New York, Rhode Island, and Washington—have enacted anti-SLAPP laws. (None directly follows the Pring-Canan model.) Most took intensive effort to pass, because business interests fought aggressively to prevent the anti-SLAPP laws from going into effect.

"In California, it took years of political struggle for California's law to become enacted," says the bill's author and president of the California senate, William Lockyer. The influential building lobby worked hard to defeat the measure, as did the Association of California Tort Reform, an organization financed by insurance, banking, and other large corporate interests. It is especially ironic that this "tort reform" group opposes efforts to curb SLAPP suits, because the group claims that it opposes frivolous lawsuits! Two governors in a row, George Deukmejian and Pete Wilson, vetoed the anti-SLAPP law before Wilson finally signed a watered-down version in 1992.

Rather than attempting to ban SLAPP suits, a difficult task that itself might chill public participation in controversies, the better anti-SLAPP laws—those in California, Delaware, Massachusetts, Minnesota, Nebraska, New York, and Rhode Island—instead place a significant procedural hurdle in front of SLAPPers. Under these laws, persons claiming that a suit brought against them is, in actuality, a SLAPP may file a motion in court at the start of the case before they have incurred major legal bills. The alleged SLAPPer must then present sufficient evidence to convince a judge that there is a reasonable chance that the lawsuit is winnable. Otherwise, the judge will dismiss the case. Some of these statutes also make it easier for SLAPPed defendants to win SLAPP-back suits by easing their burden of proof. (In Washington and Nevada, the anti-SLAPP laws have fewer teeth. In these states, a SLAPPed person may use his public participation only as an affirmative defense to the suit.)

These state laws making SLAPPs more difficult to prosecute are already having a positive impact on public participation. Jane Haines, the lawyer who represented Alice and Walter Mosher in the Salinas plant controversy, told us, "The pall has lifted. At least in my community, the fact that SLAPP suits are being routinely dismissed has made a noticeable difference." Indeed, Lloyd Lowrey, the corporate lawyer who wrote the threatening letter to the Moshers, told us that because of the Lockyer statute, he would not have written the same letter today. Mark Goldowitz agrees, although he worries that in California at least, court interpretations are beginning to weaken that state's law by making it easier for SLAPPers to present sufficient evidence to go forward with the lawsuit.

Of course, judges will continue to play a key role in preventing SLAPPs. They must look carefully at SLAPP-type actions and dismiss cases that appear to be an attempt to punish activities protected by the First Amendment. Courts should also impose severe sanctions on SLAPPers and their lawyers.

The best way to eliminate SLAPPs is the establishment of a nonprofit public-interest law firm that both provides assistance to anti-

SLAPP litigators around the country and pursues its own cases directly. The presence of such an institution would provide a greater incentive for corporate attorneys to perform their duties in an ethical manner.

Zealous representation of a client does not require lawyers to bring actions they know, or should know, are not justified, and which are merely intended to harass or oppress. Indeed, according to Professor Canan, it is *lawyers* who are most responsible for this improper use of the civil litigation system. In all her study of SLAPP suits, she has yet to come across a case in which the lawyer told the client that filing a suit would be improper and the client ignored that conclusion and filed anyway.

Many lawyers will respond with the old saw that it is their obligation to "vigorously represent their client" and that the courts exist to sort out such questions. But that isn't an accurate depiction of the lawyer's ethical duty, nor is it an excuse for abuse of process or malicious prosecution.

Lawyers are officers of the court. As stated in the preamble to the American Bar Association's current ethics guide, the Model Rules of Professional Conduct, lawyers are "public citizens" with a "special responsibility for the quality of justice." In that sense, they represent the public as well as their own clients. Lawyers who willingly file SLAPPs are attacking the foundations of the very system of governance they are duty-bound to protect.

Moreover, under state ethics codes, a lawyer is directly prohibited from bringing a frivolous lawsuit, one that has no genuine legal basis and whose primary purpose is to harass or intimidate others.[30] A SLAPP suit clearly falls under this prohibition. If a lawyer is found to have filed a SLAPP, it should be cause for an investigation by the state legal ethics board. If the board determines that the lawyer acted with knowledge that the suit was frivolous, it should impose strong sanctions.

BULLYING

Although SLAPPs are the most obvious way that large companies misuse the legal system as an instrument of corporate power, citizen-activists are not the only victims of aggressive corporate legal efforts. Corporations frequently sue each other. Indeed, nearly half of all civil cases filed in the federal courts are lawsuits between corporations.[31] Many of these lawsuits are legitimate attempts to resolve difficult business disputes. But some big companies and their lawyers use litigation as a bludgeon to bully smaller businesses or entrepreneurs with fewer resources, so as to stifle competition. Too often, this creates circumstances where might makes right, and depth of financial resources, rather than the merits of a case, is the most important factor in determining which party prevails.

THE CASE OF THE PESKY ENTREPRENEURS

Consider the case of *Alcon Surgical Inc. v. Surgin Surgical Instrumentation, Inc.* Surgin is a business started by two entrepreneurs, Armand Maaskamp and Theodore Wortrich, in 1981. The company makes and markets medical instruments and supplies.

During the 1980s, advances in medical technology gave surgery to remove cataracts from patients' eyes a tremendous boost, transforming the field into a growth industry. One major improvement was the ability of doctors to surgically insert a plastic lens directly into the eye to replace the natural lens, which is removed during the procedure. This development eliminated the need for the thick glasses that cataract surgery patients once needed. The medical advances, coupled with the aging of the population, increased the demand for cataract surgery. According to Armand Maaskamp, Surgin's president, while in 1983 there were 250,000 cataract surgeries per year, by 1990 the number was more than 1 million.

One key to the new-and-improved cataract surgery was a phacoemulsification machine and disposable cassette device developed by Alcon, a subsidiary of Nestlé S.A., the giant Swiss-based multinational corporation. (In 1994, Nestlé, the world's largest food and beverage company, reported $2.8 billion in net profits on $42 billion in sales.) The machine is used to dissolve the natural lens and then, by using suction, to remove it from the patient's eye. The cassette incorporates all the tubing necessary to transport fluid into and out of the eye during the operation. Each surgery requires a new cassette.

Having developed the machine, Alcon was the only company manufacturing the disposable cassette. It could sell a cassette for every cataract surgery performed, which in and of itself grossed the company tens of millions of dollars per year.

But the cassette also gave Alcon a tremendous leg up in the even more profitable and highly competitive ancillary-product market, which included items needed in cataract surgery such as the lens, saline solution, sutures, and the like—a market worth approximately $800 million a year. Rather than sell its ancillary products and the cassette separately as just one company in a very competitive market, Alcon "bundled" its cassette device, which cost very little to manufacture, with its ancillary products for approximately the same price as other companies were selling the supplies without the cassette. Thus, it was significantly less expensive for hospitals that owned an Alcon phacoemulsification machine to buy the bundled products from Alcon than it would have been to buy the cassette from Alcon and ancillary supplies from one of its competitors. This made Alcon the number-one supplier of cataract devices.

Surgin saw great potential to make inroads in Alcon's business if it could develop a cassette device of its own that would be compatible with the Alcon machine. Not only could Surgin sell the cassette to hospitals by undercutting Alcon's price, but it also hoped to sell its cassette to Alcon's ancillary-product competitors so that they could compete with Alcon's bundled products program.

Surgin had to be careful when entering the field. Alcon's cassette was duly patented. If Surgin infringed Alcon's patent, Alcon would surely sue.

Maaskamp was well aware of patent issues. He directed his company's effort to develop a device that would be compatible with the Alcon machine but that would not infringe on Alcon's patent. In his view, Surgin was successful. The Surgin cassette eventually passed the grueling patent search process and obtained its own federal patent.

In 1989, Surgin entered the cassette market in competition with Alcon. The company gained a 5 percent market share within a few months. More significant, Surgin was in active negotiation with other ancillary product providers who wished to bundle the Surgin cassette with their own supplies. Surgin also intended to undercut Alcon's price for the cassette alone, offering their product for one half Alcon's price. As a result, Maaskamp had reasonably hoped that Surgin would eventually obtain a 25 percent market share.

All this did not sit well with Alcon. In 1990, Alcon sued Surgin in federal court. Alcon, represented by the Los Angeles firm Munger, Tolles and Olson, claimed, among other allegations, that Surgin infringed the patent on its cassette.[32] Alcon, by convincing a judge that it was likely to prevail in the case, obtained a preliminary injunction blocking Surgin from selling its product. Surgin turned to its liability insurance carrier, Truck Insurance Exchange, part of the Farmers Insurance Group, which specifically insured the company against claims of liability, including patent infringement suits, and requested it defend the company and its two principals, pursuant to its obligation under the policy. The company refused, placing Surgin in the financially difficult position of paying for its own attorneys. (Surgin later sued the insurer and, in one of the most important insurance litigation cases in recent years, won a large verdict. That case is discussed in Chapter 8.)

Alcon pressed its patent infringement claim, and discovery commenced. "That's when the lawyers for Alcon really turned up the heat," Maaskamp says. "As my deposition was being taken, there was shouting and fighting between both sides about the propriety of the questions. I have never been in anything as tense. My first deposition took eight hours and essentially nothing was accomplished."

Then, according to Maaskamp, one of Alcon's lawyers calmly told him that his deposition alone would take *thirty days*. And that wasn't all. "The Alcon attorney looked straight at me and told me that they were ready to settle this case," Maaskamp says. "But if we didn't settle they were going to take depositions on a national basis and really put the pressure on." Maaskamp claims that Alcon's lawyer threatened Surgin with a war of attrition, which would have had the effect of breaking the company's financial ability to litigate the case and interfering with the entrepreneur's ability to run his business.[33]

The prospect of unlimited litigation was taking a personal toll on Maaskamp, who did not view it as merely being an ordinary part of doing business. He had suffered intense stress as a result of being personally named as a defendant, from the refusal of Surgin's insurance carrier to meet its obligation to defend him and his company, and from the financial worries of being sued by a subsidiary of one of the world's largest corporations. Prior to the deposition, Maaskamp had been hospitalized for stress illness, and he was near the end of his rope. Now, he faced a grueling discovery process that promised to take months, with his company paying the entire bill, including lawyers' fees, costs, and travel expenses, not to mention the productive time Maaskamp and other employees would have to take away from the business. "I asked my lawyer how much this case was going to cost if we fought it to the very end," Maaskamp told us. "He told me one million dollars."

"We didn't want to settle," Maaskamp recalls. "We were convinced we were in the right. We pleaded with Farmers to come to our aid. They never responded and totally stonewalled us. Finally, we decided that we had no choice. We simply could not afford the legal fees or the time away from our business."[34]

Surgin realized it was no match for Alcon, the proverbial eight-hundred-pound gorilla. The case settled confidentially. Surgin removed its cassette device from the market. Other issues between the companies were quietly resolved. Maaskamp is bitter: "We had obtained an independent patent. We had a just defense and could have prevailed. But we were bludgeoned out of the market by sheer litigation overkill."

"Nestlé got what it wanted," agrees attorney Daniel Callahan, who later represented Surgin in its lawsuit against Farmers Insurance arising out of the company's refusal to pay for Surgin's defense. "It now has a monopoly in the market. They accomplished the feat by taking a company to court and bleeding them to death."[35]

The Surgin case is not unusual. Corporate lawyers know that, like private individuals, small businesses often do not have the ability to withstand an all-out legal assault by a large company, since even if they are insured, the time and effort taken away from business extracts a burdensome toll. Pounding smaller would-be competitors into submission also serves a larger corporate business purpose. "If entrepreneurs were permitted to compete against the conglomerates, and more specifically their attorneys," Maaskamp says, "the American public would save a bundle. Instead, a system has been fostered to prevent innovative and cost-effective products from entering the marketplace."

No one knows which party would have prevailed had the Alcon-Surgin dispute been tried on the merits. But there seems little reason to doubt Maaskamp's claim that the case was settled early because of Alcon's vast superiority of resources and the legal firepower it could purchase.

In this case, taxpayers also may have come up losers. Most cataract operations are paid for with Medicare funding. Surgin's entry into the market as a competitor of Alcon could very well have brought costs for cataract surgery down because of price competition. Now, with Surgin pushed to the sidelines, Alcon is once again the sole manufacturer of the cassette device. It has little incentive to keep prices down.

THE CASE OF THE OBSTINATE DAIRIES

The Monsanto Company is a large chemical conglomerate with tremendous power in the marketplace. For the first half of 1995, it reported $4.8 billion in revenues and more than half a billion in profits. In recent years, Monsanto has invested substantial capital for research and development into the emerging field of biotechnology.

Monsanto developed an artificial bovine-growth hormone, rBST, also known as rBGH. When rBST is injected into cows, it increases the animals' milk production by approximately 20 percent. On November 3, 1993, the federal Food and Drug Administration approved Monsanto's use of rBST, but the U.S. Congress acted to delay this approval for ninety days, until February 3, 1994, to provide time for a government study on the hormone's economic impact. The day after that,

Monsanto began marketing rBST under the name Posilac, and, as of this writing, the company remains the only firm that sells rBST.

Posilac is controversial. Monsanto contends that milk from injected cows is safe; indeed, that it is no different from milk produced by noninjected cows. The FDA agrees with Monsanto. But many in the consumer movement disagree. These opponents contend that cows injected with rBST show increased rates of a bovine infection known as mastitis. This infection, in turn, forces dairy farmers to inject cows with more frequent doses of antibiotics. Opponents worry that the increased use of antibiotics in milk cows will make it more likely that people who drink milk will develop resistance to antibiotics, a position that has received some support from a study by the General Accounting Office (GAO), the investigative arm of Congress.[36] Increasing instances of bacterial resistance to antibiotics cause great concern among doctors, because infections that do not respond to antibiotics are very difficult, if not impossible, to treat. Medical authorities fear that bacteria in humans could become fully resistant to antibiotics, thus making bacterial infections the major killers they once were. Consumers Union, the publisher of Consumer Reports, has pointed out that, in addition to such serious questions about possible health risks from rBST, there are also strong doubts about the benefits of using the hormone. Because there has been a milk surplus for many years, and retail milk prices are subject to strong government regulation, it is unlikely that rBST use will reduce the cost of milk to consumers. Instead it will lead to the production of more and more surplus milk—milk that, under federal law, the government will be forced to purchase at taxpayers' expense.[37]

Whether or not milk produced from rBST-treated cows is, given present knowledge, an unacceptable risk is beyond the scope of this book. What is of concern, however, is Monsanto's use of the court system to stifle the free speech of dairies that merely wish to inform their customers that the milk they sell does not come from rBST-treated animals.

On February 10, 1994, the FDA issued interim guidelines, "Appropriate Labeling Statements," with respect to rBST. These guidelines, which are advisory in nature rather than mandatory, make it clear that the FDA frowns at milk producers or sellers advising customers that the milk they sell is not treated with growth hormone. Misguidedly, the agency has even warned against milk sellers making truthful statements such as "rBST free," since such a label might "imply a compositional difference between milk from treated and untreated cows rather than a difference in the way the milk is produced." Further, according to the FDA, it would also be potentially false advertising to advertise milk as not being produced from rBST-treated cows unless a state government "require[s] that firms that use such claims establish a plan and maintain records to substantiate the claims, and make those records available for inspection by regulatory officials."[38]

The FDA's guidelines are intended to discourage labeling. But many consumers want the ability to exercise choice when buying milk products, preferring to buy milk from untreated cows. In order to do so, they have to be able to identify such milk. If labels are discouraged or prevented, consumers are denied the ability to make a free choice. This prevents the forces of the marketplace from rewarding those dairies that choose not to inject their cows. That, in turn, induces dairies to use the hormone, because treated cows produce more milk. If, instead, dairies could alert milk consumers that their products are rBST free, and a significant number of consumers purchased only such milk, it would discourage dairies from using Posilac. That would lead to fewer farmers injecting their cows, which could derail the profit-making machine that Monsanto hopes Posilac will become.

Not surprisingly, Monsanto would rather not risk consumer rejection of its product. It is therefore intent on discouraging dairies from labeling their milk as rBST free. Its lawyers have filed lawsuits to drive that point home, suing at least two companies for doing so.

One of the dairies that Monsanto sued is Pure Milk and Ice Cream Company of Waco, Texas, a small dairy that claims to control milk production from the hay that goes in the cow to the milk that comes out, and beyond to the bottling and sales to markets. Shortly after the FDA approved rBST, Pure Milk began to advertise that its milk comes from nontreated cows. One such advertisement, printed on jug hangers the company had attached to its milk bottles sold in grocery stores, read:

THE PURE TRUTH ABOUT OUR MILK

We offer Pure Milk because they raise their own cows and milk them. Pure maintains absolute control over quality and purity . . . and you can just taste the freshness of their milk. Also, you can be confident Pure's cows are not BGH treated and that Pure Milk is free from impurities, antibiotics and unnatural BST. No other Texas dairy will make that statement.

Buy the brand you can trust.

The jug hanger ad also contained the words "no unnatural BST" in a red circle with a slash through it.

In addition, Pure Milk ran a print advertisement with "No BST cows" in a circle with a slash through it. The ad stated:

WHAT MAKES PURE MILK DIFFERENT?

Pure is the only dairy in this market that can make these statements . . .

- We raise and own all of our own cows
- We feed them, milk them, care for them
- We package only milk from our own cows
- We have sole responsibility for our quality
- We do not treat our cows with rBST or rBGH

The U.S. Food and Drug Administration has found no significant difference between milk derived from rBST and non rBST treated cows.

Buy the brand you can trust.

We care about our cows because we care about the quality of our milk. Milk we confidently serve our own children and grandchildren. Milk guaranteed by the Pure family of dedicated dairymen.

s/
Joe Gore, Chairman

Even though this ad included a statement advising consumers of the FDA's position, Monsanto's lawyers immediately reacted by seeking to prevent Pure Milk from advising its customers that its cows are not treated with artificial bovine growth hormone. On February 9, 1994, attorney S. William Livingston of the 301-lawyer firm Covington & Burling, one of the largest and most prominent corporate firms in the nation's capital, fired off a letter threatening Pure Milk for making labeling statements "likely to mislead consumers into believing that milk from BST treated cows is less safe or less nutritious, or otherwise inferior to milk from untreated cows."

Attorney Benjamin F. Yale, on behalf of Pure Milk, responded to the letter on February 11, 1994, stating that the jug hangers which did not contain the disclaimer about the FDA's safety determination had been discontinued from use but that Pure Milk would continue to advertise its product as coming from cows free of rBST. He concluded the letter by stating, "Pure Milk will act responsibly and lawfully within its right to free speech. Any effort to thwart that by coercion, threats, or frivolous litigation techniques will not be tolerated."

The battle had been joined. On February 18, 1994, Monsanto filed suit in federal district court in Texas, represented by the Atlanta-based power firm King & Spalding and two Texas firms. The suit claimed damages for false advertising, libel, injury to Monsanto's business reputation, and commercial disparagement. Pure Milk was in for a potentially long and very expensive fight.

Monsanto's actions and ensuing lawsuit appear to be a new twist in libel litigation where *telling the truth* is contended to be actionable. If Pure Milk truly sells milk that comes from uninjected cows, to so state is the truth. Yet, Monsanto claims that a statement of factual truth can be false advertising.

We attempted to reach Monsanto's lawyers for comment. We first called attorney Livingston from Covington & Burling. He stated he was not authorized to comment and referred us to King & Spalding. An attorney at King & Spalding also declined comment and referred us directly to Monsanto. We left word with Monsanto about the nature of our inquiry. Tom McDermott, the director of biotechnology communications for Monsanto, returned the call.

McDermott justified Monsanto's actions by saying, "We are not opposed to voluntary labeling. We are not opposed to statements that milk comes from cows not treated with rBST. However, to say that alone is insufficient. We strongly believe that the claim has to be put in proper context.

"Imagine a person in a store to buy milk who sees a 'No rBST' label on a carton of milk. That individual might think, 'I'll buy this milk instead of other milk because there is nothing in it.' But if the label had additional language that there is no significant difference between milk produced with and without rBST, that individual might not make the same choice."

When we pointed out to Mr. McDermott that Pure Milk made that *very statement* in its print ad and was sued anyway, Mr. McDermott said that he would not comment on pending litigation.

As the litigation proceeded, Pure Milk's chairman, Joe Gore, told us that standing up to a multibillion-dollar corporation and its lawyers is anything but fun. "Our family's whole life's work was riding on this issue," he said. "The lawsuit has taken tremendous time away from our business and we have been restricted from aggressively entering markets we believe would be profitable. Emotionally, we have been torn up inside. It really keeps you up late thinking into the night." Gore added, "We don't have a quarrel with Monsanto. Never have. But they are asking us to refrain from telling our customers the truth. And we just won't give in to that."

Attorney Yale also felt the pressure. "This case is very trying," he told us. "These are people who are not only clients, but friends. Besides, the case is very important. I believe Monsanto's lawyers are using Pure Milk and a few others as test cases. If they prevail, they will bring actions against other dairies all across the country who advertise their milk as being free of rBST." Yale warned of "the real danger facing free speech in American commerce and the adverse impact that has on Americans' right to know." He worried that, in light of suits like the rBST cases, "free speech is only free to those who can afford to defend it."[39]

The day before it sued Pure Milk, Monsanto sued another company, Swiss Valley Farms of Davenport, Iowa, for advertisements that touted the rBST-free nature of its milk products and noted that questions had been raised about the possible negative effects of the hormone. The lawsuit, filed in federal district court in Illinois, contended that such advertising "undermines consumer confidence in milk, and dairy products derived from milk, from cows receiving Posilac, injures the good will of Posilac, adversely affects Monsanto's ability to sell Posilac, and directly undermines Monsanto's attempts to sell Posilac. Because production is in its current marketing stage, Swiss Valley's advertisement and promotional activities threaten Monsanto's entire investment in Posilac." Among the remedies sought, in addition to money, was a court order requiring Swiss Valley to "sponsor and pay for advertising which corrects the false and misleading advertising and promotion and which retracts the false and misleading claims."

Monsanto's actions, designed and carried out by its lawyers, are a serious threat to freedom of speech, the consumer's right to know, and the rights of independent businesses to pursue a business strategy that conflicts with a huge corporation's desires. The theory is novel: Facts might induce consumers into a *belief* with which Monsanto does not agree, and thereby cost the company money. Dairies will be punished for telling the truth, and those who might wish to label their milk will be deterred for fear of litigation.

But winning these lawsuits was probably not the point for Monsanto. Monsanto's suits appeared aimed at scaring dairies who use nontreated cows from advertising that fact or forcing these dairies to get Monsanto's prior approval for the content of such ads. Indeed, Monsanto is reported to have made just such a demand for prior approval to The Natural Way, a food store in Texas that ran a radio ad promoting its sale of milk products made from cows not treated with rBST.[40]

Executives and attorneys from Swiss Valley declined to be interviewed. The head of Swiss Valley said he would *love* to talk about the tactics of Monsanto and its lawyers but could not while the litigation was ongoing.

In June 1995, Monsanto and Pure Milk settled out of court. The terms are confidential, but attorney Yale reports that "under the terms of the settlement, Pure Milk will continue to advise its customers that its cows are not injected with rBST." The Swiss Valley case also settled confidentially.

While Monsanto sought to keep two dairies from trumpeting their rBST-free status, the state of Vermont adopted legislation *requiring* milk from cows treated with rBST to include labels that alert the public to the use of the hormone, while at the same time noting that the FDA had found no significant difference between milk treated with rBST and milk without it. Despite the state-imposed reference on labels to the FDA position, a group of national trade associations, including the International Dairy Foods Association and the Grocery Manufacturers of America, sued in federal district court to block the law. Their lawyers: Covington & Burling, the same firm that represents Monsanto. On September 5, 1995, a federal appeals court rejected their request to stop implementation of the law before it went into effect. At this writing, the case is back before the district judge.

Corporate SLAPP suits against activists and bullying lawsuits against competitors arise from the same insight: Forcing opponents to spend time and money on lawsuits can be very good business. The power lawyers who bring these types of actions aid, abet, and facilitate the concentration of business power, earning big fees as they stifle competition and even chill freedom of speech. The current "tort reform" movement, backed by large corporations, hysterically, and without providing substantiation beyond phony anecdotes, denounces lawsuit abuses (see Chapter 8) but rarely, if ever, criticizes this corporate-style abuse of the right to go to court. But all concerned citizens should take offense at groundless, frivolous lawsuits that waste the valuable time of our courts, twist the legal system, and distort the political process. And those who bear the greatest responsibility for this mess, even more than the avaricious corporations that demand these actions, are their crafty corporate lawyers, who ignore their ethical duties to counsel rather than supinely serve and who thereby abandon their professional standards.

CHAPTER 6

THE GAMES CORPORATE LAWYERS PLAY

W
HY DO AMERICANS FEEL A GROWING HOSTILITY TOWARD the legal system in general and lawyers in particular? Many of us probably have an idealized image of what lawyers and the law should be. We might think of great lawyers like Abraham Lincoln or Clarence Darrow (or Darrow as portrayed by Spencer Tracy in the film *Inherit the Wind*). Or purely fictional lawyers like Perry Mason, Matlock, and *The Firm*'s Mitch McDeer, who represent the hunger for truth and justice that we always hope to find in the profession. Or think of the movie *Twelve Angry Men*, in which a jury struggles toward a just verdict, portraying an ideal court system, one where people of goodwill work to determine the facts and reach the proper result.

Many of the corporate law tactics described in this book could not be more different from those idealized views of the law's role in our society. And although many of the abuses take place far from public view, people know that something is wrong. They sense the imbalances, the unfairness in the justice system. They suspect that the playing field and the rules of the game favor the rich and powerful, but they may not know what to do about it. Unfocused anger can be destructive, because it can be manipulated by organized interests with hidden agendas and often leads to support for measures that will ultimately prove harmful.

Citizens *should* act to bring meaningful and effective reforms to the legal system. In previous chapters we examined the misdeeds of corporate power lawyers and considered proposals for change. But we haven't finished opening the windows onto this misconduct. This chapter examines still more areas of power-lawyer influence and manipulation, conduct that usually stays hidden in the shadows. These are the games corporate lawyers play to ensure that they are on the winning side when the final buzzer sounds.

KICKING PLAYERS OUT OF THE GAME

One potent tactic sometimes utilized by corporate lawyers is maneuvering to have someone who knows unpleasant truths or is perceived as an impediment to winning removed from involvement in the matter. As we shall see, the list of the removed includes witnesses, plaintiffs' lawyers, and, with increasing brazenness, even judges.

THE CASE OF THE EMPLOYEE WHO KNEW TOO MUCH

Can a corporation prevent a witness from telling the explosive truth about its products? In the case of the General Motors Corporation and Ronald Elwell, corporate lawyers tried to make it happen—they tried to bar from the courtroom a crucial eyewitness to corporate decisions, decisions that resulted in numerous deaths and injuries.

Since 1973, more than thirteen hundred people have been killed in fiery crashes involving pickup trucks that General Motors manufactured between 1973 and 1987. More than 650 of these deaths were caused by fire rather than trauma—that is, the occupant of the truck survived the crash but was burned alive by the subsequent fire.[1] Critics contend that the location of the fuel tanks in these trucks renders them unsafe. During those model years, GM placed the fuel tank outside the truck's steel frame rails rather than in a more protected area. As a result, critics claim, when a direct side-impact accident occurs, the energy generated in the crash goes undeflected into the gas tank, which can then rupture, leading to a fiery explosion. In a sideswipe or angled front impact, critics further charge, sharp edges of sheet metal, bolts, or other objects can easily puncture the five-foot-long gas tank, again leading to fire. But GM has continued to insist that the trucks in question are safe.

A number of aspects of this controversy have generated headlines:

- On November 17, 1992, the television newsmagazine program *Dateline NBC* aired a report on the GM truck dispute that included two side-impact demonstrations. On February 9, 1993, GM filed suit in Indiana state court, alleging that NBC had rigged the tests to ensure that the trucks would ignite. The next day, NBC, which is owned by industrial giant General Electric, issued a widely publicized apology, referring to the televised crash tests as "inappropriate."
- In December 1992, the National Highway Traffic Safety Administration launched an investigation into the safety of GM trucks to

determine whether the government should order a recall. As a result of the investigation, U.S. Secretary of Transportation Federico Pena determined in October 1994 that the trucks were unsafe and that a recall was appropriate. But on December 2, 1994, in an action that shocked safety advocates and some members of Congress, Pena agreed to close the investigation and cancel an imminent scheduled public hearing on the matter in exchange for a GM commitment to provide between $21 million and $51 million in cash and in-kind support for auto safety programs. GM, represented by the 401-lawyer firm Kirkland & Ellis, had sued to block the hearing.

- On April 17, 1995, the United States Court of Appeals for the Third Circuit rejected a settlement agreement, previously approved by a Philadelphia federal trial judge, of a class-action lawsuit brought on behalf of GM truck owners to compensate for the reduction in GM truck resale values caused by the gas tank problems. Under the proposed settlement—a cynical arrangement between corporate and plaintiff lawyers if there ever was one—owners of the trucks would have received only a coupon providing for a $1,000 discount on the purchase of a new GM truck, while their lawyers would have received $9.5 million in cash fees. Rejecting the arguments of GM's power-lawyer team from Kirkland & Ellis, the court of appeals said the agreement did not adequately protect the interests of GM truck owners and was, instead, "arguably . . . a GM sales promotion device."[2] GM, represented by Kirkland partner Kenneth Starr, sought Supreme Court review. The high court declined, sending the case back to the trial court for further proceedings.

Meanwhile, more than three hundred accident victims or members of their families have individually filed suit against GM over the alleged pickup truck defect. Of these cases, only eight have gone to trial, with GM losing five and winning three. But the nonprofit Center for Auto Safety[3] estimates that over the years GM has paid more than $200 million to settle lawsuits conditioned on the plaintiffs' agreeing to confidentiality, with settlements as high as $20 million.[4] GM repeatedly follows the same strategy in these lawsuits—prolong the litigation until the arm of the law is about to descend in the form of sanctions for discovery abuse or the emergence of evidence that GM knew of and concealed the dangers of its trucks—and then settle, confidentially. One case that settled in September 1995, *Bishop v. General Motors*, was discussed in Chapter 3 because it highlighted the obfuscation tactics employed by GM lawyers in many of these cases.

One of the other cases that GM settled in September 1995 was *Moseley* v. *General Motors*. In 1989, seventeen-year-old Shannon Moseley of Snellville, Georgia, dropped off his girlfriend on the night before college entrance exams and headed home in his 1985 GMC Sierra pickup. As he entered an intersection, a Chevrolet pickup that had run a red light smashed directly into the side of his Sierra. Moseley's truck skidded 150 feet and burst into flames. The coroner concluded, and eyewitnesses at trial confirmed, that Shannon Moseley had survived the crash but died in the fire.

The boy's parents sued. After a one-month trial in January 1993—some readers may have watched the proceedings on the cable network Court TV—a Fulton County jury awarded the Moseleys $105 million, $4 million in compensatory damages and $101 million in punitive damages. On appeal, GM was represented not only by Kenneth Starr and Kirkland & Ellis but also by the 294-lawyer Atlanta firm King & Spalding and one of its top partners, Griffin Bell—a former United States attorney general. The Georgia Court of Appeals ordered a new trial because it concluded that the Moseleys' lawyer made inappropriate references before the jury to other lawsuits involving GM pickups and because it found that the trial judge erred in allowing the Moseleys to offer certain evidence. But the court majority, reviewing the punitive damage award, did not find the amount to be improper. The court stated:[5]

> In the instant case, there was evidence that GM was aware of the problems inherent with placement of the fuel tanks outside the frame on its full-size pickup trucks, which exposure could have been significantly reduced . . . yet it did not implement such modifications because of economic considerations. This evidence of a knowing endangerment of all who may come in contact with one of the 5,000,000 GM full-size pickup trucks still on the road, motivated by economic benefit, was sufficient to support an award of punitive damages.

One of the Moseleys' witnesses at trial was Ronald Elwell, a former GM employee who left in 1989 following a dispute with the company. For twenty-eight years, Mr. Elwell was a GM safety engineer. As part of his employment, he had worked with GM's legal teams, advising them and frequently testifying on behalf of the auto giant in product liability lawsuits brought against it. Over the years, Elwell testified in more than sixty depositions and a dozen trials on behalf of GM.[6]

Then, Elwell and GM parted company, with the company and its former employee engaging in a nasty lawsuit over Elwell's pension rights. Eventually that suit settled confidentially. Apparently, part of the settlement agreement between Elwell and GM prevented the former employee from testifying in product liability cases against his former employer.

But could GM legally shut up a witness who possessed firsthand knowledge and information about the company's business practices merely by entering into a secret agreement? And could that agreement be binding against parties injured by GM products who believed Elwell possessed information that would help prove that the company's products were defective?

GM lawyers certainly thought so, and they pressed Elwell to affirm his vow of silence. On August 26, 1992, a Wayne County, Michigan, circuit court judge issued a permanent injunction, based on an agreement between GM and Elwell, that purports to prohibit Elwell from testifying in any trial or deposition regarding GM products *without GM's written consent*. Elwell subsequently asked the judge to "clarify" this ruling to permit him to testify where a court ordered him to do so, but the judge refused.[7]

But victims of the allegedly unsafe trucks continued to ask trial judges to issue subpoenas—court orders—compelling Elwell to testify in depositions and at trials. GM lawyers tried to convince judges to cancel the subpoenas whenever they were issued, citing the settlement agreement and the Michigan court order. They claimed that Elwell's testimony would impermissibly expose business secrets and privileged conversations between him and GM lawyers.

While concerns about authentic trade secrets and privileged information are legitimate, they could have been addressed in the context of particular questions lawyers might have for Elwell; they could not have justified the blanket gag order the Michigan judge had approved. An absolute ban on Elwell's testimony without GM's permission interfered with the rights of victims to discover the truth about GM programs. Nearly all of the approximately twenty judges across the country that have addressed this issue subsequently have refused to uphold the Michigan order. Instead, these judges have ruled against GM and in favor of the right of litigants to obtain Elwell's testimony.[8] For example, Judge Dudley H. Bowen of the United States District Court for the Southern District of Georgia rejected the Michigan judge's gag order, holding that it extended "far beyond" legitimate concerns about corporate trade secrets or attorney-client privilege. And Missouri federal district judge Joseph E. Stevens, Jr., ruled that barring Elwell's testimony "amounts to concealment of relevant evidence."[9]

Anyone who may have wondered why GM lawyers worked so hard in so many cases to keep Elwell from telling publicly what he knows learned the answer in the Moseley case, where, for the first time since leaving GM, Elwell testified publicly, after the trial judge there refused GM's request to bar the testimony.

Elwell told the jury that he had often testified as the GM designated employee most knowledgeable about post-collision fires. One lawsuit in which Elwell had testified on behalf of GM was *Adams* v. *General Motors*, a case in California Superior Court in San Francisco involving a side-impact GM truck collision and subsequent fire. In that matter, Elwell had testified that the trucks were safe. But, as he told the Moseley jury, he later learned that GM had kept important information from him, their own designated safety expert: Without telling Elwell, GM had conducted extensive crash tests on the trucks to test their safety in a side impact. The plaintiff in the Adams case was also never given information about the GM crash tests, despite asking for it in discovery. Answering attorney Jim Butler's questions before the Moseley jury, Elwell recounted his experience:[10]

> Q: When you went to San Francisco in May of 1983 [to testify in the Adams matter], did you know that, starting sometime in 1981, GM had embarked on a crash testing program whereby a total of some 31 GM pickup trucks were crash-tested by having an X-car, which is a small GM car, driven into the side of the pickup trucks?
>
> ELWELL: I had no knowledge of that, no. . . .
>
> Q: When did you first learn of this '81 through '83 crash testing program?
>
> ELWELL: September of '83.

After Elwell returned from the Adams trial, a supervisor suggested he go to the GM proving grounds, where he observed the results of pickup truck crash testing.

> Q: What did you see when you got there?
>
> ELWELL: I saw a ton of pickup trucks that were just smashed. There must have been over 20 of them.

Q: Where were they smashed?

ELWELL: In the side. . . .

Q: What condition were the fuel tanks in?

ELWELL: Well, they were very badly smashed. There were holes in them as big as melons. They were split open.

Elwell recalled that this evidence left him "pretty upset." Concerned that he might have given false testimony in the Adams case, Elwell confronted his boss:

ELWELL: I said to him that I am terribly afraid that I committed perjury.

Q: What did he [Elwell's supervisor] say?

ELWELL: I don't remember. But I think it was something to the effect that, 'Don't worry about it, it's not—wasn't your responsibility,' or something like that. But I told him that it was. I was under oath. . . .

Q: Now, to your knowledge, had the existence of this crash testing program ever become known to any victim . . . or any of their lawyers . . . or to any court or to any jury before 1991, 10 years after the program started?

ELWELL: Not to my knowledge, no sir.

Butler then questioned Elwell as to whether he ever sought to inform his superiors that he now believed the truck's fuel tank placement was unsafe and not defensible. He testified that he spoke to his superiors about it but did not write a memo because he feared it would get him fired.

GM placed a plastic stone shield around the gas tank for 1985 model year trucks. Elwell testified that this was not sufficient to make the tanks safe.

Q: . . . did you discuss with your superiors at GM these changes that were made . . . ?

ELWELL: Yes.

Q: All right. What did you think of these changes?

ELWELL: Well, they were no good. They were dangerous, and they had not properly designed the guard for occupant safety, and I told them so. . . .

Q: Why?

ELWELL: . . . number one, they used plastic, not steel . . . Number two, they made it a poultice, a Band-Aid which totally encompassed the tank and would not drain. . . . [The mud and water sitting in the stone shield against the tank] rots the tank out from the bottom, outside in. And what you started off with was a fuel tank that could take 25- or 30-mile-an-hour side impact, and . . . five years later you've got a tank that won't take 15-miles-an-hour side impact because you've rusted out half the bottom of your tank. And that's what I told management we had to fix and fix right away. And that was in 1984.

Butler then asked about GM's practice of storing safety-related documents in such a way that GM's lawyers would not "find" documents that would otherwise have to be turned over in discovery—a practice akin to keeping double books. Elwell testified:

[When discovery] was served on General Motors [that] asked for documents, . . . if GM went to the engineering files, I'm afraid they would find an awful lot of . . . information carefully kept on just those subjects. . . . And we would go only to those files which were the general files that were kept. See, project information was always kept by the engineer, never by the general file system. And so they would go to the general file system and, lo and behold, they would find no documents. So, they would say, "None" [when asked by lawyers for victims whether documents existed about the safety of a GM product].

Q: Who would say "None"?

ELWELL: Legal staff.

This testimony makes plain why GM lawyers wanted so badly to fashion an agreement to keep Elwell from testifying and would work so hard to keep him bound to that promise: He can testify that the pickup trucks are unsafe. He can testify that GM's legal staff cynically manipulated the search of files so as to avoid complying with legally due discovery. And he adds credence to charges that have been made that GM's legal group shredded documents to cover up the company's knowledge that the trucks were unsafe (a matter discussed further below).

Elwell's testimony clearly hurt GM before the Moseley jury, whose substantial punitive award was clearly aimed at teaching the company a lesson. The amount GM agreed to pay in the September 1995 settlement of the case is confidential.

Court-sanctioned gag orders are not the only means power lawyers use to muzzle witnesses whose testimony threatens the interests of their corporate clients. Just as corporations and their lawyers use SLAPP suits (see Chapter 5) to neutralize troublesome activists, they sometimes consider similar types of lawsuits to deter expert witnesses whose testimony threatens their profits. Such was the case when a major pharmaceutical maker used a deft legal maneuver to neutralize a medical expert who offered a compelling case that one of its most lucrative products posed serious health risks.

THE CASE OF THE PROFESSOR WHO KNEW TOO MUCH

Ilo Grundberg, age fifty-seven, lived in Hurricane, Utah, with her mother, Mildred Coats. On June 19, 1988, the eve of Coats's eighty-third birthday, Grundberg fired eight gunshots from a .22 caliber revolver into her mother's head and then put a birthday card in the elderly woman's hand. When authorities charged her with manslaughter, Grundberg claimed that she had been acting under the influence of Halcion, the world's most popular sleeping pill.

Halcion has been a cash cow for its manufacturer, the Michigan-based Upjohn Company, generating more than $2 billion in sales since it was introduced in 1977. (It has been sold in the United States since 1983.) Halcion's success is owed to the fact that the user of the medication will normally awaken without feeling hungover, tired, or groggy, effects that often result from taking other sleeping aids. But a very disturbing side effect appears to be associated with Halcion. Some medical authorities have alleged that the drug drives some people crazy, even that its use has caused suicides and murders.

Ilo Grundberg was one of those people. In February 1989, Utah prosecutors asked the judge to dismiss the charges against her after two court-appointed psychiatrists concluded that the shooting was an involuntary reaction to Halcion and other prescription drugs. Grundberg then filed suit against Upjohn in federal district court in Salt Lake City. Her lawyer, Edward H. Kellogg, Jr., struggled with Upjohn to obtain company documents through discovery. Eventually he gained access to previously undisclosed information about Upjohn's knowledge of Halcion's side effects. These materials indicated that Halcion was more likely than other sleeping medications to cause such side effects as depression, amnesia, paranoia, and hallucinations. In August 1991, on the eve of trial, Upjohn settled the case for an undisclosed sum, reportedly $8 million, with no admission of liability.[11] In a sad postscript to the tragedy, Ilo Grundberg committed suicide six years to the day she shot her mother. "She couldn't get over killing her mother," attorney Kellogg told us.[12]

Before Ilo Grundberg settled her suit against Upjohn, she had retained as an expert witness Dr. Ian Oswald, professor emeritus of psychiatry at Edinburgh University in Scotland. Dr. Oswald, an expert in sleep disorders, reviewed the Upjohn documents produced in discovery, compared the raw data with Upjohn's published reports, and gave a pretrial deposition in which he contended that Upjohn knew that Halcion could cause mental illness and had engaged in a lengthy cover-up.

The deceit, according to Oswald, began with Upjohn's very first Halcion study, which occurred in 1972 among Michigan prison inmates, twenty-eight of whom took Halcion while nineteen others took placebos. Seven Halcion users displayed paranoia, but Upjohn reported to the Food and Drug Administration that only two did so. Only one of the inmates who had taken placebos demonstrated signs of paranoia, but Upjohn reported that two had. Oswald found that in one early 1980s clinical trial, 188 participants, out of a total of 1,567, vanished from the records without explanation. Upjohn also appeared to have concealed evidence of at least one suicide by a Halcion user.[13]

A subsequent FDA staff investigation produced an internal memorandum that concluded that Upjohn sought

> to gain approval for long term use of the drug even though available evidence indicated that long term use was both dangerous and medically untenable. The motivation for this is documented in an internal Upjohn memo dated 4-21-82 which stated that ". . . a 14 day limit could reduce projected sales by 50% over a 10 year period." A 3-4-82 memo . . . stated that "if we are unsuccessful in appealing the 14 day upper limit, it will be necessary to redo the analysis omitting [certain] protocols." This is perhaps the most incriminating evidence found at Upjohn, because it shows that the firm chose to disregard the potential harm of inappropriate use, in order to gain additional sales profits. . . . It appears that Upjohn misrepresented the data in order to persuade FDA reviewers to waive the pro-

posed 14 day duration of use limit. The only caution statement regarding usage in the original package insert is the statement "it is recommended that Halcion not be prescribed in quantities exceeding a one-month supply."

Whether Professor Oswald's testimony was crucial to Upjohn's decision to settle the Grundberg case is not known. However, it has become abundantly clear that the company had long been *very* unhappy with the professor and his opinions and wanted to silence him.

Back in 1972, when it was developing Halcion, Upjohn sought to hire Oswald because, according to Upjohn documents, he was the only "big name" who had conducted long-term EEG (electroencephalogram) sleep tests. But instead of allying himself with Upjohn, Oswald became a Halcion critic, eventually publishing two studies in the 1980s that concluded that the drug's risks were greater than its benefits.

The FDA investigation cited above found that Upjohn "conducted a continuous, on-going campaign to discredit or neutralize any individual or publication reporting adverse information about Halcion." According to the FDA investigation (released pursuant to a Freedom of Information Act request), Upjohn "vigorously sought to suppress the publication of unfavorable studies, and attempted to silence Halcion critics."

As part of its campaign, Upjohn worked behind the scenes to try to prevent publication of Oswald's studies, and it paid doctors to criticize Oswald and his work. According to a 1982 Upjohn memo, the company paid one British psychiatrist, Dr. Anthony Nicholson, $5,000 to help "ascertain the best way to counter any contributions by Ian Oswald which are inimical to our interests." Nicholson wrote letters to *The British Medical Journal* that branded Oswald's articles "misleading." The letters did not disclose that Nicholson was on Upjohn's payroll. Another Upjohn memo noted that Nicholson criticized Oswald's methods rather than openly advocating for Halcion so as "not to appear to be an Upjohn man."

By 1987, Oswald had produced a study documenting anxiety, weight loss, depression, and paranoia among Halcion users. He submitted a paper based on the study to the journal *Archives of General Psychiatry*. The editor, UCLA professor Daniel X. Freedman of Los Angeles, sent a copy to Upjohn for review and subsequently rejected the article, which was eventually published in another journal. Oswald later learned that Freedman, too, was a paid consultant to Upjohn.[14]

Oswald's willingness to serve as an expert witness in the Grundberg case, and the fact that his analysis helped convince British authorities to ban Halcion in October 1991,[15] appeared to persuade Upjohn that it had to do more to neutralize Oswald, that it had to open a new front in the war against the professor. It was time to unleash the power lawyers.

On January 20, 1992, *The New York Times* published an extensive front-page report headlined MAKER OF SLEEPING PILL HID DATA ON SIDE EFFECTS, RESEARCHERS SAY. The article reported some of Oswald's conclusions about Halcion and Upjohn's conduct and quoted Oswald, from an interview he gave the *Times,* as saying that Upjohn had been involved in "one long fraud" and had known of Halcion's adverse effects for twenty years but "concealed these truths from the world."

Only a few days later, Upjohn responded by suing Oswald for libel based on the article. But instead of filing suit in the United States, where Upjohn is headquartered and where almost all copies of *The New York Times* are published, the company brought its case in Britain. Why Britain? Because that country does not have an equivalent of the freedom of speech and freedom of the press clauses of the First Amendment to the United States Constitution. In Britain it is far easier to obtain injunctions and damages based on claims of defamation. The burden of proof in Britain is the reverse of that in the United States. In the United States, Upjohn would have had to prove that the alleged libelous statement was false. In Britain, Professor Oswald would be compelled to attempt to prove that his statement was true. Because approximately one hundred copies of the offending *New York Times* made it to Britain (in addition to republication of the article and Oswald's allegations in British periodicals), the British court deemed the case suitable for resolution in Britain.

Revealingly, Upjohn did not sue *The New York Times*, which would have been potentially liable as the publisher of Oswald's remarks. If the true purpose of the lawsuit was to collect damages to compensate for an egregious wrong, that would be an odd omission, perhaps even legal malpractice if the decision came from Upjohn's lawyers. After all, why would the company not sue the "deep pocket," a wealthy party like The New York Times Company, if it felt it had suffered damages because of alleged libel?

It wasn't odd, nor was it malpractice, however, if obtaining financial redress was not the true purpose for filing the lawsuit. It appears, at least, that Upjohn's motive was to punish Professor Oswald and deter him from criticizing Upjohn in Halcion lawsuits and other public forums.

After Upjohn filed its suit, Oswald cross-sued Upjohn for libel, based on the company's published allegations that he had a financial motive for his opinions and had engaged in "junk science." More claims followed: In an interview included in a British Broadcasting Corporation documentary, Oswald had contended that Upjohn official Royston Drucker lied to the U.S. FDA about what he knew about Halcion's effects. Drucker sued Oswald, but not the BBC, while Upjohn sued the BBC and one of its reporters, but not Oswald, over those statements.

On May 27, 1994, following a lengthy nonjury trial, the British judge found that every alleged claim of libel was valid—everyone had libeled everyone else. Upjohn won its case against Oswald and was awarded £25,000 ($37,500). But the court specifically noted that it had reached no conclusion as to the safety or effectiveness of Halcion. Instead, it based its judgment on the fact that Oswald was unable to prove that Upjohn had engaged in an intentional cover-up of Halcion's side effects.[16] Oswald also won *his* case against Upjohn for twice the amount the company had won against him, £50,000 ($75,000), because the court found that Oswald had not acted out of improper motive or practiced "junk science." But Oswald and the BBC lost the related suit, with Oswald ordered to pay Drucker £75,000 ($112,500) and the BBC ordered to pay Upjohn £60,000 ($90,000), because the court found that Drucker did not lie to the FDA.

Upjohn lawyers achieved their ultimate goal: keeping Professor Oswald from testifying as to his opinion about the safety of Halcion. The professor told us that as a result of the litigation, "I intend to take no new Halcion cases."[17] Who could be surprised? Few people would want to spend their retirement years locked in legal battles with an international corporate giant.

Beyond intimidating Professor Oswald out of being an expert witness, Upjohn may have had an additional motive for suing him. In a 1991 internal Upjohn memo that we obtained, the company's "Halcion Business Team" appears to recommend that litigation be used as a component of the Halcion sales strategy. The memo discusses the "business ramifications" of suing critics. Upjohn consultants and medical customers, according to the memo, were saying that Upjohn "appears unwilling to defend Halcion in the medical or public arena." Settling the Grundberg case, the memo says, exacerbated the problem. Filing suit against critics, the memo says, "would publicize our intent to defend Halcion against unjust action." It would also "encourage both the thought leaders and primary care physicians to continue writing Halcion prescriptions" and "retain physician influence on the regulatory process." There you have it in relatively plain English: The lawsuit as marketing tool.

At least two parties have petitioned the FDA to take Halcion off the market or require better warnings about its potential side effects.[18] The FDA has not yet acted on the petitions, although it has reduced recommended doses for the medication. On May 31, 1996, an FDA task force composed of outside specialists recommended that the Justice Department consider whether Upjohn committed crimes by failing to report to the agency on Halcion side effects. Although the task force found that "information . . . suggests" that Halcion is safe when prescribed as directed by the manufacturer and did not propose its removal from the market, it called for further safety assessments. Upjohn, now known as Pharmacia & Upjohn, Inc., acknowledged that "mistakes were made in the past" but said that it "has always strived to present accurate information." The company continued to insist that Halcion is safe and effective.

Meanwhile, there have been more than 130 lawsuits, according to one estimate, filed against Upjohn alleging Halcion-related injuries and deaths. Many have settled confidentially, and pending cases have protective secrecy orders firmly in place. Paris, Texas, lawyer Michael Mosher, who has brought several Halcion cases, says, "Whenever they think they are going to lose, Upjohn settles."[19] Of the cases that have gone to trial, Upjohn has won at least three and had a fourth verdict, a $1.8 million judgment for the plaintiff—a former police officer who, while under the influence of Halcion, shot a good friend on a hunting trip—reversed on appeal because the trial judge instructed the jury incorrectly.

Big corporations and their lawyers are not content to try to throw out expert witnesses and put them on the sidelines. They also want to neutralize opposing lawyers who have succeeded in exposing or punishing corporate misconduct. Such lawyers are major threats to corporate wrongdoers because they have institutional memory. They know which closets hide the most horrifying corporate skeletons. And they can take this knowledge and apply it in other cases.

To combat this situation, corporations will often try to buy off a knowledgeable lawyer with what is known as a "global settlement." In a global settlement, in return for a large payment, a lawyer will agree never to bring another case against the defendant corporation.

Proposing a global settlement can be risky from a public relations perspective if no agreement is reached. For example, Upjohn claims that Michael Mosher, attorney for plaintiffs in Halcion litigation, offered to take $15 million in return for getting out of the Halcion business. But Mosher contends that it was Upjohn who wanted to buy him off.[20] Sometimes, however, a lawyer will take the deal. During the 1960s, California attorney David Harney, worn down by General Motors' litigation tactics, agreed, as part of the settlement of more than forty cases involving the Corvair automobile, never to bring another similar suit. A more recent example involved a suit between competing product distributors. A lawyer representing the plaintiffs in the case told us that, at his client's urging, he accepted a deal under which he agreed, as part of the case settlement, to stop representing the plaintiff and become a paid adviser to the defendant. He showed us a written agreement to that effect. He was not expected, he says, to do any work for his new "client." Rather, he contends, the purpose of the agreement was to neutralize him, his experience, and his knowledge, thus reducing the threat of litigation against the defendant.

And in May 1996, Texas federal judge Paul Brown fined attorney E. Todd Tracy $2,500 and referred him to the Texas State Bar for abruptly withdrawing from representation of a client suing Chrysler Corporation. The client contended she was injured by exposure to chemicals released when her air bag deployed in a collision. According to Judge Brown's opinion, Tracy claimed that Chrysler told him that "if he wished to continue his success at getting favorable treatment for his clients from Chrysler, he should withdraw" from the air bag suit. Chrysler denied the allegation, but Judge Brown said he was concerned about "the propriety of the conduct of Chrysler and its attorneys" and urged the State Bar to investigate. Tracy appealed the fine, saying Chrysler's alleged demand left him with "the most egregious legal and ethical dilemma I have ever seen in my practice."

SEEKING JUSTICE IN DELAWARE

Powerful corporations and their lawyers have not been content to remove troublesome witnesses and opposing lawyers from the legal landscape. Sometimes, in their quest for legal dominance, they try to get judges off a particular case or even off the bench for good.

One instance where questions were raised regarding a power law firm's role in removing a judge involved 968-lawyer Skadden, Arps, Slate, Meagher & Flom, the largest-grossing U.S. law firm. Skadden came to prominence during the takeover wars of the 1980s, when many corporate CEOs and board members spent much of their time pursuing or resisting various mergers and acquisitions, sometimes at the expense of paying sufficient attention to their core business operations. Skadden was there to facilitate the action, to devise the tender offers, draft merger agreements, and litigate court disputes among corporate titans and shareholders. Skadden maintains offices in many of the world's most important cities—New York, Washington, Los Angeles, London, Paris, Moscow, Wilmington, Beijing, Hong Kong, Tokyo. . . .

Just a moment. Wilmington? Wilmington, Delaware? Why? Because for decades the Delaware legal system has been structured to favor the interests of corporate CEOs and other insiders, sometimes at the expense of outside shareholders and the public. Thus big businesses rush to incorporate in Delaware and gain the advantages of sympathetic Delaware corporate law.[21] Nearly half of the Fortune 1000, the largest industrial companies in America, are Delaware corporations. And when the big companies come to blows, particularly when two giants compete to acquire a third company, frequently they turn to the Delaware state courts for resolution. Some of the richest corporate clients rely on Skadden, Arps for representation in these hard-fought lawsuits before Delaware judges.

The governor of Delaware appoints justices to the state's highest court, the Delaware Supreme Court, for terms of twelve years. In 1977, Governor Pete DuPont created a nine-member judicial nominating commission to send lists of candidates for judgeships to the governor for consideration. The commission was established with the aim of insulating judicial selection from the political process.

In 1994, the first twelve-year term of Justice Andrew G. T. Moore II was coming to an end. He wanted to be renominated for a second term. By tradition and practice, that is what was expected. For sixty years, no sitting justice had ever been rejected for an additional term. The rules of the judicial nominating commission provided that the votes of only four of the nine members were needed to submit a sitting justice's name to the governor for renomination. In addition, although some complained that Justice Moore was an arrogant questioner of lawyers in oral argument, there was no serious debate about his competence, intelligence, or integrity.

But Justice Moore was not renominated. And some critics believe that Skadden, Arps pulled the strings that led to this extraordinary result.

One member of the judicial nominating commission is Rodman Ward, Jr., the head of Skadden, Arps's Wilmington office. Press sources contended that Ward led the effort to defeat the justice, whom the commission rejected by a 6–3 vote, one vote short of the four Moore needed to get his name to the governor.[22]

Whom did the commission recommend instead? Delaware Chancery Court Judge Carolyn Berger, who prior to being appointed to the bench in 1984 had spent five years practicing law as an associate at Skadden, Arps. Indeed, Berger and Rodman Ward had worked at another Delaware firm before leaving together to set up the Skadden, Arps Wilmington office. Although a long-standing Delaware tradition held that a state judge should not apply to take away another judge's seat, Berger sought Moore's. She later explained that "there was always the possibility that Justice Moore was not going to seek reappointment,"[23] although she did not explain why she never bothered to ask him. And she acknowledged that, at the time she submitted her application, she "made a courtesy call on [Rodman] Ward."[24]

Although the commission's guidelines, as revised in 1993 by Governor Thomas R. Carper, directed the commission to submit at least three names for each opening unless there were not enough "appropriate" candidates, the commission recommended only one candidate: Carolyn Berger. Governor Carper endorsed the recommendation and sent it to the Delaware senate. After some direct questioning, including worrying aloud by the chairman of the judiciary committee about public complaints that "Skadden Arps is locking into the Delaware Supreme Court their own people . . . that all of a sudden some law firm has got some kind of influence or stranglehold on the Delaware Supreme Court," the senate unanimously confirmed Berger.

Skadden, Arps, Governor Carper, and members of the selection commission all denied that there was a collaboration to replace Moore with Berger. Skadden, Arps leader Joseph Flom, in fact, had written to the commission urging that Moore, a friend of Flom's, be renominated. And Berger supporters stressed the judge's credentials. Defenders of the appointment also said it was time for a woman to serve on Delaware's top court, previously an all-male bastion. But the chain of events raised eyebrows in the legal community and prompted complaints from corporate investors and others who contended that Skadden, Arps was wielding too much power in the state in pursuit of its corporate clients' interests.

Ward was not the only Skadden lawyer close to the center of government power. A former Skadden associate served as Governor Carper's chief legal counsel. Another Skadden partner was a key Carper fund-raiser. And the Skadden Wilmington office provided legal advice to the 1992 Carper campaign.

Justice Moore, meanwhile, had twice joined in unanimous state Supreme Court decisions reversing Chancery Court rulings in favor of a powerful Skadden client, business executive Ronald O. Perelman. Perelman's Revlon Corporation gave $1,200, the maximum contribution, to Carper's 1992 campaign. James Cotter, whose company opposed Perelman in other Delaware litigation, suggested that Moore's removal might send a powerful signal to his former judicial colleagues: "If you live in that close-knit, insular environment, and you see a Supreme Court judge get defrocked . . . the message is clear: 'Hey, watch out! You be nice to Skadden, Arps.' "[25]

Delaware Attorney General Charles M. Oberly III said that, although Justice Moore could be a "sharp" questioner, other judges could be harsher. He surmised that Justice Moore had "stepped on the toes of a higher echelon—some of the higher-priced corporate lawyers." William Prickett, an attorney well known in the state, cautioned Governor Carper that "the perception is widely held that the important function of nominating judicial officers for the Supreme Court of Delaware has been subverted to achieve your political ends."[26]

After refusing to comment on the events for nearly a year, Justice Moore told *The New York Times*, "The citizens of Delaware and the corporate community should have grave concern about the circumstances that prevailed in the selection of state judges. If the process was designed to insulate the courts from political influence, unfortunately it does not appear to have done so."[27] Justice Moore told us he had no comment beyond what he told the *Times*. (We also requested comment from Justice Berger. Her clerk asked that we state the topics we wished to address in writing. We did, summarizing the matters described above. Justice Berger had no comment.)

Whatever occurred behind the scenes—whether or not Skadden, Arps lawyers deliberately placed the firm's interest ahead of the public interest in participating in the judicial selection process—the case illustrates a common phenomenon that goes beyond mere appearances: the ability of a wealthy, well-connected law firm to place its members and allies into the centers of government power.

In July 1995, critics of Skadden's role saw their worst fears borne out: The Delaware Supreme Court, now minus Justice Moore, reversed course to issue a ruling favorable to Skadden, Arps client Ronald Perelman in a key case.

Cinerama, Inc. v. *Technicolor, Inc.* concerned Perelman's 1983 acquisition of Technicolor, the movie-print-making company. Cinerama, a shareholder in Technicolor, claimed that Technicolor's board of directors had agreed to sell the company to Perelman at too low a price and without adequate deliberation. (Perelman sold Technicolor to Carlton Communications in 1988, reportedly for about five times what he paid for it.[28]) In October 1993, a three-judge Supreme Court panel, consisting of Justice Moore and Justices Henry Horsey and Randy Holland, agreed, ruling, in an opinion by Horsey, that the directors had not lived up to their duties. They sent the case back to the trial court for reconsideration.[29] But the trial judge, Chancellor William Allen, apparently miffed, essentially reaffirmed his earlier decision in favor of Technicolor.

Cinerama went back to the Supreme Court, expecting it to overrule Chancellor Allen again. Horsey and Holland were again on the panel, joined, with Moore gone, by Superior Court Judge Henry du Pont Ridgely. (Justice Berger had a conflict of interest due to her

Skadden connection.) But the court this time ruled that Technicolor's directors had acted properly in approving the deal with Perelman.[30] *Corporate Counsel Magazine* (CCM) quoted a "prominent Delaware expert" as saying, "It doesn't take a genius to see that the only thing that changed between the two Supreme Court rulings was the removal of Moore from the court. That fact lies behind this latest, otherwise inexplicable opinion." CCM reported that Moore was the "driving force" behind the October 1993 opinion and that he was greatly dismayed by the reversal.[31]

THE LANDLORD, THE TENANT, THE JUDGE, AND HER HUSBAND

Of course, the political process is not the only means power lawyers consider to push aside pesky judges who rebuff their clients. Chapter 1 revealed how tobacco industry lawyers managed to persuade a federal appellate court to remove from their case Judge H. Lee Sarokin, who had strongly condemned industry misdeeds and ordered disclosure of industry documents.

Another corporate lawyer attempt to remove a judge occurred in a case previously discussed in Chapter 4, the dispute between Louisiana landowners Lorraine McGuire and Jack Valley and their polluting tenant, the giant Fina Oil and Chemical Company. Shortly after the judge in that case, Edith Brown Clement, held Fina and one of its lawyers in contempt of court and imposed sanctions for discovery abuses, the company's in-house lawyer, Cullen M. Godfrey, hired *the judge's husband's law firm*, Locke, Purnell, Rain and Harrell, to represent the company in the case. That created an inherent conflict of interest, and Judge Clement announced that she would recuse herself from further involvement in the lawsuit.

Godfrey insists that the purpose of the hiring was not to force the judge to recuse herself, although he admits he knew that would be the consequence: "The firm I had hired was not doing a good job, and I felt they were responsible for [the controversy over the discovery abuses]. I felt we needed a new attorney. The firm I often use had a conflict. I tried Wilmer, Cutler & Pickering, but we mutually agreed that they were not the best choice. There are not a lot of good environmental litigators around. Fina had once been represented by a Dallas firm with a good environmental litigator. They had a Louisiana branch. They analyzed the case and I was ready to hire them, when I was asked who the judge was. That was the first I found out that the judge's husband was even a lawyer, much less a lawyer in the firm I wanted to hire in the case."

But once he knew the facts, we asked, wasn't it then wrong to proceed to retain Judge Clement's husband's firm? Godfrey responded, "In
remote hindsight that is easier to call than it was at the time. I have
never had a litigation so out-of-control in my life as that case. I was
under a terrible time constraint. I was down to a precious few alternatives. We knew that there was an ethical issue. We researched the law
and concluded that it was not an unauthorized substitution, even
though it would result in the disqualification of Judge Clement. It
turned out we were mistaken."[32]

Indeed, the recusal did not stick. McGuire and Valley, noting that
Judge Clement had not only ruled against Fina on discovery issues but
also had decided against Fina on a number of substantive issues in the
case before trial, charged that Fina was simply hoping that a new judge
would bring them better luck. They asked the court to disqualify the
Locke, Purnell firm from representing Fina and allow Judge Clement
back on the case. On January 19, 1994, one of Judge Clement's colleagues, United States District Judge Peter Beer, granted that request.[33]
He wrote:

> I've got to say that it is pretty hard to imagine a scenario where
> disqualification [of a law firm] would be more justified than
> here. This litigation wasn't going well for Fina when it got rid
> of Judge Clement. . . . Any party finding itself in [Fina's] cir-
> cumstances would want to try another judge. . . .
>
> Locke, Purnell contends that prior representation of Fina
> in environmental matters was its primary motivation in ac-
> cepting employment by Fina. I find this to be a sham. Locke,
> Purnell clearly was aware that this case was before Judge
> Clement's section and understood exactly what action this
> outstanding judicial officer would take, thus confronted.

So, Fina was chastised for its brazen gambit, and Judge Clement was
back on the case. But, as often happens, the corporation and its power
lawyers found a silver lining. Their maneuver forced another round of
discovery, leading, by Judge Beer's description, to "voluminous depositions . . . several thousand pages of testimony" as to whether Fina hired
Locke, Purnell primarily to force Judge Clement's recusal. This discovery delayed the case and forced the parties to spend more on legal fees,
factors that, time and time again, favor corporate defendants like Fina.

Most corporate lawyer attempts to remove offending judges from
cases are less imaginative than the approach Fina tried. Normally, the
approach is more straightforward: Insist that the judge is biased against

your client. An example is General Motors' successful removal of a trial judge in one of the lawsuits involving its pickup trucks.

THE CASE OF THE JUDGE AND HIS JEST

As we discussed in Chapter 3, many of the lawsuits involving 1973-to-1987-model-year GM trucks have become bogged down in discovery disputes and allegations by lawyers for plaintiffs that GM and its attorneys have obstructed discovery or destroyed evidence harmful to GM's defense. One such case is *Cameron v. General Motors*, filed in April 1993 in the United States District Court for the District of South Carolina.

The case arose on May 5, 1990, in Summerfield, Kansas, where two brothers, Mark and Steven Cameron, were driving a 1977 Chevrolet pickup. The truck collided with another vehicle, turned over, and burst into flames. Both brothers suffered serious burns, and Steven Cameron lost his right arm.

Once again GM hired Kirkland & Ellis, including former federal judge and solicitor general Kenneth Starr, and King & Spalding, including former U.S. Attorney General Griffin Bell. And once again the victims turned to Jim Butler's firm.

Butler alleged that GM hid crash test results and destroyed documents that proved that its pickups were unsafe. Specifically, he contended that in 1981 and 1982, GM brought young attorneys from different law firms around the country to Detroit and paid their salaries, housing costs, and other expenses while the lawyers reviewed and systematically purged GM files of documents that showed GM's knowledge of the defects in its pickup trucks. GM staffers allegedly nicknamed these attorneys the "Fire Babies."

Among the documents that the Camerons' lawyers claimed were missing, in addition to safety tests, were GM Safety Review Board meeting minutes from 1970 to 1971, the period in which GM officials would have discussed the design of the 1973-model-year trucks; depositions from various relevant cases; supporting documents; and other such paperwork.

Former GM attorneys admitted in deposition testimony that in 1981–82 GM did gather about a dozen attorneys from around the country who did nothing but search through files and collect GM fuel tank documents. The attorneys filled out a form for each document that they reviewed, identifying the document and providing other pertinent data. GM has admitted that these forms were discarded. GM initially claimed that the lawyers reviewed documents pertaining only to cars, but officials later admitted in deposition that the lawyers also reviewed truck files. But GM insisted that the lawyers were simply making a good faith effort to review documents in order to comply with discovery in pending lawsuits and were not involved in destroying evidence.

But at least one witness appeared to contradict GM's claim. In November 1991, retired GM engineer Ted Kashmerick gave a deposition in an employment dispute between GM and its former employee Ronald Elwell (a case discussed above). Kashmerick's testimony was recorded on videotape because he was seriously ill at the time. (He has since died.) Kashmerick testified that in the early 1980s—the same period when, the Camerons' lawyers contended, the Fire Babies were about the task of purging damaging GM documents—he had discarded numerous documents, dating as far back as 1953, that concerned the design of GM trucks:

> My problem was I stored too many documents . . . The sales department and the legal department always came to me for information. . . .
>
> What I did was get rid of every damn thing I had in my files in my office. I even had the guys in this group [legal group] and one of the ladies that worked in there come to my office, and they sat down and took my desk and chair and went through my file cabinets and they took every damn thing they thought was a problem. . . . To the best of my knowledge they took everything they wanted and it was shredded. It's long gone. . . .
>
> The legal staff was involved in some kind of lawsuit when they went through. I told them, "You're responsible for throwing that away, not me." Well, they did, they went through there and cleaned them out. . . .
>
> The papers were put in a great big trash bin outside my office in the hallway, and the guy was given strict instructions by the legal people, take those downstairs and put them in the shredder, and we are going to take these with us. They had two briefcases full of documents they took with them. . . .
>
> There was one other reason [they did this] and I think it was the main one: They wanted them, they wanted to go through them and see if there was anything they could use in lawsuits they were working on. They didn't just cover one lawsuit . . . they were working on five or six or eight or ten of them. . . . They were doing it to a lot of fellas, a lot of people

who were there. They were concerned that some of the stuff could be detrimental because of the way it was worded.

All in all, Kashmerick testified, five or six filing cabinets full of documents were reviewed and, but for two briefcases of material, all the documents were shredded.

GM argued that Kashmerick's testimony was flawed and should be disregarded because GM had not cross-examined him on the issue of document destruction, since that was not the central issue in the Elwell employment case.[34] But the fact that the deposition might not be admissible at trial did not mean it was untrue. Kashmerick had no apparent motivation to lie. He wasn't involved in a dispute with GM.

Judge G. Ross Anderson, Jr., presiding in the Cameron case, learned about the Kashmerick deposition and other allegations of document destruction. "I'm going to get to the bottom of all the facts in this case," he warned GM attorneys in court on December 10, 1993, when the parties met to argue the Camerons' motion to compel discovery of GM documents. "This business of deception is not going to fly."[35] Judge Anderson appeared to take a very dim view of improper discovery tactics, whether from plaintiffs or defendants. Indeed, in the Cameron case, he had previously chastised both plaintiffs and defendants for their wrangling over discovery and, in fact, had ordered the plaintiffs' lawyers to pay a $50,000 sanction for bringing an improper discovery motion.

Judge Anderson vowed that if he determined that GM had destroyed documents, "the whole world would know about it" and that he would take severe action. Similarly, if the charges were frivolous, the judge promised the plaintiffs' lawyers that they would regret having made them. The judge felt the charges were so serious and so important that it was a "matter of national concern." If GM was found to be innocent, he stated, "the whole world should know about it and General Motors should be exonerated."

But exactly one week before the December 10 hearing at which he warned the lawyers to shoot straight, Judge Anderson had made public remarks of his own that would change the course of the litigation. Attending a South Carolina Trial Lawyers Association–sponsored seminar for personal injury plaintiff lawyers, he delivered comments about computer animation and the rules of evidence. Jim Butler, one of the lawyers representing the Camerons against General Motors, was present. Butler also made a presentation at the seminar, but Judge Anderson did not attend. Judge Anderson had similarly attended seminars sponsored by corporate defense lawyers. During his speech, Judge Anderson made some mildly jesting comments at the expense of defense lawyers, including this one:[36]

> I just got back from the defense trial lawyers meeting in Sea Island, Georgia. You know, most of those fellows are pretty nice. They really are. . . . But while we were down there, you know, we all accept the fact that fish is brain food. You know what they serve three times a day at the defense lawyers? Whale. The only exercise some of them get is stretching the truth. . . .

This mild ribbing and the judge's attendance at the seminar would become the basis for a defense motion to throw him off the case.

GM did not move immediately for recusal; it waited until after Judge Anderson's ruling. On January 4, 1994, Judge Anderson ruled against GM. The Camerons would be able to conduct further discovery on their claims of document destruction. Only then, on January 18, 1994, did GM file its motion for recusal, accusing Judge Anderson of "continuing, pervasive and manifest bias."

One month later, the judge filed a fifty-nine-page opinion.[37] He began by recounting the progress of the litigation:

> This case has been primarily a discovery war of unprecedented magnitude laced with acrimony bordering on open hostility between the disputatious attorneys. To appreciate the extent of the tortured history, there have been a total of sixty-nine (69) motions filed. . . . Hardly a document has been produced without a claim of privilege. Literally thousands of documents have been reviewed which has necessitated time consuming court hearings and countless hours of document examination by the court. Paper accumulated to date fills three (3) cabinet drawers in my chambers, yet discovery is still in its infancy. Both parties have been repeatedly warned against filing frivolous discovery motions. The defendants have been non-responsive and evasive in practically all discovery requests. . . .

Then Judge Anderson discussed the remarks that General Motors considered disqualifying:

> As a frequent speaker, I have found that humor is an effective educational tool. By mischaracterizing statements patently intended to be humorous, the defendant attempts to cast doubt

upon the ability of this court to render a fair and unbiased trial. The defendant literally cuts and pastes statements from different portions of the speech, strategically placing them together in a manner designed to make the innocuous appear sinister. . . . The defendant attempts to fabricate "bias or prejudice" against defendants and defense attorneys by pulling sentences out of context and ignoring the humor that was intended . . .

The judge then addressed the merits of the discovery motions:

A review of the thousands of documents in this case including *in camera* reviews of documents for which an attorney-client privilege was asserted[38] reveals a substantial likelihood that perhaps perjury and systematic destruction of documents involving gross misconduct by General Motors' regional counsel occurred. Evidence of the commission of such activity by and with the knowledge of these General Motors regional counsel would defeat the attorney-client and work-product privilege[39] asserted by General Motors.

Judge Anderson found that, as a matter of law and fact, he was not prejudiced against defense lawyers or General Motors and that his attendance at the seminar and remarks given there did not constitute prejudice. However, the judge acknowledged that legal ethics required him to avoid not only actual impropriety but even the appearance of impropriety. Bowing to this principle, Judge Anderson recused himself from the case, stating:

Public confidence in the impartiality and fairness of the judiciary must forever remain inviolate. This concept transcends all other considerations. Therefore, I find that a reasonable person could possibly view my mere appearance on the same legal education program with Mr. Butler and Mr. Few, attorneys for plaintiffs in a case pending before me, as compromising the fairness and impartiality of the presiding judge. Now, therefore, for this reason and this reason only, and further out of a super abundance of caution, I hereby recuse myself from further participation in these cases.

GM's lawyers had won the round. Judge Anderson was out of the case. As his last act, he vacated his previous orders concerning discovery. The plaintiffs were almost back to square one. They would have to attempt to educate a new judge about the nature of the discovery disputes, the importance of the Fire Babies, and other matters of dispute that had already consumed years of time and effort.

Postscript: On November 4, 1994, the new judge, Charles H. Haden II, issued his own order, finding some documents to be privileged, but substantially reinstating Judge Anderson's original decision, including authorizing the depositions of corporate lawyers alleged to be Fire Babies and rejecting GM's claim of privilege over key documents.[40]

GM responded by quickly settling the Cameron case. Once again, the terms are confidential.

So the Cameron case was put quietly to rest, as were the Moseley and Bishop suits against GM described in this chapter and Chapter 3. But 4.7 million 1973–87 GM trucks (out of 10 million manufactured), with gas tanks ready to ignite in the event of collision, remain on the road. Such are the costs of the games power lawyers play. They are measured not only in the months and years of justice delayed and the waste of judicial resources but sometimes also in the lives of people placed unnecessarily at risk of death or serious injury. Veteran auto-safety expert witness Byron Bloch says that efforts to remedy defects like the placement of GM truck gas tanks "are usually delayed ten to twenty years. The primary reasons for this time-lag are litigation delaying tactics, confidential settlements, and protective orders and other such corporate law strategies."[41]

Ted Kashmerick knew too much. So GM tried to suppress the deceased man's candid recollections. Ronald Elwell knew too much. So GM sought to keep him from testifying even where courts had issued subpoenas demanding his appearance. Truly, one of a major corporation's biggest nightmares is the emergence of an employee who blows the whistle on unsafe, improper, or illegal company practices. Corporations seeking to hide the truth and avoid embarrassment or punishment have gone to great lengths to neutralize corporate whistle-blowers before they can tell their stories of corporate misconduct to government agencies or the press. This chapter concludes with two such cases.

CRUSHING THE ETHICAL WHISTLE-BLOWERS

They are unsung heroes, people who serve as the conscience of American enterprise and government. They expose misconduct by defense contractors, oil companies, airlines, auto companies, insurance companies, food and drug makers, utilities, and government. These whistle-blowers, usually low- or mid-level employees of giant corporations or enormous government bureaucracies, are sometimes the only protection the public has against threats to health, safety, fiscal integrity, and fundamental fairness.

But whistle-blowing often extracts a very heavy price. Whistle-blowers can face intimidation, harassment, firing for frivolous or bogus reasons, or threats of physical harm to themselves or their families. They are cheated out of promotions or job awards, blackballed from their industries, or otherwise confronted with the prospect of financial ruin. Fellow workers ostracize them under pressure from management to "teach them a lesson" or because managers have told them that the whistle-blowers' activities threaten their jobs. Sometimes, their former employers undertake a vendetta to destroy their livelihoods even after they have left their jobs. (Sometimes, however, citizen organizations, government, and/or the media acknowledge their courage and contributions.)

Whistle-blowers who refuse to back down to such pressures often seek redress in the courts or through administrative proceedings. When they seek such help, they sometimes come face-to-face with power lawyers, who may already have been working closely with employers, advising them how to legally "get" the whistle-blowers, or who may use hardball litigation tactics to stonewall any legal action brought by the whistle-blowers.

THE CASE OF THE NUCLEAR WATCHDOG

Over twenty-one years, Paul Blanch had built a successful career as an engineer with Connecticut's Northeast Utilities (NU). He worked on the firm's nuclear power plant operations and moved up through the ranks to the position of supervisor of instrumentation and control engineering. Blanch also served on nuclear power plant safety commissions and enjoyed the esteem of his employer and the nuclear power professional community.

But Blanch's fortunes were to change when he came upon a serious safety hazard. In 1988, he concluded that an electronic transmitter used to measure crucial temperatures and pressures in one of Northeast's nuclear reactors, as well as in other U.S. nuclear plants, had a propensity to malfunction and do so without giving any signal of failure. As a result, control room operators might receive incorrect readings without knowing anything was wrong. He has likened it to "an airplane altimeter that tells the pilot the plane is at 30,000 feet no matter what the actual altitude."[42] The problem, he believed, was so bad that a meltdown could be in process and the operator might not be aware of it. According to Blanch, this problem with the transmitter, made by Rosemount, Inc., of Eden Prairie, Minnesota, "increased the risk of failure by a projected 6800%!"[43]

Blanch notified the Nuclear Regulatory Commission (NRC), the federal agency charged with regulating the nation's nuclear power plants, about his discovery. The deadly consequences of a meltdown being what they are, one would have thought that NU chairman and chief executive officer William B. Ellis and the NRC would have been extremely grateful to Blanch. But in testimony that is typical for its depiction of the mistreatment to which many whistle-blowers are subjected, Blanch told a United States Senate committee in December 1991 how he became a victim of on-the-job harassment, intimidation, and interference with professional activities and growth:

> As a result of identifying this sensor failure to NU management and the NRC, I have been subjected to an internal audit conducted by NU internal auditing personnel using false credentials, had subordinates suspended without a fair and impartial hearing, suffered poor performance reviews and was chastised by my management with false accusations which they refused to support. Further, I had outside contract work cancelled due to direct influence by an NU Vice President and was otherwise "black-balled" in the nuclear industry.

Faced with these retaliatory actions by his employer, in 1989 Blanch filed a complaint with the U.S. Department of Labor, which sustained his claims that NU had subjected him to improper treatment in retaliation for his whistle-blowing. But NU appealed the Labor Department decision, and, according to Blanch's testimony, the utility's outside lawyers began to subject him to harassment.

In January 1990, NU and Blanch reached a settlement of his claims. The agreement is confidential. However, in a February 1990 letter to an NRC official, Blanch asserted that he did not sign the agreement "due to its terms, but . . . only due to the extreme personal financial pressure imposed upon me by NU. Had I the financial resources, I would have continued my complaint against NU." In the letter, Blanch estimated that pursuing the case against NU would have cost him $100,000 in legal fees.

Thus Blanch found himself in a typical situation: Companies with massive resources direct their lawyers to financially exhaust whistle-blowing employees by waging a war of attrition, using every legal option—litigation, appeal, and administrative processes—until finally, the whistle-blower faces the prospect of the poorhouse, which forces a settlement or capitulation. "You have an individual who has been terminated and unemployed now fighting a legal battle with his own funds against a company or utility with unlimited dollars who can hire the best, most expensive lawyers in the country," Blanch told us. "He doesn't have the money to pursue the case because of all the money being thrown against him."[44] To add insult to injury, at tax time the employer deducts its legal fees as a cost of doing business, while the whistle-blower may receive no such relief.

Blanch's lawyer, Ernest C. Hadley of Wareham, Massachusetts, who has represented other whistle-blowers, agrees with this dismal view. "Whistle-blowing almost always involves very acrimonious litigation. You are going to see objections, motions, appeals, as well as allegations of misconduct and unacceptable performance. In many ways, it's like divorce court. It gets very ugly."[45]

According to one published report, NU has spent more than $10 million on legal fees fighting various whistle-blowers.[46] And who pays the lawyers to battle those attempting to heighten the safety of nuclear power plants? Ultimately, consumers are the ones, when they pay their utility bills.

Corporations mount such expensive, elaborate defenses in order to force the whistle-blower to shut up and settle. The settlement agreements are almost always strictly confidential as to terms, often preventing the whistle-blower from speaking out against the former employer.

This seems to be the scenario that ensnared Paul Blanch. His agreement appears to prevent him from public criticism of NU. A June 1993 letter from NU attorney Nicholas S. Reynolds, of the national power law firm Winston & Strawn, advised Blanch that his settlement agreement with NU "does place limitations on your ability to disparage or criticize the Company and its employees in a public way . . ." Indeed, in speaking with us, Blanch refused to criticize NU or the company's treatment of him.

But Blanch spoke to us generally about his experiences: "It has been demonstrated that everything that I contended was, in fact, true. Yet today, if someone asked me whether to blow the whistle or play along, I would tell them to think twice and consider keeping their mouths shut because whistle-blowing extracts such a terrible emotional and financial price."

Blanch resigned from NU in February 1993. In July 1993 he told a Senate committee that, as a result of his whistle-blowing, "I have been isolated by the industry that I have given my entire professional career to. There is virtually no chance that I will ever work in my chosen field again."[47] He has filed a lawsuit against Rosemount, maker of the transmitter, contending that it pressured NU to go after him because of the company's fears that its prior knowledge of the problem would be uncovered. Rosemount denies the charge. As this is written, that matter remains in litigation.

In May 1993, the NRC determined that the Rosemount transmitter problem and other safety violations raised by Blanch were significant, that the company wrongfully retaliated against Blanch for pressing his concerns, and that the company improperly delayed reporting a problem that could have caused accidents at reactors across the country. It fined NU $100,000.[48] The utility issued a lengthy rebuttal disputing the agency's findings but agreed to pay the fine.[49]

With corporate executives and lawyers able to exercise such power over the lives and careers of individuals, and with corporate lawyers ready, willing, and able to engage in litigation tactics that have the effect—and often the design—of emotionally exhausting and financially draining the whistle-blower and his or her family, it is a tribute to human courage that there are any whistle-blowers at all.[50]

HARASSING WHISTLE-BLOWERS— COURTESY OF UNCLE SAM

The United States government often enters into contracts with the private sector to perform vital government services. These contracts usually receive little public scrutiny. In fact, most citizens are probably unaware of many expensive deals made in their name.

Incredibly, sometimes your tax dollars are used to pay the legal fees for private companies, working as government contractors, in their litigation battles against conscientious whistle-blowers. One example is the saga of Ed Bricker. In 1977, he went to work at the Hanford Nuclear Reservation in Washington State.[51] Hanford processes plutonium for the production of nuclear weapons. The federal facility is administered by the Department of Energy (DOE). Under contract with the government, Rockwell International Corporation operated portions of Hanford from 1977 until 1987, when Westinghouse Electric Corporation took over these contracts. That same year, Bricker reported what he considered safety violations at the plant. Instead of receiving a medal, he got the fight of his life.

Private DOE contractors at Hanford and at other such facilities don't have to worry about the legal costs associated with squaring off in court against whistle-blower employees. Why? The United States government pays their legal fees incurred in disputes with third parties, such as employees. This indemnification scheme for Department of Energy contractors costs taxpayers approximately $30 million in legal fees and costs each year.[52]

How can this be? How can DOE contractors use federal funds to battle workers who report unsafe conditions, when such reporting is required by DOE's own regulations? To attract private sector companies to run its nuclear weapons programs, the DOE enters into deals that specifically protect contract companies from certain liabilities, meaning that in addition to paying these company's legal fees, the government may be responsible for money damages arising from a company's improper operations. The DOE accepts such a bad deal in part because it fears that, if contractors were responsible for their own legal costs and liabilities, they might frequently turn around and sue the government, claiming that government negligence or misconduct caused the harms alleged. By assuming the costs up front, DOE hopes to maintain greater control of litigation decisions.

Unfortunately, the way this tends to work in real life is that the DOE allows its contractors to decide whether to defend the case, to choose the lawyers (subject to approval by the DOE), and to exert tremendous influence over decisions about the whistle-blower's case, e.g., whether to settle or go to trial. Then, the government rubber-stamps the company's legal bills.[53] This often forces whistle-blowers into protracted litigation, fighting a company that wants to beat them into the ground and that has little incentive to quit, because the taxpayers, including, of course, the whistle-blowers themselves, are paying the bills. Meanwhile, whistle-blowers frequently must pay their own legal fees, even as they risk losing their jobs. This was the reality facing anyone at Hanford who considered blowing the whistle on safety violations.

Hanford has been a busy place since World War II, when it processed the plutonium in the atomic bomb that the United States dropped on the Japanese city of Nagasaki. Plutonium processing was a growth industry throughout the Cold War, but business really took off in the early 1980s, when President Reagan decided to massively increase military spending and accelerate the growth of the U.S. nuclear arsenal.

Bricker, a third-generation Hanford worker, helped restart an old processing facility brought back on-line when business expanded. Soon thereafter, however, he became disturbed by what he perceived to be acute problems, problems that he believed threatened the health and safety of Hanford workers.

Bricker could have kept his mouth shut and collected his pay-check. He had done that once before—with tragic consequences. He recalls, "Back in 1977, I had a buddy killed, literally cut in half, due to a safety problem I knew about but which I had done nothing to cure because I was concerned about job pressures. After my friend's funeral, I vowed that would not happen again."

Bricker's friend died in a crane accident, not due to nuclear material. This time, however, Bricker observed what he thought were safety deficiencies that could have exposed workers directly to plutonium, one of the most dangerous carcinogens known to humankind. "The area where we worked had alarms that would warn us if we were exposed to radiation," Bricker reports. "But the alarms weren't working correctly. They were being set off merely by the background radiation of concrete. So, they were often disconnected because they had become such a nuisance."[54]

If Bricker was correct, there was an insidious problem. Workers, exposed to unsafe levels of radiation, would not be aware of the contamination. And Bricker's concern about the disconnected alarms was heightened when he discovered an additional hazard. Hanford workers observed plutonium processing and used insulated gloves to reach into sealed processing areas at so-called hood windows. Bricker concluded that these windows were leaking air, thus exposing workers to increased radiation risks. He was alarmed. "Can you imagine hearing the hiss of air that may contain specks of plutonium, whistling around you?" he asks.

That wasn't all Bricker believed he had discovered. "I noticed that the actual layout of the plant did not match the schematics. Over a period of thirty years, there had been no configuration control to make sure that the updating process matched the drawings." That meant that the actual layout of the plant would not have been recorded. The company had even allowed the governor of Washington to drive through a contaminated area while on an official visit without warning him of the danger.

The last straw for Bricker came one day when he walked into the plant control room and there was no plant operator at the controls. "The only person in the room was an engineer. He told me that he had things under control. I asked him what he would do if a sudden problem developed, and it became clear to me that he didn't know what to do in an emergency. It was as if the whole plant was on auto-pilot. That was when I decided to nail my 'Ten Theses' to the church door."

Bricker complained about the safety deficiencies he had observed. "I went up the chain of command and got nowhere." So he decided to take his complaints to *The Seattle Times*, which reported them. "That," he says, "is when the campaign of harassment began."

In the wake of his public statements, Bricker says, he was subjected to myriad forms of intimidation, some minor, some more serious. He was denied good work assignments. He believes his phone was tapped. His wife began to receive obscene phone calls, but only when Bricker was at work. "I was called a nitpicker and a troublemaker. I was called a 'government mole.' I was told that if I didn't stop complaining, the facility would be shut down and everyone would lose their jobs. I began to receive poor work performances. I was threatened with firing for being two minutes late. I was ordered to see a psychologist who wanted to know about my nervous breakdown, when in fact, I had never had one. My security clearance was threatened. Petitions were circulated with management's active involvement stating that I had mental health problems. The icing on the cake came when my air equipment was sabotaged that allowed me to go safely into contaminated areas. I held my breath and ran out of the facility and passed out. If I had breathed the air I could have contracted lung cancer."[55] Tom Carpenter, an attorney for the nonprofit Government Accountability Project who eventually became Bricker's lawyer, concluded that Bricker's claims of safety risks were fully warranted.[56]

Bricker filed a formal complaint against Rockwell and Westinghouse with the Department of Labor, contending he was being harassed on the job because he had engaged in legally protected whistle-blower activities. After an extensive investigation, John R. Spear of the Occupational Safety and Health Administration, an agency within the Labor Department, concluded:

> There is . . . little question that Bricker suffered adverse employment action. He received negative performance appraisals; he was directed to be evaluated by a DOE contractor psychologist on three occasions under the perceived threat of losing security clearance and job; he received written disciplinary actions for alleged misconduct; he was the subject of a continuing investigation by contractor security officials; and, a decidedly hostile work environment developed between Bricker and his managers and among fellow employees. . . . Based on the above it is concluded by this investigator that Bricker was discriminated against by the Rockwell Hanford company in retaliation for his safety and health complaints filed with his management, Congress and the DOE. The reprisals

were in the form of an investigation by security officials of his protected activities which were designed to result in his termination. . . . There was some carry-over of these hostilities after Westinghouse took over the contract due to the continuation of lower level managers, but it appears that Westinghouse management has attempted to correct the situation.

Bricker contends that if Westinghouse upper management did indeed attempt to correct the problem, their efforts were short-lived. For, while the Labor Department report led to an agreement by Westinghouse Hanford officials to cease all harassment, Bricker says the intimidation continued unabated.

"Westinghouse was ordered to purge all incorrect appraisals that had been made because of my labor actions," Bricker recalls. "When I found my requests for transfer hampered because of my reputation as a whistle-blower, I asked to see my files. Lo and behold, nothing had been purged." Bricker also reports that the harassment continued. "I was denied good worker awards I had earned. I was still under continual scrutiny. I was forced to take yet another medical and psychological examination, which did not result in my losing my clearance. The company was thumbing its nose at the Department of Labor and sending the message to other workers that it did not pay to blow the whistle because the government could not protect you."[57]

Finally, after suffering years of abuse, for the good of his family, his health, and his own peace of mind, Bricker gave the officials of Hanford what they so dearly wanted: He quit and took a job working for the State of Washington. Perhaps fittingly, he now is a state regulator overseeing some of Hanford's health and safety practices.

In August 1990, Bricker brought a lawsuit in Yakima, Washington, federal district court against both Rockwell and Westinghouse alleging that the companies engaged in a campaign of illegal harassment because of his legally protected whistle-blowing activities. Despite the earlier Department of Labor finding in his favor, and despite substantial reporting by the media on Hanford's campaign of harassment,[58] Rockwell and Westinghouse, with the support of the DOE, denied the charges and fought Bricker every step of the way.

Here's where the corporate lawyers come in. According to materials supplied by the DOE under the Freedom of Information Act, the agency paid two Seattle law firms, Helsell, Fetterman, Martin, Todd & Hokanson, and Davis Wright Tremain, more than $1 million in taxpayer money for legal fees and expenses to fight Bricker's claim. What makes that especially outrageous is that Bricker offered to settle his entire dispute with the companies for $65,000, which would have done little more than cover his legal fees, but the DOE rejected this offer, according to Bricker's lawyer, as "outrageously high"!

How could these law firms spend so much money? First, Westinghouse and Rockwell appear to have authorized, and the DOE appears to have approved, a full-bore, all-out, spare-no-expense litigation. Then, the company representatives merely sent the legal bills on to the general counsel at the Richland, Washington, DOE office for rubber-stamp approval, after which the DOE accommodatingly wrote a check.

We reviewed the lawyer billing sheets charged in the Bricker litigation. They reveal that each month, the two Seattle firms billed the taxpayers (through Westinghouse or Rockwell) between $18,000 and $45,000. Thus, two or three months' worth of lawyering more than equaled the entire amount for which Bricker had been willing to settle his case. The bills show how many hours corporate lawyers, billing at high hourly rates, are willing to devote to cases, with inordinate amounts of time spent on reviewing records, pleadings, correspondence, deposition notices, responses to discovery, writing memoranda, revising memoranda, conferring, telephoning, etc.

That isn't all. Whatever the propriety of the specific bills submitted by the law firms fighting Bricker, recent analysis by Congress's investigative arm, the General Accounting Office (GAO), indicates that DOE has repeatedly paid more for outside legal fees than federal regulations permit or the market would require. On July 13, 1994, Victor S. Rezendes, director of Energy and Science Issues, Resources, Community and Economic Division, for the GAO, told a congressional committee:

> We found that DOE is paying significantly higher costs than guidelines allow. For example:
>
> —The Federal corporations [government operated corporations such as the FDIC] require that discounts on fees for legal services be sought. . . . DOE does not require that contractors seek discounts for outside legal fees.
>
> —The federal corporations' criteria limit document duplication to $0.08 per page. All of the law firms retained by DOE contractors were charging more—as much as $0.25 per page. This could be significant, as duplication costs for one firm over a 3 year period were over $175,000.
>
> —The federal corporations' criteria require that facsimile transmissions—faxes—be billed at actual cost. DOE is reimbursing some contractors' law firms as much as $1.75 per page

plus telephone charges for faxes. For one firm, the charges for faxes totaled over $48,000 during a 3 year period.

—The federal corporations' criteria limit travel costs to coach airfare, moderately priced hotels, and federal per diem rates for meals. Travel costs reimbursed by DOE were significantly higher. For example, two firms billed first-class airfare for their senior partners. Additionally, some firms billed for meals costing almost $100 per person.

(These kinds of billing practices, shocking as they seem, will become quite familiar to the reader in Chapter 7.) As to the Bricker matter, the GAO says that the Richland DOE chief counsel approved bills "on the basis of billing summaries" which "lacked the specificity that would enable a reviewer to determine what the costs actually were for and their appropriateness."

We recently asked the DOE whether it had tried to recover any of the overcharges documented in the GAO report. In August 1995, the DOE provided a written response that stated in part:

> In the summer of 1994, DOE made an attempt to recover some of the overcharges billed by contractors to the Department. In those instances where charges were clearly unallowable under the provisions of [federal regulations], costs were disallowed or restitution was made. However, most of the overcharges involved past costs or activities for which the Department had issued no clear guidance to contractors. In those instances minimal or no recovery was made.

The DOE also reports that it has implemented reforms to control litigation costs in the future.

But what of the more fundamental issue—government backing of corporate legal battles against whistle-blowers? President Clinton's energy secretary, Hazel R. O'Leary, seems to take a somewhat more whistle-blower-friendly approach than her predecessors from the Reagan and Bush administrations. She committed the department to protecting whistle-blowers and asked her subordinates to develop policies to ensure such protection. In April 1994, DOE official Thomas F. McBride wrote in a letter to Ed Bricker:

> As you may know . . . Secretary O'Leary set up a working group to make specific recommendations to carry out the Whistleblower Protection commitments she has made. . . . I

can tell you that [the group's report] calls for an expeditious review of pending cases, such as yours, to ensure that DOE is not
reimbursing contractors for legal expenses for defense of cases
where the contractor is at fault and where opportunity for reasonable settlement exists.

Legal expenditures on the Bricker case had achieved their desired
effect: stalling a final resolution of Bricker's claims. In September 1991,
Hanford lawyers convinced the federal trial judge that Hanford employees, who worked for a private company rather than the government, had no right under federal law to recover damages for
whistle-blower harassment. Because all of Bricker's other claims arose
under state law, the federal judge ruled that he had no jurisdiction to
hear the case. Two years later, the U.S. Court of Appeals for the Ninth
Circuit affirmed that decision, and in October 1994 the U.S. Supreme
Court refused to review the lower court rulings.[59] Bricker would have to
start all over again, with fewer legal claims, in state court.

DOE settled these remaining state law claims against Rockwell and
Westinghouse in December 1994 by paying Bricker $200,000. As late
as August 1994, the DOE Richland field office had offered only
$25,000. Bricker's lawyer, Tom Carpenter, reports, "It was only through
Washington Headquarters' intervention that a reasonable settlement
figure was offered."[60] (The defendants admitted no wrongdoing. Officials at the DOE Richland office did not make themselves available for
comment.)

Why the increase from Bricker's original $65,000 demand to a final
settlement agreement of $200,000? Four years came and went after
Bricker's offer to settle for $65,000. Years of bitter and expensive litiga-
tion caused Bricker severe emotional distress, ulcers, stress-induced
skin rashes, and inability to sleep, forced him to quit his job, give up his
seniority and other benefits, and leave his home in Richland. According to Carpenter, "We engaged in a major, bitterly contested litigation
with a lot of discovery, depositions, motions, and other trial work. Our
out-of-pocket costs alone to pay for the litigation were more than
$50,000. Yet, if in 1990 Westinghouse had undertaken a good faith ef-
fort to transfer him and undo the negative effects of the hostile work
atmosphere that had been created, the matter would have been quickly
resolved."[61]

But that course of action did not reflect the purposes of Rockwell,
Westinghouse, and the DOE, before being forced into sweet reason by
Secretary O'Leary. Bricker and his lawyer believe that the obstinance
and retaliation they faced were designed to deter any inclinations by

other would-be whistle-blowers to do their public duty. Hardball litigation conducted by corporate lawyers at great taxpayer expense was the primary tool.

"This is the public policy importance of the Bricker settlement," Carpenter says. "Workers have to feel that, like Ed, they can take on the system and win. It is not about the money but the vindication. If Ed had lost this fight, the signal was going to be heard by the workforce. People would not speak out as Ed did."

And herein lies a bitter irony. Ed Bricker lost, even as he won. "Ed was a foot soldier for a safer work environment," Carpenter says. "He got worn down, abused, and damaged but, in the end, at least he has the satisfaction of knowing that his sacrifice served the public interest." Meanwhile, the government also lost, spending more than $1 million on outside attorneys' fees and costs in resisting the whistle-blower's legitimate claim—plus costs incurred by assigning DOE's own in-house lawyers to the matter. Only the corporate lawyers, who received fat fees for throwing legal obstacles in the way of a clearly meritorious case, suffered no adverse consequences from the litigation.

There was at least one public benefit resulting from the Bricker litigation: the release, through discovery, of important information regarding operations at Hanford. "Freedom of Information Act[62] requests are not enough to watchdog government," Carpenter says. "The government often does not provide the information in a timely manner that is helpful. Legitimate litigation helps us promote the public interest because we can often get through discovery that which might be denied in a FOIA [request]. What we discovered in this case led directly to beneficial reforms."

In December 1994, the Hanford Joint Council was created as a nonprofit corporation partially funded by Westinghouse. The council is a mediation board composed of public interest activists, such as attorney Carpenter, as well as Westinghouse managers. It is designed to resolve whistle-blower disputes before they turn bitter and get out of hand. "Because of the council, it is now much safer to be a whistle-blower at Hanford," Carpenter says. Given the growing public record of Hanford's environmental toxic contamination from radioactive and other materials in past years, this is a welcome assurance for the exercise of employee conscience.

Bricker's case also led Congress, in 1992, to improve the legal protections available for whistle-blowers who work for DOE contract companies. "Congress expanded the law to explicitly provide whistle-blower protection to contractor employees such as Ed," Carpenter happily reports. Indeed, Representative Ron Wyden of Oregon specifically cited the court decision in the Bricker case as the catalyst for the change in the law. (Thirty-five states have enacted statutes providing protections for whistle-blowers. Twenty-four cover only government employees, but eleven extend some protections to workers for private companies.)

This chapter has provided just a small sampling of the tricks power lawyers use to bring misfortune upon people who get in the way of powerful corporate clients. The next chapter will demonstrate why power lawyers are so fond of playing these games: It pays.

CHAPTER 7

THE "BUTS" PRINCIPLE

ORPORATE LAW PRACTICE IS ONE OF THE MOST PROSPEROUS sectors of our economy. The large firms are well-oiled machines that can rack up profits year after year, through economic recession as well as boom times. The reader will be familiar with some of the following figures from previous chapters, but they are worth repeating here: The legal services industry in the United States generates more than $108 billion in revenue annually,[1] and the one hundred top-grossing law firms take in about $15 billion of that amount.[2]

In the most recent year surveyed, the giant New York–based 968-lawyer firm Skadden, Arps, Slate, Meagher & Flom had $582 million in gross revenues, resulting in $820,000 in profits per partner. Elsewhere in New York, 262-lawyer Cravath, Swaine & Moore had $186 million in gross revenues, producing a whopping $1,225,000 in profits per partner. Profits per partner at two other big New York firms, 195-lawyer Cahill Gordon & Reindel ($1,200,000) and 382-lawyer Sullivan & Cromwell ($1,185,000), were close behind. A smaller New York firm, 109-lawyer Wachtell, Lipton, Rosen & Katz, home of former White House counsel Bernard Nussbaum, boasts probably the highest profits per partner in the nation: $1,400,000.

Baker & McKenzie, with 1,642 lawyers spread across the world, had $546 million in gross revenues, $425,000 in profits per partner, while another global firm, 1,072-lawyer Jones, Day, Reavis & Pogue, also implicated in the savings and loan investigations, had $384 million in gross revenues, $375,000 in profits per partner. Chicago's 401-lawyer Kirkland & Ellis took in $215 million in gross revenues, producing $800,000 in profits per partner. Boston's 237-lawyer Hale and Dorr had $109 million in revenues, $410,000 in profits per partner, while Los Angeles's 538-lawyer O'Melveny & Myers had $257 million in revenues, $605,000 in profits per partner. Meanwhile, in Washington, D.C., 329-lawyer Arnold & Porter brought in gross revenues of

$150 million, with $390,000 in profits per partner, 301-lawyer Covington & Burling had $135 million gross revenues, $490,000 profits per partner, and 230-lawyer Wilmer, Cutler & Pickering had $102 million in gross revenues, $460,000 in profits per partner.[3]

But there is a dark side to this success story. As attorney Joseph W. Cotchett has written, the intensity of the business imperative in the practice of law, especially in large corporate firms, has caused the public to view "a once great profession . . . as a tank of sharks, with little if any morals."[4] Unfortunately, there is much to support this perception, as we learned through discussions with men and women who work in some of the largest corporate law firms in the world, including firm partners, associates, and support staff. These attorneys and staffers had much on their minds and consciences, particularly about the extent to which money seems to drive the corporate legal culture, creating a bottom-line mentality under which what is best for the financial interests of the law firm is confused with what is best for the legal needs of the client. Worse, this hyperkinetic commercialism sometimes leads to egregious billing abuses and even outright fraud, at the expense of corporate and, particularly, government clients, who rarely take the time to effectively monitor their legal bills. Some of our sources were understandably reluctant to speak on the record. As one of them said, "It is a matter of my job, not only at my firm . . . I could be blackballed in the industry."[5] Where we rely on a source that asked to remain anonymous, out of fairness we do not name the firm that the source discussed.

One attorney, once idealistic but now angry and cynical about his profession, is incensed at the billing practices he observed at a prominent California firm. Our source wrote, "I worked for [firm name] for five years and observed the type of billing abuses that your book will undoubtedly chronicle. I coined an acronym that I thought you might like to use in your book . . . 'The BUTS principle.' BUTS stands for 'Bill Until They Squawk.' "[6]

"I feel wrong about our billing and really want this information to come out," another lawyer, who works for a large firm representing insurance companies before regulatory agencies, said. He gave us a typical example of dishonesty in his firm: "We had a couple of partners. One was a senior partner charging $250 per hour, and another charged $220 per hour. They had a practice of billing four tenths of an hour [twenty-four minutes] per service, even though the retainer agreement [the contract between the firm and its client] provided for a one-tenth [six-minute] minimum. If I came in to ask them a question, even if it took a minute or two, they would charge the client twenty-four minutes. I know. I saw the bills."[7]

Another disgruntled power lawyer wrote, "Many of my colleagues decide ahead of time how much they want to bill and they fill in the time sheets to get to that spot. Or, if a service takes two hours to perform but the lawyer believes the value to the client was more, they will bill for four hours or more, especially if the client has the reputation of rubber-stamping the bills that are sent."[8]

Yet another correspondent related this tale from large-firm practice: "Once, while I was going through our accounting department's files in order to prepare a motion for fees in bankruptcy court, I came across the monthly billing records of the partners. I discovered that several of the partners had billed over three thousand hours per year to clients for a period of several years. There is no way those partners could have billed those hours because they were rarely in the office when the [billing] entries showed they were working on motions, research, and various pleadings." This writer added bitterly, "The people who got the biggest bonuses were the highest billers, not necessarily the ones who put out the best work product and certainly not the efficient ones. In fact, these associates were actually the slowest, most inefficient ones. It's no wonder they billed so many hours! This must be the only industry that worships and rewards inefficiency."[9]

Then there's this story, which, while involving a relatively small amount of money, has to win a prize for sheer nerve. "I am a secretary for [one of the largest firms in Los Angeles]. We used to charge clients for the flowers we sent to their own funerals! The amount was on a sliding scale depending on the size of the estate since we were going to handle the probate."

This secretary also illustrated how the nation's largest and most prestigious firms bill anything that moves. "We charged for everything. If we offered a client a doughnut, we would charge it to the bill. We would charge the client for soft drinks. We would charge for secretarial overtime. We made a profit on faxing and photocopying. Our lawyers were always padding their bills. I once saw a memo from one of the partners who said if you even *think* about a file, whether in your car, in the shower, or on the golf course, it gets a minimum fifteen-minute charge."[10]

Thomas D. Barr is one of the leaders of Cravath, Swaine & Moore, which reports the highest profits per partner of any of the biggest one hundred U.S. law firms. A few years ago, he actually bragged about the intensity with which he sees to it that clients are billed for every expense: "[I]f you tell me you won't pay for one cost, then I will charge you more for another cost, if that's the kind of shell game we are playing."[11] Of course, declining to pay for certain expenses is not a "shell game"; charging a client for one expense by disguising it as another expense is.

Are the many anecdotes of overbilling and false billing exaggerations of the disgruntled or mere anomalies, examples of rare rotten apples in an otherwise healthy barrel of lawyers? Unfortunately, no. The practice of inflating charges to clients appears endemic throughout much of legal commerce—attorneys operating their cash registers with premeditated thievery. "Hourly rates now guarantee that clients will be overcharged for almost any conceivable legal service," writes Washington, D.C., lawyer Donald E. deKieffer, who served as general counsel at the Office of the United States Trade Representative during the Reagan administration. The reason? Corporate attorneys in big firms "are under intense pressure to bill as many hours as possible and are strongly motivated to maximize their hours by fair means or foul."[12]

There are three primary ways that lawyers cheat their clients. First, there is overbilling, i.e., charging for more hours or at higher rates than is warranted by contract and by the facts, such as when a lawyer claims more hours than she worked. Second, there is overlawyering, i.e., performing and billing for unnecessary tasks, such as when a firm brings an extra associate or two to the courthouse just to carry a briefcase and fetch lunch. And, third, there is padding of expenses, i.e., charging the client for every conceivable cost and often including an outrageous markup. These practices seem to have become a major source of income for many unscrupulous lawyers.

THE CASE OF THE OUTRAGED INSURANCE COMPANY

A few years ago, squeezed by the recession and looking for ways to reduce costs, some corporations began to scrutinize the billing practices of their outside lawyers. What they discovered caused many a breach in long-standing, highly profitable corporation-law-firm relationships.

One of the first company executives to pursue systematically overbilling by attorneys was James P. Schratz, vice president for major claims at Fireman's Fund Insurance Company. Schratz, concerned by what he perceived as overbilling against his company, saw it as his duty to his employer to investigate and put an end to it. But when he contacted the law firms that Fireman's Fund had retained, all he received back was arrogance. "Their attitude was, 'You are not going to change this institution,' " Schratz recalls. " 'You are a flyspeck as far as we are concerned. Your fees represent only a small base of our revenue.' "

Fine, Schratz thought, if that's the way you want it, that's the way it will be. "I decided to make it so uncomfortable to cheat us that lawyers would stop trying to take advantage of Fireman's Fund," he told us.[13] Fireman's Fund decided to challenge several of its law firms, including 518-lawyer Latham & Watkins ($263 million annual gross revenues, $550,000 in profits per partner), based in Los Angeles, and the San Francisco firm Tarkington, O'Connor & O'Neill.

Fireman's Fund refused to pay any questionable bills without an audit. In November 1988, Latham & Watkins sued Fireman's Fund for $664,000 in disputed unpaid bills arising out of a case in which a Fireman's Fund customer was accused of unlawfully firing two of its employees. Fireman's Fund cross-complained against Latham for fraud and malpractice, claiming that the firm had built up a $1.1 million fee by "churning" the case and engaging in unnecessary scorched-earth tactics designed to pad the bill.

Fireman's Fund accused Latham of a broad array of bill-padding and improper charges, including putting up a partner in a hotel rather than have him drive thirty minutes to the courthouse during the six-week trial, billing $1,500 for having a partner watch a trial in the next town (the partner testified that he considered this activity legal education), billing $176.46 for dinner for a partner, his assistant, and a jury expert at a luxurious seaside restaurant, billing for $50 stolen from a lawyer's hotel room, billing for tobacco, and other such abuses. There was even a photograph discovered of Latham paralegals wearing T-shirts with the slogan BORN TO BILL.

The Latham case ultimately settled. Although the settlement is confidential, *The Wall Street Journal* reported that the firm paid Fireman's Fund $1.5 million in damages to reimburse the insurer for the amount it paid to the plaintiffs in the underlying employment case and that Latham also waived its unpaid $664,000 fee.[14] Latham did not admit wrongdoing in the settlement and claimed that its billing practices were "conservative" and "mainstream." According to *The Wall Street Journal* report, if anyone from Fireman's Fund discusses the Latham case, Fireman's Fund must pay Latham $75,000.

Fireman's Fund's dispute with the Tarkington firm raised more billing issues. A former Tarkington partner, Stephen Pahl, claimed that one of his ex-colleagues, working on an asbestos-related case, billed thirty-three hours in a single day—a grueling pace, to say the least. There was also evidence that a Tarkington partner billed a paralegal's time at the partner's hourly rate, as if the partner had done the work.

The Tarkington firm and Fireman's Fund went to arbitration over their billing dispute. The arbitrator, Robert H. Kroninger, concluded that Tarkington's billing practices violated its agreement with Fireman's Fund and "resulted in exaggerated unjustifiable time being billed." The arbitrator found that Tarkington lawyers billed 20-hour days, 23-hour days, and even a 29-hour day—reduced from a time sheet showing 32.3 hours—by allocating increments of time to multiple clients. "It is inescapable," he wrote, "that over the years invoices were submitted for payment by the insurers with representations of time and task and case designations which were untrue." The arbitrator did not find the kind of "extreme case of fraud" that would justify total disallowance of the firm's fees. But he did find that a Tarkington senior partner generated bills by simply adopting another employee's time sheets, a practice that was "wilfully and knowingly false."

In the end, of the $870,241 outstanding fees requested by Tarkington (out of a total bill of about $2.9 million), the arbitrator disallowed as improper $463,579, or more than half of the amount in dispute.[15]

Tarkington, however, has admitted no wrongdoing. Members of the firm continue to insist that they did nothing wrong other than commit clerical billing errors or innocent mistakes. Tarkington partner Steven F. O'Neill asserts, "The entire auditing experience tended to focus entirely on the minutiae of billing details rather than the overall quality and efficiency of the representation."[16]

Meanwhile, Tarkington sued former partner Pahl in California state court and managed to keep much of the litigation secret—so secret, in fact, that in court records the official name of the case is simply two pseudonyms, Roe v. Doe. The case settled confidentially on the eve of trial.[17]

Tarkington was not done. It subsequently sued Schratz, Fireman's Fund, and the auditing firm used by Fireman's Fund for libel, breach of confidentiality, and other causes of action. (Tarkington also sued the lawyers who represented Fireman's Fund in the arbitration, but later agreed to dismiss them from the case.) All defendants deny Tarkington's charges. In fact, Schratz claims the suit is, in reality, a SLAPP suit (see Chapter 5) and has vowed to fight it to the end. He insists that he will never resolve this new suit by entering into a confidential settlement. As this is written, the case is pending.

When we asked Schratz why companies so often tolerate overbilling by their own lawyers, he blamed the corporate culture: "People working for corporations become risk averse," he told us. "They will do anything to avoid making a decision that might cause them trouble. For example, I have never seen an [insurance] adjuster called on the carpet for paying a legal bill—no matter how fraudulent. However, dispute a bill and there could be trouble when the well-connected lawyer creates a stink [with upper corporate management] about his integrity being impugned. The typical adjuster will see this and be intimidated into silence. That creates a culture that is quite fertile for lawyer abuse."[18]

Billing disputes between corporate clients and firms, such as those involving Fireman's Fund, Tarkington, and Latham, have been growing in recent years. They are the talk of the defense and corporate legal industry throughout the country, and for good reason. Allegations of billing abuses, whether warranted or not, can destroy a firm's reputation. The Tarkington firm shrunk from about eighty attorneys to twenty-one in the four years after the controversy with Fireman's Fund was first reported in the media, primarily, according to a Tarkington lawyer, as a result of the bad publicity.

These disputes have grown so pervasive that a new business has developed around keeping lawyers honest in their billing practices. Known as legal bill auditing or litigation consulting, it has created lawyer watchdogs who have gone into business with the purpose of saving corporations millions of dollars in legal fees by preventing abuses, helping corporations make the best use of lawyers, and negotiating better retainer agreements.

How do law firms go about cheating their clients? We interviewed Jim Schratz, who left Fireman's Fund Insurance to form his own legal auditing company, Jim Schratz & Associates of Santa Rosa, California; John Toothman, founder of The Devil's Advocate of Alexandria, Virginia, one of the best-known practitioners in the field; Gary Greenfield of Litigation Cost Management in Oakland, California; and other bill auditors.

"Clients have to watch out for both overbilling and overlawyering," says Toothman.[19] According to Schratz, "The only thing that will slow down billing abuses is aggressive case management by clients. Just letting firms know that attention is being paid deters much overbilling."[20] Greenfield reports that he is ever "on the watch for excessive overhead charges designed to turn photocopying and faxing into profit centers."[21] Law firms may charge clients $1 per page for faxes, sent or received, and 25 cents or more for in-house photocopies, even though the local copy service will do it for 7 cents a page.

Another tactic that may not be visible to the uninformed eye is using multiple law firm personnel to attend depositions or court hearings. "Multiple billing really adds up," Schratz told us. "Sometimes it may be necessary, but, then again, it may just be a way of charging the client for training younger lawyers."

The auditors with whom we spoke all agreed that the following practices, if not routine, were not rare either, demonstrating that some lawyers believe that dishonesty is the best policy:

- Lawyers billing unworked hours, sometimes more than there are in the day.
- Senior partners billing their time for work actually performed by support personnel, work that therefore should have been billed at a substantially lower rate.
- Firms charging for filling in the blanks in legal "forms," documents preprepared and used repeatedly, as if the lawyer had created the document from scratch.
- Lawyers advising clients not to accept reasonable settlements so that the case, and the billing, can continue.
- Lawyers taking unnecessary depositions.
- Firms taking a markup for business expenses such as secretarial overtime, fax charges, long-distance phone calls, and the like. (Expense markups can quickly add up to big profits for the firm. For example, real estate attorney Jay Dushoff tells the story of a large New York firm typesetting and printing fifty copies of a final loan document, without request or consent, and then charging the client $13,000. The client paid, because as Dushoff put it, "We had no choice. We were in the economic position of being coerced."[22])
- Lawyers living in luxury at the client's expense, such as using limousine services, staying in four-star hotels, and eating at the most expensive restaurants.
- Firms charging for using staff personnel to unnecessarily "messenger" materials that could have been mailed or commercially messengered for a lower price.
- Firms failing to provide detailed billing statements, making it impossible for the client to monitor the accuracy of the charges.

Even auditors or sophisticated clients may be unable to audit bills for accuracy because some law firms so garble their bills that it cannot be determined whether they are fairly computed. For example, law professor Robert Fellmeth, a former California state legal ethics overseer, was involved with the probate of a large estate, and had retained the New York corporate firm Reid & Priest to assist him with vital legal work. He was shocked by the firm's billing practices. The first bill he received "was a single line for services rendered, requesting an amount in six figures, a sparsely worded but lucratively enriching bill." When

Fellmeth objected, the firm sent an itemized bill, but not one that he found sufficient.[23]

Increasing press attention has focused on lawyers accused of over-billing:

- OVER-BILLED BY $57 MILLION? was the headline in a 1994 article in *The American Lawyer* about an internal Citibank audit alleging billing abuses by the bank's outside lawyers, the New York 522-lawyer firm Shearman & Sterling ($268 million gross revenues, $625,000 profits per partner). The audit, conducted by Citibank vice president John Roche—a former Shearman & Sterling partner!—concluded that about half of the $57 million in questionable charges were indeed excessive. The bank told Shearman & Sterling that it would not pay similar charges in the future. The firm was charging for services like photocopying, faxes, utilities, and use of conference rooms, all of which were often marked up.[24]

- Another *American Lawyer* report coined the phrase "Skadden-omics" to describe the billing practices of the country's top-grossing firm, Skadden, Arps. The article reported, for example, that a senior associate in the Washington, D.C., Skadden office ordered breakfast for four—coffee, juice, and Danish—from Skadden's own in-house cafeteria. The cafeteria price was $23.80, which seems like plenty. But it wasn't enough for the firm, which added a 40 percent markup and charged a client, the South Florida Water Management District, $33.60 for the meal. Skadden also charged this client a $2.50 per minute fax charge—on top of the long-distance phone charge—so that, for a thirty-one-minute outgoing fax, which incurred $7.51 in phone charges, Skadden billed $85.01. Skadden also billed $22 to send its in-house messengers ten blocks, even though a commercial service would have delivered for $5. After the client complained about various charges, Skadden agreed to reduce its bill from $1.6 million to $500,000—but admitted no wrongdoing.[25]

- The Los Angeles firm Buchalter, Nemer, Fields & Younger agreed to cut a $16 million legal bill by $3 million after a client, American International Group, complained. In addition to the familiar markups for things like photocopies, AIG claimed that a Buchalter partner billed it for a personal trip to Rome (an accusation the lawyer denied). Buchalter also charged AIG $200,000 for work by a partner's brother, an attorney, who allegedly summarized depositions and attended sessions where documents were exchanged. When it reviewed the materials, Buchalter reportedly found no deposition summaries.[26]

- On August 30, 1995, Maryland state judge Ann S. Harrington concluded that, in the 1980s, Weinberg and Green, one of Maryland's largest firms, had engaged in an "utterly reprehensible" scheme to inflate the bills of one client. Judge Harrington found that Weinberg and Green partners were guilty of "an organized systematic billing fraud," which came to include a computer program that automatically increased hours by 15 percent.[27]
- Also in August 1995, Webster Hubbell, formerly the third-ranking official in President Clinton's Justice Department, began serving a twenty-one-month federal prison term after pleading guilty to charges of fraud and income tax evasion. The bright-light scrutiny that enveloped top Clinton officials helped reveal the fact that, while a partner at Little Rock's Rose Law Firm (as was Hillary Rodham Clinton), Hubbell had overbilled fifteen clients, including the Federal Deposit Insurance Corporation and the federal Resolution Trust Corporation, by claiming bogus expenses. All in all, between 1989 and 1992, Hubbell stole $482,410 from these clients and from his own law firm partners, who were not implicated in the misconduct.

Unfortunately, these stories do not appear to be isolated anecdotes blown out of proportion by an irresponsible media into an industry-wide scandal for the purpose of selling newspapers. Rather, billing abuses appear to be pervasive and ingrained, costing corporations, and ultimately consumers, untold millions.

Washington lawyer Donald E. deKieffer has written a 199-page book exposing the many ways in which lawyers cheat their clients. *How Lawyers Screw Their Clients* presents in excruciating detail the many and varied ways in which lawyers dishonestly pad their bills, creating a system where the amount billed "has little relationship to the value of the legal services to the client or the amount of time it should have taken competent counsel to accomplish the result."[28]

William G. Ross, a law professor at Samford University in Birmingham, Alabama, has twice conducted intensive studies of billing abuse. After surveying 272 private practitioners and eighty corporate counsel in 1991, he was shocked at what he found. He wrote us, "My survey revealed that a substantial proportion of attorneys engage in billing practices that most lay persons probably would regard as unethical. I estimate that most large corporate clients would receive ninety-eight percent of the benefits they now obtain if their lawyers invested fifty percent of the time for which they now bill."[29] If true, these practices are no less dishonest than the butcher who puts his thumb on the scale in order to increase the price of meat or the taxi driver who intentionally takes the long way to a destination in order to increase the fare. It is the same misconduct—only on a larger scale. It is not merely unethical; it is criminal behavior that has most of society's sentinels looking the other way. When Professor Ross conducted a new survey of 197 in-house and outside counsel in 1995, after much discussion in the legal and financial press about attorney overbilling, he was surprised to find that very little had changed. Three quarters of in-house lawyers he contacted reported occurrences of inappropriate timekeeping by law firms.[30]

A survey of executives from the country's one thousand largest companies revealed that 49.25 percent believed that their companys' legal bills had been padded by at least 10 percent, with 13.16 percent believing that the padding exceeded 20 percent.[31] Considering the size of legal bills incurred by large corporations, this degree of bill padding, if true, costs stockholders well into the tens of millions of dollars each year. Imagine the outcry if such sums were stolen at the point of a gun or knife rather than obtained surreptitiously through improper billing practices. It's time for authorities to convene grand juries to investigate these practices.

Rarely do corporate billing practices come under formal scrutiny, but one place where they do is in federal bankruptcy court. Padded bills sometimes come to light when a conscientious bankruptcy judge refuses to be a rubber stamp and carefully examines legal fees submitted in bankruptcy proceedings, as in the following two cases involving two of the nation's most well known law firms—the kind of firms the media often calls "prestigious."

THE CASE OF THE BLOATED BANKRUPTCY FEES

Big-business bankruptcies cost nearly everyone. Stockholders may lose their entire investment; employees may face reduced wages or job loss; creditors' debts will not be paid on time or in full. But not everyone loses. Many corporate law firms make big money helping companies use the bankruptcy laws to reorganize debts or otherwise attempt to get their fiscal affairs in order. Lawyers also represent creditors seeking to enlarge their piece of the corporate asset pie. Bankruptcy has become an especially lucrative area of law in the wake of the go-go 1980s, when corporate raiders got rich taking over companies, stripping them of assets, and running them into the ground—assisted, of course, by corporate lawyers.

One recent big-business bankruptcy involved Spreckles Sugar, Inc., a holding company with ten wholly owned subsidiaries. Spreckles sought protection in the United States Bankruptcy Court for the Northern District of California under Chapter 11 of the federal bankruptcy code. In a Chapter 11 reorganization, a company's debts are rescheduled but it is allowed to stay in business. A creditors' committee was established to represent the interests of unsecured creditors (creditors holding no collateral from Spreckles) in the bankruptcy proceeding. The committee hired the Los Angeles–based 550-lawyer firm Gibson, Dunn & Crutcher. (Gibson, Dunn's most recent annual gross revenues are $278 million, with $520,000 profits per partner.)

There were legal and accounting disagreements between Spreckles and the committee. The committee, relying on legal advice, made the process difficult for Spreckles, filing lengthy objections to the company's disclosure statement. The court denied most of these objections, after which the parties arrived at terms for the Spreckles reorganization and the case moved swiftly to a conclusion.

Under the law, Gibson, Dunn was entitled to a court order awarding it reasonable fees for the work performed on behalf of the committee. Accordingly, it filed a fee application with the court requesting $1.353 million in fees and $169,000 in reimbursed expenses. Unfortunately for Gibson, Dunn, the court had this fee request audited, as a result of which it reduced the firm's request by approximately 50 percent ($665,930), and the firm suffered a very public and embarrassing scolding for its billing techniques.[32]

United States bankruptcy judge Edward D. Jellen's ruling in the case is notable for the specificity of its criticisms, and serves as a good illustration of the kind of fee problems billing auditors uncover with disturbing frequency.

Judge Jellen stated:

> Sadly, Gibson did not exercise any billing judgment in this case. Rather, its Application is bloated with many hundreds of hours that cannot reasonably be justified, and which Gibson would not have spent had it exercised billing judgment. Indeed, this Application presents a prime example of too many people aggressively billing too many hours for doing the unnecessary and redoing that [work which] has already been done.

The court found that Gibson, Dunn had made demands that were "unobtainable" and had made "lengthy arguments" that were "not only not at issue, they were generally not even well grounded as a matter of law." In other words, Gibson, Dunn had spent time and effort pursuing a legal agenda that had no chance of success. And not only were Gibson, Dunn's legal arguments and tactics off the mark, but also the time the firm charged for pursuing the failed strategy was unreasonable:

> The objection Gibson prepared is 55 pages in length, and is supplemented by five declarations plus an appendix. The $289,527 Gibson requests for the project represents 1,356 hours of time expended by 20 billers, whose efforts included repeated, duplicative, and seemingly endless reviews and revisions of the ill-conceived objection, the proposed disclosure statement, and the factual reports on which some of the objection was based. . . . Gibson expended this time without any risk-reward analysis.

The court also found that Gibson, Dunn had apparently pursued, in part, a legal strategy designed for its own enrichment rather than for the client's benefit.

> Gibson was apparently willing to see the estate engage in lengthy and expensive cash collateral litigation which, if unsuccessful, would have needlessly damaged the very clients Gibson was purportedly representing, and if successful, would have led to nothing more for Gibson's clients than that which had already been negotiated. . . . The court must assume that the bulk of this was for Gibson's reckless and misguided effort on its own behalf.

The court also found that Gibson, Dunn had taken too much time to retain certain professionals on behalf of the creditors' committee:

> The documents required [concerning reporting to the court about the hiring of professionals] are not complex. Most attorneys with prior bankruptcy experience use a form containing boilerplate language to which the attorney adds the information relevant to the specific case. In the court's experience, this normally requires no more than 30 minutes, and certainly can be done within an hour.
> Gibson requests $32,094.50 for the 196.5 hours that 13 persons billed for retaining the committee's professionals.

Gibson, Dunn had advised the court that the reason the hours billed were so high was the need for it to interview the professionals and negotiate their fees, a reasonable explanation, according to the court. Still, the court found that, even allowing for negotiations and the like, Gibson should have taken, at most, fifty-five hours for the work, including arranging its own retention. What, then, of being paid for the remaining 141 claimed hours?

> The balance will be disallowed. A review of the time Gibson billed for preparing its own retention papers is illustrative of the reason. On October 28, 1992, attorney Trundle billed four hours to "draft and revise G D & C. application for retention." On the next day, attorney Cohen, a partner at the firm who charges $235 an hour billed .8 hours for reviewing the application and a full hour to "oversee filing the application with the court." The same day, attorney Ricciardi, a senior attorney who bills at the rate of $265 an hour, billed 2.3 hours for reviewing the same application. The application together with related papers . . . totals only 10 pages, much of it boilerplate. This means that if senior attorney Ricciardi's time records are accurate, he reviewed boilerplate . . . plus the additions, at the incredible rate of 14 minutes per page, or 4.3 pages per hour.

On and on the decision goes, documenting Gibson, Dunn's overbilling, with the judge finding that the firm repeatedly engaged in "duplicative efforts" and billed for "working up several potential lawsuits and motions in the absence of any existing legal or factual controversy," or, as the judge put it, "shadowboxing in the absence of any realistic threat." Further, Gibson, Dunn charged "hourly rates that materially exceed[ed] the market."

Gibson, Dunn did not appeal the court's ruling. We contacted the firm and asked for a response to the judge's opinion. A Gibson, Dunn attorney named John Landers responded by leaving a message stating, "I am sorry to tell you that I simply can't help you in any way on this project. Best of luck and thanks for calling."

On the other side of the continent, the well-paid lawyers of New York's Cravath, Swaine & Moore were taken to task by a federal bankruptcy judge in comparable circumstances.

Cravath represented the General Development Corporation, which between 1983 and 1989 built more than ten thousand houses in Florida and sold them, at well-above-market prices, to lower-income families. Cravath earned as much as $5 million in a single year representing GDC. The company, run by a former Cravath lawyer, used various tactics to convince customers the homes were worth more than their actual value. A federal grand jury indicted GDC executives for conspiracy and fraud. Their defense at trial was that they relied on Cravath's advice every step of the way and thus acted responsibly—the Cravath partner in charge testified that he advised GDC that it was legal to charge the high prices. The jury, however, convicted the executives on August 5, 1992, and they were sentenced to five-to-ten-year prison terms. But on April 16, 1996, the Eleventh Circuit Court of Appeals reversed the convictions, finding that there was insufficient evidence of a scheme to defraud.[33]

Meanwhile, GDC's business was collapsing, and claims by homeowners and creditors led the company, in April 1990, to file for Chapter 11 protection in the federal bankruptcy court in Miami. In August 1990, GDC fired Cravath. The next month, Cravath submitted to the bankruptcy court a request for $323,230 for "professional services" rendered to GDC subsequent to the bankruptcy filing. As documentation, Cravath submitted a long computer printout that gave no explanation as to who performed the work or what work they performed. When pressed for more details, Cravath submitted a revised application that revealed that more than one third of the amount requested for "professional services" went to nonlawyers billing at high rates: For paralegals, Cravath requested $65 to $75 per hour; for records clerks, $70 per hour; for librarians, $60 per hour; for secretaries and typists, $44 per hour; for copy machine operators, $30 per hour. In November 1990, Judge A. Jay Cristol responded by awarding only $34,266 in fees, about 12 percent of what Cravath sought. Cristol found not only that Cravath's prices were high, but also that their work was less than vital: "Cravath, Swaine & Moore have not demonstrated any significant benefit to [GDC] as of the time of this application. Many cost items are neither proper nor allowable." *The American Lawyer* magazine, which reported this decision, sought comment from the Cravath lawyer representing GDC as well as from the firm's presiding partner. Neither returned the reporter's phone calls.[34]

When lawyers overcharge corporate clients, the larger public ultimately loses through higher consumer prices. But sometimes private law firms engage in similar troublesome billing practices when the client is a government agency. In those cases, such as the one that follows, again involving top earners Cravath, Swaine & Moore, power lawyers unjustly take money directly out of the pockets of U.S. taxpayers.

THE CASE OF THE OVERBILLED AGENCY

Although thousands of lawyers work in-house at the various agencies and departments of the United States government, each year the government pays approximately $600 million to outside lawyers to represent it in litigation or to provide other legal services. (This represents more than the twice the amount the government provides to the federally chartered Legal Services Corporation to provide basic legal representation to millions of low-income people.) More than 120 agencies are permitted by law to hire outside lawyers.[35] These include every cabinet department, the Office of Management and Budget, the African Development Foundation, the Consumer Product Safety Commission, and the Federal Election Commission. But, by far, the most hiring of outside lawyers has been done by two agencies with key responsibilities for regulating financial institutions: the Resolution Trust Corporation (RTC) and the Federal Deposit Insurance Corporation (FDIC). (The RTC went out of business in 1995.)

When agencies like the RTC and the FDIC retain outside lawyers, they usually turn to the same large firms that represent the country's major corporations. One such firm is Cravath, Swaine & Moore.

The RTC and FDIC contended that the investment banking firm Drexel Burnham Lambert and its employee Michael Milken had fraudulently rigged the market for high-risk "junk bonds," resulting in, among other things, the collapse of forty-five federally insured savings and loans. Drexel and Milken were already in deep, documented trouble. The agencies, alleging more than $2 billion in damages, sought to recover $6.8 billion from Drexel and another $6.8 billion from Milken and other Drexel and savings and loan executives (including punitive damages as provided by federal antitrust and racketeering laws).[36] They hired Cravath and its top litigators, Thomas Barr (the lawyer who was quoted earlier complaining about billing "shell games") and David Boies. In March 1992, Cravath concluded a settlement that resulted in a $500 million payment from Drexel and Milken to the government— only 25 percent of the actual damages and a tiny fraction of the total claim.

The government's agreement with Cravath guaranteed the firm's senior partners a $300 hourly billing rate, other partners $250 per hour, associates $180 per hour, and paralegals $50 per hour. But there was a major bonus built in: If the Cravath lawyers obtained $200 million or more for the government in the case (10 percent of the claimed damages), senior partner fees would double to $600 per hour, partner fees would increase to $425 per hour, associate fees to $270 per hour, and paralegal fees to $85. Tallying up all its efforts, Cravath submitted a bill for about $40 million.

Considering the extremely high hourly rates, Cravath might have been satisfied with a straightforward accounting of reasonable time and necessary expenses. But it wasn't, as an investigation by the RTC's Office of the Inspector General (the office in charge of RTC internal investigations) made clear. The investigation spot-checked the overall bill. Although the inspector general's office concluded that Cravath "typically verified through supporting documentation" that expenses billed were accurate and related to the case, it questioned many of the charges. For the three months, out of a seventeen-month representation, that were closely reviewed, the inspector general challenged or found improper $272,000 in fees and expenses. The inspector general also questioned $165,069 in "overhead" charges over the entire seventeen months, as well as $60,000 for five months' worth of undocumented photocopying charges. The report added that "a detailed review of charges relating to other months would undoubtedly reveal additional unallowable charges."[37]

Included in the disputed $165,069 for "overhead expenses" were charges for use of Cravath's in-house computer systems ($58,494), office supplies ($57,314), transmitting document facsimiles ($1 per page for all outgoing transmissions, totaling $45,924), and binding documents ($3,337). According to the report, Cravath had billed the government in the same manner it billed its corporate clients, despite restrictions in the retention agreement with the government prohibiting such charges. Cravath also charged the federal agencies for a New York hotel room for a lawyer who lived in the New York area and for a weekend hotel stay for a lawyer not working on government matters over that weekend. Out of $43,526 claimed for three months' travel expenses by Cravath, the RTC inspector general disallowed $10,763 and further recommended that Cravath's $308,081 seventeen-month travel claim be subjected to further auditing.

The inspector general also found that Cravath had overbilled hours. One energetic Cravath attorney charged for a twenty-six-hour day. In that instance, the inspector general reduced the allowable hours by two, allowing a twenty-four-hour billing day, along with other twenty-to-twenty-four-hour billed days, despite "serious reservations about the effectiveness of individuals working these type of hours." Cravath also charged $22,095 for "learning curve costs" and $9,639, according to the report, "for services rendered by employees who were on vacation or sick leave."

Cravath eventually agreed to reduce its bill, although we have been unable to confirm the amount it ultimately received. The RTC advised us that it has performed no further audits of the Cravath bill. Cravath declined to respond to our repeated requests for comment.

Government payouts of taxpayers' money to corporate lawyers are not, of course, limited to controversies involving the savings and loan debacle or to contract companies reimbursed by the Department of Energy for their legal fees. For example, when health care corporations are denied Medicare benefits for services rendered, the government pays their legal fees. Tens of millions of taxpayers' dollars are spent each year to pay the lawyers for health care corporations involved in Medicare disputes with the government—whether the corporations win or lose. In a four-state area study conducted by the General Accounting Office, these payments amounted to 3.3 percent of total Medicare payouts to nursing homes and home health care providers surveyed.[38] Eleven percent of one company's Medicare payments were reimbursed legal fees. (The company's name was kept confidential by the GAO.)[39] Since the government picks up the legal tab, the corporations have nothing to lose by contesting every instance where their billings are disallowed.

It is important to emphasize that the government does not conduct detailed audits of every law firm with which it does business, nor do all audits that are performed uncover significant overbilling. However, what the Cravath audit and other reviews like it do indicate is that a great deal of money is wrongfully charged to taxpayers and put into power-lawyer coffers.

REINING IN THE ABUSES

Four years after its 1991 article coining the term "Skaddenomics," *The American Lawyer* magazine obtained a document indicating that, notwithstanding the controversy about billing and the supposed increased vigilance of clients, the practice of marking up ordinary office costs had not gone away, at least among some big New York firms. According to an article in the October 1995 issue of the magazine, 320-lawyer Debevoise & Plimpton ($181.5 million in annual revenues, $805,000 profits per partner) quietly produced a "disbursement survey" on behalf of thirty top New York firms, including Cravath, Swaine & Moore, so that the firms could compare billing practices. Although the leaked document did not say which firms were charging what prices, it did report that eleven of the thirty firms were charging at least $2 per page for an outgoing fax sent within the United States, that twenty-one of the firms placed a markup on phone charges, and that thirteen of the firms marked up charges for the use of computer on-line research services by as much as 50 percent. The article also quoted clients of big firms as saying that the law firm bills they received still failed to itemize expense charges. "Right now I cannot tell you if I'm paying fifty cents a page for a fax or two dollars," one said. "[The law firms] could be making a three hundred percent profit."[40]

Jed Ringel, president of Law Audit Services, Inc., in Wilton, Connecticut, reviews ten thousand legal bills per month for insurance company clients. He recently told *The Wall Street Journal* that 20 to 25 percent of the bills he sees include expense markups that are clearly prohibited by agreed-upon billing standards: "The agreement says ten cents a page for copying, and they charge twenty cents. It means the firm just doesn't give a damn."[41]

Concerns about attorney overbilling have reached the very top of the legal hierarchy. Chief Justice William Rehnquist, for one, has worried out loud that lawyers who are expected by their firms to bill more than two thousand hours per year may fall prey to the temptation to "exaggerate the hours actually put in."[42]

Legal bill auditor Jim Schratz contacted a number of law firms with the proposal that he provide internal audits as a kind of "Good Housekeeping" seal regarding billing practices to show clients. He got no takers. Schratz told *The Wall Street Journal* that, over beers, one managing partner explained his firm's refusal in this way: "Off the record, we're making a lot of money and we don't want to know how."[43]

Are we claiming that most large-firm lawyers are crooked? No. There has not been the kind of systematic investigation of the entire industry to permit such a broad-brushed criticism. But that is no cause for complacency. It is evident that all too many lawyers seem willing to steal from clients through intentional overbilling or, at the very least, give themselves the benefit of every billing doubt. Indeed, according to Professor William Ross, outright billing fraud is "much more common than most lawyers are willing to admit."[44]

Overbilling does not arise in a vacuum. Rather, the incentives to overbill are built in to the prevailing method most corporate law firms use to compute their fees: the hourly rate billing system.

"Hourly billing is a blank check from client to lawyer," says litigation consultant John Toothman. "The client bears both the risk and expense of litigation, and there is no inherent limit to the fees and expenses that can be charged." In such a system, lawyers may be less likely to curb unnecessary work, since to do so is to reduce their own compensation. It can also lead to the problem of firms "leveraging" staff time, that is, throwing more associates and paralegals at a problem than is required to get the job done, and billing all the way.[45]

Added to the built-in, self-managed conflict between what should be done for a client and what a lawyer may wish to bill is the unfortunate reality that many firms judge their lawyers' performance and levels of compensation almost exclusively on the amount of hours they bill clients. "Each year the minimum required annual billing hours for associates goes up and partners' year-end bonuses often depend on the amount their departments have billed," one disgruntled corporate lawyer complained to us in a common refrain. "That means that associates wanting to make partner will bill anything and everything to make sure they don't fall behind. Partners will not 'waste time' training associates because it takes away from billable work. That leads to an atmosphere where money is the most important thing, and if the client pays, forget ethics."

Harry Maue, a member of the St. Louis legal audit firm Stuart, Maue, Mitchell & James, gave The Wall Street Journal this description of the dilemma the billable hours system poses for corporate attorneys: "You either work sixty or seventy hours a week and have no personal life or you're going to synthesize those bills. Most bills [I see] are padded, whether intentional or not."[46]

In recent years, some of the most biting criticism of big-firm culture, including the race for billable hours, has come from a monthly faxed satirical publication called The Rodent, produced by a Los Angeles–based lawyer who formerly worked at 1,642-lawyer Baker & McKenzie and who keeps his identity a secret.[47] He told us, "Too many lawyers get sucked into the belief that the way to gauge your worth as a lawyer is based on your billing scores, not your legal talent. My old firm used to put out a monthly tally of billed hours for all the associates to see. It was like a billing derby. It created intense competition, as if the firm were a car dealership and the lawyers were salespersons. Often, the lawyers who made partner weren't the skilled professionals but the best rainmakers, who knew how to bill and work a cocktail hour to garner clients."[48]

Similarly, University of Wisconsin law professor Marc Galanter says, "Something of a Frankenstein's monster has been created in many of the big firms. People are experiencing this incredible pressure to bill. This has corroded firm collegiality. Lawyers within the same firm are competitive with each other, adding to the pressures that result in billing abuses."[49] An anonymous former partner of a large Chicago-based firm lamented in The American Lawyer about his working environment, "It's a law firm of the eighties and nineties. You have a bunch of people tied together by money, and that's it."[50] There is no reason why such amoral, mercantilist firms should receive so much business. If corporate executives were more careful about the firms they retained, "hiring a lawyer instead of the firm," in corporate attorney William Langston's words,[51] and came to realize that big companies can often be better represented by smaller, "boutique" firms with different billing imperatives, the marketplace could abate the current billing scandal.

The incentive to bill can create a conflict of interest between client and attorney that is resolved, according to Professor Ross, by seeing what is good for the firm's coffers and what is good for the client's legal problem as synonymous. "Excessive billing is primarily the result of delusions by attorneys about what is in the best interests of their client. Having an incentive to overbill clients, most big firm attorneys, particularly litigators, appear to have convinced themselves that their Herculean hours serve their clients' interests."

Many experts on billing, as well as wise corporate lawyers, agree that the hourly rate system is the culprit behind much of this abuse. It is a system that, as Professor Ross puts it, "encourages inefficiency, excessive litigation, and fraud." John Toothman says that clients have come to realize that "all too often, hourly billing translates into billing all the client can afford to pay. As a result, many are looking for alternatives as a way to keep their legal costs within reason."

The once unassailable hourly billing system is under unprecedented scrutiny and, according to some, may be giving way to what is known as "alternate billing." Many of the emerging alternate billing schemes can be compared with the system of "managed care" currently in vogue in the field of health care. In place of hourly billing, alternate billing uses a form of capitated billing, meaning one price pays for all.

The simplest form of capitated legal billing is the flat fee, meaning that a firm and a client will agree on the total fee for a given litigation or other legal task or series of tasks. Flat-fee billing is growing in popularity. A number of major corporations, including Chrysler Corporation and Aluminum Company of America (ALCOA), have begun to hire law firms on a flat-fee basis.[52] The flat fee can benefit the corporate bottom line. There is greater predictability about legal costs. Lawyers who accept cases on a flat-fee basis have no incentive to run up unnecessary hours. And a long-term flat-fee arrangement, where an outside law firm handles a substantial portion of a corporation's litigation for an extended period, can encourage outside lawyers to suggest internal corporate reforms to reduce future legal skirmishes—because the lawyer will not make additional money from such skirmishes.

An even more compelling reason to support flat fees is the benefit society in general, and the legal system in particular, will reap from such a system. Many of the systemic problems addressed in this book are spurred by the dual incentives of client and law firm to "work the system." However, once a law firm's compensation is limited to one price, the firm, at least, loses its own incentives to engage in excessive legal work.

Flat fees might well curb obstructionist discovery tactics because, although clients may continue to urge them, lawyers will no longer have the same automatic incentives to go along. After all, how many lawyers are going to want to spend the many grueling and boring hours it takes to play bad-faith games with discovery when they won't be paid extra for it? Judges will also benefit from a flat-fee system, since they will be relieved from having to read some of the volumes of pleadings associated with discovery disputes and meritless motions. Frivolous claims and defenses will also likely be reduced. In a system where the longer a case lasts, the less profit is made, it would not make any financial sense for lawyers to "churn" cases and keep them going for years if a reasonable outcome is obtainable in a shorter period of time.

A flat-fee system is not without its problems. Flat fees are to law firms what a health maintenance organization is to health care consumers. In general, HMOs are paid a flat fee by the member and in return are required to provide all necessary health care. Just as the financial incentive of an HMO may tempt the company to provide too little medical care rather than too much, so too the financial incentive for the flat-fee-compensated lawyer is to do less work rather than more. Clients paying their attorneys a flat fee need to be vigilant to ensure that their lawyers do not cut too many corners.

Many clients recognize this potential pitfall in the flat fee and look to another form of alternative billing that provides their lawyers with a financial incentive to perform well. "Clients are increasingly looking for value and a system that promotes efficiency," says attorney Lee Fifer of the four-hundred-lawyer firm McGuire, Woods, Battle & Boothe. "Hourly billing tends to be arbitrary. It reinforces the already existing incentive for lawyers to be thorough. But alternative billing adds in the important factor of efficiency. It is economically rooted and will lead to more use of electronics, paralegals, and other forms of keeping bills down."[53]

The most popular alternative is what is known as "value billing." The purpose of value billing, according to John Toothman, is to reduce fees while rewarding quality legal work with financial incentives. Thus, a lawyer may receive a lower hourly rate with a bonus earned for obtaining a good result or the right to bill at a higher rate for each successful legal maneuver. "Value billing shifts some of the risk of paying legal fees and expenses from the client to the firm," Toothman says.

"The object is to pay just enough in fees to obtain the optimal net result, considering the legal expenses and the amount at stake in the underlying transaction." With value billing, says Fifer, "what you are doing is taking the risk along with the client, with the idea that everybody shares in the endeavor's success." Of course, this kind of reward system raises its own set of ethical concerns—if the real earnings come only with victory, and not simply with responsible, zealous representation, win-at-all-cost tactics may actually increase.

Indeed, flat fees and value billing will not deter a client who is willing to pay whatever is necessary to induce lawyers to obfuscate and stonewall. But if these methods become widespread, they will reduce the likelihood of law firms putting unsuspecting clients through the overbilling mill.

BILLING ABUSES AND PROFESSIONAL ETHICS

Reforming the prevailing legal billing system is only a partial answer to the problem of overbilling. Such larcenous conduct requires a much more rigorous response, including professional discipline and criminal sanction.

Unfortunately, most state legal ethics boards have generally failed to punish lawyers who overbill. "There is no doubt that billing abuses are unethical," New York University law professor and ethics expert Stephen Gillers says. "The problem is, grievance committees view it as more of a business dispute than an ethics violation. You can count on two hands the number of cases brought because of billing violations."[54] With the bar association cops winking at or ignoring the practice, unscrupulous lawyers have little to fear from overbilling. If they get caught, in most cases they are able to feign shock that they "mistakenly" overcharged and quickly agree to grant restitution for all overcharges. At worst, a client is lost, but the lawyer or firm remains free to bait the hook for other victims.

This complacency by ethics boards, as well as state bar associations, must be challenged. "Attorneys need to recognize that unethical time-based billing practices harm not only the client but also the legal profession, the courts, and the public," Professor Ross says. "It calls into question the integrity of the judicial system and weakens public faith in the quality of the nation's justice."[55]

The American Bar Association appears to have come to the same conclusion. On December 6, 1993, it issued a formal opinion on billing for professional fees that seeks to prevent a lawyer from billing "more time than she actually spends on a matter" and requires invoices to "fairly reflect the basis on which the client's charges have been determined."[56] While it is sad that such basic honesty must be set forth in an ethics opinion, the opinion at least establishes the bar's recognition that a problem exists and, in the opinion's words, that a "contributing factor to the discouraging public opinion of the legal profession appears to be the billing practices of its members."

State ethics codes, modeled on the ABA's Code of Professional Responsibility or the ABA Model Rules of Professional Conduct, contain only broad prohibitions against unreasonable, excessive fees.[57] When asked about deterring lawyer billing abuses, Columbia University law professor H. Richard Uviller responded that the professional responsibility obligations of lawyers should be expanded. "It is time for lawyers to accept the principle that their profession requires absolute honesty about everything in all circumstances in which they act professionally. The current professional codes only require that level of integrity in the courtroom. I would like to expand that to include false statements to colleagues and clients and to the public at large." However, as for enforcing the expanded ethics through bar discipline, Professor Uviller expressed doubts, saying, "It is a sad day if we have to rely on a police force to keep lawyers in line. Insofar as the profession has departed from a sense of professionalism, there is very little that the code can do to make up for it."

The appropriate response to dishonesty in attorney billing cannot be a mere wringing of hands. Instead, victims of billing abuse should complain loudly to authorities, even if offered restitution from their overbilling lawyer. Otherwise, the perpetrator will likely victimize others. Honest leaders of the bar need to issue a clarion call that fraudulent and padded billing will result in sure and swift professional discipline and, if warranted, referral to criminal authorities for prosecution. Intentional billing fraud is theft and should be treated as such. Prosecutors have to treat complaints about billing fraud as seriously as they do other forms of theft.

Unless fee abusers come to perceive that their dishonesty will incur very serious costs, it is doubtful that overbilling will abate. Bad habits are often hard to break, and dysfunctional cultures are difficult to reform. Clients, including government clients, must aggressively monitor both the activities and the bills of lawyers to prevent massive overcharging and fraud.

CHAPTER 8

THE CORPORATE SCHEME TO WRECK OUR JUSTICE SYSTEM

*I*N THE LARGE UNITED STATES SENATE ANTEROOM ADJACENT TO the Senate floor, lobbyists frequently gather, waiting to corner senators during debates on pending legislation. On June 28, 1994, the Senate was considering S. 687, a bill to impose, for the first time, sharp federal restrictions on the rights of individuals injured by defectively manufactured products when they sue the corporate wrongdoers who harm them.

Two dozen business lobbyists patrolled the anteroom that evening, coordinating strategy and buttonholing senators and Senate staffers. These well-paid peddlers of influence, many of them attorneys, represented big corporations in the automobile, aircraft, drug, tobacco, food processing, chemical, insurance, and other industries. They were optimistic about the bill's chances of passage. They believed that their longtime, extensive drive to gut the common law of torts—the legal rules that govern lawsuits seeking justice for wrongful injuries—(a campaign they call "tort reform") was about to pay off. But these tort deformers, as we shall call them, remained concerned that senators might be swayed by opponents of the bill.

One of these opponents had come from Gainesville, Florida, at her own expense. She was Marlo Mahne, age twenty-four. Nine years earlier she had been riding in a Ford Mustang when it was rear-ended and burst into flames. She suffered severe burns and was left disfigured and blind in one eye. She alleged that the Mustang was defectively designed and sued Ford Motor Company, which agreed to an out-of-court settlement. Mahne believed that had S. 687 been in place at the time of her suit, Ford's potential liability would have been greatly reduced and the automaker might never have offered her a fair settlement to compensate for her injuries.

Mahne's presence outside the Senate chamber irked one of the leading lobbyists for the bill, Alfred W. Cortese, Jr., then a pugnacious partner in the corporate law firm Kirkland & Ellis. Cortese, so aggressive that his colleagues nicknamed him "Hector," apparently saw Mahne's efforts on behalf of tort victims as a violation of the usual rules of the game. To millionaire moguls and corporate mercenaries, "real people" like Marlo Mahne are not supposed to be so intimately involved in the legislative struggles that take place on Capitol Hill. She should have been at home nursing her wounds and contemplating her 103rd plastic surgery for her face, arms, and the rest of her body. Why, Senator William S. Cohen, Republican of Maine, after hearing her story firsthand, had been near tears as he talked with her on the way back to his office. And Senator Bob Graham, Democrat of Florida, said in a speech on the Senate floor that Mahne's "story speaks volumes about the reasons the product liability bill . . . should be defeated." Unlike Cortese, Mahne was not paid to be in the Senate anteroom. She was there out of a sense of civic responsibility, because she felt, in her words, a "moral commitment to millions of innocent motorists to let them know how unfair" the proposed legislation was.[1]

Unable to control himself any longer, Cortese strode over to Mahne's escort, Pamela Gilbert, then the director of the nonprofit group Public Citizen Congress Watch, pressed a quarter into her hand, and said, "Here is a quarter, Pam, for your sideshow."

Word of Cortese's cruel remark quickly spread, but he remained unrepentant, telling a reporter, "It's a disgusting display. They exploit those poor victims. I mean, my heart goes out to those poor people. But they [consumer groups] ought to know better. They should be ashamed of themselves for doing that kind of thing. . . . It's a disgrace. An absolute disgrace. It's sickening. What are they running? A circus? We want to trade freaks? It's disgusting."[2]

Not all tort deformers are so personally callous and insensitive. Indeed, Victor Schwartz, a partner at the D.C. law firm Crowell & Moring and the legal counsel for the American Tort Reform Association (ATRA), a corporate front group that has spearheaded the tort deform effort, told us that he strongly disapproved of Cortese's statement. But Schwartz's relentless, two-decades-long lobbying effort to limit injured victims' rights speaks much louder than a few words upbraiding a colleague. In the public policies they advocate, policies that would seriously weaken the ability of the Marlo Mahnes of the world to pursue justice in court and obtain adequate compensation from wrongdoers, the wealthy corporate lawyers who press for tort deform are, in effect, saying to victims, "Here's a quarter for your sideshow. Your agony is not important in the relative scheme of things. The injustice done to you must not get in the way of business."

Marlo Mahne is on to them. "I have undergone over one hundred and fifty medical procedures," she told us, "most of them painful skin grafts and reconstructive surgery. My fingers have been amputated to the second knuckle on both of my hands. I have little hair. My earlobes were completely burned off. I am unable to see out of my left eye. I have obvious scarring over most of my body and all of my face." Mahne can't talk about the details of her case because after six years of struggle, she was forced to agree to a confidential settlement in order to receive compensation. But she can and does speak out against attempts to weaken the law so as to make it difficult for victims like her to sue for damages, attempts sponsored in part by the very company that caused her injuries. Having been there, Mahne is enraged by the ongoing attacks on the civil justice system. "If laws like S. 687 become law, people like me would never have a chance to seek justice against the corporate wrongdoer who caused our injury," she says.

The day after Alfred Cortese branded Marlo Mahne's sincere, principled lobbying effort a "sideshow," he and his fellow tort deformers, to their shock and dismay, lost the Senate vote on the bill, coming up three votes short. But in May 1995, following the Republican party takeover of Congress, the tort deformers had their way in the Senate, which passed a new version of the bill. The tort deformers had even greater success in Newt Gingrich's House of Representatives, which adopted legislation that went even further, weakening the tort law rules of the states not only as to product liability but also as to liability for medical malpractice casualties.

On May 2, 1996, President Clinton, who has wavered on the tort deform controversy, found the courage to veto a bill that would have sharply limited the right to recover damages in product liability cases. But the tort deformers' lobbying push continues, both at the federal and the state level.

This organized attack on the civil justice system is a direct assault on victims. Led by corporate lawyers, corporation-financed "think tanks," front groups, and campaign-contribution-hungry politicians like Speaker of the House Newt Gingrich (Republican of Georgia) and Christopher Dodd (chairman of the Democratic party and Democrat of Connecticut), it seeks a radical dismembering of the justice system's ability to hold corporations accountable to people they have wronged.

At its foundation, it is anticonsumer and anti–individual rights. As the nonprofit Alliance for Justice has put it, its agenda seeks to "elevate corporate profits and private wealth over social justice and individual rights as the cornerstones of our legal process,"[3] or, as Marlo Mahne so aptly states, to make "financial profits of corporations more important than people's lives." The tort deform movement is a brazen effort by corporations and politicians beholden to corporate interests to pull off—under the guise of a "common sense" reform—a nationwide perpetual bailout for polluters, swindlers, reckless health care providers, and makers of tobacco, defective vehicles, dangerous drugs, and many other hazardous consumer products.

The effort to wreck the civil justice system has grown over recent years into a veritable industry. This isn't grassroots politics, generated from and driven by the people. Behind the various front groups agitating for tort deform in Washington and state capitals are the usual suspects: America's richest industrial and insurance companies and their power-lawyer lieutenants from such big firms as Gibson, Dunn & Crutcher, Covington & Burling, and LeBoeuf, Lamb, Greene & MacRae. As a comprehensive review in the Washington, D.C.–based publication *Legal Times* of the most prominent tort deform groups concluded: "The money trail typically leads back to a few dozen of the nation's largest corporations."[4]

For example, the American Tort Reform Association includes among its members chemical and pharmaceutical firms like Dow Chemical, Eli Lilly, Exxon, Johnson & Johnson, Mobil, Monsanto, Pfizer, and Union Carbide; tobacco maker Philip Morris; alcohol purveyors like Anheuser-Busch and Miller Brewing; insurance companies like Aetna and GEICO; weapons makers like General Electric, Boeing, Honeywell, and Rockwell International; health care businesses like Humana, Inc.; trade or professional groups like the Chemical Manufacturers Association, the Beer Institute, and the Sporting Arms and Ammunition Manufacturers Association; and the American Medical Association and many other doctors' groups. Another proud member of ATRA is the Washington, D.C., power law firm Covington & Burling, which represents the interests of so many big companies in regulatory and litigation matters. Although ATRA includes small businesses, most of its money is provided by large corporations.[5]

Another tort deform lobbying group, the Product Liability Coordinating Committee, includes Exxon, Monsanto, General Motors, Ford, TRW, Aetna, and other big corporations, plus business lobbying groups like the National Association of Manufacturers, the United States Chamber of Commerce, and the Chemical Manufacturers Association.

Again, most of the funding comes from big business. And PLCC's chief
counsel is Victor Schwartz, the same lawyer who serves as general
counsel for ATRA.[6] PLCC has paid Schwartz $18,000 a month for his
efforts, with additional monthly checks of $20,000 and $15,000 going
to two other Washington corporate lawyers.[7]

Yet another tort deform operation, the Civil Justice Reform Group,
is made up of the top in-house lawyers from forty of the biggest U.S.
corporations, including General Motors, Ford, Exxon, Dupont, Johnson & Johnson, Caterpillar, Metropolitan Life, and Aetna. This group
is sometimes called the $100,000 club, because that is the minimum
amount most members pay to join.[8] CJRG is directed by Theodore B.
Olson, a partner at the Washington, D.C., office of 550-lawyer Gibson,
Dunn & Crutcher and once a top Reagan administration Justice Department official.

A former tort deform lobbyist told Legal Times, "In a true sense, the
PLCC, ATRA, and CJRG are all financed by the same people."[9]

Had enough? What about Americans for Lawsuit Reform (formerly
Citizens for Civil Justice Reform), which has counted among its members insurance companies Aetna, Allstate, and New York Life; drug
and chemical giants Eli Lilly, Chevron, and Texaco; tobacco makers
Philip Morris and R.J. Reynolds/Nabisco; defense contractors Rockwell
and General Dynamics; health giant Humana, Georgia Pacific Corporation, Amway Corporation, the American Petroleum Institute, the
American Corporate Counsels Association, the giant law firm Skadden, Arps, Slate, Meagher & Flom, and ATRA itself.[10]

There's also Lawyers for Civil Justice Reform, directed by none
other than Alfred Cortese; the Coalition for Uniform Product Liability
Law; and the Product Liability Alliance. And all of these groups get
support in their lobbying efforts from the dozens of corporate, medical,
accounting, and securities lobbying groups already in Washington and
state capitals to influence legislation on business issues.

And that's just the lobbying outfits. The tort deform propaganda
campaign, intricate in design and broad in scope, is waged on other
fronts as well. Corporations finance indentured "think tanks" such as
the Manhattan Institute for Policy Research and the Heritage Foundation, whose members author books and opinion pieces, appear as "experts" on radio and television talk shows, testify before legislative
committees, and present their views to newspaper editorial boards, selling their corporate sponsors' agenda.

Tort deform organizations are often quite candid about the quid pro
quo contributors can expect. For example, William M. H. Hammett,
president of the Manhattan Institute, wrote to potential contributors

in November 1992, "Our entire effort [to change the legal system] depends on the voluntary contributions from corporations and foundations. . . . We feel confident that any funds made available to the Judicial Studies Program will yield tremendous returns at this point— perhaps the *highest 'return on investment'* available in the philanthropic field today." (Emphasis added.)[11]

Corporations and their front groups also spend millions on propaganda advertising on television and radio, in newspapers and magazines, and on billboards to attack lawsuits against them, the courts, and the lawyers who represent the injured and the defrauded. Editorials and features in publications like *Forbes* echo these views.

Politicians who toe the big-business line are fed corporate campaign contributions. They add fuel to the tort deform fire, demanding change to "save the economy." Speaker of the House Newt Gingrich, a leading advocate for tort deform, receives extensive financial and political support from those business interests who will most benefit from the weakening of tort law, as do many of his pro–tort deform colleagues.[12]

Corporate-sponsored nonprofit law firms such as the Pacific Legal Foundation use tax-exempt moneys donated by corporations to represent their tort deform agenda in court, particularly in appellate court proceedings on crucial legal issues. By financing these nonprofits, corporations take two bites out of the apple: first with their in-house and power-law-firm attorneys and then with surrogates masquerading as altruistic public-interest advocates.

The tort deformers' strategy is straightforward: Play on Americans' suspicions about greedy "shyster" lawyers, i.e., those lawyers who represent individuals seeking compensation for personal injuries. Take the few lawsuits each year where juries award large punitive damages and distort the facts beyond recognition. Spread fears of job loss, of high insurance premiums caused by lawsuits, and of a national economy crippled by a litigation "explosion."

Such scare tactics were employed in March 1996 when Silicon Valley mega-millionaires and other business tycoons financed three initiatives in California designed to take rights away from consumers and give them to corporations. Proposition 200 would have instituted a radical form of no-fault auto insurance, denying consumers nearly all access to the courts if injured in an accident and forcing drivers into mandatory arbitration proceedings over compensation disputes with their own insurance companies. Proposition 201 would have made it harder for people cheated in securities transactions to bring suit in state court by compelling small investors to post a bond to cover a corporation's attorney fees and by instituting a system, known as loser pays (discussed later in this chapter), designed to deter cheated consumers from seeking redress. Proposition 202 would have cut attorney contingency fees, thereby making it harder for consumers to find an attorney they could afford.

This was a battle the business community desperately wanted to win. But industry representatives knew the initiatives would never be accepted on their merits. So, the tactic of the backers was to avoid focusing on the content of the initiatives and instead launch an unremitting attack on lawyers. Not all lawyers were attacked, however. Big corporations and insurance companies like their own lawyers. Thus, only lawyers who represent individuals were vilified. (None of the ballot initiatives would have restricted the activities of corporate or insurance company attorneys, only attorneys representing consumers.) Proving that the tort deform movement springs from the corporate roots and not the grass roots, all three propositions were defeated by California voters, 200 and 201 by very large margins.

The very people screaming the loudest about the need to "free" the market by reducing government's ability to protect consumers through regulation of business are often the same advocates who seek to foist upon society the deeply uncapitalistic notion that business need not take full responsibility for its own injurious acts. *The National Law Journal*, a publication devoted to covering legal news, has recognized how destructive the tort deform restriction agenda is, editorializing that it is "essentially, Stage Two of the unfinished Reagan revolution, the first stage of which was deregulation. But less stringent supervision of the workplace and the environment [has] made the courts more necessary as recourse for the injured and as a brake on corporate negligence. Exploding Pintos and baby toys that kill expose the gaps in existing regulation. Ergo, tort 'reform' which would restrict access to the courthouse and enable corporations to relax their guard."[13]

A DISINFORMATION CAMPAIGN

Money, hype, sloganeering, scapegoating, sound-bite advocacy, and the power of repetition can effectively obfuscate the truth. The relentless propaganda campaign pressed by tort deformers is omnipresent in the United States today. A series of myths about tort law are accepted as reality by many busy citizens who don't have the time to cut through the noise and separate fact from fiction. Have you had the wool pulled over your eyes? Have you accepted corporate disinformation as proven truth? It depends on whether you believe to be true any of the following statements, each of which is, in fact, false:

> Myth No. 1: There has been a "litigation explosion" by individuals suing businesses in recent years.

> Myth No. 2: Juries tend to have an antibusiness bias and look for ways to punish corporations with "deep pockets" full of cash.

> Myth No. 3: Punitive damages awards are designed to and frequently do punish companies that meant no harm but simply made good-faith mistakes.

> Myth No. 4: Lawsuits against doctors are out of control and are far out of proportion to the deaths or major injuries actually caused by medical malpractice.

> Myth No. 5: Forcing consumers to settle their disputes with businesses through binding arbitration, rather than the court system, allows for quick and effective justice.

> Myth No. 6: The reason plaintiffs' lawyers work on a contingency fee basis—getting paid out of the proceeds of a judgment rather than by the hour—is because they are greedy and want to take both defendants and their own clients for all they are worth.

> Myth No. 7: The proposal to require the loser of a lawsuit to pay the winner's attorney fees will prevent frivolous lawsuits and allow meritorious claims to go forward.

Let's examine these dangerous myths—dangerous because they threaten to mislead the public into supporting laws that will ultimately weaken our economy as well as our system of justice—one by one.

THERE IS NO "LITIGATION EXPLOSION"

"I believe that litigation is causing unnecessary hemorrhaging of the American economy," Barry Keene, former president of the Association for California Tort Reform, says.[14] Indeed, a major thesis of the tort deform movement is that corporations have been increasingly assailed by frivolous lawsuits and therefore, in the name of jobs and the economy, they need new laws to protect them from being victimized.

This false concept has been peddled relentlessly throughout the nation. "There has been a mass public relations campaign by manufacturers, marketers, insurance companies, and others to persuade the general public and many legislators that the tort system is somehow bad for the economy," says Suffolk University law professor Charles P. Kindregan. "And I don't think the public has effectively heard the other side."[15]

Are corporations truly being victimized by an ever-increasing number of frivolous lawsuits? Has the civil justice system really caused a "hemorrhaging" of the American economy?

Simply, no. "Despite all the rhetoric about litigiousness, empirical research shows that Americans are not all that litigious," Deborah R. Hensler, director of the Rand Institute for Civil Justice (part of the nonprofit, nonpartisan Rand Corporation), told a seminar of corporate lawyers meeting in San Francisco in 1994. Mark Silbergeld, codirector of the Washington office of Consumers Union, the group that publishes *Consumer Reports* magazine, agrees. "There is no litigation crisis," he told us. "The supporters of tort reform use the argument as one in a series of ploys to convince people to accept their proposals. They have used it at times and abandoned it at other times. But the data just doesn't support the argument."[16]

Here are the facts. Professor Marc Galanter, director of the Institute of Legal Studies at the University of Wisconsin, found that between 1985 and 1991, aside from asbestos suits (an area that experienced substantial growth in this period when it was discovered that numerous workers had been exposed to cancer-causing materials) product liability cases in the federal courts declined from 8,268 cases to 4,992 cases, a reduction of more than 40 percent.[17]

U.S. Representative Christopher Cox, Republican of California, is a key member of Speaker Newt Gingrich's leadership team. Appearing on PBS's *MacNeil/Lehrer NewsHour* in February 1995, he complained, in a debate over the tort deform agenda, that there were 100 million lawsuits filed annually in the United States.

But this 100 million figure was extremely misleading—it had almost nothing to do with tort law. The National Center for State Courts reports that 93,786,499 cases were filed in state trial courts in 1992. But their breakdown reveals that only 19,707,374 of these were civil cases at all—the rest were traffic and other ordinance violations (59,102,861), criminal cases (13,245,543), and juvenile adjudications (1,730,721). Only 9 percent of the civil cases—less than 2 percent of all cases—were tort cases. (The largest category in the civil case docket is domestic relations—35 percent.) Only 4 percent of tort cases—less than one tenth of 1 percent of all cases—were product liability cases, and only 5 percent of tort cases were for any form of malpractice. (Fifty-

eight percent of tort suits concerned the operation of motor vehicles—
cases that have little to do with the corporate tort deform agenda.)[18]

We wrote and called Representative Cox on March 6, 1995, asking
him to clarify his misleading remark prior to a key House vote on tort
deform legislation. He did not respond.

According to a study by the Rand Corporation, a think tank that
receives substantial corporate support, only 10 percent of people who
are injured in accidents ever use the tort system to seek compensation.[19] Minneapolis attorney G. Marc Whitehead, who cochaired a
1992 conference at the Brookings Institution (another mainstream
think tank) on the future of jury trials in civil cases, told a reporter that
lawyers sense "that litigation is actually down overall. People find it's
too expensive, slow and difficult."[20] Even a November 1995 study by a
corporate consulting firm acknowledged that since 1985 the cost of
tort liability has increased no faster than the growth of the overall
economy.[21]

Tort deformers would have you believe that one area of particularly
out-of-control litigation growth is the securities field. They claim that
a rabid army of plaintiffs' lawyers bring constant fraud lawsuits aimed at
bringing down the most responsible companies and brokers of stocks
and bonds. Congress passed a bill—modeled on the provisions in Newt
Gingrich's Contract with America—to make it much more difficult for
investors to sue for securities fraud. The bill, pushed by Senator Dodd,
makes it harder to prove fraud and otherwise skews securities suits in
favor of defendants. It became law in December 1992 when Congress
overrode a veto by President Clinton.[22]

But, in light of massive financial debacles like the savings and loan
crisis (see Chapter 1), is there really justification for changes in the law
that make it easier for unscrupulous and irresponsible brokers, bankers,
lawyers, and accountants to swindle small investors? Is there really a
reason to weaken legal remedies available to individual investors,
when, as Herbert J. Stein, chairman of the Council of Economic Ad-
visers in the Nixon and Ford administrations and a fellow at the conservative American Enterprise Institute, puts it, such remedies ensure
"that the passive investor [is] willing to put his money in private enterprise," a condition "essential to the efficient functioning of our economic system"?[23]

The truth is, as a USA Today editorial noted, there is "no litigation
explosion" in the securities field.[24] According to the Securities and Exchange Commission, barely 1 percent of publicly traded companies are
sued by investors each year.[25] Herbert J. Stein, who strongly opposes
the tort deformers' agenda on securities laws, notes that in 1993 there

were 238 securities fraud suits organized as multiple-plaintiff class actions filed in the entire country.[26] Securities cases make up about one tenth of 1 percent of federal court civil suits and an even lower percentage of cases in state court. The number of such cases has held steady for two decades.[27]

How about the malpractice field? Aren't more and more people suing doctors and hospitals over minor mishaps? There is no convincing evidence for that proposition. New York State Justice Helen E. Freedman, who has presided over numerous malpractice trials, told a reporter, "In medical malpractice, if anything, the quality of cases has gotten better. Plaintiffs know that these cases are very costly and time-consuming, and I think they've become more reluctant" to file lawsuits.[28]

If there has been any kind of litigation explosion, it has not been fueled by personal injury victims, investors, or other individual citizens. Rather, it has been in businesses suing businesses. Indeed, nearly *half* of all federal lawsuits filed between 1985 and 1991 involved interbusiness disputes.[29] But tort deform groups generally do not propose restricting the rights of businesses to sue one another.

JURORS ARE ACTUALLY INCLINED TO RULE IN FAVOR OF BUSINESS

Another constant cry of the tort deform movement is that juries are biased against business. Jurors are alleged to be so antibusiness and/or so sympathetic to injured claimants that they are likely to exploit a "deep pocket"—a business or person perceived to have a lot of money—regardless of the validity of the lawsuit.

According to the deep-pocket theory, juries decide cases based on emotion and hostility toward big business rather than the facts of each case. To illustrate their contentions, tort deformers are fond of using "horror stories," brief tales of supposedly frivolous lawsuits that led to huge, unwarranted jury verdicts. The goal is to make people angry at the justice system.

THE CASE OF THE SCALDED GRANDMOTHER

The mother of all "horror stories" used by tort deformers to support their attack on individual rights is the case of Stella Liebeck, the woman who sued McDonald's over hot coffee. This is the story you usually hear from the tort deform movement: An elderly woman bought a cup of coffee at a McDonald's drive-through window. She opened the cup on her lap and spilled coffee. She sued McDonald's. In August 1994, a New Mexico jury found McDonald's liable for $2.9 million, including $2.7 million in punitive damages.[30]

Here was the kind of case that tort deformers love to use as proof that the civil justice system has run amok. The U.S. Chamber of Commerce, an industry group, created radio ads bellowing, "Is it fair to get a couple of million dollars from a restaurant just because you spilled your hot coffee on yourself? Of course not. It's ridiculous. But it happened." The American Tort Reform Association's ad was similar: "A jury awarded a woman $2.9 million in a lawsuit against McDonald's. She spilled coffee on her lap while sitting in her car and claimed it was too hot." Mobil Oil, in an advertisement in *The New York Times*, whined that "nearly $3 million was awarded to a customer who spilled hot coffee on herself."[31] Newspaper and magazine editorials, influenced and driven by corporate propaganda, attacked the jury. Talk radio listeners around the nation called their favorite shows to sneer, complain, and mock the elderly Mrs. Liebeck. In his *Tonight Show* monologues, Jay Leno offered a relentless series of jokes about the case. The popular situation comedy *Seinfeld* depicted the manic Kramer character, spurred by a cynical, greedy lawyer, suing after he stuffed a Styrofoam coffee cup in his pants to sneak it into the movies.

But the actual facts of the case tell a very different story than the one popularized in tort deform myth: It is the story of a verdict based on serious injury and hard evidence of indifference and callousness by McDonald's employees and executives. And it is not a case where somebody got "nearly $3 million"—the trial judge upheld the jury's decision that McDonald's should be made to pay punitive damages, but he reduced the total damages—compensatory and punitive—to $640,000. McDonald's then, in exchange for dropping an appeal, settled the case for an undisclosed amount, perhaps less than $640,000. (ABC News correspondent John Stoessel, a fervid advocate of business nonregulation, ended a one-sided television segment on the McDonald's case by stating that Liebeck, in an interview, refused to disclose the amount of the settlement. What he failed to mention was that it was McDonald's that had insisted, as a condition of settlement, that Liebeck agree not to reveal the sum she received.)

Mrs. Liebeck, according to her daughter, Judy Allen, views the relentless carping and lying about her case "as a very personal attack on her."[32] The architects of the smear campaign against Stella Liebeck don't want you to know what actually happened.

In February 1992, Liebeck, a seventy-nine-year-old former department store clerk, was a passenger in her grandson's car. She bought coffee at the drive-through window of a McDonald's in Albuquerque, New Mexico. She opened the Styrofoam coffee cup while the car was stationary—not in motion, as some false accounts of the case allege—for the purpose of adding cream and sugar. When she removed the lid of the small cup, all of the coffee spilled out. She suffered third-degree burns on 6 percent of her body, including her groin, inner thighs, and buttocks. She spent eight days in the hospital and received skin grafts. She suffered tremendous pain. Indeed, Mrs. Liebeck's physician testified that her case was one of the worst burn injuries he had ever seen. It took her over two years to recover from her injuries. There is permanent scarring over 16 percent of her body.[33]

After she was injured, Liebeck, who had never filed a lawsuit before, did not rush to court demanding a multimillion-dollar judgment. Instead, she spent six months attempting, without retaining a lawyer, to convince McDonald's to cover her medical and other expenses— $15,000 to $20,000, not much, considering that she was obligated to reimburse Medicare for about $10,000 out of any settlement—and to reconsider its coffee temperature so others would not be harmed. McDonald's responded with a letter offering $800.[34]

After she finally filed suit in state court, a court-appointed mediator recommended that McDonald's settle the case for $225,000. The company refused. Just before trial, Liebeck's attorney offered to settle for $300,000. McDonald's again refused.[35]

As trial began, Stella Liebeck faced a jury with typical juror doubts about such a lawsuit. "I was very skeptical of the case," one juror told us. "It seemed strange to me to have a coffee spill as the center of a lawsuit. In my mind, the plaintiff was really going to have to prove her case."[36] This juror asked to remain anonymous to avoid the media spotlight, so we'll call her Juror A.

Betty E. Farnham, another of the jurors, agrees. "I was definitely not biased against McDonald's," she told us. "When I first heard about the case, I thought, yeah, right. A cup of coffee. Why are they wasting our time?"[37]

As the evidence unfolded in the one-week trial, the jurors' skepticism toward Liebeck was overcome by evidence that the temperature of McDonald's coffee was so high that it created an unreasonable risk of very serious third-degree burns. When such burns occur, the affected skin is literally burned away down to the muscle or fatty-tissue layer. In Liebeck's case, this skin obliteration took just a few seconds. McDonald's required by corporate directive that all its coffee be served at between 180 and 190 degrees Fahrenheit. Evidence Liebeck introduced at trial showed that, at 190 degrees, third-degree burns occur in less than three seconds. At 160 degrees, a temperature at which many other restaurants hold their coffee, it takes twenty seconds to cause third-degree burns—enough time in most cases to wipe away the coffee.[38]

"When I heard how hot they kept the coffee," Juror A told us, "it started me thinking. I began to realize that people could buy coffee at the drive-up window and not realize how very hot the coffee was and how seriously they could be burned. And in a car, once the coffee spills, there is nowhere to go to avoid injury. It's not like being in a restaurant, where you can stand up and try to brush the hot coffee off you."

The jurors found McDonald's liable for keeping their coffee too hot for human consumption and for failing to warn consumers of the inherent danger. (They apparently decided that the phrase "Caution contents hot" in small gold writing on the cup was insufficient in relation to the danger.) They concluded that $200,000 was appropriate to compensate Liebeck for her expenses and pain and suffering, but they reduced their actual award of compensatory damages to $160,000, concluding that Liebeck's own negligence in spilling the coffee contributed to her injuries.

Why did the jury hit McDonald's for $2.7 million in punitive damages? "If the media had been privy to the facts as we were, there would not have been an uproar," insists Betty Farnham. "The thing that impressed all of us was that there had been a long history of people being severely burned by McDonald's coffee." The jury learned that there were seven hundred other burn cases between 1982 and 1992, including cases of children burned when McDonald's employees dropped or knocked over coffee cups. McDonald's had settled a number of these cases out of court.[39] The Shriners Burn Institute in Cincinnati had reported to fast-food chains like McDonald's about serious injuries caused by hot coffee. P. Robert Knaff, a safety consultant for McDonald's, testified, however, that there was no cause to turn down the heat. The reason: With billions of cups served annually, less than a thousand burn injuries over a decade was statistically insignificant. McDonald's thought it was worth keeping up the heat allegedly to improve taste and ensure that coffee stayed hot for later consumption.

"McDonald's tried to play down the significance of these cases as statistically trivial," Farnham said, "but did not seem to appreciate that behind each case was a human being who had gone through one of the most painful injuries that one can receive."

Similarly, juror Jack Elliot, a retired real estate agent, told The Washington Post that he was skeptical of Liebeck's case until he "heard the callous testimony" of McDonald's witnesses. The claim of McDonald's expert Knaff that the many documented burn cases were statistically insignificant among the billions of cups McDonald's has sold "did not set well with the jury."[40]

"The idea behind the punitive damages was not to enrich the plaintiff," Juror A says, "but to get McDonald's attention. They knew their coffee was served so hot that it could severely hurt people. But McDonald's employees did not care about the people being burned. They knew there was a problem, there had been at least seven hundred cases over many years, and yet they had taken no action to study the matter or adequately warn their customers. Their callous disregard was very upsetting."

Betty Farnham echoes the point. "McDonald's serves five hundred million cups of coffee through the drive-up window each year. That is a very high degree of consumer risk, and I think the company was totally insensitive to the safety of their customers. If this had been the first case or the tenth case, and if McDonald's had made any effort to reduce the danger, if they had shown they even cared about the seven hundred cases, we might have looked at things differently."

The jurors had ample ground for concluding that McDonald's had failed to take adequate steps to remedy known dangers. One of the witnesses called by McDonald's was one Christopher Appleton, a McDonald's quality assurance employee since 1976. On cross-examination by Reed Morgan, Liebeck's attorney, Appleton admitted that the coffee kept by McDonald's at between 180 and 190 degrees is hazardous:

> Q: [Y]ou know, as a matter of fact, that coffee is a hazard, selling it at 180 to 190 degrees, don't you?
>
> A: I have testified before, the fact that this coffee can cause burns.
>
> Q: It is hazardous at this temperature?
>
> A: At that high temperature the coffee is a hazard. . . .
>
> Q: If customers attempt to swallow that coffee, isn't it a fact that it will scald their throat or esophagus?
>
> A: Yes, under those conditions, if they could get the coffee in their throat, that could happen, yes.[41]

After Appleton testified that he knew more about the safety of hot coffee than anyone else at the McDonald's corporation, he acknowledged that in 1988, in another burn case, he had seen pictures of a young woman severely injured by McDonald's coffee:

> Q: Isn't it a fact that back in 1988, when I showed you the pictures of the young lady that was burned in that situation, that you were appalled and surprised that coffee could cause that kind of burn?
>
> A: Yes, I had never seen photographs like that before.
>
> Q: All right. In those six years, you still have not attempted, yourself, or know of anyone within the corporation that has attempted to find out the rate of speed, the lack of margin of safety in serving coffee at this temperature right? . . .
>
> A: No, we have not.[42]

Appleton also boasted of the "very good insulating properties" of McDonald's Styrofoam coffee cup, which keeps liquids hotter than ceramic cups used at home: "When you are holding it in your hand, it is not going to be readily apparent that you have very hot liquid in the cup. It does an excellent job of insulating."[43]

This testimony and other evidence of indifference by McDonald's, and the company's failure to warn its customers adequately of how badly they could be burned by spilling its superhot coffee, led the jurors to award punitive damages in the amount of $2.7 million—an amount the jury selected because it was equal to two days' worth of McDonald's coffee sales. It is a settled rule of law, in New Mexico and elsewhere, that a jury may take into account a defendant's wealth as one factor in setting an appropriate punitive damage award. As the New Mexico Supreme Court has explained, "To be an effective punishment, the award must be high enough, in relation to the defendant's assets, to hurt."[44] At the time of the jury verdict in the Liebeck case, McDonald's was reporting annual worldwide profits of $1.083 billion.[45]

"McDonald's lawyer [Tracy E. McGee of Albuquerque] did a good job trying to defend an untenable case," Betty Farnham told us. "But we had a duty. The main thing we in the jury wanted to do was to get a message out to the company that 'you have a problem and you have a responsibility to fix it.' That is something they are going to have to take into account when they make corporate policy."

It wasn't just the jury who found McDonald's behavior suitable for punitive damages. A month after the jury verdict, trial judge Robert Scott, a conservative Republican, reduced the punitive damages award because he concluded that $2.7 million was out of proportion to the injuries suffered. But he denied McDonald's motion to set aside the verdict, and he upheld $480,000 of the punitive damages award—three times the compensatory damages awarded. Moreover, he, too, weighed in against the corporation:[46]

> I think that there was evidence and argument about the Defendant's knowledge that the coffee could cause serious, third degree, full tissue burns. The Defendant McDonald's knew that the coffee, at the time it was served, was too hot for human consumption. . . .
>
> [T]he written transcript is not going to reveal the attitudes of corporate indifference presented by demeanor or of the witnesses for the Defendant McDonald's as well as their employees, but the jury was exposed to it and I think that they properly considered it in their deliberations. And let me say that with knowing the risk of harm, the evidence and testimony would indicate that McDonald's consciously made no serious effort to warn its consumers by placing just the most simple, adequate warning on the lid of the cup in which the coffee was served . . . This is all evidence of culpable corporate mental state and I conclude that the award of punitive damages is and was appropriate to punish and deter the Defendant for their wanton conduct and to send a clear message to this Defendant that corrective measures are appropriate.

So, what was presented by tort deformers as an unjust verdict by a runaway, antibusiness jury turns out to be a reasoned decision based on true corporate indifference to the safety of consumers. "I feel as if I have done my duty," Juror A says. "The coffee at my local McDonald's is definitely cooler. That means people are safer. I feel good about that." Indeed, after the verdict, McDonald's in Albuquerque was serving its coffee at 158 degrees,[47] certainly hot enough to satisfy drinkers but cool enough to reduce the risk of injury.

If the jury, and the judge who ratified part of the punitive damages award, had acted so improperly, or if McDonald's felt that the facts of this case justified a rethinking of the law of punitive damages in New Mexico or nationwide, it could have pursued an appeal. Instead, McDonald's settled with Mrs. Liebeck, with a condition that the terms be confidential.

But tort deformers haven't allowed the truth to get in the way of their disinformation campaign. They continue to use the McDonald's

spilled coffee case as "evidence" that biased, incompetent juries dominate the court system.

It's not as if the tort deformers don't know the truth. Many national publications, including *Newsweek* and the business staple *The
Wall Street Journal*, have reported on the facts behind the verdict. And
Jay Leno has stopped joking about the case, a *Tonight Show* staffer told
us, because he now knows the real facts. Indeed, Reed Morgan, Mrs.
Liebeck's lawyer, reports that Leno went so far as to call him to express
his appreciation of the need for a strong civil justice system and the
need to hold corporations accountable for their wrongdoing.

The McDonald's case is only the most recent example of tort deformers twisting the facts to mislead the public about tort law and civil
juries. In truth, most juries will only return big verdicts against corporations when a party solidly demonstrates a compelling case of corporate irresponsibility leading to serious injury. But that doesn't stop the
corporate propaganda. Consider a pair of tales told by former president
Ronald Reagan.

In May 1986, Reagan addressed the American Tort Reform Association, which had recently been founded by a former Republican congressman and Reagan White House aide, James K. Coyne. He brought
along one of his trademark anecdotes, tailor-made for the occasion:[48]

> In California, a man was using a public telephone booth to
> place a call. An alleged drunk driver careened down the street,
> lost control of her car, and crashed into the phone booth. Now,
> it's no surprise that the injured man sued. But you might be
> startled to hear whom he sued: the telephone company and as-
> sociated firms.

It sounded like another tale of a tort system gone mad, of unscrupulous
plaintiffs and ambulance-chasing, deep-pocket-picking lawyers. But it
never sounded that way to the man in the phone booth, Charles Bigbee, who suffered severe injuries, including the loss of a leg, in the accident.

In 1974, Bigbee, a custodian working for the city of Los Angeles,
was in a phone booth located in a liquor store parking lot, about twelve
feet from busy Century Boulevard. When a car came speeding toward
the booth, Bigbee tried to flee. But he couldn't. The phone booth door
jammed.

After the devastating crash, Bigbee learned that twenty months
earlier the same phone booth had been hit and destroyed by another

car. The phone company simply erected a new one in the same spot without installing a guardrail or other barrier. The combination of the sticky door and the dangerous location put Bigbee at the mercy of the errant driver.

The accident left Bigbee unable to walk and severely depressed. He couldn't work. The driver's insurance company paid compensation, but not nearly enough to cover Bigbee's medical expenses. He was broke.

The trial judge dismissed Bigbee's lawsuit before trial, but in 1983 the California Supreme Court ruled, six votes to one, that Bigbee was entitled to at least make his case before a jury.[49] In 1985, eleven years after the accident, the phone company and the firms that built, installed, and maintained the booth agreed to settle the case for an undisclosed amount.

In July 1986, Bigbee came to Washington to testify at a congressional hearing on tort law. He sought the opportunity to meet and discuss his case with the man who had publicly ridiculed him. But President Reagan never responded. Instead, Reagan officials continued to tell the president's misleading version of the story. Bigbee died in 1994 at age fifty-two.[50]

In April 1987, Reagan offered another tort deform anecdote, again tailored to its audience, this time the College of Physicians and Surgeons:[51]

> Last year a jury awarded a woman a million dollars in damages. She'd claimed that a CAT scan had destroyed her psychic powers. Well, recently a new trial was ordered in that case, but the excesses of the courts have taken their toll.

The facts show, once again, that this version of the case, repeated again and again by tort deformers for a decade, is incomplete and misleading.

In September 1976, Judith Haimes, age thirty-three, was referred by her doctor to Temple University Hospital in Philadelphia for a CAT scan. While awaiting the procedure, Haimes warned the radiologist, Dr. Judith Hart, that she had previously suffered a strong allergic reaction to a dye frequently used in CAT scans and that she had been cautioned to avoid the dye in the future. According to Haimes, Dr. Hart told her that she was being "ridiculous." Dr. Hart proposed that Haimes receive a small test dose of the dye first, and she readied a dose of drugs to administer if problems arose. Haimes finally consented to the injection. Seconds later, she suffered pain, as she later testified, "as if my head was going to explode." She experienced difficulty breathing, lost control of her bladder, and began vomiting. Welts and hives appeared on her body. Over the next two days, she suffered from nausea, vomiting, and headaches. She had welts for three days and hives for two or three weeks. Thereafter, she testified, she suffered severe, debilitating headaches when she tried to perform tasks involving intense concentration.

Haimes did indeed work as a professional "psychic" and was even retained by police agencies to assist in solving crimes. And, in addition to claiming for the symptoms she experienced right after the dye injection, she did seek compensation against the hospital and Dr. Hart for loss of her purported psychic abilities. (She closed her psychic business a month after the CAT scan.) But the Pennsylvania state court judge, Leon Katz, who presided in the 1986 trial of her case, instructed the jury not to consider this component of her claim for damages, because Haimes had failed to offer expert testimony linking the administration of the dye to her chronic headaches. Judge Katz told the jury that it could *not* award damages for chronic headaches, loss of concentration, or loss of earning power—only for pain and suffering during and immediately following the dye injection.

After a four-day trial, the jury awarded Haimes $600,000 in damages. Pennsylvania law would have raised Haimes's actual award to $986,000, because it entitled her to interest accruing from the incident to the date of the verdict—eleven years. However, in August 1986, Judge Katz threw out the award, calling it "grossly excessive." After Haimes presented her evidence at a second trial, a different trial judge, Bernard Goodheart, dismissed the case. The Pennsylvania Supreme Court affirmed the dismissal in February 1991. Haimes never received a dime from the justice system.[52]

These twin anecdotes—the phone booth and the CAT scan tales—and many others like them are not relics of the bygone Reagan era. Like the case of Stella Liebeck, they continue to make the rounds in industry statements, on talk radio, and through other outlets for tort deform information.[53] Corporate propagandists simply refuse to let the actual facts get in the way.

Where frivolous and phony lawsuits are filed, there are sufficient checks and balances in the legal system to ensure that the vast majority of such claims are defeated, soundly and promptly. (If only more judges would act so swiftly when faced with frivolous corporate defenses and delaying tactics.) If a plaintiff has no solid legal claim or can offer no facts to fully support a claim, the judge can dismiss the case on a defendant's motion before any trial. Judges have authority under court rules to punish lawyers who make unsupported claims in court. And, in those cases that do make it to trial, where juries make occasional errors of judgment, the many safeguards in the system usually change the outcome. For example, federal case law provides that a trial judge may set aside a jury verdict where it is clear that the jury was influenced by passion or prejudice or where the verdict has no reasonable relation to the actual damages.[54] Similar principles govern lawsuits in state courts. While the definition of *frivolous* varies according to whose ox is being gored, the suits that are clearly without merit, such as suing a football team for losing, are not numerous, if only because of the potential damage to the career reputation of attorneys by outraged judges; most judges were once business lawyers.

Arbitrary tort "reforms"—like placing statutory limits on the amount of punitive damages a party can recover, eliminating compensation for pain and suffering, deconstructing "joint and several" liability rules that permit an injured party to receive full compensation for harms from multiple wrongdoers, reducing the amount of time parties have to file suit after their injuries, destroying "strict liability" standards for hazardous products, and making compliance with often obsolete government regulatory standards an affirmative defense to victims' claims—strike indiscriminately at both good and bad claims. Such provisions do little to deter unwarranted suits but could unjustly penalize innocent victims with valid claims based on very serious injuries caused by the most flagrant wrongdoers.

In any case, the facts belie the claim that jurors are proplaintiff and antibusiness. A review of ninety thousand jury verdicts from 1992 and 1993 by Jury Verdict Research, a Pennsylvania legal publishing company that compiles court statistics, indicates that juries have increasingly sided with business defendants. Each year from 1961 to 1991, plaintiffs won personal injury cases between 57 and 63 percent of the time. But in 1992, juries ruled for plaintiffs only 52 percent of the time. In product liability cases, plaintiffs' verdicts dropped from 59 percent in 1989 to 41 percent in 1993. In medical malpractice cases, jurors found for plaintiffs 31 percent of the time in 1992, down from 48 percent in 1989.[55]

Tort deformers like attorney Victor Schwartz insist that even a 52 percent success rate by plaintiffs shows that the system is skewed against business. "Where there is a marginal chance" of losing, he told a reporter, defendants are settling. "The cases that are going to a jury are cases where defendants are reasonably certain they are going to win."[56] Defendants may have strong incentives to settle cases before trial in order to control the outcome and avoid disclosure of wider patterns of recklessness affecting other harmed persons. But most plaintiffs' lawyers work on a contingency-fee basis, earning no money unless they obtain a favorable verdict or a settlement for the client. Few of them are likely to spend hours of uncompensated time through discovery and trial, dealing with the sophisticated tricks of opposing corporate lawyers in cases so thin that a defendant would be "reasonably certain" of victory.

A far more likely explanation for the many defendant victories in product liability and medical malpractice cases is that such claims are very difficult to prove, and a determined defendant, aided by power-lawyer tactics, can often pull out a victory in spite of the actual merits of a case. As previous chapters in this book have shown, a plaintiff claiming injury from a defective product or malpractice usually faces a well-funded defense effort. The defendant controls the evidence—the internal corporate deliberations and safety tests or the medical records—and may fight hard to prevent disclosure, claiming privilege, hardship, or that the documents sought never existed or are no longer available. Most of the witnesses who can testify to facts related to potential negligence or misconduct work for, or otherwise depend on financial relationships with, the defendant. The defendant knows the relevant engineering or medical field, and controls or has influence over many of the relevant experts. Many plaintiffs' lawyers lack detailed expertise in technical areas and simply cannot afford to compete with the array of lawyers and experts assembled on the defense side. The defense needs just a small minority of jurors (sometimes just one) to deadlock a jury and prevent a damage award; once that has happened, the chances that an individual plaintiff or plaintiffs' attorney will finance a retrial are slight. In this no-contest world, usually only the most easily provable claims have a chance of succeeding.

Another reason why defendants do so well at trial is that juries tend to tilt, if at all, toward a pro–big business position. The likely explanation for such a tilt is that tort deform propaganda has persuaded some citizens that the tort system is costing consumers and that only bleeding hearts on a jury would believe the claims of injured victims. Brian Shenker, editorial director of Jury Verdict Research, told *The New York Times*, "There's been such a campaign by the insurance industry, by people like Dan Quayle, saying these big awards are killing our society. People see this in the media, and when they get on juries they think, 'I'm not going to contribute to this.' "[57]

"Approximately four out of every five jurors asserted that there are too many frivolous lawsuits today," Professor Valerie Hans, a professor of sociology at the University of Delaware, says, citing a study of the issue that she and a colleague made about the attitudes of actual jurors in business cases.[58] Professor Hans interviewed 269 jurors who had entered a verdict in a case involving a corporation. She also conducted mock jury trials and conducted a public opinion survey to measure public attitudes toward business. The results offer a revealing picture of how everyday people who sit on juries view the civil justice system.

According to Professor Hans, rather than expressing an anti-business bias, jurors actually tend to be antagonistic toward litigation. "The idea that there is a litigation explosion has fallen on fertile soil," she reports. "In general, there is a lot of belief among people sitting in cases that there are a lot of frivolous suits, that there really is a need to hold the line." The research also found that "[t]hose who expressed greater belief in the litigation explosion tended to decide on lower verdicts."

Professor Hans says she had "read the literature about how juries were hostile to business and ever-ready to find against deep pockets. But I found that there was a great deal of scrutiny [by jurors] of the plaintiff. Had the paraplegic plaintiff done enough to rehabilitate herself? What was the assumption of the risk? I found that the 'Robin Hood' jury theory is exaggerated. There may be a few cases where a jury is overwhelmed by sympathy for a badly injured plaintiff, but it is definitely more the exception rather than the rule."[59]

Terence Dunworth, a senior associate at the Cambridge, Massachusetts, consulting firm Abt Associates (and a former Rand Corporation researcher), and Joel Rogers, professor of law, political science, and sociology at the University of Wisconsin, Madison, School of Law, have conducted a major study of federal court cases over twenty years involving the nineteen hundred largest corporations in America. They found that these big businesses are overwhelmingly the winners in lawsuits, whether they are plaintiffs or defendants. When they are plaintiffs, they win 79 percent of judgments, compared with a 62 percent win rate for all plaintiffs. As defendants, they win 62 percent of the time, compared with 33 percent for all defendants.[60]

The evidence, as opposed to the hysteria of the tort deformers, is that, in reality, jurors approach cases against big corporations with caution and skepticism. They are not antibusiness. They don't see a corporation's money as theirs to give away. Juries rarely let pure sympathy sway their ultimate verdict. Indeed, most jurors sincerely attempt to do their duty, based on facts and the law. If their perceptions have been distorted at all, it is by the tort deform propaganda blitz itself.

For example, tort deformers claim the tort system is draining corporate and individual pocketbooks for the benefit of "lucky" victims and their lawyers. That is untrue. Product liability verdicts and settlements in the United States against all manufacturers in 1993 cost $4.1

billion[61]—less than Americans spend on dog food ($5.1 billion, according to the Pet Food Institute[62]), and less than the annual profits of a single corporation such as Ford Motor Company ($5.3 billion)[63] or Royal Dutch/Shell ($6.2 billion).[64] Actuary J. Robert Hunter, a former federal insurance administrator (under Presidents Ford and Carter) and later the Texas insurance commissioner, now studies liability and insurance issues for the Consumer Federation of America. In a 1995 report, he found that the total cost of product liability insurance premiums and other product liability costs in 1993 was only 19.9 cents for every $100 in retail sales.[65] In inflation-adjusted, real terms, the cost of product liability insurance fell 45 percent between 1987 and 1993. Hunter told a U.S. Senate committee, "The current system of product liability is an exceptional bargain for America: it serves as a deterrent to unsafe products in a free market way, with no bureaucratic regulation, it takes care of persons injured by unsafe products, and it costs remarkably little."[66] Similarly, a 1995 study by the Risk & Insurance Management Society, Inc., an organization of corporate and nonprofit risk managers, and Tillinghast-Towers Perrin, a business consulting firm normally inclined to defend corporate agendas, found that the cost of "liability risk"—insuring against not only product liability but also other employment discrimination, shareholder suits, and other claims—amounted to 25.5 cents for every $100 in revenue in 1994 (a 22 percent drop from the 1993 cost). Not much of an expense to provide protection for all Americans from dangerous and defective products and other corporate misbehavior. A *Wall Street Journal* report on the study noted that its "findings are intriguing in light of the widely-held view that American employers are being held hostage by litigation."[67]

PUNITIVE DAMAGES ARE RARELY IMPOSED EXCEPT IN CLEAR CASES OF EGREGIOUS BEHAVIOR

A prime target of tort deformers and corporate apologists is the punitive damage system, against which no hyperbole is too strong and no weakening scheme is too severe. "Punitive damages have replaced baseball as our national sport," Theodore Olson of Gibson, Dunn & Crutcher and the so-called Civil Justice Reform Group, roared. "The system is a perverse combination of lottery and bullfighting, selecting beneficiaries and targets almost at random and inflicting brutal punishment on the latter if they wander into the arena . . ."[68] Likewise, Texas

Governor George Bush, Jr., has complained, "Punitive damages are used to terrorize small business owners and force higher and higher settlements."[69]

All of this wailing and gnashing of teeth does not change the facts. Empirical data, known in legal parlance as "evidence," show that punitive damage awards are rare. Some states do not even permit juries to award punitive damages, and those that do often require high standards of proof or impose limits on any such award.[70] Under the instructions of judges, juries follow the law and impose punitive damages only in cases of willful misconduct, grossly negligent conduct, or outrageous misbehavior that is intentional or callously indifferent to human suffering.

Punitive damage awards play a vital role in our system of justice, especially considering that there is so little criminal prosecution of corporate crimes. They are one of the few effective deterrents to misconduct by multibillion-dollar corporations, and as such are, in the words of Professor Marc Galanter, "perhaps the most important instrument in the legal repertoire for pronouncing moral disapproval of economically formidable offenders."[71] Yet, this truth is ignored by tort deformers, who seek to free the very rich and powerful from the one punishment for their conduct that has proved effective.

Suffolk University law professor Michael Rustad and Northeastern University sociology professor Thomas Koenig conducted a national study of product liability cases involving punitive damages in both federal and state courts between 1965 and 1990. For the entire twenty-five-year period, Professors Rustad and Koenig could find only a minuscule 355 reported verdicts in which punitive damages were awarded, out of tens of thousands of product liability cases nationwide. Ninety-one of these awards came in the busy asbestos area—where workers have repeatedly obtained relief against companies for cancer-causing workplace conditions—and when those cases are removed there were an average of less than eleven punitive damages cases per year in the entire nation! The professors discovered that, contrary to tort deform propaganda, punitive damages are awarded only in cases of truly egregious conduct, with most cases involving serious injury or death where the victim was not at fault. There was also usually a "smoking gun," evidence proving that the wrongdoer knew it was engaging in misconduct. Seventy percent of the cases involved a corporation's failure to warn of a product danger it knew about. Most of the other cases involved inadequate testing (12 percent), knowing violation of safety standards (7 percent), or outright fraud (5 percent).[72]

According to the professors, "The popular perception of vast wealth being awarded in the form of punitive damages to greedy or extremely careless plaintiffs" contrasts sharply with the empirical evidence found in their study. "The typical plaintiff was permanently disabled or killed by a product *known* [emphasis in original] by the manufacturer to be unnecessarily hazardous . . . Few manufacturers were assessed punitive damages unless they failed to take remedial action in the face of a developing or existing danger or risk to the public." Further, they found that "[d]ocumented sacrificing of the public welfare on the basis of cost-benefit analysis . . . was a common profile leading to punitive damages."[73]

The study also refuted the claim that punitive damage awards are becoming larger and more frequent. "There is no dramatic increase in punitive damages," Professor Rustad says. "In fact, my research indicates that punitive damages are infrequently awarded. And while there has been some increase in the last few years, the increase is built on a very small base."

Professors Rustad and Koenig continue to update their research. As of mid-1995, the total number of product liability punitive damages awards in the United States since 1965 stood at 379—less than thirteen cases per year, including asbestos actions.[74]

In July 1995, the United States Department of Justice released the results of a review of state court civil cases in the United States' seventy-five largest counties for the twelve months ending June 30, 1992. The review found that plaintiffs won only 40.5 percent of product liability cases, and, of those victorious cases, juries awarded punitive damages only 2.2 percent of the time. Punitive damages were awarded in 6.2 percent of cases involving toxic substances (such as asbestos), and in only 3.2 percent of medical malpractice cases.[75]

A 1987 Rand Corporation study, analyzing civil trials in Cook County, Illinois, and San Francisco County, California, reached similar results. The study found in those jurisdictions only six awards of punitive damages in product liability cases over a twenty-five-year period. According to the Rand report, "Punitive damages continue to be rarely assessed in personal injury cases, and most frequently assessed against defendants who were found to have intentionally harmed plaintiffs. In most of these cases the damages were modest."[76]

The Rand study also found that punitive damages in business contract cases, which include cases brought by major corporations against business competitors, have become significant. In these business versus business cases, punitive damage awards "were larger and given more frequently."[77]

Consider this: Using the Rustad-Koenig data, the aggregate total of all punitive damage awards in product liability cases between 1965 and

1995 is estimated at $1,337,832,211—$1.3 billion over a thirty-year period.[78] That is less than half of the $3 billion in punitive damages a Texas jury awarded in a single dispute between two oil companies—Pennzoil and Texaco—in November 1985.[79] Yet, there has been no hue and cry from Newt Gingrich and his associates about businesses abusing the legal system by making huge damage claims against each other. Even the $1.3 billion total likely overstates the actual amount of punitive damages actually paid in product liability cases. Such punitive damage cases, and indeed many tort suits in which substantial compensatory damages are awarded, are frequently settled after the verdict by the plaintiff accepting an amount substantially smaller than what the jury awarded, in exchange for the defendant agreeing to drop a lengthy, burdensome appeal that would increase the legal costs to the plaintiff's side and greatly delay payment of compensation.

Rand has continued to study punitive damages and, in March 1995, published preliminary results. The updated study reports that "the actual number of punitive damage awards [in all types of cases] in each of the jurisdictions was quite modest. The number of awards grew during the 1980s but fell back considerably within the most recent five-year period."[80] The preliminary results also show that punitive damages are most likely to be awarded in intentional tort cases and, as in the earlier study, in business and contract disputes. According to the preliminary report, the actual amount of punitive damages awarded in most cases is usually quite modest. The median punitive damage award in San Francisco County was only $97,000, while it was $250,000 in Cook County. The average award was $1.6 million in San Francisco County and $6.8 million in Cook County, but according to the study, the average figures are skewed higher because of "a few extremely large punitive damage awards."[81]

In another study, Stephen Daniels and Joanne Martin of the American Bar Foundation reviewed 25,627 reported jury awards in forty-seven jurisdictions between 1981 and 1985 and found that in 967 product liability verdicts, punitive damages were awarded only thirty-four times—only 3.5 percent of the cases (8.9 percent of cases plaintiffs won). In 1,917 malpractice cases, punitive damages were awarded in only eighteen—less than 1 percent of cases (2.9 percent of the cases plaintiffs won). The median punitive damages award was only $30,000.[82]

Tort deformers will respond by claiming that even if the number of punitive damage awards is low, and the amount of many such awards is small, the mere possibility of facing a multimillion-dollar punitive award paralyzes corporate managers with fear. But since experience shows that punitive awards are made and affirmed only where there is compelling evidence of deliberate misconduct or grossly negligent behavior, responsible and ethical business executives have little reason to be afraid.

The empirical evidence reveals that the so-called punitive damage crisis does not exist. It is merely a mirage erected by corporate-financed propagandists to shield companies and their executives from responsibility—and poetic justice. After all, "High punitive damage awards hit *homoeconomicus* where it hurts: an eye for an eye, a tooth for a tooth, a bottom line for a bottom line."[83]

THE CASE OF THE DEADBEAT INSURANCE COMPANY

Punitive damages, while rarely applied, serve an important function. They deter and punish wrongdoing so egregious that it demands an extraordinary legal response, as in the following case.

Chapter 5 described a patent infringement lawsuit brought by Alcon Surgical, Inc., against Surgin Surgical Instrumentation, Inc. Alcon, a subdivision of the giant conglomerate Nestlé, sued Surgin, an independent business, for patent infringement over a cassette medical device used in cataract surgery.

Armand Maaskamp, Surgin's president, maintains that Surgin had a good case but was bludgeoned into settling by Alcon's lawyers, who threatened to make Surgin's defense unaffordable through burdensome discovery tactics. Unable to afford what Surgin's lawyers predicted would be a million-dollar defense, Surgin settled with Alcon, even though it contended it had not infringed Alcon's patent. It stopped selling a cassette device that competed with Alcon's.

Surgin was forced to pay for its own lawyers, which was the main reason for settling without a fight, because Truck Insurance Exchange, part of the Farmers Insurance Group, refused to pay for Surgin's defense, even though it was contractually bound to do so. Maaskamp and his partner did not think that was right. Consequently, in November 1994, Surgin filed suit in Orange County, California, superior court against Truck and Farmers for the legal fees incurred in its aborted defense of the Alcon suit.

The case started simply enough. "All we wanted initially was to collect the $280,000 attorneys' fees we incurred fighting Alcon," Maaskamp told us.[84] Surgin retained the Irvine, California, firm Callahan and Gauntlett. But Truck and Farmers refused to acknowledge their obligations. "After Surgin had incurred another $300,000 in fees [trying to collect the initial $280,000 from Farmers], all Farmers would offer the company was $75,000," Surgin's lawyer, Daniel Callahan, says. "That was a ridiculous offer. It wasn't as if we even wanted payment for lost profits [arising from the fact that Surgin was forced to capitulate to Alcon]. All we wanted was payment of attorneys' fees as required in the insurance contract."[85]

Surgin claimed that Truck and Farmers had acted in "bad faith."[86] A bad-faith action is a tort, allowing a wronged party to sue an insurance company for punitive damages, as well as for actual out-of-pocket losses.

The legal battle quickly grew intense and bitter, involving the worst kind of discovery war. Surgin claimed that Truck had destroyed documents, while Truck contended that the alleged documents never existed.

The insurance companies' legal tactics dramatically increased Surgin's attorneys' fees. Callahan told us, "Farmers put three law firms on the case against us. They did everything in their power to stonewall us. Surgin's fees [to Callahan's firm] really added up fast."

Ultimately, it almost became a case of déjà vu. Just as Surgin had been unable to financially proceed with the case brought against it by Alcon, the Truck and Farmers' defense tactics succeeded in financially exhausting Surgin's ability to prosecute its case against the giant insurance companies. This almost resulted in the same capitulation as had occurred in the controversy with Alcon.

If Truck and Farmers' lawyers and executives intended this result, they underestimated Callahan's resolve. "We made a decision," he recalls. "When Surgin could simply not pay any more of our fees, we switched the case to a contingency fee so they could keep up the fight."

Farmers, arguing that Surgin's real complaint was with Truck alone, managed to get itself dismissed from the case, but Truck continued its campaign of obfuscation. Eventually, Truck's misconduct was more than Superior Court Judge C. Robert Jameson could bear. He imposed sanctions limiting Truck's defense in the case, ruling that "Truck Insurance Exchange and Lictman & Bruning [of Pasadena, California—Truck's trial lawyers] willfully and repeatedly disobeyed this Court's Order by failing to produce documents despite repeated requests . . ."[87]

When the defense asked Judge Jameson to reconsider, he expressed outrage:[88]

Truck has not complied with this court's discovery orders in that Truck has refused and failed to produce documents, answer interrogatories, or provide complete further responses . . . Truck's defiance of the discovery demands and court orders in this case is cool and calculating, to say the least. To say that Truck's conduct was willful is an understatement. Truck's misconduct was in defiance of court orders, blatant, willful and in bad faith.

Meanwhile, Callahan uncovered evidence of unethical practices in Farmers' own legal department. For example, a former Farmers assistant vice president, Michael Douglas Conn, who had been fired by the company, gave a deposition. "He admitted under oath that Farmers had a pattern and practice of destroying evidence," Callahan recalls. "The legal department in Los Angeles would call up a file, destroy damaging records, and then send it back to the adjuster. Then, when the records were subpoenaed, the file would be turned over without worry about damning evidence."

Specifically, Conn testified under oath as follows:[89]

Q: Isn't it true that in lawsuits where Farmers Group, Inc. was named in addition to Truck Insurance Exchange, the corporate legal department would dictate how the litigation was handled?

A: Yes.

Q: Isn't it also true that the corporate legal department would make the decisions about what internal documents of Farmers or Truck would be produced in discovery?

A: Yes.

Q: When a plaintiff suing Truck Insurance Exchange requested documents, did anyone at Truck remove documents from the file before turning them over to Plaintiff's counsel?

A: It is my understanding that occurred, yes. . . . We knew of specific instances where they were in fact removing documents from files in discovery prior to turning it over to plaintiff's counsel.

Q: And, therefore, not turning those documents over to plaintiff's counsel?

A: That is correct. . . .

Q: Was that common knowledge at Farmers?

A: As a matter of fact it was. It was common knowledge, in my understanding, at the time, that this type of process was taking place. . . .

Conn testified that he did not believe that the documents that Truck removed from its files were solely those covered by attorney-client privilege. He continued:

Q: When a plaintiff's counsel subpoenaed the records of Farmers or Truck and requested the custodian of records, how would Truck respond?[90]

A: I've been involved in litigation where I observed the custodian of records identified by Farmers or Truck to be an individual that didn't have anything to do with the records presented. I was advised by counsel or defense counsel that this tactic was used to limit plaintiff's counsel's cross-examination . . . because the individual, basically, didn't know anything.

Q: So, when he said he didn't know anything, he wasn't lying?

A: He wasn't lying, no.

Q: But he actually really wasn't the custodian of the records that were being sought by that plaintiff?

A: He was appointed custodian of records by Farmers at that time, but I mean—

Q: You mean he was custodian for a day?

A: Custodian for a day. . . .

Q: Did Truck make a practice of hiding documents during discovery in litigation to avoid disclosure of the truth?

A: It is my understanding that both Truck and Farmers did exactly just that.

After the case was tried, Truck, which denied any discovery abuse, was indeed faced with a substantial verdict for its willful refusal to assist Surgin in its hour of need. But not by one of those emotional, anti-deep-pocket juries prevalent in tort deform myths. Instead, the verdict was reached by a conservative judge appointed by California's Republican, pro-corporate governor George Deukmejian. (As sometimes happens in lawsuits, each party had waived its right to a jury trial and asked the judge to decide the case himself.)

After trial, Judge Jameson chose on October 7, 1993, to deliver his decision orally in the courtroom, rather than quietly issuing a written opinion. The judge's decision included this denunciation of the tactics of the insurance company:[91]

> We have an insurance policy which created a contractual relationship between Truck Insurance and Surgin Surgical. Both had duties to each other in the contract. . . .
>
> Truck, upon notice of [Surgin's] claims, was dilatory, unreasonably responded to their claims, . . . and unrealistic in their approach to a patent case and the timing of the case. They failed to investigate the claims, they failed to provide a defense, they failed to authorize . . . representation. They consciously and in bad faith and in derogation of the rights of Surgin avoided their responsibilities under the policy. Truck clearly takes its own interests ahead of its insured. . . .
>
> . . . (W)ithout any contradiction and by more than clear and convincing evidence, the record is replete with despicable, vile, malicious, fraudulent, oppressive conduct on the part of Truck Insurance. This conduct warrants a substantial award of punitive damages. . . . With respect to despicable conduct, on a scale of one-to-ten, Truck Insurance rates an eleven. . . . Truck has lied, cheated and tramped on the rights of the insured to escape its own responsibilities. All of this in the most flagrant fashion. And it appears to be consistent with a pattern and practice within the industry for Truck Insurance.
>
> This conduct is even more aggravated because of two other factors. One is the oppressive ability of the huge economic and other resources of Truck to have advantage over a relatively small business:
>
> "Litigate the hell out of the little guy until he can't go any further," seems to be the theory. Second, Truck is in a fiduciary relationship, a position of trust.

Surgin had presented evidence at trial that the total net worth (called "surplus" in the insurance industry) of the fourteen property and casualty insurance companies of the Farmers Group, the third-largest property and casualty insurer in the United States, was nearly

$2.62 billion. Because of the way the Farmers Group was structured, Truck could draw on this huge pool of funds to pay damage awards.[92] In order to ensure that Truck received a message about its egregious conduct, Judge Jameson awarded Surgin $572,143.79 in damages for unpaid attorneys' fees plus $57.23 million in punitive damages. The judge specifically rejected awarding $1.5 million in punitive damages, three times the compensatory damages, the formula for punitive damages that many tort deformers want to impose on the nation. Why? Because it would have had *no impact* on Farmers. It would have neither punished the company nor deterred it—or other insurance companies, for that matter—from engaging in such flagrant abuse. As the judge noted in his opinion, "Expert testimony [at trial] indicated that a million and a half dollars wouldn't even make a bleep in the balance sheet and would not even [have] been brought to the attention of administration and the board of directors at Truck." The amount of punitive damages Judge Jameson actually awarded constituted 2.18 percent of the Farmers Group combined net worth—a major wake-up call, but, under the circumstances, not a disproportionate punishment.

Truck filed an appeal, which, as we write, is pending.

Limiting punitive damages to a formula such as three times compensatory damages would defeat the important societal purposes behind allowing punitive awards. Three times the compensatory damages in the Surgin case, $1.5 million, would certainly be enough to deter many a small business from future wrongdoing. But it would be chump change, and thus an empty threat, to conglomerates the size of Farmers, General Motors, Exxon, General Electric, or other similarly situated companies.

If the anti–punitive damage campaign succeeds, if punitive damages can no longer, in Judge Jameson's words, "make a bleep on the balance sheet," the awards will no longer be an effective deterrent in many cases, particularly against big companies. As Professor Rustad writes, "If punitive damages are capped or limited to a defined multiple of compensatory damages, a firm can calculate with certainty how large a penalty a judge might impose."[93]

That could lead to tragic results. Imagine the potential for harm if punitive damage awards are limited to a predictable formula. Many corporate leaders make business decisions based on cost-benefit analyses. If punitive damages were legally limited and made predictable, unscrupulous lawyers and business executives could easily base their business decisions on a utilitarian determination about what best served the bottom line of their corporation: to knowingly market an unsafe product or engage in other reprehensible conduct and pay the legally limited consequences, or to act ethically. And if illegal or unethical conduct best promoted corporate profits? Well, that would give new meaning to the old term *caveat emptor*—buyer, beware!

Consumers Union's Mark Silbergeld worries about the impact of limiting punitive damages. "We believe that punitive damages have to be proportional to the wrongdoer's ability to pay and they have to be sufficient to deter," he told us. "To cap them means the larger the wrongdoer, the less likely the wrongdoer will be deterred from the same type of conduct in the future."[94]

Even some prominent tort deform advocates see the danger inherent in taking the worry about a big punitive damage award for intentional misconduct out of corporate and legal decision making. For example, University of Virginia law professor Jeffrey O'Connell, co-author of *The Blame Game: Injuries, Insurance and Injustice*,[95] supports both restricting plaintiff lawyer contingency fees and implementing a national "no fault" system for injury compensation. He is a well-paid consultant and spokesman for insurance companies and other tort deformers. Yet, when it comes to capping punitive damages, he parts company with them. "I don't think it makes sense to restrict punitive damages," he told us. "When you are dealing with quasi-criminal conduct, there should be severe punishment. Often, compensatory damages are not sufficient to deter such conduct."

Punitive damages are an extraordinary remedy, rarely applied, designed to punish, in the classic legal formulation, "conduct that is outrageous, because of the defendant's evil motive or his reckless indifference to the rights of others."[96] This isn't just theory. Liability insurance generally does not pay for punitive damage awards, and thus the actual wrongdoers must usually pay for their misconduct out of their own pockets. To take this arrow out of the civil justice quiver, especially when criminal and regulatory sanctions against wrongdoing corporations are so weak and ineffective, would emasculate justice and free unscrupulous corporate lawyers and executives to engage in intentional misconduct without fear of effective sanction. That is a "reform" that this country simply cannot afford.

Postscript: The Surgin versus Farmers case influenced the political struggle over tort deform efforts. In 1994, the Association for California Tort Reform planned to place an initiative on California's ballot that if passed by voters would have restricted attorney contingency fees. Farmers Insurance, a major financial backer of tort deform efforts, planned to be a primary sponsor.

Opponents of the proposed measure decided on a preemptory strike. They produced a commercial that quoted Judge Jameson's words in the Surgin case about how Truck Insurance had "lied, cheated, stonewalled and tramped on the rights" of its insured. Before it was aired, a copy of the commercial found its way to the managing executives of Farmers.

Their response was immediate. A source close to the events who would speak only on condition of anonymity told us, "There was a lot of talk in the back rooms. It was agreed: If the commercial was not aired, Farmers would not sponsor the initiative." Whether such a quid pro quo was agreed upon cannot be stated unequivocally. Farmers Insurance has not stated that the proposed commercial was the cause for its backing away from the proposed initiative.[97] However, Farmers *did* pull its financial support from the proposed initiative in late 1993, and the commercial never aired.

Looking back on the controversy, Robert Forsythe, media director for Consumer Attorneys of California, believes the proposed commercial had a major impact on the debate. "It was a hard-hitting tape on point in terms of fact," he told us. "It told the truth about how the tort system protects consumers from abuse. Those in control of corporate America and the insurance carriers did not want that truth told."[98]

The enlightening effect of publicized truth can, once in a while, thwart even the most powerful opponents.

MEDICAL MALPRACTICE IS WIDESPREAD AND EFFECTIVE REMEDIES FOR VICTIMS ARE NEEDED TO PROTECT THE PUBLIC

The wedge issue in the campaign to limit victims' rights has been medical malpractice. Throughout the country, laws have been passed to shield physicians and their malpractice insurance companies from paying full damages for the harm caused by destructive medical negligence. For example, in California, for nearly twenty years state law has imposed a $250,000 ceiling on awards for past and future pain and suffering, even if admitted malpractice causes serious brain damage or quadriplegia. The law also limits fees plaintiffs' attorneys in medical malpractice cases can earn and places various technical rules in the path of malpractice victims to discourage them from seeking redress.[99]

But efforts to weaken legal protections against malpractice are cruelly misguided and unfair. The real malpractice crisis is not a flood of lawsuits but the epidemic levels of negligent medical practice itself.[100] Medical malpractice is a primary cause of preventable deaths in the country. Charles B. Inlander, president of the People's Medical Society, one of the largest patient advocacy groups in the country,[101] says, "This whole malpractice issue is a smoke screen to divert attention from the real issue, which is the extent of malpractice that is committed." *Business Week* has recognized that there "is not a malpractice insurance crisis. Nor, contrary to popular mythology, is the problem a lawsuit crisis. The real crisis is the degree of malpractice itself."[102] Vice President Al Gore has said it most succinctly: "The malpractice crisis is malpractice."

Medical malpractice is far worse than most people realize or the media generally report. According to a study published in 1990 by the Harvard Medical Practice Study Group and conducted at Harvard's School of Public Health, one of the most comprehensive and objective studies of medical malpractice ever performed, more than 98,000 patients in hospitals located in New York State suffered "adverse events," injuries from medical care rather than disease, in one year, 1984. Twenty-seven percent of these adverse events were the result of medical negligence—failure by health practitioners to meet reasonable standards of care—the study found. Such negligence resulted in 6,895 patient deaths in the state's hospitals that year.[103] Projecting its figures nationwide, the study's authors estimated in subsequent testimony that approximately 80,000 people die from medical negligence each year, with another 150,000 to 300,000 injured.[104] And those figures represent deaths only in hospitals; they do not include deaths caused by malpractice in clinics or physician's offices, which have not yet been analyzed. Eighty thousand hospital deaths from medical negligence amount to more annual deaths than are caused by automobile accidents (43,000),[105] homicides (23,730),[106] suicides (32,400),[107] or AIDS (41,930).[108] And other published estimates of yearly deaths caused by medical malpractice go as high as 150,000 per year.[109]

The human toll extracted by medical malpractice is daunting, creating enormous suffering and heartache. But that has not gotten in the way of the juggernaut to limit victims' rights. Rather than seeking better ways to prevent malpractice and seeking to ensure that victims or their families receive adequate compensation from wrongdoers, lawmakers, under pressure from the insurance industry and the doctors lobby, have instead passed laws to limit the liability of physicians and insurance companies from the free-market consequences of malpractice.

If the tort deformers really want to protect insurance companies and doctors from the cost of malpractice, they could do so without further victimizing the already victimized. This could be accomplished by, among other steps, enhancing the authority and capacity of state med-

ical licensing boards to take away the licenses of the relatively few doctors who are responsible for most of the malpractice.

Studies show that most physicians who engage in malpractice are
repeat offenders. For example, a 1985 analysis found that in Pennsylvania just 1 percent of physicians accounted for 25 percent of losses
paid over a ten-year period.[110] Similarly, a 1987 study by the nonprofit
group Public Citizen[111] found that 7.5 percent of all practicing physicians in Texas were responsible for 65 percent of the reported claims
filed between 1978 and 1984.[112]

Instead of dealing with this crisis, tort deformers propose legislation that would make matters worse. Instead of trying to stop medical
negligence, they want to try to obstruct people from seeking compensation for medical negligence.

The U.S. Congress's Office of Technology Assessment (OTA)
concluded, after comprehensive research, that the federal medical
malpractice "reform" legislation tort deformers have proposed would
not reduce national health care expenditures.[113] OTA found that the
health care industry spent $4.86 billion on malpractice premiums in
1991—less than two thirds of 1 percent of total U.S. health care
spending.[114] (A study by J. Robert Hunter of the Consumer Federation of America found, similarly, that malpractice premiums from
1985 to 1994 averaged seventy-seven one hundredths of 1 percent of
health care costs—with the 1994 figure being sixty-five one hundredths of 1 percent.[115] Total payout by insurance companies to satisfy medical malpractice judgments and settlements in 1994 was
about $3 billion.[116]) Because premiums were so small in relation to
the size of the industry, the OTA concluded that legislation to restrict
the rights of malpractice victims could save money only if doctors
regularly ordered extra tests and procedures simply because of the demands of the current malpractice liability system—what tort deformers denounce as "defensive medicine." The OTA accordingly
proceeded to examine this very question. It concluded that there was
no optimal means of measuring defensive medicine but, using its best
judgment, found that only a small percentage of diagnostic procedures—"certainly less than 8 percent"—is conducted primarily out of
concerns over malpractice. The OTA thus further concluded that
proposed malpractice reforms were unlikely to significantly reduce
unwarranted defensive medicine.

Troyen Brennan, an MD and professor of law and public health at
the Harvard School of Public Health, has taken the analysis a step further. He concludes that, rather than reducing health care costs, medical malpractice law "reform" would actually raise costs by reducing

doctors' concerns about malpractice and thereby increasing the frequency of injuries caused by malpractice.[117] Research he and his colleagues have conducted indicates that the risk of negligent injuries decreases as malpractice claims increase.[118] Thus, he has told Congress, malpractice suits "may accomplish the task for which it is primarily intended, that is the prevention of medical injury."[119]

The careful analyses of the question of defensive medicine by Dr. Brennan and the OTA stand in sharp contrast to the wild, unsubstantiated claims of tort deformers. President George Bush, in a 1991 speech at Johns Hopkins University, claimed that defensive medicine costs up to $75 billion per year.[120] Philip K. Howard, author of *The Death of Common Sense*, a book critical of government regulations, writes, with no documentation cited, that "the cost of 'defensive medicine' has been estimated to be as high as $200 billion annually, or close to 5 percent of America's [Gross Domestic Product]."[121] One wonders how such estimates become part of tort deform lore, when even the American Medical Association, a strong proponent of restrictions on malpractice liability, offers their latest, highest guess of a $35 billion per year price tag for the medical malpractice liability system, including the costs of so-called defensive medicine.[122]

Extrapolating from the Harvard study of New York hospitals and other research, Dr. Brennan estimates that the yearly cost of the liability system, including defensive medicine, is actually no more than $20 billion to $30 billion—less than half of his estimate of the yearly costs of injuries caused directly by medical treatment itself: $60 billion.[123]

Claims that exorbitant defensive medicine costs are driven by the tort system are without foundation. As the OTA study notes, many tests and procedures that tort deformers want to label defensive medicine are actually good medicine—second opinions, diagnostic screenings, etc.—that benefits patients.[124] And, if doctors and hospitals perform tests and procedures that are unnecessary, it is likely, for many of them, that their main motivation is financial—the more tests they run or operations they perform, the more money they collect from patients and insurance companies.[125] Limiting the rights of malpractice victims does nothing to address this problem. Finally, as neurosurgeon and attorney Harvey F. Wachsman argues in his book *Lethal Medicine: The Epidemic of Medical Malpractice in America*, if a medical test is not necessary to treatment of a patient's illness, it is difficult to see how the fact that it was conducted could assist a doctor or hospital in defending against a malpractice suit.[126] Indeed, completely unnecessary invasive tests and procedures conducted only out of cynicism, far from protecting against malpractice, are themselves malpractice, he concludes.

One reason that the malpractice recovery system costs so little is that so few victims of medical negligence seek compensation for their injuries. The Harvard School of Public Health study of New York hospitals found that only one in eight negligence victims files a malpractice claim and that only one in sixteen receives compensation through the tort system.

A second reason for the low cost is that, even when patients do file suit, juries rarely give large damage awards except in cases of egregious misconduct. Neil Vidmar, a professor at Duke University Law School, has extensively studied medical malpractice lawsuits from around the country. He reports the following:[127] Plaintiffs win less than three out of ten malpractice cases that reach a jury. The vast majority of judges believe that juries make competent and responsible decisions in malpractice cases. And most awards are only to cover medical bills; damages for noneconomic injuries, i.e., pain and suffering, probably represent no more than 20 percent of jury awards.

A comprehensive review by Professor Vidmar of malpractice suits filed in North Carolina between 1984 and 1990 found that juries decided for the defendants in 79 percent of cases. Among the 21 percent of cases where plaintiffs prevailed, the median jury award was $36,500. The average award was a much larger $367,737, but this amount reflected a handful of large verdicts. Vidmar looked carefully at these big verdicts to see whether they were justified. One involved a child born severely brain damaged as a result of medical negligence. Medical costs over the child's short two-and-one-half-year life were $680,000. Another involved a second brain-damaged baby, this time expected to live a long life, requiring constant medical attention. The medical insurance company's own expert estimates of expenses ranged between $2.1 million and $4.2 million. The jury awarded $1.5 million. A third case involved a hospital that inserted a feeding tube, a relatively simple procedure, into the lung rather than the stomach of a thirty-five-year-old patient. The lung had to be partially removed, after which the hospital inserted the feeding tube in the other lung. The patient ended up confined to a nursing home. The jury awarded $750,000.

Malpractice is not mostly about tiny errors in complex procedures. It is usually about egregious misbehavior by men and women who have taken an oath to protect the health of their fellow citizens. According to Dr. Wachsman, the most common cause of malpractice is "a physician's simply not showing up"—ignoring or dismissing patient telephone calls for help. The second biggest cause of malpractice, he says, is failing to take the time to establish a patient's complete medical history. The study by professors Rustad and Koenig found four major categories of cases in which punitive damages were awarded: sexual assaults by doctors; intentional injuries, including fraud and false imprisonment arising from treatment; extreme violations of medical standards of care; and abandonment, neglect, or failure to treat when there was a duty to provide care.[128]

These facts are not a secret. Members of the medical and legal defense establishment know that restricting victim's rights does not save insurance companies or society a great deal of money, with the little money that may be saved coming at a terrible cost to injured individuals and their families. A few will even say so publicly. Unfortunately, as the following case demonstrates, such candor often comes at a terrible price.

THE CASE OF THE BLACKBALLED LAWYER

Robert C. Baker is a partner in the Santa Monica, California, law firm Baker, Silverberg and Keener. Baker is a trial lawyer who has represented defendants in medical malpractice cases for more than twenty years. He is also the former president of the American Board of Trial Advocates, an organization of defense and plaintiff lawyers.

On June 22, 1994, Baker provided written testimony to the United States House of Representatives Judiciary Committee, then looking into the issue of medical malpractice and its costs in relation to the Clinton administration's health care proposal. He wrote about California's experience under its medical malpractice "reform" legislation. His testimony, coming as it does from his experience within the malpractice defense establishment, is a persuasive and powerful argument against restricting victims' rights. Baker testified:

> In my view, the [California] malpractice reforms have aided insurance companies and physicians, but have, to a significant extent, been detrimental to persons injured by medical negligence. As a result of caps on damages, as well as limitations on attorneys' fees, most of the exceedingly competent plaintiff's lawyers in California simply will not handle a medical malpractice case. . . . [T]hose attorneys that choose to handle medical malpractice cases concentrate on only those cases that have high economic damages . . . such as . . . wrongful death of a breadwinner, or cases involving demonstrable brain damage. There are entire categories of cases that have

been eliminated since malpractice reform was implemented in California. The victims of cases that have a value between $50,000 and $150,000 are basically without representation.

   . . . Medical malpractice premiums have not diminished in California, nor to my knowledge have they in any state that has enacted alleged medical malpractice reform. There can be little doubt that with caps on pain and suffering and limitations on attorneys' fees there are fewer cases being filed.

   It is my opinion that malpractice reform has not worked in California for the injured victims of medical negligence. Physician groups report that there has been no reduction in their medical insurance premiums. As the number of case filings has diminished and dollar amounts of awards have decreased, one can assume medical malpractice reform is benefiting some entity, but it most certainly is not benefiting the average citizen in our country. . . . It is my view, based on a significant amount of experience in the California experiment, that a reduction in health care costs is not going to be achieved by some of the far-reaching medical malpractice reform proposals now being considered by the Congress. What will occur is that victims of medical negligence will have a decreased opportunity for redress.

To put it mildly, the insurance establishment did not appreciate this refreshing public candor by one of their own leading trial lawyers. "There is no question about it, I was blackballed," Baker says. "I think most lawyers on either side of the courtroom would agree that my testimony was accurate. The difference is that most defense lawyers are afraid to say anything."

According to Baker, within two weeks of his testimony, one of his law partners received a call from a senior claims executive with the Doctors' Company, a doctor-owned malpractice insurance enterprise: "My partner was told that our firm would receive no more cases from Doctors' because of my testimony before Congress. He was also advised that it was all the claims executive could do to keep the board of directors from pulling all of the existing cases with the firm."

Could there have been another reason for the company to withhold future business? For example, was Baker's firm doing a bad job for Doctors'? "We had always been told the company was pleased with us," Baker recalls. "In fact, we had never lost a trial verdict for the Doctors' Company in the years we had represented their insureds. In 1993, we had won at least ten, maybe twelve defense verdicts. The company did not pay out one dime because of an adverse verdict."[129]

Doctors' was not the only insurance company that apparently began boycotting Baker's firm. The HMO company Kaiser withdrew business from the firm, as did other insurance companies. Within months, the loss of fees forced the firm to significantly downsize and, as of our interview with Baker, it was fighting merely to stay in business.

Baker now painfully understands the might of the insurance industry. "After all this occurred," he recalls, "I had a meeting with a head executive of a large firm who shall remain nameless. When I complained about how our firm was being retaliated against for expressing truth, he said, 'What you don't understand is that insurance companies have always had the power. We are just now using it.' "

We repeatedly attempted to contact the Doctors' Company claims representative for a response. Our messages, left on voice mail, went unanswered. We spoke with Trish O'Hanlon at the Pasadena office of Kaiser, the woman identified by Baker as one of his firm's two Kaiser business sources. When asked if Kaiser had blackballed Baker's firm because of his congressional testimony, she replied, "It is a firm we are no longer using. We haven't blackballed the firm. We are not going to comment further."

Big health care companies and wealthy doctors are determined to quell attacks on California's restrictive 1975 malpractice law for one reason: It restricts the rights of victims, thus freeing health care providers and their insurance companies from the full consequences of their misconduct. Consider, for example, the case of Steven A. Olsen of Chula Vista, California.

On February 29, 1992, Olsen, a healthy two-year-old boy, was walking with his family in the Laguna Mountains. He fell down, and his face hit a twig, which lodged between his upper lip and his gums. His parents brought him to San Diego's Children's Hospital, where his wound was cleaned. A week later, Steven was suffering from fevers and headaches. After two visits to the doctor, he reentered the hospital. The resident pediatrician correctly diagnosed Steven as possibly suffering from a central nervous abscess. However, despite the family's specific request, hospital personnel failed to verify the diagnosis by performing a CT scan. Steven was diagnosed with viral meningitis, treated, and released.

The next day he was returned to the hospital unconscious, by paramedics. His brain herniated from the pressure of the abscess. He was left blind, mentally handicapped, and suffering from seizures.

Steven's family sued the Sharp-Rees Stealy Medical Group, which provided doctors for the Olsens' HMO, and the University of California, which provided one of the hospital residents. Sharp-Rees settled with the family for $2 million, but the state-run university decided to go to trial. The family charged that, had the proper diagnosis been pursued, Steven could have been successfully treated. They further contended that the doctors decided not to follow up with a CT scan in order to save the HMO the cost. (The health providers denied that the CT scan was needed or that cost was a consideration in their decision.)

In November 1994, a San Diego Superior Court jury concluded that the circumstances required the defendant to pay Steven's family $7 million for the lifetime of pain and suffering caused by the misdiagnosis, plus $4.3 million to compensate for medical bills and lost future earnings. What the jury had not been told was that California's malpractice law caps pain and suffering damages at $250,000 (with no adjustment for inflation since the law was passed in 1976). The law required the presiding judge to reduce the award by $6.75 million.

To compensate for a lifetime of lost vision and lost opportunities, Steven was left with about $4,000 per year for pain and suffering, assuming he lives to age sixty. The amount the jury awarded for economic damages, as Steven's father has written, "is merely money to keep his damaged body alive,"[130] as well as to compensate for the fact that he will never be able to earn a living.

"Until this happens to you," Steven's mother, Kathy Olsen, told the San Diego Union-Tribune, "you never realize what a position you can be in. The damage limits don't take into account catastrophic injuries like Steven's."[131] Tort deforms had seen to it that health providers were held only partially responsible for their negligence and that an innocent victim was left with far less compensation than the circumstances warranted. And yet Newt Gingrich's House of Representatives, buffeted by the lobbying and campaign contributions of major medical organizations and companies, has passed and wants the country to adopt legislation to extend this $250,000 malpractice cap nationwide.

ALTERNATIVE DISPUTE RESOLUTION IS DESIGNED TO BENEFIT THE POWERFUL

Alternative dispute resolution (ADR) refers to various methods developed to help individuals and businesses resolve their legal disputes outside of the court system. There are several forms of ADR. Mediation is one example. In a mediation, a professional facilitator, called a mediator, assists parties in resolving their dispute. Mediators have no power; they cannot decide who is right and who is wrong. But a mediator will have the training and personality to help disputants voluntarily reach an agreement.

Another form of ADR is arbitration. In some respects, an arbitration is similar to a trial, since the dispute is "decided" by the arbitrator or panel of arbitrators hearing the case. But there are significant differences between an arbitration and a trial. In an arbitration there is no judge and no jury. The rules of evidence tend to be less strict, and the hearing will usually take place in an office rather than a courtroom. Also, unlike judicial proceedings, arbitrations are handled in complete privacy and confidentiality.

A hard core of ADR believers, which includes some law professors, lawyers, and judges, idealize ADR as a less costly and quicker way to settle disputes than going to court.

ADR can sometimes achieve such goals in certain kinds of disputes if—and it is a big "if"—the proceedings are voluntary, if both sides have affirmatively agreed to settle the dispute through an arbitration rather than in court. But business executives are increasingly seeing to it that ADR becomes mandatory through the way their corporate lawyers draft small-print contracts that bind individual consumers and employees. In legal parlance, these are called "contracts of adhesion," preprinted, standardized written agreements composed by a party with superior bargaining power, which give the weaker party only the opportunity to accept or reject them. As consumers, we see them all the time—when, for example, we purchase airline or interstate bus tickets, apply for a credit card, take out a loan, or obtain health insurance. These contracts of adhesion are legal, but courts have the authority to refuse to uphold them where the terms are unconscionable.

Lawyers for the nation's powerful business institutions are increasingly writing binding arbitration clauses into their one-sided, preprinted contracts, on a take-it-or-leave-it basis. If the trend continues, consumers will not be able to enter into bank, insurance, and other financial transactions, sign employment agreements, or enter into other contracts with corporations without giving up their access to the justice system. But in these circumstances, as corporations and their power lawyers well know, ADR stacks the deck in company management's favor, at the expense of employees and consumers. Compulsory arbitration has become a cornerstone of power attorneys' carefully crafted, no-contest structure, aimed at ensuring the legal dominance of large corporations.

Unscrupulous loan companies and securities swindlers are among the leaders in forcing ADR clauses on unsuspecting or powerless customers. But more "respectable" big corporations also want in on the action, as the following case illustrates.

THE BIG BANK AND THE SMALL PRINT

In June 1992, the Bank of America inserted a notice in the monthly statements it sent to its millions of checking account and credit card customers telling them that they could no longer sue the bank in the event of a dispute; instead, their only recourse would be binding arbitration. The bank's own research before the mailing indicated that less than 4 percent of its customers read such notices.[132] Even if a customer bothered to read the notice, it offered no invitation to respond, to disagree, or even to consent to this substantial curtailing of customer rights.

A group of depositors hired the four-lawyer San Francisco firm Sturdevant & Sturdevant and sued the bank, claiming that the notices were incomplete and misleading, were unconscionable, and were not sufficient to incinerate customers' constitutional right to a jury trial. Bank of America retained the 500-lawyer San Francisco–based firm Morrison & Foerster. The case was entitled *Badie* v. *Bank of America*.

Why didn't the Bank of America customers who sued—people who apparently had the time, resources, and experience to read and understand the bank's unilateral decision to demand binding arbitration—simply agree with the bank that such procedures, and not lawsuits, were the best way to resolve serious disagreements? Because mandatory ADR almost always favors a big institution over individuals. ADR can cost as much as or more than court litigation, can prevent aggrieved parties from finding facts essential to their cases, can conceal important information of broad public concern, and can keep the individual disputant, even if victorious, from obtaining an effective remedy. Patricia Sturdevant, attorney for the customers, explains, "There may be no right to discovery in a dispute. The arbitrator decides whether or not to permit it. Moreover, since the consumer has to pay for half of the arbitrator's fees, it significantly raises the cost of resolving a dispute. Finally, the arbitrator is not bound to follow the law or precedent. They are empowered to make a decision and don't even have to explain its basis. Even if the decision results in a manifest injustice, it is still final and binding." That is, an arbitrator's decision cannot be appealed to the court system. And, unlike judges, arbitrators do not have the power to issue and enforce injunctions that direct the parties to act or forgo actions. Mandatory arbitration, Sturdevant says, "promotes an ethic that you are only entitled to the amount of justice you can afford to buy."[133]

While Bank of America and its suing customers were squaring off over the arbitration notices, another dispute over mandatory arbitration, involving a very different kind of financial institution, was taking shape in the same San Francisco County trial court.

In 1990, two misfortunes befell a Glen Park, California, woman named Geneva Bell. She lost her clerical job at the University of California Medical Center. And she made a deal, what seems a terrible deal, with a company called Congress Mortgage Co. of San Jose. Bell sought a loan to pay some taxes and overdue mortgage payments. The Congress Mortgage agent who visited Bell's home told her to sign the agreement and that he would return with more papers. The papers, according to Bell, turned out to be additional contract provisions she had never seen. The loan turned out to be for substantially more than Bell said she actually requested. Bell was unable to keep up with the payments and was headed toward foreclosure.[134]

Bell was probably unaware that some mortgage companies thrive by encouraging individuals to borrow sums that are larger than they will likely be able to afford to repay. A primary purpose of such lending, in addition to charging high loan fees and interest rates, is to enable the companies to foreclose on the debtors' homes, thereby obtaining the properties for a price—the loan amount—well below the fair-market value. Congress defended its practices by asserting that its foreclosure rate was about average for the state of California.[135]

Fortunately for Bell and other homeowners who had obtained loans from Congress Mortgage, the San Francisco law firm Jenkins and Mulligan was willing to represent them. In 1993, they filed a lawsuit in state court against Congress Mortgage and other companies involved in similar actions, alleging that these lenders had repeatedly engaged in illegal, unfair, and fraudulent business practices, including failing to disclose actual loan terms, imposing exorbitant fees, retaining funds required to be disbursed to borrowers, and improperly granting loans to people who had no hope of repaying them.

Congress Mortgage demanded that the case be immediately dismissed. Why? Because Geneva Bell and the other borrowers had agreed to keep any dispute out of court and instead to resolve their differences through binding arbitration. And, indeed, there it was, albeit in an inconspicuous, unhighlighted fine-print passage in the middle of the page—the handiwork of corporate lawyers—buried in a document, an appeals court later found, "whose every other significant provision was a recitation of rights guaranteed the borrower":[136]

> All disputes to this agreement and accompanying loan docu-
> ments or remedies of default herein shall be settled by arbitra-
> tion in accordance with the rules of the American Arbitration
> Association.

Whatever that meant. "I don't know what an arbitration clause is,"
Geneva Bell told a reporter, "but I imagine they threw something at
me."[137]

They sure did. Binding arbitration clauses are attractive to some
lenders because an arbitrator cannot issue an injunction to prevent
foreclosure; only a judge has that power. And if the borrower sues, a
judge may determine that the court has no power to act because of the
binding arbitration clause. In such cases, the property can be foreclosed
upon and sold long before the dispute gets to arbitration.

The homeowners' attorneys urged the judge to put aside the arbitration clauses in these contracts of adhesion because they were, in the
circumstances, utterly unconscionable. Congress Mortgage Company
agents had never explained the clauses, never explained that, as one
price of obtaining the loans, borrowers would agree to sign away their
fundamental constitutional rights to access to the justice system. Many
borrowers were inexperienced in financial matters and never even read
the agreements, a practice, plaintiffs' lawyers alleged, that Congress
Mortgage did nothing to discourage.

The trial court, backing the homeowners, issued a temporary injunction against foreclosure and ruled that the court case could proceed rather than being dismissed in favor of arbitration. On May 17,
1994, a unanimous panel of the California Court of Appeal, in an opinion by Judge Richard Hodge, affirmed the trial judge's decision that the
arbitration clause was unenforceable:[138]

> The trial court record is replete with evidence that appellants
> engaged in practices which were both unlawful and designed to
> deceive unsophisticated and inexperienced borrowers as to
> their essential contractual rights. We recognize that the allega-
> tions are not yet proven in the crucible of trial, but they estab-
> lish a nexus of facts consistent with the trial court's finding of
> unenforceability.
>
> Acceding to arbitration necessarily entails a waiver of the
> right to a jury trial secured by . . . the California Consti-
> tution. . . . We conclude . . . that an adhesion contract must
> elicit a clear and informed waiver of that constitutional right . . .

The appellate court then attempted to lay down a rule to clarify the duties of lenders in the future and help prevent further disputes about whether or not a given case belonged in court or in arbitration. In order to be enforceable, the court ruled, an arbitration clause in a contract of adhesion must "appear in clear and unmistakable form by highlighting, bold type, or with an opportunity for specific acknowledgment by initialing. Enforceability requires a clear recitation that the parties knowingly waive their right to a jury trial." In imposing this requirement for arbitration clauses, the court took its cue from similar requirements in state statutes governing medical and real estate contracts.

Congress Mortgage, still hoping to send the case to arbitration, sought review by the California Supreme Court. But meanwhile, other, larger companies quickly developed an interest in the case, and they set out to manipulate state law to restore their dominance over consumers and employees. One big fish was particularly anxious to minimize the impact of the Bell decision: the Bank of America. The trial in *Badie v. Bank of America* over the arbitration notices stuffed into Bank of America customer statements concluded on May 19, 1994—two days after the appellate court's decision in *Bell*. The trial judge in *Badie*, Thomas Mellon, Jr., told the parties that he would be watching for developments in the Bell case. Judge Mellon's decision could have come at any time, and state rules required the judge to rule by August 19, 1994, three months after the trial had ended. Bank of America wanted desperately to get rid of the appellate court's *Bell* decision, and do so fast, so that it would not bind Judge Mellon in deciding *Badie*. Otherwise the bank's scheme to force arbitration clauses on its customers would be imperiled. (Not only was the appellate court's decision in *Bell* binding on all trial judges within that appellate court's regional district, it also could be cited by lawyers around the state as persuasive authority.)

But what to do? The bank had no standing in the Bell case, since it was not a party. Nor, presumably, did it relish coming to the rescue of the allegedly unsavory Congress Mortgage Company. But Bank of America's power lawyers had a plan.

Instead of urging the Supreme Court to reverse the appellate decision and rule in Congress Mortgage's favor, the bank's lawyers decided to see if the Supreme Court could be persuaded to wipe the Court of Appeal decision off the books by ordering it "depublished." Depublishing would not affect the outcome of *Bell* itself. But depublishing, an unusual procedure that is not even permitted in many states, would obliterate the precedential value of the opinion in future proceedings before state trial and appellate courts.

Bank of America's attorneys devised a clever strategy to achieve their aim, and it worked. Instead of approaching the Supreme Court directly, they convinced the office of the California attorney general to do their work for them. In June 1994, Bank of America Assistant General Counsel June Arne Wagner called Chief Deputy Attorney General M. David Stirling, urging his office to petition the Supreme Court to depublish the decision. Later that month, Kathleen Fisher of the Morrison & Foerster firm wrote Stirling on behalf of the bank, again asking that the attorney general seek depublication. Stirling told a reporter for the legal publication *The Recorder* that neither Wagner nor Fisher even mentioned the Badie case; instead they stressed the profound public-policy impact the Bell decision might have on cases involving businesses across the state. (Asked by the same reporter why its lawyers didn't raise the Badie case in its discussions with the attorney general's office, a Bank of America spokesman, Peter Magnani, explained that the bank's interests were broader. "I don't think *Badie* is the issue," he said.)[139]

The bank's argument regarding the threat to business interests would not have been lost on California's strongly procorporate attorney general, Republican ex-congressman Dan Lungren. It probably also didn't hurt Bank of America that it was negotiating, along with other banks, to cosign a $4 billion loan the state government needed to meet its budget requirements (a loan issued on July 20, 1994), or that the bank was among Lungren's top twenty campaign contributors that year, giving $5,000.

In an interview with *The Recorder,* Stirling denied that Lungren's office was doing the Bank of America's bidding. He said that the office was acting to uphold the state's interest in promoting arbitration. But he admitted that the office was unaware of *Bell's* implications until Bank of America's lawyers came calling.

On July 18, 1994, the attorney general's office wrote the Supreme Court a letter requesting that it depublish the Bell decision because, the office argued, it was up to the legislature, not courts, to issue specific standards for adhesion contracts.[140]

The bank's lawyers pursued their plan on other fronts as well. They convinced the California Manufacturers Association to write a similar letter to the Supreme Court urging depublication. And more letters taking the same side arrived at the court from the California Bankers Association, the California League of Savings Institutions, and the California Employment Law Council, an association of the state's largest employers. Yet another letter taking the pro–big business position in support of depublication came from a group that might have been expected, under the circumstances, to stay on the sidelines: the leading U.S. arbitration organization, the American Arbitration Association (AAA)—the very group that both Congress Mortgage and the Bank of America had designated, in their fine-print notices, as the neutral overseer of disputes between these businesses and their customers.[141]

On July 28, 1994, Bank of America got what it wanted. The California supreme court denied Congress Mortgage's request to review the Bell case, thereby allowing to stand the Court of Appeal's ruling that Geneva Bell and the other homeowners could pursue their claims in court, rather than in arbitration. But, at the same time, the Supreme Court, without comment, agreed by a 7-1 vote to depublish the decision.[142] *Bell* ceased to be binding on other courts. Lawyers representing consumers or workers could no longer cite it as a valid case authority. (A trial of Geneva Bell's claims against Congress Mortgage Company appears to be months or years away, mostly because of legal maneuverings by defense lawyers.)

There was only one chapter left to be written in this tale of power-lawyer manipulation. On August 18, 1994, California Superior Court Judge Thomas J. Mellon, Jr., freed of the shackles of the *Bell* precedent, decided the Badie case by ruling for the Bank of America. He held that alternative dispute resolution was favored by state public policy and that, although the bank had not provided "the best possible notice," it had acted within its rights.[143] As of this writing, the customers' appeal to a higher court is pending.

We contacted attorney Fisher of Morrison & Foerster and asked why Bank of America was so intent on getting the Bell case depublished. She told us, "I really cannot comment on the issue other than to state that the decision was depublished, which you already know." Bank of America in-house counsel Wagner did not respond to our request for comment.

If the customers and employees of Bank of America and other large businesses are stuck with forced arbitration, they are in trouble. Not only can arbitrators decide to bar or sharply limit discovery, even if discovery is allowed, the arbitrator has little power to enforce it. "Arbitrators are simply not going to be able to force disclosure," attorney Sturdevant told us. "And if you have a discovery dispute, you are going to have to pay the arbitrator for the privilege of contesting the issue."

This puts less-affluent litigants at a potentially devastating disadvantage. As we showed in Chapters 2 through 4, corporate lawyers will only reluctantly disclose evidence of their clients' wrongdoing. It may take years of fighting the discovery wars, hundreds of court hours reviewing the matter, and tens of thousands of dollars in costs merely to obtain information that the law requires to be disclosed. Indeed, it often takes the most harsh court-imposed sanctions to convince corporate lawyers and their clients to fully obey the rules.

What a judge can do to punish discovery abuse and compel disclosure, an arbitrator cannot do. Arbitrators generally cannot dismiss a claim because of discovery abuse, issue injunctions, impose monetary sanctions, or hold parties in contempt of court for disobeying an order. In short, while binding arbitrators possess tremendous and unreviewable power to decide cases, they have virtually no power at all to guarantee a fair process.

Claims that arbitration saves individuals money as compared with litigating in the court system do not stand up. Individual taxpayers pay for the courts, allowing access to jurisprudence for modest fees, which can be waived if necessary. Not so arbitration. Arbitrators charge both parties for their services—usually $200 or more per hour—half of which must be paid by consumers. This places consumers in the unenviable position of paying taxes for court services from which they are barred, while at the same time being forced into paying high arbitrator's fees when seeking justice, in addition to other expenses associated with litigation, such as attorney's fees.

In California, courts have upheld the rights of health providers to use fine-print contracts to force malpractice disputes out of the courts and into arbitration. Each arbitration typically has three arbitrators, with the injured claimant required to pick up half the tab. As one plaintiff's lawyer explained, "Those arbitrators charge $250 an hour apiece. If you go eight hours a day, that's $6,000 dollars a day for the arbitrators. [Health care giant] Kaiser has billions of dollars. If they take ten days and spend $30,000, that's no problem . . . And remember, in a jury trial, if you're indigent, you get a jury for free."[144]

ADR certainly has a place in resolving disagreements. For example, it can work well in settling disputes between parties of relatively equal power who wish to maintain a business or personal relationship. ADR certainly makes sense where both sides know well the pros and cons of obtaining a resolution out of court and mutually agree to it. But use of ADR in such circumstances is not at the heart of the tort deformers' agenda. Rather, they want to use ADR because it can help protect them from punitive damage awards for egregious behavior, limit corporate embarrassment by shielding proceedings from public view, and deny future victims of corporate misconduct the benefits of relevant trial records and judicial precedents.

Big companies are forcing not only their customers into giving up their rights to sue. Increasingly, they are insisting that their employees agree, in order to obtain or keep their jobs, that any dispute with the employer—whether the subject is on-the-job injuries, racial or gender discrimination, sexual harassment, failure to pay wages or benefits, etc.—must be resolved through mandatory arbitration rather than through the civil justice system. Ralph Hurvitz, an in-house labor lawyer with weapons contractor Lockheed, gave a reporter his version of the reason why: "Arbitrators are more familiar with the realities of the workplace and are less subject to emotion."[145] Since most judges and jurors have plenty of workplace experience, and judges have at least as much as arbitrators, what could Hurvitz mean?

A lawsuit brought by J. Meg Olson, a former sales executive at NCR Corporation in Dallas, offered a slightly different hypothesis for why employers are herding aggrieved employees into arbitration. Olson claimed she was sexually harassed on the job. When she sought relief in court, claiming intentional infliction of emotional distress, NCR got the case dismissed by pointing to the mandatory arbitration clause in her employment agreement. In 1994, she went to arbitration under the auspices of the American Arbitration Association and lost. Before the arbitration had begun, Olson filed a suit claiming that arbitrations conducted by the AAA are biased because the group usually assigns white male corporate lawyers as arbitrators. AAA denied it was biased. A Texas federal district judge, and then the Fifth Circuit Court of Appeals, rejected Olson's claim.[146]

AAA receives corporate contributions, and individual arbitrations are usually financed by the employer.[147] Even where the costs of paying for the arbitration are split, an arbitrator might see more reason to please a big corporation than to satisfy an individual disputant or smaller business: The corporation, unlike most individuals, is routinely in litigation and thus is far more likely to be a repeat customer. "If you get an arbitrator or an arbitration decision you don't like, you don't pick him again," T. Warren Jackson, corporate counsel for Hughes Aircraft, admitted to a reporter.[148]

Orrick, Herrington & Sutcliffe, a 291-attorney San Francisco corporate firm, recently circulated a report on arbitrations of employment discrimination cases in the securities industry. Out of the eight cases discussed in the report, employers won six. In the other two, the workers received awards of $300 and $5,822.[149] Arbitration appears to keep awards to plaintiffs down. "It's the existence of jury trials which is the major impetus toward arbitration agreements," Los Angeles corporate lawyer Paul Grossman acknowledged to *The New York Times*.[150]

Two federal agencies, the National Labor Relations Board and the Equal Employment Opportunity Council, contend that mandatory arbitration clauses in employment contracts violate workers' civil rights.[151] The AAA and other arbitration groups are facing increased pressure from worker and consumer representatives to develop more diverse, open-minded panels of arbitrators—and to stop cooperating with companies that require employees to sign mandatory arbitration clauses.[152] But until that occurs, and unless arbitration is completely informed and voluntary, it cannot be an acceptable substitute for the right to file suit to redress injuries.

The best way to keep down the costs of resolving disputes is to preserve the constitutional rights of citizens to have their day in court, if they so choose, in the event of wrongdoing. The possibility of facing public trial and accountability assists in keeping powerful corporations and individuals from misbehaving in the first place and helps facilitate sufficient out-of-court settlements when they nevertheless engage in misconduct. If corporations knew that the worst result of their wrongdoing would be a confidential scolding and slap on the wrist from a sympathetic arbitrator, incentives to sell defective products and worthless securities, to trick and mislead consumers, and to mistreat and discriminate against employees would surely increase.

CONTINGENCY FEES ARE NECESSARY TO EQUALIZE ACCESS TO THE COURTHOUSE

Many of the individuals whose cases have been described in this book would not have had access to justice or the courts but for the contingency fee. For example, look at what happened to Surgin when it sued Farmers Insurance. After incurring $300,000 in fees, Surgin was at the end of its rope, even though, as the courts later affirmed, it had an excellent case. The company would have had to give up its pursuit of the case in court and drop the matter but for its attorneys agreeing to switch to a contingency fee. Similarly, the individuals who have sued General Motors over the terrible casualties that they contend were caused by dangerously designed and positioned gas tanks in pickup trucks could not have challenged GM without lawyers working for them on contingency. The Miller family, whose twin sons were catastrophically injured by a defect in a Ford Motor Company vehicle, could not have litigated against Ford and obtained their just settlement but for an attorney willing to take the case on contingency. The same is true for tens of thousands of individuals who are able to seek justice only because they don't have to pay an upfront fee and a high hourly rate. In other words, the contingency fee allows average people access to justice that normally is available only to the fattest of cats.

The corporate establishment knows that the contingency fee empowers individuals and expands access to justice. That is why so much corporate money is donated to finance various aggressive efforts to regulate and restrict the contingency fee in the legal marketplace, while leaving undisturbed the amounts corporate defense attorneys on the other side of the aisle can charge.

This attack on the contingency fee is broad and pervasive. It comes from corporate-financed think tanks, such as the Manhattan Institute and the Heritage Foundation. It comes from people such as John C. Scully, counsel with the corporatist Washington Legal Foundation, who has written that contingency fees "are fuel that feed the litigation explosion."[153] It comes from Newt Gingrich and company, one of whose highest priorities for the legal system is to restrict contingency fee arrangements.

The contingency fee is quite simple. A lawyer agrees to take a case without any money upfront and without requiring the client to pay an hourly or flat fee. In return, the lawyer is entitled to receive a percentage of the actual amount of money collected, generally 33 percent, but sometimes 40 percent if the case has gone through trial and/or appeal. Unlike hourly fees charged by corporate lawyers, in a contingency the lawyer takes a risk. If the case is lost, the lawyer will collect no fee. For that reason, most contingency-fee lawyers will only take cases they believe have a good chance of success. Moreover, unlike lawyers being paid by the hour, attorneys working on contingency have no financial incentive to overwork the case or flood the court with unnecessary, delaying motions and paperwork, since that will not increase the amount of money they are paid.

Opponents of the contingency fee contend that it somehow promotes frivolous lawsuits because, they say, lawyers take bad cases knowing that insurance companies will settle for the nuisance value. But even one Heritage Foundation staffer, attorney James L. Gattuso, once admitted in a *Wall Street Journal* article that the contingency fee "acts to provide the services of attorneys to injured people who may not be able to otherwise afford legal representation," and he added, "[T]here is no incentive for a lawyer to file a losing [contingency] case—he gets paid only if he wins. It is consequently difficult to persuade a lawyer to risk his time and resources on what seems a losing cause. Thus, rather than encourage baseless lawsuits, the contingent fee actually helps screen them out of the system."[154] Moreover, the charge that contingency fees encourage frivolous suits ignores a basic fact about insurance companies: They are not in the business of giving away their money on bad claims. Indeed, it can be very tough to get them to settle meritorious claims fairly. Even Barry Keene, former president of the Association for California Tort Reform, says that lawyers who work on contingency "reject many cases simply because they require too much work or are difficult to prove."[155] Most contingency-fee lawyers are not in the business of offering free legal services and are reluctant to accept cases with little real chance of recovery.

Keene and Professor Jeffrey O'Connell of the University of Virginia, both supporters of restrictions on individual rights within the civil justice system, say that they don't want to eliminate all contingency fees—merely end abuses. "Many contingency fees are earned," Professor O'Connell told us. "But some are unearned. For example, if someone is involved in an accident and rendered a quadriplegic, and the only assets of the wrongdoer is a $50,000 liability policy, the full amount is going to be paid. An injured party should not have to pay a lawyer one third to get these damages because that money will not have been earned."[156]

That is true, as far as it goes. And it is certainly true that consumers need to question lawyers about the difficulty of a prospective case when determining whether to hire them on contingency and, if so, at what percentage. And it is also true that some unscrupulous lawyers will take one third of a "slam-dunk" case, even if it requires very little work.

In reality, however, few significant injury cases are easy. Most require detailed investigation, fact finding, and research about whether there is any liability—whether the victim has a strong enough case to justify filing suit. It is usually important to let time pass after the injury in order to evaluate the full extent of a victim's damages. Experts must be located and retained.

Tort deformers know that. But they choose to use the slam-dunk scenario as an excuse to sow confusion and distrust between the public and plaintiffs' lawyers, and to justify legislation to enact price controls that would apply only to one side: those tort lawyers representing individuals against powerful corporations. The truth is that plaintiffs' lawyers generally earn less than the corporate defense attorneys they face in court. According to a Consumer Federation of America study, for every $1 paid to plaintiffs' lawyers from 1984 to 1993, defense lawyers received $1.31. The average fee for a plaintiff's lawyer was about $6,000 for a *successful* claim[157]—and remember that a plaintiff's lawyer working on a contingent fee usually earns nothing if the claim is unsuccessful. Research by Herbert Kritzer, professor of political science and law at the University of Wisconsin, indicates that lawyers working on contingency fees earn about the same as those paid by the hour.[158]

As to the concern that consumers are sometimes overcharged by lawyers who take a contingency fee when no real contingency exists, that problem can best be overcome through effective and widespread consumer education. There are many consumer books published that teach clients how to hire a lawyer and obtain a fair fee. Most bar associations also publish free client guides to assist them in hiring contingency-fee lawyers. David Schrager, a former president of the American Trial Lawyers Association, a leading plaintiffs' lawyer group, has stated repeatedly his view that no contingent fee should exceed one third of the judgment, no matter how complicated or time-consuming the case. We urge state bar associations to finance an advertising campaign alerting consumers to their rights to negotiate the level and terms of contingency fees.

"LOSER PAYS" IS DESIGNED TO DETER INDIVIDUAL ACCESS TO JUSTICE

Another item in the tort deform catalog, one aimed, like the effort to abolish contingency fees, at increasing the risk of bringing a lawsuit against a wrongdoer, is enactment of the so-called "English Rule," also known as "loser pays." Various versions of this proposal would require the losing party in a lawsuit to pay some or all of the winning side's attorney fees.

Tort deformers say this proposal is fair, since both plaintiffs and defendants would bear the same burden under the law—paying for the victor's attorney fees. But there is an obvious hidden agenda, in a country where individual consumers and workers are up against Dupont, General Motors, or Aetna.

William L. Fry, the director of HALT, a national group that critiques lawyers, said in an interview, "We are totally against loser pays. The English Rule is designed to scare people away from seeking redress."[159]

Professor Jeffrey O'Connell, who supports many aspects of the tort deform agenda, agrees: "What has happened in England is that the poor can get representation because of Legal Aid, but the middle class cannot because they cannot afford to pursue their rights, because if by chance they lose their case—and it is often a matter of chance—they face an additional financial penalty."

Loser pays could deter people not only from seeking redress for personal injuries but also from standing up for the basic rights that are guaranteed by the Constitution and laws of our nation. Abner J. Mikva has served in all three branches of the federal government: as a congressman from Illinois, as a federal judge on the District of Columbia circuit court of appeals, and, most recently, as White House counsel. His comment on loser pays: "If the English rule had been in effect here, none of the civil rights cases would have been brought. If they had lost, a single lawsuit would have wiped out their treasuries."[160]

Loser pays, while appearing to apply equally to all litigants, would have a profoundly unequal impact. This is best illustrated by what is known in law school as a "hypothetical." It assumes a common variant of the loser-pays proposal, one that, according to loser-pays proponents, acts to blunt the harsh impact of the rule. Under the modification, the losing side would be liable for the other side's attorney fees—but only up to the amount the loser himself has spent or, in the event the loser's attorney worked on a contingency fee, up to the reasonable value of the losing attorney's services.[161]

> Assume that a lawsuit is brought alleging a defect in a Conglomerate Amalgamated (CA) automobile, which the victim claims exploded, leaving him a paraplegic. CA, a company worth $8 billion, denies the car is defective, and its lawyers dig in for a protracted legal battle. Its executives and lawyers believe that the case poses grave risks for the company. They know that if the suspect vehicle is actually proved defective, the company will face a potential government recall that could cost it at least $100 million. They can also expect other injured consumers to sue, potentially costing the business giant tens of millions more in damages. Then, there is the potential for a lot of lost business if the public comes to believe that CA sells unsafe cars. An immediate budget of $10 million is authorized to litigate the case.
>
> Bob, the accident victim, lives on a disability check, since at present he has been unable to return to work because of his injuries. His most valuable asset is $25,000 equity in his home. He has $12,000 in the bank and another $8,000 in his children's education fund. He also has a credit line of $10,000.

Bob's attorney, who has obtained two professional opinions from auto safety experts, believes she can prove that the CA car is defective. However, CA can be expected to fight the case with every weapon in its legal arsenal. She expects the case to take several years, at least a half million dollars in litigation expenses, which she will advance, and thousands of hours in attorney time. The victim's lawyer is willing to take the case on contingency, but because of the English Rule, which is now the law in every state, she must tell her client that if he loses the case, which is always possible, he will owe CA perhaps $1 million in attorneys fees, based on the time she and her firm will have to invest in the case, what with the discovery wars, research, trial, and probable appeal.

Bob is horrified. He has been severely injured, and he believes, with some justification, that defects in his car were the cause. Yet, that informed suspicion remains to be proved. If it cannot be proved—perhaps because CA's power-lawyer tactics keep the crucial evidence under wraps—or if the jury makes a mistaken decision, and the case is lost, he faces, at best, bankruptcy, and, at worst, homelessness.

Meanwhile, CA's corporate attorneys must also tell their client that if CA loses, it too may have to pay the accident victim about $1 million in attorneys' fees. "Yeah, so?" the executive in charge might say. "We are willing to spend $10 million to win this case in order to avoid spending more than $100 million. Another tax-deductible million bucks isn't going to bother us one bit." (To add insult to injury, payment by corporations like CA of the other side's attorney fees could be deducted from corporate income on tax returns; payments by consumers like Bob could not.)

Loser pays is a loser for consumers. It does not deter the rich and powerful or the corporate executive whose own money is not on the line. Rather, it is individuals, people forced to risk their own standard of living or their children's futures, who cannot deduct legal fees from income taxes, who are likely to be dissuaded from pursuing their legal rights in such an oligarchic system.

Proponents of the English Rule know this, of course. They also know that abundant remedies already exist to punish frivolous suits. For example, in federal court, Civil Procedure Rule 11 allows a judge to award attorney fees to a party if the opposing party has filed a frivolous claim. State judges possess similar authority. In addition, as Chapter 5 illustrated, parties that file frivolous suits can themselves be held subject to countersuit for abusing the legal system. Given these safeguards, it is apparent that loser pays is just one more tort deform item that would do little to cut down on frivolous or unfair suits against business but would deter meritorious, genuine claims. It would, in short, result in another unwarranted bonanza for big business at the expense of the public.

THE TORT SYSTEM BENEFITS ALL OF US

No doubt, the tort law system needs to be improved, particularly to respond efficiently to the many injured people who, in today's system, are deterred from seeking relief because of costs and delays. But what is definitely *not* needed is to go backward, to effect a wholesale dismantling of rights that tort deformers seek. Stephen Gillers, New York University law professor and legal ethics expert, recently noted that, at a time when Congress is reducing the power of the government to regulate corporate and other perpetrators of harm, an effective tort system becomes even more important. If Congress limits tort awards and lawyers thereby lose their incentives to take cases, "we are going to leave people without adequate remedies."[162] Senator Fred Thompson, a Tennessee Republican, is a former trial lawyer. Although he voted under party and corporate pressures for the Senate tort deform bill, he admitted to *The Washington Post*, "In the overwhelming number of cases, the bad ones are ferreted out early on, the good ones go through the system, lawyers don't charge exorbitant fees, juries do their job . . . and the system works."[163]

The evidence shows that the tort system works when used and that the tort "reforms" proposed by industry are nothing but efforts to reduce corporate accountability and jack up corporate profits.

There is one additional but crucial point to consider in evaluating the debate over tort law. Tort litigation, although it is almost always financed by private parties, provides substantial societal benefits beyond the effects of damage awards. Consider, for example, the cigarette litigation discussed in Chapter 1. It was through these suits that the public gained access to secret documents revealing the cynical and deceitful behavior of the tobacco industry. These records and other disclosures from the cases have helped shape public debate and spurred federal safety agencies, investigators, and the U.S. Congress to act. Malpractice suits can inform the public and enforcement officials as to medical practices generally and bad doctors in particular. Securities suits can perform the same function with respect to dealers in stocks and bonds. Automobile defect cases do the same with the respect to the auto industry. And so on. Tort deforms that discourage parties from bringing suit weaken this important public alert function. Consider some other examples of how tort suits helped protect the public from harm, at a cost, for the entire tort liability system, of only 26 cents per $100 in retail sales:[164]

- In the landmark case of *Borel v. Fibreboard Paper Products Corp.*, the United States Court of Appeals for the Fifth Circuit held in 1973 that a manufacturer of asbestos could be held liable if its products were unreasonably dangerous and it failed to adequately warn workers.[165] Evidence in the case showed that asbestos makers had known of and deliberately concealed evidence that asbestos causes cancer. The immediate effect of the decision was to provide compensation for the widow of insulation worker Clarence Borel, who had died of asbestos-caused lung cancer after thirty years of exposure. The long-term effects, however, were broader. Many more suits were filed, and asbestos makers were made to pay for their misconduct. Asbestos insulation was withdrawn from the market.[166]

- From 1970 through 1979, Ford Motor Company manufactured several models with defectively designed transmissions. The vehicles appeared to be in "park," but would slip into reverse when a vibration, such as the slamming of a car door, occurred. At least eighty-nine people were injured as a result. Ford took no action until after two 1979 jury verdicts, the second one awarding $400,000 in compensatory damages and $4 million in punitive damages to the family of a Bay City, Texas, woman, Anna Nowak, who was killed when her 1977 Ford reversed and ran her over. (Judgments in both cases were affirmed on appeal.[167]) Evidence produced in the Nowak case suggested that Ford knew of the problem by 1971.[168] A few months after the verdicts, Ford fixed the problem.

- According to *Sports Illustrated*, in response to liability suits brought by injured student athletes, football helmet manufacturers have improved helmet designs, and in the later 1970s and early 1980s, high school and college leagues adopted helmet safety standards. In 1968, thirty-six student football players died from game-related injuries. By 1990, not a single such death was reported.

- In 1970, a four-year-old Minnesota girl, Lee Ann Gryc, suffered third-degree burns over her upper body when her pajama top caught fire. She required several skin graft procedures, experienced severe pain, and was left with permanent scarring on her face and body. Her family sued the pajama manufacturer, Riegel Textile Corporation, and proved, as the Minnesota Supreme Court later found, that the company was "uniquely aware" that its product was highly flammable, particularly in light of earlier claims filed against it. A state court jury awarded $750,000 actual damages and $1 million punitive damages, and this award was affirmed on appeal.[169] After the verdict, the company stopped selling the pajamas. The dangerous pajamas at issue in the case actually met the lax federal standards then in effect, and Congress subsequently amended the Flammable Fabrics Act to provide for more stringent regulation of children's sleepwear.

- Airco, Inc., the world's biggest maker of anesthesia equipment, sold a machine that assisted patient breathing during surgery. The family of Georgia Huchingson, an Arkansas woman, sued the company after she suffered brain and lung damage as a result of being connected to the device during a May 1980 operation. (Huchingson died in January 1982.) A jury concluded that the machine was defectively designed because it included a switch that made it easy for operators to inadvertently misuse the machine, resulting in oxygen deprivation to the patient. The jury awarded $1 million in compensatory damages and $3 million in punitive damages. The Arkansas Supreme Court, in July 1982, upheld the award[170] (the first time the court had approved a punitive damage award in a product liability suit), finding proof that Airco "knew from the outset, by its very own testing, that an unnecessary component of the product was so deadly that it should never have been made available to the public." Such proof, the court ruled, was sufficient to justify punitive damages. In the wake of the ruling Airco voluntarily issued a medical device alert through the U.S. Food and Drug Administration, warning physicians and hospitals nationwide of the potential for misuse of the product.

- A New Jersey auto body mechanic used a utility lamp made by the Carol Cable Company while removing a gas tank from a damaged car. Gasoline vapors caused the lamp to explode. The man suffered third-degree burns over 45 percent of his body and could no longer work as a mechanic. After the man won a jury verdict in 1984,[171] Carol Cable began including written warnings with its lamps telling users not to put the lamps near flammable vapors.

- Betty O'Gilvie, a Kansas woman, died in 1983 from toxic shock syndrome after using Playtex super-absorbent tampons. As a federal appeals court later found, there was "abundant evidence that Playtex deliberately disregarded studies and medical evidence linking high-absorbency tampon fibers with increased risk of toxic shock at a time when other manufacturers were responding to this information by modifying or withdrawing their high-absorbency products." The appeals court also found "evidence that Playtex deliberately sought to profit from this situation by advertising the effectiveness of its high absorbency tampons." In 1985, a federal district court jury, having heard the evidence, awarded O'Gilvie's family $1.5 million in compensatory damages and $10 million in punitive damages. Playtex promptly removed the tampons from the market, improved its warnings on other products about toxic shock syndrome, and began an effort to increase public awareness of the problem. The presiding judge told the family's attorney that the suit had "literally changed an industry."[172]

- Vitek, Inc., developed a synthetic jaw implant, made of Teflon, for persons suffering from mandibular joint syndrome. Between 1983 and 1990, more than 26,000 people received the implants. Experience showed that the implants tended to fragment, leading to deterioration of the skull and debilitating pain. Patients began filing suits against Vitek and physicians that inserted the implants. In 1988, Vitek stopped selling the implants, but other companies continued to do so. In 1990, Vitek declared bankruptcy. The next year the FDA issued a safety alert and recalled the implants.[173]

- Jean Kinder, a St. Louis woman, was driving with her daughter to a bowling alley on January 19, 1989, when a Domino's Pizza delivery driver ran a red light and struck her car. She suffered severe head and spinal injuries. She sued Domino's, the world's largest pizza delivery business, alleging that the company's promise to deliver pizzas in thirty minutes spurred driver recklessness. On December 17, 1993, a state court jury awarded her $78 million in punitive damages. Four days later, Domino's dropped its dangerous thirty-minute guarantee, which had been in effect for a decade. Domino's president, Thomas S. Monaghan, acknowledged that the verdict was what led to the company's decision to drop its delivery pledge. By then, hundreds of accident victims had filed claims against Domino's. (The company settled the Kinder case out of court for an undisclosed amount.)[174]

The more one analyzes the real source of opposition by industry and commerce (including physicians and hospitals, HMOs, and insurance companies) to American tort law, the more one realizes that the very modest amount of money paid out in verdicts and settlements each year for hazardous products and negligent medical treatment is only a small part of the story. It is the national public disclosure of misdeeds, cover-ups, and crimes that triggers the bitter corporate assaults on the rights of injured Americans. It is the deterrence that often leads to redesign of products, changes in service qualities, expansion of duties to notify, and, in general, changes in the ways companies have to do business. And it is the evolving framework of responsibility for harm done that the common law of torts has produced over the decades. The United States has come a long way from the days when awards for injuries were grossly inadequate, when there was no compensation for horrible pain and suffering, and when there were no punitive damages for criminal-type behavior.

Early in this century, a Mississippi worker lost his leg due to the negligence of the railroad company that employed him. He sued and won a $3,000 verdict from the jury. The judge reduced the award to $1,000, saying to the worker standing before him: "Your disability is for life, but for life only."

The cruelty in those old judicial words is echoed in the modern tort deform drive. This campaign is relentless, chipping away human rights each state legislative session and coming back for more destruction, now aimed at the U.S. Congress as well. The corporations that fund this assault on a pillar of American democracy will not be satisfied with merely curbing compensation, keeping crucial evidence secret, and superimposing one-sided legislative restrictions on judges and juries alike. Their goal is to maximize their immunities by getting rid of jury trials completely in personal injury cases. They care not for the Seventh Amendment to the Constitution, which provides that "the right of trial by jury shall be preserved," nor do they care for the importance that the protestors in the American colonies gave to trial by a jury of their peers when they listed their grievances to King George III. Nor do their legal spear-carriers care. Attorney Richard K. Willard, a top Reagan administration Justice Department official and now a partner with the 190-lawyer Washington, D.C., firm Steptoe & Johnson, scarcely concealed his contempt for the jury system when he recently said on CNN, "Juries today are overwhelmingly composed of people who are civil servants, retired, or have nothing better to do with their time."[175] So much for the only obligation of citizenship in the United States Constitution.

The current product liability system is not simply the only system that is faithful to our constitutional principles. It also benefits American industry by spurring innovations of safe products while deterring the production of dangerous products. Professors Nicholas Ashford and Robert Stone of the Massachusetts Institute of Technology have studied the impact of the product liability system on safety and innovation in the chemical industry. These are their conclusions with respect to that industry: (1) tort liability promotes safety and health; (2) tort liability tends to encourage safer innovations and discourage unsafe innovations; and (3) strengthening the tort liability system to allow greater recovery for injured parties would lead to safer products and more socially desirable innovation.[176]

In 1987, an industry-funded research organization, the Conference Board, published a survey of risk-management executives at 232 major U.S. corporations. It concluded:[177]

> For the major corporations surveyed, the pressures of product liability have hardly affected larger economic issues, such as revenues, market share or employee retention. . . . Where product liability has had a notable impact—where it has most significantly affected management decision-making—has been in the quality of the products themselves. Managers say products have become safer, manufacturing procedures have been improved, and labels and use instructions have become more explicit.

Tort deform legislation erodes corporate deterrence by significantly reducing the financial incentive for manufacturers to produce safe products. The tragic result is more injuries, more uncompensated victims, and greater overall costs to society. The horrors that thousands of victims have lived through, and continue to live with, as a result of dangerous products and medical malpractice illustrate the need for stronger, not weaker, safety rules and for letting the common law of judge, jury, and appellate courts remain independent to decide the facts of individual cases.

So, the next time you hear someone waxing eloquently on the need to "reform" tort law, ask yourself these questions: Who is paying for the advertisement or the spokesperson's salary? How much is actually being paid out in verdicts and settlements each year? What percentage of wronged people receive any compensation? What will be the corporate agenda's impact on the health and safety of our citizens? Get those answers right and we are confident you will tell the tort deformers that you've read the package label and are just not buying.

CHAPTER 9

FINDING THE COURAGE
TO CHANGE THE SYSTEM

*I*N CHAPTER 1, WE MET WASHINGTON ATTORNEY LLOYD CUTLER, the consummate power lawyer and a master at manipulating the system to suit his ends while repeatedly proclaiming himself a "person of integrity." But Cutler has passed his prime, and, as we saw, even he, in his brief tenure as President Clinton's counsel, was unable to completely escape the tarring brush of the Whitewater controversy.

It is, in fact, Whitewater that confirmed the new king of corporate law practice, a man we have encountered briefly in previous chapters: Kenneth W. Starr, a partner in the Washington, D.C., office of 401-lawyer Kirkland & Ellis. Starr has not only passed Cutler in influence, he also exceeds him in sheer audacity.

Starr served as a federal appeals judge from 1983 to 1989 and U.S. solicitor general from 1989 to 1993. Since leaving government, he has become the power lawyer of choice for corporate interests. He also became the Whitewater special prosecutor, the man in a position, if he found sufficient evidence, to bring down the president of the United States. Ignoring the standards set by the independent counsels in the other major investigations implicating presidential conduct—Leon Jaworski in the Watergate case, Lawrence Walsh in Iran-contra, and Robert Fiske, Starr's predecessor as Whitewater counsel—Starr steadfastly refused to suspend his private practice while investigating Whitewater, as was his right under the independent counsel statute, even though his conduct raised troubling questions about the potential for misuse of power.

From the time of his appointment as Whitewater independent counsel in August 1994, critics have attacked Starr for brushing aside potential conflicts of interest arising from his role as a partisan conservative Republican. Starr served as a political appointee in the Reagan and Bush Justice Departments, had considered seeking the 1994 Republican nomination for the Senate from Virginia, and sits on the advisory board of the conservative Washington Legal Foundation. Just prior to his appointment, he had publicly considered filing, at the invitation of the conservative Independent Women's Forum, a legal brief opposing President Clinton's claim of immunity from a sexual harassment suit brought by former Arkansas state employee Paula Corbin Jones. In 1995, he agreed to defend Wisconsin Governor Tommy Thompson against a court challenge contending that the governor's plan to use state funds to pay religious-school tuition fees violated the Constitution. Starr's fee in the case—$390 per hour—was paid for by the Lynde and Harry Bradley Foundation, also a client of Starr's. The conservative Bradley Foundation, meanwhile, was providing major grants to three of Clinton's leading Whitewater antagonists: the Landmark Legal Foundation, *American Spectator* magazine, and the cable television network NET.

But as disturbing as these potential conflicts seemed—Starr the conservative beacon versus Starr the impartial prosecutor—they were probably not as troublesome as a second set of conflicts: Starr the prosecutor versus Starr the corporate power lawyer. Starr earned $1.1 million from his law firm in 1994, even though he served as independent counsel for five months of that year. Far from reducing his private practice options, Starr became an increasingly attractive magnet for big corporate clients as his Whitewater investigation grew. No independent counsel could boast of such a wide-ranging practice, covering dozens of high-stakes matters, many intersecting with key political and regulatory issues directly involving the Clinton administration:

- Starr became the key lawyer for the tobacco industry while it faced unprecedented government pressure, as described in Chapter 1: a Justice Department criminal investigation; proposed Food and Drug Administration regulation; increased congressional scrutiny; and lawsuits brought by states seeking reimbursement for Medicare expenses incurred for smoking victims. He was not only the lead attorney in the crucial New Orleans class action suit, he also represented Philip Morris and Brown & Williamson in other matters, including a lawsuit to force two Democratic congressmen to return internal Brown & Williamson files they had received.
- Starr represented Bell Atlantic in Supreme Court litigation contesting the constitutionality of a law that blocked telephone companies from selling video programming. The case essentially became moot when Congress, at the behest of the Clinton admin-

istration, repealed the law in February 1996, thus giving Bell Atlantic and Starr what they had sought through the lawsuit. Starr's
work for Bell Atlantic, however, got off to a rough start. In the last
week of the Bush administration, Justice Department attorneys produced an internal memo concluding that Justice officials were free,
after leaving government, to sign legal briefs for private parties in
cases where the United States was also a party. This was the department's interpretation of a criminal conflict of interest law prohibiting top officials, for one year after leaving office, from
appearing before and seeking to influence their former agencies.

Whether Starr ever saw this memo, which reversed the department's long-standing position on this issue, or indeed played a role
in preparing it, is unclear, but in April 1993, three months after
ending his tenure as Solicitor General, Starr signed a brief on behalf of Bell Atlantic in its suit against the United States. Clinton
Justice Department officials, including Associate Attorney General
Webster Hubbell, advised Starr that Justice was once again concerned that such action was illegal; the department later ratified
this conclusion in a formal opinion. Starr stopped signing the papers until after the year had passed. (In August 1995, Hubbell
began serving a twenty-one-month federal prison sentence after
pleading guilty to fraud and tax evasion charges brought by Starr in
the Whitewater probe.)

- While Starr, as independent counsel, by statute has the "full power
and independent authority to exercise all investigative and prosecutorial functions and powers of the Department of Justice," two
months after his appointment he sought to convince the Supreme
Court to review a criminal conviction and a $3.5 million fine ob-
tained by the same Department of Justice against his client Hughes
Aircraft. A federal jury in California had convicted Hughes of
conspiring to defraud the Defense Department by falsely certifying
that weapons components had been adequately tested. (The
Supreme Court, as it does 99 percent of the time, declined to hear
the case.)

In February 1996, Starr again asked the high court for relief for
Hughes, this time after an appellate court had refused to dismiss
claims against the company brought by a former employee who says
Hughes committed fraud against the Air Force on the B-2 bomber
program. Starr contended that a federal law allowing workers who
blow the whistle on employers to keep a portion of taxpayer savings
resulting from their actions is unconstitutional; the Clinton Justice

Department had previously taken precisely the opposite view. (Indeed, so had Starr when he served as solicitor general.)

- Starr's work for General Motors also raised conflict issues. His first major assignment for Kirkland & Ellis was the Moseley case, discussed in Chapter 6, in which he convinced the Georgia Court of Appeals to throw out, on procedural grounds, a $105 million verdict against the automaker in a case involving a GM side-saddle-fuel-tank light truck. (The case later settled, confidentially, for a substantial sum.) In another GM light-truck case described in Chapter 6, Starr prevailed on a motion to have the trial judge, who had joked about corporate lawyers while making a public speech, recuse himself—on conflict of interest grounds!—after the judge had ruled against GM on a discovery issue.

While Starr was rescuing GM in the courts, his closest law firm colleague, Paul Cappuccio, was successfully resisting the Clinton administration's effort to recall the side-saddle trucks. As noted in Chapter 6, Secretary of Transportation Federico Pena announced plans for public hearings and a tentative decision to recall the trucks. But on December 2, 1994, Pena suddenly reversed course, agreeing to drop the recall in exchange for GM's promise to fund some traffic safety programs.

What had happened? While some cited possible difficulties in proving safety risks in the trucks, others focused on the effective efforts of Kirkland & Ellis. On October 31, 1994, GM's general counsel and senior vice president, Thomas A. Gottschalk (himself a former Kirkland & Ellis partner), wrote to the Transportation Department warning that public hearings on the pickup matter "will generate considerable acrimony and emotion" and create "the potential for lasting rancor." On November 17, 1994, GM sued to prevent the recall. Although Starr himself had no part in the settlement, Kirkland attorney Cappuccio played a key role, representing GM both in court and in negotiations with the Clinton administration to resolve the matter. Cappuccio, a former law clerk to Justice Antonin Scalia and a Justice Department official under President Bush, has known Starr for a decade, and the two came together to Kirkland and are extremely close.

In June 1995, Starr again went to GM's aid on the pickup trucks, asking the Supreme Court to restore a settlement in which owners of the side-saddle vehicles would receive only a $1,000 coupon toward the purchase of a new GM truck, while GM would pay $9.5 million to the lawyers purportedly representing the own-

ers. A federal appeals court had rejected the settlement as unfair to
the truck owners. (The high court turned Starr down.)

- Starr represented Dean Witter in a closely watched, high-stakes antitrust case. Dean Witter sought up to $1 billion in damages against
Visa U.S.A. over Visa's refusal to allow a Dean Witter–owned bank
to issue Visa cards. After Dean Witter lost before the Tenth Circuit
Court of Appeals, Starr, working with another former appeals judge
and solicitor general, Robert Bork, sought review in the U.S.
Supreme Court. Although Starr did not personally lobby the Justice Department, the Dean Witter legal team made efforts to have
the department support its position before the court. (The department took no position, and the court rejected Dean Witter's petition in June 1995.)

- In 1996, Starr represented National Football League players in the
Supreme Court in a suit against the league owners, notwithstanding a potential conflict: According to court papers, Jerry Jones,
owner of the Dallas Cowboys NFL team, invested in properties related to the Whitewater affair. In this matter, the Justice Department argued before the Supreme Court alongside of Starr in
support of his clients' position. (Starr's clients lost the case.)

- As noted in Chapter 8, Kirkland & Ellis has played a key role in
lobbying for so-called "tort reform," efforts by manufacturers to federally limit the authority of state judges and juries to impose liability for personal injuries from defective products and medical
malpractice—a matter of intense concern to the Clinton administration, as evinced by the lengthy decision process undertaken by
President Clinton before vetoing a product liability bill in 1996.

Among other items on Starr's very full corporate law plate: representing Suzuki Motor Co. against findings by a federal appeals court
that its lawyers had provided false and misleading answers in the discovery process (see Chapter 3); representing financier Victor Posner
after a federal trial judge in Manhattan concluded that Posner had violated federal securities laws, "repeatedly abused [his] positions in public companies," and "enriched [himself] at the expense of public
shareholders"; and representing controversial labor practices at a
Delaware steel mill by the mill's owner, the People's Republic of China.
Other Starr clients included Amoco, Apple Computer, Chiquita
Brands, Siemens Corp., and United Airlines. In 1996 his firm was also
representing: Dupont, after a federal judge fined the chemical giant
$115 million for allegedly misrepresenting and "consciously, willfully,
intentionally and deliberately" withholding key scientific test results in

a lawsuit over the herbicide Benlate; Charles Keating, in his efforts to set aside his previous criminal convictions and avoid additional con-victions for looting customer accounts at the savings and loan he once controlled, Lincoln Savings (see Chapter 1); and Dow Corning Corp., in suits brought by women alleging injuries from the company's silicone breast implants (see Chapter 2).

Avoidance of conflict of interest is a bedrock principle of the ethi-cal and legal standards governing both the practice of law and the con-duct of government officials. Under canons of ethics promulgated by the American Bar Association, "a lawyer shall not accept employment if the exercise of his professional judgment on behalf of the client will be or reasonably may be affected by his own financial, business, property or personal interests." An attorney generally must avoid representing a client if that representation will be directly adverse to the interests of another client or if the representation may be limited by the interests of another client or the attorney's own interests; otherwise there is the concern that an attorney will favor the interests of one client to the detriment of the other. All government officials, attorneys or not, owe their primary duty to the public; conflict-of-interest laws and regula-tions prevent them from acting instead in their own financial interests.

As independent counsel, Starr's primary responsibility was that of any prosecutor: to "do justice," i.e., to ensure that the guilty are pun-ished and the innocent go free. One could fairly ask whether his private law interests could potentially have interfered with that duty.

Many of Starr's clients sought relief from government regulation—relief that could have saved them millions or even billions of dollars. The concern is that an unscrupulous prosecutor in Starr's position could use the Whitewater investigation—focusing on the president, his wife, and his aides—as leverage to exact favors for his law firm and its clients from the government. It is not just that such a prosecutor, or underlings in the independent counsel's office or the corporate firm, could issue threats, implicit or explicit, that failure to grant regulatory relief to clients could lead to a more aggressive Whitewater probe, while extension of favors could prompt the prosecutor to go easy. The very status of such a conflicted arrangement sends improper signals all by itself. Such a circumstance not only perverts justice in the White-water case, it could also interfere with the honest functioning of gov-ernment with respect to business regulation. Even if the independent counsel and his colleagues were incorruptible and thus never tempted by such a possibility, the targets of his investigation or their zealous sub-ordinates might nevertheless extend leniency to Starr clients in hopes of curbing the Whitewater probe.

Although his supporters insisted that Starr is a highly ethical person, above reproach, his treatment of the ethics concerns was less than sensitive. In 1996, journalists reported a conflict involving conduct by Starr's own law firm. In May 1993, the federal Resolution Trust Corporation had sued Kirkland & Ellis for aiding and abetting financial misconduct by one of its clients, a Colorado savings and loan. Although RTC officials believed that Kirkland was liable for $1 million and that the agency could obtain a judgment of $770,000 against Kirkland at trial, it settled the case in January 1995 in exchange for a $325,000 payment from the firm. Kirkland, however, also insisted, and the RTC agreed, that the settlement be kept secret.

As Kirkland was quietly seeking a favorable resolution of the charges leveled by the RTC, Kirkland partner Starr was, as Whitewater special prosecutor, investigating officials of the very same agency. Indeed, one of the first aspects of the Whitewater matter pursued by Starr after his appointment was the allegation that the RTC, that same month, had improperly suspended one of its investigators for aggressive tactics in the Whitewater case. Thus Starr was bringing to bear prosecutorial authority against an agency and individuals that had brought suit against his own law partnership.

After the press exposed the apparent conflict, Georgetown University law professor Samuel Dash, paid by Starr's independent counsel office to serve as an ethics adviser, said that Starr was unaware of the suit until March 1995, notwithstanding the fact that Starr has served on Kirkland's management committee since he arrived at the firm in February 1993. Dash said he advised Starr that it was unnecessary to recuse himself even from the investigation of RTC. Dash's interpretation, on which Starr relied, was premised on a virtual wall beyond Starr and his law firm partners: Starr could go forward because he had played no role in representation of the Colorado bank or the secret settlement of the suit. Starr followed Dash's advice and did not recuse. But Dash conceded that a judge in similar circumstances would be required by the judicial ethics code to recuse, and it is troubling that a public prosecutor in Starr's position would not have felt obligated to do the same.

Starr's silence in another matter was also disturbing. Conservative members of Congress and the editorial page of The Wall Street Journal had sought to remove his predecessor Robert Fiske in part on the ground that Fiske had a conflict of interest: He had, years before, represented International Paper Co., a firm that once sold land to the Whitewater Development Company. What Starr chose not to say was that he himself was representing International Paper in a lawsuit at the time of his appointment as independent counsel. (He withdrew from the representation after being appointed. Dash said he learned of Starr's representation of International Paper by reading about it, along with the rest of the public, in an April 1996 magazine article.)

Starr, the son of a minister and himself a part-time Sunday school teacher, continued to insist that there was no problem with his unprecedented status. He had inherited not only Lloyd Cutler's influence and earning power but also his mantra: Trust me. But his apparent indifference to this multiconflicting status and its ethical ramifications—while being hailed as a person of integrity and a key counselor to leading corporations—threatened to further erode already crumbling standards of propriety for the profession. Starr had broken new and dangerous ground, blurring the separation of government and business. He had undermined the very integrity of government by imperiling its arm's-length relationship with the industries it regulates. As of this writing, neither the organized bar nor any of its leaders have done much, if anything, to question, let alone strongly protest, Starr's wayward behavior. To what extremes must a special prosecutor go before elders of the bar are moved to action?

Starr's unfortunate judgments, and the bar's failure to rebuke him, came at a particularly inauspicious time, when the legal profession had reached a low point in the public perception of its commitment to enhancing the quality of justice in this country.

Indeed, the leaders of the bar, who are so proficient as attorneys in making connections for their clients, seem unwilling to make connections between the excluded majority and the justice system. They seem unwilling to address concretely how to achieve, in the words of one ABA president, "a system of justice that is open to the many, not just the monied."

The mainstream media have chronicled the epidemic of business violations and disreputable practices in areas like banking, insurance and other financial frauds, product defects, medical malpractice, toxic harm, government contracts, corporate welfare, and regulatory nonenforcement. *The Wall Street Journal, Business Week, Barron's Financial Weekly,* and television magazine programs such as *60 Minutes* and *Prime Time* are in the business of exposing abuses, yet criminal prosecutions are still rare. Toothless consent decrees, weak settlements, bailouts, voluntary bankruptcies, and many other clever amortizations of payouts and misdeeds highlight the creativity of corporate attorneys and mask some hard realities. Corporate crime does pay, in terms both of the small percentages disgorged from wrongdoers and returned to the defrauded or harmed and of the routine escapes from mandated corporate restructuring. The taxpayer bailouts of the savings and loan scandals—about half a trillion dollars in principal and interest—utterly overwhelms what those scoundrels had to pay back to their customers from their own pockets.

Legislation and regulation to forestall future looting and violations are weak. As of this writing, Congress is going in the opposite direction—dismantling the modest strengthening of the banking laws enacted in 1990 and 1991 that were designed to protect savers and other financial consumers. The Republican majority in Congress has weakened the security fraud laws, overriding President Clinton's veto, and is driving to limit the state common law of torts—all this in the midst of documented abuses in the financial industry and among product manufacturers. Even the tobacco companies, guided by their lawyer-lobbyists, are finding little criticism from the established bar in their maneuvers not just to avoid regulation but to achieve outright immunity from products liability.

One would think that the "professionals" closest to these corporate recidivists or pattern violators would have something to say as lawyers about the chronic inefficacy of the law, about the supremacy of power, and about the diminishment of their own professionalism and all that is meant by that status. These practitioners seem so much more comfortable drafting legislation, regulations, or contracts of adhesion than they are using the First Amendment to take a stand or thinking through what needs to be done systematically to elevate the rule of just law and its democratic utilization over the reign of raw power. Unlike the media, which limits itself to reporting the abuses, corporate lawyers have a far deeper grasp of the structural origins of the misbehavior and the changes required to foster corporate accountability. As such, they can be viewed as a substantial unused national resource.

Mere candor by legal insiders in the public forums and publications of the profession requires too much common courage to occur with any frequency. Outsiders are almost never invited to major ABA sessions or other gatherings of corporate bar leaders to knowledgeably take them to task.

A CULTURE BUILT ON GREED
AND DECEPTION

But if you ask corporate attorneys for their private opinions, some will display poignant forthrightness. A very few will even do so publicly. One is Ansel B. Chaplin of Boston, a Harvard-educated corporate lawyer practicing for over thirty-five years. With the sadness bred of three generations of proud lawyers, he says that corporate attorneys "are spin control artists. That is to say, they are either putting the best spin they can on outrageous or close-to-outrageous behavior by their clients, or they are putting the best spin they can on bad news that has to go into a prospectus. That is the service clients are paying for. They want a hired gun."[1]

Chaplin harbors deep reservations about this state of affairs. "The system seems to promote a kind of fundamental moral dishonesty," he laments. "It is very hard to avoid that in the corporate arena. A friend of mine, who is an enormously successful corporate lawyer, says that the way to get ahead is to drive over the center of the road and pull back just before you get hurt. That is what makes a good corporate lawyer, going as far as possible and then having the instinct to pull back just in the nick of time."

Judging by what corporate attorneys can get away with—as described in the foregoing chapters—there are not that many "nicks of time." For there are very few resources and little resolve by either government grievance agencies or the various bar associations to uncover, stop, and discipline callous or unethical or sometimes criminal attorneys. Moreover, there is far less attention paid to the merciless way these attorneys deploy their clients' power when they act as lobbyists working to twist or displace the public legal systems that otherwise would provide their opponents with a chance for justice.

The assumption of professionalism that would animate such monitoring is itself under de facto repudiation. Even the mythical symbolism of the profession as a calling requiring specialized knowledge under strict ethical standards and public service responsibilities has been lost. Observations gathered in our research indicate a swell of disgruntled resignation. Like many we interviewed, one lawyer who practices with one of Chicago's largest firms wished to remain anonymous—telling in itself. Asked about the basis of the go-for-the-jugular methods of contemporary power attorneys, he replied, "Quite frankly, our power and authority comes from our clients. That's our business. It begins and ends there. That sometimes leads to things that maybe shouldn't be done. But that is the way the game is played."[2]

A corporate lawyer who practices at one of the largest East Coast firms wrote to us, stating, "Whatever happened to the belief that being a lawyer was a public service? On some days, I wonder why I went to law school. Many of us who have gone through the big firm experience are sick of the hypocrisy, the overbilling, and the ethical violations." She gave an example from her own practice. "At my former firm," she wrote, "I was asked to render an environmental opinion regarding the level of cleanup that needed to be done on a piece of contaminated property. I carefully did my research and wrote a ten-page, single-spaced memorandum to the client. When I showed it to the partner in charge of the matter, he wanted me to change the memorandum and tell the client (a large company) that they would not have to spend the millions of dollars cleaning up the property. The partner wanted me to render an opinion advising a lower level of cleanup. He changed my memorandum and they are now building condominiums, townhouses, recreational centers, and playgrounds on this site! I keep my original memorandum and the floppy disk bearing this memo . . . in a safety deposit box just in case in the future the federal government discovers the truth about what's going on."[3]

A young associate at another of the nation's biggest firms reports, "The only thing that counts in my firm is being 'productive' which translates to mean billing—not necessarily giving good legal advice. The message sent to young lawyers is loud and clear: Just bring in paying clients and give them everything they want, including false opinions."[4]

Such attitudes do not go unnoticed by staff members of large law firms. "I worked nine years at a hundred-plus lawyer insurance defense firm," says one legal secretary. "The whole premise at the firm was for the attorneys to find any reason possible to keep their client from having to make payments [to insurance claimants]. I never once saw or heard of the firm reviewing a claim or lawsuit and telling their client, 'This looks righteous.' Rather, they would war-game the ways in which they could resist, come up with anything to say, 'It wasn't our client's fault.' " This secretary says she quit this firm because she was so disgusted by what she saw behind the scenes.[5]

Another lawyer, a partner in one of the world's largest firms, who said he feared speaking on the record because of the impact he perceived it would have on his career, says, "The largest corporate law firms have a depth of resources that perhaps only government can match. This permits us to accomplish what small firms or individual lawyers could never hope to." This attorney acknowledges that the strong sense of professional ethics needed to mitigate the power of the big firms and inhibit abuses is often lacking among these corporate lawyers. Consequently, he sees the justice system as "heading in the wrong direction"—a direction that will facilitate unchecked growth of corporate power.[6]

The ultimate attitude of resignation belonged to a Los Angeles corporate lawyer who quit practicing law altogether in 1995. First she gave up a huge salary at her law firm and joined one of the firm's large clients—a real estate development corporation—as in-house counsel.

It was not long before she left that company, commenting that she was sick of being "a yes person with a J.D."

But are corporate lawyers any more likely to engage in such questionable or improper conduct than lawyers who represent individuals? To Seattle attorney Leonard Schroeter, who started his practice of law working with Thurgood Marshall when the late Supreme Court justice was counsel to the NAACP, the answer is a definite yes. "The big law firms are the butlers to big business," he says. "Unlike lawyers who work for individuals or smaller business concerns, they abdicate their own professional judgment and place it in the hands of their clients."[7]

Says legal ethicist Geoffrey C. Hazard of the University of Pennsylvania, "Corporate lawyers develop a siege mentality. Of course it is supposed to be the attorney's job to rise above those feelings. But if the consequences are severe and you tell the truth, you might make the situation worse for your client. It has the effect of making life very difficult for the conscientious lawyer. You sometimes wake up feeling like you have a compulsion to do something wrong. You add this up and it extracts a substantial price."[8]

The likelihood of rebellion within the large law firm ranks is reserved to commercial, not professional, coup d'états. If you do not like how the controlling rainmakers—those who bring in the clients—are running the firm, you either become a technician, stay with your long-time clients as a niche specialist, or leave. The authoritarian nature of corporate firm culture can no longer be denied when dissenters have nowhere to go but the exit.

Young law firm associates generally must meet billing quotas, often two thousand billable hours a year, and the number actually expected of lawyers who hope to advance in the firm may be even higher. Experienced law firm bill auditors say that to tally two thousand hours legitimately chargeable to clients in a year, a lawyer must put in six or seven full days of work a week, virtually without break. (Chief Justice William Rehnquist noted in a May 1996 speech that average billable lawyer hours in the 1960's totalled 1450 per year—a far more manageable load than today's 2,000.) And even though, as described in Chapter 7, some attorneys have experimented with alternatives to hourly billing, the hourly charge, plus ample expensing, remain the bread and butter of most major firms.

The pressure to bill extracts a terrible toll on health, energy, and family life. As a consequence, many of these young attorneys end up padding bills or doing unnecessary work simply to feed the voracious billing quota monster. This situation makes their stomachs—and their consciences—queasy. The idealistic reasons for which the lawyer may have entered the profession are easily swept away in a blizzard of time sheets, late nights working on minutiae, and lost sleep worrying about whether all of the hard work will pay off with a lucrative partnership.

Chapter 7 mentioned *The Rodent,* an "undercover" newsletter that wickedly satirizes the culture and foibles of the corporate megafirms as viewed by low-level associates. Its creator, a former associate of sprawling 1,642-lawyer Baker & McKenzie, is in continuing contact with a multitude of big-firm associates and agrees that the law firm environment bears much of the blame. He says, "I hear from associates from all over the country. Many are very disappointed with the practice of law. They like the money, but they hate the long hours, the pressure to overbill, the legal gamesmanship and getting sucked into the big firm culture. They begin to feel like bottom-line items and billing machines rather than professionals. Many find that they have lost the reason why they went to law school in the first place."[9]

Joseph Calve is a commentator on legal matters who often writes for the Washington, D.C.–based industry newspaper *Legal Times.* He, too, has chronicled the path many new lawyers take from idealistic youngsters to cynical and sometimes alienated corporate firm bigwigs. "It's not just the associates who are unhappy," he says. "Partners also get discouraged. They talk about the difference between law as a profession and as a business. They bemoan the loss of collegiality. They become concerned when the simplest matters turn into Armageddon."[10] Indeed, a partner we interviewed from one of the world's most prominent law firms says that corporate lawyers tend to be the unhappiest people he knows. Typical of too many self-censoring attorneys, he asked that even this general comment not be identified with his name or even his law firm.

There seems to be little question that money is driving the worst aspects of the system, creating a runaway train effect in which everyone is preoccupied with holding on for their lives. University of Wisconsin professor of sociology Marc Galanter, director of the Institute for Legal Studies, has written much about large firm practices in scholarly articles and in his book *Tournament of Lawyers* (coauthored by Thomas Palay).[11] He described the situation as follows: "Associates are in a mad race to become a partner, a process that can take many years. That has left many with a sense that lawyers have lost their civic virtue and the ideal that they serve as officers of the court."[12]

Even though many grow weary of the journey, few manage to get off the train. The opportunity cost of leaving is usually a major drop in income. The large firms need to bill in order to grow and stay ahead of the competition. Associates need to bill in order to make partner. This need to perform work, without regard to whether the work is really necessary, becomes the engine of abuse. The firms and their lawyers develop a material stake in driving the system's dysfunction.

Young lawyers at big firms also face substantial pressure to specialize—and specialize early—in a very narrow area of law. They become experts on a single provision in federal pension law or the tax code. They become part of an insular, myopic community. They never gain the kind of breadth of legal experience, not to mention other types of human experience, that produces better public citizens. They also become more anxious in their drive for partnership, fearing that their narrow sets of skills may limit their options if they are thrown back into the job market. They lose sight of the larger issues of justice and lawyerly responsibilities to the system.

Added to these pressures are the changing dynamics of the corporate attorney-client relationship. Whereas in the 1970s, Charles Tillinghast, the CEO of Trans World Airlines, could wearily reply to the question, "How are earnings?" by saying, "Not bad—seven times legal fees," corporations are increasingly becoming tough customers. Years of soaring legal bills, periods of recession, and corporate restructuring have shifted the market for legal services more in favor of buyers. Where once big corporations maintained long-term relations with their law firms, many corporate lawyers now find, to paraphrase Ira Gershwin, that loyalty is a sometime thing, particularly as in-house corporate counsel operations grow in influence and size. Corporations are increasingly ready to replace outside lawyers who do not toe the party line. Recall from Chapter 8 the case of attorney Robert Baker, whose firm lost major insurance and health care clients after he spoke his mind about the detrimental effects of changes in California's medical malpractice laws. The state of the market puts increased pressure on corporate lawyers and big firms to do the bidding of their clients, even when it crosses the ethical line and shatters their independence.

Competition for client dollars and the steady creep of crass commercialism into every sector of our society has eroded professional standards and professional values among lawyers. The brazen behavior of now bankrupt firms like New York's giant Finley Kumble, whose sheer greed, overbilling, corruption, and savage infighting, described in Kim Isaac Eisler's book, *Shark Tank*, have made it a metaphor of decay and criminality, cannot be so easily dismissed by partners in other law firms who routinely say: "Oh, that's Finley Kumble."[13]

There are Finley Kumble traits in many "prestigious" law firms, and that genotype is perpetuated when no reforms or enhanced enforcement come from the organized bar and state disciplinary agencies. As

Seattle attorney Leonard Schroeter observes, "In most of the large firms, there's not even a pretense of professionalism. For them, law is a business, and that is all it is. In that atmosphere, the abuses, the lying, the destruction of evidence, are simply rationalized as 'helping our clients' or 'giving our client what he wants.' "[14]

THE PERILS AND PROMISE
OF THE LAW SCHOOLS

To the rapidly absorbing minds of law students at the more prominent and heavily recruited law schools, the ways and means of big-firm practice cast a heavy shadow. From their friends already practicing, reading the legal newspapers, summer jobs, and numerous visits and firm interviews, law students learn what it takes to succeed in those spacious and richly decorated office suites. The acculturation process is dramatic during the three years from entering school to graduation. Robert Granfield, a sociologist who teaches at the University of Denver, wrote an insightful book published in 1992 titled *Making Elite Lawyers* about what happens to Harvard Law School students between their acceptance and the time they graduate. Granfield says that legal education often turns idealists into amoral pragmatists: "A lot of people who go into law school have a strong sense of right and wrong and a belief in moral truths. Those values are destroyed in law school, where students are taught that there is no right and no wrong and where such idealistic, big-picture concepts get usurped. The way the majority of students deal with this is to become cynical. They actually come to disdain right-versus-wrong thinking as unprofessional and naive."

This amoral view suits the agendas of the corporate firms and their clients well. "Part of the school culture becomes corporate," Granfield says. "The first-year students see the second- and third-year students interviewing with corporations and corporate firms. They hear about the big money that can be made and the perks, the six-figure income down the road. Even the most 'socially progressive' students begin to rationalize working for the large corporate firms. They think that is the way to power and that they will be able to reform perceived wrongs from the top down. The only problem is that by the time they get there, they don't push for change because they have become part of the very power system they once disdained."[15]

Granfield's description is echoed by other observers of the law school scene. Professor H. Richard Uviller teaches legal ethics at Columbia University School of Law. He says, "Professors try to keep the ideals of the students high. But when they learn that their highest obligation is to the client, students begin to think of the rest of it [duty to society and the justice system] as wimpy and soft and not what clients respect. One reason they get that message is because it is true."[16] And, of course, many professors in fact do not attempt to instill idealism in their students. They come from corporate law backgrounds and, indeed, some law professors maintain lucrative corporate law practices on the side. Others, even critics of corporate power, are simply cynics who see little chance of reforming the legal profession. Such cynicism is infectious and convinces many students, often burdened with large tuition debts in the tens of thousands of dollars, to avoid idealistic pursuits and simply maximize income.

But there is another side to law students—a good number take clinical courses that deal with serving the poor, children, or other needs affecting housing, health care, the environment, consumer protection, immigration, and other civil rights and civil liberties. They publish journals covering the environment and human rights, draft model reform legislation, and take on clients under lawyerly supervision. They usually enjoy these clinics and experiences more than their traditional courses because they are given the opportunity to help real people, learn practical skills, and grapple with significant ongoing issues in society. Some students involved with these programs aim to devote their professional careers to these noncommercial practices.

But for many, reality sets in with their debt load, the lack of public interest law jobs, the shrinking of federally funded legal services programs for the poor, and the paucity of law school teaching positions. There is little to balance the expensive recruitment drives by partners in the big firms. The amount of time that many law students spend just flying out to or back from law firm interviews, all expenses paid, massaging their résumés, and worrying and speaking with their friends about the "hottest" firms, is astounding.[17] There are times during the year when second- and third-year classes at the leading law schools are half empty because the students are out of town interviewing at corporate firms. So, while more law schools are expanding their programs to support students in public interest work (with, for example, financial support, course choices, or credits for field internships), the majority of the lights at the end of the law school tunnel are those that flicker from the luxurious office buildings of corporate law practices.

Law students today do not recognize the effect they can have on veteran attorneys. A tighter job market and the burden of their student loans make these students more supplicants than stimulants. Back in the late sixties and early seventies, students at some law schools, such as Harvard, sent questionnaires to recruiting law firms about their pro bono and minority hiring practices. Quite a few law firms took these questionnaires seriously and prepared elaborate responses that, in turn, led to a heightened focus on these professional duties. Together with the enlightening impact of urban fires and disturbances, law students played a major role in challenging many firms to formalize their pro bono programs and respect those young associates who took such responsibilities seriously.

That was twenty-five years ago. Now those law students are senior partners. Many recall their student days as the time when they were idealistic about the law, when they believed that the law could generate justice for the people and help solve social problems. Today's students should be aware of the higher missions of the law and legal institutions. Unfortunately, to understand these missions before they are conditioned by the law firm's conventional ethos, these students need to read legal history. Most do not. They also need legal scholarship and teaching that, in the words of Harvard law professor Gary Bellow, a pioneer in clinical legal programs, "should be much more concerned than is now the case with the actual functioning of the legal system and its institutions, *particularly the institution of counsel as a lawmaking, law-enforcing, law-nullifying activity.*"[18] (Emphasis added.)

A glimmer of how law students can inspire their elders is seen every year at the annual meeting and dinner of the nonprofit National Association of Public Interest Lawyers (NAPIL) in Washington, D.C. There the efforts of NAPIL in expanding its yearlong public interest fellowships, encouraging student summer internships, and nudging law schools to establish loan forgiveness programs for new graduates in such work draw almost wistful admiration by the corporate attorneys in attendance.

Students at law schools should know that they can do more to quicken the conscience of the legal profession, in both small and large ways. But they would be in an even better strategic position to influence were the few outstanding law professors supporting such exemplary student initiatives joined by the larger number of teachers who are essentially on the sidelines. These faculty members are often too busy with their moonlighting business consultantships. Or they are pursuing their own critical legal studies, which, while taking apart conventional assumptions about the law, have also generated much cynicism among students about the law ever being able to restrain power. The other discernible school of thought on the law school campus is the empirically starved, narrow ideology of "law and economics," which provides business with convenient formulas to block health and safety regulations and antitrust enforcement. This dogma also provides handsome fees for a sizable number of its professorial adherents.

So, the law school environment, taken as a whole, is awash in cynical apathy or commercialism. But it can also be aware of its potential. The job market now favors buyers, and the core course curriculum reflects the existing commercial practice of law rather than the civic practice of law. Law schools need to be pushed toward new alliances within the profession and with the communities surrounding them to move in a public-spirited direction. Instead of merely servicing corporate attorneys and their world of business, some of the nation's 177 ABA-accredited law schools at least could make more concrete the ethical precision of their graduating students and heighten their institutions' expectations for corporate legal practice. The galvanizing words of attorney and former diplomat Sol Linowitz suggest the appropriate course. He urged that lawyers must:[19]

> see and thus . . . create the possibility of a legal profession that is once again independent, willing to sacrifice money for pride, eager to reassert its role as the guarantor of rights. To make the contribution only lawyers can make to the future of our country and the world, we must accept rather than simply assert our responsibilities. When we look at our fellows and we decide whom we respect, civic leadership should count for more than hourly rate, the sense of justice for more than a record of victories at trial, service to those who need the law for more than representation of those who merely use the law.

It is worth noting that many of the harmful practices engaged in by corporate attorneys are not recent inventions. To be sure, times have changed. There is more gold and more deals to be greedy about, and large clients are more adept at manipulating the way law firms have to compete, which results in indentured client relationships. But the existing nexus between power law firms and corporate power goes back to the industrial revolution of the late nineteenth century. A. A. Berle, Jr., an eminent New York corporate lawyer, prolific author, and professor of law at Columbia University, wrote the section on the modern legal profession in the celebrated *Encyclopaedia of the Social Sciences*, published in 1933. To dispel the notion of some critics of the corporate bar that the past was a period of nobler business law practices, it is worth quoting Professor Berle at some length:[20]

> The manipulations of the railroad builders, the oil pioneers, the utilities and traction magnates, and the accompanying political corruption were tolerated by the community because

they seemed to be connected with an unparalleled rise of the mechanisms of industry, transportation and urban life. In defending, legalizing and maintaining this exploitative development the legal profession found its principal function. Many of the great American law firms of today, recognized as the leaders of the bar, owe their origin to the safe navigation of clients through some scandal of the latter part of the nineteenth century: the defense of the Tweed ring, the safe-guarding of the interests of Jay Gould in Erie, the wreck of the Pere Marquette railroad and the violences of the Harriman administration, the wreck of the Rock Island railroad. The impression grew that the lawyer existed to serve and not to counsel his clients.

The law firm became virtually an annex to some group of financial promoters, manipulators or industrialists; and such firms have dominated the organized profession, although they have contributed little of thought, less of philosophy, and nothing at all of responsibility or idealism. What they have contributed, however, is the creation of a legal framework for the new economic system, built largely around the modern corporation, the division of ownership of industrial property from control and the increasing concentration of economic power in the industrial east in the hands of a few individuals.

There are, of course, important differences between the past that Berle describes and the present. It is one matter to represent crassly the power-hungry early industrialists who were producing useful products; it is quite another to so serve the abstract paper economy of currency speculation, derivatives, empire-building mergers, and leveraged acquisitions that produce no new wealth or jobs while hugely increasing corporate debt, the risks of taxpayer bailouts, and the loss of lifetime savings. It is one matter to have opposed the progressive reforms of the past; it is another to be the spear-carriers for rolling back these successful legal frameworks that serve the justice needs of ordinary people as workers, consumers, and taxpayers. And it is one matter to service domestic corporations within one jurisdiction of American law and quite another to become the architects of an evolving globalization where large corporate clients can escape or avoid our jurisdiction and pit the lures of crueler regimes against the higher living and legal standards of the United States, using the GATT and NAFTA systems of autocratic governance. In short, for these and other more recent aggregations of power, capital, and technology, the stakes are higher for present and future generations when the influential leaders or, to use Berle's phrase, the "great commercialists" of the corporate bar become mere adjuncts to the captains of industry and finance.

THE PRO BONO LANDSCAPE

There is another difference that corporate or business attorneys are sure to point out. Today, the large firms engage more extensively in pro bono (or largely no-charge) activities for clients who cannot afford to pay. Some of the firms, like Hale and Dorr in Boston, display booklets trumpeting their pro bono efforts.[21] Other firms, without much activity to warrant such a compilation, show their written policy to encourage pro bono hourly commitments by their partners and associates and list their monetary contributions to legal and other charities. There are still other firms who think it is none of the public's or bar's business to set standards, even if voluntary, in minimum pro bono time per attorney. Not surprisingly, these collections of attorneys often operate on the lower rungs of pro bono ladders.

There is, indeed, the endemic kind of unequal access to justice that flows from the inability to afford a lawyer. The American Bar Association estimates that 80 percent of the legal problems faced by poor citizens—problems that include the most basic areas of adequate food, decent shelter, and protection from abuse—go unassisted.[22] In a time of shrinking government contributions to the Legal Services Corporation—the federally financed nonprofit that provides staff attorneys in civil cases for low-income Americans—and as the middle class has been substantially priced out of the legal system unless their claims seem sufficiently large to lend themselves to a contingency fee, each law firm, and each individual lawyer, ought to strongly consider, as part of a lawyer's duty to the justice system, the obligation to perform legal work on behalf of those unable to pay for the legal services they need.

"There is no way to avoid the conclusion that every lawyer should be required by the courts to devote some substantial time each year to pro bono representation," Ansel Chaplin asserts. "If such were the prevailing climate in the legal system—a situation where the best trial lawyers, for example, were defending the needy, on an occasional but regular basis—we would witness a sea change in the public's perception of the worth of lawyers to society."

A corporate lawyer who is personally committed to and has experience in representing individuals can develop empathy for real people. That empathy would serve the ideals of professionalism—aiding society as well as clients—too often lacking today in lawyering for impersonal corporations. Such pro bono involvement, by pricking their consciences, may make it harder for lawyers to stomp on the little guy and still get a good night's sleep.

Harrison Wellford, a partner in the 518-attorney Los Angeles–based firm Latham & Watkins, and chairman of the firm's International Practice Group, believes that too many corporate lawyers come to their work with insufficient life experience to be the best attorneys possible for themselves and their clients. "Corporate lawyers need the expanded life experience that pro bono or other noncorporate legal work would bring them," he says. "Latham & Watkins only interviews the top two percent of law students from the nation's best schools. The work [by the student] necessary just to obtain an interview doesn't leave a lot of room for obtaining balanced life experience necessary to keep one from becoming a mechanical servant of the client."[23]

Wellford believes that this lack of broad experience could be offset by a required internship for all new lawyers, giving future corporate attorneys experience representing individuals, small companies, nonprofit organizations, and others not part of the corporate power structure as part of their preparation for the pressures of large-firm practice. "Lawyers often make ethical mistakes because they believe they have limited choices," he says. "Having such broad experience is important for corporate lawyers. It will help get them out of the tunnel vision that 'trying to make partner' or working to meet billing quotas that working in a large firm can force lawyers to adopt. They will know they have other choices in life, and I believe that will enable them to escape the thinking that all they must do is meet the immediate demands of the client in exactly the terms that the demand is made."

Wellford contends that the broader experiences gained by working in the noncorporate world would better enable corporate lawyers to use the critical faculties that they will have developed to bring a larger context to the client's problems, leading to the lawyer giving better legal advice. "We often see very successful people make the most stupid mistakes," Wellford says. "I think that is because they get sealed within fairly narrow groups, dealing with partners and associates, all coming from similar backgrounds and having similar outlooks. That often makes them unaware of potential adverse consequences." Lawyers who may have worked within a consumer organization or on behalf of people injured by defective products may be better at spotting potential pitfalls than those who have primarily seen life through a corporate client's prism of privilege and power.

Expanded life experiences would also encourage what Wellford calls "personal line-drawing," better enabling lawyers to toe the proper ethical line. Diligent commitment by lawyers to ethical standards "will prove to the executive that the lawyer has the client's best long-term interests in mind," Wellford says, "making for a better client rapport and a reduction in the troubles and harm that can be caused by corner-cutting or doing the wrong thing." Thus, rather than simply being "zealous advocates" for their clients, corporate lawyers would return to a more truly professional approach to their representation, better balancing their private and public functions, for the betterment of all.

The American Bar Association has in recent years rejected the concept of mandatory pro bono work. But the ABA has taken steps to increase the public visibility of voluntary pro bono. In February 1993, the ABA promulgated a new model ethical rule suggesting that all lawyers perform at least fifty hours of pro bono legal work each year. But the rule is, for now, simply a nonbinding prescription; no state has yet adopted it as part of its legal ethics code.[24] In April 1993, the ABA challenged the nation's five hundred largest law firms to begin contributing, no later than the end of 1995, pro bono work in an amount equal to 3 to 5 percent of the firm's billable hours—an amount the ABA figures will lead to at least fifty hours of pro bono work per year for each attorney. Within a month of the challenge's announcement, 155 firms had signed on.[25] But by December 1995, according to the ABA, only 171 of the biggest five hundred firms were on board. Many of the largest, highest-earning firms in the country, including New York's Cravath, Swaine & Moore, Sullivan & Cromwell, Davis Polk & Wardwell, and Simpson Thacher & Bartlett; Washington's Williams & Connolly; Boston's Ropes & Gray; Cleveland's Jones, Day, Reavis & Pogue; Houston's Fulbright & Jaworski; and Los Angeles's Latham & Watkins, declined to participate.[26] "It's a bit disappointing," the program's chair, Jim Jones of D.C.'s Arnold & Porter, told a reporter.[27]

Three styles of pro bono illustrate the range of such activity as well as its self-containment from the other commercial operations of these law firms. Hale and Dorr is still inspired by its first managing partner, Reginald Heber Smith, the architect of private legal aid in America and author of the seminal book *Justice and the Poor*, published in 1919. The firm describes its pro bono work to include "criminal defense for the indigent, drug treatment programs, death row cases, representation of handicapped advocacy groups, public policy cases, and cases involving freedom of speech . . . real estate work for community development corporations and other organizations dedicated to providing shelter to low-income and homeless individuals, battered women, the elderly, and people with HIV/AIDS."[28] In 1992, Hale and Dorr attorneys contributed $2 million to the Legal Services Center of Harvard Law School. The funds were used to purchase and renovate the Jamaica

Plain building where the clinics are now housed. The center is the major defender of tenants in Boston's housing court, and its staff and students work with those Hale and Dorr attorneys who have specialized in "cases brought by tenants for rent overcharges, violation of the warranty of habitability and other causes, such as home improvement scams, and have defended tenants in actions brought by landlords for eviction and nonpayment of rent." While legitimate questions can be raised about the risks of such private legal business influence over the programs of an academic institution, the value of Hale and Dorr's contribution cannot be denied.

Type-two pro bono comes from the nation's highest-earning firm—New York's Skadden, Arps, Slate, Meagher & Flom. In 1989, flush with enormous profits, the firm set aside $10 million to fund twenty-five annual public interest law fellowships. For two years, the firm's contribution would pay the awardees about $33,000 plus benefits and absorb their student loan payments. Skadden had expected some other large firms to follow suit with similar no-strings-attached commitments. None did. Some managed much more modest contributions. Hunton & Williams, a Richmond, Virginia, firm that received deservedly bad publicity in 1995 for assuming the roles of Republican congressional staffers, by the latter's consent, in the internal drafting and negotiating process of federal health and safety deregulation legislation, announced in December 1995 that it would pay for one fellow to work a two-year stint, mostly at the local Legal Aid Society. (Public relations deficits can be a stimulus to some pro bono forays.)

Type-three pro bono is the New York Lawyers for the Public Interest (NYLPI)—a twenty-year-old partnership involving dozens of New York corporate law firms and corporate legal departments. With five attorneys, NYLPI provides a clearinghouse of pro bono cases for these firms to choose from and also directly represents clients—both individual and institutional—who need legal assistance. Led by energetic executive director Joan Vermeulen, NYLPI describes its activities and that of its participating firms this way: "Together we represent low-income co-ops; community-based organizations providing social services, recreation, education, neighborhood planning and employment assistance in low-income communities; children and adults with disabilities; victims of home equity and other consumer fraud; people with AIDS; the homeless; communities suffering environmental degradation; and children in foster care."[29]

These pro bono initiatives are not typical. In the scheme of things, they represent the ripples of a drop in the bucket. Although the occasional corporate-firm pro bono effort results in meaningful reform, most such projects are one-shot, isolated efforts that help cloak the other work that dominates the corporate law firm agenda. The top one hundred law firms in the United States gross more than $15 billion a year. Yet not even 1 deductible percent a year is contributed in cash to focused public interest law efforts. As far as hours are concerned, pro bono time per attorney is notoriously difficult to verify unless the firm is submitting its hours to obtain an attorney fees' award from the court. And pro bono efforts almost never stray from traditional legal charity and move toward challenging corporate power structures—any such proposal will be deemed to conflict with the firms' corporate clients, their clients' policy agendas, or even possible future clients. These are severe limitations not just because representation of clients supersedes pro bono advocacy when there is a conflict, but also because the large size of the firms means that with more companies and conglomerates as clients, the likelihood of perceived conflicts is all the greater.

But as the Skadden fellows and the NYLPI innovations demonstrate, ambitious pro bono can be supported through one-step-removed mechanisms that avoid the pretext of client conflicts, while corporate firms themselves can also find meaningful pro bono projects that do not pose such problems.

However, as practiced, pro bono activities, by and large, have not drawn on the firms' greatest strengths—their influence and their specialties. Several hours' time from a well-placed senior partner making calls to and meeting with movers and shakers for a systemic or institutional change—the genuine pitting of power against power—can be worth far more than piecemeal charitable efforts undertaken with one hand tied behind the back. Preventive law and systemic policies should be the touchstone for pro bono, not interminable stitching that doesn't stop the bleeding. Strategic thinking to establish systems to foresee and forestall problems and facilitate initiatives is what big-time corporate attorneys do for their regular clients. Surely they can apply some of this intellectual energy for problem solving and then apply some of their power on recognized patterns of abuse.

On some subjects, these firms could even press their corporate clients into action. Many major firms and bar associations bemoan the efforts in Congress to destroy or debilitate the Legal Services Corporation, provider of basic legal needs of the poor. The annual budget for this public institution is now less than $300 million, and it is now under restrictions as to what kinds of cases its attorneys may bring. By comparison, the federal government pays more than $600 million annually for outside law firm services—mostly with the larger firms. A few corporate attorneys testified before Congress in favor of preserving

Legal Services in 1995, and bar groups sent detailed written expressions of support. But no real muscle was applied.

In an unheralded but passionate address by Supreme Court Justice Sandra Day O'Connor before the 1991 American Bar Association annual meeting—the day before Vice President Quayle's highly publicized showboating in favor of restricting victims' rights—she emphasized some sobering data:

> The American Bar Foundation has estimated that nearly one quarter of all poor people each year have a civil legal problem deserving a lawyer's attention. But publicly funded attorneys can handle only 12 percent of the load. According to the ABA, 80 percent of poor people's civil legal needs go unmet. . . . The legal needs of poor people involve the most basic necessities of life, needs like food and shelter. . . . Every day, all over the country people lose their homes or apartments when the law says they should keep them, and people can't feed their children when the law says they should be able to feed them. People don't know the rights they have; even if they know the rights they have, they don't know how to enforce them. And it all has one cause—many people desperately need legal services but can't afford to pay.[30]

The major firms could have organized more of their corporate clients to urge their friends in Congress to maintain this modest governmental pledge to make equal justice under law a little more realistic to America's poor. There was reason to believe this could have been done. In 1981, three of the most hard-boiled CEOs in the nation, those of General Motors, Dupont, and General Electric, wrote President Ronald Reagan urging him to let Legal Services continue. That letter was not lost on congressional Republicans, who stopped short of invoking all the available procedural tools to block its fiscal renewal.

It is the nonuse of their specialties for pro bono endeavors that merits more introspection by the firms. It is too easy an exit for a real estate lawyer to say he or she is conflicted from being a catalyst for citizens who wish to have critical building codes enforced or who are struggling to stem the tide of property tax abatements for large office buildings or want help with city hall's subsidy giveaways to professional sports teams shopping for welfare packages. It is too easy for tax attorneys to say their allegiances to clients prohibit doing anything about the injustices of the tax code and its administration. Recall the words of the tax attorney Randolph Paul in our introduction about the tax lawyer as citizen. When, in 1970, one of the authors asked Ernest Jennes, a prominent communications attorney and practitioner before the Federal Communications Commission, why he had not used his widely recognized FCC expertise to propose, if not to advocate, ways to improve the agency's procedures so as to serve the public better, the Covington & Burling attorney replied: "It does not suit my taste." (In the mid-sixties, a legendary and brilliant workhorse for Arnold & Porter, Dennis Lyons, remarked that in representing a client against an action by a regulatory agency "the last thing I want is administrative due process"—meaning he preferred instead to find grounds for appeal and, therefore, delay.)

And so it has been over the decades, a sadly barren record of pro bono initiatives in the very area of expertise that affords these attorneys an early, inside view of what is wrong that can be improved throughout our political economy. Even with the pro bono opportunities that one would believe should unite these law firms—as defenders of our democracy—corporate lawyers followed with few exceptions the motto "Mum's the word." While one of their own, Hale and Dorr's Joseph N. Welch, was taking on the then powerful Senator Joseph McCarthy in 1954 while representing, without charge, the U.S. Army before the famous Army-McCarthy hearings, and while one of their favorite deans, Harvard Law School's Erwin Griswold, was out front criticizing McCarthyism, and even when their brethren were under attack, these firms were mostly silent. These same firms for decades heard themselves at bar association conventions speak of the glorious Constitution, yet on the whole did nothing to open up law schools and their firms to women and minorities—seemingly a kind of pro bono work that was free of client-conflict excuses.

For practitioners who can think of the most unlikely ways to get their clients out of tight spots, these corporate attorneys present their firms' conflict problems and say they are pessimistic about finding solutions. Pessimists do not look for solutions, almost by definition. But solutions abound. Two modest options were just described—the one by Skadden and the one by the New York Lawyers for the Public Interest. Once these attorneys decide that they are primary human beings, not secondary human beings whose lives are tied to their retainers with invisible chains, the imagination connects to the urgency of their liberation for society's benefit. To achieve justice, one must desire justice and, when one feels institutionally trapped by golden handcuffs, that desire invites moral courage. What fuels this sequence is a sense of injustice, whether spurred by close experience or observation or a cool process of thinking through who you are and what you should do about something you believe is not right. It helps to recall that the *nonuse* of legitimate power by these firms has rarely been publicly evaluated for accountability compared with their wrongdoing or abuse of power. It was the British mathematician-philosopher Alfred North Whitehead who put the challenge concisely when he wrote: "Duty arises from our potential control over the course of events."

This sense of professional duty can have many sources of nourishment, going back to childhood. Quite obviously there is a narrow range of present variation already at work in these otherwise comparable firms. The difference in pro bono commitments between the two large Boston firms Ropes & Gray ($140 million in annual gross revenues; 284 attorneys) and Hale and Dorr ($110 million; 237 attorneys) can be substantially explained by the differing views of their firms' relation to the world around them held by the leaders of those institutions. The outside pressures on them are certainly not different . . . not so far.

Quite apart from these self-limiting conceptions of pro bono work and the present small likelihood of dealing with causes, not just symptoms, there is the lack of any discernible effect on the way these firms have been practicing corporate law—in short, the absence of any enduring crossover effect. As described earlier, the power lawyering goes on—the radical concealment of vital health and safety information, the chronic delay, obstructionism, corporate destruction of documents, makework, overbilling, the stifling of competition against inventors and small business, the hamstringing of proper law enforcement, the merger deals driven by the enrichment of a few at the expense of workers and investors. The refusal to say no or counsel restraint to the most outrageous demands of lucratively paying clients also goes on. Rather than trying to dissuade their corporate clients from becoming too involved in their own claims, as Sol Linowitz believes was more likely a generation ago when he was practicing, these lawyers now, in Linowitz's words, "find it emotionally satisfying or profitable—or even (for they have been mistaught) professionally correct—to make their clients' causes their own."[31] Presently, the tobacco industry's attorneys would make a useful case study to test this critique. (See Chapter 1.)

As was made clear by the bar ethics and disciplinary committee responses to the outside law firms' behavior in the savings and loan enforcement actions, recounted in Chapter 1, the tension between the obligations to the legal system and the public on the one hand, and vigorous guarding of the client's position and secrets on the other hand, is most often resolved not on the balancing of the merits but on the imbalance of power. And the power undisputedly almost always favors putting the corporate client first, even in the extreme cases—the result of a combination of economic incentives, peer group bonding, and lawyer domination of the ethics reviews.[32]

In most instances, the economic rewards that favor siding with might rather than right signal far and wide not to come to the side of attorneys who go by the ethics book and clearly take the right and courageous course of action. Consider what happened to Illinois attorney Roger J. Balla.

THE CASE OF THE WHISTLE-BLOWING LAWYER

In March 1980, Balla, licensed to practice law in Illinois, went to work for Gambro, Inc., the United States subsidiary of a Swedish company called Gambro Lundia, AB. Gambro, Inc., sold the parent company's kidney dialysis equipment—machines that filter excess fluid and toxic substances from the blood of persons whose kidneys do not function properly.

Balla's title was director of administration, and his duties included advising and representing the company on legal matters and ensuring company compliance with applicable laws and regulations, as well as overseeing personnel policies.

In July 1985, Gambro's German subsidiary informed Gambro, Inc., that it was about to ship some dialysis machines from Germany. The German subsidiary noted, however, that these particular machines could put dialysis patients at risk because they could leave "continuous high levels of potassium, phosphate and urea/creatine" in a patient's system. Balla advised Gambro, Inc.'s president, David Maupin, to reject the defective machines because they did not meet regulations issued by the U.S. Food and Drug Administration and that Gambro would have to report such importation to the FDA. Maupin promptly told the German subsidiary that he would not accept the shipment.

However, one week later, Maupin reversed course. He informed the German subsidiary that he would accept the dialysis machines and sell them to a customer that he believed cared only about price rather than quality.

According to Balla, Maupin did not even tell him of this reversal. Instead Balla learned of it through other Gambro employees. Balla was appalled. Use of the defective machines would place already-vulnerable kidney patients at serious risk. Balla told Maupin that he would do whatever was necessary to stop the sale of the machines.

On September 4, 1985, as a reward for Balla's good advice and ethical practice, Maupin fired Balla. Later that day, Gambro shipped some of the defective dialysis machines to customers. The next day, Balla reported the shipment to the FDA, which quickly seized the shipment and declared the machines to be defective.

Balla was out of a job for saving lives. He had done not only the right thing but also, under the circumstances, the legally required thing. The ethical rules governing attorney conduct in Illinois require an attorney to "disclose information about a client to the extent it appears necessary to prevent the client from committing an act that would result in death or serious bodily harm to another person."[33] The rules also permit—although they do not require—a lawyer to reveal the intention of a client to commit a crime.[34]

On March 19, 1986, Balla sued Gambro in Illinois state court for retaliatory discharge, a tort that protects workers who are fired in retaliation for their activities—such as filing a worker's compensation claim or reporting company wrongdoing to government authorities—where the firing violates valid public policies. Balla's claim was a compelling one. If companies were free to fire their in-house attorneys who insisted on compliance with the law, it would place tremendous power in the hands of wrongdoing company executives to stifle dissent and suppress misconduct.

Before Balla could get his case to a jury, Gambro interposed a legal issue: It claimed that, given the special nature of the relationship between a corporation and its attorneys, a lawyer serving as a legal adviser to a corporation could *never* sue for retaliatory discharge, no matter how egregious the case was.

The case was litigated all the way to the Illinois Supreme Court, which rendered its decision on December 19, 1991.[35] Writing for the majority of the state high court, Justice William Clark agreed with Balla that the evidence indicated that Gambro fired Balla in retaliation for his activities and that this discharge conflicted with "clearly mandated public policy." Indeed, Clark wrote, "there is no public policy more important or more fundamental than the one favoring the effective protection of the lives and property of citizens." And, he concluded, under the ethical rules, Balla "had no choice but to report to the FDA Gambro's intention to sell or distribute" the dialysis machines. The use of the machines, Justice Clark accepted for purposes of the decision, would have caused death or serious bodily injury.

So the Illinois supreme court ruled . . . for Gambro, Inc. For, Justice Clark reasoned, if a lawyer like Balla "had no choice" but to expose Gambro's wrongdoing, then Illinois courts had no need to protect lawyers against retaliatory discharge. Lawyers could be counted on to do the right thing—even if it meant losing their jobs. And lawyers had to accept such risks as a necessary part of pursuing their noble profession. Thus, the court believed it had no need to protect lawyers from discharge. It did, however, have an obligation to bolster the attorney-client relationship: If corporate lawyers could sue their employers for retaliatory discharge, the court said, "employers might be less willing to be forthright and candid with their in-house counsel."

In a tough dissent—an opinion disagreeing with his colleagues—Illinois Justice Charles Freeman said, essentially, "Be realistic." In Justice Freeman's view, to say, as Justice Clark had, that the existence of a clear ethical rule is enough to ensure that lawyers will obey it "simply ignores reality." Alluding to abundant evidence in recent years of attorney misconduct in his state, Freeman said that attorney ethical obligations alone were not a sufficient safeguard against threats to public welfare.

The Illinois court majority was certainly right to worry about upsetting the attorney-client relationship. Only if confidentiality is the general rule can clients be encouraged to be candid with their lawyers, providing enough facts to permit lawyers to do their jobs properly. But the majority paid insufficient attention to the countervailing need to protect society from corporate-client wrongdoing and to the real-life incentives that confront lawyers who learn of corporate misconduct. After the Balla decision, Illinois lawyers know the score: If they follow their ethical responsibilities they may be out of work, and the legal system will do nothing to help them keep their positions, nothing to vindicate the legal and ethical principles they fought to uphold. Nor is it likely that any protest group of fellow lawyers will come to their assistance.

(The Illinois Supreme Court majority apparently welcomed the opportunity to come down on Gambro's side. While the case was pending, before the Illinois Supreme Court had issued its decision, Gambro and Balla reached an out-of-court settlement. Since the case was now moot, they jointly requested that the Supreme Court dismiss the appeal. The court refused. The parties settled anyway. The terms of the settlement are, we need hardly add, confidential.[36])

New York University law professor Stephen Gillers, a scholar on legal ethics, criticized the Illinois court majority opinion. "If we're going to tell lawyers they have to do something," he told *The American Lawyer,* "we must protect them when they do it." Moreover, he pointed out, if, as the majority stated, lawyers must—and will—disclose corporate misconduct, then it is the potential exercise of that duty that chills the attorney-client confidential relationship; permitting lawyers to sue for retaliatory discharge won't lower the temperature much further.[37]

Although courts in other states have issued opinions at odds with that of the Illinois court,[38] the Balla decision appears to express the prevailing ethic among corporate lawyers, as suggested by the brief filed in the case by the American Corporate Counsel Association, a professional association of in-house corporate lawyers. Rather than support a wronged in-house lawyer, the association filed a legal brief in favor of Gambro. According to the association's brief, a ruling on behalf of Balla would have destroyed the confidence of corporate executives in their in-house lawyers and deprived them of "the opportunity to police corporate activities and advise their corporate clients to comply with our laws."[39] The association might also have been concerned that corporations would stop hiring in-house lawyers and shift more work to outside counsel, independent contractors who would never be able to claim retaliatory discharge.[40]

The Balla case presented extraordinary circumstances crying out for attorney whistle-blowing—there was a genuine threat to human life if the corporation's lawyer did not expose his company's wrongdoing. Indeed, the circumstances facing Balla fell squarely under one of the few exceptions provided in the American Bar Association Model Rules of Professional Conduct to the preservation of client secrets (an exception partially modified in the Illinois code): "to prevent the client from committing a criminal act that the lawyer believes is likely to result in imminent death or substantial bodily harm."[41] (As noted in previous chapters, the model rules are the result of the ABA's 1983 effort to craft a legal ethics code for state authorities to adopt. Every state's ethics code is modeled on either the model rules or the 1969 ABA Model Code of Professional Responsibility, although many states have modified these ABA model laws in certain respects.)

The model rules—which are designed to govern conduct by both in-house corporate attorneys and those who work in outside firms—allow a lawyer to expose wrongdoing only in such extreme situations. And, even then (unlike under Illinois law), a lawyer is only *permitted*, not required, by the model rules to reveal client secrets. Moreover, the ABA's official comments, attached to the model rules, warn attorneys against reaching too hasty a judgment because it "is difficult for a lawyer to 'know' when such a heinous purpose will actually be carried out, for the client may have a change of mind."[42] If a client's wrongdoing falls below the threshold of causing imminent death or substantial bodily harm, the lawyer must keep silent. The model rules do permit a lawyer to go up the corporate hierarchy to the CEO or board of directors to try to stop wrongdoing,[43] but what good is that provision if these are the very people driving the wrongful conduct? If the misconduct is sufficiently serious and "is likely to result in substantial injury to the organization"—injury to some third party is not enough—and if, but only if, no one at the company will listen after repeated, discrete efforts, the ethical rules permit the attorney to resign,[44] but there will likely always be another eager, less "ethically obsessed" attorney available to take over. And such withdrawal from representation does not free the attorney from the ethical *obligation* to keep secret the client's misconduct.[45] Even if attorneys know that a corporation is stealing millions of dollars from unsuspecting consumers, *at least under the provisions of the model rules*, they may not tell others, including potential victims or the government.

These ethical rules make it very difficult for lawyers to restrain unscrupulous corporate management, creating a disturbing mentality of accommodation. "There is no question that the incentives, as they exist now, are for lawyers to wink at wrongdoing," University of Arizona law professor Ted Schneyer, an expert on corporate lawyer ethics, says. "There is an awful lot of evidence of lawyers being in a very good spot to recognize wrongdoing but doing nothing to stop it."[46]

The rules do not upset the majority in the corporate legal establishment. They want to tie their own hands—so as to better meet the improper demands of clients. Indeed, the original version of the rule permitting lawyers to reveal confidences—drafted by an ABA commission—would have allowed lawyers to expose client secrets not only where lives were at stake but also to prevent clients from committing crimes likely to cause "substantial injury to the financial interests or property of another." In 1983, the ABA House of Delegates, by a 207–129 vote, rejected this provision, with corporate lawyers leading the charge.[47] (Some state legal ethics codes, however, have restored the provision in some form.[48])

A great deal of harm—to individuals, to society at large, and to corporations themselves—might be prevented by giving corporate lawyers more ethical support and legal rights to expose client wrongdoing. Much litigation against corporations might never take place if attorneys were truly empowered to dissuade business executives from acting improperly and contrary to law.

Ted Schneyer believes that the time has come for dramatic change in the current system that inhibits lawyers from deterring corporate misdeeds. Make it permissible, he advises, for lawyers to breach corporate confidences when their clients engage in gross misconduct.

Codes of ethics for other professionals are much more responsible in recognizing the overriding need to protect the public against danger and dishonesty. For example, the Code of Ethics for United States Government Service, approved by Congress to govern the conduct of federal civil servants, says, "Any person in Government service should: Put loyalty to the highest moral principles and to country above loyalty to persons, party, or Government department. . . . Expose corruption wherever discovered." The ethical code of the National Society of Professional Engineers requires members, as a last resort, to report to the appropriate authorities illegal conduct by their employers or clients that threatens public health or safety. Whatever other practical obstacles there are to taking action, at least professionals governed by such ethical duties can invoke them as the first step.

The first step a lawyer takes in response to evidence of grave corporate misconduct should be internal. But if that proves futile, merely resigning provides insufficient protection to society. That is why ethical rules should *require*—not merely permit—a corporate lawyer, whether in-house or retained, to notify the proper authorities in specifically defined and limited circumstances. These circumstances, while remaining relatively restricted, should include instances in which, for example, the lawyer is reasonably certain that the corporation is involved with criminal conduct, whether or not it is likely to cause "imminent death," or in cases where the public health and safety is likely to be substantially harmed, such as the marketing of a known dangerous product or the serious violation of pollution laws. In addition, if the circumstances justify whistle-blowing, the law should protect in-house attorneys from suffering job sanctions merely for complying with their ethical responsibilities.

Adopting these conscience-releasing reforms would create a powerful deterrent to corporate wrongdoing. Ethical executives would be unaffected, since there would be no misconduct to expose. At the same time, those willing or tempted to cross the ethical or legal line would face additional risks in doing so. Depending on the misconduct, labor, consumers, the community, or others affected would be better protected. Stockholders would be the ultimate beneficiaries, less exposed to internal decay, lawsuits, damages, and regulatory punishments suffered because management knowingly engaged in serious misconduct and no one—lawyers included—lifted a finger to stop them.

Many corporate attorneys would howl in protest if confronted with this proposal. These defenders of an unacceptable status quo will claim that unscrupulous executives will respond by simply keeping corporate attorneys in the dark about their plans. But few major decisions in corporate America are made without some lawyer participation. Executives would surely open themselves up to personal liability if they eschewed legal advice on important transactions for the purpose of concealing fraud. Moreover, other professionals, such as engineers and civil servants, also need access to information to do their jobs properly. Yet they function under ethical codes that demand greater disclosure of wrongdoing.

The corporate law establishment will add, as the American Corporate Counsel Association did in the Balla case, that protecting attorney whistle-blowing would create a climate of distrust between lawyer and corporate client. But that is unlikely to occur except where corporate executives are conducting or concealing improper or illegal acts. In such circumstances, an atmosphere of honest distrust and deterrence is preferable to one of harmful collusion.

Corporate lawyers and the executives who hire them need reminding that as licensed professionals, lawyers owe important duties to the public as well as to their clients. As New York University professor Gillers says, "If business executives want the benefit of lawyers' services, they have to be willing to have their lawyers subscribe to the ethics of their profession."[49]

The reason that weak ethical rules—rules that make it unlikely that corporate lawyers will prevent client wrongdoing—remain in effect is that they scratch the backs of both executives and corporate attorneys. If the ethics standards were strong and the enforcement resources adequate, then the Balla case might have become a consequential cause célèbre within the legal profession. Significant change is needed to replace the remarkably complacent position of the ABA's Committee on Ethics and Professional Responsibility, which on December 6, 1993, prefaced a formal opinion on billing practices by declaring: "[T]he profession has spent extraordinary resources on interpreting, teaching and *enforcing* these ethics rules"[50] (emphasis added.)

One place to start is for the bar, the courts, and agencies to consider whether it continues to make sense to have a single code of ethics govern across the broad range of legal practice—from divorces to bank examinations to environmental reviews. Historically, the strong tilt in the ethical rules and the interpretations of those rules in favor of zealous client representation and away from responsibility to the justice system is grounded in the needs of counsel for individual defendants in criminal cases. But this "lowest-common denominator" approach to ethics (as Sol Linowitz describes it[51]) gives unnecessary leeway to lawyers for irresponsible corporations. As noted earlier, some government agencies, such as the Federal Deposit Insurance Corporation and the Securities and Exchange Commission, have issued regulations that demand of attorneys greater devotion to telling the truth and aiding the justice system than the ethical rules of the various states might otherwise require. But, as Linowitz suggests, more needs to be done in this area, so that disclosure rules and other ethical obligations are more closely tailored to the genuine demands in each area of legal practice, with a "core" code of ethics guiding the moral principles governing the conduct of all attorneys.[52]

IMPROVE LAWYER DISCIPLINE

Many commentators believe the time has come for state lawyer disciplinary panels to start taking tough action to restrain the anything-goes ethic found in corporate law today. One such observer is Steve France. As editor of the newsletter *Bank Lawyer Liability*, he saw how irresponsible corporate attorneys helped drive or condone the savings and loan debacle, requiring bailout legislation that is costing taxpayers hundreds of billions of dollars.

France believes the foundation of the problem lies with corporate executives. "A lot of companies don't want lawyers with a conscience," he says. "What amazes me is how widely this ethic is embraced. It has gone way beyond what is tenable."

Reversing and correcting this sad state of affairs is essential, but it will not be easy. "Solving the ethical problems in the profession is a tall order," says Professor Gillers. "Lawyers are trained to be aggressive, trained to believe that winning is the most important thing. The culture of practice reinforces that view. Unless you make it too expensive to get caught, nothing is going to change."

As matters stand now, the lawyer disciplinary system is focused on the little guys, solo practitioners or small-firm lawyers who cheat clients or negligently fail to perform basic tasks in the course of representation. At the same time, the big shots who may be more crooked usually remain untouched.[53]

This reflects a problem with the system. Ethics investigations by disciplinary committees tend to be complaint driven. That is, ethics board investigators usually do not act unless some outsider reports a lawyer. Individuals who have been wronged by their lawyers are far more likely to file a complaint with legal ethics authorities than are corporate executives. Where attorney misconduct has benefited the corporation or was undertaken at the behest of the corporation, the corporate managers involved are most unlikely to complain. And even where the attorney misbehavior was at the corporate client's expense, executives will often opt simply to fire the lawyer quietly, rather than grouse publicly and face embarrassing public exposure of the company's errors.

Even if corporate lawyer misconduct is discovered, bar disciplinary committees may be reluctant to tackle powerful, well-known lawyers whose large-firm power bases may overmatch the meager resources available to ethics enforcers. Also, as we indicated in discussing the Kaye, Scholer matter, in ethics matters the legal establishment clearly and repeatedly resolves the tension between the obligation to provide "zealous advocacy" and obligations to truth and the integrity of the justice system by favoring the former. Complaints about attorney misrepresentations, about destroying evidence and the like are swept aside by the corporate attorneys who dominate ethics boards.

To help overcome these systemic obstacles to effective lawyer discipline, entire law firms—not just individual lawyers—should be held accountable for attorney misconduct before bar disciplinary committees.[54] Ted Schneyer is a strong proponent of this change. He says, "We need to give ethical enforcers jurisdiction to proceed against firms as targets. If you make the firm vicariously responsible for unethical practice by individual members, you will create an incentive for firm lawyers to watchdog their own members. If you can show that there has been improper supervision or that the firm itself created the impetus to the unethical behavior, then sanctions could apply."

If a large firm adequately supervised its members, if it had an ethics overseer in place responsible for the firm's procedures and practices, if it informed its associates and partners on proper practice and created a firm culture that valued ethical practice, it would be free from disciplinary sanctions when an individual lawyer from the firm acted wrongly. On the other hand, if management was lax, if the creed was "please the client, whatever the cost," if members were insufficiently educated on ethical issues, then the firm itself could be punished or its principals disciplined for failure to properly supervise.

Given the increased size, power, and wealth of firms, this is a necessary reform. And while many in the legal establishment will resist it, there is nothing radical about the concept. If airlines can be punished by the Federal Aviation Administration for allowing employees to engage in lax safety procedures, and corporations can be held civilly liable and criminally culpable for the wrongdoing of management, then surely law firms (many of which today are themselves structured as professional corporations rather than partnerships) can be held responsible for the unethical conduct of their individual members. To do less is to permit law firm managers to shirk responsibility and countenance the ethical indifference, if not outright ethical and criminal violations, occurring in the practice of corporate law today. In May 1996, New York became the first state to authorize professional discipline against entire firms for failure to adequately supervise their attorneys.

ABOLISH THE CONFIDENTIAL SETTLEMENT

If secrecy is the mortal enemy of civil justice, then the confidential settlement is secrecy's squire. It is time for these confidential settlements to go. They promote wrongdoing by keeping it in the shadows well past the time when, in a system not choked by secrecy, disclosure would have ended it. Confidential settlements force desperate injury victims and their lawyers into a wrenching, corrupt bargain: personal remuneration at the expense of the public good. Confidential settlements also stymie the justice system's vital role of warning society about safety hazards and stigmatizing, and thereby deterring, unethical conduct.

The public would surely benefit, especially if, at the same time, judges insisted that secrecy orders routinely put in place before trial be limited to those occasions where genuine trade secrets or other legitimate interests justified confidentiality. Consumers and workers would enjoy heightened protection, both because regulators and lawmakers would learn of potential hazards earlier and because increased access to information about the safety of products would enable consumers to make more informed choices in the marketplace.

Take an example from Chapter 2 of this book: the breast implants case. If court secrecy had not kept the documented dangers of silicone implants out of the public eye for so long, hundreds of thousands of women would have avoided misery and Dow Corning might well have avoided going into voluntary bankruptcy. The FDA would have been alerted to the potential hazards of those products that much sooner and would have initiated studies earlier to assemble comprehensive data. Some women, informed about the problems associated with implants that the manufacturers were able to keep quiet using secrecy orders, might have decided not to take the risk, leading to fewer potential victims. Those women who did decide to have implants would have made their decision based on greater knowledge of the potential hazard. This, in turn, could have reduced the potential liability of manufacturers and diminished the likelihood of punitive damage claims based on proof that manufacturers hid information about implant risks from women and doctors.

With greater likelihood of disclosure, market incentives would promote safe product design and manufacture. Service providers would approach their work with greater training and diligence. The potential costs of unscrupulous conduct would increase, thereby providing a greater incentive toward honesty and proper ethics. At the same time, a company wrongly accused of misconduct could look forward to a very public vindication.

In 1980, attorneys from the Public Citizen Litigation Group submitted to the United States District Court for the District of Columbia—the federal trial court in the nation's capital—a proposed amendment to the court's rules to limit confidentiality orders and confidential settlements. The proposed amendment provided that any time parties to a lawsuit submitted to the court a request to seal documents, court records, or other information relating to a case and that request was not opposed by any other party in the case, the party seeking the order would have to file a notice in a local legal publication, briefly explaining the case and the proposed order. Anyone who opposed the order would have the opportunity to express disagreement in a filing with the court. This simple, clear proposal would be a sensible addition to the rules of every state and federal court. It would at least let the public know when parties sought to use the public courts for secret business and provide a chance to be heard.[55] Unfortunately, this proposal was never adopted. Instead, most recently, judicial authorities actually sought to increase the hospitality toward secret orders by the federal courts. Two committees of the United States Judicial Conference proposed that the Federal Rules of Civil Procedure, which govern all federal courts, drop the requirement that a judge must find "good cause" for a confidentiality order before issuing one. Under the proposal, judges could issue a protective order whenever both sides in a case wanted one. At its March 1995 annual meeting, the Judicial Conference, faced with protests by public-interest and plaintiffs' attorneys, dropped the proposal,[56] but corporate attorneys, backed by Assistant Attorney General Frank Hunger (brother-in-law of Vice President Al Gore), continue to press for changes that would enhance their ability, both at the federal and state level, to hide court cases behind judicially approved screens.

THE EVER-EXPANDING NO-CONTEST REGIME

We have described the oppressive conduct of many corporate attorneys and their unsavory tactics. Where there are resourceful adversaries on both sides of a case, these attorneys argue, as did Kaye, Scholer's Peter Fishbein, they are under no obligation to do anything that might aid the opponent. This view, which has been a long-standing rationale for the mailed fist theory of advocacy for corporate clients, sidesteps both the contemplation and application of an ethical critique. Legal historian Berle long ago spotted this departure from the historic view "that a lawyer was an officer of the court and therefore an integral part of the scheme of justice." He observed in 1934: "Reliance is placed on the fact that the opposing interest may pull an opposite set of levers and that in the resulting equilibrium approximate justice will be performed." Ever the empirical realist, Berle declared: "In the field of the large corporations, with their great concentration of power in the hands of a few men, this point of view has been disastrous for professional standards and public welfare. The financial interests are amply represented by legal skill, while the vast disorganized public, composed of investors, workers and consumers, is not represented at all."[57]

Given the great number of actions by corporations, whether in formal dispute or policy forums spanning the three branches of government at the federal, state, and local levels, or in the private sector, this state of affairs, described by Berle, is largely still the norm. It was expressed by John Douglas, a lawyer with Covington & Burling who wrote in 1969, "Our nation must assure legal representation for consumers before the federal agencies—representation which they do not now have. Without their own lawyers, the consumers' interests are not assured adequate attention. . . . Even where agency members and staff personnel have the best of intentions, the scales are tipped against the public. Those scales now favor the regulated industries."[58] Covington then had more than 125 corporate attorneys (the firm now has 301 attorneys), representing dozens of large companies and industries before these agencies, so Douglas spoke with a special credibility on this absence of contest. To be sure, the growth in the number of plaintiffs' attorneys specializing in tort (personal injury) and securities fraud in cases involving money damages has improved the "other side's" representation since the 1930s. And over the past twenty-five years, several hundred public interest lawyers have strained to fill a few of the usually empty chairs on the other side of consumer, environment, and access-to-justice disputes. Still, the ethical dilemma for those corporate lawyers who observe and treasure their "officer of the court" status remains.

This dilemma occupied the thoughts of an eminent constitutional law professor at Harvard in 1965. Professor Paul Freund urged that "Where the adversary process does not operate, the lawyer has a wider scope and obligation to see around a problem unconstrained by what may be too parochial concerns of his clients, and to advise accordingly."[59] As an indication of how remote such sensibilities are from the king rainmakers of the megafirms, the most powerful partner at Kirkland & Ellis in the seventies, Chicago attorney Donald Reuben, told an audience, "[A]s Mr. Kirkland used to say, a good lawyer is like a good prostitute. If the price is right, you warm up to your client."[60] Surely said partly in jest but, as Professor Freund used to say to his students, "in humor there is truth."

Would a dramatic expansion of the number of public interest lawyers and institutions relieve corporate attorneys of the need for such sensibilities to "draw that wider scope and obligation"? In the unlikely event that their opponents or opposing interests before agency, court, and legislature always are represented by counsel, could these attorneys be free ethically to act as parochially as their business clients demand? Recent history indicates that once the corporate attorney succumbs to his client, the clients up the ante. The ethical gravities become more serious because these lawyers are now on missions of taking away, generically, the rights and remedies of people and weaker institutions so they do not have a chance to plead for justice.

The degrading role of the corporate attorney as a clever hired hand supinely following orders so long as the big checks keep flowing has been demonstrated recently in three areas of the law.

First is the campaign, described in Chapter 8, to take away the rights—piece by piece—of tort victims by preemptive legislation, greased by campaign contributions from both attorney and client, that regulates judges and juries in ways that expressly favor immunizing or further limiting the liability of defendants. These include caps on pain-and-suffering and even economic damages, restrictions on expert witnesses for the plaintiffs, abolishing punitive damages, terminating three-hundred-year-old doctrines of joint and several liability, specific immunities for certain products and privileges for certain information, and dozens of other one-sided substantive and procedural nullifications or limitations on the legal tools that have been available to wrongfully injured Americans for many years. The codification downward and backward of the extraordinary common-law tradition of our country, devoted to decision making by the only people who see, hear, and evaluate the evidence—judge and jury (subject to appellate review)—is not part of the law firm description pamphlets that Gibson, Dunn & Crutcher, Covington & Burling, Crowell & Moring, and Kirkland & Ellis—to mention a few—send to law school placement offices for law students to peruse. This reactionary drive is based on contentions, illustrated by manufactured anecdotes, of a civil justice system wildly out of control, including frivolous suits, unrestrainable trial lawyers, pliant judges, runaway juries, irrational verdicts, and astronomical litigiousness in product liability, medical malpractice, and securities fraud.

Corporate attorneys leading this charge are aware of studies by the General Accounting Office, the Rand Institute for Civil Justice, University of Wisconsin Law School scholars, the Harvard School of Public Health, the Justice Department, the National Center for State Courts, and even corporate consulting firms, among others, that undermine the tort deform lobbyists and insurance industry horror stories and allegations with hard data. Two new books by impeccable scholars, with no axes to grind, further expose the myths about jury incompetence, deep pockets, and high damage awards. They dispassionately parse the rhetoric as compared with the reality in the debate over civil justice and analyze how the corporate defendant lobby sets both the legislative and political agenda. These studies, heavy with empirical research, are *Civil Juries and the Politics of Reform* by Stephen Daniels and Joanne Martin and *Medical Malpractice and the American Jury* by Neil Vidmar.[61] They draw attention to long-available documentation that corporate attorneys have refused to recognize in their zeal to fashion false and lurid portrayals of courts and juries into evisceration of the system.

These corporate attorney efforts amount to counseling on and participating in a massive propaganda assault on a major pillar of our democracy. The preamble of the American Bar Association Model Rules of Professional Conduct urges lawyers "to improve the law and the legal profession and to exemplify the legal profession's ideals of public service." That would seem to mean reforms that widen the access to justice by the majority of the wronged who now are outside the system. It does not mean working to dissolve existing rights for the few who are able to exercise them against the perpetrators of their harm.

The second area in which corporate attorneys are presently working to strengthen their no-contest hold on the justice system is, like tort deform, embedded in Newt Gingrich's "Contract with America." This scheme was put forth by House Republicans in H.R. 9—the "Jobs Creation and Wage Enhancement Act." The measure has nothing to do with jobs or wages. It is, rather, a cynical effort to hamstring the presently modest federal health, safety, and environmental regulation by adding mountains of bureaucratic hurdles and new opportunities for industry-inspired litigation. And it was written and fine-tuned by squads of high-priced corporate lawyers on behalf of virtually every major industrial sector.

Corporate executives and their attorney supplicants still allege, after twelve years of Reagan and Bush, no less, that "reform" is needed because government mindlessly churns out regulations harmful to business and that the public is tired of "red tape." Americans may dislike regulation in the abstract, but we do value clear air, pure water, and safe food, drugs, and automobiles and the other benefits of health and safety regulation that private markets ignore. The power lawyers know that the public would not stand for explicitly dismantling the Clean Air Act, the Food, Drug and Cosmetic Act, the Safe Drinking Water Act, the Highway Safety Act, or the Occupational Safety and Health Act. So they are trying a sleight of hand: trying to cripple these laws by enacting neutral-sounding procedural burdens on agencies that would make effective regulation impossible. That is, they seek no-law laws.

The House of Representatives passed H.R. 9 in March 1995. The Senate has considered a number of proposals, including one sponsored by then–Majority Leader Bob Dole that was initially even more draconian than H.R. 9 but remains a close counterpart. More moderate proposals put forth by Republican Senator William Roth and Democrat John Glenn have already been rejected by the Republican majority.

There are four fundamental components of both H.R. 9 and the Senate bill. First, both proposals try to make nearly universal the requirement that rules be subjected to highly burdensome and intricate cost-benefit analyses and risk assessments. Although agencies have been required to weigh costs and benefits for many years, the proposed legislation would compel agencies to try to quantify all likely costs and benefits, which builds in a bias against regulation. Cost data, generally submitted by industry, is readily available in dollars and cents, although industry typically overstates considerably the true compliance costs. On the other hand, there is no hard data on most of the benefits that flow from regulation. Suffering and casualties are real, but they defy easy quantification. As EPA administrator Carol Browner poignantly asked, "How should I value the loss of IQ points by children exposed to lead?" Economic analysis also tends to ignore "soft" benefits, such as the joy of experiencing a wilderness. As former EPA administrator Doug Costle has observed: "That which can be measured tends to receive more weight than less tangible, though perhaps more important, effects which cannot be quantified."

Compounding the problem, agencies would be required to prepare elaborate risk-assessment documents for virtually every rule of significance. This makes little sense. For instance, the FDA has proposed a rule to require that iron tablets come in childproof containers to curb the epidemic of iron poisoning in children, who often mistake the vitamins for candy. In recent years, more than 100,000 children have been poisoned. The risks of iron toxicity have been known for literally centuries. What sense does it make to require the FDA to spend $100,000 or more to conduct a risk assessment on iron poisoning? Yet that is what these bills would require.

Both bills pervert an honorable scientific institution—peer review. True peer review is professional review conducted by disinterested parties. Under the bills, agencies would submit risk assessments and cost-benefit analyses to panels that could be composed of industry scientists. Conflicts of interests are no barrier, provided that the panelists disclose their financial ties to industry. Since public interest groups usually lack the resources to supply scientists, the process would guarantee industry representatives an early opportunity to attack a proposed new rule's economic and scientific underpinnings. And at a minimum, the reviews will delay rule making and drain away scarce agency resources.

The bills would force agencies to engage in regulatory triage. The new procedures required by the legislation would cost agencies tens of millions of dollars. Yet, at the same time that corporate lobbyists have proposed to add immeasurably to agencies' workloads, their allies in Congress have moved to slash the agencies' already modest budgets. The clearly intended result is that agencies will have to scale back dramatically their safety efforts.

Perhaps most critically, these Rube Goldberg–type proposals increase exponentially the opportunities for frivolous industry litigation, even before regulations are issued. At present, anyone affected by a rule can sue to overturn it if it is arbitrary or unsound. But industry wants to be able to tie agencies up in court for years, regardless of the need for or ultimate rationality of the rule. Under the proposed bills, a court would be free to set aside a rule if the agency had committed an error in its risk assessment or cost-benefit analysis—even if the rule was nonetheless rational. And industry would be given the right to compel agencies to re-review all of their existing rules to ensure that the rules meet current risk-assessment and cost-benefit criteria.

If industry disagrees with an agency over the outcome of the agency's review, the industry would be free to sue. Nearly all of the major rules issued over the past twenty years have been subject to detailed cost and risk analysis. While agencies certainly ought to reexamine rules on a selective basis, this universal requirement is a recipe for a colossal waste of resources—which is precisely what the bills' proponents have in mind. If agencies are tied up reevaluating existing rules and defending those evaluations in court, they will not be able to respond at all to many new threats to health, safety, or the environment.

Serious students of regulation have concluded that, by the time of the Reagan presidency, the rule-making process had already become ossified with new procedural and analytical requirements. The updating of weak safety standards and the issuance of new standards have slowed greatly since 1981. From a comparatively efficient tool for making and implementing government policy, agency rule making has become a bloated, plodding process. The even more burdensome and pointless requirements of the proposed legislation—a cruel caricature of reform—would bring the regulatory process to a halt. Such procedural gridlock is precisely the objective of these corporate attorneys; it serves the twin goals of their clients' license and their own drive for billable hours.[62]

A third area in which power lawyers are expanding corporate advantage can be described as a runaway privatization of the law that reduces consumers, workers, physicians, nurses, and many small businesses to a modern form of bondage. Through coercive fine-print clauses, companies and their attorneys escape the public civil laws that give you the right to sue or speak out to correct or stop an injustice.

Assume you are a longtime customer with the giant Bank of America in California. In June 1992, you receive your regular checking account and credit card account statement. Also inside the envelope is an insert containing less than scrutable language that amounts to a unilateral imposition of an amendment of your agreement with the bank: Henceforth, any dispute you have with the bank can be resolved only through binding arbitration before a private panel to be financed jointly by you and the bank. The paper notice does not require an affirmative consent by the consumer. Presto! As described in Chapter 8, millions of Californians, mostly without their knowledge (the bank's own readership survey found that less than 4 percent of its customers would read "stand alone" inserts), gave up the right to a judge and jury should they, or a class of consumers, believe they were deceived or defrauded. Not a meaningless coup on the bank's part or a meaningless concession on the part of customers—the very same Bank of America had previously been caught charging unconscionable fees and had to refund millions of dollars to its customers.

The right to sue is a powerful tool to bring misbehaving companies to justice or to deter disreputable practices. Even unexercised, it stands as a deterrent against abusive practices by companies. Mandatory arbitration privatizes the dispute and, as we discussed earlier, places the weaker party at an extreme disadvantage. When such arbitration is in reality nonconsensual and unilateral, and is based on no affirmative agreement by the customers, it becomes a ball and chain. You can leave and go to another bank with the same policy or you can sue, once there is a dispute, and hope that some court will find that the arbitration notice was not consensual or, if it was, that the agreement is unenforceable because it is unconscionable. In the meantime, the bank's attorneys will change a few things and start the coercive, sly maneuver all over again.

Broad compulsory arbitration clauses imposed by nonunionized employers on their employees also have been spreading in recent years.

You are a physician or nurse under contract with a managed health care organization owned by a large insurance company. HMOs (health maintenance organizations) are dominating the medical markets in various cities, and the merger trend is leading to more corporate concentration. The HMO has the bargaining power; so it has an explicit indemnification or "hold harmless" provision permitting the HMO to shift any liability resulting from a policy that withholds necessary care from a patient onto the physician or nurse. Attorneys for the HMOs draft joint-hold harmless rules that appear to the untutored eye like reciprocal agreements between physicians and HMOs. They are in reality very one-sided. As Dr. Harry L. Greene II of the Massachusetts Medical Society testified before the Massachusetts legislature's Joint Committee on Insurance: "Currently [HMOs] with hold harmless clauses may aggressively deny services to [HMO patients] without fear that [HMOs] shall be liable." He argued that "individual physicians have very little ability to negotiate out terms of a contract with an insurance company. We probably have about the same leverage you would have in dealing with a car dealer and asking for the removal of just one clause in a General Motors financing contract."[63]

There is more. The same HMO has a "gag rule" clause in the contract to curb a doctor's right of free speech. Of course, the attorneys do not call it a "gag rule" in the fine print. Here is how one health insurer phrases the shut-up: "Physician shall agree not to take any action or make any communications which undermines or could undermine the confidence of enrollees, potential enrollees, their employees, their unions, or the public in [name of insurance company] or the quality of care which it provides." So, for example, if a patient complains about being undertreated, the physician would be barred by contract from telling him about financial incentives given doctors to keep down treatments.

You can get fired for speaking about bad conditions or sleazy practices within your health insurer's domain. Take Dr. David Himmelstein, who teaches at the Harvard School of Medicine. In 1994, he simply criticized U.S. Healthcare's gag rule on the *Donahue* show and his HMO gave him the pink slip. All this in the land of the free, home of the brave—the handiwork of corporate power and its unblinking attorneys.

You want to run your own business, and you have some life savings to get started. You figure if you hook up with a national franchisor, you'll be able to use its logo and benefit from its supply networks, advertisements, know-how, management, and marketing skills. You go to an exposition, ponder your choices, decide on the franchise you'd like, and make contact with the franchisor. Welcome to one of the most one-sided, unfair commercial agreements in the marketplace. And these one-sided provisions are becoming uniform in more and more of the four thousand franchise systems in the United States, which, the Department of Commerce reports, accounted for about $800 billion in retail sales in 1994. During the rabid antiregulatory atmosphere at the White House Conference on Small Business in 1995, the delegates voted for only one exception: They wanted more federal regulation over the franchise relationship. Attorney Peter Lagarias, a former Federal Trade Commission attorney whose clients now are often franchisees facing financial ruin, explains why the delegates supported more regulatory legislation: "An examination of the increasingly uniform franchise agreements . . . reveals a dark secret. These agreements systematically abrogate franchisor duties and eviscerate most franchisee rights and remedies. Leading the charge have been lawyers specializing in representing franchisors. These franchisor lawyers have, individually and collectively, systematically taken an obscure area of trademark law and developed a laboratory for outrageously unfair adhesion contracts."[64]

What would the franchisor attorney say in reply? That they are protecting the interests of their clients. They are doing so by including an escape clause in most franchisor obligations, by stripping franchisees of many of their rights, and by rigging the dispute-resolution system in their favor. Obviously, franchisors vary in the degree of their scruples. But all franchisors have the power; therefore they make their own private law—what the former CEO of Midas Muffler, Gordon Sherman, called a "modern form of feudalism." This does not mean that franchisees are all cowering vassals squeezed to the nth degree. Some are multimillion-dollar operations with multiple outlets. But they are the exceptions.

What passes for public laws requiring disclosures by franchisors were considered far too weak by the 1995 White House Conference participants. Franchisors have blocked specific legislation, except when automobile dealers and service stations rebelled to get their watered-down Automobile Dealers Day in Court Act of 1956 and Petroleum Marketing Practices Act of 1978 through Congress. These laws dealt chiefly with providing some due process for unfair terminations by the franchisors. Since then, franchisors and their aggressive counselors have learned even more about how to imbalance greatly their relationships with franchisees through take-it-or-leave-it conditions imposed by their unilateral private legislatures. They have created mechanisms to vitiate the effects of existing public laws.[65]

All this was too much for one prominent attorney for franchisors, Robert L. Purvin, Jr., who used to enjoy "being able to pull out all the stops in the preparation of a lawsuit against franchisee defendants unable to afford even an 'inadequate' defense." His growing concern over the "inequity of the franchise relationship" led him to tell a *Wall Street Journal* reporter, "I had never written or read a franchise agreement I could recommend a franchisee to sign." (Purvin now represents as an attorney—and crusades as a lawyer for—franchisees who are seeking a fairer, more balanced franchising industry.)

What can be said of these and other systemic erosions of fairness in both substance and procedure of laws and legal arrangements that affect the health, safety, economic and civil liberties, and civil rights of millions of people?

First, the corporate attorneys are the lead architects, riding high astride the chariots of power. They are providing expanded meaning to what Professor Gary Bellow described as "the institution of counsel as a law-making, law-enforcing, law-nullifying activity."

Second, these attorneys are using that power extensively, and exert little professional restraint on their clients.

Third, that power arrayed against essentially defenseless and vulnerable persons takes away their very chance to protect their rights or have their government do so. In centuries past, indentured servants and serfs were said to have concurred in their status. Corporate attorneys should be able to cease and desist when their corporate clients demand the destruction of basic rights of the American legal system and the ability of the various authorities to protect the public health and safety.

Unable to do so on their own, these attorneys may require external jolts. One jolt may have been spurred by the 2,300-member National Employment Lawyers Association, which, in October 1995, authorized a limited boycott of alternative dispute-resolution firms if these firms continue to hear cases from corporations that place mandatory arbitration clauses in the preprinted agreements they require their employees to sign. In February 1996, one of the nation's largest alternative dispute-resolution firms, JAMS/Endispute, committed to promote voluntary rather than mandatory employee arbitration. The employment lawyers' group promptly dropped its threatened boycott of the firm. (At this writing, the larger American Arbitration Association had not taken a similar step, but the company denies that it promotes binding arbitration to the exclusion of other approaches.) As Chapter 8 notes, both the federal Equal Employment Opportunity Commission and the National Labor Relations Board have recently expressed their opinions that such clauses violate the civil rights laws, but their legal challenges now under way have not yet been resolved. These agencies are concerned that these clauses would permit employers to opt out unilaterally of federal antidiscrimination laws and other statutory protections for workers by essentially conditioning employment on a waiver of the substantive and procedural provisions of these statutes.

Following the fall of communism, the American Bar Association's Central and East European Law Initiative (CEELI) swung into detailed advisory activities for the newly emerging legal systems of these national governments. A concept paper on consumer protection for Bulgaria was prepared by CEELI for Bulgarian officials in 1992 by a group of corporate lawyers and law professors. Free of any corporate client shackles, the group proposed a "plan of action for the Bulgarian government": "First, enact a law that generally prohibits unfair contract terms and provides a relatively short, nonexclusive list of clauses that are prohibited. . . . Second, when laws concerning specific types of consumer transactions are under consideration, such as laws governing insurance, banking, consumer credit, product liability or warranty, provide that consumer rights and remedies granted by the law cannot be diluted by contract."[66] One can wonder and wait for the ABA to recommend to the U.S. Congress a similar set of generic prohibitions of unconscionable contractual impositions by those with wealth and power over those without either.

The role of the law in saying no to unjust power and yes to the legitimate rights of those without power is part of the legal profession's responsibility. That means significant energies in that direction must come from the responsible efforts of lawyers who are not restricted by retainer-induced myopia. We know how much good effect a few hundred public interest lawyers have produced in persuading courts and regulatory agencies to recognize fairer procedures and rights for consumers and others against whom, as John Douglas noted, the scales were tilted. It is long overdue for the mainstream bar to begin directing lawyer energies toward improving our perfectible democracy. But how?

Sol Linowitz worked more than five years to prepare a jarring critique and recommendations for a changed profession, particularly with respect to the business bar. His book, *The Betrayed Profession*, while broadly reviewed, was not nearly as widely read among attorneys as one of John Grisham's novels. But books like Linowitz's do not come around every year; they are, in fact, quite rare, especially coming from a charter member of the corporate law establishment. We asked Linowitz whether his colleagues were listening.[67] He said that he had expected to be clobbered by the bar associations, but quite the opposite happened. He gave a keynote address to the ABA's annual meeting and was received with warm enthusiasm and applause, more pointedly from the young lawyers. State bar associations are inviting him to address their gatherings. When asked what they should do, he urges them to form councils of high standing to come up with some answers. That is starting to happen in some states, he added.

Just why are these bar associations responding to Linowitz? He says lawyers have had it up to here with lawyer-bashing, with being the butt of jokes leading to a loss of their dignity and respect. (Certainly William Ide III, president of the ABA in 1993, would agree. He has lamented that "Jay Leno puts America to bed with jokes about us. Movie audiences cheer as dinosaurs devour us. Beer commercials show rodeo cowboys roping us." How ironic, said Ide, that all this goes on in ignorance of the historic fact that since "the first meeting of the First Continental Congress until today, lawyers have been the champions of popular justice and the primary agents of popular freedom." But Ide failed to note that many of the laudable, heroic contributions of individual lawyers came over the opposition of business lawyers.) To Linowitz, corporate law firm attorneys are fearful of losing more business to in-house corporate counsel. They are also worried that, unless deserving public expectations are met, they could start, like physicians, facing demands for more federal and state regulations.

We find these to be inadequate motivations for any basic reorientations and initiatives to improve the ways the law delivers justice in our country. They are inadequate because they cannot provide the needed stamina to counter the expected reactions and conflicts that such initiatives would have to endure. The bar associations are vague about what needs to be done, how to get it done, and who needs to do what. Simply saying that the poor need more legal aid or that law schools should have more memorable ethics courses is not going beyond the talk even for these relatively unthreatening objectives. Linowitz, who insists he is not kidding himself, has found that young lawyers and old-timers were more receptive to his call to action than those middle-aged attorneys presently running the firms. Could this be a start—youthful idealism and elderly wisdom—to expand the "professionalism" of the legal trade?

It became clear to some classmates from the Harvard Law School class of 1958 that such a combination could work. On the eve of their thirty-fifth reunion, they formed the Appleseed Foundation, whose chief purpose is to help establish, with young lawyer organizers, centers for law and justice in state after state throughout the country.[68] (The foundation's statement of purpose can be found in Appendix 2.) Instead of waiting on bar associations, a new and potentially dynamic mechanism has emerged—law alumni classes. Appleseed, which has already started, in its brief tenure, centers in Massachusetts, New Jersey, and the District of Columbia, is focusing on systemic change, on systemic approaches to pervasive problems, not on individual legal aid. In Appleseed's statement of purpose, the classmates wrote:

> Most of us who are now lawyers grew up believing in the law—in its power and its capacity for justice. The social movements of our time—for civil rights, women's rights, environmental protection, and economic justice—harnessed the aspiration for equality to a belief that the law could remedy what was wrong in our society. We knew then, and still know now, that the law could remedy what was wrong in our society. We knew then, and still know now, that the law can help satisfy peoples' just demands for safety, dignity, and equity.
>
> Today, however, many of us have all but surrendered our vision of justice. Our legal system often seems neither willing nor able to serve the public demand for a just society. The law and lawyers are widely perceived as serving only the privileged few. . . . One large private law firm employs more lawyers than all of the full-time private sector public interest law firms in the country put together.
>
> The Appleseed Foundation is born of a desire to reclaim the law as a vehicle for achieving justice for all of this country's citizens. It is driven by a need to confront the *most basic causes of the significant problems we face, not the isolated symptoms of these problems*. We understand that the law must be shaped and served not only in the courts, but in legislatures, government agencies, board rooms, and civic associations. We also know that lawyers cannot work alone, but must join with other professions and with the community at large, to fashion more general and lasting solutions. [Emphasis added.]

Most of the class of 1958 are business attorneys. Most of Appleseed's board are business attorneys. They are determined to place the challenge of building these centers on the shoulders of the mainstream bar to demonstrate that attorneys can leave their clients back in their offices when they do the work of lawyers. Building democracy under law makes the lawyer a primary human being, worthy of the word "professional," because what is being professed are the ideals of this learned body of knowledge, experience, and service, which can be effectively applied in community and society.

Many young lawyers are looking for sustainable opportunities in public interest law—positions that are not there. The older lawyers have the resources and status to make those opportunities happen for the young and for themselves. With more senior corporate attorneys retiring early to seek second careers, or being asked to leave, the available human resources are plentiful. They are free at last. Peter Libassi, former general counsel to the U.S. Department of Health, Education and Welfare and later to the Travelers Insurance Co., believes that many of these retired attorneys in their fifties and sixties are "looking for useful pursuits." "They have money and good pensions," he cheerfully added from his present location as dean of the Business School at the University of Hartford.

Achieving a critical mass of enduring lawyer energy to expand public interest law, and to organize it in conjunction with millions of citizens, demands a desire for fundamental self-renewal.[69] In his book *On Leadership*, John W. Gardner quotes Jean Monnet, the celebrated citizen for a united Europe: "Nothing is possible without individuals; nothing is lasting without institutions."

Once the process of professional regeneration is under way the challenge becomes one of restructuring abusive power systems—public and private—and not simply becoming another legal charity, sponsoring palliatives and congratulatory dinner ceremonies.

Lawyers understand power, its sources, its machinations, its ways of intimidation and beguilement, and its vulnerabilities to change or displacement. They understand what law can mean to the construction of democracy as the best problem-solving mechanism yet developed and as a work in continual progress against authoritarian forces of capital, technology, bureaucracy, and brute force. But they must also understand that from the commons and from the aroused citizenry come the pressure, the trusteeship, the sensitivity, and the challenge for lawyers bent on building the future.

If there are eyes reading these words that belong to members of the legal profession who want to view their lives as moving from success to significance, whether wealthy or not, young or old, and who believe that their finest accomplishments are still ahead of them, then what awaits these lawyers is the greatest work of human beings on earth—justice.

THE TOP-GROSSING LAW FIRMS IN THE UNITED STATES

Below is a list of the one hundred law firms in the United States with the highest gross incomes in 1994. The list was compiled by the journal *The American Lawyer* and published in its July/August 1995 issue.

Rank by Gross Revenue	Firm & Base City	Gross Revenue	Total Number of Lawyers/ Number of Partners
1	Skadden, Arps, Slate, Meagher & Flom New York	$582,000,000	968/227
2	Baker & McKenzie Chicago	$546,000,000	1,642/500
3	Jones, Day, Reavis & Pogue Cleveland	$384,000,000	1,072/252
4	Weil, Gotshal & Manges New York	$311,000,000	600/152
5	Sullivan & Cromwell New York	$298,000,000	382/108
6	Gibson, Dunn & Crutcher Los Angeles	$278,000,000	550/212
7	Shearman & Sterling New York	$268,000,000	522/115
8	Cleary, Gottlieb, Steen & Hamilton New York	$265,000,000	451/122
9	Latham & Watkins Los Angeles	$263,000,000	518/218

Rank by Gross Revenue	Firm & Base City	Gross Revenue	Total Number of Lawyers/ Number of Partners
9	Mayer, Brown & Platt Chicago	$263,000,000	570/259
11	O'Melveny & Myers Los Angeles	$257,000,000	538/184
12	Sidley & Austin Chicago	$254,000,000	608/179
13	Davis Polk & Wardwell New York	$254,000,000	377/99
14	Morgan, Lewis & Bockius Philadelphia	$241,500,000	625/245
15	White & Case New York	$232,500,000	501/137
16	Fulbright & Jaworski Houston	$227,000,000	609/269
17	Simpson Thacher & Bartlett New York	$216,000,000	364/100
18	Kirkland & Ellis Chicago	$215,000,000	401/93
19	Pillsbury Madison & Sutro San Francisco	$211,000,000	527/186
19	Vinson & Elkins Houston	$211,000,000	495/219
21	McDermott, Will & Emery Chicago	$208,500,000	495/171
22	Morrison & Foerster San Francisco	$200,000,000	500/192
23	Cravath, Swaine & Moore New York	$186,000,000	262/69
24	Debevoise & Plimpton New York	$181,500,000	320/80
25	Paul, Weiss, Rifkind, Wharton & Garrison New York	$175,500,000	331/89
26	Milbank, Tweed, Hadley & McCloy New York	$172,500,000	332/88
27	Willkie Farr & Gallagher New York	$172,000,000	335/107
28	Baker & Botts Houston	$171,000,000	398/145
29	Proskauer Rose Goetz & Mendelsohn New York	$169,000,000	400/121
30	Dewey Ballantine New York	$164,000,000	361/105
31	Akin, Gump, Strauss, Hauer & Feld Dallas/Washington, D.C.	$162,500,000	478/190

Rank by Gross Revenue	Firm & Base City	Gross Revenue	Total Number of Lawyers/ Number of Partners
32	Fried, Frank, Harris, Shriver & Jacobson New York	$162,000,000	363/122
33	LeBoeuf, Lamb, Greene & MacRae New York	$161,000,000	459/145
34	Rogers & Wells New York	$158,000,000	357/104
35	Brobeck, Phleger & Harrison San Francisco	$157,000,000	389/123
35	Paul, Hastings, Janofsky & Walker Los Angeles	$157,000,000	378/134
37	Kaye, Scholer, Fierman, Hays & Handler New York	$153,000,000	311/100
38	Arnold & Porter Washington, D.C.	$150,000,000	329/139
39	Stroock & Stroock & Lavan New York	$148,000,000	310/102
40	Winston & Strawn Chicago	$146,000,000	430/85
41	Foley & Lardner Milwaukee	$145,000,000	437/237
42	Hunton & Williams Richmond	$144,500,000	418/164
43	Ropes & Gray Boston	$140,000,000	284/129
44	Covington & Burling Washington, D.C.	$135,000,000	301/111
44	Hogan & Hartson Washington, D.C.	$135,000,000	401/128
46	Jenner & Block Chicago	$131,500,000	370/169
46	Squire, Sanders & Dempsey Cleveland	$131,500,000	360/130
48	Howrey & Simon Washington, D.C.	$129,500,000	360/130
49	King & Spalding Atlanta	$126,500,000	294/118
50	Baker & Hostetler Cleveland	$125,000,000	439/150
51	Katten Muchin & Zavis Chicago	$124,000,000	306/81
52	Chadbourne & Parke New York	$122,000,000	252/74
53	Coudert Brothers New York	$121,000,000	328/99

Rank by Gross Revenue	Firm & Base City	Gross Revenue	Total Number of Lawyers/ Number of Partners
54	Heller, Ehrman, White & McAuliffe San Francisco	$120,000,000	329/152
55	Cadwalader, Wickersham & Taft New York	$118,000,000	288/87
55	Sonnenschein Nath & Rosenthal Chicago	$118,000,000	336/125
57	Cahill Gordon & Reindel New York	$117,000,000	195/55
58	Orrick, Herrington & Sutcliffe San Francisco	$116,000,000	291/109
59	Bryan Cave St. Louis	$113,000,000	395/181
60	McGuire, Woods, Battle & Boothe Richmond	$111,500,000	405/109
61	Hale and Dorr Boston	$109,500,000	237/101
62	Kelley Drye & Warren New York	$108,000,000	296/100
62	Wachtell, Lipton, Rosen & Katz New York	$108,000,000	109/57
64	Dechert Price & Rhoads Philadelphia	$107,000,000	302/128
65	Dorsey & Whitney Minneapolis	$106,500,000	340/182
66	Seyfarth, Shaw, Fairweather & Geraldson Chicago	$106,000,000	340/152
67	Perkins Coie Seattle	$104,000,000	310/133
67	Reed Smith Shaw & McClay Pittsburgh	$104,000,000	348/156
69	Brown & Wood New York	$102,000,000	287/94
69	Wilmer, Cutler & Pickering Washington, D.C.	$102,000,000	230/84
71	Wilson, Sonsini, Goodrich & Rosati Palo Alto	$101,000,000	248/72
72	Graham & James San Francisco	$100,000,000	275/145
72	Wilson, Elser, Moskowitz, Edelman & Dicker New York	$100,000,000	385/88
74	Holland & Knight Tampa	$98,500,000	383/124
75	Andrews & Kurth Houston	$95,500,000	261/85

Rank by Gross Revenue	Firm & Base City	Gross Revenue	Total Number of Lawyers/ Number of Partners
76	Mudge Rose Guthrie Alexander & Ferdon New York	$93,000,000	243/59
77	Goodwin, Procter & Hoar Boston	$91,000,000	260/80
78	Alston & Bird Atlanta	$88,500,000	258/86
79	Arter & Hadden Cleveland	$88,000,000	310/149
79	Honigman Miller Schwartz and Cohn Detroit	$88,000,000	226/110
79	Winthrop, Stimson, Putnam & Roberts New York	$88,000,000	235/72
82	Keck, Mahin & Cate Chicago	$87,000,000	290/101
82	Lord, Bissell & Brook Chicago	$87,000,000	315/112
82	McCutchen, Doyle, Brown & Enersen San Francisco	$87,000,000	240/106
85	Mintz, Levin, Cohn, Ferris, Glovsky & Popeo Boston	$86,500,000	225/76
86	Kirkpatrick & Lockhart Pittsburgh	$85,000,000	351/158
86	Shaw, Pittman, Potts & Trowbridge Washington, D.C.	$85,000,000	246/98
88	Anderson Kill Olick & Oshinsky New York	$84,500,000	209/102
89	Steptoe & Johnson Washington, D.C.	$84,000,000	190/83
90	Gray Cary Ware & Freidenrich Palo Alto/San Diego	$83,000,000	249/124
90	McKenna & Cuneo Washington, D.C.	$83,000,000	245/73
90	Piper & Marbury Baltimore	$83,000,000	259/107
93	Sheppard, Mullin, Richter & Hampton Los Angeles	$82,000,000	209/97
94	Pepper, Hamilton & Scheetz Philadelphia	$81,500,000	263/96
94	Sutherland, Asbill & Brennan Atlanta/Washington, D.C.	$81,500,000	233/108
96	Greenberg, Traurig, Hoffman, Lipoff, Rosen & Quentel, Miami	$80,500,000	194/67
97	Hughes Hubbard & Reed New York	$78,000,000	240/80

Rank by Gross Revenue	Firm & Base City	Gross Revenue	Total Number of Lawyers/ Number of Partners
97	Rosenman & Colin New York	$78,000,000	221/75
97	Williams & Connolly Washington, D.C.	$78,000,000	135/60
100	Thompson, Hine and Flory Cleveland	$76,000,000	313/155

Notes: Estimated numbers for gross revenue are rounded to the nearest $500,000. Firms that are tied in the rankings are listed alphabetically.

THE APPLESEED FOUNDATION STATEMENT OF PURPOSE

The Appleseed Foundation
733 15th Street N.W.
Suite 700
Washington, DC 20005
(202) 393-1223

STATEMENT OF PURPOSE

If we are to keep our democracy, there must be one commandment: Thou shalt not ration justice.

—Learned Hand

Last spring, at our thirty-fifth reunion, the Harvard Law School Class of 1958 established the Appleseed Foundation to plant the seeds for a new model of lawyering for the public interest. Galvanized by the belief that lawyers can and should contribute more significantly and more institutionally to ensure "equal justice under law," our alumni class created the Appleseed Foundation for the purpose of organizing statewide Appleseed Centers for Law and Justice. These centers will be more than mere litigation firms, and will embrace the widest sweep of the law's potential in the service of a better society. By mobilizing the resources, knowledge, and commitment of alumni, private and public interest lawyers, and community organizers, these centers can prove powerful catalysts for remedying the systemic ills in our society.

The Appleseed Foundation represents the first time that a law school alumni class, or any Harvard alumni class, has harnessed its energy to build institutions to serve the public interest. For years, alumni classes have united around reunion activities, sporting events, fund-raising functions, or academic conferences to renew social bonds among classmates and to support school programs. Appleseed was born of a conviction that graduates can and must serve the broader public good.

We, the directors and supporters of the Appleseed Foundation, are lawyers in large and small law firms, government officials, academics, and officers in corporations and nonprofit civic organizations. Our fields of practice, our interests, and our politics differ widely, but we also have much in common. We came of age together. We are the beneficiaries of an exceptional education and opportunities in life that are not available to many. To Appleseed, we bring our legal and life experiences, our financial resources, and our commitment to justice.

Appleseed is a vehicle through which we can all work together in realizing our common goals. Because Appleseed is an organizer—not a provider—of legal services in the public interest, we need not agree on—or with—the substantive work to be done. These matters will be decided by the board of directors and staff of each center. Those who wish to become more involved in the legal projects of an individual center will have the opportunity to provide assistance on specific cases, or to spend sabbaticals or some time following retirement to work with the centers.

In coming together to help build a more just and prosperous democratic society, we hope to provide a model of engagement for other alumni classes, not only in the law but in other fields as well. Perhaps, in the not-too-distant future, business leaders, engineers, scientists, physicians, accountants, and architects can forge public interest initiatives from their own alumni classes. When these professionals, together with lawyers, apply their collective experience to healing, improving, and rebuilding our society, then we shall have taken a significant step toward a better future.

THE NEED

Most of us who are now lawyers grew up believing in the law—in its power and its capacity for justice. The social movements of our time—for civil rights, women's rights, environmental protection, and economic justice—harnessed the aspiration for equality to a belief that the law could remedy what was wrong in our society. We knew then, and still know now, that the law can help satisfy peoples' just demands for safety, dignity, and equity.

Today, however, many of us have all but surrendered our vision of justice. Our legal system often seems neither willing nor able to serve the public demand for a just society. The law and lawyers are widely perceived as serving only the privileged few. Most lawyers represent a small percentage of the population. One large private law firm employs more lawyers than all of the full-time private-sector public interest law firms in the country put together. In the meantime, an estimated 80 percent of the legal needs of the poor are ignored.

Even those legal institutions dedicated to helping the broader public—legal aid societies, public defender offices, and public interest law centers—usually address the symptoms, but not the causes, of our shared problems. While serving an essential purpose, these legal service organizations have always had a limited mission: to provide personal legal services to indigent clients in housing, public assistance, domestic relations, or criminal cases. Legal service lawyers have neither the mandate nor the resources to challenge most of the underlying societal failures—abuses of power, gross waste, and ineffective public and private institutions, to name only a few—that have brought, and continue to bring, clients to their doors in overwhelming numbers.

The few other legal organizations that are generally accessible specialize in certain areas. Public interest lawyers have focused their work either on the problems of a particular group, defined by gender, race, ethnicity, age, or occupation, or on a particular issue, such as the environment, voting rights, or health care. But in our increasingly complex society, public and private wrongs rarely sort out along a single issue or constituency. Beyond specialized legal institutions providing legal services for aggrieved clients, we need private-sector law centers that are capable of developing comprehensive solutions to their communities' most urgent problems.

The Appleseed Foundation is born of a desire to reclaim the law as a vehicle for achieving justice for all of this country's citizens. It is driven by a need to confront the most basic causes of the significant problems we face, not the isolated symptoms of these problems. We understand that the law must be shaped and served not only in the courts, but in legislatures, government agencies, boardrooms, and civic associations. We also know that lawyers cannot work alone, but must join with other professions and with the community at large to fashion more general and lasting solutions.

THE METHOD

If Appleseed's vision were distilled to an existing model, it would be community groups that shape and revitalize political and economic institutions from the bottom up. In neighborhoods across the country, people are finding new ways to address their problems. Brought together by geography and shared interests, individuals organize across a variety of issues and groups to improve their lives. Depending upon their needs, members of the same group might seek an adequate health care system, fight zoning violations or merchants who create hazardous conditions, and develop new start-up businesses. These are the fibers of a democratic resurgence.

Appleseed-sponsored Centers for Law and Justice represent a groundbreaking approach—one that unites the energy, diversity, and creativity of these civic associations with the abilities and institutional access of lawyer-organizers. Drawing upon their strength as grassroot state organizations, and their reach as part of a national network, the Centers for Law and Justice have the potential to transform the legal landscape for many people in this country who are denied justice.

What makes this endeavor unique is its capability to bring about fundamental reform in our social institutions:

- *The centers will work systemically* to challenge the practices, conditions, and regulations that underlie our social problems. Rather than representing a consumer injured by a faulty product, the center would work with community groups to fight for improved methods to ensure public safety, and insist that the entities charged with protecting the public are both effective and accountable. Instead of battling a single unfair eviction, a center would help expand the stock of housing by helping to resolve the legal, financial, and political obstacles to such development.

- *The centers will work inclusively* with community groups to identify areas of concern and develop solutions. No issues or actors will be off-limits: injustices involving government, business, labor, and the professions, including the legal profession and the courts, all would be within the potential purview of the centers. Areas of concern include human rights, economic development, government and corporate accountability, consumer and environmental protection, school reform, criminal justice, and health care. The Appleseed Foundation has broadly designated these areas of concern to allow the centers freedom to respond to the most important and otherwise unmet needs of the states in which they work. Because the unmet needs of each locality differ, the issues and strategies chosen by each center will also vary.

- *The Centers will work creatively* through a variety of working tools beyond litigation, such as public education and advocacy, institution building, and direct action. The centers will adopt a "task force" approach—combining litigation with campaigns to increase public awareness of the problem, grievances before regulatory agencies or legislative committees, legislative drafting or advocacy, arbitration, institution building, and any other effective means of assistance. Thus, a center working in the field of school reform could not only file class-action lawsuits, or draft an alternative legislative scheme, but, at the same time, could provide communities with the legal assistance needed to develop their own magnet school. In addition, the centers will build links with other professions, drawing upon the skills and assistance of their members in addressing the issues they undertake. For example, a center involved in criminal justice reform, as a matter of course, would involve experts in public health, education, social work, and other related fields.

In selecting the areas in which they work, the centers should choose projects that:

- lend themselves to systemic or institutional approaches;
- are not addressed by other legal groups working effectively in this same, institutional manner;
- are within the resources and power of the center to change;
- allow the center to adopt a multidisciplinary approach, working with community groups and members of other professions to craft a solution to the problem;
- have exemplary visibility and clear potential for motivating citizens or alerting similar institutions to reform themselves.

Working within these criteria, the centers will be autonomous. The specific priorities and projects of each center will be determined by its board of directors, which will include a diverse group of Harvard alumni, public interest and private lawyers, and community organizers from that state. A national advisory council, made up of alumni, organizers, and lawyers from across the country, will advise the centers in their areas of expertise and link the centers into a national network.

To carry out its substantive work, each center will hire lawyer-organizers, committed to combining legal advocacy with community organizing. In addition, the centers will establish support networks of local lawyers with expertise in the centers' areas of concern, who will handle projects on their own, or lend their expertise to particular aspects of a project. The centers will also tap the resources and energy of law students who enroll in clinical programs, connecting each center to law schools in their home state.

THE FUTURE

Within a decade, we anticipate that there will be Centers for Law and Justice in more than two dozen states. Under Appleseed's umbrella, the centers will share information and ideas, coordinate strategies, and meet, along with the advisory council, to consider projects that might be undertaken on a national level. Through this organizational network, local efforts can be leveraged into national campaigns with a more powerful impact. With local roots and a national scope, the centers will form a connected movement that is much more than the sum of its parts.

In the past, in times of great social need, individuals have worked creatively and concertedly to make our system more fair and just. Lawyers and organizers—litigating, demonstrating, advocating, and advising for change—have achieved fundamental reforms. Only a generation earlier, few would have imagined it possible that Congress would enact workplace and consumer safety measures, which have dramatically improved peoples' lives. Civil rights laws, enacted only twenty-five years ago, have increased the opportunities available to women, people of color, and other groups suffering discrimination.

Today, similarly fundamental and far-reaching change is both imperative and within our reach. Working creatively, constructively, and systemically, we can generate reforms that will become basic elements of a society that will be better for our efforts. To bring about such change, we must create a new, more expansive vision of the legal system, and the sustaining role we play in it. The Appleseed Foundation represents a historic opportunity to renew our dedication to the law as an agent of change and as a servant of justice.

$\mathcal{N}$otes

1 *Washington Post* editor Bob Woodward, of Watergate reporting fame, told us the following story: William Casey, then the Central Intelligence Agency chief, went to see the *Post's* executive editor, Ben Bradlee, in 1986 and informed him that he would recommend criminal prosecution of the *Post* if it ran a story about certain technical collection capabilities of the National Security Agency, the supersecret federal agency that monitors foreign electronic communications. Edward Bennett Williams served at that time in the following roles: member of President Ronald Reagan's Foreign Intelligence Advisory Board, informal adviser to Casey, legal counsel to *The Washington Post*, and personal counselor to Woodward. Woodward asked Williams, "Ed, how do you possibly sort all this out?" Williams replied, "Bobby, I represent the situation." Williams did resign from the presidential board, and the *Post* did print some of what it had. Woodward says that Williams thought that this straddling of the various parties was the highest aspiration of a lawyer, i.e., to make independent judgments representing all the parties in order to come up with a solution that makes all sides fairly happy. Williams got Casey calmed down, Casey got most of what he wanted, and the *Post* still got some of its story printed.

2 Monroe Freedman, "Brandeis' Lawyer for the Situation," *Legal Times*, April 1, 1996.

3 Ruth Marcus, "Mikva to Take On New Role as Counsel at White House After Court, Hill Career," *The Washington Post*, August 12, 1994.

4 Ruth Marcus and Helen Dewar, "Call for Hearings Grows in Congress," *The Washington Post*, March 9, 1994.

5 Robert Schmidt, "Lloyd Cutler's Deal," *Legal Times*, March 14, 1994.

6 *Ibid*. In fact, one of the authors of this book did publicly object to the arrangement.

7 Ruth Marcus and Dan Balz, "President Picks Capital Insider as Counsel," *The Washington Post*, March 8, 1994; Ruth Marcus, "Cutler's Stance Creates a Stir, Legal Colleagues Angrily Disavow His Public Support for Bork," *The Washington Post*, September 14, 1987.

8 Andrew Ferguson, "Not Ready for Prime Time," *The Washingtonian*, September 1994.

9 Mark J. Green, *The Other Government: The Unseen Power of Washington Lawyers* (New York: Grossman/Viking, 1975), p. 58.

10 Ruth Marcus, "Good Counsel: More Judge than Witness," *The Washington Post*, July 27, 1994.

11 *Ibid*.

12 Stephen Labaton, "Ex-Official Spars with Whitewater Panel," *The New York Times*, November 10, 1995; Letter from Lloyd N. Cutler, "That Was No Whitewater Evasion," *The New York Times*, December 11, 1995.

13 Green, *The Other Government*, p. 58.

14   Public Citizen was founded by Ralph Nader.

15   *Motor Vehicle Manufacturers Assn. v. State Farm Mutual Automobile Ins. Co.*, 463 U.S. 29 (1983).

16   An extensive chronicle of Cutler's advocacy for business groups through the mid-1970s is contained in Green, *The Other Government*.

17   *Ibid.*, pp. 171–80.

18   *Ibid.*

19   Hedrick Smith, *The Power Game* (New York: Random House, 1988), p. 253.

20   *Lloyd Corp. v. Tanner*, 407 U.S. 551 (1972).

21   Saundra Torry, "Two Former FDA Lawyers Come to Tobacco's Defense," *The Washington Post*, May 9, 1994.

22   Green, *The Other Government*, p. 163.

23   *Ibid.*, pp. 119–20.

24   *Ibid.*, p. 117.

25   *Ibid.*, p. 248.

26   John H. Cushman, Jr., "Forced, U.S. Sells Gold Land for Trifle," *The New York Times*, May 17, 1994.

27   Green, *The Other Government*, p. 169.

28   *Ibid.*, p. 243.

29   "The Small World of Big Washington Law Firms," *Fortune*, September 1969.

30   "The Am Law 100 Firms," *The American Lawyer*, July 1995; Margaret Cronin Fisk, "What Lawyers Earn," *The National Law Journal*, July 10, 1995; "Annual Survey of the Nation's Largest Law Firms," *The National Law Journal*, October 3, 1994. When we cite similar facts and figures regarding firm sizes and lawyer earnings elsewhere in the book, we rely on these same sources, unless otherwise noted.

31   "Who Represents Corporate America?" *The National Law Journal*, July 3, 1995; for Covington & Burling's tobacco clients: "Florida Gov. Chiles Cancels Contract with Law Firm over 'Conflict of Interest,' " *Political Finance & Lobby Reporter*, August 9, 1995.

32   Economic census data shows that the legal services industry had $108.4 billion in revenues in 1992. Marianne Lavelle, "Lawyers Are Top Earners," *The National Law Journal*, August 28, 1995.

33   "The Am Law 100 Firms," *The American Lawyer*, July 1995.

34   Fisk, "What Lawyers Earn," *The National Law Journal*, July 10, 1995.

35   "Annual Survey of the Nation's Largest Law Firms," *The National Law Journal*, October 3, 1994.

36   The Joseph and Edna Josephson Institute of Ethics, located in Marina Del Ray, California, is named for Michael Josephson's parents.

37   Michael S. Josephson, interview with authors, February 1, 1994.

38   Steve France, interview with authors, April 13, 1994.

39   Mary Ann Glendon, *A Nation Under Lawyers* (New York: Farrar, Straus and Giroux, 1994).

40   See, for example, the U.S. Supreme Court's decision in *United States v. Zolin*, 491 U.S. 554 (1989).

41   These excerpts from cigarette advertising are found in the Third Circuit Court of Appeals' decision, *Cipollone v. Liggett Group, Inc.*, 893 F.2d 541 (3rd Cir. 1990), affirmed in part and reversed in part, 505 U.S. 504 (1992).

42   *Ibid.* Although the Third Circuit Court of Appeals voided the jury verdict and remanded the case to the district court for a new trial, the appellate judges ruled in Cipollone's favor on a number of issues where Judge Sarokin had instead ruled for the tobacco defendants.

43   *Haines v. Liggett Group, Inc.*, 140 F.R.D 681 (D.N.J. 1992).

44 See *Cipollone v. Liggett Group, Inc.*, 893 F.2d 541 (3rd Cir. 1990), affirmed in part and reversed in part, 505 U.S. 504 (1992).

45 *Cipollone v. Liggett Group, Inc.*, 822 F.2d 335 (3rd Cir. 1987).

46 *The Wall Street Journal*, March 4, 1994.

47 *Cipollone v. Liggett Group, Inc.*, 505 U.S. 504 (1992).

48 *Haines v. Liggett Group, Inc.*, 975 F.2d 81 (3rd Cir. 1992).

49 David Margolick, "Judge Ousted from Tobacco Case over Industry's Complaint of Bias," *The New York Times*, September 9, 1992.

50 *Cipollone v. Liggett Group, Inc.*, 799 F.Supp. 466 (D.N.J. 1992).

51 This account of the Budd Larner firm's hardships relies on Alison Frankel, "Was Budd Larner Another Smoking Victim?" *New Jersey Law Journal*, July 12, 1993, as well as a brief filed by Budd Larner in the U.S. Court of Appeals in the Haines case.

52 Frankel, "Was Budd Larner Another Smoking Victim?" *New Jersey Law Journal*, July 12, 1993.

53 Tracy Schroth, "Sifting Through Cipollone Litigation's Ashes," *The Recorder*, November 18, 1992.

54 Charles Strum, "Major Lawsuit on Smoking Is Dropped," *The New York Times*, November 6, 1992.

55 *Haines v. Liggett Group, Inc.*, 814 F.Supp. 414 (D.N.J. 1993).

56 Patricia Bellew Gray, "Tobacco Firms Defend Smoker Liability Suits with Heavy Artillery," *The Wall Street Journal*, April 29, 1987.

57 *Ibid.*

58 As of October 1995, the highest rate for attorneys at Cravath, Swaine & Moore was reportedly $525 per hour. Karen Dillon, "Dumb and Dumber," *The American Lawyer*, October 1995.

59 Gail Appleson, "U.S. Probe of Tobacco Industry Began in 1992 Case," *The Reuter Business Report*, July 27, 1995.

60 Milo Geyelin and Timothy Noah, "In Fighting the FDA, Tobacco Industry Gets Expert Help from Ex-FDA Lawyers," *The Wall Street Journal*, January 16, 1996.

61 See Lisa Bero, Deborah E. Barnes, Peter Hanauer, John Slade, and Stanton Glantz, "Lawyer Control of the Tobacco Industry's External Research Program," *Journal of the American Medical Association*, July 19, 1995.

62 John Schwartz and Saundra Torry, "Anti-Tobacco Activists Hope to Put Industry's Legal Tactics on Trial," *The Washington Post*, September 26, 1995.

63 Alix M. Freedman, "Tobacco Firm Shows How Ammonia Spurs Delivery of Nicotine," *The Wall Street Journal*, October 18, 1995.

64 John Schwartz, "1973 Cigarette Company Memo Proposed New Brands for Teens," *The Washington Post*, October 4, 1995.

65 "Tobacco Firm's Documents Note Smoking-drug Analogy," *USA Today*, October 6, 1995.

66 Schwartz, "1973 Cigarette Company Memo Proposed New Brands for Teens," *The Washington Post*, October 4, 1995.

67 Ellen J. Silberman, "GOP Senators Grill Outspoken Nominee on Judicial Advocacy," *The Record*, August 4, 1994.

68 Jane Fritsch, "Tobacco Companies Pump Cash into Republican Party's Coffers," *The New York Times*, September 13, 1995.

69 Lana Ambruster, interview with authors, January 18, 1994.

70 *Ibid.*

71 Gary Gwilliam, interview with authors, August 22, 1993.

72 Paul Tobias, interview with authors, October 4, 1994.

73 "Practice Areas of NLJ 250 Law Firms," *The National Law Journal*, October 9, 1995; "Who Represents Corporate America?" *The National Law Journal*, July 3,

1995; Ariel Sabar, "With Workplace Rules in Flux, Littler Plots National Expansion," *The Recorder*, May 15, 1995; Kevin Kelleher, "S. F. Law Firm Employs National Expansion Strategy," *San Francisco Business Times*, May 5, 1995; Julie Triedman, "Labor Lawyers 'R' Us," *The American Lawyer*, January/February 1996; Barbara Steuart, "Littler Opens Atlanta Office," *The Recorder*, March 27, 1996.

74   Quoted in Rich Arthurs, "Unfriendly Climate Leads to New Union Tactics," *Legal Times*, June 4, 1984.

75   *Huettig & Schromm v. Landscape Contractors Council*, 582 F.Supp. 1519 (N.D.Cal. 1984).

76   *Hudson v. Moore Business Forms, Inc.*, 609 F.Supp. 467 (N.D.Cal. 1985), affirmed in part and vacated in part, 836 F.2d 1156 (9th Cir. 1987); subsequent proceeding, 898 F.2d 684 (9th Cir. 1990).

77   *Worrell v. Uniforms To You & Co.*, 673 F.Supp. 1461 (N.D.Cal. 1987).

78   Jorge Aquino, "On the Defensive," *The Recorder*, December 12, 1994; Bill Kisliuk, "Chutzpah and Hardball Mark Littler Malpractice Case," *The Recorder*, August 9, 1994.

79   Stephen G. Hirsch, "Something Nasty in the Air," *The Recorder*, April 28, 1993.

80   Aquino, "On the Defensive."

81   *Tonry v. Security Experts, Inc.*, 20 F.3d 967 (9th Cir. 1994).

82   Aquino, "On the Defensive."

83   *Ibid.*; Hannah Nordhaus, "Firm Is Off the Hook, but Littler's Lawyers Aren't," *The Recorder*, June 13, 1994.

84   Arthurs, "Unfriendly Climate Leads to New Union Tactics."

85   Aquino, "On the Defensive."

86   According to government figures, a total of 143 savings and loans closed between 1934 and 1979. Two hundred and eighty-four closed between 1980 and 1987, and 882 closed between 1988 and 1993. "Recovering From Keating: How His Defrauded Investors Are Faring," *Los Angeles Times*, October 24, 1993.

87   Undated ACC document obtained from the National Association of Securities and Commercial Law Attorneys (NASCAT).

88   *In re American Continental Corporation/Lincoln Savings & Loan Securities Litigation*, CIV 90-0566-70, 74, 90-1270, Reporters Transcript of Proceedings Before Richard M. Bilby, Presiding Judge, Volume 5 (United States District Court for the District of Arizona, March 13, 1992).

89   Rita Henley Jensen, "Jones Day: Behind the Settlement," *The National Law Journal*, July 5, 1993.

90   The federal Office of Thrift Supervision provided us with these figures.

91   *In re American Continental Corporation/Lincoln Savings & Loan Securities Litigation*, CIV 90-0566-70, 74, 90-1270, "Sixth Consolidated Amended Class Action Complaint for Violations of the Security Exchange Act of 1934, The Securities Act of 1933, and the Racketeer Influenced and Corrupt Organizations Act (RICO)."

92   Jensen, "Jones Day: Behind the Settlement."

93   See Susan Beck and Michael Orey, "They Got What They Deserved," *The American Lawyer*, May 1992.

94   Harris Weinstein, "Attorney Liability in the Savings and Loan Crisis," *University of Illinois Law Review*, 1993, p. 53.

95   The regulation is codified at 12 Code of Federal Regulations 563.180(b) (1992).

96   David Margolick, "Last Year the Government Brought a Law Firm to Its Knees. Should It Have?" *The New York Times*, November 26, 1993.

97   Peter Fishbein, interview with authors, August 3, 1994.

98   *Ibid.*

99   Brian Toohey, interview with authors, September 15, 1994.

100 American Bar Association Working Group on Lawyers' Representation of Regulated Clients, "Laborers in Different Vineyards?: The Banking Regulators and the Legal Profession," February 8, 1993.

101 Karen Donovan, "Feud Between Bar and Thrift Officials Continues at ABA," *The National Law Journal*, August 23, 1993.

102 Letter dated August 9, 1993, from Hal R. Lieberman, chief counsel for the Departmental Disciplinary Committee, Supreme Court Appellate Division, First Judicial Department, to Peter M. Fishbein.

103 The American Bar Association has twice developed a code of ethical conduct for lawyers. All states follow some variant of one of these, either the 1969 ABA Model Code of Professional Responsibility or the 1983 Model Rules of Professional Conduct. The classic formulation of the lawyer's duty to a client is in Canon 7 of the Model Code of Professional Responsibility: "A lawyer should represent a client zealously within the bounds of the law." Rule 1.6 of the Model Rules of Professional Conduct forbids a lawyer from revealing confidential information conveyed by a client unless doing so is necessary to prevent the client from committing a criminal act that will result in death or serious bodily injury. Some states that have adopted the Model Rules have amended this provision to permit a lawyer more leeway in exposing ongoing client crimes of various kinds.

Other rules impose demands on lawyers when clients are involved in ongoing misbehavior. Rule 1.2(d) forbids a lawyer from knowingly assisting a client in committing fraud. Rule 1.13 authorizes a lawyer who has discovered an ongoing fraud by a client to try to talk the client out of proceeding. Rule 1.16(a) requires a lawyer to withdraw from representation of a client who is using the lawyer's services to further criminal or fraudulent conduct. Rule 3.3 forbids a lawyer from making false statements or failing to disclose material facts to a tribunal when disclosure is necessary to avoid assisting a criminal or fraudulent act by a client. Rule 3.4 prohibits a lawyer from destroying or falsifying evidence. Rule 4.1 prohibits a lawyer from knowingly making a false statement to a third party. Rule 8.4 prohibits a lawyer from engaging in behavior involving dishonesty, fraud, or deceit.

104 Margolick, "Last Year the Government Brought a Law Firm to Its Knees."

105 Weinstein, "Attorney Liability in the Savings and Loan Crisis."

106 David B. Wilkins, "Making Context Count: Regulating Lawyers after Kaye, Scholer," *The Southern California Law Review*, Vol. 66, No. 3, March 1993.

107 France interview, *supra.*

108 Fishbein interview, *supra.*

109 Sources for penalties and practice restrictions are Rita Henley Jensen, "Jones Day Pact Sets Conditions in Representing Thrifts," *The National Law Journal*, May 3, 1993; Mark Hansen, "Yet Another S & L Settlement: New York Law Firm's Payment of $45 Million Not Quite a Record," *ABA Journal*, January 1994; Susan Beck, "A Look Back at Big Suits," *The American Lawyer*, March 1994; Robyn Meredith, "OTS Seeks $18.6 Million from Ex-Thrift Director," *The American Banker*, March 24, 1994; "The 'Keating Six'" *The National Journal*, September 26, 1992; Stephanie B. Goldberg, "Kaye Scholer: The Tremors Continue Part I," *ABA Journal*, July 1992.

110 Karen Dillon, "Brand Names at the Brink," *The American Lawyer*, May 1995.

111 John Kaplan, "That's How the Money Changes Hands," *The New York Times Book Review*, January 27, 1985; Jacob A. Stein, "Real Litigators of the '80s Also Wouldn't Eat Quiche," *Legal Times*, February 21, 1983; Joseph W. Cotchett with Stephen P. Pizzo, *The Ethics Gap* (Carlsbad, CA: Parker & Son Publications, Inc., 1991).

112 See Claudia MacLachlan, "Butler Knows His ABCs and CBSs," *The National Law Journal*, August 14, 1995.

113 "The Best Paid Corporate Lawyers," *Forbes*, October 16, 1989.

114 Dillon, "Brand Names at the Brink."

115 "The 1994 Power List," *The National Law Journal*, April 4, 1994; Margaret Cronin Fisk, "Profiles in Power: The 100 Most Influential Lawyers in America," *The National Law Journal*, March 25, 1991; Emily Couric, "Profiles in Power," *The National Law Journal*, May 2, 1988; Emily Couric, "Profiles in Power," *The National Law Journal*, April 15, 1985.

116 See Edward T. Pound, *The Wall Street Journal*, April 27, 1984; Lyn Bixby, "Arms Exports Grounded in the Dirty Deal of Traders," *The Hartford Courant*, October 27, 1992.

117 "Who Represents Corporate America?" *The National Law Journal*, July 3, 1995.

118 Robert J. Beck, "OGJ300 Population Shrinks, but Assets Total Grows," *Oil & Gas Journal*, September 4, 1995.

119 Quoted in "Former Ashland VP Alleges Improper Transactions," *Platt's Oilgram News*, December 17, 1984.

120 United Press International, West Virginia Editorial Roundup, wire compilation, January 8, 1988.

121 "Moore Has Colorful History of Controversy, Investigations," United Press International wire story, April 12, 1990.

122 Zachary Schiller, "Ashland Just Can't Seem to Leave Its Checkered Past Behind," *Business Week*, October 31, 1988.

123 "Ashland's Days in Court," *Platt's Oilgram News*, January 10, 1991; United Press International, West Virginia Editorial Roundup, wire compilation, January 8, 1988.

124 See "Judge Denies Request to Add Defendants to Ashland Suit," *The Sunday Gazette Mail* (Charleston, W. Va.), April 17, 1994; "Ashland Settles 96% of Refinery Lawsuits," *The Oil Daily*, February 23, 1993; "Ashland Settles Emissions Lawsuits," United Press International wire story, February 22, 1993.

125 See "Atkins Given Probation for Ashland Scam," *Los Angeles Times*, December 1, 1990; Stephen Labaton, "Ex-Ashland Chief Pleads Guilty," *The New York Times*, September 15, 1989.

126 This account of the payments by Ashland and their repercussions draws on information contained in Robert Safian, "Say It Ain't So, SAM," *The American Lawyer*, November 1988. It also incorporates information from the following: Zachary Schiller, "Ashland Just Can't Seem to Leave Its Checkered Past Behind," *Business Week*, October 31, 1988; Morton Mintz, "SEC Draws Fire for Handling of Bribery Charges Against Ashland Oil After Private Lawsuits Succeed," *The Washington Post*, July 10, 1988; Terry Carter, "What Did Ashland's Lawyer Know," *The National Law Journal*, June 27, 1988; Morton Mintz, "How Saudi Businessman in McLean Put Oil Company in Quandary," *The Washington Post*, August 23, 1987; Morton Mintz, "$17 Million in Fees Prompt Allegations of Kickbacks," *The Washington Post*, August 16, 1987; Morton Mintz, "Scarce Oil, Disputed Deals—and a Corporate Revolt," *The Washington Post*, August 9, 1987; and letter from Morton Mintz to authors, November 11, 1995.

127 "Who Has the Chairman's Ear? Fortune 250 Companies with Directors from Law Firms the Company Uses," *Corporate Legal Times*, January 1995; "Who Represents Corporate America," *The National Law Journal*, July 3, 1995. A comment included with the American Bar Association's 1983 Model Rules of Professional Conduct, Rule 1.7, provides the following ethical guidelines with respect to this issue:

> A lawyer for a corporation or other organization who is also a member of its board of directors should determine whether the responsibilities of

the two roles may conflict. The lawyer may be called on to advise the corporation in matters involving actions of the directors. Consideration should be given to the frequency with which such situations may arise, the potential intensity of the conflict, the effect of the lawyer's resignation from the board and the possibility of the corporation's obtaining legal advice from another lawyer in such situations. If there is material risk that the dual role will compromise the lawyer's independence of professional judgment, the lawyer should not serve as a director.

CHAPTER 2: I'VE GOT A SECRET

1 Nicole Schultheis and Arthur Bryant, "Unnecessary Secrecy in Civil Litigation: Combating the Threat to Effective Self-Governance," *Journal of Contemporary Legal Issues*, Vol. 3, No. 1 (Fall 1991). Nicole Schultheis is a lawyer who practices in Baltimore, Maryland. Arthur Bryant is the executive director of Trial Lawyers for Public Justice.

2 Leonard Schroeter, interview with authors, February 22, 1994.

3 Federal Rule of Civil Procedure 26(c).

4 GM eventually agreed to a settlement of the Green case on terms that are confidential.

5 *Confidentiality Orders* (New York: John Wiley & Sons, Inc., 1988).

6 *Republic of the Philippines* v. *Westinghouse Electric Corporation*, 949 F.2d 653 (3rd Cir. 1991).

7 Public Citizen and Essential Information are public advocacy nonprofit organizations based in Washington, D.C. Both were founded by Ralph Nader.

8 An intervenor is a person or entity that claims an interest in the subject matter of a lawsuit and therefore seeks to be heard and obtain relief from the court. In this matter, the intervenors did not have a direct interest in whether Westinghouse bribed President Marcos but intervened as organizations with an interest in investigating and disclosing corporate corruption.

9 *Republic of the Philippines* v. *Westinghouse Electric Corporation*, 139 F.R.D. 50 (D.N.J. 1991).

10 *Republic of the Philippines* v. *Westinghouse Electric Corporation*, 949 F.2d 653 (3rd Cir. 1991).

11 See *Republic of the Philippines* v. *Westinghouse Electric Corporation*, 43 F.3d 65 (3rd Cir. 1994); Fred Pieretti, "Jury: Westinghouse Did Not Bribe Philippine President Marcos," Associated Press wire story, May 18, 1993; Jeffrey Kanige, "Jury Clears Westinghouse in Marcos Bribery Case," *New Jersey Law Journal*, May 24, 1993.

12 "Westinghouse Makes First Payment in Nuclear Plant Settlement," Associated Press wire story, October 25, 1995; "Westinghouse Settles Row on Philippine Nuclear Plant," *Asian Economic News*, October 23, 1995.

13 *Sieracki* v. *Ford Motor Company*, slip op. (S.D.Ill. June 6, 1978).

14 E. S. Grush and C. S. Saunby, "Fatalities Associated with Crash Induced Fuel Leakage and Fires," Ford Department of Environmental and Safety Engineering Inter-Office Memorandum, undated. The Ford memo purportedly relied on NHTSA calculations for the $200,000 figure, but NHTSA officials later criticized the use of this formula; they said it was intended only to estimate a person's productivity, not his or her overall value to society. Elsa Walsh and Benjamin Weiser, "Court Secrecy Masks Safety Issues; Key GM Fuel Tank Memos Kept Hidden in Auto Crash Suits," *The Washington Post*, October 23, 1988.

15 Mark Dowie, "Pinto Madness," *Mother Jones*, September–October 1977.

16   Walsh and Weiser, "Court Secrecy Masks Safety Issues," *The Washington Post*, October 23, 1988.

17   *The Chicago Reporter*, Vol. 20, No. 6, June 1991.

18   James Ylisela, Jr., interview with authors, November 24, 1993.

19   The Illinois CUB is a citizens group advocating before regulatory agencies and the courts on behalf of residential ratepayers in matters related to telephone, gas, and electric services. The Illinois CUB was created by the legislature but is funded by citizen donations. Other CUBs exist in Wisconsin, New York, Oregon, and in San Diego, California.

20   Martin Cohen, interview with authors, November 24, 1993.

21   In many cases involving personal injury or wrongful death, plaintiffs' lawyers work on a contingency fee basis, in which they usually earn a percentage, typically one third, of the actual amount collected from the defendant. If the plaintiff recovers nothing, the plaintiff's attorney receives nothing.

22   Bill Lockyear, interview with authors, August 6, 1993.

23   Leroy Hersh, interview with authors, January 27, 1994.

24   Dan Bolton, interview with authors, January 4, 1994.

25   *Ibid.*

26   Sybil Goldrich, interviews with authors, December 12, 1993, and July 7, 1995.

27   "A Restoration Drama," *Ms.*, June 1988.

28   Sybil Goldrich interview, July 7, 1995.

29   The major U.S. breast implant manufacturers were: Baxter Healthcare Corporation, Bioplasty Inc., Cox-Uphoff (CUI), Dow Corning, McGhan Medical Inc., Mentor, and Surgitek. The breakdown of complaints was as follows:
     —Dow Corning: 16,232 complaints (60.92% of all complaints received).
     —Surgitek (Bristol-Myers): 5,263 complaints (19.75%).
     —Baxter: 1,716 complaints (6.44%).
     —McGhan: 1,709 complaints (6.41%).
     —Mentor: 1,065 complaints (6.41%).
     —CUI: 490 complaints (1.84%).
     —Bioplasty: 169 complaints (.63%).

30   Paul Valentine, "Implant Maker Loses Bid to Block FDA," *The Washington Post*, February 15, 1992.

31   *Hopkins v. Dow Corning Corp.*, 33 F. 3d 1116 (9th Cir. 1994).

32   Statement by David A. Kessler before the Subcommittee on Human Resources and Intergovernmental Relations, Committee on Government Reform and Oversight, U.S. House of Representatives, August 1, 1995. See also Marcia Angell, "Are Breast Implants Actually OK?" *The New Republic*, September 11, 1995, p. 17.

33   ABC News *Nightline*, August 17, 1995, transcript.

34   "A New Study of Breast Implants Says Gel on the Surface Indicates a Rupture," *The New York Times*, November 28, 1995.

35   Nancy Hersh, interview with authors, January 27, 1994.

36   Ralph Nader, *Unsafe at Any Speed: The Designed-in Dangers of the American Automobile* (New York: Knightsbridge Publishing Co., 1991); *Auto Safety Oversight Hearing—Corvair Heater: Hearing Before the Senate Committee on Commerce*, 92nd Cong., 1st Sess. (1972).

37   Federal government regulations are promulgated by regulatory agencies such as the National Highway Traffic Safety Administration for automobiles and the Federal Aviation Administration for aviation. Most rules become law in the following manner: An agency publishes a Notice of Proposed Rule Making in a daily publication called the Federal Register. The public, including regulated industry

groups and concerned nonprofits, then has an opportunity to comment on the proposed rules. A final rule, if the agency decides to issue one, may be identical to the proposed rule or it may be modified. In this case, the agency decided not to issue any rear shoulder belt rule.

38 Jim Miller, interview with authors, August 3, 1993.

39 *Ibid.*

40 Patricia Miller, interview with authors, August 3, 1993.

41 Letter from Craig R. McClellan, attorney at law, to Roswell Page III, attorney at law, March 20, 1990.

42 Letter from Roswell Page III to Craig R. McClellan, March 25, 1990.

43 Letter from Craig R. McClellan to Roswell Page III, March 29, 1990.

44 Jim Miller interview, *supra.*

45 *Decker v. American Motors Corp.*, Case No. 474278, Superior Court of San Diego County, State of California.

46 *Wilson v. American Motors Corp.*, 759 F. 2d 1568 (11th Cir. 1985).

47 "New Ruling Lifts Veil of Secrecy in Civil Cases," *Los Angeles Times*, September 9, 1990.

48 Judith McConnell, interview with authors, November 30, 1994.

49 Marlin Applewick, interview with authors, March 22, 1994.

50 Letter in opposition to SB711, a California state senate bill that would have made it more difficult to agree to a confidential settlement, June 7, 1991. The American Tort Reform Association has more than 375 members, including: Aetna Insurance, Bethlehem Steel Corporation, Boeing Company, Clorox Company, Dow Chemical Company, Eli Lilly and Company, Exxon Company, U.S.A., GEICO, General Electric Company, Hartford Insurance Company, Liberty Mutual Insurance Company, Litton Industries, Inc., March & McClennan Worldwide, Merck & Company, Inc., Minnesota Mining & Manufacturing Company, Monsanto Company, Pfizer, Inc., Rockwell International, Sears, Roebuck & Company, State Farm Insurance Companies, TRW Inc., Transamerica Insurance Company, Travelers Companies, and Union Carbide Corporation. See John Gannon, "Tort Deform: Lethal Bedfellows," paper published by Essential Information, Washington, D.C., 1995.

51 February 24, 1992.

52 April 5, 1992.

53 March 9, 1993.

54 January 21, 1992.

55 January 15, 1992.

CHAPTER 3: THE OBSTRUCTIONISTS

1 Roscoe Pound, later to become dean of the Harvard Law School, criticized this "sporting theory of justice" in a famous 1906 speech that helped trigger subsequent legal reforms. R. Pound, "The Causes of Popular Dissatisfaction with the Administration of Justice," 29 American Bar Assn. Reports 395 (1906).

2 *Hickman v. Taylor*, 329 U.S. 495, 507 (1947).

3 *United States v. Procter & Gamble*, 356 U.S. 677 (1958).

4 Robert Aronson, interview with authors, March 14, 1994.

5 Jim Butler, interview with authors, May 23, 1994.

6 Stephen Gillers, interview with authors, April 29, 1994.

7 Ted Schneyer, interview with authors, May 2, 1994.

8 Geoffrey Hazard, interview with authors, March 16, 1994.

9   Model Code Disciplinary Rule 7-109(A).

10 Gillers interview, *supra*.

11 Aronson interview, *supra*.

12 The following account of the litigation is based on interviews with plaintiff's lawyer Lynne Bernabei and on Sarah M. Hodder and Jonathan Groner, "Discovery Spat Erupts in Charges," *Legal Times*, December 20, 1993.

13 *Anderson v. Children's National Medical Center*, Plaintiff's Motion for Order to Show Cause Why Default Judgment Should Not Be Entered Against Defendant for Serious Abuse of the Discovery Process and Motion for Evidentiary Hearing.

14 This authority derives from the Federal Rules of Civil Procedure, particularly Rule 37, and from the inherent power of federal judges, see *Chambers v. NASCO, Inc.*, 501 U.S. 32, 46 (1991). The Federal Rules of Civil Procedure are rules enacted by the Supreme Court that govern the various aspects of federal litigation: filing complaints and motions, engaging in discovery, etc. Congress can amend the rules by legislation. Each state has similar rules to govern procedures in its courts.

15 *Anderson v. Children's National Medical Center*, Transcript of Evidentiary Hearing, Testimony of Mary C. Dollarhide-Lutz, February 23, 1994.

16 In most cases, defendants have the right to remove cases from the state or local court and send it to federal court if federal law would have permitted a plaintiff's claims to have been brought in federal court in the first place. 28 United States Code section 1441.

17 *Shepherd v. ABC*, 151 F.R.D. 194 (D.D.C. 1993).

18 *Shepherd v. ABC*, 862 F.Supp. 486 (D.D.C. 1994).

19 "The District's Largest Law Offices," *Legal Times*, September 25, 1995.

20 *Shepherd v. ABC*, No. 94-7141, No. 94-7186 (D.C.Cir., slip op. Aug. 25, 1995).

21 Benjamin Weiser, "ABC and Tobacco: The Anatomy of a Network News Mistake," *The Washington Post*, January 7, 1996.

22 Mark Landler, "ABC News Settles Suits on Tobacco," *The New York Times*, August 22, 1995.

23 ABC was represented in the cigarette litigation by Wilmer, Cutler & Pickering. But "sources" told the journal *Legal Times* that Wilmer, Cutler lawyers were "itching" to go to trial rather than settle the case. *Legal Times* reported that because of potential conflicts between ABC's interests and those of the reporter and the producer on the offending news report, settlement talks were conducted by ABC's in-house general counsel, Alan Braverman. Braverman was previously a partner at Wilmer, Cutler & Pickering. "Inadmissible," *Legal Times*, August 28, 1995.

       A brief filed by Wilmer, Cutler prior to settlement, sealed by the court but later obtained by *Legal Times* and posted on the Internet, used Philip Morris documents disclosed through the litigation to show that the company added a nicotine-containing solution to batches of its tobacco. The brief also charged that fourteen months after the judge in the case had ordered disclosure of documents, Philip Morris had failed to fully comply. *Philip Morris v. American Broadcasting Company*, Virginia Circuit Court for the City of Richmond, No. 760CL94X00816-00, Defendants' Memorandum in Support of Summary Judgment, July 10, 1995. Philip Morris continues to deny manipulating nicotine levels.

24 *Malautea v. Suzuki Motor Corp.*, 148 F.R.D. 362 (S.D.Ga. 1991), affirmed, 987 F.2d 1536 (11th Cir.), cert. denied, 114 S.Ct. 181 (1993).

25 Bill Rankin, "Suzuki Decides to Fight, Loses," *The National Law Journal*, July 24, 1995.

26 Benjamin Weiser, "Judge Imposes a Rare Sanction on GM in Upcoming Pickup Truck Trial," *The Washington Post*, September 10, 1995.

27 In the month of August 1995, Judge Burrage had issued a series of rulings adverse to GM. He directed GM to produce a wide range of documents requested by the Bishops' lawyers, including copies of all settlement checks paid in other cases involving the GM pickups and GM records regarding proposed modifications in the design of its pickups. He also denied GM's motion to prevent a former GM engineer, Ronald Elwell, from testifying at trial. Chapter 6 details GM's many efforts to keep Elwell out of court.

28 *Rozier v. Ford Motor Co.*, 573 F.2d 1332 (5th Cir. 1978).

29 James B. Stewart, *The Partners* (New York: Simon and Schuster, 1983).

30 With new lawyers representing Kodak, the antitrust verdict was later reversed on appeal.

31 David Margolick, "The Long Road Back for a Disgraced Patrician," *The New York Times*, January 19, 1990.

32 Bruce Schafer, interview with authors, March 22, 1994.

33 James Lobsenz, interview with authors, March 9, 1994.

34 Schafer interview, *supra.*

35 *Ibid.*

36 Aronson interview, *supra.*

37 Stuart Taylor, Jr., "Sleazy in Seattle," *The American Lawyer*, April 1994.

38 *Washington State Physicians Insurance Exchange & Association v. Fisons Corporation*, 858 P. 2d 1054 (Wash. 1993). The court also ruled that it was improper for the trial judge to allow the parade of lawyers to offer testimony as expert witnesses on the law itself. The judge, aided by the arguments of the attorneys for the parties, is supposed to be the resident expert on the law.

39 Schafer interview, *supra.*

40 Lobsenz interview, *supra.*

41 Butler and his firm have also been charged with discovery misconduct resulting from their efforts to unearth and introduce evidence of corporate wrongdoing. Butler was fined $100 by the trial judge in the Malautea case for "attempting to compel a non-party law firm to produce documents which they knew had been sealed." In 1994, a Michigan federal judge charged that Butler's firm had obtained a document in violation of a protective order, *Grace v. Center for Auto Safety*, 155 F.R.D. 591 (E.D.Mich. 1994), a charge Butler denies. The decision is being appealed. See Ann Woolner, "Firm in GM-Moseley Case Is Banned in Boston," *The Recorder*, February 3, 1995.

42 Aronson interview, *supra.*

43 Ann Pelham, "Forcing Litigants to Share," *Legal Times*, May 3, 1993.

44 Randall Samborn, "Districts' Discovery Rules Differ," *The National Law Journal*, November 14, 1994.

45 Gillers interview, *supra.*

46 In 1986, state legislation established the position of California State Bar Discipline Monitor. The bar discipline monitor was given the task of analyzing the state bar's system of receiving, investigating, prosecuting, and adjudicating complaints against licensed attorneys by that state's attorney general and directed to make recommendations for legislative and administrative changes to improve the bar's discipline system.

47 Robert C. Fellmeth, "Final Report of the State Bar Discipline Monitor," *The California Regulatory Law Reporter*, Vol. 11, No. 4 (Fall 1991).

48 Schneyer interview, *supra.*

49 Berkeley Rice, "Why You Aren't Shielded from the Law's Bad Apples," *Medical Economics*, July 20, 1992.

50 Stewart, *The Partners.*

51 Mark J. Green, *The Other Government: The Unseen Power of Lawyers in Washington* (New York: Grossman/Viking, 1975).

52 Mary Ann Glendon, *A Nation Under Lawyers: How the Crisis in the Legal Profession Is Transforming American Society* (New York: Farrar, Straus and Giroux, 1994).

CHAPTER 4: BURNING THE TAPES

1 "Comment," *The New Yorker*, August 21 & 28, 1995; Kaye Northcott, "I Reminded Everybody of Lyndon," *The New York Times Book Review*, November 26, 1989.

2 ABC News *Primetime Live*, June 6, 1991, transcript.

3 Steve Berg, "Buchanan's ideas for the judiciary would alter Constitution," *Star Tribune* (Minneapolis), February 25, 1996.

4 Phil Gailey, "Behind the Scene with Ed Williams," *The New York Times Magazine*, April 17, 1983. In the article, Williams justified this approach as follows: "I would have advised [Nixon], before [the tapes] were ever called for, before they were ever subject to any subpoena, to make a public disposition of these things. It would have had to be premised on the fact that there were all kinds of state secrets, private conversations with heads of state that would be embarrassing to the United States worldwide if exposed. So the tapes would have to be destroyed for national security reasons." The article quotes Yale Kamisar, a University of Michigan law professor with expertise in criminal and constitutional law, as responding: "I think it would have been unethical, even though it would be difficult to prove the real reasons for destroying the tapes. I hate to say this, because I am a great admirer of Edward Bennett Williams. First of all, he would have been misrepresenting the real reasons for burning the tapes. It would have had nothing to do with national security. It would have been to put his client in a better position to prevail in a lying contest."

5 *Litton Systems, Inc. v. AT&T*, 91 F.R.D. 574 (S.D.N.Y. 1981).

6 *Combating Stonewalling and Other Discovery Abuses* (Washington: ATLA Press, 1994). Quote is from prepublication manuscript.

7 Charles R. Nesson, "Incentives to Spoliate Evidence in Civil Litigation: The Need for Vigorous Judicial Action," *Cardozo Law Review*, Vol. 13 (1991).

8 *Fortune*, April 18, 1994.

9 *McGuire v. Sigma Coatings, Inc.*, case number 91-2076, slip op. (E.D.La. Aug. 19, 1993).

10 *McGuire v. Sigma Coatings, Inc.*, slip op. (E.D.La. Oct. 29, 1993).

11 Jonathan Andry, interview with authors, June 15, 1994.

12 James Veach, interview with authors, June 1995.

13 Letter from Marilee Neff, Regional Counsel, Office of the Chief Disciplinary Counsel, State Bar of Texas, to James L. Veach, dated March 4, 1994.

14 *McGuire v. Sigma Coatings, Inc.*, slip op. (E.D.La. March 25, 1994).

15 *McGuire v. Sigma Coatings, Inc.*, 48 F.3d 902 (5th Cir. 1995).

16 Andry interview, *supra*.

17 James Gilbert, interview with authors, 1994.

18 Ted Schneyer, interview with authors, May 2, 1994.

19 Model Rules of Professional Conduct Rule 3.4 and comment (1992).

20 Moreover, in the section of the memo discussing how Westinghouse should decide which records to destroy, Bair listed a series of questions, including:

1. What are the chances of litigation? Is it pending or imminent?
2. In case of litigation, which party would have the burden of proof?
3. When does the statute of limitations run? . . .

5.   What records is the corporation required to maintain pursuant to law?

Whether these questions, in the aggregate, demonstrate a responsible recognition of Westinghouse's obligations to preserve relevant documents or, instead, signify additional concern about keeping embarrassing documents is not entirely clear. But giving Bair the benefit of the doubt, and assuming he was laying out appropriate guidelines for applying legal obligations to document retention, his blanket recommendation—to purge all older files—does not follow. Any responsible review under such guidelines would have resulted in much more detailed recommendations.

21   The New Jersey case was *Cerka v. A.C.&S., Inc.*, docket number L 13639-81 (Superior Ct., Middlesex Co.). The Texas case was *Dashko v. Fibreboard Corp.*, docket number 91-14798 (District Ct., Travis Co.). See Andrew Blum, "Westinghouse Loses on Papers," *The National Law Journal*, March 22, 1993; "New Jersey Judge Releases Westinghouse Memo Advising Destruction of Harmful Documents," *BNA Occupational Safety & Health Daily*, March 12, 1993.

22   From the cases in which courts have punished parties or attorneys for spoliation, it appears that defendants or defense lawyers are more likely to engage in the misconduct than plaintiffs or their attorneys, particularly in the personal injury area. For as attorney Leonard Schroeter notes, defendants "are the actors. The victims are often passive, who haven't done anything. In such cases, it is the corporations that have something to hide."

23   J. Patrick Wright, *On a Clear Day You Can See General Motors: John Z. DeLorean's Look Inside the Automotive Giant* (New York: Avon Books, 1979), p. 61.

24   John DeLorean, interview with authors, May 21, 1996; memorandum from John Z. DeLorean to Thomas A. Murphy, December 1972, obtained by authors; C. D. Bohon, "The Safety War," *Dealer Business*, August 1993; see also Wright, *On a Clear Day, supra.*

25   Philip Lacovara, interview with authors, 1994.

26   Schneyer interview, *supra.*

27   Claudia Maclachlan, "Bone Screw Suit Places FDA In 4-Way Squeeze," *The National Law Journal*, January 8, 1996.

28   Charles R. Nesson, interview with authors, June 20, 1994.

29   *Ibid.*

30   Stephen Gillers, interview with authors, April 29, 1994.

31   Nesson interview, *supra.*

32   *Ibid.*

33   All of these states impose liability where spoliation is intentional. Two of the states, California and Florida, also recognize the tort of negligent spoliation, i.e., destroying of evidence due to failure to exercise reasonable care to avoid such destruction.

34   Trudy Maran, interview with authors, December 1, 1993.

35   *Kelly v. New Jersey University of Medicine and Dentistry Hospital, et al.*, Docket No. UNN-L-03532-89 (N.J.Super.Ct. Law Div.).

36   This is the same firm that represented plaintiffs in the tobacco litigation discussed in Chapter 1.

37   Maran interview, *supra*; see also Jeffrey Kanige, "Battle Over Missing Evidence: Was It Spoliation," *New Jersey Law Journal*, May 4, 1992.

38   *Viviano v. CBS*, 597 A.2d 543 (N.J.Super.Ct.App.Div. 1991).

39   One of the hospital's defenses was that they believed the child's lungs were too immature to withstand a cesarean, making the lung tests vital evidence.

40   Maran interview, *supra.*

CHAPTER 5: SLAPP: TAKING CARE OF BUSINESS

1   Richard Spohn, interview with authors, May 16, 1995.
2   Michael Josephson, interview with authors, February 1, 1994.
3   Walter and Alice Mosher, interview with authors, November 23, 1993.
4   Jane Haines, interview with authors, November 23, 1993.
5   Letter from Lloyd W. Lowrey, attorney at law, to Jane Haines, attorney at law, April 18, 1990.
6   Mosher interview, *supra*.
7   Lloyd Lowrey, interview with authors, June 28, 1994.
8   Haines interview, *supra*.
9   See George W. Pring and Penelope Canan, *SLAPPs: Getting Sued for Speaking Out* (Philadelphia: Temple University Press, 1996); Penelope Canan, Michael Hennessy, and George W. Pring, "The Chilling Effect of Slapp's," *Research in Political Sociology*, Vol. 6 (1993).
10 George Pring, interview with authors, October 28, 1994.
11 Penelope Canan, interview with authors, October 28, 1994.
12 Lowrey interview, *supra*.
13 Ralph Wegis, interview with authors, August 23, 1994.
14 *Ibid*.
15 Jack Thomson, interview with authors, November 14, 1994.
16 *Ibid*.
17 *Thomson v. J.G. Boswell Co.*, No. F011230, slip. op. (Cal.Ct.App., 1986).
18 Edmond Constantini and Mary Paul Nash, "SLAPP/SLAPPback: The Misuse of Libel Law for Political Purposes and a Countersuit Response," *The Journal of Law & Politics*, Vol. 7, No. 3 (Spring 1991), pp. 461–62.
19 *J.G. Boswell v. Wegis*, 502 U.S. 1097 (1992) (denying petition for writ of certiorari).
20 Thomson interview, *supra*.
21 Howard Kim, "Accusations Against Humana Trigger Lawsuit," *Modern Healthcare*, May 19, 1989.
22 *Humana v. Hemmeter*, case number A274231, District Court, Clark County, Nevada, special verdict forms, November 25, 1991.
23 *Neal v. Griepentrog*, 837 P.2d 432 (November 1992).
24 *Leonardini v. Shell Oil Company*, Case Number 310945 (Cal. Superior Court), Reporter's Transcript.
25 *Leonardini v. Shell Oil Company*, 216 Cal.App. 3d 547 (Cal.Ct.App. 1989), cert. denied, 498 U.S. 919 (1990).
26 Mary Ann Galante, " 'Intimidated' Lawyer Wins $5.2M; Malicious Prosecution Claimed," *The National Law Journal*, May 12, 1986.
27 *Leonardini v. Shell Oil Company*, *supra*.
28 *Leonardini v. Shell Oil Company*, 39 Daily Journal D.A.R. 14860. (This portion of the opinion was not certified for publication and therefore is not contained in the casebooks.)
29 Raymond Leonardini, interview with authors, December 13, 1994.
30 See ABA Model Rules of Professional Conduct, Preamble and Rule 3.1, ABA Model Code of Professional Responsibility, DR 7-102(A)(1).
31 "Suits by Firms Exceed Those by Individuals," *Wall Street Journal*, December 3, 1993.
32 In fact, there were at least four lawsuits between Alcon and Surgin in the years 1989–90. In April 1989, Surgin sued Alcon for alleged defamation in connection with a Surgin product. Alcon filed related counterclaims against Surgin. Alcon then sued Surgin for patent infringement over another Surgin product. A month

after that, Alcon filed its patent suit over the cassette. Alcon subsequently withdrew this last complaint, only to file a new suit, with the same claims, in July 1990.

33 Armand Maaskamp, interview with authors, May 26, 1994.

34 *Ibid.*

35 Daniel Callahan, interview with authors, May 12, 1994.

36 *Recombinant Bovine Growth Hormone—FDA Approval Should Be Withheld Until the Mastitis Issue Is Resolved*, Government Accounting Office, August 1992.

37 "Consumers Union Denies 'Backing Off' On rBST," *Food & Drink Daily*, April 5, 1995.

38 "Interim Guidance on the Voluntary Labeling of Milk and Milk Products From Cows That Have Not Been Treated With Recombinant Bovine Somatotropin," *Federal Register*, Vol. 59, No. 28, Thursday, February 10, 1994, pp. 6,279–80.

39 Benjamin F. Yale, interview with authors, June 6, 1995.

40 Jim Hightower, "Monsanto: Pushing BGH On Our Kids," *The Daily Citizen*, April 28, 1994.

CHAPTER 6: THE GAMES CORPORATE LAWYERS PLAY

1 Source: Center for Auto Safety, Washington, D.C.

2 *In re: General Motors Corporation Pick-up Truck Fuel Tank Products Liability Litigation*, 55 F.3d 768 (3d Cir. 1995).

3 The Center for Auto Safety was founded by Ralph Nader and Consumers Union in 1970. It is now independent of its founders. Clarence Ditlow has been its director since 1975.

4 Center for Auto Safety, *Impact*, Vol. 18, No. 1 (September–October 1992).

5 *General Motors Corporation v. Moseley*, 447 S.E.2d 302 (Ga.App. 1994).

6 See S. Richard Gard, Jr., editor, *Side Impact: How a Jury Slammed General Motors for $105 Million* (The American Lawyer Media, 1993).

7 Trisha Renaud, "Silenced GM Engineer Still in Great Demand," *Texas Lawyer*, September 27, 1993.

8 See "Constitutional Law," *The Connecticut Law Tribune*, February 20, 1995 (reporting Connecticut Superior Court decision that upheld plaintiff's right to take Elwell's testimony and noted that twelve of fourteen federal and state court judges who had considered the issue had done the same). Clarence Ditlow of the Center for Auto Safety reports that, as of August 1995, twenty-three courts had refused to follow the Michigan order barring Elwell's testimony.

9 Renaud, "Silenced GM Engineer Still in Great Demand," *Texas Lawyer*, September 27, 1993.

10 *Side Impact, supra.*

11 Andrew Blum, "Halcion Stirs Litigation Storm," *The National Law Journal*, April 11, 1994, citing "European press accounts" for the $8 million figure.

12 Edward Kellogg, interview with authors, June 23, 1994.

13 Gina Kolata, "Maker of Sleeping Pill Hid Data on Side Effects, Researchers Say," *The New York Times*, January 20, 1992.

14 Steven R. Reed, "Sleep Merchants: The Halcion Story," *The Houston Chronicle*, September 14, 1994.

15 The British authorities informed Upjohn that they had banned Halcion because "the risk/benefit ratio of [the drug] is unacceptable" and because "Incomplete information on adverse effects and withdrawals from clinical trials was provided in the original product license application." Letter from the British Licensing Authority dated July 17, 1992.

16 *The Upjohn Co. & Another* v. *Oswald*, judgment, In the High Court of Justice, Queen's Bench Division, Case Nos. 1992-U-No. 111; 1992-D-No. 625; 1992-U-No. 112, May 27, 1994.

17 Ian Oswald, interview with authors, July 22, 1994.

18 See Public Citizen, *Petition for Revision of Doctor and Patient Labeling of Triazolam*, April 19, 1990.

19 Michael Mosher, interview with authors, November 23, 1993.

20 Blum, "Halcion Stirs Litigation Storm," *National Law Journal*, April 11, 1994.

21 The classic article on how competing state law efforts to curry favor with corporate management create a "race to the bottom" is William Cary, "Federalism and Corporate Law: Reflections Upon Delaware," 83 *Yale Law Journal* 663 (1974).

22 Karen Donovan, "Shareholders' Advocates Protest Justice's Removal," *The National Law Journal*, June 6, 1994; John Close, "Justice Denied in Delaware," *The American Lawyer*, July/August 1994.

23 "Excerpts: The Controversial Del. Court Nomination," *The National Law Journal*, July 11, 1994.

24 *Ibid.*

25 Diana B. Henriques, "Top Business Court Under Fire; Critics Say Politics Is Hurting Delaware Judiciary," *The New York Times*, May 23, 1995.

26 *Ibid.*

27 *Ibid.*

28 Carl DiOrio, "Perelman Deal for Technicolor Cleared in Court," *The Hollywood Reporter*, July 19, 1995.

29 *Cinerama, Inc.* v. *Technicolor, Inc.*, 634 A.2d 345 (Del. 1993).

30 *Cinerama, Inc.* v. *Technicolor, Inc.*, 663 A.2d 1156 (Del. 1995).

31 John Close, "When Moore Is Less," CCM: *The American Lawyer's Corporate Counsel Magazine*, November 1995.

32 John Godfrey, interview with authors, May 1995.

33 *McGuire* v. *Sigma Coatings, Inc.*, slip op. (E.D.La. January 19, 1994).

34 On this basis, GM later convinced the Georgia Court of Appeals that Kashmerick's taped testimony should not have been viewed by the jury in the Moseley case. *GMC* v. *Moseley*, 447 S.E.2d 302, 308 (Ga.Ct. App. 1994).

35 Bryan Gruley, "Suits Over GM Pickups Could Cost It Billions," Gannett News Service wire story, February 21, 1994.

36 *Cameron* v. *General Motors*, slip op. (D.S.C. February 23, 1994).

37 *Ibid.* The lengthy opinion was a substantial effort, especially considering that both of Judge Anderson's law clerks were unable to assist him. Each had already accepted, prior to the filing of the Cameron suit, future employment with, and received $2,500 "stipends" from, a South Carolina firm that represents GM. Bryan Gruley, "Judge: GM May Have Committed Perjury in Pickups Case," Gannett News Service wire story, March 3, 1994.

38 In an *in camera* review, a judge examines materials from one party in chambers to determine whether they should be disclosed to the other party.

39 The work product doctrine generally protects an attorney's notes, written memoranda, and other materials prepared in connection with legal representation from being subject to discovery.

40 *Cameron* v. *GMC*, 158 F.R.D. 581 (D.S.C. 1994).

41 Byron Bloch, interview with authors, July 14, 1994.

42 Matthew L. Wald, "Operator of Reactors Suffers Run of Trouble," *The New York Times*, March 31, 1992.

43 Letter from Paul Blanch to Senator John F. Kerry, October 22, 1993.

44 Paul Blanch, interview with authors, August 23, 1994.

45 Ernest C. Hadley, interview with authors, August 23, 1994.

46 Robert A. Hamilton, "Legal Battles Cost NU Over $10 Million," *The Day* (New London, Connecticut).

47 Jim Morris, "NRC: We're Too Slow to Protect Whistle-blowers," *The Houston Chronicle*, July 16, 1993.

48 Matthew L. Wald, "Regulator Says Connecticut's Largest Power Company Harassed Worker," *The New York Times*, May 5, 1993.

49 "Northeast Utilities to Pay Federal Fine," Reuters wire report, June 6, 1993.

50 For more information on whistle-blowing and its importance, see Ralph Nader, Peter J. Petkas, and Kate Blackwell, eds., *Whistle Blowing: The Report of the Conference on Professional Responsibility* (New York: Grossman Publishers, 1972).

51 Bricker left his job at Hanford in 1979 to attend college but returned in 1983.

52 Report of the Department of Energy Subgroup on Contractor Litigation and Outside Counsel Fees, 1993.

53 See testimony of Victor S. Rezendes, General Accounting Office, before the Subcommittee on Oversight and Investigations, Committee on Energy and Commerce, U.S. House of Representatives, July 13, 1994.

54 Ed Bricker, interview with authors, August 23 and 25, 1994.

55 *Ibid.*

56 Tom Carpenter, interview with authors, April 26, 1995.

57 Bricker interview, *supra.*

58 See, for example, Claire Safran, "We Dared Blow the Whistle!" *Good Housekeeping*, April 1991; Karen Franklin, "It's Only Plutonium," *The Progressive*, October 1991; Chris Sivula, "Persecution or Perception?" *Tri-City Herald*, July 14, 1991.

59 *Bricker v. Rockwell Intl. Corp.*, 10 F.3d 598 (9th Cir. 1993) and 22 F.3d 871 (9th Cir. 1993), *cert. denied*, 115 S.Ct. 195 (1994).

60 Carpenter interview, *supra.*

61 *Ibid.*

62 The federal Freedom of Information Act provides procedures by which requesters may obtain unreleased government information. Government officials must justify denials of requested information by reference to specific exemptions in the act, and resulting disputes can be brought to federal court. It is an imperfect system that still permits too much government secrecy, but it is far better than the pre-FOIA period. Every state has its own version of the act to apply to state government records.

CHAPTER 7: THE "BUTS" PRINCIPLE

1 Economic census data show that the legal services industry had $108.4 billion in revenues in 1992. Marianne Lavelle, "Lawyers Are Top Earners," *The National Law Journal*, August 28, 1995.

2 "The Am Law 100 Firms," *The American Lawyer*, July/August 1995.

3 "The Am Law 100 Firms," *ibid.*; Margaret Cronin Fisk, "What Lawyers Earn," *The National Law Journal*, July 10, 1995; "Annual Survey of the Nation's Largest Law Firms," *The National Law Journal*, October 3, 1993.

4 Joseph W. Cotchett with Stephen P. Pizzo, *The Ethics Gap: Greed and the Casino Society* (Calabasas, CA: Parker and Sons Publications, 1991).

5 Interview with authors, March 19, 1994.

6 Correspondence with authors, March 18, 1994.

7 Interview with authors, June 28, 1994.

8 Correspondence with authors, March 11, 1994.

9 Correspondence with authors, March 20, 1994.

10 Interview with authors, August 23, 1993.

11 Victoria Slind-Flor, "Some Just Say 'No' to Clients," *The National Law Journal,* November 2, 1992.

12 Donald E. deKieffer, Esq., *How Lawyers Screw Their Clients* (New York: Barricade Books, 1995).

13 Jim Schratz, interview with authors, December 14, 1993.

14 "An Insurer's Sleuth Sniffs Out Lawyers Inflating Their Bills," *The Wall Street Journal,* July 21, 1992. For more on the Fireman's Fund–Latham dispute, see "Everybody's Doing It," *The American Lawyer,* September 1991; and Alan Abrahamson, "Insurer's Suit Warns Lawyers to Watch Bills," *Los Angeles Times,* July 1, 1991.

15 *Tarkington, O'Connor & O'Neill v. Fireman's Fund Insurance Company,* Alternate Adjudication No. 91-3, Decision and Award of Arbitrator, March 9, 1993.

16 Steven O'Neill, interview with authors, December 6, 1994.

17 Bill Kisliuk, "Tarkington Firm, Ex-Partner Settle Slander Suit," *The Recorder,* December 2, 1994.

18 Schratz interview, *supra.*

19 John Toothman, interview with authors, March 10, 1994.

20 Schratz interview, *supra.*

21 Gary Greenfield, interview with authors, December 2, 1993.

22 Pension Rights Center, Washington, D.C., *Cutting Legal Costs for Business,* May 18, 1981.

23 Robert Fellmeth, interview with authors, January 3, 1996.

24 Roger Parloff, "Over-billed by $57 Million?" *The American Lawyer,* May 1994.

25 "Skaddenomics," *The American Lawyer,* September 1991.

26 John E. Morris, "Buchalter Agrees to Big Write-Offs," *The Recorder,* March 23, 1992.

27 Saundra Torry, "Decision Exposes the Pitfalls of Padding Legal Bills," *The Washington Post,* September 11, 1995.

28 deKieffer, *How Lawyers Screw Their Clients.*

29 William Ross, correspondence with authors, November 8, 1993.

30 Margaret A. Jacobs, "Problem of Overbilling by Many Large Firms Is Confirmed in Surveys," *The Wall Street Journal,* September 18, 1995.

31 Association of Legal Administrators, Greater Chicago Chapter, The Administrator's Advantage, Special Edition, 1995.

32 *In re Spreckles Industries Inc.,* No. 92-47497, slip op. (Bankr. N.D.Cal., April 6, 1994.)

33 See Mark Sell, "Cravath's GDC Blues," *The American Lawyer,* November 1990; Rita Henley Jensen, "A Firm Blessing," *The National Law Journal,* August 24, 1992; John C. Coffee, Jr., "If Silence Equals Fraud, the Rules Shift," *The National Law Journal,* October 5, 1992; David Lyons, "Judges Hit Feds in Fraud Appeal," *The National Law Journal,* March 27, 1995; *Brown v. United States,* slip opinion (11th Cir. April 16, 1996).

34 "Everybody's Doing It," *The American Lawyer,* September 1991.

35 General Accounting Office, *Information on the Federal Government's Use of Private Attorneys,* October 20, 1992.

36 "FDIC, RTC Seek $6.8 Billion from Milken, Keating, and Others for Junk Bond Losses," *Antitrust and Trade Regulation Report,* January 31, 1991; "Thrift Regulators Seek $6.8 Billion in Claims Against Drexel," Reuters wire story, November 14, 1990.

37 RTC Office of Inspector General, *Legal Fees Paid to Cravath, Swaine & Moore,* September 28, 1992.

38 Ralph Vartabedan, "Win or Lose, Medicare Pays the Legal Fees," *Los Angeles Times*, October 6, 1995.

39 Correspondence from Jonathan Ratner, Associate Director of Health Financing Issues, General Accounting Office, to Representative Ron Wyden, Democrat of Oregon, Ranking Minority Member, Subcommittee on Oversight and Investigations, Committee on Commerce, United States House of Representatives, July 18, 1995.

40 Karen Dillon, "Dumb and Dumber," *The American Lawyer*, October 1995.

41 Jacobs, "Problem of Overbilling by Many Large Firms."

42 William H. Rehnquist, "Dedicatory Address: The Legal Profession Today," 62 Ind. L.J. 151, 155 (1987).

43 Jacobs, "Problem of Overbilling by Many Large Firms."

44 William Ross, interview with authors, May 1994.

45 See Margot Slade, "Billable Hour, a Centerpiece of American Law, Is Fading," *The New York Times*, October 22, 1993.

46 Jacobs, "Problem of Overbilling by Many Large Firms."

47 It has been widely reported that Baker & McKenzie is where the *Rodent* publisher formerly worked, so we depart from our policy, stated above, of declining to name a firm where our source has asked to remain anonymous. The newsletter, started in 1990, has spawned a growth industry, with a monthly "Word from the Rodent" column in legal publications across the country and, in 1995, a book, *Explaining the Inexplicable: The Rodent's Guide to Lawyers* (Pocket Books).

48 Publisher of *The Rodent*, interview with authors, March 24, 1994.

49 Mark Galanter, interview with authors, March 22, 1994.

50 Emily Barker, "Winston and Strawn Gets Ruthless," *The American Lawyer*, June 1993.

51 Quoted in *Cutting Legal Costs for Business*, *supra*.

52 John E. Morris, "End of the Billable Hour?" CCM: *The American Lawyer's Corporate Counsel Magazine*, November 1995.

53 Lee Fifer, interview with authors, 1994.

54 Stephen Gillers, interview with authors, April 29, 1994.

55 Ross interview, *supra*.

56 ABA Committee on Ethics and Professional Responsibility, Formal Opinion 93-379.

57 Disciplinary Rule 2-106 of the Model Code provides that a lawyer shall not charge a "clearly excessive fee," defined as one as to which "a lawyer of ordinary prudence would be left with a definite and firm conviction . . . is in excess of a reasonable fee." Model Rule 1.5 provides "A lawyer's fee shall be reasonable" and lists several factors for determining reasonableness, including the time required, the difficulty of the issues, the experience and skill of the lawyer, and the results obtained.

CHAPTER 8: THE CORPORATE SCHEME TO WRECK OUR JUSTICE SYSTEM

1 Marlo Mahne, interview with authors, January 23, 1995.

2 "Here's a Quarter for Your Sideshow," *Liability Week*, July 5, 1994. Cortese's remark has also been reported in Catherine Yang, "Snatching Defeat from the Jaws of Victory," *Business Week*, August 1, 1994, and Stephen Labaton, "Playing With the Words in the Product Liability Bill," *The New York Times*, March 5, 1995. A few months after his "sideshow" remark, Cortese decided to leave 401-lawyer Kirkland & Ellis's Washington office for the D.C. office of Philadelphia's 263-lawyer Pepper, Hamilton & Scheetz, where he had begun his legal career. He

said, "I will continue to do the same work I've been doing in the past with no diminution in activity." "Cortese's Homecoming," *Legal Times*, August 22, 1994.

3   *Justice for Sale; Shortchanging the Public Interest for Private Gain*, Alliance for Justice, 1993.

4   "Proponents of Reform," *Legal Times*, April 17, 1995.

5   *Ibid.*

6   *Ibid.*

7   T. R. Goldman, "Business Split Spells Code Blue," *Legal Times*, July 31, 1995.

8   "Reform War Chest," *The National Law Journal*, March 21, 1994; "Proponents of Reform," *Legal Times*, April 17, 1995.

9   *Ibid.*

10 Michael Rustad and Thomas Koenig, "The Historical Continuity of Punitive Damages Awards: Reforming the Tort Reformers," 42 *The American University Law Review* 1269 (1993).

11 Fund-raising letter from William M. H. Hammett, November 1992.

12 See, e.g., David Maraniss and Michael Weisskopf, "Speaker and His Directors Make the Cash Flow Right," *The Washington Post*, November 27, 1995.

13 *National Law Journal*, "Why We Sue," October 1994.

14 Barry Keene, interview with authors, March 23, 1994.

15 Charles P. Kindregan, interview with authors, January 23, 1995.

16 Mark Silbergeld, interview with authors, February 6, 1995.

17 Testimony of Marc Galanter, Director, Institute of Legal Studies, University of Wisconsin Law School, before the United States Senate Consumer Subcommittee, Committee on Commerce, Science and Transportation, September 19, 1991.

18 The complete breakdown is: domestic relations, 35 percent; contract, 11 percent; small claims, 11 percent; real property, 9 percent; tort, 9 percent; estate, 7 percent; and other civil, 18 percent. *1992 Annual Report of the National Center for State Courts*, National Center for State Courts, 1994.

19 Hensler et al., *Compensation for Accident Injuries in the United States*, Rand Corporation, Institute for Civil Justice, 1991.

20 Richard Perez-Pena, "U.S. Juries Grow Tougher on Plaintiffs in Lawsuits," *The New York Times*, June 17, 1994.

21 Jay Mathews, "Payment Rates Ease in Jury Awards and Liability Settlements, Survey Shows," *The Washington Post*, November 13, 1995. The report, "Tort Cost Trends: An International Perspective," was produced by Robert W. Sturgis of the international management consulting firm Tillinghast Towers Perrin. Tort deformers have pointed to the firm's 1985 study, which claimed that between 1950 and 1985, tort costs increased an average of 12 percent per year, while the economy grew an average of 8 percent. But the 1995 study showed that from 1985 to 1994, both tort costs and the economy grew at an average of 5 percent annually. The 1995 report concluded that state efforts to weaken victims' rights had little impact on the down trend in tort costs. Instead, the study found, fewer parties are suing and fewer defendants have been willing to settle questionable claims.

22 Robert A. Rosenblatt and Gebe Martinez, "Senate Completes First Override of Clinton Veto," *Los Angeles Times*, December 23, 1995.

23 Herbert J. Stein, "Letting Wall Street Off Easy," *The New York Times*, February 15, 1995.

24 "Toothless Watchdog Can't Stop Investment Fraud," *USA Today*, July 31, 1995.

25 *Ibid.*

26 Herbert J. Stein, "Letting Wall Street Off Easy."

27 Benjamin J. Stein, "Tort 'Reform' Is a License to Steal," *The New York Times*, July 30, 1995.

28 Perez-Pena, "U.S. Juries Grow Tougher."

29 "Suits by Firms Exceed Those by Individuals," *The Wall Street Journal*, December 3, 1993.

30 *Liebeck v. McDonald's*, Second Judicial District Court, County of Bernalillo, State of New Mexico, case number CV-93-02419.

31 *The New York Times*, February 16, 1995.

32 Saundra Torry, "Tort and Retort: The Battle Over Reform Heats Up," *The Washington Post*, March 6, 1995.

33 Charles Allen, "Fighting Over More Than Just Spilled Coffee," *Los Angeles Times*, March 23, 1995. (Allen, of Albuquerque, New Mexico, is Stella Liebeck's son-in-law.)

34 Charles Allen, "The McDonald's Coffee Spill Case" (letter), *The Washington Post*, April 4, 1995.

35 Andrea Gerlin, "A Matter of Degree: How a Jury Decided That a Coffee Spill Is Worth $2.9 Million," *The Wall Street Journal*, September 1, 1994.

36 Liebeck case juror, interview with authors, February 8, 1995.

37 Betty Farnham, interview with authors, February 9, 1995.

38 Gerlin, "A Matter of Degree."

39 *Ibid.*

40 Torry, "Tort and Retort."

41 *Liebeck v. McDonald's, supra*, Transcript of Proceedings, August 15, 1994.

42 *Ibid.*

43 *Ibid.*

44 *United Nuclear Corp. v. Allendale Mutual Ins. Co.*, 709 P.2d 649 (N.M. 1985).

45 Paul Vitello, "A Big McThank You," *Newsday*, August 11, 1994.

46 *Liebeck v. McDonald's, supra*, Transcript of Proceedings, September 14, 1994.

47 Gerlin, "A Matter of Degree"; S. Reed Morgan, "Verdict Against McDonald's Is Fully Justified" (letter), *The National Law Journal*, October 24, 1994.

48 *Public Papers of the Presidents of the United States, Ronald Reagan*, May 30, 1986.

49 *Bigbee v. Pacific Telephone and Telegraph Co.*, 665 P.2d 947 (Cal. 1983).

50 "Victims Charge Administration Distorted Their 'Sufferings' in Tort Reform Bid," BNA *Daily Report for Executives*, July 24, 1986; Leon Daniel, "Witnesses hit insurers' claims about damage awards," UPI wire story, July 24, 1986; John Gannon, *Tort Deform—Lethal Bedfellows*, Essential Information, 1995, citing "Have You Heard the One About? . . . Here is the Rest of the Story," press release from the Association of Trial Lawyers of America, January 23, 1986, and telephone conversations with Bigbee's attorney, Thomas Cacciatore, April 1994.

51 *Public Papers of the Presidents of the United States, Ronald Reagan*, April 1, 1987.

52 *Haimes v. Temple University Hospital*, slip op. (Pa. Court of Common Pleas, August 7, 1986); "Claimed CAT Scan Stole Her Powers," *Los Angeles Times*, August 10, 1986; Michele DiGirolamo, "Judge throws out $986,000 jury award to 'psychic,' " UPI wire story, August 9, 1986; Frederic N. Tulsky, "Did Jury's Award Consider Psychic's Loss of 'Powers'?" *The National Law Journal*, April 14, 1986; Jesse Birnbaum, "Crybabies: Eternal Victims," *Time*, August 12, 1991; letter to Ralph Nader from Judge Leon Katz, Court of Common Pleas, undated, 1995; John Gannon, *Tort Deform—Lethal Bedfellows*, Essential Information, 1995, citing CBS 60 *Minutes*, Jan. 10, 1988 (segment on "Reexamination of Lawsuit Crisis"), telephone conversations with Haimes's attorney, Joel M. Lieberman, and John Vargo, "The Truth, the Whole Truth and Nothing but the Truth," *Verdict*, Summer 1992.

53 See, e.g., Peter Huber, *Galileo's Revenge: Junk Science in the Courtroom* (New York: Basic Books, 1991), p. 4 (citing the CAT scan case); W. Kip Viscusi, *Re-*

forming Products Liability (Cambridge, MA: Harvard University Press, 1991); Peter Nye, "The Great Debate," *Public Citizen*, November–December 1992 (reporting that in October 1991, Jerry Jasinowski, president of the National Association of Manufacturers, a leading industry group, offered inaccurate accounts of both the CAT scan and the phone booth cases).

54 See, for example, the following Supreme Court opinions: *Pacific Mutual Life Insurance Co. v. Haslip*, 499 U.S. 1, 24, 27 (1991) (Scalia, J., concurring in the judgment); *Gertz v. Robert Welch, Inc.*, 418 U.S. 323 (1974) (White, J., dissenting).

55 Perez-Pena, "U.S. Juries Grow Tougher"; Sally Roberts, "Plaintiffs winning fewer injury suits: Study," *Business Insurance*, March 28, 1994.

56 *Ibid.*

57 Perez-Pena, "U.S. Juries Grow Tougher."

58 Valerie Hans, interview with authors, April 1994; Valerie P. Hans and William S. Lofquist, "Perceptions of Civil Justice: The Litigation Crisis Attitudes of Civil Jurors," 12 *Behavioral Sciences and the Law* 181 (1994).

59 Hans interview, *supra*.

60 Terence Dunworth & Joel Rogers, Corporations in Court: Big Business Litigation in U.S. Federal Courts, 1971–91 (1995).

61 Source: J. Robert Hunter, Consumer Federation of America.

62 Pet Food Institute Fact Sheet 1995, Pet Food Institute, Washington, D.C. Figure is for 1994.

63 Ted Shelsby, "Ford's Newest Gamble," *The Baltimore Sun*, September 20, 1995 (1994 profits).

64 *Fortune*, August 7, 1995 (1994 profits); David Hoffman, "Russia's Economic Colossus," *The Washington Post*, December 3, 1995.

65 J. Robert Hunter, *Product Liability Insurance Experience 1984–1993*, Consumer Federation of America, March 1995; Statement of J. Robert Hunter before the Subcommittee on Administrative Oversight and the Courts of the Judiciary Committee of the United States Senate, May 2, 1995. Hunter found that in the ten-year period from 1984 to 1993, product liability cost consumers 26 cents per $100 in retail sales.

66 *Ibid.* Michael Schrage, a business writer and research associate at the Massachusetts Institute of Technology, argues that the effort to restrict tort laws is simply government interference in the marketplace—a financial subsidy to certain businesses: "When the government directly intervenes to change the legal risk-reward ratios that industry considers before designing, building and shipping a product—or making a public offering in the securities markets—it is not merely being 'pro-business,' it is penalizing some industries at the expense of others." Michael Schrage, "Tort Reform? It's Government Interference in the Marketplace," *Los Angeles Times*, March 9, 1995.

67 Ellen R. Schultz, "Large Employers Are Carrying Lighter Loads of Liability Costs," *The Wall Street Journal*, December 12, 1995; Ellen R. Schultz, "U.S. Firms Are Spending Less to Guard Against Risk for the First Time in Years," *The Wall Street Journal*, April 25, 1995. A 1986 study by the Rand Corporation Institute for Civil Justice concluded that the total cost of *all* tort litigation—not just product liability but all types of torts, and not just cases brought by individuals but also cases brought by businesses—including judgments and settlements, attorney fees on both sides, court costs, and the value of time litigants spent dealing with lawsuits, was $28 to $35 billion in 1985. (The study focused only on federal and state courts of general jurisdiction; it excluded cases in small claims court and other specialized tribunals, as well as claims paid prior to any litigation. However, the study found that about 90 percent of compensation paid in tort litiga-

tion was paid in cases arising in the general jurisdiction courts.) See Statement of James S. Kalalik, the Institute for Civil Justice, the Rand Corporation before Joint Economic Committee, United States Congress, July 29, 1986.

68 Theodore B. Olson, "The Dangerous National Sport of Punitive Damages," *The Wall Street Journal*, October 5, 1994.

69 Office of the Governor of Texas, *The Common Sense Case for Lawsuit Abuse Reform*, January 1995.

70 Twenty-five states require "clear and convincing evidence" and one state requires evidence "beyond a reasonable doubt" that the defendant's behavior was wanton, malicious, grossly negligent, or oppressive before a jury may award punitive damages. Four states—New Hampshire, Louisiana, Nebraska, and Washington—do not allow punitive damages at all, regardless of the nature of the defendant's conduct. Massachusetts juries can award them only in specific types of cases, as determined by state statute. In addition, many states impose upper limits on punitive damage awards. Thomas Koenig and Michael Rustad, "The Quiet Revolution Revisited: An Empirical Study of the Impact of State Tort Reform of Punitive Damages in Products Liability," *Justice System Journal*, 1993.

71 Gallanter and Luban, "Poetic Justice: Punitive Damages and Legal Pluralism," 42 *American University Law Review*, 1993.

72 Michael Rustad, "Keynote Address: Punitive Damages and the Public Trust," before the New Mexico Trial Lawyers Association, April 26, 1991.

73 Michael Rustad and Thomas Koenig, "Punitive Damages in Products Liability: A Research Report," *Products Liability Law Journal*, Vol. 3, No. 2 (February 1992).

74 Congressional Record, May 2, 1995, S 5951 (statement of Senator Hollings). The 379 figure—broken down by state—was provided at the request of Senator Ernest Hollings, Democrat of South Carolina, by legal expert Jonathan S. Massey, who relied on the Rustad-Koening data.

75 U.S. Department of Justice, *Civil Jury Cases and Verdicts in Large Counties*, July 1995.

76 Mark Peterson, Syam Sarma, Michael Shanley, *Punitive Damages, Empirical Findings*, the Rand Institute for Civil Justice, 1987. The Rand study found that punitive damage awards in personal injury cases were usually small, but that the largest awards had gotten larger in the mid-1980s.

77 *Ibid.*

78 Congressional Record, May 2, 1995, S 5951 (statement of Senator Hollings).

79 The $3 billion punitive award was on top of $7.53 billion in compensatory damages. The defendant, Texaco, which Pennzoil accused of interfering with a merger agreement, settled the case in 1987 by paying Pennzoil a total of $3 billion. See "Pennzoil Wins $10.53 Billion in Texaco Suit," *Los Angeles Times*, November 19, 1985; Diane Burch Beckham, "Ten Cases That Changed Texas," *Texas Lawyer*, April 3, 1995.

80 Deborah Hensler and Eri Moller, *Trends in Punitive Damages: Preliminary Data from Cook County, Illinois and San Francisco, California*, Rand Institute for Civil Justice, March 1995.

81 *Ibid.*

82 Stephen Daniels and Joanne Martin, *Empirical Patterns in Punitive Damage Cases: A Description of Incidence Rates and Awards*, American Bar Foundation Working Paper No. 8705 (1987). See also Stephen Daniels and Joanne Martin, "Myth and Reality in Punitive Damages," 75 *Minnesota Law Review* 1 (1990).

83 Gallanter and Luban, "Poetic Justice," *supra*.

84 Armand Maaskamp, interview with authors, May 26, 1994.

85 Daniel Callahan, interview with authors, May 12, 1994.

86 *Surgin Surgical Instrumentation, Inc., v. Farmers Group, Inc., et al.,* Superior Court of the State of California for the County of Orange, Case No. 662216.

87 *Surgin, supra,* slip op., March 24, 1993.

88 *Surgin, supra,* slip op., September 15, 1993.

89 *Surgin, supra,* "Deposition of Michael D. Conn," September 24, 1993, pages 10–20.

90 A custodian of records is a representative of a party charged with identifying documents turned over pursuant to a subpoena.

91 *Surgin, supra,* Reporter's Transcript, October 7, 1993.

92 Daniel J. Callahan, "Insurers' Real Net Worth Is Key to Damage Awards," *The National Law Journal,* May 22, 1995.

93 Michael Rustad, "In Defense of Punitive Damages: Testing Tort Anecdotes with Empirical Data," *Iowa Law Review,* Vol. 78, No. 1 (October 1992).

94 Silbergeld interview, *supra.*

95 Jeffrey O'Connell and C. Brian Kelly, *The Blame Game: Injuries, Insurance and Injustice* (D.C. Heath & Co., 1987).

96 Restatement (Second) of Torts § 908 (2). The American Law Institute publishes "restatements" that attempt to summarize various bodies of common law, i.e., legal rules that have evolved through judicial opinions from across the country.

97 Dan Morain, "Preemptive Strike: Farmers Insurance Was Poised to Fight for a Cut in Lawyers Fees—but the Threat of a Powerful TV Ad Shifted the Balance of Power," *Los Angeles Times,* December 27, 1993.

98 Robert Forsythe, interview with authors, March 7, 1995.

99 Specifically, California's 1975 Malpractice Injury Compensation Reform Act (MICRA):
   —Places a $250,000 cap on the amount of compensation paid to malpractice victims for their lifetime "non-economic" injuries (pain and suffering).
   —Eliminates the "collateral source rule" that requires those found liable for malpractice to pay for all the expenses incurred by a victim.
   —Permits those found liable for malpractice to pay for the compensation they owe victims in installments.
   —Enables health care providers to include in their contracts with patients provisions requiring patients to waive their right to a jury trial and submit to binding out-of-court arbitration in the event of malpractice claims.
   —Imposes a one-year statute of limitations (time within which a case can be brought).
   —Establishes a sliding scale for attorneys' fees, which discourages lawyers from accepting serious or complicated malpractice cases and leaves people with mid-level cases unrepresented.

100 See Harvey Rosenfield, *Silent Violence, Silent Death* (Essential Books, 1994).

101 The People's Medical Society has over 100,000 dues-paying members. Its main goal is to inform the public about issues of health care, empower individuals in the health care system to make intelligent decisions, and seek to reform the system to be more responsive to individuals.

102 *Business Week,* August 3, 1987.

103 *The Report of the Harvard Medical Practice Study to the State of New York. Patients, Doctors and Lawyers: Medical Injury, Malpractice Litigation, and Patient Compensation in New York* (Cambridge, Massachusetts: President and Fellows of Harvard University, 1990); T. A. Brennan, L. L. Leape, and N. M. Laird, et al., "Incidence of adverse events and negligence in hospitalized patients: results of the Harvard Medical Practice Study II," *New England Journal of Medicine,* 1991, 324.

104 Testimony of Dr. Troyen A. Brennan, Harvard School of Public Health, before the Subcommittee on Health and the Environment, Committee on Energy and Commerce, U.S. House of Representatives, November 10, 1993.

105 Matthew L. Wald, "In Reversal of 20-Year Trend, Traffic Deaths Increase in U.S.," *The New York Times*, October 27, 1995 (reporting National Safety Council figure for 1994).

106 "Murder Rate Fell in 1994 for 3d Consecutive Year," *The New York Times*, October 24, 1995 (citing Centers for Disease Control figure for 1994).

107 "Murder Rate Down but Teen Suicides Up," Reuters wire story. October 23, 1995 (citing Centers for Disease Control figure for 1994).

108 "Murder Rate Fell in 1994 for 3d Consecutive Year," *The New York Times*, October 24, 1995 (citing Centers for Disease Control figure for 1994).

109 Paul C. Weiler, a Harvard Law School professor who helped conduct the Harvard study, has estimated annual deaths caused by medical negligence malpractice events at 150,000. Statement of Lawrence H. Thompson, General Accounting Office, before the Subcommittee on Health, Committee on Ways and Means, U.S. House of Representatives, May 20, 1993. These estimates of malpractice deaths were calculated before the vast increase in the number of people in the United States who have been herded into health maintenance organizations (HMOs), as part of efforts by employers, insurers, and government to control health care costs. HMOs earn their profits by "managing care," that is, eliminating some of the caution built into the traditional fee-for-service system, often derided by tort deformers as "defensive medicine."

110 Alfred E. Hofflander and Blaine F. Nye, *Medical Malpractice Insurance in Pennsylvania*, Management Analysis Center, 1985.

111 Public Citizen is a nonprofit consumer advocacy organization founded by Ralph Nader.

112 *Medical Malpractice in Texas: Are We Covering Up the Symptoms Instead of Curing the Disease?* Public Citizen, compiled from reports by the Texas State Board of Medical Examiners, 1987.

113 Office of Technology Assessment, *Impact of Legal Reforms on Medical Malpractice Costs*, OTA-BP-H-119, October 1993; Office of Technology Assessment, *Defensive Medicine and Medical Malpractice*, OTA-H-602, July 1994. The tort-deform-minded Congress elected in November 1994 apparently did not want to hear such conclusions. It abolished OTA.

114 See also *Medical Malpractice Insurance: 1985–1991 Calendar Year Experience*, National Insurance Consumer Organization, 1993 (estimating the cost of medical malpractice premiums in 1991 at $4.9 billion).

115 J. Robert Hunter, Medical Malpractice Insurance, Consumer Federation of America, September 1995.

116 Figures provided by J. Robert Hunter, based on A. M. Best, *Aggregates and Averages*, 1995 edition.

117 Testimony of Dr. Troyen Brennan on Medical Malpractice and Health Care Reform before the United States Senate Finance Committee, May 12, 1994.

118 Paul C. Weiler, Howard H. Hiatt, Joseph P. Newhouse, William G. Johnson, Troyen A. Brennan, and Lucian L. Leape, *A Measure of Malpractice: Medical Injury, Malpractice Litigation, and Patient Compensation* (Cambridge, Massachusetts: Harvard University Press, 1993).

119 Testimony of Dr. Troyen Brennan on Medical Malpractice and Health Care Reform before the United States Senate Finance Committee, May 12, 1994.

120 Harvey S. Wachsman with Steven Alschuler, *Lethal Medicine: The Epidemic of Medical Malpractice in America* (New York: Henry Holt and Company, 1993).

121   Philip K. Howard, "Fear of Litigation Costs More Than Price of Prevention," *Corporate Legal Times*, October 1995.

122   Brian Cox, "Clinton Med. Mal. Reform Challenged," *National Underwriter, Life & Health/Financial Services Edition*, November 15, 1993.

123   Only a portion of such injuries from medical care are caused by *negligent* medical care. Health providers may meet established standards of care—i.e., not act negligently—but nevertheless injure patients. The Harvard study of New York hospitals found that about 28 percent of such injuries and about 51 percent of such injuries resulting in death were caused by negligence. Testimony of Dr. Troyen Brennan on Medical Malpractice and Health Care Reform before the United States Senate Finance Committee, May 12, 1994.

124   See Wachsman and Alschuler, *supra*.

125   *Ibid.*

126   *Ibid.*

127   Testimony of Neil Vidmar, Professor, Duke University School of Law, Senate Judiciary Subcommittee on Administrative Oversight and Courts, May 2, 1995.

128   The Rustad/Koenig finding is cited in *ibid.*

129   Robert Baker, interview with authors, January 17, 1995.

130   Scott Olsen, "California's Malpractice Cap Hits Injured Children Hardest," *The San Diego Union-Tribune*, August 30, 1995.

131   Rex Dalton, "A Painful Price," *The San Diego Union-Tribune*, May 11, 1995.

132   This research was introduced at the subsequent trial over the matter. Letter from Ann Saponara, Sturdevant & Sturdevant, July 7, 1995.

133   Patricia Sturdevant, interview with authors, April 12, 1995.

134   This account of Geneva Bell's case relies on the opinion of the California Court of Appeals, *Bell v. Congress Mortgage Company, Inc.*, 24 Cal. App. 4th 1675 (1994); and Barbara Steuart, "Banking on the Attorney General," *The Recorder*, August 3, 1994.

135   "Mortgage Company Targeted by Consumer Group," UPI wire story, April 8, 1993.

136   *Bell v. Congress Mortgage Company.*

137   Steuart, "Banking on the Attorney General."

138   *Bell v. Congress Mortgage Company.*

139   Steuart, "Banking on the Attorney General."

140   Letter from the Office of the California Attorney General to the Honorable Malcolm M. Lucas, Chief Justice of the California Supreme Court, July 18, 1994.

141   American Arbitration Association general counsel Michael Hoellering told *The Recorder* that the group supported depublication because *Bell* threatened to undermine many existing contractual arbitration provisions and because the group believed, like the attorney general's office, that guidelines like those issued by the appellate court were in fact the province of the legislature. Steuart, "Banking on the Attorney General."

142   *Bell v. Congress Mortgage Company*, 94 Cal. Daily Op. Service 5860, (Cal. July 28, 1994) (Case No. S 040252).

143   *Badie v. Bank of America*, slip op., Case No. 944916 (Cal.Super.Ct. August 18, 1994).

144   Stephen Von Till of Fremont, California, quoted in Mike McKee, "A Model for the Nation?" *Legal Times*, September 13, 1993.

145   Nina Schuyler, "Expensive Cost Cutting," *California Lawyer*, January 1995.

146   Diana Kunde, "Court Dismisses Bias Suit Against Arbitration Group," *The Dallas Morning News*, November 22, 1995; *Insurance Risk and Management*, April 26, 1995.

147 Nina Schuyler, "Expensive Cost Cutting."

148 Steven A. Holmes, "Some Employees Lose Right to Sue for Bias at Work," *The New York Times*, March 18, 1994.

149 Schuyler, "Expensive Cost Cutting."

150 Holmes, "Some Employees Lose Right to Sue."

151 Dave Thom, "Plaintiffs Lawyers Plot Boycott Over Mandatory ADR," *The Recorder*, October 3, 1995.

152 *Ibid.*

153 John Scully, "Washington Legal Foundation Brings Contingency Fee Reform to the State of Washington," *Legal Backgrounder*, March 31, 1992.

154 James L. Gattuso, "Don't Rush to Condemn Contingency Fees," *The Wall Street Journal*, May 15, 1986.

155 Keene interview, *supra*.

156 Jeffrey O'Connell, interview with authors, January 16, 1995.

157 J. Robert Hunter, *Product Liability Insurance Experience 1984–1993*, Consumer Federation of America, March 1995.

158 Testimony of Herbert Kritzer before the Senate Judiciary Committee, November 7, 1995.

159 William Fry, interview with authors, 1994.

160 Mary McGrory, "Putting People in Their Place," *The Washington Post*, March 7, 1995.

161 Such a modification was part of the version of "loser pays" that passed the U.S. House of Representatives in March 1995—a somewhat weakened version of the "loser pays" proposal contained in Newt Gingrich's Republican "Contract with America." It would establish a series of complicated and perhaps difficult-to-enforce rules for making a loser pay in some circumstances. The provision would apply to suits where one side had offered to settle. If the defendant prevailed at trial, or if the plaintiff prevailed but was awarded lower damages than the defendant had offered in settlement, the plaintiff would have to pay all the defendant's attorney fees incurred after the settlement offer. If the judge or jury awarded the plaintiff damages greater than the settlement offer, the defendant would pay the plaintiff's attorney fees incurred after the settlement offer. The amount of attorney fees the loser would have to pay the winner would be capped by the loser's own attorney fees, except that where a losing party's lawyer was working on a contingency basis, the winner would be entitled to the "reasonable cost" of such representation. Losers would not have to pay where the court found such an obligation to be "manifestly unjust" or where the case might have established an important legal rule. In addition, the provision would apply only to the cases in federal courts that arise under state law, rather than federal law. See David Hilzenrath, "House Passes 'Loser Pays' Legislation," *The Washington Post*, March 8, 1995.

162 Benjamin Weiser, "Tort Reform's Promise, Peril," *The Washington Post*, September 14, 1995.

163 *Ibid.*

164 Hunter, *Product Liability Insurance Experience 1984–1993*, *supra*.

165 *Borel v. Fibreboard Paper Products Corp.*, 493 F.2d 1076 (5th Cir. 1973), *cert. denied*, 419 U.S. 869 (1974).

166 See Stephen Solomon, "The Asbestos Fallout at Johns-Manville," *Fortune*, May 7, 1979.

167 *Ford Motor Co. v. Bartholomew*, 297 S.E.2d 675 (Va. 1982); *Ford Motor Co. v. Nowak*, 638 S.W.2d 582 (Tex.App. 1982).

168 Roger Parloff, "Bonanza," *The American Lawyer*, December 1990.

169 *Gryc v. Dayton-Hudson Corp.*, 297 N.W.2d 727 (Minn. 1980), *cert. denied*, 449 U.S. 921 (1980).

170 *Airco, Inc. v. Simmons First National Bank*, 638 S.W.2d 660 (Ark. 1982).

171 *Queiros v. Carol Cable Co.*, Case No. L-51272-81 (N.J. Superior Ct., Essex Cty.)

172 The judge reduced the jury's punitive damage award to $1.35 million, citing Playtex's posttrial action to remove the product. The U.S. Court of Appeals for the Tenth Circuit reinstated the $10 million award, holding that the judge had no authority to reduce the amount based on postverdict conduct. *O'Gilvie v. International Playtex, Inc.*, 609 F.Supp. 817 (D.Kan. 1985), *modified*, 821 F.2d 1438 (10th Cir. 1987), *cert. denied*, 486 U.S. 1032 (1988).

173 See Richard Connelly, "Jaw Implant Suit Takes the Fast Track," *Texas Lawyer*, July 17, 1995; Judy Foreman, "Danger Cited in Teflon Jaw Implants," *The Boston Globe*, June 5, 1992; Philip J. Hilts, "F.D.A. Issues Warning on Jaw Implants That May Disintegrate in the Body," *The New York Times*, June 5, 1992.

174 *Kinder v. Hively Corp.*, Case No. 902-01235 (Circuit Ct., St. Louis City). See Tim Bryant, "Angry Jury Hits Domino's Pizza Chain for $79 Million," *St. Louis Post-Dispatch*, December 19, 1993; Bruce Horowitz and Elaine Tassy, "Jury Award Ends Domino's 30-Minute Delivery Pledge," *Los Angeles Times*, December 22, 1993; Michael Janofsky, "Domino's Ends Fast-Pizza Pledge After Big Award to Crash Victim," *The New York Times*, December 22, 1993. The jury ordered Domino's and its local franchise operator to pay Kinder $750,000 in actual damages. The punitive damage award was assessed against Domino's only. From 1984 to 1986 Domino's had promised a free pizza if the 30-minute deadline was not met. Between 1986 and 1993, it offered a $3 discount if the pizza did not arrive on time.

175 *Burden of Proof*, Cable News Network, November 29, 1995.

176 See Nicholas A. Ashford, "The Product Liability Fairness Act," testimony before the Consumer Subcommittee, U.S. Senate Committee on Commerce, Science and Transportation, September 12, 1991.

177 Nathan Weber, *Product Liability: The Corporate Response; A Research Report for the Conference Board*, Report 893, 1987.

CHAPTER 9: FINDING THE COURAGE TO CHANGE THE SYSTEM

1 Ansel Chaplin, interview with authors, February 7, 1995.

2 Interview with authors, 1994.

3 Correspondence with authors, March 17, 1994.

4 Correspondence with authors, March 9, 1994.

5 Interview with authors, March 10, 1994.

6 Interview with authors, February 16, 1995.

7 Leonard Schroeter, interview with authors, February 22, 1994.

8 Geoffrey Hazard, interview with authors, March 16, 1994.

9 Publisher of *The Rodent*, interview with authors, March 2, 1994.

10 Joseph Calve, interview with authors, January 24, 1994.

11 Mark Galanter and Thomas Palay, *Tournament of Lawyers* (Chicago: The University of Chicago Press, 1991).

12 Marc Galanter, interview with authors, March 22, 1994.

13 See Kim Isaac Eisler, *Shark Tank* (New York: St. Martin's Press, 1990).

14 Schroeter interview, *supra*.

15 Robert Granfield, interview with authors, December 12, 1993.

16 Richard Uviller, interview with authors, April 14, 1994.

17 Richard D. Kahlenberg, *Broken Contract: A Memoir of Harvard Law School* (New York: Hill & Wang, 1992).

18 Gary Bellow, "Clinical Studies in Law," in Stephen Gillers, ed., *Looking at Law School*, 3rd rev. ed. (New York: Meridian Books, 1990), pp. 295–296.

19 Sol Linowitz, *The Betrayed Profession* (New York: Scribners, 1994), p. 245.

20 A. A. Berle, Jr. "Modern Legal Profession," *Encyclopaedia of the Social Sciences* (New York: The Macmillan Co., 1933), p. 341.

21 Hale and Dorr, "A Tradition of the Commitment to the Community," Boston, 1994, 30 pages.

22 William J. Dean, "The ABA's Challenge to Law Firms," *New York Law Journal*, May 24, 1993.

23 Harrison Wellford, interview with authors, February 12, 1995.

24 "ABA Approves 50-Hour Pro Bono Minimum," *United States Law Week*, February 16, 1993.

25 Dean, "The ABA's Challenge to Law Firms," *supra*.

26 Wendy R. Leibowitz, "Metting the Pro Bono Challenge," *The American Lawyer*, July/August 1995; Robert Schmidt, "Williams & Connolly Changes Its Tune," *Legal Times*, June 5, 1995.

27 Mary Voboril, "Many Lawyers in the City Are Donating Their Talents but the Need for More Is Growing," *Newsday*, October 31, 1994.

28 Hale and Dorr, "A Tradition of Commitment," *supra*.

29 Annual Report, 1994–95, New York Lawyers for the Public Interest.

30 Associate Justice Sandra Day O'Connor, "Pro Bono Work—Good News and Bad News," Remarks at the American Bar Association Meeting, August 12, 1991.

31 Linowitz, *supra*, p. 193.

32 See the *Final Report* of the State of California Bar Discipline Monitor, by Robert C. Fellmeth, Sept. 20, 1991, for instructive material on what is required to modestly improve the overall bar discipline system.

33 Illinois Code of Professional Responsibility, 87 Ill. 2d R. 401 (c).

34 *Ibid.*, 87 Ill. 2d R. 4-101 (d) (3).

35 *Balla* v. *Gambro, Inc.*, 145 Ill. 2d 492, 584 N.E.2d 104 (1991).

36 Nicholas Varchaver, "Opposite Answers in Whistle-Blower Cases," *The American Lawyer*, March 1992.

37 *Ibid.*

38 On December 27, 1991, eight days after the Balla decision, the Minnesota Supreme Court ruled that an in-house lawyer "is not, by reason of the attorney-client relationship, precluded from making a claim against the employer for wrongful discharge." *Nordling* v. *Northern State Power Co.*, 478 N.W.2d 498 (Minn. 1991). On July 18, 1994, a California state trial judge ruled that an attorney could bring an action for retaliatory discharge if the firing resulted from a lawyer's refusal to violate a mandatory ethical duty, such as the duty, implicated in the Balla case, to try to prevent death or bodily injury resulting from a client's conduct. *General Dynamics Corp.* v. *Superior Court*, No. S033640 (Cal.Sup.Ct. July 19, 1994), *United States Law Week*, August 9, 1994. In *Parker* v. *M & T Chemicals, Inc.*, 236 N.J. Super. 451, 566 A.2d 215 (1989), a New Jersey judge also recognized an attorney's suit for retaliatory discharge, although the availability of a state "whistle-blower" statute strengthened the attorney's argument. But, in *Willy* v. *Coastal Corp.*, 647 F.Supp. 116 (S.D.Tex. 1986), a federal trial judge sitting in Texas took the Balla approach, rejecting an attorney's claim of eligibility to sue for retaliatory discharge.

39 Brief of Amicus Curiae, American Corporate Counsel Association, *Balla* v. *Gambro*, Illinois Supreme Court, Case No. 70942 (1991).

40   The filing of the brief sparked a debate among association members, some of whom disagreed with it, and led the group's board in November 1991 to adopt a resolution on the matter. While the resolution did not completely reject the concept of in-house attorneys suing for retaliatory discharge, it did oppose such suits in circumstances, presumably including Balla's, where proof of the claim would require the introduction of evidence obtained through attorney-client communications. Varchaver, "Opposite Answers in Whistle-Blower Cases," *supra*.

41   American Bar Association Model Rules of Professional Conduct, Model Rule 1.6(b)(1).

42   *Ibid.*, comment to Model Rule 1.6.

43   *Ibid.*, Model Rule 1.13.

44   The attorney who wishes to halt misconduct by a corporate client must jump, carefully, through a series of hoops before Model Rule 1.13(b) permits the attorney to quietly resign:

> If a lawyer for an organization knows that an officer, employee or other person associated with the organization is engaged in action, intends to act or refuses to act in a matter related to the representation that is a violation of a legal obligation to the organization, or a violation of law which reasonably might be imputed to the organization, and is likely to result in substantial injury to the organization, the lawyer shall proceed as is reasonably necessary in the best interest of the organization. In determining how to proceed, the lawyer shall give due consideration to the seriousness of the violation and its consequences, the scope and nature of the lawyer's representation, the responsibility in the organization and the apparent motivation of the person involved, the policies of the organization concerning such matters and any other relevant considerations. Any measures taken shall be designed to minimize disruption of the organization and the risk of revealing information relating to the representation to persons outside the organization. Such measures may include among others:
>
> (1) asking reconsideration of the matter;
>
> (2) advising that a separate legal opinion on the matter be sought for presentation to appropriate authority in the organization; and
>
> (3) referring the matter to higher authority in the organization, including, if warranted by the seriousness of the matter, referral to the highest authority that can act in behalf of the organization as determined by applicable law.
>
> (c) If, despite the lawyer's efforts in accordance with paragraph (b), the highest authority that can act on behalf of the organization insists upon action, or a refusal to act, that is clearly a violation of law and is likely to result in substantial injury to the organization, the lawyer may resign . . .

45   See Rule 1.6, comment on withdrawal. The comment notes, however, that nothing in the relevant Model Rules "prevents the lawyer from giving notice of the fact of withdrawal, and the lawyer may also withdraw or disaffirm any opinion, document, affirmation, or the like."

46   Ted Schneyer, interview with authors, May 2, 1994.

47   "ABA House of Delegates Approves Revisions to Proposed Conduct Rules," *BNA Securities Regulation and Law Report*, February 18, 1983; Center for Professional Responsibility, American Bar Association, *The Legislative History of the Model Rules of Professional Conduct* (1987).

48 For example, New Jersey and Pennsylvania each *require* disclosure of such serious economic crimes. N.J. Rules of Professional Conduct Rule 1.6(b)(1) (1992); Penn. Rules of Professional Conduct Rule 1.6(c)(1) (1994).

49 Stephen Gillers, interview with authors, April 29, 1994.

50 American Bar Association Committee on Ethics and Professional Responsibility, Formal Opinion 93-379, December 6, 1993.

51 Linowitz, *supra.*

52 See also David B. Wilkins, "Making Context Count: Regulating Lawyers After Kaye, Scholer," 66 *Southern California Law Review* 1147, March 1993 (arguing for context-specific rules and enforcement practices shaped to meet conditions in specific areas of law practice).

53 See, for example, Steve Albert, "Discipline Doesn't Come Easy," *The Recorder*, May 9, 1994; Steve France, "Can the Bar Regulate Large Firms?" *New Jersey Law Journal*, February 7, 1994.

54 Federal law enforcement agencies appropriately held entire law firms responsible for the actions of firm attorneys in the savings and loan scandal.

55 Letter from William B. Schultz, Alan B. Morrison, and John Cary Sims to the Honorable William B. Bryant, June 12, 1980.

56 Eva M. Rodriguez and Robert Schmidt, "Judicial Conference Tries a Little Openness," *Legal Times*, March 20, 1995.

57 Berle, *supra*, p. 343.

58 John Douglas, *Los Angeles Times*, opinion section, August 31, 1969.

59 Paul Freund, "The Legal Profession," in R. Lynn, ed., *The Professions in America* (1965).

60 Mark Green, *The Other Government* (New York: Grossman/Viking, 1975), p. 289.

61 Stephen Daniels and Joanne Martin, *Civil Juries and the Politics of Reform* (Evanston, Illinois: Northwestern University Press, 1995); Neil Vidmar, *Medical Malpractice and the American Jury* (Ann Arbor, Michigan: The University of Michigan Press, 1995).

62 For further discussion of the legislation, see David C. Vladeck and Thomas O. McGinty, "Paralysis by Analysis," *The American Prospect*, Summer 1995.

63 Testimony of Harry Greene II, MD, before the Massachusetts State Legislative Joint Committee on Insurance, April 10, 1995.

64 For more detail, see comments to the Federal Trade Commission on 16 CFR Part 436, submitted by Jere W. Glover, Chief Counsel for Advocacy, U.S. Small Business Administration, Aug. 11, 1995, and by Peter C. Lagarias, Esq., of San Francisco, California, July 25, 1995.

65 Robert L. Purvin, Jr., *The Franchise Fraud* (New York: John Wiley & Sons, Inc., 1994).

66 The American Bar Association Central and East European Law Initiative, Concept Paper Protection for Bulgaria, November 25, 1992.

67 Sol Linowitz, interview with authors, October 5, 1995.

68 One of the authors, Ralph Nader, is a member of the Harvard Law School Class of 1958.

69 The reason attorneys give for doing different work is usually the tedium of their practice, however lucrative it may be. Clark Clifford, at age seventy-five, went into banking because he was bored, as his former partner Paul Warnke put it. Clifford said he wanted a new challenge. As if there were not enough challenges in the law writ large. Victor Schwartz switched from a professor favorably disposed to plaintiffs' tort law rights to a lobbyist for a network of corporations pressing to restrict these rights for injured persons. His reason: "I was getting bored with what I

was doing." A number of FDA attorneys left the agency and joined Washington law firms, where they represent the tobacco companies. Public Citizen Litigation Group director David Vladeck told us that when he asked them the question "aren't there better ways to make a buck than representing the tobacco industry?" he was told that money is not the issue. Instead it is the rush one gets representing a high-profile client in a high-profile case. One attorney at Arnold & Porter told Vladeck that "while I don't necessarily love my client, I love the excitement that comes from working on such a big-stakes proceeding."

Index

ABOUT THE AUTHORS

RALPH NADER is a nationally renowned consumer activist.

WESLEY J. SMITH is a lawyer and author.

ABOUT THE TYPE

This book was set in Goudy, a typeface designed by Frederic William Goudy (1865–1947). Goudy began his career as a bookkeeper, but devoted the rest of his life to the pursuit of "recognized quality" in a printing type.

Goudy was produced in 1914 and was an instant best-seller for the foundry. It has generous curves and smooth, even color. It is regarded as one of Goudy's finest achievements.